American Women in the 20TH Century
The Festival of Life

D0141098

American Women in the 20th Century
The Festival of Life

Robert L. Daniel
Ohio University

HARCOURT BRACE JOVANOVICH, PUBLISHERS

San Diego   New York   Chicago   Austin
London   Sydney   Tokyo   Toronto

To Robert, Martha, and Joseph

ISBN: 0-15-502590-2
Library of Congress Catalog Card Number: 85-82623
Printed in the United States of America

Photo Credits

Page 20, Musée des Arts Decoratifs, Paris; 36, Brown Brothers; 56, Missouri Historical Society; 69, Reproduced with permission of the A.T. & T. Archive; 89, The Bettmann Archive; 104, Photo by Ben Shahn. Courtesy of the Harvard University Art Museums. (The Fogg Art Museum.) Gift of Mrs. Bernarda B. Shahn; 123, Reproduced with permission of the Estate of Norman Rockwell; 126, UPI/ Bettmann Newsphotos; 165, Brown Brothers; 173, Carl Iwasaki Collection; 198, Courtesy of the Stroh Brewery Company; 238, © Bruce Davidson/Magnum Photos; 252, UPI/Bettmann Newsphotos; 289, Bettye Lane; 315, Bettye Lane; 335, Bettye Lane; 340, UPI/Bettmann Newsphotos; 362, © Pam Hasegaw/Taurus Photos; 381, © Richard Woods/Taurus Photos; 408, UPI/Bettmann Newsphotos; 415, Bettye Lane.

*Woman should stand beside man
as the comrade of his soul,
not the servant of his body.*

Charlotte Perkins Gilman

Preface

One of the most notable transformations of the twentieth century has been the entrance of American women into what Margaret Dreier Robins called "the festival of life." Women have substantially expanded their political roles and legal standing, pushed steadily and boldly into the labor force, broadened their access to education, and greatly altered their social and family roles.

Since the first courses in women's studies and women's history surfaced in the early 1970s, there has been a profusion of studies of American women. Most have been highly specialized monographs; precious few provide a rounded account of the vast changes that have marked the lives of American women since 1900.

This book provides a broad, balanced, systematic analysis of the transformations in women's lives thus far in the twentieth century. Several features stand out. Access to education is seen as prerequisite to expanding women's perspectives and providing women from all backgrounds with the skills and self-assurance required to undertake expanded political, economic, and social roles outside the home. Women's educational attainments are assessed in terms of those of previous generations of women, affording a measure that is free from distortion by the ups and downs that have characterized the enrollment patterns of men. In fact, the educational attainment of women has been marked by steady progress, contradicting the conventional picture of women "copping out" or even regressing at times during the past.

In evaluating women's political roles I look beyond the pursuit and utilization of the suffrage. Far more central are the tensions between those reformers who emphasized the need for legislative protection of working-class women and the middle-class reformers concerned with equal rights. I trace the reflections of this debate in constitutional law and assess the genuine gains of the 1970s and 1980s, when legislation and policy were reshaped in conformity with the principles of the Equal Rights Amendment, although the amendment itself failed to be ratified.

Major attention is devoted to women's economic roles. The text shows that structural changes in the American economy gave women increasing opportunities for roles outside the home and for greater personal autonomy. These structural changes produced a rapid growth of middle management and a concomitant need for clerical support, which in turn stimulated the steady rise in women's labor-force participation. Just as changes in the economic structure increased the demand for women in the labor force, changes in the demographic structure of the female population had major consequences for the supply of women to meet the increased demand for their labor.

In evaluating women's gains in the labor market, I rely heavily on uniform series of data from the U.S. Bureau of the Census and the Bureau of Labor Statistics to delineate the interplay of the supply of and demand for female workers. In particular, I use the labor force participation rate (LFPR) to measure changes in the propensity of women to engage in paid labor. Use of the LFPR also permits analysis of the function of age, marital status, ethnicity, and race in determining the supply of women in the labor force. A constant-share/expanded-share analysis shows how much of the numerical growth in the female labor force resulted from the growth in the nation's population and how much resulted from changes in women's share of the job market. An examination of the proportion of women employed in "female" jobs provides a clearer picture of the degree to which the labor-market experience of women has differed from or approximated that of men. In many ways the expanded public roles of women are rooted in economic forces quite independent of organized feminism. But, by the same token, these expanded roles required adjustment of women's political and social roles to keep pace.

Finally, this book assumes that because American society is pluralistic, women have not had a common shared experience. There never has been, nor is there now, an "American woman." Among Anglo-American women, the life experiences of working-class women differed from those of the middle class whose values set the norms for American society. Special attention is given to the lives of minority women—black women, to be sure, but also those of Hispanic, Asian, and American Indian heritage. These women, too, were Americans, but their lives were often guided by values that differed substantially from those of middle-class Anglo-American woman. They often bore a dual burden of balancing their efforts to improve their lot as members of an ethnic or racial minority with their desire to expand their roles as women. As a result, feminism developed many faces.

As with any broad historical study, this work draws on the monographic studies of scores of scholars, as my footnotes and bibliography attest. I wish to express special thanks to my colleague Marvin Fletcher for his insightful reading of the sections treating minority populations; to my son Joseph for lending his expertise in the sections treating legal and constitutional issues; to Judy Daso and her staff at the Ohio University Library for expediting access to government publications; and to George Hinkle for introducing me to the techniques of computer graphics. Last, but not least, I am especially grateful to Andrea McCarrick of Harcourt Brace Jovanovich for the meticulous care with which she exercised her editorial skills and to Amy Krammes for her sound judgment in the selection of the illustrations. My thanks also go to Martha Berlin, production editor; Diane Pella, designer; Schamber Richardson, production manager; and Maggie Porter, art editor. For the sins of omission or commission that survive, I must plead *mea culpa*.

Robert L. Daniel

Contents

Preface   vii
List of Figures   xvi
Introduction   1
    Notes   3

CHAPTER 1   APPROACHING THE FIRST HOUR   4

The Heritage of Woman's Place   4
The Black Community   9
    Political Status   9
    Social Status   10
    Access to Education   11
    The Black Community 1900 to 1920   13
The Heritage Challenged   15
    Charlotte Perkins Gilman   15
    Sigmund Freud   17
    Margaret Sanger   18
    The New Woman   19
Ideals and Practices: 1920   21
    Political–Legal Status   22
    Economic Status   23
    Supply and Demand   27
    Family Status   31
The Momentum of Change   33
    Social Feminists   33
    Suffrage Secured   35
Notes   41

CHAPTER 2   ENTERING THE FESTIVAL: THE 1920S   47

The First Hour   47
Equality Versus Protection   51

Flappers Frustrate   55
From Peasant to Proletarian   61
White Collar, Blue Collar   63
   A Rising Demand   64
   Supply Meets Demand   70
Access to Equality   77
Notes   81

CHAPTER 3   THE TRAUMA OF DEPRESSION:
                THE 1930S   86

Woman's Place   87
"Stolen Jobs"   92
Interracialism Versus Separatism   108
Education   110
Political Visibility   113
Notes   117

CHAPTER 4   WAR AND PEACE: THE 1940S   122

Rosie the Riveter: The War Years   122
   Wartime Demand   124
   Black Women in Wartime   125
   Wartime Supply   128
Rosie Remains: The Postwar Years   130
   Postwar Demand   132
   Postwar Supply   135
Public Policy   137
Education   145
Redefining Woman's Place   150
Notes   156

CHAPTER 5   MINORITY WOMEN TO 1950   160

The Jewish Community   161
   The Judaic Heritage   161
   The Reform Community   162
   The Orthodox Community   164
Asian Americans   167
   The Chinese American Community   168
   Japanese Americans: Issei and Nisei   171

American Indians   174
Hispanic Americans   177
Notes   182

CHAPTER 6   ENCOUNTERING THE MYSTIQUE: THE 1950S   185

An Accelerated Demand   185
A Transformed Supply   191
Rise of the "Feminine Mystique"   197
Political Roles   207
A Differentiated Education   213
Black Women   217
Other Americans   221
   Hispanic Americans   222
   Asian Americans   225
   American Indians   228
   The Jewish Community   229
Notes   231

CHAPTER 7   A NEW FRONTIER FOR WOMEN: THE 1960S   236

Black Revolution   237
Black Family   244
Other Minority Women   247
   Hispanic Americans   247
   Asian Americans   249
   American Indians   251
Equality Entices   256
   Equal Pay   257
   Civil Rights: Title VII   258
Work Proliferates   263
   The Rising Demand   264
   The Escalating Supply   266
Education in the Sixties   276
Notes   282

CHAPTER 8 THE REFORMULATION OF FEMINISM: THE 1960S 288

Friedan and the Moderates   289
   Diagnosis and Prescription   290
   The National Organization of Women   293
Radical Feminism   295
   The New Left Connections   295
   Juliet Mitchell: Woman's Estate   297
   Radical Feminists Organize   299
   Germaine Greer   302
   Shulamith Firestone   303
Black Feminism   305
   Black Liberation   305
   Black Feminists   306
Chicana Feminism   308
Sexual Liberation   309
   Anatomy and Destiny   313
   The Lesbian Connection   314
Evolving Sex Roles   316
Notes   319

CHAPTER 9 THE PURSUIT OF EQUALITY: THE 1970S 323

Reform by Amendment: The ERA   323
   Griffiths Proposes   324
   Ervin Opposes   324
Feminism and the Family   326
   Child Care   327
   Reproductive Control   328
   Abortion   329
Feminism Challenged   332
   International Women's Year   334
   Schlafly's Positive Woman   339
Reform by Statute   341
   Reform by Congress   341
   Marriage and Family Law   342
   Terms of Work   345
   Insurance, Pensions, and Taxes   347
   Criminal Law   348
   Political Status   351
Notes   353

CHAPTER 10   THE WINDS OF CHANGE:
                    THE 1970s   356

The Collegiate Majority   356
An Unprecedented Demand   364
    White-collar Occupations   366
    Blue-collar Occupations   367
    Service Workers   368
    Black Women   369
    Hispanic Women   370
    Other Americans   373
    Occupational Shares   374
A Plenteous Supply   377
    Marital Status   377
    Age   380
    Educational Attainment   380
    Labor Elasticity   382
Notes   383

CHAPTER 11   THE PRESENT HOUR: RETROSPECT
                    AND PROSPECT   387

The Character of Womanhood   387
The Character of the Family   390
Equality in the Classroom   400
Civil Rights and Privileges   404
    Abortion Rights   407
    The Shifting Debate   410
    The Expanding Presence   413
All Profitable Employments   416
    Birth Cohorts   417
    Segmented Labor Market   418
    The Meaning of Work   420
Comparable Worth   422
Notes   426

Key to Abbreviations   432

Bibliography   433

Index   463

List of Figures

1-1   Proportion of White Women by Age, 1900 and 1920   **27**
1-2   Labor Force by Industry, 1900 and 1920   **29**
1-3   LFPR for Women by Age Group, 1900 and 1920   **30**
2-1   Industrial Distribution of Labor Force, 1900–1980   **66**
2-2   Changes in Demand for Female Workers, 1920–1930   **67**
2-3   Marital Status of Female Population, 1920–1930   **73**
2-4   LFPR for All Women by Age, 1920 and 1930   **74**
2-5   LFPR for Women by Race and Age, 1920 and 1930   **75**
3-1   Proportion of White Women by Age, 1930 and 1940   **93**
3-2   Number of Children by Race, Under 5 Years Old, Per 1,000 Women 20 to 44 Years Old, 1880–1940   **94**
3-3   Proportion of Youths and Elderly Females by Race and Age, 1900–1950   **95**
3-4   LFPR for Women by Race and Age, 1930 and 1940   **96**
3-5   LFPR for Women by Birth Cohorts and Age, 1870–1960   **98**
3-6   Gainful Workers by Occupation and Sex, 1930–1940   **100**
3-7   Changes in Demand for Female Workers, 1930–1940   **101**
3-8   "Female" Occupations, 1940   **103**
4-1   Estimated Female Employment by Age, 1941 and 1945   **129**
4-2   Changes in Demand for Female Workers, 1940–1950   **133**
4-3   Female Labor Force by Marital Status and Age of Children, 1950   **136**
4-4   Employed Black Women by Occupation, 1940 and 1950   **138**
4-5   Percentage Distribution of Employed Women by Occupation and Race, 1950   **139**
6-1   Female Labor Force by Occupation, 1950 and 1960   **186**
6-2   Changes in Demand for Female Workers, 1950–1960   **187**
6-3   Major "Female" Occupations, 1950 and 1960   **190**
6-4   Female Population by Age Groups, 1950 and 1960   **192**
6-5   Marital Status of the Female Population, 1950 and 1960   **193**
6-6   LFPR for Women by Marital Status and Age of Children, 1950–1980   **194**
6-7   LFPR for Women by Marital Status and Age, 1950–1960   **195**
6-8   Women with Work Experience by Extent of Employment, 1950–1983   **196**
6-9   Rate of First Marriages and Divorces for Women Age 14 to 44 Years, 1921–1977   **205**
6-10   Fertility Rate by Race, 1940–1980   **206**
7-1   Change in Employment by Occupational Group, 1960–1970 and 1970–1980   **263**

7-2   Female Labor Force by Occupation, 1960 and 1970   **265**

7-3   Changes in Demand for Female Workers, 1960–1970   **267**

7-4   LFPR of All Women by Age, 1940–1980   **270**

7-5   Occupational Distribution by Race and Ethnic Group, 1960 and 1970   **272**

7-6   Percent of Working Women Employed 50–52 Weeks Per Year by Marital Status and Age, 1959 and 1969   **274**

7-7   LFPR for Women 18 Years and Over by Years of School Completed   **275**

10-1   Labor Force by Industry, 1970 and 1980   **365**

10-2   Occupational Distribution of Women, 1970 and 1980   **366**

10-3   Occupational Distribution of Women by Race, 1972 and 1980   **369**

10-4   LFPR for Women by Ethnic Origin, 1980   **371**

10-5   Changes in Demand for Female Workers, 1970–1980   **375**

10-6   LFPR of Women by Marital Status and Age, 1970 and 1980   **378**

10-7   Work Experience of Wives and Husbands, 1981   **383**

Introduction

Numerous historians, from Arthur Maier Schlesinger, Sr., to Gerda Lerner, have remonstrated against "the pall of silence" with which historians have shrouded the "services and achievements" of American women. Long denied a share in the "transmission and exercise of power," women have remained largely invisible to most historians. The effort to reconstruct the female past has been termed "women's history."[1]

But what is women's history? Historians are not agreed, and scholarly efforts have exhibited little unanimity in approach or content. Most of the earliest works were compensatory efforts to find "missing women" and fit them into the empty spaces of traditional history. This approach—dating to the nineteenth century—involved assembling collections of women's "contributions." Uncritical toward their sources and their criteria for selection, the authors tended to praise anything women had done. The resulting work, as Gerda Lerner has noted, was "topically narrow, predominantly descriptive, and generally devoid of interpretation." This early work was especially flawed in that it had a thoroughly white middle-class Anglo-Saxon orientation. Women who were black, Indian, Hispanic, or Asian, as well as white women who were immigrants or of the working class, continued to be invisible.[2]

Beginning with the collectively authored *History of the Woman Suffrage Movement,* women's history has been preoccupied with the woman's rights movement. Eleanor Flexner's classic, *Century of Struggle,* (1959), reinforced a view that the central theme of women's history was the decades-long campaign for the suffrage and for related political and legal rights. Flexner regarded political citizenship as "a vital step toward achieving human dignity and the recognition that [women], too, were endowed with the faculty of reason, the power of judgment, the capacity for social responsibility." Recognizing that women's history had other, nonpolitical dimensions, Flexner focused attention on women's struggle for expanded access to education and the movement out of the home and into factories. She sketched the activities of middle-class women's clubs, as well as those of working-class women in the trade union movement. Furthermore, she included black women as an element of women's history.[3]

Numerous historians have accorded the center stage of women's history to an economic interpretation. "The issue of earning a living," William Henry Chafe argued, "has been central to the definition of mass culture and feminine responses." Indeed, much of the rationale for exploring women's entrance into the labor force derived from a conviction that the suffrage amendment had "a negligible impact" on the status of women. As Carl Degler viewed it, the industrial revolution of the the nineteenth century had provided "the impetus to women's aspirations for equality of opportunity" and "carried through the first stage in the changing position of women—the removal of legal and customary barriers to women's full participation in the activities of the world." This point was challenged, however, by Lois Banner who saw industrialization as but one of a number of forces—urbanization, changing attitudes toward sex and marriage, the growing power of mass media, expansion of the economy, two world wars, depressions, and technological advances—that shaped the status of women. Nevertheless, the economic role, so important to men, operated differently for women who shifted readily from one role to another at different stages in their lives. In this connection it is essential to distinguish among their "economic status, family status, and political-legal status." What this means, as Leila Rupp reminds us, is that as there is no "homogeneous group of 'women,'" so industrialization has meant different things for different women depending on class, race, ethnicity, age, marital status, and place of residence.[4]

Feminists and Marxist-feminists have done much to broaden the conceptual framework of women's history. Under the influence of feminism, historians of women, irrespective of ideological orientation, have argued that the female experience must be considered in relation to male experiences. Thus, while examining the past in terms of traditional time periods, the historian should explain why women have a "different historical experience from men." In particular, this approach makes sex "as fundamental to the analysis of the social order as other classifications, such as class and race." To make sex a social category assumes that women form a distinct social group and that the invisibility of women in traditional history is not to be ascribed to inherent female nature. Whereas traditional Marxism embraced a deterministic doctrine of class struggle, Marxist-feminists held that it was one thing to use tools of class analysis, "another to maintain that women are a class." In reordering their ideas, these Marxist-feminists argued that "notions of caste and minority group are not productive when applied to women." "Clearly the minority psychology of women, like their caste status and quasi-class oppression, has to be traced to the universally distinguishing features of all women, namely their sex."[5]

In arguing that women experience the world about them in different terms than men, feminists have argued, first, that it would be worthwhile "to distinguish the ideas society holds at any given moment in regard to woman's 'proper place' from what was actually woman's status at that time." Accordingly, historians have been led to explore the domestic world of women and to examine the family as a basic unit of analysis. A study of the life cycle provides an especially useful tool for analyzing female roles according to age and marital grouping. Still another related set of topics growing out of sexuality includes prostitution, rape, homosexuality, illegitimacy, and the control of reproduction.[6]

The content of women's history, then, has been broadened by the concerns of the feminist movement of the 1960s and 1970s. The conceptual framework for the systematic study of women's history is still evolving. As one element of women's studies, women's history addresses a wider range of concerns than conventional political and economic history. Further, it has prompted a reassessment of the past, yielding new interpretations of old issues. While the evidence is not all in, a trial balance is in order.

NOTES

[1] Arthur Maier Schlesinger, *New Viewpoints in American History* (New York: Macmillan, 1922), 126. Gerda Lerner, "New Approaches to the Study of Women in American History," *Journal of Social History* 3 (1969): 53. Gerda Lerner, *Teaching Women's History* (Washington: American Historical Association, 1981), 2–3.

[2] Lerner, "New Approaches," 53.

[3] Elizabeth Cady Stanton, Susan B. Anthony, and Matilda J. Gage, eds., *The History of the Woman Suffrage Movement,* 6 vols. (Rochester and New York: 1881–1922). Eleanor Flexner, *Century of Struggle: The Woman's Rights Movement in the United States* (New York: Atheneum, 1968[1959]), xiii.

[4] William Henry Chafe, *The American Woman* (New York: Oxford, 1972), ix; David M. Kennedy, "Review, The American Woman by William Henry Chafe," *JAH** 60 (1973): 493. Carl N. Degler, "Revolution Without Ideology: The Changing Place of Women in America," *Daedalus* 93 (Spring 1964): 654. Lois W. Banner, *Women in Modern America: A Brief History* (New York: Harcourt Brace Jovanovich, 1974), vi; Lerner, "New Approaches," 60. Leila J. Rupp, "Reflections on Twentieth-Century American Women's History," *Reviews in American History* 9 (June 1981): 276.

[5] For Marxist-feminists see Margaret Benston, "The Political Economy of Women's Liberation," *Monthly Review* 21 (Sept. 1969): 13–25; and Sheila Rowbotham, *Woman's Consciousness, Man's World* (Middlesex: Pelican, 1973). Joan Kelly-Gadol, "The Social Relation of the Sexes: Methodological Implications of Women's History," *Signs* 1 (1976): 812–14.

[6] Lerner, "New Approaches," 61–62.

* See p. 432 for a list of abbreviations used throughout the Notes and Bibliography.

1
Approaching the First Hour

Anticipating the adoption of the Nineteenth Amendment, Margaret Dreier Robins, a leading feminist, looked forward to the event as marking "the first hour in history" for women. After centuries of disabilities and discrimination, women were "coming into the labor and festival of life on equal terms with men." Long restricted to second-class citizenship, women were on the point of attaining "virtually the same rights as men." Finally on August 26, 1920, the suffrage amendment was ratified; the "first hour" had arrived.[1]

Before evaluating the experiences of women as they entered "the festival of life," an examination of the expectations and experiences of women in 1900 is in order. First, we need an overview of the value system that shaped woman's place in the social order. Second, we need to take note of woman's roles in order to get a measure of the gap between society's ideals and its practices. Third, a review of the major activities that had absorbed the energies of woman since the start of the century provides a measure of the momentum and direction of change that women were experiencing.[2]

THE HERITAGE OF WOMAN'S PLACE

The ideological base that defined woman's proper sphere in 1900 had a lineage that included the Cult of True Womanhood and the Victorian

Lady, but most fundamental was the Judaic-Christian heritage. The creation story in Genesis invoked divine sanction for woman's subordinate role. God created Adam; then as an afterthought He fashioned Eve as Adam's helpmate. For disobeying His order, God punished Eve and all women with the pain of childbirth and banished the couple from the Garden. In spelling out the meanings and disabilities of womanhood, the Mosaic law enjoined the husband to leave his father and mother and "cleave unto his wife." Moses' injunction was that: "he shall rule over thee." Woman's sexuality was especially suspect. Menstruation was unclean: following the birth of a child, she was regarded as unclean—for 40 days if a boy, 80 days if a girl—and forbidden to touch a hallowed thing. As a sign of her restricted sphere, she had to be veiled in the presence of strangers. The family described by the Old Testament was patriarchal. Yet there were compensatory aspects of the Mosaic tradition—husbands were to love their wives; both were to forgo sexual relations outside the marriage bed.[3]

The Christian tradition refined and softened the ideal of a husband-dominated family. Jesus set an example by treating women with respect. The Apostle Paul, the first great interpreter of Christ's teachings, taught that in the eyes of God the souls of women were indistinguishable from those of men: "You are all one in Christ Jesus." Women—who had been excluded from Judaic religious ceremonies except as auditors—were admitted to the sacraments of the Christian church and could serve as deaconesses, the lowest order of church office. But Paul also decreed a separate sphere for women. Within the Church, he excluded them from the priesthood; within the family, he subordinated them to their husbands. In marriage the husband and wife became one flesh, and Paul made it clear that the husband was that one. He reaffirmed the Mosaic proscriptions on extramarital and homosexual sex. Since marriage was "for life," remarriage by a surviving spouse was permitted. Recognizing that husbands and wives did not always live happily everafter, he represented as God's decree "that the wife depart not from the husband (but should she depart let her remain unmarried or else reconciled to her husband): and that the husband leave not the wife." While he reluctantly endorsed separation, he prohibited divorce.[4]

Woven into the fabric of European culture over a period of sixteen centuries, these ideas provided the cornerstone for the new society that English colonists fashioned in the New World. As the Reformation was still underway, the puritan colonists, while accepting most of the Pauline tradition, introduced a fundamental alteration. In England, The Anglican church made policy regarding marriage and the family, but the puritan colonies, in recognition that marriage was "common to all men, whether Christian or heathen," left marriage and family matters to the government. Thus, while puritan leaders frowned on divorce, they acquiesced in letting civil law provide for divorce. In colonies controlled by Anglicans, the older traditions continued. But whether puritan or Anglican, the colonies insisted on monogamous marriage, restricted sexual relations to husband and wife, and established the wife as subordinate to her husband. Her place was in the home with her children and her husband. However, an integral part of her domesticity involved the production for home consumption of a broad variety of goods and services that later would be purchased in the marketplace. No less important, these ideas about woman's place were incorporated into statute law. Bigamy, adultery, fornication, and homosexuality were punished. The law presumed that in marriage, the couple were one and the wife's identity was submerged in that of her husband. While an adult single woman, a divorced woman, or a widow had a legal identity of her own, the married woman did not. She could not own property in her own name, make a contract or will in her own name, or sue or be sued in her own name.[5]

In 1900, woman's place and her roles were in flux. The traditional value system operated in an agrarian society. In rural society, however, there was a sexual division of work. Husbands worked outside—plowing, planting, and harvesting; wives worked inside caring for the house and children and engaging in domestic industries. In emergencies and at harvest time wives worked in the fields as well. The few males who were craftsmen or merchants typically carried on their work at home. Seldom out of calling distance from each other, even when engaged in different tasks, husbands and wives shared a common set of social contacts and experiences.[6]

The factory mode of production, the beginnings of urbanization, and the rise of an urban middle class provoked profound changes. First, it transferred the production of goods out of the home, greatly altering the relationship between husband and wife. While his workplace moved to the factory, store, or office, she remained isolated within the home. As he acquired a circle of male acquaintances at work, she developed a circle of women friends in the neighborhood. As he ceased to share in training his sons in a craft or as farmers, she shouldered increasing responsibility for mothering the children. As the husband's economic role was greatly augmented, the wife's was diminished. As he assumed the support of the family, she became his dependent.[7]

In this new economic order, because wage rates did not invariably enable working-class husbands to support their families, wives and children had to enter the labor force. Typically women began producing the goods in factories that they previously had made at home, perpetuating the older sexual division of labor. As society thought it unseemly for an adult woman to work alongside males other than her father or husband, employers assigned women to work with other women, men to work with other men, thus reinforcing the sexual division of labor. On the assumption that a woman secured her primary support from her father or husband, employers paid women less than men for the same or comparable work.[8]

By contrast, the new mode of production enabled a middle-class husband to support his family in comfort. The result was "the modern American family" in which marriage was based on the affection and mutual respect of the partners. The primary role of the wife became the care of the children and the maintenance of the home, within which she acquired an increasing measure of autonomy. Free, or isolated, from the daily temptations of business, she was viewed as the moral superior of her husband, though she remained his legal and social inferior. Compared to farm wives, whose economic roles remained relatively unchanged, the wife of the urban, middle-class male was a lady of leisure. The value system that directed the lives of these urban, middle-class women has been named the Cult of True Womanhood. Designed to make her life meaningful, it reaffirmed or redefined older traditional values.[9]

The True Woman was pious. This was the "core of woman's virtue, the source of her strength." She inculcated Christian values in her children; at the end of the day she intercepted her husband, frazzled by the dog-eat-dog ethics of the evolving business world, and helped him recover his moral equilibrium before he set forth the next morning. In the name of piety, women were permitted a limited public role in religion-related organizations.

She was pure. Isolated from her husband hours on end, she had to assume responsibility for her chastity. According to the conventional wisdom, sex was for men to enjoy, for women to endure. Society expected her to suppress all outward evidence of her sexuality. Her purity went beyond the sexual, for, as Sarah Josepha Hale pronounced, women were "God's appointed agents of MORALITY," with a responsibility to set the standards for the family and to refine man's "human affections and elevate his moral feelings."

She was submissive. At marriage she vowed to obey her husband, and she accepted expectations, without protest, that she would subordinate her interests and preferences to those of her husband. While she was not his chattel, her identity and status in society derived from him. Reflecting the "one flesh" view of Christian marriage, American law eradicated the separate civil existence of a woman when she married. Ironically, a society that prized individualism in males, suppressed individualism in females.

She was domestic. This was the crux of the new relationship. The Cult rationalized a doctrine of separate spheres—work for him, home for her.

Because of the state of domestic technology, housekeeping, cooking, laundering and ironing, sewing, and child care were inordinately time-consuming. As middle-class women gained relief from the more exhausting chores of housekeeping, they substituted equally time-consuming responsibilities for child care so that there was no time to pursue a role outside the home. The result so altered relationships between husband and wife as to produce a "new kind of family." By 1860 the Cult had become the norm for urban middle-class women.[10]

If the great majority of women accepted the formulations of the Cult of True Womanhood, a vocal minority did not. Meeting at Seneca Falls, New York, in 1848, a group of women and men endorsed a "Declaration of Sentiments" that challenged the limited domestic role prescribed by the Cult. First on the list was the demand for the suffrage—political equality with men. But no less important were demands for an independent legal status for married women, equal access to education, access to jobs, and divorce reform. The Declaration did not attack the family or marriage; it did envisage a marriage in which husband and wife were equal partners. Although the Declaration claimed these rights as natural rights—the same rationale that underlay the Declaration of Independence—these demands were regarded as radical.

In the period following the Civil War, traditional values were further modified to suit the needs of the Victorian Lady. Pious as ever, the lady worked through the Women's Christian Temperance Union to hasten the realization of her vision of a Christian society. Pure as ever, she supported first the Purity Crusaders who sought to suppress prostitution and then Anthony Comstock in his effort to vanquish vice. Submissive as ever, she acknowledged her husband's headship of the family, but she ruled the household. Domestic she was, but with a difference. By 1900, young women from middle-class families could enter the labor market prior to marriage, although the variety of employments thought suitable was limited, and none of the jobs—teacher, nurse, retail clerk, secretary, or telephone operator—paid well enough to permit her to support herself independently at a middle-class level of living. Few middle-class women sought careers; those who did generally had to forgo marriage.[11]

Work outside the home by a married woman remained taboo except in cases of dire economic necessity. But a slowly increasing variety of purchasable goods and services combined with the availability of domestic servants and smaller families reduced the physical burden of homemaking, enabling middle-class wives time to participate in "one of the most important sociological phenomena of the century"—the newly appearing women's clubs. And in the 1890s, middle-class women's groups lobbied for social, economic, and political reforms that touched on the lives of women, children, and family. Without sacrificing her womanhood, the Victorian wife acquired a public role not open to her grandmother's generation. Nonetheless, the place accorded the Victorian Lady was far more limited than the place envisaged by the Seneca Falls Declaration.[12]

THE BLACK COMMUNITY

Black women in 1900 had a heritage that differed substantially from that of Anglo-American women. Their ancestors had come from Africa not Europe. Uprooted from their "cultural and family moorings," they arrived in America in chains to be sold as slaves. Black values, customs, traditions, and culture were pushed aside as white owners gave them new "American" names and forced them to use English, to dress in the European mode, to eat strange foods, to live in assigned shelters, and to perform whatever tasks their owners requested of them. As slaves—male or female—they could not own property, make contracts, or sue or be sued. Nor could they contract a legally binding marriage; as a slave, the black woman had no rights that her master was obligated to respect. Overall, slavery had "a crippling effect" on the establishment of normal patterns of family life either by Anglo-American or African standards. The great majority of mature black women in 1900 had been born slaves; only the children were likely to have mothers (or fathers) who had been born free. Nonetheless, the black community had put down roots: their numbers exceeded 9,000,000— 90 percent of whom lived in the South.[13]

Political Status

At the start of the century, the black community was still struggling to fashion a new set of values. The black woman faced severe limits on her political, social, and economic roles that put her at a disadvantage vis-a-vis white women—limits that were tied to her race as much as to her sex. The political position of blacks, men and women, was deteriorating. In their bid for political power in the 1890s, the Populists had made the blacks— long subjected to a variety of informal discriminatory practices—scape-goats for the South's economic troubles. Once in office, the Populists mandated racial segregation in public accommodations and services and adopted a variety of legislative ploys to disfranchise the blacks. In 1896 in *Plessy* v. *Ferguson,* the U.S. Supreme Court acquiesced in racial segregation with its "separate but equal" doctrine. Cities and states vied with one another in curbing the political roles of blacks by use of grandfather clauses, poll taxes, and literacy tests to deny the black male access to the vote or to public office. For black women in 1900, the constitutional guarantees of equal protection of the laws were often empty phrases.[14]

Social Status

At the social level, black women—and their menfolk and children— were confronted at every turn by a broad range of informal social practices that excluded them from participating fully in the social and cultural life of the community. They were required to use separate drinking fountains and restrooms and were denied access to restaurants, theaters, or hotels. Most doctors and hospitals refused to serve them. Interracial marriage, a measure of the process of integration and social assimilation, was barred by law. The realities of her political impotence meant that while a black woman could file charges if she were physically or sexually assaulted, white authorities were not likely to take her complaints seriously. Many white males regarded the black woman as fair game for sexual exploitation. Though white males were not adverse to sexual liaisons with black women, the black man who made sexual advances to a white woman put his life at risk.[15]

As in the white community, the husband–wife family was the norm for the black community. Formal marriages, as opposed to consensual marriages, were becoming more common. The proportion of black children born out of wedlock was subsiding, but the rate was far higher than in white society. The fact that black women bore their first child at a relatively young age and most single mothers were under 30, strongly suggests that most of these single mothers eventually married, following a pattern with long historical antecedents. The research of Herbert Gutman amply documents that in the early twentieth century, "nine in ten blacks lived in households that had at their core two or more members of a black nuclear family." A husband or father was present in most households: fathers who were in unskilled occupations headed families as frequently as did fathers who were artisans or who pursued middle-class occupations.[16]

Nevertheless, the black woman was more likely than the white woman to be husbandless: she was three times more likely to be divorced and was half again as likely to be a widow. Widows at least 40 years old headed most of the father-absent households. The proportion of female heads of family increased as blacks moved from the farms to towns and cities of the South. As women were more mobile than men, serious imbalances of the sexes occurred in the urban communities—the average was 118 women per 100 men—and seriously reduced their prospects for marriage and family life. The tradition of the extended family in which mothers, daughters, and sisters shared one another's burdens, however, provided means for care of children in fatherless families and emotional support for the female heads of household. Neither in the rural South nor in the northern cities was an extended, matriarchal family—the mother, her daughter, and the daughter's children—common.[17]

Given the adverse conditions that blacks had faced in the post–Civil War period, the black family in 1900 was a surprisingly supportive institution over which the individual black had a degree of control. That the incidence of female-headed households was higher in the black than in the white community reflected not so much the destructive force of the slave heritage as the hostile environment within which blacks functioned— the difficulties faced by black males in attempting to support their families and the higher level of violence to which black males were exposed.[18]

While black women faced more restricted economic opportunities than Anglo-American women, they did not live in a homogeneous society. The black community, like the white, was differentiated by socio-economic classes. Living conditions were stark for the great majority of black women. Their homes reflected the abject poverty in which they lived. Fully three out of four women lived in the rural South, raising a family as best they could in a one- or two-room house. Glass windows were an exception, so that there was little light and almost no ventilation. "Stale sickly odors" assaulted the visitor. Roofs leaked. There were either "no privies or bad ones"; there were poor facilities for washing the face and hands, none for other parts of the body. Facilities for preparing food were primitive.[19]

Perhaps one family in five lived in a "village" of at least 1,000 persons. The homes ranged from structures "rudely constructed of logs or boards" to frame houses with two or three rooms and a porch. Even cities such as Atlanta, Charleston, Savannah, and Washington offered few amenities. A fifth of the urban populace lived in slums, a crowded home "14 or 15 feet square and 8 or 10 feet high. The furniture is scarce—a bed or two, a few chairs, a table, a stove or fireplace, a trunk or chest." Water was obtained from a well or a street hydrant; several homes shared an outhouse. For a very small elite—families of teachers, mail carriers, merchants, and professional men—there was a degree of comfort.[20]

Access to Education

As compared with white women, black women were disadvantaged in terms of education. Reconstruction and Bourbon governments, hard-pressed to create a public school system for white children, begrudgingly supported segregated elementary schools for blacks. In 1900 approximately one third of the nonwhite females between 5 and 19 were enrolled, a marked improvement over the 10 percent who went to school a generation earlier. Even this modest gain in access to school reduced the level of illiteracy from 79.9 percent to 44.5 percent during the last three decades of the nineteenth century. But it meant that as of 1900, most of the older black women and many of the younger ones were ill-prepared to compete politically, economically, or socially with women of the white community.[21]

While blacks slowly secured access to elementary schools, the white South did little to enable blacks to secure a secondary education. As late as 1920 there were but 62 public, black high schools in the South; the number of students, less than 20,000. The most significant developments lay in private schools, such as Hampton, Calhoun, Penn, and Tuskegee. Hampton, the model, aimed at a "comprehensive system of moral and industrial education" to "train these people not only to make a living but to live honestly and decently." Initially boys worked on the school farm a few hours every day; later on they worked two days a week. Girls spent four days at classwork and two days at paid labor in the school kitchen and laundry; they made and mended clothing and took care of the students' quarters. In time the school added a cooking class and kitchen–garden instruction. In 1913 all the trade courses at Hampton were placed on a high school level.[22]

Schools on the Hampton pattern were founded in Alabama and South Carolina. The Calhoun School in Lowndes County, Alabama, founded by Charlotte R. Thorn and Mabel Dillingham, operated primary and secondary departments and taught the trades and agriculture. Like Hampton, it trained girls to be homemakers. The Penn School in South Carolina, founded at the end of the Civil War, originally emphasized academics. Coming under the spell of Hampton in 1890, it reorganized as an agricultural, industrial, and normal high school.[23]

By far the most important of the black secondary schools, Tuskegee Institute was founded by Booker T. Washington, a graduate of Hampton. At the turn of the century, most of the pupils were either teachers or persons preparing to teach. Concerned with designing a curriculum that would enable the southern black to achieve a place of dignity in an unfriendly, even hostile environment, Washington pursued a policy of "learn, work, earn respect." As one aspect of this, "the gospel of the toothbrush," he taught his charges cleanliness and self-reliance. He resisted "the craze for Greek and Latin learning" and insisted that students combine the adademic with mastering the techniques of modern farming and skilled trades. After 1900 the emphasis shifted to vocational instruction, which was conducted at a high school level; in 1920 a college program was added. Every girl took classes in domestic science and in "women's industries" regardless of her other studies. These black schools did not aim at directing female students away from conventional paths; they did aim at equipping them to provide leadership to their own people.[24]

Booker T. Washington experienced substantial success in his efforts to prepare rural, southern black youth to compete in American society. As Tuskegee added to the pool of trained black teachers, the level of illiteracy among blacks dropped, reaching the 30 percent level by 1920. At the same time, farm ownership among blacks increased four times more rapidly than the black population. Washington, himself, wielded much political influence as the person the white community was most likely to consult in regard to policy issues affecting the black community.[25]

The Black Community 1900 to 1920

Despite the leadership of Booker T. Washington, the political position of blacks—men and women—was deteriorating in 1900. Black males bore the direct thrust of disfranchisement as no southern state in 1900 permitted any woman to vote in state or national elections. But black women were affected indirectly as their membership in a politically powerless class was made explicit. They suffered, too, as segregation in schools and in the work place narrowly restricted them, and their children, in the development and utilization of their innate talents.

Given the limitations they faced in the South, blacks migrated to northern cities. Even in 1900, Philadelphia and New York City were home to more blacks than any city of the old Confederacy except New Orleans. While the black population of the South increased 12 percent between 1900 and 1920, the number of blacks in the Northeast increased by 65 percent and in the Midwest by over 50 percent. In part, the attraction of the city was the hope of "more and better work." But "of signal importance" to parents was the chance to get a better education for their children. Life in the northern cities was not easy. William E. B. DuBois noted that typically black men migrated north first, their families following later. While some blacks succeeded, urban life overwhelmed many. Housing was costly; the jobs, not secure. Many blacks lacked marketable skills. Caught between low wages and high rents, many sent their wives and children back South; others, unable to support their families, deserted. Illegitimacy rates were high. Certainly the position of black women in northern cities was far different than it had been in the South. The pace of urban life was strange. As newcomers, they were often resented.[26]

The rising tide of racist rhetoric, which carried Populist politicians to victory, exposed the black community to mob violence. Individuals, usually males accused of offenses against whites, were murdered by lynch mobs, and some 2,500 blacks lost their lives in this fashion during the last 16 years of the nineteenth century. But at times the entire black community was the target of mob violence. To a handful of young northern blacks, Booker T. Washington seemed ineffective and too accommodating to the white community. Rejecting Washington's leadership, they met at Niagara Falls, Canada, in June 1905 under the leadership of William E. B. DuBois and William M. Trotter and drafted a program demanding full manhood suffrage, "now, henceforth and forever." They demanded that "discrimination in public accommodation . . . cease." They vowed to "fight against any proposal to educate black boys and girls simply as servants and underlings, or simply for the use of other people. They have a right to know, to think, to aspire."[27]

In the aftermath of a particularly vicious riot in Springfield, Illinois, in 1908, William English Walling and Oswald Garrison Villard took the lead in fashioning the National Association for the Advancement of Colored People (NAACP) to defend black rights in the courts. The national officers were white with one exception, the director of publicity, W. E. B. DuBois. Black women such as Mary Church Terrell and Ida Wells-Barnett participated in the organizational meeting, Terrell becoming a member of the executive committee. The NAACP program called for anti-lynching laws, legislation to end debt slavery among sharecroppers, enfranchisement of blacks, abolition of injustices in criminal procedures based on color, equitable distribution of funds for public education, abolition of segregation, and equality of work opportunity.[28]

A year later, northern community leaders, black and white, joined forces to create the National Urban League. Working chiefly in northern cities, the Urban League operated community centers, day nurseries, well-baby clinics, and child-placement services. It also undertook social casework, dealing with problems of delinquency, illegitimacy, unemployment, illness and old age. Special attention was given to persuading employers to make available more jobs and better jobs to blacks.[29]

While the NAACP and the Urban League would do notable work, black women had been organized for a decade and a half. In the wake of a particularly brutal lynching in 1892, Ida Wells-Barnett and Mary Church Terrell organized campaigns against lynching. Wells-Barnett carefully researched her cases and fearlessly mounted a campaign that had a direct impact in stemming the number of killings. Subsequently, several dozen black women's clubs joined forces in 1896 as the National Association of Colored Women (NACW), marking "a watershed" in the history of black women. The counterpart of the General Federation of Women's Clubs, the NACW represented local groups from Denver and Omaha to Boston and New York and to New Orleans. Its leaders included Victoria Earle Matthews, whose White Rose Working Girl's Home was a precursor of the Urban League; Susan McKinney, the leading black woman medical doctor; Margaret Murray Washington, a leading black educator (and wife of Booker T. Washington); and Josephine St. Pierre Ruffin, suffragist editor of *The Woman's Era*. The NACW was concerned with both the status of black people and of black women. It was both feminist and suffragist. By the time the NAACP held its organizational meeting, NACW clubs had a record of accomplishment in the area of child care. By World War I, the NACW represented 50,000 women and over 1,000 clubs.[30]

With the coming of World War I, conditions for blacks changed substantially. The ravages of the boll weevil, the westward drift of the cotton economy, and the drought of 1916 and 1917 pressed southern blacks to look for new opportunities; at the same time, the drafting of white workers, the curtailment of immigration, and wartime prosperity forced northern employers to recruit blacks. The wartime migration moved 250,000 blacks out of the South. By 1920, 84 percent of the blacks were still in the South, but Harlem had become the cultural capital of black Americans.[31]

THE HERITAGE CHALLENGED

As women entered the twentieth century, serious challenges attacked one or another of the traditional views of woman's place. The result was a "vast dissolution of moral authority." Of special importance were the critiques of Charlotte Perkins Gilman, Sigmund Freud, and Margaret Sanger. At the same time, journalists, social critics, and historians identified a reformulation of values that guided a group they termed the New Woman.

Charlotte Perkins Gilman

At a time the organized woman's movement was focusing on the suffrage as the means to enlarge women's sphere of action, Gilman defined women's issues in economic terms. The question that most interested her was "how to achieve full equality for women in an industrial society." Following a childhood scarred by economic and psychological insecurity and a marriage marred by severe depression and terminated by divorce, she achieved independence as a writer and lecturer. Attracted to the utopian socialism of Edward Bellamy, she developed a feminist ideology that argued for female economic independence.[32]

Gilman's work, *Women and Economics* (1898), addressed the economic bondage of women to men. She argued that human beings were "the only animal species in which the female depends on the male for food, the only animal species in which the sex-relation is also an economic relation." A wife's domestic activities enabled her husband to maximize his productivity by enabling him to work without interruption. As between two women whose husbands had equal incomes, the skillful cook, thrifty shopper, and expert mother fared no better in terms of her keep than the wife who was a poor cook, careless shopper, and neglectful mother. A wife's level of living depended solely on her husband's economic position. The restrictive roles assigned to women cost society dearly "in limiting her ideas, her information, her thought-processes, and power of judgment. . . . But this is innocent in action compared with her restricted expression, the denial of the freedom to act." In fact, society's further growth would be threatened if the range of economic activity open to women were not broadened.[33]

If Gilman's economic views were radical, her views about marriage and the role of sex in marriage were conventional. "Wifehood and motherhood" she termed as "the normal status of women, and whatever is right in woman's new position must not militate against these essentials." She recognized sex as natural and needful to procreation, but she saw women as exploited through the sexual relationship. Accepting an older nineteenth-century view, she thought that frequent sexual intercourse was physically harmful. In later years she made her view explicit that sex was for procreation, not recreation. "Motherhood," she asserted, was "the common duty and the common glory of womanhood."[34]

Gilman's major contribution to feminist thought, however, was in positing ways by which a woman might fulfill her role as a wife and mother while fully realizing her humanity. The key to this lay in separating woman's role as wife and mother from her role as housekeeper and child raiser. Noting that the home had ceased to be the locus for laundering and baking, Gilman predicted: "the cook stove will follow the loom and [spinning] wheel, the wool-carder and shears." Homes would become "places to live in and love in, to rest in and play in, to be alone in and to be together in." She proposed to rationalize homemaking and child raising. Each family would have a private apartment that it would keep tidy on a day-to-day basis, but the cleaning, laundry, ironing and other household chores would be performed by professionals for pay. Meals would be prepared in community kitchens by professionals. Infants would remain with their mothers, but child care, too, would be professionalized, with preschool children cared for in community day-care centers while older children attended school. Families would benefit by receiving a higher quality of care than hitherto; wives could pursue careers along with marriage. As a contributor to her family's support, the married woman would earn a share in family management.[35]

Women and Economics promptly established Gilman as the leading intellectual of the feminist movement, and she remained so for the next two decades. *The Nation* hailed her work as "the most significant utterance on the subject [of women] since Mill's *Subjection of Woman.*" In the succeeding years she lectured widely, wrote innumerable articles, authored nine books, and edited and published *The Forerunner,* a monthly journal that treated the role of women in an industrialized society. Her work, however, was overshadowed by the attention focused on the reforms of the social feminists and the suffrage movement.[36]

Sigmund Freud

A second critique of woman's position came from Sigmund Freud whose lectures at Clark University in 1909 accorded him a forum for his ideas on the pervasive influence of sexuality on human beings. Though others—notably Richard von Krafft-Ebing, Havelock Ellis, and G. Stanley Hall—had begun a scholarly exploration of human sexuality, Freud's work was far more revolutionary and fundamental. His essay, "Civilized Sexual Morality and Modern Nervousness" (1908), advocated an "incomparably freer sexual life." Within the next five years his *Interpretation of Dreams* and *Three Contributions to the Theory of Sex* appeared in English translations. The popular press began to present him as "a wizard, a surgeon of the soul who had a secret formula for ending mental disease and restoring social efficiency overnight. . . ." But his most receptive audience consisted of the "Young Intellectuals," avante-garde literati and bohemians such as Mabel Dodge Luhan, Lincoln Steffens, and Max Eastman who used his ideas as "a spearhead in the onslaught against Puritanism." With a revolt against the genteel tradition in literature already underway, Floyd Dell, Sherwood Anderson, Theodore Dreiser, Edgar Lee Masters, and Eugene O'Neill exploited the repression of the sex drive by parental authority and social convention.[37]

By 1920 the Freudian movement was well launched, but he had yet to develop fully his theories on the Oedipus and Electra complexes or articulate fully a concept of the ego, id, and libido. In "The Psychology of Women" (1933), he suggested that, biophysiologically, women were intellectually less able than men. The task of the analyst, he argued in the 1930s, was to aid men to develop their capacities and aid women to resign themselves to their destiny. At the end of his career, Freud was certain that anatomy was destiny, but in 1920 his message had a liberating tone. In general, his work established a causal relationship between sexuality and mental health and pushed discussion of sexuality into public forums. As his ideas reached college campuses and the general public in 1920, Freud seemed to challenge the validity of traditional standards of sexual purity. In the popular version of Freud, sex was "the central and pervasive force which moved mankind. Almost every human motive was attributable to it: if you were patriotic or liked the violin, you were in the grip of sex—in a sublimated form. The first requirement of mental health was to have an uninhibited sex life."[38]

Margaret Sanger

If Freud liberated the mind in matters of sex, Margaret Higgins Sanger liberated women physiologically. From her father, a rebel and a free thinker who espoused woman's rights in public while ignoring them at home, she acquired a sensitivity to the wrongs of the world. With her husband, William Sanger—an artist and armchair socialist—she entered the intellectual circle of rebels and bohemians of Greenwich Village. The Sanger apartment became a meeting place for "Big Bill" Haywood, Eugene Debs, John Reed, Emma Goldman, and Henrietta Rodman, along with Walter Lippmann, Max Eastman, and Will Durant. "Not at all sure" that her opinions would be accepted by "this very superior group," she was a listener and a learner. She became familiar with the ideas of Karl Marx, Friedrich Nietzsche, and Sigmund Freud.[39]

As a nurse-midwife in working-class homes, Sanger was appalled that so many women risked death in abortion to avoid adding to their families. Convinced that the sex drive—expressed in large families and unwanted babies—was a more fundamental cause of individual and social malaise than economic causes, she concluded that the Marxists had missed the connections between reproduction and poverty. But neither would the economic or the political solutions of organized feminists free a woman from her "biological subservience to man. . . ." What was needed was knowledge of the means to limit the size of one's family.[40]

Her quest for an effective method of contraception led her to rummage various libraries in Boston, New York, Washington, and Paris for information. As she began her promotion of "birth control," a term she coined, her economic and political views had their roots in romantic anarchism and revolutionary Marxism. Her slogan, "No Gods, No Masters," she borrowed from the Industrial Workers of the World. She not only repudiated capitalism but the possibility of progressive reform. Like Gilman, she saw no possibility that woman suffrage could right women's wrongs, but unlike her, she rejected traditional marriage as reducing woman to a sex chattel, and she looked ahead to its transformation into a "voluntary association." Her publication, *The Woman Rebel,* discussed and advocated birth control, but it also attacked the Rockefellers, religion, and matrimony. She also challenged the portion of the Comstock Law that prohibited the mailing, transporting, or importing of all contraceptive devices and information. At this point, 1914, Sanger's objective was to enable working-class women to control their reproduction.[41]

A second trip to Europe in 1914 to 1915 sharpened her focus. Guided by Havelock Ellis, she studied the work of the Neo-Malthusian League in England and the contraceptive methods of the Rutgers Clinic in the Netherlands. She came to realize that to succeed in promoting birth control, she would have to concentrate on a rationale and on methods acceptable to the middle class and to the medical profession. Her views matured, Sanger affirmed that women had a "special sphere"—maternity, child care, and housekeeping—while men were providers. She affirmed the sexuality of women as well as of men, but in contrast to Gilman, she denied that "the sole purpose of sexual activity is procreation." Through birth control, a woman could raise sex "into another sphere, whereby it may subserve and enhance the possibility of individual and human expression." Repeatedly she affirmed that marital happiness depended to "a high degree" on sexual fulfillment.[42]

In October 1916, in emulation of the Rutgers Clinic, Sanger opened a birth-control clinic in Brooklyn in defiance of New York's Comstock Law. She was arrested, tried, and convicted. Subsequently, on appeal, the court, while upholding her conviction, held that it was permissible for licensed physicians to dispense birth-control information and devices. Ironically, in winning this substantive victory, Sanger found herself working with and for a middle-class clientele rather than for working-class women whose plight had first prompted her efforts. By 1920 she was widely known and at the threshold of a long career as publicist for birth control as a means of liberating women.[43]

The New Woman

While Gilman, Freud, and Sanger challenged the values of the Cult of True Womanhood, the growing secular tone of society further eroded those values. Piety ceased to direct personal behavior as Protestantism, from which it had derived its vigor, lost its dominant position. Some critics explicitly rejected organized religion and moral values that derived their authority from religion. More importantly, secularization substituted a concern with the appearance of respectability for concern with the substance of one's religious values. As piety lost its importance, nineteenth-century views of purity seemed quaint, if not outmoded. Contemporary critics reacted to this change in the moral climate in articles with shock headlines

*Seeking to live life to the fullest, on completing school
the New Woman secured a job and an apartment of
her own and enjoyed a period of personal
independence before she married.*

such as "Sex O'Clock in America" and "The Repeal of Reticence." In the
latter, Agnes Repplier objected to the "obsession of sex which has set us
all a-babbling about matters once excluded from the amenities of conversation." Certainly the public print explored birth control, prostitution, divorce,
and sexual morals on an unprecedented scale. "Victorianism" became an
epithet. In his analysis of the phenomenon, historian James McGovern
emphasizes the displacement of the social controls based on "face-to-face
association," in which the "norms of family, church, and small community"
usually reinforced each other.[44]

Moved by the spirit of individualism, women, particularly those just
coming of age, rejected the submissiveness of earlier generations. Structural changes in the economy greatly expanded employment opportunities

for young, single women, enabling many to enjoy a period of independence approaching that of their brothers and to dispense with "maidenly reserve." Writing in 1914, the novelist Owen Johnson described these New Women as "determined to liberate their lives and claim the same rights as their brothers." Her viewpoint was existential. "She is sure of one life only and that one she passionately desires. She wants to live that life to the fullest. . . . She wants adventure. She wants excitement. . . ." Similarly the proliferation of housekeeping appliances created a "kitchen revolution" that enabled married homemakers, especially in the upper and middle classes, to have time for out-of-the-home activities. To be sure, marriage still meant the economic dependence of the wife on her husband, but by 1920 such dependence no longer prevented a woman from enjoying a limited life of her own, independent of her husband.[45]

Rather than reject domesticity, the New Woman revalued it. Whereas the independent-minded Victorian woman had to choose between marriage with its concomitant domesticity and a career with a celibate life, the New Woman wanted to sample both marriage and a career. Most had to compromise. Completing school, she secured a job and left home for an apartment of her own. She met and dated males who were unknown to her family, but in the end she quit her job, married one of these men, and submerged herself in home and family. Helen Campbell, a staunch defender of the working girl, spoke for the great majority when she characterized the employment of married women as "fruitful of evil."[46]

How pervasive was the New Woman or her lifestyle? Certainly she was visible enough to provoke public comment. One can agree with McGovern that "women had become sufficiently active and socially independent to prefigure the 'emancipation' of the 1920s." But the New Woman whose lifestyle included "widespread" use of the automobile, attending afternoon "trots" (dances), experimenting with birth control, using cosmetics, and wearing deep décolleté dresses at the opera and restaurant was not a typical college woman, much less a high school miss. Henry F. May's assessment of the New Woman under the rubric "Cracks In the Surface" suggests the limited scale and exploratory character of her protest. *The Nation* reinforced this assessment in identifying the New Woman with the "fluttering tastes" of the Greenwich Village intellectuals. But even though a great majority of the American middle class continued to adhere to nineteenth-century views of woman's place, by 1920 those values lacked the uncritical support and relevance of earlier times.[47]

IDEALS AND PRACTICES: 1920

Whereas the concept of woman's place focuses on social ideals rooted in the often distant past, that of woman's status is concerned with the reality of their lives at a moment in time. As women filled a variety of roles, their status not only varied from role to role but varied according to their membership in a particular social, ethnic, or racial group.

Political–Legal Status

The political–legal status of women was ambiguous that August day in 1920 when Secretary of State Bainbridge Colby announced the ratification of the Nineteenth Amendment. Henceforth no state could exclude a woman from the right to vote because of her sex. But in fact many states had long permitted women to vote. As early as 1880, one woman in five could vote in school elections; by 1890, one woman in three. In 1869 Wyoming and Utah had granted woman suffrage in territorial elections, but by 1900 women in only four states could vote in state and federal elections. As the final drive for the suffrage amendment proceeded, women in state after state secured the right to vote. Some gained experience as party workers and a few as officeholders. Thus, in 1916, Jeannette Rankin, a Montana social worker, became the first woman elected to Congress. The activities of women in lobbying for the suffrage as well as for a wide spectrum of social and economic reforms suggested the development of a "petticoat hierarchy" that professional politicians dreaded.[48]

While suffragists and politicians speculated on the extent of women's power at the voting booth, the limits on their power were overlooked. Despite the Fifteenth Amendment, black males had been excluded from the suffrage by requirements—white primaries, poll taxes, and literacy tests—which would exclude black women as well. Indian, Hispanic, and Asian Americans—male and female—were almost universally excluded from participation in the political process. Although Irish and German Americans participated in local politics, immigrants of eastern or southern European origin still had too little social or economic standing to be very active politically. Foreign-born women, as well as many native-born women, were inhibited from voting because of the belief that politics was "man's business." Even among women who felt it was their civic duty to vote, the location of the polls in fire stations and saloons—places off limits to self-respecting women—constituted an impediment. While the suffrage amendment offered potential equality between the sexes at the polls and a narrowing in the differences in political status between men and women, white middle-class women were most likely to benefit immediately.[49]

In other respects, women's legal status, though measurably improved since the Seneca Falls convention in 1848, remained well behind that of men. Severe restrictions on married women's property rights, a major concern in 1848, had been removed. By 1900 in the great majority of states, a woman could hold property independently of her husband and had limited rights to make contracts and to sue and be sued in her own name. Yet "points of grievance" remained. The law still discriminated against women in terms of grounds for divorce, although these grounds had been broadened. As late as 1930, eight states did not accord a mother the status of joint guardian of her children with the same powers, rights, and duties as the children's father. Many states still withheld from women, married or single, the right to serve on juries or to hold public office. But in 1920 most women—and men—remained unaware of the degree to which the law still restricted the legal status of married women.[50]

Economic Status

The prevailing value systems in 1900 accorded women a limited economic role and a status inferior to that of men. But the propriety of work for women varied according to ethnic group, social class, age, and marital status. The economic status of the great majority of women in 1920, as Charlotte Perkins Gilman put it, depended on that of "those men to whom they are related." Society ranked men by the work they did; women, by their family affiliation. The more prestigious the work of the father or husband, the higher the status of his wife and daughters. As Thorstein Veblen pointed out, males derived psychic rewards from being able to keep their womenfolk out of the labor force. Inevitably, then, the minority of women who entered the labor force did so with a decidedly different perspective on work than that held by men. For a white, American-born middle-class miss, a "respectable" job such as teaching school was fashionable, but manual or domestic labor remained taboo. The fact that teaching, unlike manual or domestic labor, required special training served to confirm rather than question the father's middle-class status. But prior to 1920, the individualist determined to pursue a long-term professional career had to forgo marriage and motherhood. At the same time, society preferred that adult single women, divorcées, and widows attempt to support themselves rather than be public charges. For many daughters and wives of white working-class families, as well as for nonwhite women, work was a matter of economic necessity.[51]

The economic status of women in the various ethnic groups was affected by the value systems of their respective groups. When a family operated its own business and as need required, a woman of any ethnic background or marital status could work subject to the direction of her father or husband. As girls had worked as live-in domestic servants in Ireland, the Irish American community permitted them to do similar work in America or to accept factory employment. German American culture, too, allowed girls to leave home at an early age to work as live-in domestics, and Polish American values permitted women to take factory jobs as well as domestic employment. Because of the value Italian culture attached to female purity, Italian American husbands refused to permit their womenfolk to work outside the home under the direction of a nonfamily male. Restricted to employment they could pursue within their own homes, Italian American women sewed long hours at low pay, taking in laundry, or caring for boarders.[52]

For Hispanic American, Asian American, and American Indian women, work was often a matter of necessity, seldom a means of enhancing personal status. The value systems of these groups restricted these women to working within their family group. Defeated, dispirited, and socially disorganized, American Indians were desperately poor. Most Indian families subsisted on government annuities. In exceptional Indian communities, women contributed to the support of their families by pursuing traditional crafts—the Navajo by weaving, the Pueblo by potting, the Pima by basketry. Hispanic women, isolated in their barrios, produced goods and services for consumption by their own families. Many also worked alongside their husbands and children as agricultural laborers. Chinese American women worked in family enterprises, while Japanese American women joined their husbands or fathers in truck farming in California.[53]

At the economic level, most black women lived in families in which fathers and husbands had severely limited means to support the family. A great majority of males worked as farm laborers, sharecroppers, or cash tenants. The minority of urban blacks, sharing "a uniformly depressed lower-class status," were either unskilled laborers or service workers; the handful of black artisans occupied "precarious and declining positions" in all but a few urban crafts. Only a small portion of the black males held middle-class jobs such as teacher, mail carrier, merchant, or professional that would enable them to support their families from their own earnings. As a consequence, large numbers of black women grew up expecting to share in the support of their families. Because of race, black women were barred from most white-collar and the more desirable blue-collar occupations. As a result, the great majority of these women were concentrated in two occupations—field hands in the rural areas and house servants in the cities. While Anglo-Americans had always regarded field work as unfeminine, black women found that sharecropping offered a means by which "husbands and wives retained a minimal amount of control over their productive energies and those of their children on both a daily and seasonal basis." It offered the mother optimal freedom to divide her time between field and housework in terms of family needs. Further, it allowed wives and daughters a productive economic role without exposing them to "the menacing reach of white supervisors." Of all American women, black women had the highest labor force rates at every age.[54]

World War I, the dominant event of the first two decades, disrupted the lives of millions of Americans, yet its impact on either the supply of or the demand for female labor was surprisingly limited. Relative to the American Revolution or the Civil War, America's involvement in World War I lasted a short time, and most of the adjustments in the labor market were temporary expedients. To be sure, patriotic sentiments led women, who otherwise would have stayed at home, to enter the labor force, thus increasing the supply for the moment. White women who joined the labor force for the first time took unskilled or semiskilled jobs long-defined as women's jobs, chiefly in their hometowns. Some women already in the labor force shifted from one female job to another, higher-level job. A few women secured employment as skilled workers in male jobs, operating various machine tools as well as electric and oxyacetylene welding equipment. Those women taking traditional female jobs experienced little difficulty, but employment in nontraditional jobs often entailed self-exploitation, as such women felt compelled to "prove" themselves in metalworking factories and railroad yards. To do so they tolerated sexual harassment and strained themselves physically. Black women took advantage of the war to migrate from farms to southern cities and from the South to northern cities, moves with long-term consequences. To gain access to manufacturing jobs, some black women took "dirty, dangerous, and physically demanding" jobs; others took jobs vacated by white women, especially in the garment trades, government arsenals, and in the railway industry.[55]

This wartime demand for female labor was not sustained. At the end of the war as returning servicemen reclaimed their old jobs or looked for new ones, traditional cliches respecting woman's place were revived as a means of ousting women from new-found positions in the labor force. The long-term impact, then, enabled some of those women who had been in the labor force prior to the war to emerge with better jobs. While the number of women with labor-force experience increased, the war did not significantly augment the peacetime, female labor force. At least one major employer, American Telephone and Telegraph, having learned that women could be organized into an effective union, subsequently hastened the installation of automated equipment in order to reduce its dependence on female switchboard operators, a move that checked the demand for young, white, high-school educated women in what had become a major employment opportunity. Ultimately the wartime experience confirmed the public's view of women as a labor reserve that in an emergency could fill in for men in a wide range of demanding jobs, but otherwise women should be satisfied with a limited range of employments.[56]

Given society's attitudes toward the propriety of work for women, the composition of the female labor force in 1900 differed markedly from that of the male labor force. First, the labor-force participation rate (LFPR) for all women in 1900 was 20.0 compared to 85.7 for men, but whereas the rate for males dropped off 1.1 percentage points by 1920, that for women rose a modest 2.7 points. Second, whether age 20 or 60, nine out of ten men worked, but among women, four out of ten in their early 20s and one out of six of those in their 50s were in the labor force. Furthermore, the age composition of the female labor force changed substantially between 1900 and 1920 as girls under 16 years of age dropped out of the labor force, their places taken by older girls and young women. As a result, an increase in the labor-force rate for adult women of 3.2 percentage points was modest but significant. Third, the composition of the female labor force differed substantially by race. While nonwhite males had labor-force rates similar to those for white males, nonwhite females were twice as likely to work as white females. Fourth, while a preponderance of men of all marital statuses were in the labor force, the LFPR of women varied widely by marital status. Labor-force data suggest that by 1920 a majority of young women worked briefly prior to marriage, yet the LFPR for married women was under 4 percent. Fifth, reflecting a rigid sexual division of work, women were concentrated in a small handful of predominantly "female" occupations. In 1900, 42.6 percent of the female labor force was employed in three occupations—domestic servant, seamstress, and teacher. Altogether 17 "female" occupations collectively employed 53.4 percent of all female workers. By 1920 the proportion had dropped to 43 percent, suggesting that a slight diffusion of women into a wider range of jobs had occurred.[57]

Women, however, did not operate in a single, homogeneous labor market. Age, marital status, and race, as well as social status and education, functioned as critical factors in defining relatively separate, segmented labor markets. Employers preferred young women as receptionists but sought older women as office managers. A single woman might sell girls' dresses; a married woman, women's coats. In southern cities, black women were in demand as domestic servants, while in northern cities daughters of immigrants dominated the occupation. Immigrants and their daughters swarmed the needle trades. Native-born girls with some high-school training were in demand as sales girls, typists, and telephone operators; those with a high-school diploma, as nurses or as teachers. White women did not work alongside black women; Anglo-American women seldom worked with immigrant women; and women, regardless of ethnic origin, never worked alongside men.[58]

Supply and Demand

To understand more clearly the changing status of women in the economy, it is particularly useful to study the changes in both the supply and demand for female workers. The supply of women for the labor force was a function of the size of the total female population: the larger the total female population, the larger the potential number of female workers. The supply, however, was much affected by the propensities of women of different age groups and marital statuses to enter the labor force, as well as by changes in the proportion of women in these groups.[59]

Between 1900 and 1920, the white female population age 14 and over increased by 10,349,000. As Figure 1–1 indicates during these years the proportion of women who were under age 30 declined, reducing the supply of female workers by over 400,000 (assuming no change in the propensity to work). The supply of teenage workers was further reduced by the growing societal opposition to child labor and by the gradual extension of the years of schooling, which kept girls under 16 out of the labor market. At the same time, the relative size of the female population grew

Figure 1-1
Proportion of White Women by Age, 1900 and 1920

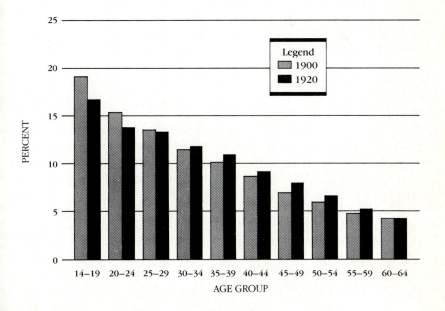

in every age group from age 30 to 65. But because of negative social attitudes toward the employment of married women or of postmenopausal women, married or otherwise, the increase in the supply of older women only partially offset the decline in the supply of younger women. Overall in 1920 the supply of white female labor was 250,000 smaller than it would have been had the age distribution remained the same as in 1900.[60]

The shift in the age mix of the nonwhite population—predominantly black—had a different outcome. The pool of teenage girls and young women under age 25 decreased, while that of older women increased. But because the labor-force rate of nonwhite women 25 years old and over was nearly as high as for the younger women, the change in the demographic mix did not add greatly to the number of women who could be added to the labor supply.[61]

The demographic shifts in the age mix had a gentle impact on the changing labor-force rates of women. Confronted by the relative decline in the supply of younger, single women, employers had to recruit more intensively from the dwindling pool of single women, causing their labor-force rate to increase. Alternatively, to the extent that employers turned to married women to meet their requirements for "female" labor, they pushed upward the labor-force rates for this group, too, whenever the increase in demand grew faster than the increase in the supply of married women.[62]

The growth of the female labor force, however, resulted less from changes in the supply of female labor than from changes in the demand that grew out of shifts in the magnitude of various sectors of the national economy. In 1900 of a total labor force of 29,025,000 workers, 10,371,000 were engaged in the primary sector—agriculture, forestry, and mining (see Figure 1–2). Another 7,729,000 were employed in the secondary sector—manufacturing and construction. The remaining 8,777,000—30.2 percent of the total—were engaged in the tertiary, or service-producing, sector. By 1920 nearly 12,900,000 persons had been added to the labor force. The increments were so uneven that in 1920 the primary sector, although it had gained 1,800,000 workers, utilized a smaller fraction of the labor force than in 1900. While agriculture was losing its relative importance in the national economy, manufacturing boomed, generating almost 4,900,000 additional jobs, so that in 1920 the secondary sector employed 30.1 percent of the total labor force. Impressive as these gains were, the tertiary sector grew even faster, adding nearly 7,000,000 jobs and employing 37.6 percent of the total labor force.[63]

These uneven changes in the structure of the economy had an enormous impact on the demand for female workers. The relative decline in the primary sector had little effect on employment opportunities for white women, for few had ever worked in that sector. But black women, who

Figure 1-2
Labor Force by Industry, 1900 and 1920

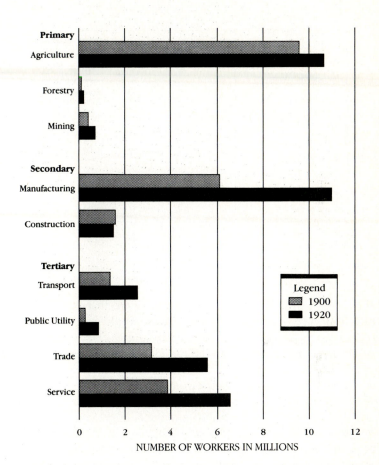

had been limited to farm labor in the rural South, faced a declining job market. The growth of the secondary sector produced an expanded demand for daughters of the foreign-born and for white women from working-class families. Most important, the growth of the tertiary sector greatly enlarged the demand for middle-class white women in professional, clerical, and sales work. Overall, these structural changes in the economy reduced the work opportunities in occupations that had never made extensive use of women while greatly increasing work opportunities in occupations that already depended heavily on middle-class white women. Accordingly the labor-force participation of adult women increased at every age level under

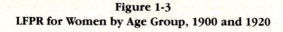

Figure 1-3
LFPR for Women by Age Group, 1900 and 1920

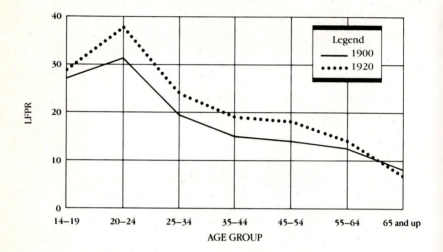

65 (see Figure 1–3). The prospects in 1920 were that the demand for women, especially middle-class white women, would continue to grow.[64]

Paid work outside the home did not invariably "liberate" the woman who worked. Historically, professional employment had offered educated middle-class women an alternative to marriage; even for a young single woman, employment might provide a taste of independence from parents prior to marriage. But for blacks and immigrants, employment was a matter of necessity, not choice. A job could provide a working-class family with extra comforts, or it might enable the family to avoid depending on charity. In either case, the working woman enjoyed an extra measure of independence and dignity. But far from liberating such women from traditional family roles, work afforded the wife–mother a means of holding her family together by a tour de force of homemaking and work. At this level, the working woman reaffirmed the traditional domestic role rather than challenged it.[65]

Women's economic status changed—improved—between 1900 and 1920. The most important changes in status occurred in the white middle class. At every age, such women encountered fewer barriers from family, friends, or employers if they entered the labor force. The relaxation of objections to work was facilitated by the proliferation of white-collar jobs.

By 1920 most young women expected to enter the labor force if they did not marry. Work remained taboo for married women whose husbands could support them and especially for mothers with young children. But even so, the proportion of married women who worked doubled between 1900 and 1920. Throughout this period, though, a woman who was committed to a demanding professional career expected to forgo marriage.

Family Status

The regard that society bestowed on women was ambiguous. Much of the nineteenth-century heritage that idealized the qualities of woman and placed her on a pedestal, while severely restricting her sphere to the home and family, still impinged on husband–wife relationships in 1920. Crucial to the evaluation of woman's status in the family was the operation of the doctrine of "two spheres" and its antithesis, the doctrine of feminism.[66]

The two-spheres concept, with the inertia of a century of acceptance, confirmed the view that woman's place was in the home. The impact on woman's status was mixed. On the negative side, marriage rather than womanhood had imposed invidious limitations on the adult woman—loss of separate civil identity, curtailment of civil and contractual rights, and preclusion of a career or economic independence. Within the family circle, the husband by custom, supported by law, spoke for the family. A decision as to where the couple lived or whether to assume a mortgage for a home was his. He might consult her, but he was not bound to do so. She might attempt to persuade him to adopt her views, but if they disagreed, his views were binding. With its special emphasis on domesticity, marriage placed a far heavier responsibility for the nurturing of family members on the wife than on the husband. Marriage, as Carl Degler observes, was "many things, but at all times a relationship of power." The inferior power position of the wife within the family acted to give her less status than her husband. "The real obstacle to equality," in the judgment of William Chafe, "was the division of spheres between men and women."[67]

This separation of spheres, however, had some positive aspects. If it gave males a free hand in the external business of the family, it gave wives supremacy within the home. Given the relative equality of the sexes in the access to public education, most women were as qualified to run their homes as their husbands were to perform their jobs. In the management of the day-to-day business of the family, the husband expected his wife to manage the budget; in fact in some working-class families, the husband delivered his unopened pay envelope to his wife, receiving back his allowance for personal expenses. She made the appointments with doctors; she talked to the teacher about school problems; she bought the food and clothes; she chose the paint and wallpaper for redecorating. In these terms, the doctrine of two spheres, by 1920, afforded married women "a degree of autonomy at home" and enough flexibility for many different activities outside the home.[68]

Counterpoised against the acceptance of the two-spheres view of woman's place were the feminists. Their numbers remain indeterminate, for they did not form a single group. Until 1920 the Seneca Falls Declaration remained the most embracing statement of feminist goals. Elizabeth Cady Stanton perceived that to be on a plane of equality with her husband, the wife must enjoy the same opportunities in marriage as her husband. Although she placed the suffrage at the top of her demands, she ticked off other objectives—a separate legal identity, married women's property rights, divorce reform, access to employment, enlarged educational opportunities, and a single standard of morals. Even by 1869 sufficient progress had been achieved in the areas of married women's property rights, divorce law, sexual standards, and women's education that many feminists regarded the suffrage as the major unfinished business, and Stanton and Susan Anthony lent their imprimatur to this emphasis in organizing the National Woman Suffrage Association. Working along parallel paths, Lucy Stone, Julia Ward Howe, and Mary Livermore organized the American Woman Suffrage Association.[69]

Although the public identified feminism chiefly with woman suffrage, women pursued a spate of interests through a wide variety of voluntary organizations. In so doing they found ways of expressing themselves, earning recognition for their achievements, and often effecting reforms that enlarged the opportunities of other women to pursue roles outside the home. Much energy was poured into informal neighborhood networks, church groups, and women's clubs. By 1900 there were major national organizations with ambitious programs—the Women's Christian Temperance Union, the Association of Collegiate Alumnae (now the American Association of University Women), the National Parent–Teacher's Association, the Young Women's Christian Association, and the General Federation of Women's Clubs. Black women had organized the National Association of Colored Women (NACW). Jewish women formed the Young Women's Hebrew Association and the National Council of Jewish Women. Membership in these groups grew enormously. Ironically, some of these women would have disclaimed being feminists.[70]

The efforts of women to have a social and intellectual life outside the home asserted a claim on the part of married women to act as autonomous individuals, as their husbands did, rather than to live vicariously through the activities of their menfolk. By expanding roles for women outside the home, feminists placed themselves "at odds" with the traditional family, in the view of Carl Degler. His unstated assumption was that an expression of personal preference or independent action by the wife was subversive to the family and the marriage, while a like assertion by her husband was not. His analysis presumes that the stability of the nuclear family lies in the exclusive leadership of a single mate—the husband. The feminist, on the other hand, implicitly assumed the workability of a democratic family in which the husband and wife, as mature human beings bound by ties of affection and shared interests, values, and experiences, could allow each other the freedom to pursue unique interests without shaking the marriage relationship apart. A young woman coming of age in the early decades of the century might well be perplexed with the contradictions between the honor accorded her as a woman and the expectation that her husband's judgments and wishes must always be valued more highly than her own.[71]

THE MOMENTUM OF CHANGE

As women went to the polls in November 1920, they took along a surprisingly broad range of political concerns and experiences that colored their use of the suffrage. Two points of view prevailed. One view emerged from the experience of the social feminists, the other from the suffragists. Both views were advanced by an elite of educated, white middle-class women.[72]

Social Feminists

Beginning in the 1890s social feminists, following the lead of Jane Addams and Lillian Wald, asserted that women should be municipal house-keepers, overseeing the public environment in which women and their families worked and lived. Of special concern were the social and economic problems that homemakers and women workers encountered. Jane Addams, the most important of these reformers, set the pace as she developed a variety of programs at Hull House to help the women of Chicago's immigrant ghetto improve the quality of their lives. More importantly, Florence Kelley, Julia Lathrop, Grace Abbott, and Alice Hamilton used Hull House as a base for studies that led to important social and economic reforms of the Progressive movement. Kelley's study of the sweating system in the garment industry persuaded the Illinois legislature to adopt a pioneer factory act. Hamilton, a medical doctor, surveyed dangerous trades, while Lathrop focused on the level of care provided in public institutions and on the treatment of delinquent children. She shared with Abbott a concern for the welfare of immigrants. Subsequently, Hamilton became the first woman awarded a tenured faculty post at Harvard; Kelley became chief factory inspector in Illinois, while first Lathrop then Abbott headed the Children's Bureau in the U.S. Department of Labor. In New York, Lillian Wald, founder of the Henry Street Settlement, promoted park and recreation facilities accessible to working people, campaigned against child labor, and founded a visiting nurse service.[73]

Social feminists also organized special interest groups that tackled specific problems of working-class women. The New York Consumers' League, founded in 1890 and led by Josephine Shaw Lowell, became a national organization under Florence Kelley, seeking to ameliorate the working conditions of young women. In the vanguard of the Progressive movement, the league campaigned for minimum-wage, maximum-hour legislation for women and for child-labor laws. Still another approach was that of the National Women's Trade Union League (NWTUL). Modeled after an English organization, the league encouraged working women to join one or another of the American Federation of Labor (AFL) unions. During a series of bitterly contested strikes, the NWTUL, led by Margaret Dreier Robins, assisted women strikers in organizing picket lines, helped union members cope with police violence, provided bail, and gave financial aid to strikers' families. Robins also trained women for union leadership roles.[74]

The social feminists quickly perceived that the social problems they addressed required legislative solutions at the local, state, and federal level. While nineteenth-century women had organized and lobbied in the cause of temperance, antislavery, and social purity, their objectives had been relatively specific and limited; their intervention in these issues had been rationalized in terms of moral concerns that were of natural interest to women. The social feminists, however, found themselves drawn into ever-widening areas of social and economic issues and into the mainstream of American politics. While the social feminists were aware that society assumed that woman's place was in the home, they recognized that millions of women worked, the great majority of them as blue-collar, domestic-service, or farm workers. The hours were unbelievably long; wages, below subsistence level; health and safety conditions, abominable. A significant number were children under 16 years of age. To curb this exploitation of women and children, the social feminists sought to invoke the police powers—the broad power to make laws to secure health and safety.[75]

The reformers found it very difficult to devise protective legislation that did not violate constitutional safeguards of property or contractual rights. In order to protect the health of bakers—all males—New York State limited them to a ten-hour workday by law. Subsequently in the *Lochner* case (1905), the U.S. Supreme Court invalidated the law as "an illegal interference with the rights of individuals, both employers and employees, to make contracts. . . ." The Court clearly thought male workers could fend for themselves. On the other hand, in the *Muller* case (1908), which challenged Oregon's ten-hour law for women, the Court acknowledged "a widespread belief that woman's physical structure, and the functions she performs in consequence thereof, justify special legislation restricting or qualifying the conditions under which she should be permitted to toil." In its analysis the Court explicitly asserted that "woman's physical structure and the performance of maternal functions place her at a disadvantage in the struggle for subsistence. . . ." It went on to conclude that because "healthy mothers are essential to vigorous offspring, the physical well-being of woman becomes an object of public interest and care in order to preserve the strength and vigor of the race. . . ." Thus the Court incorporated into constitutional law a belief that women were at a disadvantage with respect to men in ways that justified protective laws for women that it would not tolerate for men.[76]

Following the *Muller* decision, social feminists persuaded state legislators to enact an enormous body of protective legislation for working women relative to wages and hours, a day of rest, night work, meal and rest periods, as well as sweatshops and mother's pensions. They also made a concerted effort to ban child labor. In lobbying for these reforms the social feminists realized their task would be greatly facilitated if women who shared their concerns could vote. The social feminists took a major role in promoting woman suffrage, and Jane Addams became a vice-president of the national suffrage organization.[77]

Suffrage Secured

The concerns of the social feminists matured at a time when the suffrage movement was reorganizing and acquiring new leadership. In 1890 the rival suffrage organizations—the National Woman Suffrage Association and the American Woman Suffrage Association—merged, becoming the National American Woman Suffrage Association (NAWSA). As her last contribution to the cause, Susan Anthony recruited two younger women, Anna Howard Shaw, who became the chief spokesperson for the association, and Carrie Chapman Catt, its de facto executive secretary. Although Catt led successful state campaigns for the suffrage in Colorado and Idaho, the suffrage movement faced major problems involving its relationship to black women, southern whites, and social feminists.[78]

Caught up in the currents of the day, the suffragists reflected the prevailing hostility of many middle-class whites to blacks and immigrants. In fact, Stanton and Anthony had organized the National Woman Suffrage Association by way of protesting the action of Congress in enfranchising black men while refusing the vote to women. In the 1890s, white suffragists

In 1915, women in Colorado went to the polls for the first time to vote in a national election.

expressed hostility toward the immigrant. Mincing no words, Carrie Catt warned: "This government is menaced with great danger." The danger lay "in the votes possessed by males in the slums of the cities, and the ignorant foreign vote." Citing statistics, the suffragists argued that if women were enfranchised, the votes of the native-born women alone would assure the continued political dominance of native-born whites. The solution was an "educated vote," as Stanton termed it. Woman suffrage was useful, a Kentucky suffragist wrote, "as a counterbalance to the foreign vote, and as a means of preserving white supremacy in the South."[79]

In desperate need of the support of southern whites, the NAWSA gave black suffragists a cold shoulder. In her last years as a leader, Anthony refused to assist black women in organizing a branch of the NAWSA, and she urged Frederick Douglass—who had spoken in support of woman suffrage at Seneca Falls in 1848—not to attend an NAWSA convention in Atlanta. Nor did the NAWSA encourage black women to apply for membership. As a result, black women organized their own, autonomous suffrage clubs in cities such as Memphis, St. Louis, Charleston, and New

Orleans, as well as in Boston and Los Angeles and in states as diverse as New York and Idaho, Maryland and Texas. Black women's clubs and the NAACP also organized suffrage departments. At a time white suffragists were wavering, black suffragists took the high ground that the right to vote was a natural right. Nonetheless, they shared with white women a belief that the suffrage would cure many social ills, but they had their own list of problems. At the top was sexual exploitation; other items included the control of prostitution, repeal of barriers to interracial marriage, promotion of compulsory education, and protection of working women. Black women believed that with the vote, they might be listened to. In those states where women could vote, black suffragists successfully organized campaigns that elected blacks to public office and generated support for the suffrage amendment.[80]

While the social feminists generated a climate of reform in urban areas in the 1890s and at the state level in the early 1900s, their focus was on specific social problems, not the suffrage. As the reform movement grew into the Progressive movement, a few Progressives trickled into the Congress, but not until 1909 did they form an effective bloc. Even then the Progressives were linked by concerns with tariff rates, banking policy, and the regulation of big business. Theodore Roosevelt endorsed woman suffrage in the 1912 election; the General Federation of Women's Clubs, in 1914. Not until 1916 did the suffrage question enter the mainstream of American politics.[81]

As the social feminist movement matured, it caused a reshaping of the rationale for the suffrage. From the Seneca Falls convention to the end of the century, the rationale was framed in terms of natural rights. Women suffragists claimed that sharing a common humanity with men, women were endowed with an identical, inalienable right to consent to the laws by which they were governed. The argument was radical in that the suffragists claimed the right of a woman to act as an individual though society expected her to subordinate her interests to those of her family.[82]

The new generation of leaders who directed the suffrage movement after 1900 had to reckon with the concerns social feminists had developed in the course of their activities in the settlement houses, the National Consumers' League, and the NWTUL. The varied reforms of the social feminists respecting education, recreation, public health, welfare reform, and juvenile delinquency aimed at improving the health of the community at large. The social feminists further argued that women's traditional role within the home as cook, seamstress, cleaner, nurse, and teacher especially qualified them to frame legislation concerned with food inspection, sweatshops, sanitation, public health, and schools. "The individual conscience and devotion are no longer effective," Jane Addams asserted. If women were to effectively continue their old avocations, they must take part "in the slow upbuilding of that code of legislation which is alone sufficient to protect the home from the dangers incident to modern life." "City house-keeping," she insisted, had failed "partly because women, the traditional housekeepers, have not been consulted as to its multiform activities." While not repudiating the natural rights argument, the social feminists placed their emphasis on the expediency of the ballot to secure protective legis-lation. Florence Kelley advocated woman suffrage to protect working women from special hazards to their health and safety, while Catharine Waugh McCulloch, a lawyer, urged woman suffrage in order that women could help protect themselves against discriminatory man-made laws.[83]

Not the least of the difficulties in reviving the suffrage movement were the divisions among the women themselves. Carrie Catt, a woman with remarkable organizing skills, resigned the leadership of the NAWSA in 1905 to care for her fatally ill husband. Her successor, Anna Howard Shaw, though a magnificent speaker, was not a good organizer and was more interested in securing the suffrage state-by-state than by a federal amend-ment, so that the NAWSA failed to capitalize on the reform spirit of the Progressive movement. Between 1896 and 1910 the suffrage movement, afflicted by lackluster leadership and an aging membership, passed through "the doldrums."[84]

The movement gained new life in 1914 as Alice Paul, supported by Harriot Stanton Blatch and Lucy Burns, organized the Congressional Union. All three women had participated in the militant English suffrage move-ment. Paul had initially secured an appointment from Anna Howard Shaw to lobby with Congress on behalf of the NAWSA, but once in Washington, she organized her own group. Her confrontation tactics, while offending the NAWSA leadership, put the suffrage cause on the front pages of the nation's press. In 1916 Carrie Catt, once more president of the NAWSA, spurred that group to renewed vigor with a comprehensive "winning plan." Although not so intended, Paul's organization, reorganized as the National Woman's Party, ran interference for the more sedate NAWSA, contributing substantially to the success of the final drive.[85]

While Paul's group prodded the NAWSA by its militancy, southern suf-fragists questioned the desirability of a federal amendment. Recognizing that a federal suffrage amendment would undercut white supremacy, they committed themselves in 1913 to securing woman suffrage by amendments to state constitutions that would enfranchise white women only. To this end, Laura Clay in Kentucky, Kate M. Gordon in Louisiana, and Belle Kear-ney in Mississippi organized the Southern States Woman Suffrage Conference. When the NAWSA committed itself in 1916 to the adoption of a federal amendment, Clay, Kearney, and Gordon split with the NAWSA and campaigned against it.[86]

As Catt laid her plans for the "final drive," she made woman suffrage a near panacea. The NAWSA endorsed Progressive reforms designed to increase popular participation in government—the initiative, referendum, and recall. Reflecting the concerns of the social feminists, NAWSA called for child-labor laws, pure food legislation, equal pay for equal work, and protective labor laws for women. Enfranchisement of women would hasten realization of these Progressive reforms. At another level, the suffragists embraced the argument that women had a unique point of view that derived from their role as guardians of the public morality. They regarded the liquor industry not only as a threat to women, per se, but believed that liquor interests in alliance with commercial vice and big business manipulated government and corrupted society. Alice Stone Blackwell claimed that had women been able to vote in New York City in 1903, the excesses of Tammany Hall, the Democratic machine, would have been checked. In making these arguments the suffragists raised two expectations: first, that women had a set of interests unique to themselves, and hence they could be expected to vote as a bloc; second, that because of their unique moral qualities, women voters would purge the political process of corruption and make government serve the interests of all the people.[87]

As the final drive got under way, popular support for the suffrage was growing. Beginning in 1910 with Washington, eight western states granted women the vote. The objections of the southern women to a federal amendment was an obstacle to work around, but the militancy of Alice Paul's National Woman's Party, rather than undercutting the NAWSA, served to focus attention on woman suffrage. America's entrance into World War I posed a problem, for Catt and many of the other suffragists had been active, long-time pacifists. While the National Woman's Party and a minority of other suffragists including Jeannette Rankin and Jane Addams opposed the war, Catt and the NAWSA supported it, a tactic pleasing to a host of middle-class women who were actively involved in volunteer work—selling war bonds, conserving food, and organizing benefits for troops—and whose support the NAWSA needed.[88]

As the "final drive" neared its climax, the rationale for woman suffrage was refined further. A pragmatist, Catt acknowledged that she did not know whether the vote was a right, a duty, or a privilege, but that "whatever it is, women want it." Her arguments were eclectic, designed to appeal to as broad a constituency as possible. Arguing that it was unwise to withhold the vote from women whose war work was needed, she urged adoption of woman suffrage as a "war measure," an argument of expediency. When

President Wilson spoke of making the world safe for democracy, she argued that the fight for democracy began at home, an argument reaffirming the suffrage as a natural right. Remembering the time and energy that social feminists had poured into two decades of reform, she insisted that woman suffrage would hasten the process.[89]

Catt's approach worked. Her moderate stance on woman suffrage and her support of the war gave the suffrage movement an aura of respectability that won the endorsement of President Wilson. First in 1917 and again in 1918 the president urged the Senate to pass the suffrage amendment as "vital to the winning of the war." While the Senate demurred, New York state approved woman suffrage in November 1917, becoming the first state east of the Mississippi to give women the vote. In January 1918 the House of Representatives adopted a suffrage amendment; by the time the Senate followed suit in June 1919, women in 14 states had secured full suffrage, and in 13 other states they could vote for president. With victory in the offing, the NAWSA redoubled its efforts in a massive round of speeches, marches, and meetings in support of ratification. State after state ratified the amendment. Ultimately the decision lay with the Tennessee legislature, with Catt pitting her skills as a lobbyist against those of Clay and Gordon. When the final vote was taken, the federal amendment had the necessary votes. In November 1920, for the first time, no American woman could be excluded from voting because of her sex.[90]

Where, then, did women stand in August 1920? First and foremost, women's access to the suffrage was on everyone's mind. In terms of the suffrage, women had achieved equality with men. For some suffragists, victory had been achieved, and it was time to rest; for others it was a time to act. Social feminists eagerly looked forward to enacting social reforms to which the male leadership had been indifferent, and they expected that women would move quickly into major positions of party and governmental leadership. Second, structural shifts in the economy had increased the demand for women in jobs that white middle-class women regarded as suitable. Black women were just beginning their flight from the rural South and farm labor to work as domestics in the cities of the South and North. Child labor, endemic in the workplace in 1900, was in the process of being supplanted by adult labor, but the complete eradication of child labor was a major item of unfinished business. Third, the pool of college-trained women who might seek leadership roles in later life remained limited, and women seeking professional careers expected to forgo marriage. Finally, the New Woman had challenged traditional sex roles just before the war, but as of 1920, advocates of a new order were neither numerous nor in the mainstream of society. Traditional nineteenth-century values respecting sex roles retained enormous momentum; only a few youth flirted with the still radical ideas of the New Woman, of Gilman, Freud, or Sanger.

NOTES

[1] Quoted in William Henry Chafe, *The American Woman* (New York: Oxford, 1972), 49.

[2] Aileen S. Kraditor, *The Ideas of the Woman Suffrage Movement, 1890–1920* (New York: Norton, 1981[1965]), 44 ff.

[3] Genesis 2:7–25 gives the conventional Adam and Eve story; Genesis 1:26–27 presents the alternative account in which God created male and female together. The Mosaic code is scattered throughout Leviticus 12. Exodus 20 outlines the restrictions on the behavior of women. *Human Sexuality: New Directions in American Catholic Thought,* Anthony Kosnik, Chair (New York: Pauline Press, 1977), 7–17.

[4] I Corinthians 14:34–35; 6:18; 7:11. *Human Sexuality,* Kosnik, Chair, 17–29. William O. Walker, Jr., "First Corinthians 11:2–16 and Paul's Views Regarding Women," *Journal of Biblical Literature* 94(March 1975): 94–116.

[5] Arthur W. Calhoun, *A Social History of the American Family,* 3 vols. (New York: Barnes and Noble, 1960[1917]), vol. 1, 48.

[6] Barbara Welter, "The Cult of True Womanhood: 1820–1860," *American Quarterly* 18(1966): 151–74.

[7] Carl N. Degler, *At Odds* (New York: Oxford, 1980). Louise A. Tilly and Joan W. Scott, *Women, Work, and Family* (New York: Holt, Rinehart and Winston, 1978), 2–88 explores this transformation in England and France.

[8] Hannah Josephson, *The Golden Threads* (New York: Duell, Sloan and Pearce, 1949).

[9] Degler, *At Odds,* 8–9; Welter, "True Womanhood," 152.

[10] Degler, *At Odds,* 189.

[11] Annie Nathan Meyer, ed., *Woman's Work In America* (New York: Holt, 1891), offers a contemporaneous assessment; chap. 11 focuses on women in the professions and industry. Robert W. Smuts, *Women and Work in America* (New York: Columbia University Press, 1959), chap. 2. Sheila M. Rothman, *Woman's Proper Place: A History of Changing Ideals and Practices, 1870 to the Present* (New York: Basic, 1978), chaps. 1–3. Alice Kessler-Harris, *Out to Work* (New York: Oxford, 1982), pt. 2.

[12] Charlotte Perkins Gilman, *Women and Economics* (New York: Harper & Row, 1966 [1898]), 164. Karen J. Blair, *The Clubwoman as Feminist: True Womanhood Redefined 1868– 1914* (New York: Holmes & Meier, 1980). Gerda Lerner, "Early Community Work of Black Clubwomen," *JNH* 59(April 1974): 158–67.

[13] Andrew Billingsley, *Black Families in White America* (Englewood Cliffs: Prentice-Hall, 1968), 37, 59–61, 68–69.

[14] C. Vann Woodward, *The Strange Career of Jim Crow* (New York: Oxford, 1955), chap. 2.

[15] Ibid.

[16] Jessie Bernard, *Marriage and Family Among Negroes* (Englewood Cliffs: Prentice-Hall, 1966), 2–5. Herbert Gutman, *The Black Family in Slavery and Freedom* (New York: Pantheon, 1975), 443.

[17] W. E. Burghardt DuBois, *The Negro American Family* (Westport: Negro Universities Press, 1969[1908]), 29, 36.

[18] Frank F. Furstenberg, Jr., Theodore Hershberg, and John Modell, "The Origins of the Female-Headed Black Family: The Impact of the Urban Experience," in *The Black Family: Essays and Studies,* 2nd ed., ed. Robert Staples (Belmont: Wadsworth, 1978), 43–57.

[19] DuBois, *The Negro American Family,* 50–54.

[20] Ibid., 55, 59.

[21] Bureau of the Census, *Historical Statistics of the United States, Colonial Times to 1970,* Bicentennial ed., Part 1 (Washington: GPO, 1975), ser. H 433–41, ser. H 664–68.

[22] Charles William Dabney, *Universal Education and the South,* 2 vols. (Chapel Hill: University of North Carolina Press, 1936), vol. 1, 456–66.

[23] Ibid., 487–89.

[24] See Booker T. Washington, *Up From Slavery* (New York: Bantam, 1956[1901]), 77, chap. 7.

[25] August Meier, "Toward a Reinterpretation of Booker T. Washington," *Journal of Southern History* 23(May 1957): 220–27.

[26] Bureau of the Census, *Historical Statistics of the United States, 1789–1945* (Washington: GPO, 1949), 31; William E. B. DuBois, *The Philadelphia Negro* (Philadelphia: University of Pennsylvania Press, 1899), chap. 6, 192–96. E. Franklin Frazier, *The Negro Family in the United States* (Chicago: University of Chicago Press, 1939), 250–55. See also Gilbert Osofsky, *Harlem: The Making of a Ghetto, Negro New York, 1890–1930* (New York: Harper & Row, 1966) and Seth M. Scheiner, *Negro Mecca: A History of the Negro in New York City, 1865–1920* (New York: New York University Press, 1965).

[27] Elliott M. Rudwick, "The Niagara Movement," *JNH* 42(1957): 177–200.

[28] Robert L. Jack, *History of the National Association for the Advancement of Colored People* (Boston: Meador, 1943).

[29] L. Hollingsworth Wood, "The Urban League Movement," *JNH* 9(1924): 117–26.

[30] Paula Giddings, *When and Where I Enter* (New York: Morrow, 1984), 89–95.

[31] Louise V. Kennedy, *The Negro Peasant Turns Cityward* (New York: Columbia University Press, 1930) and Henderson H. Donald, "The Negro Migration, 1916–1918," *JNH* 6(1921): 383–498.

[32] James R. McGovern, "The American Woman's Pre-World War I Freedom in Manners and Morals," *JAH* 55(1968): 318. Carl N. Degler, Introduction to Gilman, *Women and Economics,* vii. See also Mary A. Hill, *Charlotte Perkins Gilman: The Making of a Radical Feminist: 1860–1896* (Philadelphia: Temple University Press, 1980) and Charlotte (Perkins) Gilman, *The Living of Charlotte Perkins Gilman; an Autobiography* (New York: Appleton-Century, 1935).

[33] Gilman, *Autobiography,* 5, 66.

[34] Charlotte Gilman, "The New Generation of Women," *Current History* 18(Aug. 1923): 735, 736 and *Forerunner* 7(1916): 287; Gilman, *Women and Economics,* 246.

[35] Gilman, *Women and Economics,* 267. See also, Susan J. Kleinberg, "Technology and Women's Work: The Lives of Working Class Women in Pittsburgh, 1870–1900," *Labor History* 17(1976): 58–72 and Ruth Schwartz Cowan, "The 'Industrial Revolution' in the Home: Household Technology and Social Change in the Twentieth Century," *Technology and Culture* 17(Jan. 1976): 1–23.

[36] *The Nation* 68(June 8, 1899): 443.

[37] Sigmund Freud, *Collected Papers,* Joan Riviere, ed., 5 vols. (London: Hogarth, 1953), vol. 2, 76–99. Sigmund Freud, *Three Essays on the Theory of Sexuality,* James Strachey, trans. (London: Hogarth, 1962), 7–14, 85–86; Henry F. May, *The End of American Innocence* (Chicago: Quadrangle, 1964[1959]), 235.

[38] Sigmund Freud, *New Introductory Lectures on Psycho-Analysis,* W. J. H. Sprott, trans. (New York: Norton, 1933), chap. 5. Frederick Lewis Allen, *Only Yesterday* (New York: Bantam, 1959[1931]), 69.

[39] David M. Kennedy, *Birth Control in America: The Career of Margaret Sanger* (New Haven: Yale, 1970), 8–10. Madeline Gray, *Margaret Sanger: A Biography of the Champion of Birth Control* (New York: Marek, 1980). Linda Gordon, *Woman's Body, Woman's Right: A Social History of Birth Control in America* (New York: Grossman, 1976), chap. 9. Margaret Sanger, *An Autobiography* (New York: Norton, 1938), 66–67, 85.

[40] Margaret Sanger, *The Pivot of Civilization* (New York: Brentano's, 1922), 8, 51–52, 163–64; Sanger, *Autobiography,* 107–109.

[41] Kennedy, *Birth Control,* 65; Margaret Sanger, *The Woman Rebel* (New York: Archives of Social History, 1976) reprints vol. 1, no. 1–7 of Sanger's 1914 periodical. Joan M. Jepsen, "The Evolution of Margaret Sanger's 'Family Limitation' Pamphlet, 1914–1921," *Signs* 6(1981): 548–57, includes the 1914 edition.

[42] Sanger, *Autobiography,* 135; Havelock Ellis, *Man and Woman* (Boston: Houghton Mifflin, 1929), 468–69, 479.

[43] Kennedy, *Birth Control,* 83–88; Sanger, *Autobiography,* 238–50; *NYT,* 6 Feb. 1917; People v. Sanger, 222 NY 102 (1918).

[44] "Sex O'Clock in America," *Current Opinion* 55(Aug. 1913): 113–14. Agnes Repplier, "The Repeal of Reticence," *Atlantic Monthly* 113(March 1914): 298. McGovern, "American Woman's Pre-World War I Freedom," 319. See also June Sochen, *The New Woman: Feminism in Greenwich Village* (New York: Quadrangle, 1972).

[45] Owen Johnson, *The Salamander* (Indianapolis: Bobbs-Merrill, 1914), foreword n.p.

[46] Helen Campbell, *Women Wage-Earners* (New York: Arno, 1972[1893]), 91.

[47] McGovern, "American Woman's Pre-World War I Freedom," 318; May, *End of American Innocence,* 333.

[48] Eleanor Flexner, *Century of Struggle: The Woman's Rights Movement in the United States* (New York: Atheneum, 1968[1959]), 283. Degler, Introduction to Gilman, *Women and Economics,* vii.

[49] Elizabeth Cady Stanton quoted in Carol Hymowitz and Michaele Weissman, *A History of Women in America* (New York: Bantam, 1978), 274. See also Ida Husted Harper, ed., *History of Woman Suffrage,* (New York: NAWSA, 1922), vol. 5, 269. Elizabeth Cady Stanton in *Woman's Journal,* 1 Sep. 1894. Elizabeth Cady Stanton, "Universal Suffrage a Pretense," *Woman's Journal,* 23 Oct. 1897; Martin Gruberg, *Women in American Politics* (Oshkosh: Academia, 1968), 10.

[50] Nancy F. Cott, "Feminist Politics in the 1920s: The National Woman's Party," *JAH* 71(1984): 46. Women's Bureau, "State Laws Affecting Working Women," *Bulletin 16* (Washington: GPO, 1921). Sue Shelton White, a lawyer, made a survey of sex discrimination in state legal codes for the Woman's Party in "Women and the Law," *Nation* 112(1921): 402.

[51] Gilman, *Women and Economics,* 10; Thorstein Veblen, *Theory of the Leisure Class* (New York: Modern Library, 1934[1899]), chap. 3. Carl Degler, "Charlotte Perkins Gilman on the Theory and Practice of Feminism," *AQ* 8(1956): 21–39. Carol Ruth Berkin, "Private Woman, Public Woman: The Contradictions of Charlotte Perkins Gilman," in *Women of America: A History,* ed. Carol Ruth Berkin and Mary Beth Norton (Boston: Houghton Mifflin, 1979), 150–73.

[52] Virginia Yans-McLaughlin, "Patterns of Work and Family Organization: Buffalo's Italians," *JIH* 2(1971): 299–314. Laurence A. Glasco, "The Life Cycles and Household Structure of American Ethnic Groups: Irish, Germans and Native-born Whites in Buffalo, New York, 1855," in *Family and Kin in Urban Communities, 1700–1930,* ed. Tamara K. Hareven (New York: New Viewpoints, 1977), 122–43. Elizabeth B. Butler, *Women and the Trades: Pittsburgh, 1907–1908* (New York: Charities Publication Committee, 1909) provides a superb treatment of the working-class woman; Kessler-Harris, *Out to Work,* 123–28.

[53] Institute for Government Research, *The Problem of Indian Administration,* Lewis Meriam, Dir. (Baltimore: Johns Hopkins Press, 1928).

[54] Gutman, *The Black Family,* 442–43; Jacqueline Jones, *Labor of Love, Labor of Sorrow*

(New York: Basic, 1985), 46. In the post–Civil War adjustment, black farmers had attempted to withdraw their womenfolk from field labor, but white landowners insisted that "every member of his family who is able to carry a hoe or plow to clean out the crops," Jones, *Labor of Love,* 82–83.

[55] Maurine Weiner Greenwald, *Women, War, and Work: The Impact of World War I on Women Workers in the United States* (Westport: Greenwood, 1980), 234–43, 13–25. Mary E. Jackson, "The Colored Woman in Industry," *The Crisis* 17(Nov. 1918): 12–17. William J. Breen, "Black Women and the Great War: Mobilization and Reform in the South," *Journal of Southern History* 44(1978): 421–40.

[56] Greenwald, *Women, War and Work,* 210–26.

[57] Gertrude Bancroft, *The American Labor Force* (New York: Wiley, 1958), 30–32. Smuts, *Women and Work in America,* 56–57; the basic studies of women in the labor force are Joseph A. Hill, *Women in Gainful Occupations, 1870–1920* (Washington: GPO, 1929) and Sophonisba Breckinridge, *Women in the Twentieth Century* (New York: McGraw-Hill, 1933). See Edith Abbott, *Women in Industry* (New York: Appleton, 1910). Valerie Kincade Oppenheimer, *The Female Labor Force in the United States* (Westport: Greenwood, 1970) employs the analytical concepts of the labor economist. Bancroft, *American Labor Force,* provides uniform census data. Also indispensable are John D. Durand, *The Labor Force in the United States, 1890–1960* (New York: SSRC, 1948); Smuts, *Women and Work in America;* and Julie A. Matthaei, *An Economic History of Women in America: Women's Work, The Sexual Division of Labor, and The Development of Capitalism* (New York: Schocken, 1982). For the most part, I have made my own analysis using Bancroft's data where applicable, otherwise using relevant Census Bureau or Labor Department data.

[58] Oppenheimer, *Female Labor Force,* chap. 3.

[59] Ibid., 19–24. Hazel Kyrk, "Who Works and Why?" *The Annals* 251 (May 1947): 44–52, sets forth the basic argument for approaching women's labor force participation in terms of a supply and demand analysis.

[60] Bancroft, *American Labor Force,* Table D-1.

[61] Ibid. Given the dynamic character of the population and the labor force, comparisons of the labor force participation rates (LFPR) offer the best index of the degree of involvement of women of various ages, races, and marital conditions in the labor force.

[62] Durand, *Labor Force in the United States,* chap 3. Bancroft, *American Labor Force,* 41–43. S. L. Wolfbein and A. J. Jaffe, "Demographic Factors in Labor Force Growth," *ASR* 11(Aug. 1946): 393–96.

[63] The concept of the primary, secondary, and tertiary sectors of the economy is developed in Stanley Lebergott, *Manpower in Economic Growth* (New York: McGraw-Hill, 1964), 100–114. See also Oppenheimer, *Female Labor Force,* chap. 5.

[64] Bancroft, *American Labor Force,* 35–38. Kessler-Harris, *Out to Work,* 148. Elizabeth Beardsley Butler, *Saleswomen in Mercantile Stores, Baltimore 1909* (New York: Charities Publications Committee, 1912), 144. The proportion of women workers employed as clerks, cashiers, typists or stenographers increased from 2 percent in 1900 to over 12 percent in 1920.

[65] Leslie Woodcock Tentler, *Wage-earning Women: Industrial Work and Family Life in the United States, 1900–1930* (New York: Oxford, 1979). Kessler-Harris, *Out to Work,* 119–20. Margaret Byington, a social worker, estimated that in Homestead, Pennsylvania, in 1907–1908 an immigrant family could survive on $11.55 a week, whereas an unskilled worker normally earned less than $10.00 a week.

[66] Degler, *At Odds,* 26–29.

[67] Ibid., 29. Chafe, *American Woman,* 246.

[68] Degler, *At Odds,* 342.

[69] E. C. Stanton, S. B. Anthony, and M. J. Gage, eds. *The History of Woman Suffrage,* vol. 1, 70 ff. The Seneca Falls Declaration is widely reprinted, e.g., Henry Steele Commager, *Documents of American History,* 9th ed. (New York: Appleton-Century-Crofts, 1973), 315–17.

[70] David J. Pivar, *The Purity Crusade* (Westport: Greenwood, 1973) treats a wide variety of social reform efforts that were precursors of the Progressive movement. Marlene Stein Wortman, "Domesticating the Nineteenth-Century City," *Prospects: An Annual of American Cultural Studies* 3(1977): 31–572. Jill Conway, "Women Reformers and American Culture, 1870–1930," *Journal of Social History* 5(1971–72): 164–77. Estelle Freedman, "Separatism as Strategy: Female Institution Building and American Feminism, 1870–1930," *FS* 5(1979): 512–49.

[71] Degler, *At Odds,* 341, 355, 471 ff.

[72] J. Stanley Lemons, *The Woman Citizen: Social Feminism in the 1920s* (Urbana: University of Illinois Press, 1973).

[73] Jane Addams, *Twenty Years at Hull House* (New York: Macmillan, 1910) and *The Second Twenty Years at Hull House* (New York: Macmillan, 1930). Lillian Wald, *The House on Henry Street* (New York: Holt, 1915). Allen F. Davis, *Spearheads for Reform: The Social Settlements and The Progressive Movement, 1890–1914* (New York: Oxford, 1967). David Morgan, *Suffragists and Democrats: the Politics of Woman Suffrage in America* (East Lansing: Michigan State University Press, 1972), 61 ff.

[74] Lloyd C. Taylor, Jr., "Josephine Shaw Lowell and American Philanthropy," *New York History* 44(Oct. 1943): 336–64. Maud Nathan, *The Story of an Epoch-making Movement* (Garden City: Doubleday, 1926). Nancy Schrom Dye, *As Equals and Sisters: The Labor Movement and the Women's Trade Union League of New York* (Columbia: University of Missouri Press, 1980). Robin Miller Jacoby, "The Women's Trade Union League and American Feminism," *FS* 3(1975): 126–40. Josephine Goldmark, *Impatient Crusader: Florence Kelley's Life Story* (Urbana: University of Illinois Press, 1953). Gladys Boone, *The Women's Trade Union Leagues in Great Britain and the U.S.A.* (New York: Columbia University Press, 1942). Allen F. Davis, "Women's Trade Union League," *Labor History* 5(1964): 3–17.

[75] Louis D. Brandeis and Josephine Goldmark, *Women in Industry: Upholding the Constitutionality of the Oregon Ten Hour Law for Women and Brief for the State of Oregon* (New York: National Consumers' League, 1908).

[76] Lochner v. New York, 198 U.S. 45 (1905). Muller v. Oregon, 208 U.S. 412 (1908). In Bunting v. Oregon, 243 U.S. 426 (1917), the Court sustained a law establishing a ten-hour maximum for factory workers, but permitting overtime at a time-and-a-half rate. In effect, the ruling overturned Lochner, but the Lochner philosophy more or less persisted.

[77] "A Program of Principles and Standards for Protective Labor Legislation in America," *American Labor Legislation Review* 9(March 1919): entire issue. Judith A. Baer, *The Chains of Protection: The Judicial Response to Women's Labor Legislation* (Westport: Greenwood, 1978). By 1919, 39 states had pensions for mothers; 14 states and the District of Columbia had minimum-wage laws. Morgan, *Suffragists and Democrats,* 65.

[78] Flexner, *Century of Struggle,* 237–38. Anna Howard Shaw, *The Story of a Pioneer* (New York: Harper, 1915). Mary Gray Peck, *Carrie Chapman Catt* (New York: Wilson, 1944). See also, Morgan, *Suffragists and Democrats,* chaps. 5–6. Anne F. Scott and Andrew M. Scott, *One Half the People: The Fight for Woman Suffrage* (Philadelphia: Lippincott, 1975), chap. 3. William L. O'Neill, *Everyone Was Brave: A History of Feminism in America* (Chicago: Quadrangle, 1971[1969]), chap. 5.

[79] Flexner, *Century of Struggle,* 248, 257, 262. Giddings, *When and Where I Enter,* 119–31.

[80] Giddings, *When and Where I Enter,* 119–31.

[81] Flexner, *Century of Struggle,* 248, 257, 262.

[82] Kraditor, *Ideas of Woman Suffrage Movement,* 46–52. Degler, *At Odds,* 341. Ellen DuBois, "The Radicalism of the Woman Suffrage Movement: Notes Toward the Reconstruction of Nineteenth-Century Feminism," *FS* 3(Fall 1975): 66. See E. C. Stanton, "The Solitude of Self," *Woman's Journal,* 23 Jan. 1892.

[83] Catharine Waugh McCulloch, "The Protective Value of the Ballot," *Woman's Journal,* 24 Feb. 1900. Florence Kelley, "The Young Breadwinner's Need of Women's Enfranchisement,"

Woman's Journal, 22 July 1905. Ross Evans Paulson, *Women's Suffrage and Prohibition* (Glenview: Scott, Foresman, 1973), 132–43. Jane Addams, "Why Women Should Vote," *Ladies' Home Journal,* 27(Jan. 1910): 121–22. Kraditor, *Ideas of Woman Suffrage,* 69. Jane Addams, *Newer Ideals of Peace,* quoted in Kraditor, *Ideas of Woman Suffrage,* 69.

[84] Flexner, *Century of Struggle,* 238, 248. See also O'Neill, *Everyone Was Brave,* chap. 3.

[85] Harriot Stanton Blatch and Alma Lutz, *Challenging Years: The Memoirs of Harriot Stanton Blatch* (New York: Putnam's Sons, 1940). Inez Haynes Irwin, *The Story of the Woman's Party* (New York: Harcourt, Brace, 1921). Maud Wood Park, *Front Door Lobby* (Boston: Beacon, 1960), 15–18, details Catt's plan. Flexner, *Century of Struggle,* 280–81. James R. McGovern, "Anna Howard Shaw: New Approaches to Feminism," *Journal of Social History* 3(Fall 1969): 135–53. Abigail Scott Duniway, *Path Breaking: An Autobiographical History of the Equal Suffrage Movement in the Pacific Coast States* (Portland: James, Kerns & Abbott, 1914). Ruth Barnes Moynihan, *Rebel for Rights, Abigail Scott Duniway* (New Haven: Yale, 1983).

[86] Giddings, *When and Where I Enter,* chap. 7. Belle Kearney, "The South and Woman Suffrage," in Aileen S. Kraditor, *Up from the Pedestal* (Chicago: Quadrangle, 1970), 262–65. "Laura Clay," *NAW* 1:346–47. Paul E. Fuller, *Laura Clay and the Woman's Rights Movement* (Lexington: University of Kentucky Press, 1975). Kraditor, *Ideas of Woman Suffrage,* 125. See also Rosalyn Marian Terborg-Penn, *Afro-Americans in the Struggle for Woman Suffrage* (Ann Arbor: University Microfilms, 1978).

[87] Hymowitz and Weissman, *History of Women in America,* 273–74. *Woman's Journal,* 15 Dec. 1894. Kraditor, *Ideas of Woman Suffrage,* 63.

[88] Carrie Chapman Catt and Nettie Rogers Shuler, *Woman Suffrage and Politics: The Inner Story of the Suffrage Movement* (New York: C. Scribner's Sons, 1926). Morgan, *Suffragists and Democrats,* chaps. 7, 8.

[89] Kraditor, *Ideas of Woman Suffrage,* chap. 3. Flexner, *Century of Struggle,* chap. 23. Morgan, *Suffragists and Democrats,* chap. 10.

[90] Flexner, *Century of Struggle,* 306–324.

2
Entering the Festival: The 1920s

Suffrage leaders hailed the millennium when the Nineteenth Amendment was ratified. Sharing in that enthusiasm, Governor Cox, the Democratic candidate for president, extravagantly announced, "the civilization of the world is saved," an evaluation that presumed that women voters would "stay the hand of war." Other appraisals, scarcely less restrained in tone, stressed that the victory "completes the political democracy of America," that it marked "the final triumph" of justice. Many old-line suffragists looked forward to a period of calm following the years of persistent campaigning. For their part, the social feminists looked forward to entering "the festival of life" and to completing some unfinished business. Many eagerly anticipated achieving great works of social justice and lasting peace. Alice Paul, while pleased with the adoption of the suffrage amendment, sounded a warning note, reminding the celebrants that despite the suffrage, "women are not yet on an equal basis with men."[1]

THE FIRST HOUR

During the "final drive," suffragists made an impressive showing of political strength. As participants in temperance and social feminist groups, women exhibited a high level of skill as lobbyists. Furthermore, in states with woman suffrage, a cadre of women acquired experience in party organization and campaign techniques. Women gave evidence of their potential as voters when in 1915 Chicago women bloc-voted "Big Bill" Thompson out of the mayor's office; in 1918 Massachusetts women purged John Weeks, an antisuffragist senator, while women in Columbus, Ohio, ousted a sixteen-year incumbent from the mayor's office. This political potential grew as state after state granted woman suffrage.[2]

As ratification approached, women hastened to consolidate their political power and the parties began to court them. As a first step, the NAWSA transformed itself into the nonpartisan League of Women Voters, and the league in turn developed procedures for studying public issues at the local level and articulating a national consensus. For their part, both major parties appointed women to their national committees and placed equal numbers of men and women on state party committees. In the national party conventions in 1920, both of which had women delegates, Republicans endorsed five league proposals; the Democrats, 15. In the campaign that followed, Warren Harding, the Republican candidate, invited women leaders to his Marion, Ohio home and endorsed the principles of equal pay for equal work, an eight-hour workday, maternity and child-welfare legislation, and a federal department of social welfare.[3]

Next the social feminists moved to secure legislation reflecting their concerns. First on the agenda was establishment of a Women's Bureau to formulate "standards and policies which shall promote the welfare of wage-earning women." Lacking substantive power to achieve its ends, the bureau, headed by Mary Anderson, orchestrated the lobbying activities of the major women's organizations—the Women's Trade Union League, the National Consumers' League, the League of Women Voters, the Women's Christian Temperance Union, the Young Women's Christian Association, the National Parent–Teacher Association, the General Federation of Women's Clubs, the American Association of University Women, and assorted church and labor organizations that had allied themselves in the Women's Joint Congressional Committee.[4]

Next on the agenda was the Sheppard–Towner Act, a measure establishing public health centers and prenatal clinics with an initial appropriation of $1,250,000. Enactment of the bill illustrated the strength of women's political power in the early 1920s. Mary Anderson and Julia Lathrop of the Children's Bureau made common cause, arguing that infant mortality and ill health followed directly from low wages, crowded housing, and parental ignorance. Congressmen generally did not want the bill, fearing that its passage would lead to other demands for federally financed social-welfare programs. But the women were insistent. Anderson pointed out that 250,000 infants died each year in the United States. Under the title "Herod Is Not Dead," *Good Housekeeping* detailed the toll in infant lives, while Harriet Upton, vice-chairman of the Republican party, threatened congressmen with retaliation at the polls if they did not approve the measure. It passed by a wide margin.[5]

In 1922 women persuaded Congress to rewrite the citizenship laws for women. Under the principle of *feme covert* an American-born woman lost her citizenship upon marrying a citizen of another country. To give "dignity and individuality to citizenship," the Cable Act established the principle that a woman secured citizenship independently of her husband. Thus, an American-born woman retained her citizenship when she married an alien. But a foreign-born woman could no longer acquire citizenship automatically by marrying an American citizen or through the naturalization of her husband. She had to qualify for citizenship on her own, as he did.[6]

A fourth victory seemed in the offing in 1924 when Congress approved a child-labor amendment. Social feminists had long worked to abolish child labor; they were appalled by the long hours and low pay, the abominable conditions of employment, and the hazards of accident and ill health to which working children were exposed. In 1916 they secured enactment of the Keating–Owen Act that in effect prohibited the labor of children younger than 14 years, set a maximum eight-hour day, and outlawed night work for children aged 14 to 16. But after the Supreme Court struck down that act in June 1918 and a subsequent measure in 1922, the social feminists were compelled to seek a constitutional amendment if they were to achieve their goal. Led by Florence Kelley, opponents of child labor persuaded Congress to submit an amendment to the states.[7]

The struggle for ratification of the Child Labor Amendment disclosed the limits of women's political power. Unlike the Cable Act or the Sheppard–Towner Act, child-labor legislation had immediate consequences for employers dependent on a supply of cheap child labor. While the National Association of Manufacturers financed opposition to the amendment in the cities, the National Farm Bureau Federation and the Grange made common cause against it in rural areas. Capitalizing on still vivid memories of the Red Scare, opponents charged that the amendment had been drafted in Moscow and was financed with Bolshevik gold. Led by William, Cardinal O'Connell, the Roman Catholic hierarchy fought it, alleging there was "never a more radical or revolutionary measure," that it "would set aside fundamental principles of states rights and at the same time would destroy parental control over children. . . ." Defeat of the amendment was assured in early 1925 as the New York State Assembly rejected it.[8]

With the defeat of the Child Labor Amendment, party leaders lost their fear that women would act as a bloc. Although experienced in organizing, campaigning, and lobbying, few women had experience, much less status, in the all-male political organizations. Before women could reach the inner circle of party leadership, they would have to work their way through successive levels of party structure, building a political following as they climbed upward. Recognizing this problem, the League of Women Voters organized classes on the election processes for prospective women voters. In 1928 women, stirred over prohibition and the Catholicism of Al Smith, campaigned extensively for the first time in a presidential contest. While 75 percent of the eligible men voted in 1928, only 56 percent of the women did so. Yet some observers claimed that women's votes provided Hoover with his comfortable margin of victory.[9]

As increasing numbers of women voted, some became poll watchers, others sought public office. During the 1920s a few thousand women attained local offices as aldermen or councilmen. A dozen women became mayors. At the county level, some served as county school superintendent, others as county clerk, treasurer, auditor, or recorder. At the state level, 149 women became legislators, Connecticut alone counting 20. An occasional woman became a state auditor, treasurer, or secretary of state. In New York State, Belle Moskowitz exerted great influence as a political adviser to Governor Al Smith, while Nellie Tayloe Ross of Wyoming and Miriam Ferguson of Texas, became governors. Miriam Ferguson experienced the indignity of having to secure her husband's consent as well as that of the county court to gain *feme sole* status so that she could make binding contracts as governor. The influence of these women officeholders was seriously undercut as they affirmed traditional female roles while pioneering new roles themselves. Governor Ross repudiated the notion "that there is any real difference in the manner in which men and women approach intellectual or practical problems," but she confided that "it is the realm of the home, in wifehood and motherhood, that woman fulfills her highest destiny and finds her greatest happiness." Belle Moskowitz, at the height of her influence, told a forum at Columbia University that "women have qualities of mind peculiarly feminine, but they are not the intellectual equals of men."[10]

Similar changes were occurring at the federal level. By 1930, 13 women had become members of Congress. Jeannette Rankin, the first to be elected, was caught between suffragists, who thought she did not do enough to promote women's interests, and antisuffragists, who thought she neglected the general electorate. The 11 women who went to the House during the 1920s included Ruth Hanna McCormick, daughter of one senator and wife of another; Ruth Bryan Owen, daughter of William Jennings Bryan; and Edith Nourse Rogers, the first congresswoman to have her name attached to a major piece of legislation. Succeeding her husband in June 1925, Rogers continued in the House until her death 35 years later. An American Red Cross worker during World War I, she maintained a continuing interest in veterans' affairs, becoming a sponsor of the GI Bill of Rights in the 1940s. Rebecca Latimer Felton, the first woman in the United States Senate, received an interim appointment as a reward for party service. A spritely 87 when appointed, she served but a single day.[11]

At other levels in the federal bureaucracy women won a scattering of positions. From 1921 to 1934 Grace Abbott provided the Children's Bureau with careful, painstaking administration. Mary Anderson directed the Women's Bureau from 1920 to 1944, making it an effective agency through the force of her own personality and intelligence. Louise Stanley headed the Bureau of Home Economics, while Mabel Walker Willebrandt became an assistant attorney general of the United States.[12]

Despite the expanded political activities of women at the end of the 1920s, foes of woman suffrage pronounced it a failure; friends apologized for its modest achievements. Carrie Catt spoke of the old prejudices that still barred women's freedom of action within parties. Although she believed that women had progressed, she conceded they had only gotten "into the outside vestibule in politics." Concurring, Charlotte Perkins Gilman noted that women were restricted to "a sub-zone" where "only routine and mechanical labor" was required. A later generation of scholars wrote of "The Hope Deferred," "The Great Withdrawal," and "the failure of feminism." These adverse evaluations failed to account how difficult it was for older women, most of whom had no more than an elementary education, to overcome their conditioning that "women have no business voting." These assessments also overlooked the substantial legal bars confronting women who aspired to public office. Ratification of the Nineteenth Amendment had not explicitly conferred rights other than the suffrage. An Arkansas court held in 1920 that despite the suffrage amendment, women could not be elected to public office. Iowa amended its state constitution to permit women to hold state office, while Georgia—which had opposed ratification of the amendment—enacted legislation barring women from elective office. As late as 1942, the Oklahoma constitution barred women from major public offices. When an antisuffragist sued to bar a woman from serving as justice of the peace, a Michigan court held that the Nineteenth Amendment settled the matter: a woman could hold public office; by contrast, New Hampshire officials held that the amendment "applies solely to voting." Although women had the suffrage, they still had to earn their way to political power. The gains, though real, were dimmed by the extravagant expectations that accompanied ratification of the suffrage amendment.[13]

EQUALITY VERSUS PROTECTION

As part of the mainstream of the woman's movement, social feminists collaborated to support one or another political, economic, or social reform; the National Woman's Party, led by Alice Paul, traveled a different path.

Notwithstanding the Nineteenth Amendment, Paul emphasized that women remained "subordinate to men before the law, in the professions, in the church, in industry, and in the home." Her point was fully documented in a painstaking survey of the legislation of all the states, made for the National Woman's Party by Burnita Shelton Matthews. The vote per se seemed of limited value; the need was to transform the attitude of society toward women. Paul objected to protective legislation that, in according women special treatment or protection, implied they were less able than men to care for themselves. She wanted absolute equality for women and rejected all special privileges. At her urging, the National Woman's Party in 1921 endorsed an equal rights amendment (ERA): "Men and women shall have equal rights throughout the United States and every place subject to its jurisdiction." To Paul, an ERA would provide women a shortcut to full equality, and on December 2, 1923, the ERA was first presented to the judiciaries committees of the House and Senate.[14]

To the social feminist majority, however, the ERA was anathema, threatening to erase most of the hard-won protective legislation for women. Mary Anderson, head of the Women's Bureau, took the lead in opposing the ERA:

> In the first place it was unsound from the legal point of view. There was no definition of 'rights.' There was no definition of 'equality.' If a state law had different standards for men and women, would the amendment mean that the men should have the women's standards, or the women have the men's? No one knew the answer. In the second place it was unnecessary because most of the real discriminations against women were a matter of custom and prejudice and would not be affected by a constitutional amendment. In the third place it was dangerous because it might upset or nullify all the legal protection for women workers that had been built up through the years, which really put them on a more nearly equal footing with men workers.

Subsequently Anderson condemned the ERA as "vicious," "doctrinaire," and "a kind of hysterical feminism with a slogan for a program."[15]

Anderson's objections were seconded by others—Florence Kelley, Carrie Chapman Catt, and Alice Stone Blackwell. Roscoe Pound, dean of the Harvard Law School, offered authoritative support for Anderson's central concern—the threat to protective legislation. "There is no surer method of repealing all legal protection for women," Pound declared, "than to substitute for the laws now in force general statutes covering all persons." Pound's judgment would be repeated over and over as debate on the ERA dragged on.[16]

To the protectionists, working-class women were vulnerable to exploitation in the job market. With limited education or skill but with great need to work, women had to take whatever employment was available; without special legislative protection their health and safety were in jeopardy. Having devoted 20 years of hard work to lobbying for protective legislation for women and children, Florence Kelley denounced Alice Paul as "a fiend come to destroy."[17]

In rebuttal, Paul argued that she was not against an eight-hour day or prohibitions against night work, but that "protective legislation [should] be made to apply to everyone alike so that industrial conditions may be definitely improved." Paul was especially aware of the sex discrimination that women encountered in state laws.[18]

The quarrel between protection-minded feminists and equality-minded feminists rested in part on constitutional law, which by the mid-1920s was deeply sexist. As early as 1872 in the *Myra Bradwell* case, the U.S. Supreme Court, in upholding an Illinois statute that barred women from the practice of law, declared "that God designed the sexes to occupy different spheres of action. . . . Man is, or should be, woman's protector and defender." By contrast, "the domestic sphere . . . belongs to the domain and functions of womanhood." This being so, the Court concluded that a "distinct and independent career" for a wife was "repugnant" to the "harmony, not to say identity, of interests and views" that should characterize a marriage. The Court reaffirmed its sexism in the *Lochner* decision as it insisted that however hostile the working environment, men must fend for themselves. On the other hand, in the *Muller* case the Court allowed protective legislation for women and children to stand, but on the grounds that because of "woman's physical structure and the functions she performs in consequence thereof," the physical well-being of the woman was "an object of public interest and care. . . ."[19]

By 1920 thousands of social feminists had invested uncounted hours over a period of a decade and a half to secure protective legislation for working women and children, and the effort was ongoing in 1920. Top priority had gone to the regulation of wages and hours. After Massachusetts adopted the first minimum-wage law, 11 other states followed suit. These minimums were set industry-by-industry, occupation-by-occupation. Statewide minimums did not exist anywhere; the amounts varied from a high of $20 per week for office workers in North Dakota to a low of $7.50 per week in Utah and Arkansas. Regulation of hours, the issue in the *Muller* case, had become general. But the variations were enormous. Whereas Indiana limited only the nighttime hours of women in manufacturing, California set an 8-hour day, 48-hour week as the statutory standard for a wide range of employments. Generally, however, the workday was restricted to 8 or 10 hours; the work week, to 54 to 56 hours. Domestic servants and farm laborers—workers most vulnerable to exploitation—were not covered.[20]

A dozen states specifically required that employers work women no longer than 5 or 6 hours straight without a rest or meal break. Likewise, 12 states specified that women might work no more than 6 consecutive days without a day of rest. Night work was interdicted in 13 states. The prohibitions were specified by industry so that in Ohio, for example, night work was banned for ticket-takers only. The home sweatshop, which had been condemned for decades as unhealthy and exploitive, was regulated or prohibited in a dozen states. Ten prohibited it entirely except for members of the immediate family who were engaged in the manufacture of clothing, trimmings, and tobacco, which, of course, had been the chief areas of abuse. Other protective laws set standards for cleanliness, adequate lighting, and ventilation.[21]

The whole corpus of protective legislation for women received a severe check in 1923 when in the *Adkins* case a new conservative majority on the Supreme Court declared the District of Columbia's minimum-wage law unconstitutional. Speaking for the Court, Justice Sutherland held that the Nineteenth Amendment had ended the need for protective legislation for women. The Court reasoned that equality at the polls meant equality at work. In the wake of the *Adkins* decision minimum-wage laws for women were struck down in Arizona, Kansas, and Wisconsin. Elsewhere such laws fell into disuse. Outraged, Florence Kelley denounced the Court for guaranteeing the "inalienable right of women to starve." The knowledge that the National Woman's Party had filed a brief urging the Court to invalidate the District's minimum-wage law dissipated whatever harmony had lingered in the woman's movement after the drafting of the ERA. The consternation of the protectionists was well-founded.[22]

Three points stand out. First, the Women's Bureau, the chief defender of protective legislation, documented the case that most of the female labor force, far from working to secure "pin money" with which to buy personal luxuries, worked to support themselves, a husband, children, or other dependents just as most men did. Second, the bureau insisted that harsh conditions on the job were more harmful to the working woman than to the working man, because at the end of the workday, he was through for the day, while she still faced several hours of child care and housework. To the Women's Bureau this meant: women needed protective legislation. But because of the multiplicity and diversity of protective legislation, any effort to render it sex-neutral—that is applicable alike to men and women— would necessitate revising a substantial portion of law in each of the 48 states. To Alice Paul this meant: an ERA would foster sex-neutral legislation. Third, in the *Lochner* decision the Supreme Court had ruled out general protective legislation for men, while in the *Adkins* decision it had ruled against special protective legislation for women; to the Court, the conclusion was clear: protective legislation—whether restricted to women alone or applied to both sexes—was of doubtful constitutional validity. The rift in the ranks of organized women was deep and, for the time being, unbridgeable. Alice Paul, with her tiny following, kept alive the idea of equal rights and sex-neutral legislation; Mary Anderson and the Women's Bureau, the de facto center of the woman's movement, kept alive the ideals of social feminism.[23]

FLAPPERS FRUSTRATE

If the suffragists and feminists were disappointed with their political progress during the twenties, far more disillusionment stemmed from the flapper. To Lillian Hellman, on the threshold of a career as a distinguished playwright, "the emancipation of women, their rights under the law, in the office, in bed," seemed "stale stuff." Although the term antedated the twenties, "the flapper" is firmly identified with the "revolution in manners and morals" of the early twenties. The flapper "smoked, drank, worked and played side by side with men. She became preoccupied with sex—shocking and simultaneously unshockable. She danced close, became freer with her favors, kept her own latchkey, wore scantier attire which emphasized her boyish athletic form, just as she used makeup and bobbed and dyed her hair." If the New Woman was identified with the bohemian set and literary rebels of Greenwich Village, the far more numerous flapper was identified with the daughters of the middle class from New York to Muncie. This revolution in manners and morals took "the two fold form of more permissive sexuality and diminished femininity." Behavior that was exceptional in the prewar years, became common in urban America in the twenties, and it disturbed not only the respectability, but also feminists as varied as Jane Addams and Charlotte Perkins Gilman. The flapper "bemused, outraged, and frustrated."[24]

The indictment of the flapper as a self-centered, hedonistic person pointed as much to sins of omission as of commission. The value system by which she was measured was that of the earnest social feminist and career woman, many of whom had forgone marriage and motherhood as the price of personal self-realization. At the political level the flapper was indifferent to the suffrage, regarding politics as a "sordid and futile" business. For her indifference she was blamed for the reaction that brought the flood of social legislation to an end, for the failure of women to vote in anticipated numbers or as a bloc, for the inability of the League of Women Voters to enroll more than ten percent of the membership of its parent organization, for the loss of their vitality by the WTUL and the National Consumers' League. To Jane Addams, the disintegration of the

The flapper—the turned-on miss of the early 1920s—shocked her elders by her antics.

woman's movement was "associated in some way with the breaking down of sex taboos and with the establishment of new standards of marriage." This was a heavy burden of responsibility to be borne by a person whom F. Scott Fitzgerald characterized as "lovely and expensive and about nineteen."[25]

Again the flapper symbolized the new consumer economy that became conspicuous in the twenties. The automobile, electric refrigerator and washing machine, and the radio became necessities of the middle class.

The cosmetic industry emerged; lipstick and rouge, which had been taboo for the self-respecting in 1920, were obligatory for dress occasions a decade later. To safeguard profits, the business community hired experts to publicize their products, others to assure that the goods were attractively packaged. Installment accounts facilitated purchase of the more expensive items, while advertising to stimulate sales began the transition that "transmuted soap from a cleansing agent to an aphrodisiac." Factory production permitted the working class, at least in dress, to emulate the middle class. If the flapper had little responsibility for initiating these changes in the character of industry and business, she conspicuously embraced those changes that had to do with fashionable dress and cosmetics. To an older generation with roots in the nineteenth century, thrift was still a virtue; to the flapper generation, virtue consisted of consumption. It was a Muncie (Indiana) editor, not a flapper, who declared "Consumption is a new necessity."[26]

The flamboyant flapper attracted attention; the press found her exciting copy and egged her on. The *Ladies' Home Journal,* a bastion of respectability, as early as around 1915 displayed "calves, arms, and shoulders and bobbed hair." Responding to the popularization of Freud, nearly one fourth of the high-brow journals approved the doctrine that sexual release was healthy for both sexes. By the end of the decade, two fifths of the mass magazines endorsed the idea. A "bumper crop" of sex magazines and confession magazines developed "to a nicety the gentle art of arousing the reader without arousing the censor." Reinforcing the sexual message of the magazines, the cinema "diligently and with consumate vulgarity" publicized the new order. Women were presented as sex symbols. Impressionable moviegoers copied the hairstyles, dress, and manners of screen heroines. Even the silent screen of the twenties illustrated "the new priority of twentieth-century women: attracting the male through sexual allure." By 1930 the star of the moment provided "the standard of sexual attractiveness" by which the women in the audience could measure their personal worth. The images varied, ranging from Mary Pickford, "the virginal child woman incarnate" to Theda Bara, the vamp, "the eternal temptress, the Eve, who led men astray and lived for sex." Variations of this theme emphasized "the seductress pure and simple," the flapper, "the flirt, the sex tease, eternally promising sex play but not mature passion," and the *femme fatale,* who was "sophisticated . . . subtle and mysterious." None of these representations was feminist. Far from developing mature personalities these women lived for one thing—a man.[27]

Central to the criticism of the flapper was her openness with respect to sexuality. By 1920 Freud reached the college campuses; novelists such as Fitzgerald and Hemingway hailed the existential pursuit of self-realization; and Margaret Sanger busily popularized birth control. If the flapper had "a widely pervasive obsession with sex," she lived in a society that touted sex. The rebellion of the youth of the twenties was directed at tearing "the cloak of shame and hypocrisy from sexual behavior and from the public discussion of sex." At the least, "modesty, reticence, and chivalry were going out of style: women no longer wanted to be 'ladylike.' . . ." From Muncie, the Lynds reported that over half of the junior and senior girls agreed that "petting" was nearly universal at teenage parties. The most adventurous women "were hungry for experience rather than commitment." "Virginity, once a young woman's most treasured asset," became a liability. And the studies of Lewis Terman, Katharine B. Davis, and Alfred Kinsey confirm that women who came of age around 1920 were twice as likely to experience premarital sex as their mother's generation had. Yet there was more smoke than fire. The double standard was bent, not broken. For women, sexual activity outside marriage remained illicit. Affairs had to be kept secret; "marriage alone legitimatized woman's sexuality."[28]

Public interest in sexuality was stimulated in part by the birth-control movement. For a decade or more, radicals, led by Emma Goldman, Eugene Debs, and Elizabeth Gurley Flynn, actively advocated birth control, while the National Birth Control League, an organization of upper-middle-class women and led by Mary Ware Dennett, aimed at repealing laws that made the dissemination of contraceptive information and devices illegal. Margaret Sanger, however, was the most visible proponent. She spoke, she organized, she wrote. Her *Woman and the New Race* (1920) sold 250,000 copies, reaching primarily the middle class.[29]

As a feminist, Sanger was at odds with many of her contemporaries. She rejected the suffrage as failing to affect directly "the most vital factors" of woman's existence; the solutions of the Progressives and social feminists, she dismissed as "superficially useful." The basic problem was "the unrestricted maternity and overpopulation that permitted the waste of human life." Presenting the case for family limitation in personal terms, Sanger's basic premise was a woman's right "to own and control her own body," to "choose consciously whether she will or will not be a mother." Her argument was existential: as a woman "goes through the vale of death alone" in each birth, neither man nor state had a right to decide whether she must risk pregnancy. Without access to birth control, woman was but "a breeding machine and a drudge." Furthermore, the woman who experienced one pregnancy after the other lost "all opportunity of personal expression outside her home. . . . She can contribute nothing to the well-being of the community." Children suffered. The "tired, nervous, irritated and ill-tempered" mother was often a hindrance instead of a help to her children. Unrestricted maternity also adversely affected husbands. A wife who avoided intercourse to prevent additional pregnancies risked driving her husband to consort with prostitutes or to turn to alcohol. "Enforced continence," Sanger argued, was "injurious—often highly so."[30]

Sanger also argued that overpopulation resulting from unrestricted maternity contributed to many fundamental social problems. She attributed wars, peonage, child labor, low wages, unemployment, famine, and plague to "too prolific mothers." Likewise, she charged such women with generating "slums, filling asylums with insane, and institutions with other defectives," with "replenishing the ranks of prostitutes, furnishing the grist for the criminal courts, and inmates for prisons."[31]

Implicit in Sanger's argument was the thesis that the maternal role was a prime one for women and that motherhood in turn imposed domestic responsibilities. She urged birth control not to free women from motherhood and domesticity in order to pursue alternative careers, but rather to improve the quality of the mother–wife–homemaker role. But in freeing women from fear of unwanted pregnancies and in denying that sexual activity was intended for procreation alone, Sanger greatly facilitated the sexual liberation of women.

The flapper was common enough in the twenties, but for the most part she was a symbol who "loomed larger in the public imagination than in the everyday life of the average American." That the flapper smoked, drank, danced close, and wore scanty attire shocked; that most women modeled themselves after her is doubtful. In reexamining the twenties, Paul Carter insists that there was "a broad continuum of Americans" in the 1920s who did not participate in the jazz age, "attractive, high-spirited" women who were not flappers. Frederick Lewis Allen made explicit that "the shock troops of the rebellion were . . . the sons and daughters of well-to-do American families." What initially were the excesses of some middle-class youth peaked by 1922; the sequel was "a children's party taken over by adults." The change in women's appearance often reflected the requirements of work, and to the extent that new hairstyles and clothing were functional, the changes were consistent with feminist demands for dress reform that had as long a history as the demand for the suffrage. The physical freedom of dress was "the superficial mark of a new social equality."[32]

The flapper was not the only young woman who caught the public's attention. During the twenties, American women acquired another role model—the woman athlete. In former times, as Elizabeth Halsey has pointed out, "nice girls did not play games in public"; now they did. Yet there was pressure to restrict these activities to intramural competition. Writing in *Hygeia,* a journal of the American Medical Association, Henry Curtis argued: "It is not good social policy to have girls travel about the country for interschool contests." Girls were untrained in "the traditions of sportsmanship"; they would be exposed to "discourteous or even insulting" comments by spectators. The ultimate put-down came from "Big Bill" Tilden, the preeminent tennis player of the day. While conceding "the full equality of women in art, science, business, the theater, music, and the movies," Tilden thought there was no contest in athletics. But in August 1926, 19-year-old Gertrude Ederle shattered that view as she swam the English Channel, besting the time of everyone, males as well as females, who had attempted the feat before. Ederle's performance gave women a "new physical dignity." Commenting on Ederle's achievement, Carrie Catt recalled that a feminist of the 1880s had predicted that "woman's freedom would go hand in hand with her bodily strength."[33]

In the same summer that Ederle won her first long-distance race, 1922, a combination of businessmen and promoters staged the first Miss America contest. Nineteenth-century males put women on a pedestal, worshipping their "superior" qualities, while deprecating their capacity to perform effectively in the "real" world. In 1900 the pedestal had been labeled "motherhood"; in the twenties the label was changed to "sex." The simultaneous emergence of Ederle and Miss America posed the paradox of womanhood. On the one hand, the one-piece swimsuit "changed *bathing* to *swimming*," opening to women a thoroughly wholesome physical activity long available to men. On the other hand, it could be the means of attracting the opposite sex, of becoming a sex object. The Miss America contest, similarly, gave young women an enlarged public presence, albeit in circumstances that reinforced the public perception of women in a sexual rather than intellectual or moral character. Young women were conditioned to emulate the swimsuit queens with "their standardized smiles and bodies and their equally standardized conversations." And in doing so they were again conditioned to accept a restricted range of activities.[34]

What occurred in the twenties was the shedding of "a spectrum of taboos," so that women were permitted a broader range of behavior that society had long tolerated in men. In the judgment of Carl Degler, the new sexual freedom—particularly for women of the upper and middle classes was the "most significant" change. The "easier sexuality outside of marriage," however, was only "the most sensational side." The more important development was the "new, informal, equal relationship between the sexes, culminating in a new conception of marriage." Even Degler's assessment overstates the degree of change. Lois Banner comes closest to placing the flapper generation in perspective. The rebellion, she argues, was a "typically adolescent one: it came from the heart and spirit, not from the mind. When it had played itself out, its adherents fell back on the standards that their parents and their culture had set for them—marriage and motherhood. In no way had this generation overcome women's greatest difficulty: the profound sex-role conditioning that was an integral part of their upbringing." The permissiveness of the bohemian New Woman of the pre-war years was adopted in part by the sons and daughters of the upper and middle classes during the twenties. Yet in 1930 the distinctions between male and female roles remained.[35]

FROM PEASANT TO PROLETARIAN

The trickle of blacks leaving the South from 1915 to 1918 became a stream in the twenties. As a result, two-thirds of the growth in the black population occurred outside the South. With Harlem as a focus, the Northeast gained nearly 300,000 migrants, while the Midwest, including Chicago, Detroit, and Cleveland, received nearly 350,000. This migration of two thirds of a million blacks, almost entirely to urban areas, had significant implications for the educational opportunities of black women and was marked by frustration and despair as well as by a remarkable outburst of creativity.[36]

During the twenties, educational opportunities for black women became less restricted, but especially so in the northern cities. In states with segregated schools, chiefly in the South, little effort was made to fund schools for blacks on a basis of parity with the whites. In the mid-twenties neither Alabama nor South Carolina, both of which had substantial black populations, had a single state-supported high school for blacks that offered a four-year curriculum. In 15 southern states, just under 10 percent of the black youth of high-school age were enrolled, a condition that would limit the capacity of the other 90 percent to function competitively in American society the rest of their lives. The black schools that did exist were generally inferior. "A poorly trained and poorly paid Negro woman" had to "control and teach a group of children from a poor and uncultured home background, in an overcrowded, dilapidated, one-room school house, where she must perform at least some of the janitorial and administrative duties." In northern communities, blacks often inherited schools in older sections of the city that the whites had abandoned for more up-to-date facilities in newer residential neighborhoods or even in the suburbs, but the blacks did have access to schools.[37]

For some blacks in the early 1920s the prejudice, the segregation, the lynchings, and the resurgent Ku Klux Klan were too much. Such blacks rallied behind Marcus Garvey—a "Black Moses" who, renouncing all hope of help or understanding from whites, insisted that blacks must help themselves. A British West Indian by birth, Garvey denounced American black leadership and was in turn denounced. Arguing that blacks should create a nation of their own, he proclaimed an "Empire of Africa" and organized a provisional government of which he was the president. The movement came to an inglorious end as Garvey was convicted of mail fraud. The significance of his movement lay in its baring, for those who would look, the deep-seated unrest among blacks, the feeling of hopelessness of ever achieving a full life in America.[38]

For other blacks, particularly a talented minority of individuals centered in Harlem, the early twenties seemed full of promise. Led by blacks such as W. E. B. DuBois of the NAACP, Charles Johnson of the Urban League, and Alain Locke, a Howard University professor, the black community burst with creative vitality in what has been variously termed the Harlem Renaissance and the New Negro Movement. Blacks began to explore their African origins and culture by way of affirming their worth. In fact the social distance between blacks and whites half pushed, half necessitated the development of autonomous black communities within the larger white metropolis, producing a market for the talents of black craftsmen, merchants, and professionals.[39]

The Harlem Renaissance, however, was primarily a cultural movement marked by the creative outpourings of Claude McKay, Jean Toomer, Countee Cullen, and Langston Hughes. Black women, too, contributed. Among the ablest of the black novelists was Jessie Redmond Fauset whose *There is Confusion* (1924) helped "to carry Negro fiction above the complex problem of race and place it in the company of general American literature." Nell Larsen, in *Quicksand* (1928) and *Passing* (1929), explored the social problems of young black women in their effort to struggle upward. The black theater, too, achieved a vitality, since black actors playing to black audiences could undertake every type of play. A number of able, popular performers emerged, including Anita Bush, Abbie Mitchell, Ida Anderson, Laura Bowman, Cleo Desmond, Rosa McClendon, and Edna Thomas. Florence Mills scored "a signal triumph" in the revue *Blackbirds* with her pantomiming, singing, and dancing. Subsequently Ethel Waters, Adelaide Hall, and Ada Ward continued the tradition. Nor was the Renaissance confined to New York City. Georgia Douglas Johnson of Washington, D.C., achieved distinction as a poet as did Angelina W. Grimke. The circle included Anne Spencer, a poet of Lynchburg, Virginia, and Zora Neal Hurston, an anthropologist who wrote short stories and novels.[40]

The personal lives of blacks during the twenties were affected unevenly by the Harlem Renaissance, for the black community was far from homogeneous. In part because of segregated housing and racial prejudice, the black community created its own institutions and its own middle class. This middle class, "affluent conformists," gained economic stability from the dual employment of husbands and wives, both of whom ordinarily worked in the public sector. Both had equally long employment records—the work being steady. Their families were small and stable. The husband and wife shared in the housework. Members of this group contributed to and participated in the Renaissance.[41]

Far more numerous were working-class families, "innovative marginals," in which both husbands and wives were locked in a continuous struggle to stay out of poverty. The families—often five or more children—were larger than those of the black middle class. Family cohesion was based less on understanding and tenderness than on "heroic effort to stave off adversity." Racial discrimination combined with limited education to restrict employment opportunities. The migration to northern cities, however, allowed black women to shift from private domestic work to institutional custodial work. Such black families prized the "owned" home and clean living, that is "puritan" values. In such families, sex roles tended to be clear cut: the husband decided finances, looked after household upkeep, and advised the sons; the wife cooked, cleaned, and advised the daughters.[42]

At the bottom were the "struggling poor," the lower class who, in the severe struggle to pay the bills, "hope for little and expect less." Their lives were characterized by much movement between jobs, houses, and cities. Unemployment was a constant specter. Wives worked as domestics, husbands as unskilled factory hands or as maintenance men. The transformation of domestic service from live-in work to day work permitted married women to combine homemaking with employment as a domestic. At best this permitted the woman to adjust her work load to her family's needs; at worst it forced her to combine a job with homemaking. Marriage and motherhood still came as early as 16, the first child often born out of wedlock. Fierce love existed between mothers and children; the siblings and grandparents were mutually supportive. As most parents had been school dropouts, so the children frequently did not complete high school. Severely limited in economic and social competition, the parents exhibited escape behavior—drinking and gambling; the children might be found in neighborhood gangs.[43]

WHITE COLLAR, BLUE COLLAR

At the end of the twenties, Frederick Lewis Allen reported that in the wake of the suffrage amendment, middle-class girls had "poured out of schools and colleges into all manner of new occupations." He saw them escaping the authority of the home by taking a job and an apartment of their own as the means to the "headlong pursuit of freedom." Echoing this theme, William Leuchtenburg pointed to the 10,000,000 women in the labor force in 1930 and concluded that "nothing did more to emancipate them." This "floodtide" of women pouring into the labor force, according to George Mowry, swept away "traditional institutions, morality, and folkways."[44]

Historians, moved by the woman's movement of the 1970s, have looked beyond the aggregate figures—the addition of 2,150,000 women workers to the labor force during the twenties—and have drawn a cautious, even dismal, picture. William Chafe argued that earlier historians "overstated the amount of economic change" during the 1920s and that there was "very little progress toward the goal of economic equality" for women prior to 1940. At most he conceded changes in the composition of the labor force and in the distribution of jobs that women performed. The majority of women remained limited to menial "female" jobs at "inadequate pay." Sharing this view, Lois Banner saw the numerical growth in female employment as "primarily a reflection of the general population growth." With the exception of the movement of women into clerical work, she argued "women did not substantially improve their position in the labor force in the 1920s." Professional women became more numerous, but they secured jobs that were "less prestigious and lower paid." Despite the widespread prosperity, working women fared little better. Taking a sweeping view of the changes the century had brought, Mary Ryan characterized "the major transformation" in the pattern of female employment prior to 1940 as a "simple shift" from manufacturing and domestic services into white-collar jobs. Common to these analyses is the conclusion that the promise of 1920 was not fulfilled.[45]

A Rising Demand

In evaluating the degree and direction of change in the economic roles of women, several factors need to be examined. First is the connection between feminism and women's economic roles. The Seneca Falls Declaration, to be sure, called for the removal of barriers to employment, but while Elizabeth Cady Stanton envisaged broader employment opportunities for women, the logic of the suffrage movement did not. To social feminists such as Jane Addams, Mary Anderson, and Julia Lathrop, a career was incompatible with marriage. Their concern was with protecting working-class women from exploitation, not with enlarging the career opportunities of middle-class women. When the suffrage was secured and the flapper generation opted for employments that posed fewer conflicts with marriage, the older social feminists expressed dismay. Charlotte Gilman, of course, had pointed out the need to restructure housekeeping so that women might be able to pursue the same range of employments as men, but the suffragists and social feminists alike had ignored her. However bright the world seemed in August 1920, jubilant suffragists were not anticipating a massive movement of women into the labor force.[46]

Second, whether a "floodtide" of women entered the labor force in the twenties raises several subsidiary questions: How did the number of women in the labor force in 1930 compare with the number in 1920? Did the increase simply echo the growth of the general population or was there a significant change in the LFPR? Because of the segmented composition of American society, one needs to study the nature of the demand for women workers as well as the elements of the female population that responded to that demand.

In the course of the twenties the labor force added 7.1 million workers, of whom 2.2 million were women. The labor-force rate of adult women in 1930 stood at 23.8, up 2.1 points from 1920. Although women joined the labor force at a faster rate than men, it is difficult to conclude that a "floodtide" of women inundated the labor force. But if women did not flood the labor market, the fact that 10,500,000 women, approximately one adult woman in four, was in the labor force was itself significant. So, too, is the fact that the labor rates increased, an indication of a growing acceptability of employment for women.[47]

Structural changes in the American economy were largely responsible for reshaping and expanding the demand for female labor. The primary sector, agriculture, continued to shrink relative to the rest of the economy, though the level of total employment in that sector remained stable. After two decades of steady growth, the secondary sector, manufacturing and construction, reversed direction. While its share of the total labor force dropped 5 percentage points, the number of workers remained steady; yet major changes occurred within the secondary sector. Rationalization of automobile production—which made new cars widely available to the middle class and used cars to the working class—stimulated growth in the rubber, plate-glass, nickel, lead, and steel industries, promoted construction of paved roads, and extended the housing boom to the suburbs. New techniques of assembly-line production in turn revolutionized the output of new consumer products that transformed housekeeping as the urban middle class outfitted their homes with electric vacuum cleaners, washing machines, refrigerators, irons, and toasters. Nevertheless, because of the introduction of new tools and production techniques, the number of persons employed in manufacturing declined by 1,200,000 during the decade. The most dramatic structural changes occurred in the tertiary sector, notably in employments relating to trade and service, which absorbed 4,400,000 additional workers in the course of the decade (see Figure 2-1). These structural changes, then, produced a declining job market in agriculture and manufacturing, areas that primarily hired men, while the expansion

Figure 2-1
Industrial Distribution of Labor Force, 1900–1980

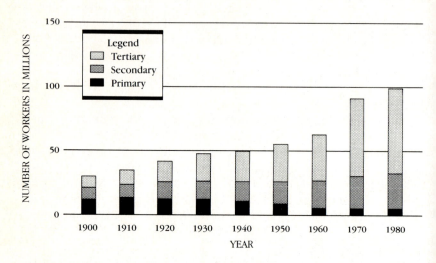

occurred chiefly in the white-collar employments, which welcomed middle-class women.[48]

Since the total labor force increased by 17.5 percent during the decade, the female labor force had to expand by 1,400,000 workers just to maintain a constant share of the labor market. The other 710,000 women added to the labor force constituted an expanded share. In short, two thirds of the increase in the female labor force reflected the general population growth, one third reflected the growing acceptability of employment to women. But because of the separate labor markets for men and women, changes in the demand for female labor varied unevenly from occupation to occupation. Figure 2-2 summarizes the change in the demand for female workers during the twenties. Altogether in five of the seven working-class occupations—crafts, operative, nonfarm labor, private-household service, and farm labor—women failed to maintain a constant share of the jobs. These "losses" ranged from 155,000 jobs as operatives and 127,000 as farm laborers to 12,300 as craftspersons. In service work within private homes—a job that was transformed from live-in to day work—the number of women employed increased even though their share of the occupation declined, while in the relatively more-attractive service work outside private homes, women increased both the number of jobs and their occupational share. In only two of these seven occupations—farmer and service other than in

Figure 2-2
Changes in Demand for Female Workers, 1920–1930

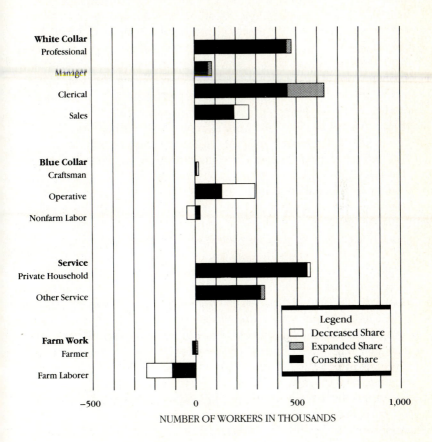

a private household—did women end the decade with a larger share of the occupational market than they had enjoyed at the start of the decade. Furthermore, total employment in two occupations, farmer and farm laborer, was contracting, causing women to lose 17,500 jobs as farmers and 119,000 jobs as farm laborers. The result was a net loss of nearly a quarter of a million jobs as farm laborer, very modest changes in employment opportunities as farmer, craftsperson, or nonfarm laborer, and substantial increases in the two service categories.[49]

By contrast, three of the four white-collar occupational groups were markedly receptive to women during the twenties. Only in sales did women's share of the job market decline, costing an estimated 68,000 jobs. In the other three groups women increased their share of the jobs. For women in professional and managerial jobs, the increased share added approximately 22,000 jobs each, but among clerical workers—a market open to women with a high-school diploma—the increases exceeded 177,000 jobs. Prior to the 1890s, the office was predominantly male, with a male bookkeeper at the very center. The concentration of business enterprise prior to World War I required an "army of clerks" to handle "business facts." Although office machines became important during the war, management—especially in insurance, banking, and finance—continued to rely more heavily on platoons of secretaries than on office machines. But by 1930, some 30 percent of the women in offices used a machine other than a typewriter at least part of the time. Two further observations are in order. First, within each of the major occupational groups, demand for women changed unevenly. Thus, within the professional occupations, for example, women increased their share in specific occupations such as architect and lawyer, while they lost ground as dentist and physician. Second, the dramatic increases in employment opportunities for women were scored in service-producing rather than goods-producing jobs.[50]

In a society whose values made it more difficult for a woman than for a man to enter and remain in the labor force, the demand for "female" labor remained the critical factor in determining the size of the female labor force. In 1920, of the 8,500,000 women who were gainfully employed, 3,714,000, or 43.4 percent, were concentrated in predominantly "female" occupations. During the course of the decade, the degree of concentration increased to 49.4 percent. In this respect, 518,000 jobs or roughly one third of the net increase in the female labor force resulted from the increase in the demand for "female" labor.[51]

Altogether there were 20 "female" occupations in 1920, 25 in 1930, and even within this select group, women were concentrated in 4 occupations—domestic service, teacher, stenographer, and launderer. The increase in the concentration of women in "female" occupations during the course of the decade resulted from sizable additions to the ranks of domestic servants and to all of the "female" white-collar occupations—teacher, trained nurse, and stenographer. By contrast, demand declined in the more traditional "female" service jobs such as boardinghouse keeper, launderer, untrained nurse, as well as in blue-collar occupations in clothing and textile production. In general, the growth in demand for women grew—domestic service excepted—in occupations that placed a premium on education, literacy, and skill training; it declined in occupations that sought women for their traditional homemaking skills.[52]

Basic to the persistence of this sexual division of labor was the demand for labor with specific qualities. The decisive factor in the preference for

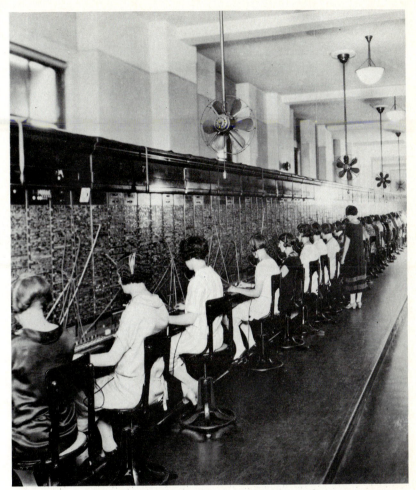

In 1925, several hundred thousand young women had "minicareers" as telephone operators.

women in white-collar employments was cheapness in combination with a fairly high level of general education or special skill training acquired before entering the job market. This was a factor in the demand for women as elementary teachers, as well as for clerical workers, librarians, nurses, and social workers. Demand was also related to traits that employers perceived as sex-linked and desirable for particular occupations. Initially employers hired women to work in textile mills and clothing factories to take advantage of their familiarity with spinning, weaving, and sewing.

Other qualities included the greater manual dexterity and patience attributed to women, as well as their feminine appeal. These characteristics differed substantially from those required for "male" occupations—physical strength, high motivation, geographic mobility, and career continuity. Once labeled a "female" occupation, a job remained a female occupation. During the twenties the demand for "female" labor shifted in the direction of employment that placed a premium on possession of a high-school diploma or a baccalaureate. Such jobs were genteel and hence consistent with stereotypical views of the feminine character, while few of the jobs required either a long-term commitment to a career or led to demanding work.[53]

Supply Meets Demand

The changing supply of female labor in the 1920s was shaped by several factors, some positive, others negative. On the positive side, popular explanations attributed the increase in the supply to "a substantial amelioration" of household work resulting from the electrification of homes, the proliferation of appliances, and the availability of processed foods. A reduction in the magnitude and duration of home responsibilities of women accompanied the ongoing decline in the child–woman ratio. Between 1900 and 1920 the ratio dropped by 10 percent; in the twenties alone it declined another 16.5 percent. No less important, the shift from live-in domestics to day workers greatly increased the number of families having access to domestic service in the course of the week.[54]

The positive potential of electrification, the new appliances and food products, the smaller families, and the availability of part-time domestic service were offset by the persistence of conventional social attitudes. The time saved by the new appliances and services offered women choices: they could participate in market work or leisure-time activities, or they could strive for a higher standard of homemaking. However, middle-class social ideals of woman's place led women, as well as husbands, to regard market labor by wives, especially those with young children, with disdain. Couples less accepting of those ideals still faced the disapproval of family and friends. For most couples the choice was between greater leisure for the wife—club activities enjoyed a higher level of social acceptance than market labor—and a higher standard of homemaking and child care. Married women with children could be expected to follow the older formulations of woman's place and to choose some combination of additional leisure and a higher level of homemaking, while women who married and began a family in the twenties would be most tempted to combine homemaking and market labor.[55]

Social attitudes toward the responsibility of the father–husband for the support of his family also affected the decision of wives in choosing among homemaking, leisure, and work. Among the urban middle-class where the husband–father had the means to support his womenfolk "in sheltered idleness," it seemed clear that industrial work might "destroy women's femininity and, by constantly throwing them into the company of men, lead to their demoralization." Furthermore, middle-class males continued to regard the employment of their wives and daughters as questioning their adequacy as providers. They were least likely to object when their wives took white-collar jobs, whose prestige compensated for the intrusion in homemaking activities. Nonetheless, the realities of a long workday, child bearing and rearing, and the burdens of housekeeping combined to discourage outside employment "as either a feasible or morally responsible activity" for a married woman whose husband could support her. As a result, the socially mobile working-class male derived great satisfaction from being able to withdraw his wife from the labor force as soon as he acquired a degree of economic well-being. Since the great majority of adult women were married, the social attitudes toward the propriety of married middle-class women entering the labor force controlled the supply of female laborers.[56]

Society was far less disturbed by the presence of single women in the labor force. Farm families accepted the domestic work by daughters as part of the normal order. In the black community, daughters remained under great pressure to share in the support of the family, but their job choices were narrowly restricted. White working-class families, unable to subsist on a single income, acquiesced in the employment of daughters and wives outside the home. For those with little or no high-school training, there was factory work. For the better educated, the choice was between sales and clerical work, and employment as a sales person enabled the single girl to be "the inviolate mistress of herself," as O. Henry phrased it. Nor were such girls condemned to a "scarcely habitable room" as had been the case at the turn of the century. But during the twenties, unlike in 1900, most young women entered marriage possessing at least limited experience in the labor force.[57]

Part-time sales jobs—a five hour workday—suited the needs of married women, Frances Donovan reported. Half the salesladies of the New York department store where she worked were married, and in fact most had worked prior to marriage. Indeed, she concluded, a part-time job facilitated marriage, since with two incomes the couple could survive. And there was some occupational mobility—a chance to become head of stock, assistant buyer, or even buyer. Even so, many single women preferred employment as an office girl. Such work paid better than sales work, and, more importantly, it provided contacts with men and the possibility of marrying the boss. The realities, though, were that advancement was slow; unmarried bosses, few in number.[58]

The supply of female laborers was further constrained by the discrimination against married and older women that society countenanced. During the twenties, numerous states excluded married women from public employment. Among the worst offenders were the public schools. One school-board president spoke for many when he declared: "The institution of marriage is mainly for one purpose—the establishment of a home and raising a family. . . ." The rationale also included assertions that a married woman had less need for employment than single women or men, that being less dependent on her job, she was less amenable to supervision by school authorities and thus had less professional commitment. By 1930, school boards generally refused to hire married women as teachers, and one-half the systems required a woman teacher to resign if she did marry. Private policy and practice varied but were often hostile to the married woman. Women over 40, married or single, were special objects of discrimination on the assumption that they were less able physically and were inclined to be "unreliable, inefficient and frequently 'neurotic.' Younger women were preferred as more easily trained, more inclined to accept company policy, more alert mentally, more attractive, and available in quantity at lower wages."[59]

Compared to the preceding two decades, changes in the age distribution of women did not greatly alter the supply of white females. The proportion of women under age 35 declined slightly; that of women 35 and over increased, but seldom by more than a fraction of a percentage point. The decreases in the supply of women occurred in age groups with low labor-force participation, while one third of the increases were concentrated in age groups beyond the conventional working age. The effect of these shifts in the age mix was to induce employers to make more intensive use of the younger women and to turn increasingly to older ones.[60]

For nonwhite women, the shifts in the age distribution were smaller in magnitude than they had been in the first two decades. The trade-offs between a relatively small pool of women under 30 and a large pool of older women had the effect of decreasing the pool of teenagers, who had very low labor-force rates, and of increasing the pool of nonwhite women in age ranges with relatively high labor-force rates. The net effect was to increase the supply of adult, nonwhite female labor.[61]

Changes in the mix of single, married, widowed, and divorced women affected the female labor supply to a modest degree. Despite the popular view of the flapper as choosing marriage in preference to a career, the proportion of women 20 to 24 years old who were single grew slightly during the twenties (see Figure 2-3). In every other age group under 55, however, the proportion of single women declined, while—excepting women in their early 20s—the proportion of married women in the general population increased on the order of 1 percent. It is relevant to the choices faced by employers of women that there were 8,350,000 women in the labor force in 1920 compared to 5.5 million single women age 20 and over. Clearly the pressure was great to maximize the recruiting of single women, for whom supply was short, and to turn to married women to make up the difference, especially where the need was for mature workers. During the decade, the number of married women in the labor force passed 3,000,000, a gain of over 1,000,000; the proportion of women in the labor force who were married jumped from 22.8 percent to 28.5 percent.[62]

On the surface there was little change in women's involvement in the labor force, as the aggregate labor-force rates rose by .9 of a percentage point during the decade. As in the first two decades of this century, this change was deceptive, for it disguised the continuing replacement of teen-

Figure 2-3
Marital Status of Female Population, 1920–1930

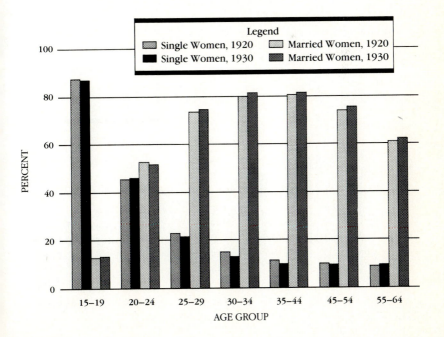

age women with adult women. During the twenties, the labor-force rate
of teenage women dropped by 5.6 percentage points, reflecting the success
of the high schools in retaining an ever-larger proportion of the youth
until graduation. There was also a ripple effect, as each successive cohort
of women from 1880 onwards entered the labor force in higher proportions; as these cohorts matured, their labor-force rates were higher at each
stage in the life cycle than the rates of earlier cohorts of women. For
women in their early 40s, for example, the labor-force rate rose 2.3 percentage points between 1920 and 1930. This graying of the female labor
force, reflected in Figure 2-4, offset the sharp decline in labor-force rates
of teenage women, so that the aggregate rate remained virtually steady. It
is also the case that the female labor force increasingly consisted of adult
women.[63]

Despite social values that continued to discourage married women
from entering the labor force, an increasing proportion of them sought
employment. Thus, of the 2.28 million women added to the labor force in
the twenties, 1.15 million, or 50.4 percent, were married women. This
compares to less than 30,000 married women added to the labor force in
the preceding decade. Census data does not permit separating the single

Figure 2-4
LFPR for All Women by Age, 1920 and 1930

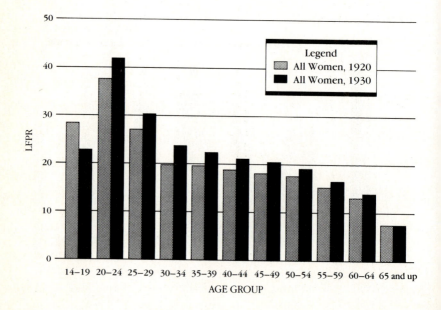

women from those who were widowed or divorced. However, as the proportion of widows remained constant and the number of divorced women constituted but 1 percent of the adult female population, neither group had a significant impact on the size or shape of the labor market.[64]

In the restructuring of the female labor force, black women had a proportionate role. Their numbers rose by 289,000, an increase of nearly 20 percent. Here too, their aggregate labor-force rates, which dropped from 40.6 to 40.4 during the decade, disguise the replacement of teenage girls with adult women. Compared with white women, the age-specific labor rates for postmenopausal black women dropped 1 to 2 percentage points. Without exception, as Figure 2-5 illustrates, the age-specific labor rates for black women ran higher than those for native-born white women, the magnitude of the differences increasing from age 20 until age 50. As single women, blacks were slightly more inclined to enter the labor force

Figure 2-5
LFPR for Women by Race and Age, 1920 and 1930

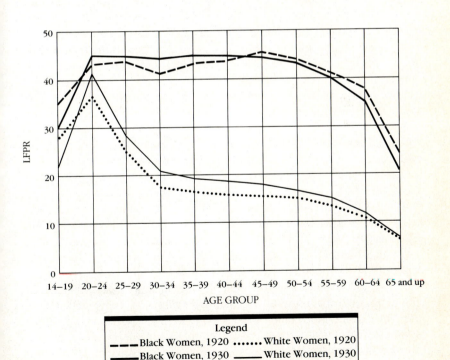

Legend
- - - Black Women, 1920   ••••••• White Women, 1920
——— Black Women, 1930   ——— White Women, 1930

than whites; but as married women, at any age, blacks were three times more likely to be in the labor force than white women.[65]

Black women continued to escape the low-paying, back-breaking toil as farm laborers that had been the lot of so many, while the shift from live-in domestic service to day work enabled black women in the cities greater flexibility in their work arrangements as domestics. Further, the shift from the rural South to city dwelling gave their children access to schooling, which a generation hence would enable them to compete for blue-collar and even white-collar employments, a most significant advance.[66]

These changing labor-force rates do not support the effusive reports of a "floodtide" of women pouring into the labor force, but neither do they describe a picture of little or no change in women's employments. The changes in the size of the female labor force in the twenties were modest, but changes in age-specific labor-force rates reflected a continuing decline in reliance on child labor and a growing acceptance of employment for adult women in all age groups, especially married women. Declining birth rates along with the introduction of labor-saving home appliances unquestionably eased the physical demands on women, enabling some to take employment outside the home, but social values, which in 1900 had inhibited all but single women, the poor, and the black from taking jobs, were refocused to inhibit mothers—especially those with young children—from entering the labor force. The structural changes in the economy also shifted the demand for female labor away from industries that used women as manual laborers or for their housekeeping skills to industries that required a degree of literacy and intellect. The decline in manufacturing and domestic employments and the rise in white-collar employments did not cause a simple transfer of personnel. Certainly there is no evidence that women who entered the labor force as domestics or factory hands subsequently became white-collared sales or office personnel. Rather changes in the structure of the economy contracted the number of jobs in the blue-collar area while expanding those in the white-collar area and hence created jobs that urban middle-class women could accept with the least difficulty. Older women in blue-collar occupations stayed on or dropped out of the labor force; younger women, benefitting from their higher levels of education, took jobs in the expanding white-collar occupations. Employers, however, remained leery of engaging women in professional and managerial positions that required extensive commitments of time and energy, and they discouraged women from seeking such employments. The freer attitudes of the twenties made it slightly easier for a woman to combine marriage and market labor. This expansion of jobs, thought suitable for the middle-class woman, was of major importance. Finally, the declining proportion of young single women in the population put pressure on employers to put aside their reluctance to employ older and married women.

ACCESS TO EQUALITY

Access to education—a key feminist objective in the days of Mary Wollstonecraft—remained important, though seldom spoken of by feminists. Since the disappearance of the frontier, schools had become the principal means for social mobility. During the twenties, secondary and collegiate education afforded the primary means of preparing for white-collar and professional employments; restricted access impeded employment opportunity, but the chief failing lay in the degree to which schools were a major source of sex-role stereotyping.

During the twenties, Americans congratulated themselves for having fashioned a public school system that reached a larger proportion of young people than schools anywhere else in the world. The elementary school was almost universally available. The appearance of all-weather roads and motor vehicles permitted the consolidation of rural schools and the enriching of school curriculums, especially in rural areas. College-trained teachers began to supplant those with no more than a high-school diploma. Curriculums were enriched. At the elementary level, music and art instruction afforded new avenues of self-expression. Field trips to the local library, post office, bank, or fire station broadened students' outlooks. The life sciences became more meaningful through the medium of school gardens. At this level the curriculum was sex-neutral; girls were as prepared to enter secondary school as boys.[67]

Developments in secondary education were even more significant. High schools, which hitherto had functioned as college preparatory institutions for a select white middle-class population, experienced major curricular changes prompted by the Smith–Hughes Act: rural schools introduced agricultural and home-economics programs, while many village and city high schools inaugurated vocational training especially attractive to boys and commercial programs for girls. As most high schools were comprehensive, students, whether enrolled in an agricultural, home-economics, vocational, commercial, general, or college-preparatory program, shared a common teaching staff and some common courses.[68]

The broader curriculums served to democratize the high school. This broadening of the high school was particularly important in enabling young women from white working-class families to prepare themselves for white-collar employments and entry into the middle class. Blacks, Indians, and Hispanics did not fare as well. Throughout the twenties, educators expressed concern with increasing the educational opportunities for blacks, while at the end of the decade the Meriam report called attention to the need for reforming educational programs available to Indian youth. Little was said about the schooling of Hispanics. In each case, however, the concern was with the ethnic or racial group as a whole rather than with the program for girls per se. Even so, by the mid-twenties about one half of all high-school-age youth were enrolled, and the percentage was still rising. American women enjoyed wider educational opportunities than the women of any other country.[69]

Remarkably little discussion occurred with respect to the education appropriate to girls as opposed to boys. Long before the first day of school, parents, older siblings, relatives, and neighbors drummed into a child a sense of sexual identification and of the behavior appropriate to his or her sex. Although the curriculums of elementary schools were ostensibly sex-neutral, the schools unwittingly reinforced differentiated sex roles. Children came to school in clothes that identified their sex and that tended to deter girls from the most vigorous activities. In school, boys carried chairs and arranged tables; girls passed out papers. In class, girls undertook "arty" projects; boys hammered, sawed, and painted. At recess, girls played jacks, jumped rope, and swung; boys played ball or soccer. Elementary teachers taught boys more mathematics, gave them more explicit directions, and encouraged them to try new experiences. Teachers tolerated, if not encouraged, aggression in boys, while rewarding neatness, conformity, and obedience in girls. Subtle forms of sex-role conditioning slipped unobtrusively into teaching materials that emphasized endlessly that males are doers, achievers, protectors; that females are homebodies, dependent, and supportive. Junior- and senior-high-school curriculums made differentiated sex roles even more explicit. Physical education was scheduled separately for girls and boys. Girls' locker rooms provided a degree of individual privacy altogether lacking for boys'. Girls took courses in sewing and cooking; boys took shop. At the time, this sex-role conditioning went unchallenged.[70]

During the twenties the high school became "a fairly complete social cosmos." As the center of teenage society, it became "a place from which they go home to eat and sleep." The extracurricular program provided the young an informal training for the future. The purely social clubs, a counterpart of adult clubs, were often both exclusive and single-sex organizations. Girls might achieve social recognition and status through such club membership or alternatively through coed organizations, such as the school paper, the senior yearbook, the school orchestra or glee club, a class play, or the student council.[71]

The high school developed another social function of critical importance—promoting social mobility. Access to middle-class employments increasingly required a high-school diploma. Working-class parents regarded the school as "an open sesame" that would "mysteriously admit their children to a world closed to them," while the business community perceived it as "a heavily sanctioned aid in getting on further economically or socially in the world." Community leaders spoke warmly of "the habits of industry," the "friendships formed," and "the great ideals of our nation" nurtured by the schools.[72]

Completion of high school in the twenties stamped the graduate as possessing better-than-average intelligence, a degree of literacy, and a modicum of stick-to-itiveness. For a male, a high-school diploma afforded direct access to white-collar employments and middle-class status or admission to college and an even wider range of careers and still-higher status. For a girl, the diploma operated differently; the range of middle-class employments was more restricted—sales work, office work, or telephone operator. With additional schooling she might become a nurse or teacher. But the overriding expectation was that her long-term status would be derived from that of the fellow she married. The social value of her high-school diploma was measured by the degree to which it enhanced her ability to marry an upwardly mobile male.[73]

The democratization of secondary education greatly increased the pool of high-school graduates, but these were not equally prepared for college-level work. And in this respect women operated at a severe disadvantage as compared with men. Whereas high-school advisors urged college-bound boys to take a third year of mathematics along with chemistry *and* physics, girls were often counselled that business math was more useful than algebra or that general science would be as good a choice as chemistry or physics. The college-bound miss might have to insist on taking Latin or a third year of mathematics and physics as well as chemistry. In short, although unnoticed at the time, girls were often not as well prepared to enter college as boys.[74]

Women also had more difficulty being admitted to the college of their choice than men. Some schools limited the female contingent to 40 percent of the total in order to reduce competition among women students for male escorts. Selective coed colleges frequently required the woman applicant to meet a more exacting admissions standard than the male. If admitted, she had less chance to secure financial aid. Although a woman determined to attend college could find some undergraduate institution that would admit her, prevailing family attitudes and institutional values often combined to inhibit her from entering college or, having entered, from completing her degree. Thus in 1920 women recorded 282,943 enroll-ments compared to 314,938 by men. The numbers of college students increased impressively during the decade, but whereas women increased their enrollments by 70 percent, men increased theirs by 98 percent. Women sustained higher attrition rates than men, but in the course of the decade, the disparities between men and women declined. The proportion of young women completing baccalaureates increased from 17 per 1,000 twenty-three-year-olds in 1920 to 45 in 1930, a substantial increase.[75]

Women who earned baccalaureate degrees fared well at the master's level but not so in the quest for a doctorate. Both in 1920 and 1930, women earned master's degrees at about the same rate as did men. The proportion of women who pursued the far more demanding doctorate lagged that of men, but whereas for every 1,000 women who received a baccalaureate in 1900, 7.7 earned doctorates; by 1920, the rate was 9.4 and in 1930, 21.2, refuting the complaints of older feminists that the flapper generation was less serious than their mother's generation had been. The achievement was remarkable in view of the higher admissions requirements graduate and professional schools set for women and their niggardliness in award-ing financial support to them. Medical schools, the worst offenders, com-monly limited female enrollments to 5 percent of an entering class.[76]

Whether one was considering undergraduate, graduate, or profes-sional training, women tended to receive a different training than men. Women tended to be concentrated in teacher-training programs or the liberal arts; men, in the applied sciences, business, engineering, and agri-culture. At the professional level, the men monopolized the classrooms in law and medicine. The discrimination women encountered, combined with the differences in training and in social values, had long-term effects on the use to which women put their education. Reflecting the difficulty women had in combining professional careers with marriage, in 1920, 75 percent of the nation's professional women were single. In the course of the decade Lewis Terman's studies further revealed that whereas 86 per-cent of the "highly gifted" males found successful careers, 61 percent of the outstanding women ended as full-time homemakers.[77]

In the heady prosperity of the twenties, women's leaders lost sight of the key role that access to education had had in enlarging opportunities for women. The achievement in opening the public schools to so large a proportion of American youth blinded critics to the limited access enjoyed by blacks, Indians, and Hispanics. Furthermore, it obscured the degree to which the public schools reinforced sex stereotypes that limited a young woman's perception of her abilities and options. Nonetheless, the propor-tion of women enrolling at the collegiate, graduate, and professional levels edged upward. However solid this progress was, it remained the case that women encountered more difficulty than men in continuing their education beyond high school at a time when a collegiate degree was increasingly prerequisite to any but routine white-collar employments.

At the end of the twenties, the attention of society was rudely shifted away from the zany antics of the flapper to the uncertainties that followed the stock-market crash. The suffrage had not brought the millennium. Checked in their campaign to abolish child labor, women's leaders were bitterly divided—the majority group defending a program of protective legislation to which they had devoted three decades of effort, the minority insisting on an ERA. While on the surface the woman's movement seemed in disarray, Mary Anderson and the Women's Bureau had become de facto the focal point of the woman's movement, turning for help as needed to a wide range of women's organizations. The woman's movement, while on the defensive, had the tacit support of the white middle class. Its ideology was that of social feminism; its basic assumption, that women differed from men in ways that required special legislative protection for women. Their divisions notwithstanding, in 1930 women had a wider share in public life—whether it be political affairs, jobs, or social life—than they had enjoyed in 1920.

NOTES

[1] *NYT,* 19 Aug. 1920.

[2] William Henry Chafe, *The American Woman* (New York: Oxford, 1972), 26.

[3] J. Stanley Lemons, *The Woman Citizen* (Urbana: University of Illinois Press, 1973), 50–54.

[4] Clarke A. Chambers, *Seedtime of Reform* (Ann Arbor: University of Michigan Press, 1967[1963]), 76.

[5] Editorial, *Good Housekeeping* 71(Dec. 1920): 4.

[6] John L. Cable, "The Citizenship of American Women," *Atlantic Monthly* 145(1930): 649–53.

[7] Chambers, *Seedtime of Reform,* 29–37.

[8] Ibid., 38–43. O'Connell quoted in Lemons, *Woman Citizen,* 211.

[9] Eunice Fuller Barnard, "Women in the Campaign," *Woman's Journal* 13(Dec. 1928): 7–9, 49. See also editorial, *Woman's Journal* 13(Dec. 1928): 26. Martin Gruberg, *Women in American Politics* (Oshkosh: Academia, 1968), 115. Paul Carter, *Another Part of the Twenties* (New York: Columbia University Press, 1977), 96–100, argues that when some women entered the speakeasies and campaigned for repeal, they broke their united front on the prohibition issue and politicians lost their fear that women would bloc vote.

[10] Carter, *Another Part of the Twenties,* 158. Nellie Tayloe Ross, "Governor Lady: An Autobiography," *Good Housekeeping* 85(Aug., Sep., Oct., 1927). Duncan Aikman, "Politics and Ma Ferguson in Texas," *Independent* 115(Dec. 19, 1925): 703–704. "Calls Her Own Sex Inferior Mentally," *NYT,* 28 Apr. 1926. See editorial, *NYT,* 29 Apr. 1926.

[11] "Rebecca Ann Latimer Felton," *NAW* 1: 606–607. Gruberg, *Women in American Politics,* 151–68. Rudolf Engelbarts, *Women in the United States Congress, 1917–1972* (Littleton, CO:

Libraries Unlimited, 1974), 120. Willa Louise Morris, "Women in Congress, 1921–1933," master's thesis, Ohio University, 1960.

[12] "Grace Abbott," *NAW* 1: 2–4.

[13] Carrie Chapman Catt, "'Woman Suffrage Only an Episode in Age Old Movement," *Current History* 27(Oct. 1927): 6. Charlotte Perkins Gilman, "Woman's Achievements Since the Franchise," *Current History* 27(Oct. 1927): 9. William L. O'Neill, *And Everyone Was Brave* (Chicago: Quadrangle, 1971[1969]), viii. June Sochen, *Movers and Shakers* (New York: Quadrangle, 1973), chap. 3. Jane S. Jaquette, ed., *Women in Politics* (New York: Wiley, 1974), xv. Gruberg, *Women in American Politics,* 169. Peter Geidel, "The National Woman's Party and the Origins of the Equal Rights Amendment, 1920–23," *Historian* 42(1980): 557–82. Nancy F. Cott, "Feminist Politics in the 1920s: The National Woman's Party," *JAH* 71(1984): 43–68. Susan D. Becker, *The Origins of the Equal Rights Amendment: American Feminism Between the Wars* (Westport: Greenwood, 1981).

[14] Chafe, *American Woman,* 114, 112. Lemons, *Woman Citizen,* 181–91.

[15] Mary Anderson, *Woman at Work* (Minneapolis: University of Minnesota Press, 1951), 168.

[16] Pound quoted in Clara Mortenson Beyer, "What is Equality?" *The Nation* 116(Jan. 31, 1923): 116. Harriot Stanton Blatch, "Can Sex Equality be Legislated?" *Independent* 111(Dec. 22, 1923): 301. See also, Cott, "Feminist Politics in the 1920s," 60.

[17] Quoted in Sochen, *Movers and Shakers,* 118. Cott, "Feminist Politics in the 1920s," 60–61.

[18] Sochen, *Movers and Shakers,* 118–19.

[19] Bradwell v. The State, 16 Wall 130 (U.S. 1872).

[20] Women's Bureau, "State Laws Affecting Working Women," *Bulletin 16* (Washington: GPO, 1921).

[21] Women's Bureau, "Health Problems of Women in Industry," *Bulletin 18* (Washington: GPO, 1921).

[22] Adkins v. Children's Hospital, 261 U.S. 525 (1923). Kelley quoted in Chafe, *American Woman,* 80. Chambers, *Seedtime of Reform,* 75–76. See also Judith A. Baer, *The Chains of Protection: The Judicial Response to Women's Labor Legislation* (Westport: Greenwood, 1978).

[23] Anderson, *Woman at Work,* 139–140. Inez Haynes Irwin, *The Story of the Woman's Party* (New York: Harcourt, Brace, 1921). Mary Anderson, "Should There Be Labor Laws for Women? Yes." *Good Housekeeping* 81(Sept. 1925), 53. "Call on Miss Paul to Drop Campaign," *New York World,* 27 Feb. 1922, 2.

[24] Hellman quoted in Lois W. Banner, *Women in Modern America: A Brief History* (New York: Harcourt Brace Jovanovich, 1974), 146. Frederick Lewis Allen, *Only Yesterday* (New York: Bantam, 1959[1931]), chap. 5. Robert S. Lynd and Helen Merrell Lynd, *Middletown* (New York: Harcourt, Brace, 1956[1929]), 137–38. Sheila M. Rothman, *Woman's Proper Place: A History of Changing Ideals and Practices: 1870 to the Present* (New York: Basic, 1978). Estelle Freedman, "The New Woman: Changing Views of Women in the 1920s," *JAH,* 61(1974): 372–93.

[25] William E. Leuchtenburg, *Perils of Prosperity* (Chicago: University of Chicago Press, 1958), 172.

[26] Allen, *Only Yesterday,* 75. Leuchtenburg, *Perils of Prosperity,* 168. Lynd and Lynd, *Middletown,* 88. Preston William Slosson, *The Great Crusade and After 1914–1928* (New York: Macmillan, 1930), 136–37.

[27] Mary P. Ryan, *Womanhood in America* (New York: New Viewpoints, 1975), 264. Allen, *Only Yesterday,* 70, 71, 72. Banner, *Women in Modern America,* 162, 165. See Marjorie Rosen, *Popcorn Venus: Women, Movies, and the American Dream* (New York: Coward, McCann & Geoghegan, 1973).

[28] Allen, *Only Yesterday,* 83, 78. Paula S. Fass, *The Damned and the Beautiful: American Youth in the 1920s* (New York: Oxford, 1977). Carol Hymowitz and Michaele Weissman, *A History of Women in America* (New York: Bantam, 1978), 290–91. Lynd and Lynd, *Middletown,*

138–39. Lewis M. Terman, *Psychological Factors in Marital Happiness* (New York: McGraw-Hill, 1938), 321. Katharine Bement Davis, *Factors in the Sex Life of Twenty-two Hundred Women* (New York: Arno, 1972[1929]). Alfred C. Kinsey et al., *Sexual Behavior in the Human Female* (Philadelphia: Saunders, 1953), 422–23.

[29] Lawrence Lader, *The Margaret Sanger Story and the Fight for Birth Control* (Garden City: Doubleday, 1955). Linda Gordon, *Woman's Body, Woman's Right: A Social History of Birth Control in America* (New York: Grossman, 1976). See also, chap. 1, 20 n. Daniel Scott Smith, "The Dating of the American Sexual Revolution: Evidence and Interpretation," in *The American Family in Social-Historical Perspective,* 2nd ed., ed. Michael Gordon (New York: St. Martin's, 1978), 426–38.

[30] Margaret Sanger, *Woman and the New Race* (New York: Blue Ribbon, 1920), 6, 53, 94, 100, 104, 152.

[31] Ibid., 4.

[32] Allen, *Only Yesterday,* 61. Leuchtenburg, *Perils of Prosperity,* 174. Frances R. Donovan in *The Saleslady* (Chicago: University of Chicago Press, 1929), 185, expresses thanks for the changes in women's wear between 1910 and 1929. In the earlier years "women decked themselves out in white drawers with ruffles and embroidery, starched corset covers, flounced petticoats, stiff shirt waists and high stocks. Praise . . . to the one who invented silk undies that . . . can be washed in five minutes and worn without ironing [and] for the knee skirt in which one can flip up and down the stairway of a bus, run for a streetcar, or hang by a strap in the subway without danger to life or limb." Carter, *Another Part of the Twenties,* ix–x.

[33] Elizabeth Halsey, "The New Sportswoman," *Hygeia* 5(Sep. 1927): 446–48. Henry Curtis, "Should Girls Play Interschool Basketball?" *Hygeia* 6(Nov. 1928), 607–608. William T. Tilden II, "Can Women Compete with Men in Sports?" *Country Life* 42(Aug. 1922): 43–44. Carter, *Another Part of the Twenties,* 115–19. "How a Girl Beat Leander at the Hero Game," *Literary Digest* 90(Aug. 21, 1926): 52–67.

[34] See *NYT,* 5 Sept. 1922. Helen Wainwright, "Swim and Grow Beautiful," *Collier's Weekly* 78(Aug. 14, 1926): 8–9. "Feminine Laurel Bearers," *American Review of Reviews* 74(Sept. 1926): 314–15. "Best Sports for Women," *Literary Digest* 82(Sept. 13, 1924): 70–74. Collett was the ranking woman golfer of the day.

[35] Carl Degler, "Revolution Without Ideology: The Changing Place of Women in America," *Daedalus* 93(Spring 1964): 658. Banner, *Women in Modern America,* 153. See also Henry F. May, "Shifting Perspectives on the 1920's," *MVHR* 43(1956): 405–407. Dorothy Dunbar Bromley, "Feminist—New Style," *Harper's* 155(Oct. 1927): 552–60.

[36] Bureau of the Census, *Historical Statistics of the United States, 1789–1945* (Washington: GPO, 1949), 31.

[37] Gunnar Myrdal, *An American Dilemma* (New York: Harper, 1944), 947.

[38] E. David Cronon, *Black Moses: The Story of Marcus Garvey and the Universal Negro Improvement Association* (Madison: University of Wisconsin Press, 1955).

[39] Alain Locke, ed., *The New Negro: An Interpretation* (New York: Boni, 1925) is the contemporaneous statement. Margaret Just Butcher, *The Negro in American Culture* (New York: Knopf, 1956) is based on Locke's notes.

[40] Nathan Irwin Huggins, *Harlem Renaissance* (New York: Oxford, 1971), 146–48, 157–61, 290. John Hope Franklin, *From Slavery to Freedom,* 3rd ed. (New York: Knopf, 1967), 505–513.

[41] James D. Blackwell, *The Black Community, Diversity and Unity* (New York: Dodd, Mead, 1975), 7–28. Elizabeth Herzog, "Is There a 'Breakdown' of the Negro Family?" in Charles V. Willie, *The Family Life of the Black People* (Columbus: Merrill, 1970), 331–41. J. Richard Udry, "Marital Instability by Race, Sex, Education, Occupation and Income," in Willie, *Family Life,* 143–55. Charles V. Willie, "The Black Family and Social Class," in *The Black Family: Essays and Studies,* 2nd ed., ed. Robert Staples (Belmont: Wadsworth, 1978), 236–43.

[42] Willie, in *Black Family,* 236–43.

[43] Ibid.

[44] Allen, *Only Yesterday,* 68. Quoted in Chafe, *American Woman,* 50. Leuchtenburg, *Perils of Prosperity,* 160. George E. Mowry, *The Urban Nation* (New York: Hill & Wang, 1965), 23. Mowry avers that the number of women working in 1928 was five times the figure of ten years before. Arthur S. Link, *American Epoch,* 2nd ed. (New York: Knopf, 1963), 274.

[45] Chafe, *American Woman,* 51. Banner, *Women in Modern America,* 155. Ryan, *Womanhood in America,* 314.

[46] Jane Addams, *The Second Twenty Years at Hull House* (New York: Macmillan, 1930), 192–98. Charlotte Perkins Gilman, *Women and Economics* (New York: Harper & Row, 1966[1898]), 242–46.

[47] Gertrude Bancroft, *The American Labor Force* (New York: Wiley, 1958), tab. D1-a.

[48] John M. Peterson and Ralph Gray, *Economic Development of the United States* (Homewood: Irwin, 1969), 279–80. Susan Strasser, *Never Done: A History of American Housework* (New York: Pantheon, 1982) explores the impact of technological change. Bureau of the Census, *Historical Statistics, 1789–1945,* ser. D, 69.

[49] See Howard Davis, "Employment gains of women by industry, 1968–78," *MLR* 103(June 1980), 3–9, for the method used in making these calculations. Bancroft, *American Labor Force,* tab. D2.

[50] Bureau of the Census, *Abstract of the Fifteenth Census of the United States* (Washington: GPO, 1933), tab. 3, pp. 306–320. C. Wright Mills, *White Collar The American Middle Classes* (New York: Oxford, 1956), 190–93.

[51] A predominantly "female" occupation is one in which 70 percent or more of the employees are women. See Valerie Kincade Oppenheimer, *The Female Labor Force in the United States* (Westport: Greenwood, 1970), 75.

[52] The calculations are based on raw data in Bureau of the Census, *Abstract of the Fifteenth Census,* tab. 3, pp. 306–320.

[53] Oppenheimer, *Female Labor Force,* 97 ff.

[54] David M. Katzman, *Seven Days a Week: Women and Domestic Service in Industrializing America* (New York: Oxford, 1978), 177. Sigfried Giedion, *Mechanization Takes Command* (New York: Oxford, 1948), 512–627. Oppenheimer, *Female Labor Force,* 30–37. See Preston William Slosson, *The Great Crusade and After 1914–1928* (New York: Macmillan, 1930), 135 ff., for the traditional view that these new household appliances "liberated" women. Oppenheimer, *Female Labor Force,* 33, challenges this view.

[55] Robert W. Smuts, *Women and Work in America* (New York: Columbia University Press, 1959), chap. 4.

[56] Oppenheimer, *Female Labor Force,* 41–42. Banner, *Women in Modern America,* 154. Chase Going Woodhouse, "Married College Women in Business and the Professions," *The Annals* 143(May 1929): 341.

[57] Alice Kessler-Harris, *Out to Work* (New York: Oxford, 1982), 233.

[58] Donovan, *The Saleslady,* 176–77. Genieve Gildersleeve, "The Private Secretary—To Be or Not To Be?" *Bulletin of the National Committee of Occupations* 1(Oct. 1920). Margery Davies, "Women's Place Is at the Typewriter, The Feminization of the Clerical Labor Force," in Richard Edwards et al., *Labor Market Segmentation* (Lexington: Heath, 1975), 274–96. "Demand for Women in Office Work Now Exceeding Supply," *NYT,* 19 Oct. 1924, 9.

[59] Oppenheimer, *Female Labor Force,* 127–30. Lois Scharf, "Employment of Married Women in Ohio, 1920–1940," in *Women in Ohio History,* ed. Marta Whitlock (Columbus: Ohio American Revolutionary Bicentennial Commission, 1976), 19, 21. "Married-Women Teachers Problem," *American School Board Journal* 75(Nov. 1927): 46. See Lorine Pruette, *Women and Leisure: A Study of Social Waste* (New York: Dutton, 1924), 6. Quote is from Ryan, *Womanhood in America,* 315.

[60] Bancroft, *American Labor Force,* tabs. D-1, D-1a, p. 202. The Bancroft data for LFPRs is the best available for the period 1890 to 1950.

[61] Ibid. The data is for "nonwhite," most of whom were blacks.

[62] Bureau of the Census, *Statistical Abstract of the United States: 1971* (Washington: GPO, 1971), tab. 39. The data is for women 14 years and over. The number of married women in the labor force rose during the decade from less than 2,000,000 to over 3,000,000. Kessler-Harris, *Out to Work,* 229.

[63] Bancroft, *American Labor Force,* tab. D1-a.

[64] Bureau of the Census, *Abstract of the Fifteenth Census,* tab. 28, p. 378. The Census Bureau reported single, widowed, divorced, and unknown as a unit in 1920.

[65] Bancroft, *American Labor Force,* tab. D1-a, for the labor force rates. Bureau of the Census, *Abstract of the Fifteenth Census,* tab. 30, p. 379. Bureau of the Census, *Fifteenth Census of the United States: 1930 Population,* vol. 5, *General Report on Occupations* (Washington: GPO, 1933), tab. 3, pp. 76–85. Data is for persons 10 years old and over.

[66] Elizabeth Ross Haynes, "Two Million Negro Women at Work," *The Southern Workman* 51(Feb. 1922): 64–72. Women's Bureau, Negro Women in Industry," *Bulletin 20* (Washington: GPO, 1922).

[67] Slosson, *Great Crusade,* 320–21. Frank Alexander Ross, *School Attendance in 1920,* Census Monographs V, Bureau of the Census (Washington: GPO, 1924), 11, 20, 63–66.

[68] Charles H. Judd, "Education," in *Recent Social Trends in the United States,* 1 vol. ed. (New York: Whittlesey House, 1934), 333.

[69] Ibid., 324. Lynd and Lynd, *Middletown,* 189, compares the curriculums of 1890 and 1924. Judd, "Education," 325–38, 341–42.

[70] Marie Richmond-Abbott, "Early Socialization of the American Female," in *The American Woman Her Past, Her Present, Her Future,* ed. Marie Richmond-Abbott (New York: Holt, Rinehart, & Winston, 1979), 118–19. Judd, "Education," 330 ff.

[71] Lynd and Lynd, *Middletown,* 214–20.

[72] Ibid., 219–20.

[73] Ibid.

[74] James B. Conant, *The American High School Today* (New York: McGraw-Hill, 1959).

[75] National Manpower Council, *Womanpower* (New York: Columbia University Press, 1957), 193–95. Patricia Albjerg Graham, "Expansion and Exclusion: A History of Women in Higher Education," *Signs* 3(1978): 759–73. Roberta Wein, "Women's Colleges and Domesticity, 1875–1918," *History of Education Quarterly* 14(1947): 31–47.

[76] S. P. Breckinridge, "The Activities of Women Outside the Home," *Recent Social Trends in the United States,* 1 vol. ed. (New York: Whittlesey House, 1934), 724–25.

[77] Chafe, *American Woman,* 102. Lewis Terman, *Genetic Studies of Genius,* 5 vols. (Stanford: Stanford University Press, 1925). U.S. Office of Education, *Biennial Survey of Education, 1928–30,* vol. 2, bulletin 1931, no. 20 (Washington: GPO, 1932), 355, 360.

3

The Trauma of Depression: The 1930s

When the stock market crashed in October and November 1929, the nation plunged into the trauma of the depression. Scarcely any Americans—men or women, white or black, young or old, white-collar or blue-collar—escaped the impact. To the homemaker the depression meant the loss or threatened loss of her husband's job; to the working woman it often meant the loss of her own. To the woman who came of age during the thirties, it imposed an austere style of life and uncertainty about whether she could finish school, whether she could find employment, whether she should defer marriage, or if married, whether she should have a child. More than in any other decade of the century, economic considerations overshadowed all else. At a time the economy failed to afford work to all adult males, the propriety of women competing for scarce jobs was debated. The old formulas that had assumed that males could fend for themselves in the marketplace were challenged in the political arena. As pundits asked themselves what went wrong, the place of women in society was reexamined in an effort to delineate the kinds of feminine behavior most appropriate to the economic realities of the depression. Although Herbert Hoover assured the public that renewed prosperity was just around the corner, the depression continued to dominate American life until World War II.

WOMAN'S PLACE

The crisis that the depression introduced in the lives of Americans called into question traditional sex roles. The alleged excesses of the flappers and the intrusion of women into the labor market provoked a reaction at the end of the twenties. Women's magazines—the *Ladies' Home Journal* and *McCall's*—repeatedly reaffirmed traditional views of woman's role as wife and mother. Homemaking, the *Journal* asserted, "Is today an adventure—an education in color, in mechanics, in chemistry." *McCall's* reminded women that only as wife and mother could a woman "arrive at her true eminence." A corollary of this celebration of domesticity was an assault on feminism. "The office woman," *McCall's* declared knowingly, "no matter how successful, is a transplanted posey." The liberated woman, far from being admired for her daring, was condemned for destroying the "deep-rooted, nourishing, and fruitful man-and-woman relationship."[1]

As the depression closed in, man's role as breadwinner was more immediately and directly threatened than woman's role as homemaker. Men tried desperately to find work for both economic and psychological reasons. Male identity and self-regard was tied to a man's capacity to support his family, and the loss of employment was devastating, resulting in remorse and self-doubt, throwing his relationship with his wife and children into disorder. Nathan Ackerman, a Columbia University psychiatrist who studied unemployment in Pennsylvania coalfields, reported that men were loath to report their layoffs to wives. For their part, some wives "punished the men for not bringing home the bacon, by withholding themselves sexually, by belittling and emasculating the men, undermining their paternal authority, and turning to the eldest son." Mirra Komarovsky, too, concluded that few husbands successfully accommodated themselves to the realignment of power and prestige wrought by unemployment. On revisiting Muncie in the mid-thirties, the Lynds were told that "men should behave like men, and women like women." The value system of Muncie in the 1930s with respect to sex roles did not differ greatly from that of the Victorian culture. Being out of a job cost a man his "sense of manhood"—a loss that could "never be measured in dollars."[2]

To revive badly damaged male egos seemed a prerequisite to recovery. In consequence, rugged individualism was exalted. The popular heroes of the day were the individuals who achieved in spite of adversity—men like Joe Louis, the black heavyweight champion, and Dizzy Dean, the unpredictable farm boy who pitched the "gas-house gang" of St. Louis to glory. The superheroes of the younger generation—Tarzan, Tom Mix, the Lone Ranger, and Flash Gordon—triumphed over disorder and chaos by "sheer power and grit" of masculinity. In the movies, John Wayne demonstrated male forcefulness and courage in *Stagecoach,* while in *Public Enemy* James

Cagney asserted his masculinity by smashing a grapefruit into Mae Clark's face. In a society in which the male had lost control of his own destiny, these heroes and superheroes provided models with whom the discouraged could identify and achieve vicariously in fantasy what they could not in real life.[3]

Tradition-minded authors lamented the loss of male influence and the feminization of American culture. John Erskine condemned the New Deal's approach to social welfare as "rampant feminine sentimentalism" and an abandonment of the old masculine values of individual responsibility for one's own welfare. Robert Rogers, an MIT professor, charged that overzealous women teachers "discouraged the development of natural and manly attributes for the sake of artificial discipline and learning." Still others, such as Stewart Holbrook, mourned the passing of the old he-man. The ascendancy of effeminate pacifism led Americans to reject the heroic moments of war. Gadgetry made males docile; beards, the sign of nineteenth-century virility, disappeared. Finally, a few writers suggested that the fathers' role had become nebulous to the point that they were little more than "star boarders" in their own homes. Foreshadowing Philip Wylie's attack on American "moms" during World War II, Lois Boyliss, Alice Kelley, and Gordon Shipman charged that mothers spoiled their sons and thwarted the development of self-confidence by over-protective care.[4]

Dismay over the alleged emasculation of males prompted a reaffirmation of traditional female roles. The sociologist Maxine Davis reported that youth were "hunting comfort and hope and stability in marriage." Writing at the end of the thirties, Pearl Buck thought that women's interest in work and a profession had never been "lower in the last half century."[5]

Women were enjoined to practice the old values by sources as varied as movies, career women, and marketers of goods. As a medium of popular entertainment, the movies reached a mass audience, permitting it to live vicariously through a variety of images of women. The Vamp, a figure of the mid-1910s, was refashioned. As blonde as possible, she combined innocence with guile, emerging as a sex symbol. At one end of the continuum, Marlene Dietrich in the *Blue Angel* was the "vamp turned temptress"; at the other, Janet Gaynor in *Seventh Heaven* was the "sweet virginal blonde." At another level, in the dance extravaganzas mounted by Busby Berkeley, "the master salesman of the sexy feminine," women were exploited as sex objects. In *Footlight Parade,* Berkeley lined up scores of female bodies to project images of "mechanical dolls wound up by male dancers, slaves of old Africa, occupants of honeymoon suites, Singapore prostitutes, and, of course, water nymphs."' Berkeley's women were "fully unveiled, her body titillatingly exposed, molded into one standard, infinitely replicable shape, displayed en masse, and put up for sale."[6]

Other approaches were less blatant in the exploitation of women, but they too denied women power outside of sex. Katharine Hepburn, Bette Davis, and Joan Crawford portrayed a series of hard-nosed career women, each of whom was taught by a man that marriage was all that mattered. Hepburn, for example, was an aviatrix in *Christopher Strong,* a woman's rights crusader in *A Woman Rebels,* and an international columnist in *Woman of the Year.* These women were usually "masculine and aggressive" until they fell in love with the "right" man, who "softened them, feminized them, and tamed them." The portrayals were such that the "forceful, decisive woman who had a separate identity and purpose in life" lingered. For the married woman, for whom the larger life seemed out of reach, the movies afforded some vicarious satisfaction as even the dynamic heroine capitulated at the last moment into a conventional marriage. The domestic comedies—those of Carole Lombard, for example—often presented a girl "on the make," a dizzy blonde who seemed clear-headed only when in pursuit

Katharine Hepburn (shown here in Woman of the Year*) played numerous roles as the aggressive and decisive heroine who, at the last moment, abandons the career for the home life and her husband.*

of a man. The implications were that women enjoyed the romantic chase but always wanted to be caught. Still other themes—the teary melodramas with which Bette Davis was identified—offered emotional catharsis. If the films of the thirties were generally antifeminist, the "intelligence and strength" of the career women were underscored. Lois Banner argues that the high-school girls of the thirties responded positively to these images, a point the Lynds confirm in their study of Muncie.[7]

While movie queens had the larger impact, women athletes also competed for popular attention, projecting quite a different image. Much attention continued to be focused on Helen Wills (Moody) and, in turn, Helen Jacobs and Alice Marble, all of them tennis champions of distinction. The 1932 Olympics marked the emergence of "Babe" Didrikson (Zaharias) as the nation's preeminent woman athlete. Breaking four women's records in track and field, the 18-year-old Didrikson excelled in baseball and basketball as well. Readers of the nation's newspapers were treated to accounts of women athletes competing on a national and international field at a level in which skill, rather than sex appeal or feminine wiles, was of the essence.[8]

Women got mixed signals about woman's place from some of the nation's top journalists, a number of whom—Martha Gellhorn, Freda Kirchwey, Anne O'Hare McCormick, and Dorothy Thompson—enjoyed a national readership. While illustrating the possibilities of making a career, they often suggested that women should either settle for less than men or else pursue traditional paths. McCormick, who wrote on both domestic politics and international affairs, praised "the nobility of women" who "scrimped and saved from their meager incomes." While she encouraged women to participate in local politics, her view of political participation was limited to working through the League of Women Voters, not running for office. Thompson, whose influence as a woman was surpassed in the thirties only by Eleanor Roosevelt's, advised women to concentrate on being good mothers rather than on being secretaries, writers, or lawyers. "It's a better thing," she argued, "to produce a fine man than it is to produce a second-rate novel, and fine men begin by being fine children." While on the other hand, as editor and publisher of *The Nation,* Kirchwey expressed her concern over the treatment women received in American society.[9]

For its part, the business community suggested that the use of a particular product would facilitate the performance of wifely tasks and enhance one's personal attractiveness. In the twenties, advertisers in women's magazines suggested first the permissibility, then the desirability, if not the necessity, of using rouge. Virtually taboo for the proper woman in 1920, rouge was almost universally employed by 1930. So, too, advertisers lured women into smoking cigarettes, not as a means to enhance allure, but to be "companionable." Listerine, which in 1920 had been promoted as an antiseptic "to prevent a minor accident from becoming a major infection," by 1930, having become a mouthwash, began its pitch: "Spring! For everyone but her." The Woodbury girl had "A skin you love to touch," while the Palmolive miss was "The Prettiest Girl in her Set." To the handsoap firms, an "exquisite smooth skin" was a prerequisite if a woman were to be "really fascinating." Toothpastes, which in 1929 still warned of tartar, pyorrhea, and the need for gum massage, by the end of the thirties had become the difference between catching and losing a beau. A mother who served her family Wheaties on winter mornings was assured that she had served a "body builder," while the wife who received a new Hoover vacuum cleaner was told: "he wants to keep you young and gay—and still keep house." For all but the most obtuse, the message was clear: a woman's personal worth was wrapped up in her sexual attractiveness. Implicit in this was the assumption that she was dependent on a man for support and, by extension, that she jolly well had better be "fascinating" and otherwise fulfill the traditional wife–mother–housekeeper role with skill.[10]

Despite pressures to enforce the traditional male and female sex roles during the thirties, there were forces at work that gave feminism a continuing push. As social welfare became a major concern, the older social-feminist groups—the National Consumers' League, the NWTUL, and the settlement houses—gained renewed importance. New Deal agencies recruited their leaders, while the organizations lobbied for social reforms. The League of Women Voters fought nepotism bills designed to exclude married women from public employment, secured the extension of state civil-service laws, and urged more adequate support of public schools. At the federal level, it lobbied effectively for the National Recovery Administration (NRA), the Social Security Act, and the Food, Drugs, and Cosmetics Act. The NWTUL, long an ardent proponent of protective legislation for women, reversed itself to support sex-neutral wages and hours laws. It was unable, though, to convince the Congress of Industrial Organizations (CIO) or the AFL to follow its lead.[11]

Feminists still disagreed on the approach to equality. At the Women's Bureau, Mary Anderson sought to unite women in support of a charter of women's rights. Her draft contained the standard social-feminist demands— equal rights for women in politics, education, law, and employment. Few women's groups supported the charter. Before the League of Women Voters could reach a consensus, the time for action had passed, and Alice Paul's National Woman's Party had mounted a vigorous attack, so that the charter was abandoned. Despite the shift to support of sex-neutral protective legislation, the past divisions between the major women's groups remained too broad to bridge.[12]

Evidence began to surface that the tide of opinion about women's rights was turning. The effort to exclude married women from public employment struck at an articulate segment of the white middle class—the public school teachers—sensitizing them and, in turn, the Business and Professional Women's Clubs to the vulnerability of women in the labor force. By 1937 enough local and state organizations had become concerned that the National Business and Professional Women's Clubs endorsed the ERA. Three years later the Republican National Convention voted its support for an equal rights amendment.[13]

"STOLEN" JOBS

In the course of the thirties, woman's place was explored largely in terms of the economic role appropriate in a troubled economy. The trauma of the depression, with its concomitant wage reductions, temporary layoffs, and dismissals of male workers, prompted much resistance to the employment of women, especially married women. Although the Women's Bureau published data documenting that most women worked because of need, the view persisted that they did so for "pin money," and that, hence, women had less need for employment than men. Acting on these premises, many states adopted laws and regulations to exclude married women from public employment, and the Congress directed that no more than one member of a family might hold a federal civil-service job. In practice, the pressure to resign fell on wives. Many private firms, especially larger banks and insurance companies, dismissed married women employees. A Chicago civic organization reflected widely held views when it declared that women workers ought to be driven back to the home, for "they are holding jobs that rightfully belong to the God-intended providers of the household." These restraints on the employment of married women, according to a 1936 Gallup poll, had widespread support. To most Americans in the thirties, a job taken by a woman was a job stolen from a man. Nonetheless, economic necessity pushed women into the labor market. In fact the proportion of adult women in the labor force rose 3.12 percentage points, a substantial increase for a single decade, and by 1940 the female labor force numbered 12,574,000—1,895,000 more workers than at the start of the decade.[14]

Overall, supply and demand factors affected the size and composition of the female labor force in the thirties much the same way as in the preceding decade. Demographic changes in the white female population depressed the pool of women in nearly every age cohort under 45, with especially large reductions in the age ranges 14 to 24 and 35 to 39. The net effect of these shifts reduced the supply of white women under age 45 by 1,571,000, a loss only partially offset by the relatively larger pool of women between 50 and 64 (see Figure 3-1; compare with Figure 1-1). Among the nonwhites, the demographic shifts produced a sharp contraction in the supply of women under age 25, though the relative size of most age groups under age 50 declined during the decade. In terms of marital status, the depression produced a modest increase in the proportion of single women—not only among those in their late teens and early 20s, but in all age groups under 40—and a concomitant decrease in the proportion of married women. The interaction of these shifts was to add 330,000 single women to the female labor supply, partially offset by a loss of 186,000 married women.[15]

Underlying these demographic changes were two phenomena. First, a declining birthrate meant that each successive generation had fewer children than its parents' generation, contracting the pool of young single women (see Figure 3-2). Second, better nutrition and health care enabled a larger proportion of the population to survive to middle and old age. In the white population, the proportion of women age 65 and up grew slowly to 1930, but during the thirties it jumped ahead by 1.55 percentage points. In the nonwhite population, prior to 1930, the percentage of women over 65 was declining, while the pool of women age 35 to 64 was progressively expanding. Then in the 1930s the trend reversed, and the proportion of nonwhite women over 65 suddenly expanded. While longevity per se is a

Figure 3-1
Proportion of White Women by Age, 1930 and 1940

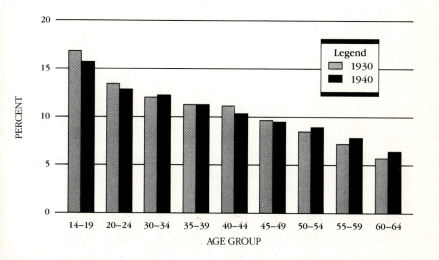

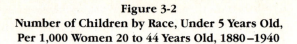

Figure 3-2
Number of Children by Race, Under 5 Years Old,
Per 1,000 Women 20 to 44 Years Old, 1880–1940

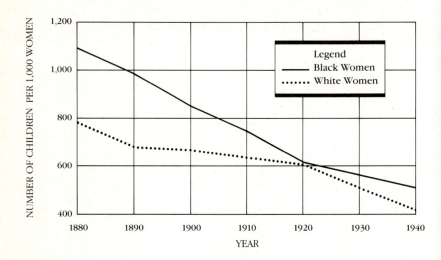

measure of general well-being, the increases in the proportion of women over 65 expanded the population least likely to participate in the labor force. The contraction in the pool of those under 19 tended to accelerate the continuing reduction of child and teenage labor; the reduction in the pool of those in their early 20s forced employers who wanted female employees in this age group to offer higher inducements or else substitute married or older women (see Figure 3-3).[16]

Whereas the demographic changes affected the size of the various pools of women potentially available to the labor force, the rise in the labor-force rate by 3.2 points underscored the increased pressure on women to enter the work force. However, the supply of women varied substantially according to age, race, and marital status.

Government policy curbed the propensity of women under 18 as well as those over 65 to enter the labor force. Supported by labor unions and social workers, public schools continued their efforts to persuade young people to complete high school. Equally important, a series of New Deal measures—the National Industrial Recovery Act, the Walsh–Healy Act, and especially the Fair Labor Standards Act—placed the power of the law behind the abolition of child labor. By 1940 the labor-force rate for all women under age 20 stood at 19.0, down 3.8 points in a decade. The Social Security

Figure 3-3
Proportion of Youths and Elderly Females by Race and Age, 1900–1950

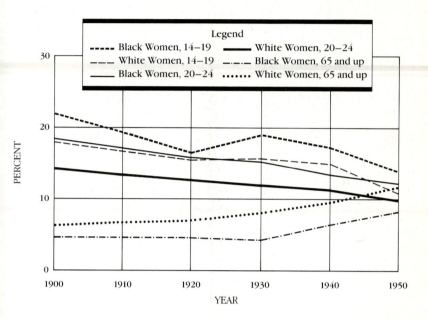

Act of 1935 underscored the view that 65 was an age at which workers could expect to retire, and although the act was not fully operational by 1940, the labor-force rate for women 65 and older dropped during the decade. The declines in the labor rates of the teenagers and women 65 and older stood in sharp contrast to a consistent pattern of increasing labor-force rates for women age 20 through 64. The increases for the decade ranged from 3.8 points for women in their early 20s to a high of 7.2 for those in their early 30s, then tapered off to .7 for those in their late 50s.[17]

The experience of white women and black women differed radically, as is illustrated in Figure 3-4 (compare with Figure 2-5). Overall adult, native-born white women, who constituted seven tenths of the total adult female labor force, increased their labor-force rate from 20.5 in 1930 to 24.8 a decade later. Women in every age group from 20 to 64 shared in these increases. Economic necessity and cultural traditions interacted such that the adult single foreign-born woman was more likely to be employed than the single native-born woman, but the married, divorced, or widowed among the foreign-born were less likely to work. Their rates remained constant. Although nonwhite women continued under strong pressure to

Figure 3-4
LFPR for Women by Race and Age, 1930 and 1940

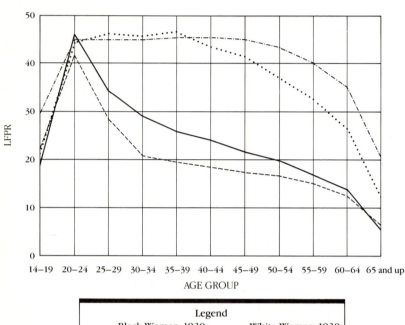

Legend

_.._ Black Women, 1930	----- White Women, 1930
...... Black Women, 1940	———— White Women, 1940

support themselves and their families, in reality the rates for those women between 20 and 35 increased only slightly, while the rates for those 40 and over dropped substantially.[18]

The propensity of women of different marital statuses to enter the labor force continued to change. The labor-force rate for single women dropped 5.0 points, and the rate for widowed and divorced women nearly as much. By comparison, the labor-force rate for married women increased 3.9 points. This increased propensity for married women to enter the labor force coupled with the growth in the female population resulted in a 52 percent increase in the number of married women in the labor force. But these aggregate figures mislead, for the rates for white married women under age 20 declined, while those for women 20 and over increased. For nonwhite women the rates dropped in every age range, the largest declines being for those 55 and over and the next largest for those under 20.[19]

To attribute the general increase in the labor-force participation of women to the depression is tempting but overly simplistic. It ignores the long-term trend since the start of the century of decade-by-decade increases in the labor-force rate of adult women and of gradual reductions in the rates for teenage women. Among nonwhite women, the labor rates for women between 20 and 45 had gradually risen while the rates for older women had peaked in 1920 and then subsided. No single answer suffices to explain the movement of women into the labor force. A variety of changes reduced the homemaking and child-care responsibilities of women. Declining birthrates, the greater availability of household conveniences, and an increase in apartment dwelling enabled some women to combine homemaking and work. More important, however, women who migrated from rural to urban areas enjoyed broader employment opportunities, while the rising level of educational attainment gave women a combination of self-confidence, skill, and interest in work.[20]

The immediate impact of these changes is reflected in the rise in the labor-force rates of successive birth cohorts of young women at comparable ages. Women born between 1876 and 1880 appeared in the 1900 census as young adults with a labor-force rate of 31.7; women born in the interval 1896 to 1900—the "flapper generation"—appeared in the 1920 census as young adults with an LFPR of 37.5; while those born between 1906 and 1910 and entered the adult scene at the start of the depression were recorded in the 1930 census with an LFPR of 41.8. These rates, established when the women, for the most part, were still single or newly married, dropped as women passed into their late 20s and assumed greater child-care and homemaking responsibilities. As the "self-indulgent" flapper generation reached their early 30s, for example, their LFPR dropped 13.9 points to 23.6; by 1940—now in their early 40s, their families completed, and the youngest child in school—their LFPR rose to 26.0. By comparison, when the "depression generation" reached their early 30s, their LFPR dropped only to 30.8, a level 7.6 points higher than that for the flapper generation at the same stage in the life cycle. Likewise, when the depression generation entered their early 40s, their LFPR stood at 36.6, over ten points higher than the comparable rate for the flappers. This pattern—an LFPR peak in the early 20s, a dip during the late 20s and early 30s, followed by a lesser peak in the early 40s and 50s and then retirement—illustrates the "two-career" pattern (see Figure 3-5; compare with Figure 1-3). But more importantly it illustrates the cumulative effects of the social, cultural, and economic changes that, having made it easier for each successive cohort to enter the labor force as young women, also made it easier to remain in or to return to the labor force in later stages of the life cycle. In short, the momentum of these long-term trends drove the aggregate LFPR for women upward decade-by-decade.[21]

Figure 3-5
LFPR for Women by Birth Cohorts and Age, 1870–1960

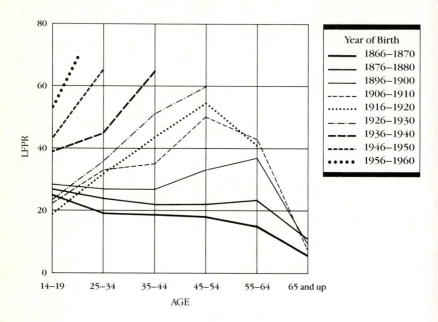

A second explanation of the rise in female labor-force rates focuses on the central role played by married women, particularly middle-class white women. In a society that insisted woman's place was in the home, the rise in the labor rates of married women was an anomaly. Nevertheless, the labor-force rate for married women, which was but 5.6 percent in 1900, had risen to 11.7 by 1930; and of the 10,390,000 million women in the labor force at that latter date, 3,900,000 combined the roles of homemaker and wage earner. By 1940 the number of married women in the labor force had grown to 4,560,000; their LFPR stood at 15.6.[22]

Society had long permitted married women to work in the event of economic necessity, but an analysis of the occupations of the husbands of working wives suggests that "economic necessity" meant different things to persons in different socioeconomic groups. In 1940, women married to men with low-paying, low-prestige jobs were more likely to be in the labor force, as might be expected, than were wives of men in high-paying, high-prestige occupations. Over half of the wives of domestic service workers were employed as were one-fourth of the wives of personal service workers. Wives of skilled craftsmen—men with experience and prestige—were much less likely to be in the labor force than the wives of factory operatives, who were paid less. Similarly in the white-collar ranks, wives of professional and semiprofessional workers were less likely to be employed than wives of clerical or sales workers. Even so, in 1940 nearly half of all wives who worked had husbands in skilled blue-collar or white-collar jobs. A significant number of these families owed their middle-class status to contributions of the working wife. In working to pay for a home, keep her children in school, or afford extras, the working wife could rationalize her work as an extension of the traditional role of homemaker. While the depression did not place these families in absolute need, it did—through wage reductions and layoffs—jeopardize their standard of living. The rise in the LFPR of married women from these white-collar, middle-income families, then, represented an effort to sustain their standard of living.[23]

A third explanation of the rising labor rates of women focuses on the increase in the demand for women, especially in occupations regarded as suitable to middle-class women. Thus, in spite of the depression, three fifths of the persons added to the labor force during the decade were women. For the economy as a whole, employments in farm work, either as owner or laborer, dwindled as did employments in two blue-collar categories—crafts and nonfarm labor. Despite the troubled economy, employment in the service occupations and as semiskilled operatives scored impressive gains. The white-collar sector fared moderately well, the smallest growth occurring at the managerial level, the largest, in the professional occupations (see Figure 3-6). These structural shifts once more benefitted women; much of the declining employment opportunities occurred in manual and blue-collar occupations thought unsuitable to women, while the largest increase appeared in white-collar jobs and in occupations as factory operative in which women already had a foothold.[24]

Of the 1,822,000 new jobs secured by women, 95 percent represented the maintenance of a constant share in the various occupations, while less than 5 percent were attributable to an increase in the female employment share in the occupation. As Figure 3-7 illustrates, there were five occupational groups in which women's employment share declined during the decade. In two—private-household service and professional and technical employments—the number of jobs held by women increased, although the proportion of such jobs declined. In the other three occupations—farm laborer, farmer, and nonfarm laborer—both the number and proportion of jobs held by women declined. Agriculture experienced extraordinary distress throughout the thirties, as changing farm technology encouraged the merger of farm units. New Deal reforms had the effect of pushing farm laborers off the land, driving blacks to the cities, and whites—the Okies and Arkies—to the West Coast. In the course of these changes,

Figure 3-6
Gainful Workers by Occupation and Sex, 1930–1940

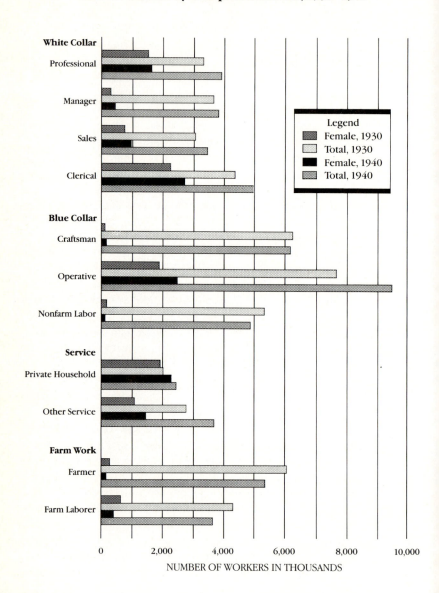

NUMBER OF WORKERS IN THOUSANDS

Figure 3-7
Changes in Demand for Female Workers, 1930–1940

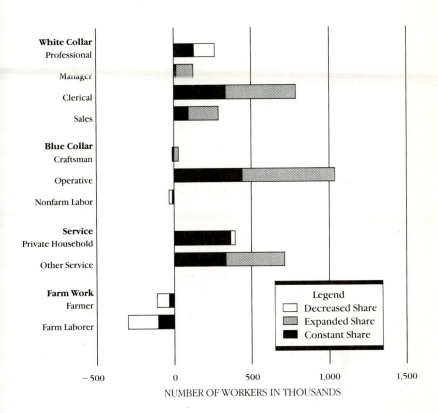

NUMBER OF WORKERS IN THOUSANDS

women abandoned agricultural employments in larger proportions than men. In the area of professional and technical employments, women failed by 130,000 jobs to maintain a constant share of the field. Contributing to this phenomenon was a loss of 81,000 teaching positions by women, while men gained 57,000. Whereas employment opportunities declined for both male and female musicians and music teachers, women lost a larger number and percentage of the positions. Another contributing factor was the counsel women received from groups such as the Institute of Women's Professional Relations, which advised women students to specialize in "feminine" occupations, such as home economics and interior decoration, in order to avoid competition with men.[25]

Substantial increases in female employment shares occurred in four occupational groups. One of these—factory operative—offered enhanced employment opportunities for working-class women. To ensure their survival, firms replaced old machinery with new, enabling them to replace skilled males with unskilled females at lower wage rates. Women "gained" 120,000 clerical jobs as the growing bureaucratization of industry required ever-larger numbers of stenographers, typists, and office-machine operatives. They also added nearly 98,000 jobs as managers and 93,000 jobs as salespersons.[26]

The demand for female labor continued to be concentrated in less than two dozen predominantly "female" occupations. The isolation of working women in this handful of "female" occupations remained startling. Of the 22 "female" occupations, 11 employed fewer than 100,000 persons, while only 4 employed as many as 500,000. Those 4, seen in Figure 3-8, accounted for nearly 30 percent of all employed women. During the decade, the proportion of women employed in "female" service occupations dropped by nearly 4 percentage points; while the concentration in "female" blue-collar occupations increased by nearly 3 points; and in the "female" white-collar occupations, it edged upwards 1 point. These gains were made in the least prestigious of the white-collar occupations—stenographer, typist, and trained nurse.[27]

While half of all women in the labor force worked in "female" occupations, the other half held jobs in which at least 3 out of every 10 fellow workers were males. Women made slight inroads into such occupations. Thus, while the number of male craftsmen declined during the thirties, the number of women so employed increased by 28,000, and by 1940 women constituted but 22 of every 1,000 persons in this prestigious blue-collar group. A second male preserve into which women pushed was the prestigious manager and administrator category, women increasing their share from 84 of every 1,000 jobs to 110. The persistence of this sexual division of labor underscores the importance of structural shifts in the economy in enlarging employment opportunities for women.[28]

Inquiries by the Census Bureau in 1890 and 1900 suggested that women were more likely to experience unemployment in the course of the work-year than men. Subsequent studies in the late 1920s confirmed that intermittent employment, even in periods of prosperity, was a common feature of female employment. As the depression deepened in 1930, unemployment rates for women soared, reaching 18.9 percent by January 1931. The highest rates occurred among factory operatives (30.3 percent) and domestic servants (24.2 percent); the lowest, among those in professional occupations (4.8 percent). Women under 20 had the highest rates; women over 50, the lowest. Foreign-born women, among whom there were relatively few very young, had exceptionally low levels of unemployment, while native-born white women had rates just below the national average. On

Figure 3-8
"Female" Occupations, 1940

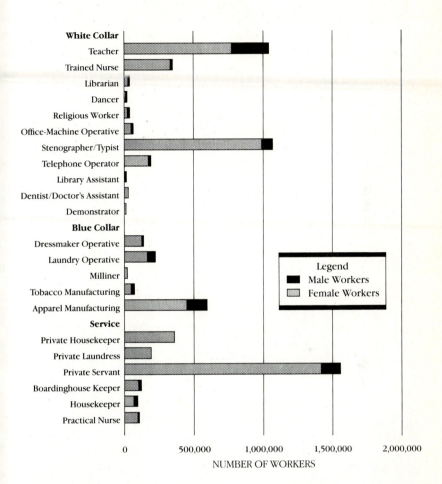

the other hand, unemployment among black women exceeded 50 percent in some communities. As vulnerable as women were in the early thirties, men generally had higher unemployment rates. Though women might be laid off temporarily, they were relatively safe from being replaced by men; masculine pride deterred males from seeking "female" jobs, but the women experienced no loss of self-regard in taking on a "man's" job. As even in good times, women often accepted employment requiring skills below their level of training; they possessed a flexibility that enabled them to shift down from semiprofessional to sales or clerical work, from white-collar to blue-collar jobs, from full-time to part-time. Of those women who sought work, perhaps 80 percent found it at some time or other. During the recession of the late 1930s, however, women experienced higher levels of unemployment than men, the impact falling chiefly on the most vulnerable—single women, older women, and minority women. To compound their difficulties, the unemployed single woman and minority woman found it difficult to secure relief from unsympathetic welfare officials.[29]

The depression hurt black Americans even more than it did whites. In the South, black farmers and agricultural laborers, especially dependent on the cotton economy, were caught by the collapse of cotton prices and the falling-off of the export market. In the North, which was hit even harder by the depression, black males experienced higher unemployment rates than did whites. And many of the blacks who held onto their jobs were beaten down to starvation wages. As the ability of black fathers and husbands to support their families diminished, black women had to work even harder to maintain the family income. The structure of the job market protected middle-class white women, since the unemployment rates for

Nearly a quarter million black women worked as agricultural laborers during the 1930s. Cotton picking was hard work for little pay.

the white-collar jobs they filled in sales, communications, and clerical work were lower than for the economy as a whole; in addition, black women were excluded from these white-collar jobs, and it was unlikely that jobless men would bid for a "woman's" job. In fact, while one third of the white female workers were employed as clerical workers, only 1.3 percent of the black women workers were so employed. At the beginning of the depression, nine out of ten black women who worked were either farm laborers or domestic servants, and much of this work was seasonal or part-time. Thus, from the start, black women were more vulnerable to the impact of the depression.[30]

The effect of the depression varied according to the kind of work women did. Federal farm programs hastened the displacement of sharecroppers, depriving both men and women of their work. Federal farm aid went to landowners who invested their scarce funds in farm machines and either evicted their tenants altogether or converted them into part-time hired hands. In such circumstances a female cotton picker in Concordia Parish, Louisiana, worked less than 90 days and earned less than $50. Some black families turned in desperation to migratory farm work. In 1940 the "A" family, as reported by the Women's Bureau, picked berries and canned tomatoes in Delaware, "grabbled" potatoes in Virginia, and harvested cucumbers in Maryland. For nine months of sporadic work, the family earned $330. Black domestic servants had to compete with white women who were desperate for employment, and white employers exploited those they hired. Some simply required longer hours of work; a few, surreptitiously turned back the clock; others failed to pay carfare. The full-time domestic might receive as little as $5.00 weekly; the day worker might receive $1.87 for an eight-hour day. Such workers felt "trapped, literally and figuratively pushed to the limits of their endurance." Many domestics must have shared the opinion of a 30-year-old woman who expressed hatred for her employers: "Dey's mean, 'ceitful, an' 'ain' hones'; but what ah'm gonna do? Ah got to live—got to hab a place to steh."[31]

The sexual and racial segregation of women employees enabled black women to slightly increase their share of factory employment during the depression decade. This owed much to the practice of assigning black women to the hard, dirty work that white women refused to take. In commercial laundries, black women did steam pressing and starching; the latter stood 10 hours a day repeatedly "sticking their hands into almost-boiling starch." In the garment industry, too, black women were pressers because of the intense heat and the "unusual strength and endurance" required. In slaughterhouses they were in the offal and chitterlings departments, which were "cold, wet, and 'vile smelling.'" Not only did black women get a disproportionate share of the unpleasant work, but, typically, they were accorded shorter lunch hours and received significantly lower wages. Unemployment rates for black women were markedly higher in the major northern cities than in southern cities and from 50 to 100 percent higher than for white women of the same city. Having access to "a smaller share of the steady and worth-while jobs," black women were more likely than white women to be on public assistance.[32]

If the depression made employment uncertain, New Deal measures, especially the NRA (1933) and the National Labor Relations Act (1935), gave organized labor and blue-collar women a boost. With respect to wages, the NRA codes authorized employers to pay women less than they paid men; but women gained, relative to the rates they had received before. In textiles, women's clothing, and cigar and tobacco making, average wages more than doubled. Gains by the poorest workers were "nothing short of phenomenal." The codes also reduced the hours of all workers, placing men and women on a plane of equality in terms of the workweek. As the nearly defunct International Ladies' Garment Workers regained strength, it succeeded in negotiating contracts that provided women operatives greater job security by reducing incentives to owners to move their plants in search of cheap, captive labor. The Committee for Industrial Organization, formed in 1935, initially focused on mass-production industries, such as auto and steel, that employed few women. Only when it organized the textile industry did it acquire a significant female membership. But the principal constituency of the CIO and the AFL was the blue-collar worker, a sector of the labor force that even in 1940 employed just over 20 percent of the women in the labor force. Men monopolized the leadership positions in local and national unions. Women members benefitted as the unions improved the position of workers generally. Women in agricultural labor, domestic workers, and clerical and sales workers, as well as nurses and teachers, remained unorganized.[33]

New Deal measures, however helpful to working-class people, did not help black women. The NRA wage agreements tended to institutionalize the racial and sexual segregation of black women, while the Social Security Act (1935) and the Fair Labor Standards Act (1938) did not cover either farm laborers or domestic servants, the occupations of 90 percent of black working women. Furthermore, to the extent that the New Deal succeeded in ending child labor, black mothers were pushed into the labor force to make up the income hitherto earned by her children.

By 1940, women workers could look back on a decade marked by economic reversals and modest gains. The demand for female labor in white-collar jobs increased with glacial slowness. Efforts to bar married women from employment had backfired, provoking middle-class women, especially the National Business and Professional Women's Clubs, to fight back. Women gained entrance to major unions, increasing their access to blue-collar employments and often to improved working conditions and wages. Moreover, New Deal reforms included protective legislation for men as well as women. Above all, more and more the female labor force was augmented by married middle-class women. Women's position in the labor force, far from having eroded, solidified.[34]

In 1940, the nation as a whole could look back on four decades that had wrought major changes in the economic roles and status of women. Children and teenagers no longer formed a significant bloc of the female labor force. Blacks and immigrant women formed a distinctly less important element than at the start of the century. In 1900 a woman worked only if she were unmarried, divorced, widowed, or had a husband unable to support her. If white, she was most likely to be a domestic servant or textile or needle-trades worker. If black, she was almost certainly either a domestic servant or a farm laborer. Only a few, talented, college-educated women pursued professional careers, but to do so they generally had to forgo marriage. Even so, a surprisingly large proportion of women had worked briefly prior to marriage.[35]

By 1940, structural shifts in the economy had enormously increased the proportion of white-collar jobs, contributing importantly to the increased employment of women. Whereas in 1900 the nation employed less than 1,000,000 clerical workers, one fourth of them women, by 1940 it utilized 5,000,000, over half of whom were women. Most of these were bookkeepers, stenographers, and typists—all "female" occupations. For young women with high-school diplomas, "the advent of the era of paper work . . . set the stage for the real breakthrough for women and their emergence from domesticity as an exclusive role." For the college-educated woman, the proliferation of public elementary and secondary schools along with the growth of professional nursing generated widely accessible employment opportunities. For women who had not completed high school, the blue-collar labor market barely kept pace with the growing economy, but the democratization of the high school in the 1920s and 1930s enabled an ever-larger proportion of young women from working-class families to compete successfully for white-collar employments. For black women, the changes in southern agriculture not only reduced job opportunities, but propelled them to cities where the variety of jobs open to them was narrowly restricted because of their limited education and the prejudices of the whites. If the structural shifts increased the demand for work that women regarded as attractive or at least consistent with their ideas of femininity, the expansion of the female labor force could not have occurred without "a radical change in the customs and attitudes of married women."[36]

INTERRACIALISM VERSUS SEPARATISM

The depression's impact on black Americans, while harsh, had unique features. First, the growth of the black population increased by little over one million persons for the decade, but nearly half of this growth occurred outside the South, chiefly in the cities of the Northeast and the Midwest. Second, because so many black Americans were still engaged in farm labor and domestic service, blacks did not gain the benefits of the Social Security Act or the Fair Labor Standards Act. Finally, the New Deal did not initially have programs designed to assist black Americans, nor were blacks initially supportive of the New Deal. Indeed, black leaders began by exploring the most efficacious ways of promoting the interests of the black community.[37]

Black club women took an active part in this search. Mary McLeod Bethune, who was by this time president of the Bethune–Cookman College and a former president of the NACW, recognized that the NACW had lost its capacity to provide the level of leadership the black community required as it narrowed its perception of women in the home as "mothers, wives, sisters, and daughters" of the men of the race. The major issue in Bethune's view was whether the black community was better served by institutions that sought interracial cooperation with the white community or by its own separate institutions. The formation a new superorganization of black club women that could "make for unity of opinion" and "insure greater coop-eration" among the various women's clubs had to be deferred until the interracialism-versus-separatism issue could be resolved.[38]

The issue was confronted first in a renewed attack on lynching. As a member of the Council on Interracial Cooperation, Bethune and other black women felt dissatisfied with their auxiliary roles in the organization. When Bethune challenged southern white women to assume responsibility for curbing racial violence, Jessie Daniel Ames responded by organizing white activists into the Association of Southern Women for the Prevention of Lynching (ASWPL). The ASWPL saw lynching as a feminist issue because, as Ames put it: "White men held that White women are their property [and] so are Negro women." The group also noted that rape was used as an excuse to subordinate blacks and that "to be industrialized," the South had "a need to assimilate 'the New Negro,' into the New Southland." But fundamental to the ASWPL's philosophy was the pursuit of racial harmony rather than equality. Ames did much to secure better housing for Dallas' black community, but her motivation was less a concern for fairness than for preventing "encroachments into white neighborhoods" by middle-class blacks. Nor did Ames invite black women to join the anti-lynching movement. When in 1935 the Costigan–Wagner Anti-Lynching Bill was before Congress, Ames declined to support it as an invasion of states' rights. The refusal of the ASWPL to support the Costigan–Wagner Bill sharpened the issue—should black women channel their energies toward interracialism or toward strengthening their own institutions?[39]

Bethune used the occasion to push to completion her proposed National Council of Negro Women. Her task was facilitated as the issue split the ranks of the NAACP leadership and W. E. B. DuBois resigned from the organization, arguing that the progress blacks had made in the previous quarter century had been "mainly in the lines" where they had been "working by and for themselves." In the belief that, for the moment, black women had more to gain from a course of separatism than from interracialism, the NACW withdrew from the predominantly white National Council of Women. Though some black leaders, such as Mary Waring, opposed the creation of an all-black women's council and others, including Mary Church Terrell and Charlotte Hawkins Brown, had misgivings, Bethune carried the day. The National Council of Negro Women came into being in December 1935 with Bethune as president and Church and Brown as vice presidents.[40]

Already the most influential leader in the black community, Bethune's influence increased greatly in the 1930s as she helped shape New Deal policies with respect to black Americans. Ironically her first contacts with Eleanor Roosevelt had been through the National Council of Women. As acquaintance ripened into friendship, Bethune helped to open Roosevelt's eyes to racial problems. In turn, Roosevelt became Bethune's most important ally. As early as 1934 Eleanor Roosevelt began taking a stand on racial issues, giving liberals in her husband's administration courage to do likewise.[41]

After blacks supported Franklin Roosevelt's bid for a second term, Bethune was appointed to a minor office in the National Youth Administration. Perceiving that the president's black advisers were "racked by internal dissension," she promptly organized this "black cabinet" into the Federal Council on Negro Affairs to "hammer out a consensus" and present "a unified front on policy." First and foremost a pragmatist, Bethune sometimes reflected the ideas of Booker T. Washington, though she refused to forgo securing equality of rights; at other times she reflected W. E. B. Dubois in believing there was merit in voluntary separation. In the conduct of her own office she brought blacks into the National Youth Administration. She had modest success in increasing student-aid funds for black college students, in helping black colleges meet accreditation standards, and in training teachers for rural black schools. She also used her influence outside the agency by recommending blacks for appointive offices, by securing White House press credentials for the *Atlanta World,* and by gaining admittance of black doctors to the staff of the Johns Hopkins Hospital. In addition, Bethune was a passionate advocate for black women with great faith in women's "possibilities." She succeeded in giving black women a greater public visibility and in making clear that their "legitimate demands . . . had to be taken into account on the national agenda."[42]

The problem of the black being judged on the basis of talent rather than race was made most vivid by Marian Anderson. Acclaimed by Jean Sibelius and Arturo Toscanini as one of the greatest singers in the world, Anderson was denied the stage of Constitution Hall by the Daughters of the American Revolution because of her color. Subsequently Harold Ickes, the secretary of the interior, invited her to sing from the steps of the Lincoln Memorial, and on Easter Sunday 1939, over 75,000 persons gathered to hear her. Even so, the Metropolitan Opera retained its unspoken rule barring blacks until January 1955, when Anderson, now in her 50s, became the first black to appear with the company.[43]

EDUCATION

Notwithstanding the depression, educational opportunities for girls and women improved in the thirties. The proportion of children enrolled in elementary school increased slightly, reaching 84.1 percent. More to the point, because of its growing importance for access to jobs, the enrollments at the secondary level increased by 6 percentage points, so that just under 80 percent of those 14 to 17 years of age were enrolled. Among the white population, females and males continued to have equal access, but nonwhites remained at a serious disadvantage. In 1930, half of the nonwhites had completed less than six years of school; by 1940 the median had risen nearly a year, but as that for whites had risen more, the disparities between whites and nonwhites increased. Illiteracy, almost nonexistent among native-born whites, ran at one in ten among the foreign-born and one in six among nonwhites. In the course of a decade, the rate among nonwhites dropped by one third. White women, then, had as good access to jobs demanding literacy as did white males and far better access than nonwhites.[44]

More and more the baccalaureate was required for professional and managerial positions, and, with jobs difficult to come by, students scraped together tuition money. College enrollments soared, and the number of women graduates increased by 57 percent in ten years. As encouraging as this showing was, undergraduate enrollment rates for men increased more rapidly than for women, so that the proportion of women eligible for a wide range of professional employments remained relatively limited. The strains of the depression also had an adverse effect on women's access to graduate education. An increasing proportion of women, to be sure, earned their masters and doctorates, but here, too, their enrollment rates increased more slowly than did those for men, and the disparity between the sexes in graduate education was greater in 1940 than a decade earlier. While it is true, as William Chafe points out, that during the depression years the percentage of all doctorates earned by women declined, a more accurate evaluation is that more women earned doctorates in the thirties than ever before and that, on a per capita basis, the number of doctorates awarded them also increased.[45]

Equally to the point is the question, to what use did women put their education? One test is the movement of women into the professions in which formal education was a prerequisite. During the thirties a few women entered male-dominated professions as architects, engineers, lawyers, doctors, and veterinarians. But there were losses, too, for in 1940 fewer women were chemists, dentists, or members of a clergy than a decade earlier. But this is not the whole of the matter. To attend college in the 1930s was not the act of derring-do that it had been prior to 1920. Before the twenties, social attitudes limited college enrollments to a select set of women highly "infused with a conscious sense of mission and obligation," but according to Virginia Gildersleeve of Barnard College, beginning in the twenties the woman student became marked by "blasé indifference, self-indulgence and irresponsibility."[46]

But if women college students after 1920 exhibited less intensity of commitment and more hedonistic desires, those who directed women's education signaled their young charges that they might legitimately pursue a home-centered curriculum. While women's colleges such as Vassar, Smith, and Wellesley sought to establish their respectability by adopting the standards of the most rigorous men's colleges, some state-supported colleges introduced home-economics instruction to attract a student clientele. In the twenties a variety of voices called for a revision of curriculums so as to prepare women for homemaking and child rearing. In 1924, Vassar—which had produced a number of distinguished scientists—created an interdisciplinary School of Euthenics to recast "education for women along the lines of their chief interests and responsibilities, motherhood and the home." The new curriculum was designed to train "gracious and intelligent wives and mothers." Vassar was not alone. Prestigious institutions such as the University of Chicago and Cornell University inaugurated programs in home economics.[47]

The negative side of the picture also included the dearth of women role models on the college faculties and positive barriers to enrollments. Women faculty, whose percentage remained constant during the thirties, were concentrated in a few special areas—home economics, women's physical education, art, music, and foreign languages. Few women became full professors; fewer chaired departments or became deans. Women's colleges employed men both as teachers and administrators. At best, women were grudgingly accepted in the professions, and major graduate and professional schools continued severe quotas on the admission of women and limited financial aid to them. Few hospitals accepted women medical students as interns or admitted them to residencies. That the New York City Bar Association excluded women from membership until 1937 underscored the reluctance of the legal profession to share the field with women.[48]

The condition of women's higher education was not as bleak as the forgoing suggests. Higher education continued, as it had for a half century, to offer women more opportunities for professional employment than law, medicine, and engineering combined. Women students in coeducational colleges—and a majority of women attended such schools—shared instruction in common with males. Junior colleges serving women took the lead in introducing individual programs to fit the needs, capacities, and interests of each student. Such programs made the extra effort to incorporate the arts into the curriculum and to promote multidisciplinary studies. Sarah Lawrence (founded 1926) and Bennington (founded 1932)—both experimental colleges for women—adopted the progressive ideals of John Dewey. The Sarah Lawrence leadership called for "more guidance, preparation and emphasis on family relationships and adjustments, human biology, housing, woman's part in the economic world, on understanding oneself, children and other people." Its curriculum, a latter-day president declared, possessed "a predominately feminine overtone" that had "little in common with the aggressive feminism" of the founders of Vassar, Smith, and Wellesley, "whose concern was with proving that women were capable of the same intellectual development as men." Opened in the midst of the depression, Bennington College emphasized progressive ideals such as "initiative, self-expression, creative work, independence, and self-dependence," and it permitted its students to explore questions relating to marriage and the family.[49]

If the depression decade brought women smaller gains in terms of expanding educational opportunities than the twenties and relatively greater gains for males, the thirties was not a time of retreat. At the secondary level, American girls continued to enjoy unparalleled opportunities, and on a per capita basis the proportion of women who completed baccalaureate, master's, or doctoral degrees in 1939 to 1940 was at an all-time high. The career-oriented curriculums of women's colleges prior to the twenties had limited appeal and operated in a milieu in which the woman who took such a degree and pursued a career had to forgo marriage. The "feminine" curriculums introduced during the twenties and thirties—the work of the older generation of women, not of "self-indulgent" flappers—broadened the appeal of college and gave many young women their first experience of living away from their families; the curriculums—even the most "feminine"—had components of English, the social sciences, natural sciences and often languages that extended the student's general fund of knowledge and outlook. By the thirties, normal schools, in which large numbers of young women had enrolled in earlier years, had extended their curriculums to become four-year colleges. But the primary fact was that most women college students attended coed colleges, sharing classroom instruction with males. The pressures on young women to eschew career-oriented professions came from their elders, and the response of young women to their educational opportunities reflected societal and family values.[50]

POLITICAL VISIBILITY

The advent of the New Deal gave women a political visibility they had lacked since the demise of the Child Labor Amendment in 1924. During the years that followed, women leaders were numerous enough—Mary Anderson, Alice Paul, Florence Kelley, and Jane Addams, for example—but they did not occupy a position that kept them or women generally in the public eye. Not until Eleanor Roosevelt entered the White House as first lady in March 1933 did any president's wife make the public role of women a major concern. Her immediate predecessor, Lou Henry Hoover, a woman of unusual intelligence and competence, had pursued an active life of outdoor activities, camping and horseback riding. Well-educated, Lou Hoover employed her knowledge of German, French, and Latin to collaborate with her husband in translating Georgius Agricola's *De Re Metallica* (1556), making a substantial contribution to the history of science. As first lady she used her "almost professional talents" in making the residential quarters of the White House more livable and in restoring the East Room. While she served as national president of the Girl Scouts and gave some public addresses, it never occurred to Lou Hoover to comment publicly on current political, social, or economic issues.[51]

Not so Eleanor Roosevelt. Conventionally raised and educated, Eleanor Roosevelt brought to the White House the interests of a dedicated social feminist, as well as exceptional experience in political affairs gained as she worked to promote her husband's political career after he was crippled by polio. In many ways Eleanor Roosevelt embraced conventional views. She believed a woman's primary responsibility was to her family. So, too, she believed that men were hard-headed, worldly, breadwinners, with an unfortunate propensity in a crisis to feel "that they must fight." By contrast, women possessed qualities of compassion, understanding, and self-abnegation and a natural pacifism needed to offset male aggressiveness. Her feminism was as conservative as her social and economic views were liberal.[52]

Having persuaded her husband to return to the political arena, Eleanor Roosevelt eschewed the conventional social activities of a woman of her position to participate actively in the work of the League of Women Voters, the National Consumers' League, the NWTUL, and the Democratic Party. Many of the reformers and social workers with whom she had become acquainted in the twenties subsequently became advisors and administrators in the New Deal. Though painfully shy, she forced herself into the political arena. As the president's eyes and ears, she toured the country as his "roving ambassador," surveying conditions in coal mines and migrant camps, talking to the unemployed and to minority peoples. Possessed of abundant energy, she wrote a syndicated newspaper column, lectured, and made radio broadcasts. Socially more aware than her husband, she lobbied for the blacks, the poor, youth, and women. She supported the efforts of Mary Dewson—a one-time colleague in the National Consumers' League and head of the Women's Division of the Democratic Party—to reactivate Democratic Women's Clubs and to secure equal representation for women on the platform committee of the Democratic National Convention. Further, she acted as a conduit for a variety of projects formulated by women for women. In particular she was responsible for calling the White House Conference on the Emergency Needs for Women and for a program of retraining for unemployed women.[53]

Eleanor Roosevelt's activities provoked considerable ridicule and disparagement; her suggestions were not always implemented. Although her position made her an effective lobbyist for women's concerns, there were sharp limits to what she could do alone. Nonetheless she was visibly more than the president's wife; she was a professional woman with her own activities and views. And she actively urged other women to emulate her. With respect to politics, she advised women to "get into the game and stay in it. . . . Throwing mud from the outside won't help. Building from the inside will." She further counseled women to leave their "womanly personalities at home" and to "disabuse their male competitors of the old idea that women are only 'ladies in business.' " Women, she insisted, must stand or fall "on their own ability, on their character as persons."[54]

While the New Deal gave women a push into public life, the impetus was nonideological. In its response to the nation's economic problems, the Roosevelt administration expanded a variety of relief agencies that utilized social workers as administrators, many of whom were women. The appointments recognized the experience of the appointee rather than reflected a feminist ideology of the appointing officer. While Grace Abbott, head of the Children's Bureau, expressed pleasure at the numbers of women added to government posts, she noted that these women encountered many difficulties with male colleagues. Whatever the impetus, Roosevelt appointed women to important offices. Ruth Bryan Owen and Florence J. Harriman became the first women ministers abroad. Florence Allen, an Ohio Supreme Court justice, became the first woman to sit on the U.S. Circuit Court of Appeals.[55]

The appointment most in the public eye was that of Frances Perkins to be secretary of labor. The first woman to hold a cabinet post, this one-time settlement-house worker had served as industrial commissioner when Roosevelt was governor of New York. Like many other social feminists, she made no effort to be a "model" to other women. Although married, she used her maiden name, not to assert her individuality but to avoid affecting her husband's career. Indeed, she thought the happiest place for most women was the home, a view Lois Banner suggests may have been a reaction to the intense publicity Perkins experienced as the first woman cabinet officer. Certainly as labor secretary Perkins bent over backwards to avoid becoming the special champion of women. Her task was particularly difficult, for as a professional social worker and a woman, labor leaders regarded her with suspicion. Ultimately, however, the United Mine Workers termed her the best of the labor secretaries since the founding of the department.[56]

Women came into public view via Congress as well as the executive department. As the decade began, there were but eight congresswomen in office, of whom Edith Nourse Rogers and Mary Norton served the entire decade. Of the nine women who joined them during the thirties, few served more than a single term; four of these succeeded to their husband's seat in the House, giving party leaders time to agree on a permanent successor. For the most part these women brought a variety of experiences to Congress. Ruth Hanna McCormick had been active first in the suffrage movement, then the Bull Moose Party. Some—like Ruth Pratt and Nan Wood Honeyman—had held local or state office. The viewpoints of these congresswomen with respect to women's issues varied from those with extensive records as suffragists to those who, like Fanny Oldfield, completed their husbands' terms out of a sense of duty but believed that a woman's place was at home. Most of the congresswomen were college-educated, and, excepting Jessie Sumner, all were either married or widows. Although few congresswomen served long enough to gain national recognition, two were visible to those who followed the activities of the House. Florence Kahn established a reputation as an outstanding parliamentarian, while Mary Norton became chairman of the House Labor Committee in 1937 and steered the Fair Labor Standards Act through the House.[57]

Women senators had as much difficulty as House members in achieving national stature. Of the three women who sat in the Senate during the thirties, Rose Long briefly replaced her husband, Huey, following his assassination, while Dixie Bibb Graves was appointed by her husband, the Arkansas governor, to occupy the seat vacated by Hugo Black until the state party machine agreed on a male successor. Only Hattie Caraway did more than serve out the unexpired term of a male senator. "A nice little old lady," Caraway seldom spoke on the floor of the Senate and did crossword puzzles during debates, but she ran for office twice, becoming the first woman to be elected to the Senate and, subsequently, the first to chair a Senate committee or to preside over the Senate. Overall, women members of Congress acquired a degree of visibility as journalists singled them out for feature stories, but their impact was limited.[58]

The broad social and economic reforms initiated by the New Deal benefitted working women. Most federal-relief measures were geared to enable males to resume their role as breadwinners, but special programs such as the National Youth Administration enabled girls and young women to complete high school and college. In addition to establishing pensions for retired workers, male or female, and retirement benefits for wives of retired workers, the Social Security Act established a program of child and maternal benefits. The New Deal addressed problems of child labor, health, and safety conditions on the job and the regulation of wages and hours, not to protect women and children per se, but to alleviate or prevent economic distress. The NRA (1933), operating through agreements between labor, management, and government, greatly curtailed the sweatshop system. It abolished child labor, thereby breaking "the chain that has bound women as wage earners to children. . . ." The codes also reduced the need for special legislation to protect women workers. Finally, the codes set minimum standards for hours and wages. While sex-neutral with respect to hours, these standards often set a lower wage scale for women than for men.[59]

The Fair Labor Standards Act (1938) made the 40-hour workweek the legal norm for persons engaged in interstate commerce and established a uniform, sex-neutral minimum wage. This legislation raised wages for one worker in four in the needle trades and in textiles, but it did not apply either to farm laborers or to domestic servants. Nor did it apply to small businesses that served a local market, so that large numbers of women in sales and clerical work were left unprotected. Nevertheless, the adoption of this sex-neutral legislation marked a significant turn in national policy, for it cut the link between protection of women workers and assertions of female inferiority.[60]

In 1937 the Supreme Court, smarting under Franklin Roosevelt's effort to "pack" the Court in order to inject fresh viewpoints in its decision making, repudiated the Adkins decision, opening the way to sex-neutral protective legislation. The Court took the first step in *West Coast Hotel* v. *Parrish* (1937) when it held that a state could invoke its police powers—the power to regulate in order to safeguard health, safety, and morals—to set a minimum wage. While the grounds for the decision were sex-neutral, tradition-minded justices pointed out that the statute applied only to women and that the state had an interest in the "health of women and their protection from unscrupulous and over-reaching employers."[61]

The second step came in 1941 with a challenge to the constitutionality of the Fair Labor Standards Act in *United States* v. *Darby*. Looking back at the *Parrish* case, the Court recognized that the sex of the worker had no bearing on the propriety of invoking the police powers to regulate wages. Thus, it insisted: "It is no longer open to question that the fixing of a minimum wage is within the legislative power and the bare fact of its exercise is not a denial of due process under the Fifth more than under the Fourteenth Amendment." The *Darby* decision, then, provided assurance to advocates of an ERA that equal rights and the protection of wages, hours, and working conditions could coexist.[62]

Traumatic as the depression decade was, women emerged with greater visibility than they had enjoyed at any earlier time. In the political arena, women were more active as voters, party workers, and officeholders. In constitutional law, women had secured a degree of parity with men as the Supreme Court upheld sex-neutral protective legislation. In the economic realm, the propensity of adult women in every age range to participate in the labor force continued to grow. Of central importance, the structural shifts in the economy generated an increasing demand for women in white-collar occupations. Although black women did not share in these gains, they were leaving the rural South and relocating in cities where at least their daughters, if they could secure an education comparable to that of whites, might bid for a wider variety of employments. Though women lagged men in undergraduate, graduate, and professional education, the proportion of women with earned degrees continued to climb, steadily enlarging the proportion of women able to take an active role in the political, economic, and intellectual life of the nation.

NOTES

[1] William Henry Chafe, *The American Woman* (New York: Oxford, 1972), 105.

[2] Studs Terkel, *Hard Times* (New York: Pantheon, 1970), 229. Mirra Komarovsky, *The Unemployed Man and His Family* (New York: Dryden, 1940), 23–43. Robert S. Lynd and

Helen Merrell Lynd, *Middletown in Transition* (New York: Harcourt, Brace and World, 1937), 410–12. Sherwood Anderson, *Puzzled America* (New York: C. Scribner's Sons, 1935), 46. Joe L. Dubbert, *A Man's Place* (Englewood Cliffs: Prentice-Hall, 1979), 209–212. See also, Ruth S. Cavan and Katherine Ranck, *The Family and the Depression: A Study of One Hundred Chicago Families* (New York: Arno, 1971[1938]); E. Wight Bakke, *Citizens Without Work* (New Haven: Yale, 1940); Eli Ginzberg, *The Unemployed* (New York: Harper, 1943).

[3]   Dubbert, *A Man's Place,* 222.

[4]   Ibid., 213–18, the words are Dubbert's.

[5]   Maxine Davis, *The Lost Generation: A Portrait of American Youth Today* (New York: Macmillan, 1936), 87. Pearl Buck, *Of Men and Women* (New York: Day, 1941), 91. Lois W. Banner, *Women in Modern America* (New York: Harcourt Brace Jovanovich, 1974), 196.

[6]   Banner, *Women in Modern America,* 106. Mary P. Ryan, *Womanhood in America* (New York: New Viewpoints, 1975), 302–303. Marjorie Rosen, *Popcorn Venus: Women, Movies and the American Dream* (New York: Coward, McCann & Geoghean, 1973).

[7]   June Sochen, *Herstory* (New York: Alfred, 1974), 330–36. Banner, *Women in Modern America,* 201. Lynd and Lynd, *Middletown in Transition,* 262–63.

[8]   "Mildred Ella (Babe) Didrikson Zaharias," in *NAW, The Modern Period,* ed. Barbara Sicherman and Carol Hurd Green (Cambridge: Harvard University Press, 1980), 756–57.

[9]   Sochen, *Herstory,* 316 ff. Ishbel Ross, *Ladies of the Press: The Story of Women in Journalism by an Insider* (New York: Harper, 1936). Marion K. Sanders, *Dorothy Thompson: A Legend in Her Time* (Boston: Houghton Mifflin, 1973).

[10]   Frederick Lewis Allen, *Only Yesterday* (New York: Bantam, 1959[1931]), 75–77. The advertisements appeared in *The Ladies' Home Journal* during the 1930s.

[11]   Martin Gruberg, *Women in American Politics* (Oshkosh: Academia, 1968), 107–108. Susan Ware, *Beyond Suffrage: Women in the New Deal* (Cambridge: Harvard, 1981).

[12]   *NYT,* 10 Jan. 1937, sec. 6, p. 6, col. 1; 7 Feb. 1937, sec. 6, p. 6, col. 1; 21 Feb. 1937, sec. 6, p. 6, col. 3. Mary Anderson, *Woman at Work* (Minneapolis: University of Minnesota Press, 1951).

[13]   Lois Scharf, "Employment of Married Women in Ohio, 1920–1940," in *Women in Ohio History,* ed. Marta Whitlock (Columbus: Ohio American Revolution Bicentennial Commission, 1976), 19–26. *NYT,* 24 July 1937, p. 17, col. 1. Susan D. Becker, *The Origins of the Equal Rights Amendment* (Westport: Greenwood, 1981).

[14]   Women's Bureau, "Women's Wages in Kansas," *Bulletin 17* (Washington: GPO, 1921), 53–82. Women's Bureau, "Women in Kentucky Industries," *Bulletin 29* (Washington: GPO, 1923), 84–85. *Literary Digest* 104 (March 1930): 12. Poppy Cannon, "Pin-Money Slaves," *Forum* 84(Aug. 1930): 98–103. See sec. 213, National Economy Act (1932). Chafe, *American Woman,* 108. The proportion of female respondents opposed to the employment of married women was lower than that for the population as a whole. Chafe gives 75 percent plus for women, 82 percent for all respondents. Compare pages 111 and 108. Hadley Cantril, ed., *Public Opinion, 1935–46* (Princeton: Princeton University Press, 1951), 1044. Alice Kessler-Harris, *Out to Work* (New York: Oxford, 1982), 255–56.

[15]   Gertrude Bancroft, *The American Labor Force* (New York: Wiley, 1958), tab. D-1, p. 207.

[16]   Ibid., tab. D-1, pp. 204, 206.

[17]   Ibid., tab. D-1a, p. 207.

[18]   Bureau of the Census, *Abstract of the Fifteenth Census of the United States [1930]* (Washington: GPO, 1933), tab. 30, p. 379. Women's Bureau, "The Negro Woman Worker," by Jean Collier Brown, *Bulletin 165* (Washington: GPO, 1938). Gerda Lerner, ed., *Black Women in White America: A Documentary History* (New York: Pantheon, 1972), 398–405.

[19]   Bancroft, *American Labor Force,* tab. D-1a.

[20] Ibid., 28–29. Robert W. Smuts, *Women and Work in America* (New York: Columbia University Press, 1959).

[21] Winifred D. Wandersee Bolin, "The Economics of Middle-Income Family Life: Working Women During the Great Depression," *JAH* 65(1978): 72. Ruth Milkman, "Women's Work and the Economic Crisis: Some Lessons from the Great Depression," in *A Heritage of Her Own,* ed. Nancy Cott and Elizabeth Pleck (New York: Simon & Schuster, 1979). Bancroft, *American Labor Force,* 53. William G. Bowen and T. Aldrich Finegan, *The Economics of Labor Force Participation* (Princeton: Princeton University Press, 1969), 114 ff., addresses the importance of education. John D. Durand, *The Labor Force in the United States, 1890–1960* (New York: SSRC, 1948), discusses cohort analysis. See also James A. Sweet, *Women in the Labor Force* (New York: Seminar, 1973), 60.

[22] Bureau of the Census, *Sixteenth Census of the United States, 1940 Population. Vol. III, The Labor Force, Part I* (Washington: GPO, 1943), tab. 6. Bureau of the Census, *U.S. Census of Population 1950, Vol. II, Characteristics of the Population, Part I, U.S. Summary* (Washington: GPO, 1953), tab. 102.

[23] Bureau of the Census, *Abstract of the Fifteenth Census [1930],* tab. 28, p. 378. Bureau of the Census, *Historical Statistics of the United States, Colonial Times to 1970,* Bicentennial ed., pt. 1 (Washington: GPO, 1975), ser. D 49–67, p. 133. Winifred D. Wandersee, *Women's Work and Family Values, 1920–1940* (Cambridge: Harvard, 1981). Lois Scharf, *To Work and to Wed* (Westport: Greenwood, 1980), chaps. 4–6.

[24] Bolin, "The Economics of Middle-Income Family Life," 69 ff. John Parrish, "Women in the Nation's Labor Market," *Quarterly Journal of Economics* 54(May 1940): 528. Broadus Mitchell, *Depression Decade: From New Era through New Deal, 1929–41* (New York: Rinehart, 1947), 261.

[25] Bureau of the Census, *Sixteenth Census of the United States: 1940, Population, Comparative Occupational Statistics for the United States, 1870 to 1940* (Washington: GPO, 1943), chap. 3. Relative to 1940, the 1930 figures overstate the size of the labor force. The 1930 statistics for "gainful workers" are not strictly comparable with 1940 statistics for the "labor force." "Gainful workers" included all persons who *usually* worked at gainful labor, regardless of *when* they worked; the 1940 "labor force" included only persons who were working, or with a job, or seeking work the last week of March 1940. Bureau of the Census, *Sixteenth Census: 1940, Comparative Occupational Statistics, 1870 to 1940,* chap. 3, pp. 7–8. John Parrish, "Changes in the Nation's Labor Supply," *AER* 29(1939): 328–30. David Eugene Conrad, *The Forgotten Farmers* (Urbana: University of Illinois Press, 1965), 76–78. Chafe, *American Woman,* 110.

[26] Bureau of the Census, *Sixteenth Census: 1940, Comparative Occupational Statistics, 1870 to 1940,* tab. 2. Kessler-Harris, *Out to Work,* 261.

[27] Kessler-Harris, *Out to Work,* 261. The comparisons are among occupations in which women constituted 70 percent or more of the workers.

[28] Ibid.

[29] "Employment Conditions and Unemployment Relief," *MLR* 38(1934): 790–95. Kessler-Harris, *Out to Work,* 262–65. Women's Bureau, "Employment Fluctuations and Unemployment of Women," by Mary Elizabeth Pidgeon, *Bulletin 113* (Washington: GPO, 1933) and Bureau of the Census, "Women in the Economy of the United States of America: A Summary Report," by Mary Elizabeth Pidgeon, *Bulletin 155* (Washington: GPO, 1937).

[30] Gunnar Myrdal, *An American Dilemma* (New York: Harper, 1944), 254. Jacqueline Jones, *Labor of Love, Labor of Sorrow* (New York: Basic, 1985), 196–200.

[31] Jones, *Labor of Love,* 200, 202–203, 205.

[32] Women's Bureau, "The Negro Woman Worker," 10. Women's Bureau, "The Employment of Women in Slaughtering and Meat Packing," by Mary Elizabeth Pidgeon, in *Bulletin 88* (Washington: GPO, 1932), 20–21. Myrdal, *An American Dilemma,* 301.

120 Chapter 3 The Trauma of Depression: The 1930s

[33] Henry Pelling, *American Labor* (Chicago: University of Chicago Press, 1960), chap. 7. Art Preis, *Labor's Giant Step, Twenty Years of the CIO* (New York: Pioneer, 1964). Benjamin Stolberg, *The Story of the CIO* (New York: Viking, 1938).

[34] Banner, *Women in Modern America,* 189. Irving Bernstein, *Turbulent Years, A History of the American Worker, 1933–41* (Boston: Houghton Mifflin, 1970).

[35] Bancroft, *American Labor Force,* 38–40. Bureau of the Census, *Sixteenth Census: 1940, Comparative Occupational Statistics, 1870 to 1940,* 9–10.

[36] Bancroft, *American Labor Force,* 33, 37.

[37] Bureau of the Census, *Historical Statistics of the United States, 1789–1945* (Washington: GPO, 1949), 31 n.

[38] Paula Giddings, *When and Where I Enter* (New York: Morrow, 1984), 204, 202. See also Elaine M. Smith, "Mary McLeod Bethune," in Sicherman and Green, eds., *NAW, The Modern Period,* 76–80.

[39] Giddings, *When and Where I Enter,* 207–209. See also Jacqueline Dowd Hall, *Revolt Against Chivalry: Jessie Daniel Ames and the Women's Campaign Against Lynching* (New York: Columbia University Press, 1979).

[40] Giddings, *When and Where I Enter,* 211–13.

[41] Ibid., 219.

[42] Ibid., 228–29, 230. Elaine M. Smith, "Mary McLeod Bethune and the National Youth Administration," in *Clio Was a Woman: Studies in the History of American Women,* ed. Mabel E. Deutrich and Virginia C. Purdy (Washington: Howard University Press, 1980).

[43] John Hope Franklin, *From Slavery to Freedom,* 3rd ed. (New York: Knopf, 1967), 519–20.

[44] Bureau of the Census, *Historical Statistics of the United States, Colonial Times to 1957* (Washington: GPO, 1960), ser. H 383–94 and H 407–411.

[45] Chafe, *American Woman,* 91.

[46] Quoted in ibid., 92–93.

[47] Ibid., 103, 104.

[48] *CHE* 8(Aug. 19, 1974): 9.

[49] Frederick Rudolph, *The American College and University* (New York: Vintage, 1965), 475–78. Constance Warren, *A New Design for Women's Education* (New York: Stokes, 1940), vii, 6, 7. Barbara Jones, *Bennington College* (New York: Harper, 1946).

[50] Mabel Newcomer, *A Century of Higher Education for American Women* (New York: Harper, 1959), chap. 5.

[51] "Lou Henry Hoover," in *NAW 1607–1950 A Biographical Dictionary,* ed. Edward T. James, 3 vols. (Cambridge: Harvard University Press, 1971), vol. 2, 217.

[52] Eleanor Roosevelt, *It's Up to the Women* (New York: Stokes, 1933), 202, 203.

[53] Tamara K. Hareven, *Eleanor Roosevelt An American Conscience* (Chicago: Quadrangle, 1968), 57, 64.

[54] Carol Hymowitz and Michaele Weissman, *A History of Women in America* (New York: Bantam, 1978), 311.

[55] Grace Abbott, *From Relief to Social Security* (Chicago: University of Chicago Press, 1941), 361–62. Gruberg, *Women in American Politics,* 144.

[56] *Independent Woman* 12(April 1933): 123. Banner, *Women in Modern America,* 179–80. Gruberg, *Women in American Politics,* 142–43.

[57] Gruberg, *Women in American Politics,* 153–58.

[58] Allan Drury quoted in ibid., 124.

[59] Maud Younger, "The NRA and Protective Laws for Women," *Literary Digest* 117(June 2, 1934): 27.

[60] John M. Peterson, "Employment Effects of State Minimum Wages for Women," *Industrial and Labor Relations Review* 12(1958): 414. Joel Seidman, *The Needle Trades* (New York: Farrar & Rinehart, 1942), 65, 218–19.

[61] West Coast Hotel v. Parrish, 300 U.S. 379 (1937).

[62] United States v. Darby Lumber Co., 312 U.S. 100 (1941).

4

War and Peace: The 1940s

Women entered the 1940s in a somber mood. While the nation had yet to free itself of the depression, Europe had slipped over the brink of war. The mood was one of "insecurity and apprehension." As the Nazis overran Norway, Denmark, the Netherlands, Belgium, and France before midyear, the likelihood of United States involvement increased, and following the Japanese attack on Pearl Harbor, the United States entered the war.[1]

The war years brought women unprecedented challenges and opportunities. Whereas in the thirties social pressures inhibited women from entering the labor force, during the war public policy required recruiting them. "Male" jobs previously closed were opened, single women were actively sought after, and married women and young mothers were at least tolerated in the work force. The wartime climate afforded women new opportunities in politics, allowing congresswomen to be taken seriously. As male students joined the armed forces, women became the principal clientele of the nation's colleges and universities. The peace that followed provided a means of testing which of the wartime changes might become permanent and which were passing expedients.

ROSIE THE RIVETER: THE WAR YEARS

Overnight the Japanese attack on Pearl Harbor transformed the United States from a country with endemic unemployment into a nation with an

*Rosie the Riveter, depicted here by Norman Rockwell,
personified the American women who swarmed into the
labor force during World War II, often taking up "male"
jobs.*

impending labor shortage, especially in job areas monopolized by men.
Government officials, who in the thirties had discouraged women from
entering the labor force, now sought to entice them into it without challenging tradition. Women without family responsibilities were to be recruited
first; married women with children, as a last resort. Expediency, rather than
any farsighted commitment to assist women in developing lifelong careers,
guided public policy. As during earlier wars, the nation's need permitted
an "expansion of women's economic role" without it being perceived as a
"feminist threat." This approach disarmed potential critics. Enunciating a
traditional Catholic viewpoint, *Commonweal* endorsed the wartime
employment of women so long as they were not "labeled and ticketed
mere units of national asset." No harm was done if a particular wife and
mother chose to work in terms of her own needs and values, but *Commonweal* warned the government against creating a milieu in which the

home was "tolerated only" or which regarded the home as keeping the wife and mother from war work. Should that happen, then, "the Soul of our society will already be lost."[2]

The leadership of organized women's groups saw the long-term implications. They realized that women were getting new opportunities not because management recognized women's ability, but rather because of the labor shortage. Helen Baker, an industrial-relations specialist, cautioned women of "the need for a responsible attitude toward their training and their work." "All too often women themselves have furnished the ammunition for attacks upon them," Mary Gilson, consultant for the War Manpower Commission, added. Repeatedly stories in the press and magazines emphasized the versatility and capability of women. The purpose seemed to be that of selling a mildly disbelieving management on taking a chance and of warning women that their future in the labor force was on trial.[3]

Wartime Demand

War caused a major shift in the demand for females as employees. Initially the expansion of war production generated a strong ongoing demand for white-collar file clerks, typists, secretaries, stenographers, and office-machine operatives. Essential and in keeping with the kinds of work that middle-class women had been undertaking in ever-increasing numbers since the start of the century, office work attracted 2,200,000 women to the labor force. Next, as the armed forces began to siphon men away from the civilian labor force, employers sought women as replacements in relatively genteel occupations—laboratories, banks, business houses, and as ticket takers at bus, train, and air terminals. Women collected taxes, operated elevators, and announced radio programs. Filing clerks, stenographers, saleswomen, seamstresses, and waitresses by the thousands moved to better-paying, higher-status jobs in war industries. Professional women—especially teachers and social workers—turned to government offices and laboratories or to organizations such as the American Red Cross, United Service Organizations (USO), Women's Army Corps (WAC), Women Accepted for Volunteer Emergency Service (WAVES), or Semper Paratus (SPAR).[4]

Psychologically the most satisfying civilian work was in defense industries where women could easily identify with the men in the armed forces. The new or expanding war industries, often operating on cost-plus contracts, paid high wages and erected few barriers to female employment. Eventually thousands of women took jobs in aircraft factories. At first they sewed fabric, a traditional female task; but as all-metal planes evolved, women shifted from the needle to the rivet gun and welding torch, to "male" jobs. Rosie the Riveter became a national symbol of women pitching in. Before the war was over, women made instruments of all kinds—from aircraft and fire-control systems to surgical and dental tools. If women seemed "particularly fitted" for light precision work, they also worked at core-making in foundries, as keel binders in shipyards, and as panmen in steel mills. Of the women added to the labor force during the war years, manufacturing took 2,500,000.[5]

This expansion of the female labor force wrought a number of far-ranging changes that outlasted the war. Labor scarcity compelled management to offer women jobs that previously had been the exclusive preserve of men, while patriotism spurred women to accept work formerly thought unbecoming to a woman. This posed a problem, for many women lacked the requisite training or familiarity with the tools used on "men's" jobs. Starting in the late 1930s, the federal government initiated vocational programs that trained women in new skills and upgraded old ones. Women learned to read blueprints, to use precision gauges, and to operate welding equipment. Major industrial firms such as Monsanto, DuPont, and Standard Oil employed their first women technicians and engineers. Sex differentiation in jobs was not eliminated, but it was reduced.[6]

Black Women in Wartime

As the United States began to rearm in 1940, black leaders were appalled to learn that although they were to be recruited in proportion to their numbers in the whole population, they would be assigned to separate units and that existing black units would have no black officers except medical officers and chaplains. Similarly, they found employers reluctant to hire them despite the impending labor shortage. Reacting to a threatened protest march on Washington organized by A. Philip Randolph, president of the Brotherhood of Sleeping Car Porters, President Roosevelt issued Executive Order 8802, declaring "there shall be no discrimination in the employment of workers in defense industries or Government because of race, creed, color, or national origin. . . ." However, defense contracts subsequently contained clauses prohibiting racial discrimination. The government's job-training programs from the start were open to blacks without prejudice, and gradually the Fair Employment Practices Commission did much to modify racial employment practices in the private sector.[7]

Though racial discrimination was not wiped out, public policy, combined with the sharp rise in the demand for female workers, had an impact on black women that William Chafe has termed the "second emancipation." Still the mudsill of the labor force in 1940, a plurality of black women were agricultural laborers, domestic servants, or cooks. Within months, the num-

*World War II enabled black women to move out of
farm labor and domestic service into jobs in plants and
industries that previously refused to employ them.
However, they were not always successful in retaining
these jobs after the war.*

ber of domestic servants declined by 400,000, and the percentage of farm
laborers was cut in half. Black women moved up to other kinds of service
work at higher wages and more regular hours. Many entered the nation's
factories. At the Brooklyn Naval Yard black women reconditioned binoc-
ulars, telescopes, and range finders; in the Washington Naval Yard they
operated drill presses, lathes, and tapping machines. Elsewhere they ran
machines, assembled parts, did inspection work, formed cables, soldered,
and tested electrical equipment. The number of black women on the federal payroll tripled. By the war's end blacks had entered plants and industries previously closed to them and had acquired experience without which
they could not expect postwar employment.[8]

The logic of the president's executive order required that the military services be open to black women. The army recruited some 4,000 black women into the WAC, but only after much delay did the navy permit black women to enlist in the WAVES. The first black woman entered the Army Nurse Corps, while the American Red Cross also enlisted black women. Yet satisfaction with these gains was offset by a variety of petty acts of discrimination; post commandants forbade the reading of black newspapers; they permitted a "whites first" policy in boarding buses; and they operated segregated post exchanges and theaters. Belatedly, in 1943 and 1944, the War Department issued orders forbidding racial segregation in recreation and transportation facilities.[9]

The "second emancipation" thesis, however cheering its promise, grossly overstates the degree of advance made by black women. The composition of the local labor force and the nature of work had much to do with the demand for the labor of black females. A United Auto Workers' (UAW) study in April 1943 reported that of 280 firms employing women as production workers, only 74 hired black women. A National Metals Trades Association study of 1943 revealed that just under half of 62 plants employing women were willing to hire black women. Generally employers were more likely to hire black women in traditional male fields of heavy industry than in female fields of clerical and sales work. Even then, employers preferred to use black women for "clerical, stock-handling, packing and wrapping work rather than for sales positions that involved public contact." Black women got the "arduous, dirty, hot or otherwise disagreeable jobs." The auto industry limited the employment of black women to low-paying service and other unskilled categories. The federal government opened some white-collar positions to black women, most of which were in Washington, D.C.—and, at that, most of these jobs were temporary—but elsewhere the old racial barriers persisted. The racial biases of coworkers bore some of the responsibility for the ongoing exclusion of black women from the labor force, but managerial intransigence was more often the decisive factor. There are also suggestions that white middle-class women, threatened with the loss of black cleaning ladies, "exerted pressure on their businessmen-husbands" not to employ black women in better-paying clerical, sales, or industrial jobs and thereby " 'spoil' good domestic servants." In the public sector, concern with expanding the opportunities of blacks took second place to maximizing war production. In consequence, neither the United States Employment Service nor the Women's Bureau aggressively assisted black women in improving their employment status. At the war's end, then, the gains of black women were limited; they remained at the bottom of the job market.[10]

Wartime Supply

Women responded impressively to the changing demand for their labor. At the start of the decade, 11,138,000 women of all ages were employed; four years later, at the peak of wartime employment, 18,830,000. The net increase in the female labor force, over 50 percent, exceeded the cumulative growth of the previous three decades. Where did this increment of 7,692,000 women come from? The conventional explanation asserts that millions of women who had never worked outside the home before flooded the labor force. Certainly patriotic feelings led women without previous work experience to take jobs. But, in fact, many of the first women came from the ranks of the unemployed of whom there were over 2,000,000 in March 1940. Because the United States had begun rebuilding its fleet and expanding its airforce in the late 1930s, the economy by 1940 was already on the upswing, and by the time the United States entered the war, at least a quarter of the unemployed women of March 1940 were back at work. Another source was the enormous pool of housewives in their 30s, 40s, and 50s who had been in the labor force as young women and for whom a return was scarcely a plunge into the unknown.[11]

The untapped female labor pool in 1940 was enormous, numbering 27,181,000 women age 20 through 64, plus another 5,985,000 girls and young women age 14 through 19. Easiest to recruit were the teenagers, most of whom expected to work when they finished school. The wartime milieu only intensified the social pressure to work. Those still in school felt pressure to work after school, on weekends, and during vacations. If such young workers could not take jobs in defense industries, they could babysit or do routine clerical and sales work, which released older women to undertake more-demanding full-time jobs. At its peak, the female labor force was augmented by nearly 1,600,000 such young women. A second major source of womanpower was the cohort of women age 20 to 24. With a labor-force rate of 45.6 in 1940, this cohort already had a larger fraction of its membership at work than any other five-year group. To provide a still-larger fraction required employing young married women, many with young children, in spite of traditional taboos. Ultimately an extra 500,000 women from this age cohort joined the wartime labor force (see Figure 4-1).[12]

The major body of new workers came from 25- to 44-year-old women, a large proportion of whom were married. By 1943, as *Fortune* magazine observed, there were "practically no unmarried women left" to recruit, and urban housewives became the principal source of additional laborers. Seventy-five percent of all new women workers were married; the number of wives in the labor force doubled. The task of recruiting them was eased

Figure 4-1
Estimated Female Employment by Age, 1941 and 1945

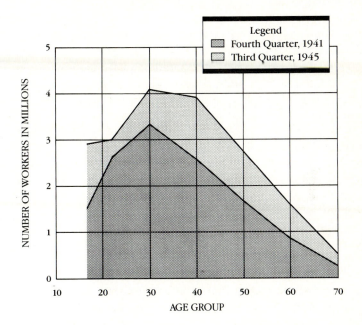

by the pattern of demographic shifts. Only the youngest women in this group, those 25 to 29, belonged to a cohort that shrank in relative size during the decade. As the cohort with the heaviest family and child-rearing responsibilities, these women had a low labor rate and the "losses" to the wartime labor supply were minimal. By contrast, the older cohorts "gained" nearly 500,000 women, most of whom were over 35. Free of responsibility for preschool children, 2,100,000 of these women entered the labor force.[13]

A final group that was tapped were women 45 and over. Prior to the war, women in this age range were the least likely to work outside the home; as postmenopausal women, they had been regarded as physically and emotionally undependable. Born before 1895, they had less education, training, or work experience than younger women. The youngest of this group, those under 50, had come of age in the era of the "New Woman," and that experience may explain the ease with which they entered the wartime labor market. Margaret Hickey, chairman of the Women's Advisory Committee to the War Manpower Commission, observed that while these older women might get sick more often than younger women, they were more responsible, and *Newsweek* concluded that though they worked less rapidly, they were more efficient. Indeed, their LFPR was as high during the war years as it had been as young women 20 years before. This group added 1,780,000 persons to the female work force.[14]

As dramatic as was the addition of 5.4 million women between late 1941 and summer 1945, the more telling statistic is the jump in the labor participation rates from 27.9 in 1940 to 36.3 in 1944. Furthermore, a rise in the rate of five to six points was shared by all age groups between 1942 and 1945. Because the magnitude of the demand exceeded the number of single women who were not already working, employers were forced to recruit married women. Feelings of patriotism and the sense of emergency allowed many wives to ignore traditional constraints and let them "do their part" by seeking work and managing as best they could with their continuing home responsibilities. The labor-force rate for married women (husband present) rose from 14.7 in 1940 to 21.7 in 1944, a major change in behavior. But other considerations also eased the way. First, by the forties, probably four out of five adult women had had some experience in the labor force, so that taking a wartime job was not a novel experience. Second, the reduction of the workweek to 40 to 44 hours, the diffusion of homemaking appliances to working-class homes, and the emergence of the smaller family that had become the norm greatly facilitated combining work with housekeeping. Third, the democratization of the secondary schools in the twenties and thirties had substantially increased the population of women qualified for white-collar employment. Fourth, the ongoing urbanization of the nation had increased the proportion of women in urban settings where a maximum of employment opportunities existed. The interaction of these factors produced an outcome in which, between April 1940 and April 1944, single women provided 800,000 of the increment in the female labor force; married women, 3,400,000. The unanswered question in the fall of 1945 was whether these women, having entered the labor force, would remain there or would resume traditional roles when the war ended.[15]

ROSIE REMAINS: THE POSTWAR YEARS

In 1944, the problems of expanding the wartime labor force largely solved, women's leaders began studying the problems of demobilization. They were certain that at the war's end many younger women who had interrupted their education to enter the labor force would return to school and that most women with young children would leave the labor force to keep house. But not all. Secretary of Labor Perkins warned early in 1943 that women must not be "unfairly accused of taking men's jobs, as at the close of the last war." In particular she noted that many women would have to stay on in place of those who failed to return from the war or who returned maimed. Reminding its readers that most working women *must* work, *Newsweek* reported in August 1943 that 56 percent of the women in the labor force expected to continue working after the war. When President Roosevelt announced his postwar goal of "full employment—the right of every American citizen to a useful and remunerative job," Mary Anderson was quick to claim this goal for "not only men but women workers whose services and sacrifices are essential factors in winning the peace." Anderson endorsed the argument of John D. Durand, the labor economist, that by incorporating women in the postwar labor force, the whole nation could enjoy a higher level of prosperity than it had ever known before.[16]

While the end of the war brought relief from wartime austerity and hazards, it also revived fears that the nation might slip back into the depressed conditions of the thirties. This uneasiness prompted a feeling that women—especially those with able-bodied fathers or husbands—should quit the labor force in favor of men. However, when the war ended, the pent-up demand for civilian goods fueled a high level of production of both durable and consumer goods. Veteran's benefits made upwards of 15,000,000 young Americans eligible for easy credit to purchase homes. Older Americans added to the demand for goods as they, too, bought new homes and replaced cars, furniture, and appliances worn out or grown shabby during the depression and war. The effort to rebuild European economies under the Marshall Plan and the emergence of the cold war between Russia and the United States further stimulated production of goods. (The cold war, however, also diverted several million young males away from the civilian labor force.) Far from slipping back into a depression, the nation enjoyed a high level of prosperity.[17]

This postwar prosperity coincided with the continuing development of the "postindustrial" economy, an economy whose expansive force derived from the production of services rather than goods. By improving its productivity, the primary sector met postwar demands for agricultural goods and minerals with a smaller number of laborers. Faced with a heavy demand for both durable and nondurable goods and a high level of construction, the secondary sector increased its share of the labor force by almost 4 percentage points, while the tertiary sector, the service-producing sector, increased its share by 3.1 points. These changes brought increases in jobs both employers and society thought appropriate for women.[18]

Initially, however, it appeared that women would flee, or be driven from, the labor force. As the nation converted to a peacetime economy, 2,500,000 women left the labor force. Employment in war industries ended;

aircraft companies alone dismissed 800,000 women within two months of the end of hostilities. Since many servicemen had a legal claim to return to their prewar jobs, their women replacements were dismissed. And, as anticipated, large numbers of teenage women (560,000) and women in their early 20s (400,000) left the labor force on their own initiative. Relatively, dropouts among women 25 to 44 were fewer (860,000), as were those of women 45 and over (430,000). For the remainder of the decade the number of women under 25 who were employed continued to ease downward.[19]

On the surface women returned to the kitchen and nursery. The annual number of marriages, which had been as few as 1,400,000 during the war years, shot upward in 1945 and again in 1946 when 2,291,000 couples wed, sending the marriage rate to 16.4 per 1,000 persons as compared to 12.1 in 1940. This rush to the altar was short-lived, and by 1950 the number of marriages—1,667,000—was in the same range as in the early forties. The number of births likewise soared, jumping from 2,735,000 in 1945 to 3,699,000 two years later, and then slipped back to 3,554,000 in 1950. Whereas the birthrate had ranged between 17.9 and 20.9 in the first half of the forties, it ranged from 23.3 to 25.8 in the last half. The question for the country was whether women with wartime work experience could or would return to the labor force and, if so, how soon.[20]

Postwar Demand

Fears that the economy would collapse or that women would be driven from the labor force did not materialize. The demand for labor in the postindustrial economy proved so strong that the labor force numbered 7,257,000 more workers in 1950 than a decade before. Of this increase 3,871,000—53.3 percent—were women. Women's share of the labor force, which had been 25.2 percent in 1940, was 28.8 in 1950, only .4 of a point below the wartime high. Structural changes in the economy continued to reshape the demand for workers. Overall, the demand for agricultural workers declined by over 2,000,000, for private-household workers by 873,000, and for nonfarm laborers by nearly 1,000,000. In the same interval, employments for semiskilled and skilled blue-collar workers increased, though at a lesser rate than for white-collar workers. This latter group of occupations generated a net increase of 5,520,000 jobs in the decade.[21]

The sectors of the economy that shrank affected women unevenly. The percentage of women farmers declined by a larger margin than did the percentage of men farmers, and the withdrawal of women from private-household service accounted for most of the decrease in the category of service employment. On the other hand, the number of women working either as nonfarm or farm laborers increased, and women's share of these occupations increased, as Figure 4-2 illustrates.[22]

In the growth sectors of the economy, women generally increased their share of employments, providing the incremental labor that enabled these sectors to grow. The number of women employed as semiskilled operatives increased by 835,000—22 percent of this increase being attributable to a growth in women's share of the occupation. Even in the category of skilled crafts, in which women had had only token representation, the number of women grew by 118,000, an increase of 104 percent. Rosie the Riveter kept working.[23]

Reflecting the development of the postindustrial economy, women scored their most impressive employment gains in the white-collar sector where they secured nearly 3,000,000 of the 5,520,000 additional jobs. The

Figure 4-2
Changes in Demand for Female Workers, 1940–1950

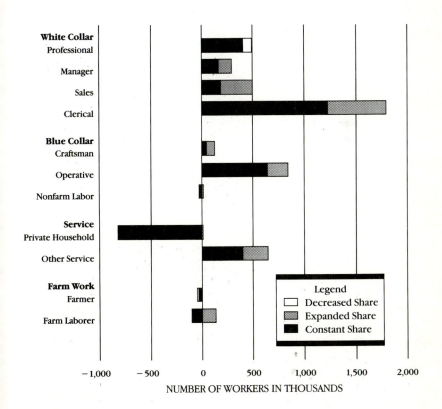

NUMBER OF WORKERS IN THOUSANDS

impact on the demand for female employees is illustrated by two comparisons. First, the increase in white-collar employments during the forties outran the increase in blue-collar employments by a factor of three—2,979,000 white-collar jobs to 965,000 blue-collar jobs. Second, the increase in white-collar employments in the forties also outran the increase in such employments in the previous decade by an even greater margin. In the aggregate, women gained about two thirds of these additional jobs. The major portion of the increase occurred in clerical employments—an area in which women were already numerous, in which a large proportion of the jobs were "female" jobs, and in which a person with a high-school diploma could qualify for most entry-level positions. The lesser part of the increase occurred in sales, managerial, and administrative work. But this is not the whole picture. In the clerical occupations, one third of the additional jobs was attributable to an increase in the occupational share of women; in managerial and administrative work, nearly one half; in sales work, over three fifths. The gains in occupational shares in managerial and administrative work reflected the growing proportions of older women with work experience and the greater acceptability of women in supervisory roles as a result of wartime experience.[24]

Women fared less well in bidding for professional and technical employments, the most prestigious white-collar work. Although the total number of women holding such jobs increased during the decade, their share of such occupations declined. Two factors were involved. First, the extent of the formal education and on-the-job experience required conflicted with the societal pressures on women to assume primary responsibility for the care of the family and household. Finding it more difficult than men to accept the demands of professional careers, women were less likely to prepare for such careers. Second, while the GI Bill subsidized thousands of veterans as they prepared themselves for professional careers, women had to finance their own education or settle for less demanding jobs.[25]

When the gains and losses are weighed, it is apparent that the forties broadened the demand for women in the labor force. The wartime crisis had led employers to place many women in men's jobs. When the war ended, however, many of the jobs ended. But inevitably some women sought alternative employment. Some who dropped out temporarily returned, while others, newly entering the labor market, sought and accepted what had been male jobs. By 1950 women held larger shares of the labor market in all three segments of the blue-collar sector—skilled crafts, semi-skilled operatives, and unskilled labor. While women remained concentrated in a small number of "female" jobs as in earlier decades, in 13 out of 23 of these occupations, women's share declined during the decade, a further indication of the diffusion of women in the labor force.[26]

Postwar Supply

In 1950 the female labor force numbered 16,445,000, up 3,871,000 from 1940; the adult female labor-force rate had risen from 25.75 to 29.25 in the same interval. Where did these women come from? The declining birthrates of white women in the late 1920s and early 1930s produced a shortfall of nearly 2.5 million women between 14 and 24 years old, while the increasing longevity of the population added an extra 1.2 million women to the 65-and-over population. A similar phenomenon produced a shortfall of nearly 300,000 black women, chiefly under 25, and an increase of 100,000 women 65 and over. Given the disparity in labor rates of young white women, as opposed to older women, the demographic changes in the white population produced a net loss of 306,000 workers. Among the black population, the tradeoffs between younger and older women evened out since the labor rates for the older women were often as high or higher than those for the younger women.[27]

Demographic changes in the marital patterns had the more important impact on the composition of the female labor force. While the declining birthrate reduced the pool of single women, the soaring marriage rate at the end of the war further depleted it. Indeed, the total number of single women in the labor force declined by 1,100,000 in spite of a rising propensity of single women to work. Whereas in 1940 single women formed 49.0 percent of the female labor force and married women, but 35.9 percent, by 1950 the proportions were almost reversed; 31.9 percent of the female labor force was single and 52.2 percent, married. Between a growing total population, a short-lived surge in the divorce rate in the mid-forties, and a rise of 2.5 percentage points in their joint labor-force rate, the widowed and divorced added nearly 700,000 persons to the labor force. But by and large the increase in the female labor force came from the nearly 4,000,000 married women added to the work force. The magnitude of this increase was made possible partly by a larger population of married women but also by a hefty rise of 7.4 percentage points in the LFPR of married women. The tug between home and marketplace is seen in the sharp variations in labor rates recorded by various categories of married women. As Figure 4-3 illustrates, for wives with no children under 18 years—newlyweds and women with grown families—the labor rate was 30.3; the rate was nearly as high—28.3—for wives whose only children were between 6 and 17 years; but for those whose children were under 6 years, the rate was only 11.9. The 85 percent increase in the number of married women in the labor force that occurred during the forties caught the public by surprise. Secretary Perkins termed it "revolutionary." Given the long-term structural changes in the economy, this development would have come anyway; the war hastened it by perhaps a decade.[28]

Figure 4-3
Female Labor Force by Marital Status and Age of Children, 1950

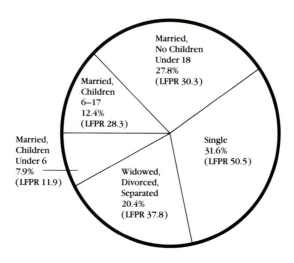

The factors that led individual women to choose to work remain elusive, yet some generalizations are possible. The propensity of women under 18 to work continued to decline as society encouraged them to complete high school before taking a job; the labor force rate of women 18 to 22 also declined as the proportion of women attending college increased. Young unmarried women expected as a matter of course to earn their own living, while many widows and divorcées had to work in order to support themselves and their families. The dynamic element in the supply of female labor was the growing tendency of married women to work. The considerations that had eased their entrance into the wartime labor force remained operative. But other factors also functioned. Experience in the wartime labor force left many women with "a taste of the higher level of living, economic independence, and broader sphere of interests," which employment offered; postwar inflation prodded some wives to work in order to offset the loss in purchasing power. Some women, especially those who had secured a baccalaureate or higher academic degree, elected to work out of a "desire for a sense of competence" or in response to a "drive for actualization." Such women, James A. Sweet suggests, may have developed more expensive tastes for consumption goods that could be satisfied only by entering the labor market. By 1950 the question about the propriety of a woman entering the labor force, a vital issue in 1900, had shifted to the propriety of work for a married woman, especially one with children.

Traditional values continued to condition women to believe that home was more important than work. Accordingly working wives showed "no strong internal commitment to work," that is they were less disposed to secure the requisite formal training for a long-term career than men. Stereotypes about male and female qualities continued to have a profound effect on the kind of work women accepted. In the economic sector women had entered the "festival of life" by midcentury and they did so in the absence of an organized feminist movement.[29]

In the conversion to a peacetime economy, black women fared less well than white women and lost part of their wartime gains. Black women were especially vulnerable to dismissal, since so many of those who had moved upward in job status had secured defense jobs that disappeared or federal positions that did not confer civil-service status. In the adjustment to the postwar labor market, some local offices of the United States Employment Service attempted to induce black women to accept work as maids, counter girls, and laundry pressers or else forfeit unemployment-compensation benefits. Unions, such as the UAW, that had championed opportunities for black women during the war, deserted them afterwards. Firms that had integrated black males into their labor force often excluded black women from postwar employment. In the scramble for employment, black women were left with the lower-level jobs, and in 1950, 42 percent of all black women in the labor force were domestic servants, an occupation in which they lacked protection either by union contracts or protective legislation. Even so, as Figure 4-4 indicates, they made "substantial progress" in securing work as operatives, especially in the apparel industry. The "greatest benefit" of the war years came from their migration from the poverty of the rural South to the possibilities provided by urban, industrial cities. There were modest gains in professional, clerical, and sales work, as well as a retreat from private domestic service and farm labor. Yet enormous disparities distinguished the place of black women from that of white women in the labor force as Figure 4-5 underscores. Blacks remained largely excluded from white-collar occupations, while they continued to be greatly over-represented in service and farm-labor occupations. The net effect of the forties, then, was to speed the migration of black women to areas of the country that offered a wider variety of jobs and to upgrade the quality of jobs available to them.[30]

PUBLIC POLICY

In his State of the Union Address in January 1941, President Roosevelt formulated his hopes for a postwar world characterized by the Four Free-

Figure 4-4
Employed Black Women by Occupation, 1940 and 1950

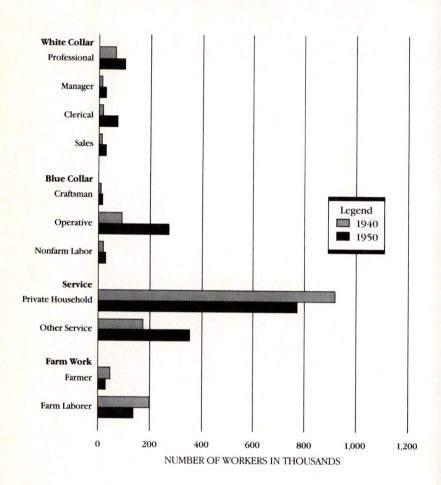

NUMBER OF WORKERS IN THOUSANDS

doms: freedom of speech, freedom of religion, freedom from want, and freedom from fear. In outlining his objectives, Roosevelt, like the framers of the Declaration of Independence, gave no thought to the implications for women. Nevertheless, the circumstances of war pushed women into positions in the economy and public life, so that issues of women's status could not be ignored.[31]

Almost immediately the place of protective legislation in public policy had to be evaluated. Having surveyed some 200 defense jobs, the United

Figure 4-5
Percentage Distribution of Employed Women by Occupation and Race,
1950

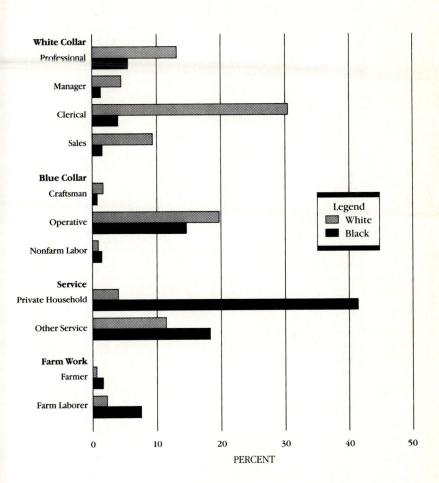

States Employment Service concluded that women could fill 80 percent of them, and the War Manpower Commission advised employers to hire women "on a basis of equality with men" and to "remove all barriers to the employment of women in any occupation for which they are or can be fitted." As a result, women ended up in jobs in heavy industry from which they had previously been excluded either by social pressure or statute. With little resistance from anyone, protective legislation that social feminists had worked so many years to secure was suspended for the duration of the war.[32]

Still committed to social-feminist concerns, the Women's Bureau urged employers to voluntarily provide one day of rest in seven, an eight-hour shift, restrooms, cafeterias, and good lighting. And industry generally complied, a task made easier as many plants were reoutfitted for war production on cost-plus contracts that provided the necessary funds. A study of war plants in the Connecticut Valley showed that machines were protected, overalls, slacks, and goggles were made mandatory, and light tools designed for the job were made available. Ironically, in the absence of protective legislation, women worked in cleaner, safer shops than had existed when such legislation was in force.[33]

A far more controversial public-policy issue centered about the need for child-care facilities for working mothers. By February 1944, some 2,770,000 mothers of 4,460,000 children under 14 years of age were at work. Many held full-time jobs in addition to already heavy family-care responsibilities. Such women generated relatively high absentee records, and they were prone to quit their jobs on short notice to the distress of employers. Social workers fretted over the number of "latchkey children"—children whom working mothers left unsupervised with a latchkey fastened to a string about their necks—and they talked darkly of a rising tide of juvenile delinquency that would follow.[34]

Sadly for the children involved, public officials failed to agree on child-care policy. Initially the Roosevelt administration insisted that the responsibility for child care lay with local communities, but local groups demurred. A Michigan child-care committee spoke for many when it complained: "The fact is that a war is a national emergency and that its effects on community life are too big and too drastic for [local governments] to handle ... on their own." Although federal resources were far more ample, federal authorities were loathe to respond. The Children's Bureau insisted "[A] mother's primary duty is to her home and children. This duty is one she cannot lay aside, no matter what the emergency." A Gallup Poll made in 1943 reflected widespread reluctance, even among working mothers, to utilize a public day-care center. In these circumstances even though General Louis McSherry of the War Production Board declared publicly that "one of the most important programs before us is the development of adequate facilities for the care of children of working mothers," he was ignored. When in 1943 the Lanham Act made available funds that might be used for day care, applicants encountered a "bureaucratic maze" that involved seven separate agencies. In the struggle for control of the program, the Children's Bureau lost out, putting wartime child care in the hands of those opposed to it. The struggle underscored the deep division that existed over the propriety of women with young children working outside the home and the desirability of community child care. By mid-

1944, child-care centers, most of which were financed with federal funds, served an estimated 140,000 children, a small fraction of those needing such aid. As a result, most working mothers had to shoulder a double burden of child care and a job.[35]

The question of equal pay for equal work gained significance as women in large numbers replaced men or began to work alongside them. The War Manpower Commission committed itself on the record to a uniform pay scale for men and women. By General Order 16, the National War Labor Board (NWLB) authorized management to adjust women's wages upward to allow equal pay "for work of comparable quantity or quality on the same or similar operations." On the other hand, the board declined to question wage rates for "female" jobs, presuming them "to be correct." New businesses and expanding defense industries often complied with the equal-pay principles; older businesses with a history of differentiated rates for men and women did not. Concerned with limiting inflation, President Roosevelt issued an executive order to "hold the line!" on wages, such that thereafter the NWLB might grant wage increases to correct substandard conditions but not to eliminate inequalities. Women's Bureau leaders quickly recognized that women would remain vulnerable to discriminatory wage rates so long as realization of the equal-pay principle rested either on the goodwill and discretion of management or an administrative board. Hence they moved to establish the principle in law.[36]

In 1945, Congresswoman Mary Norton as well as Senators Wayne Morse and Claude Pepper introduced equal-pay bills. As "women had demonstrated their ability to turn out the same day's work as men," Morse and Pepper argued, they should no longer be treated as "second class workingmen." Mary Anderson focused the issue as she insisted that the "equal pay for equal work" principle missed the mark, for, given the sexual division of labor, most women did not perform work identical to that of men. The better formula, she insisted, was "the rate for the job," a principle used by the federal civil service since 1923. In 1936, the Walsh–Healy Act adopted the principle that private employers holding federal contracts could not discriminate between men and women in pay rates. Despite the positive record of women in the wartime labor force, many industrial employers still declined to adopt an equal-wage policy. In part, resistance stemmed from the belief that women could do only light work, that they did not perform equal work. Congress adjourned without enacting either measure.[37]

Along with a demand for an equal-pay law, feminists renewed discussion of an ERA. The efforts of employers during the thirties to limit women's employment led many business and professional women to support an ERA. In 1943 a new formula—"Equality of rights under the law shall not be denied or abridged by the United States or by any State on account of sex"—was introduced to Congress with the endorsement of the General Federation of Women's Clubs, the National Association of Women Lawyers, the National Federation of Business and Professional Women's Clubs, and the American Medical Women's Association. Borrowing language from the Fifteenth Amendment, this new version of an ERA focused on legal rights rather than rights in general. It aimed at securing "equal protection of the laws."[38]

In arguing the case for an ERA, Alma Lutz inquired rhetorically: "Are women an integral part of a democratic government or are they a class apart unfit for the rights and freedoms that apply to men?" Advocates of the ERA, such as Lutz, argued that women could not expect to safeguard their rights under the "equal-protection" clause of the Fourteenth Amendment, for as construed by the courts, the equal-protection clause at most assured women of common-law rights but it did not prohibit treating women as a class in a manner different from men as a class. A second line of argument emphasized that since most states had repealed or suspended their protective laws for the duration of the war and as women had poured into the labor force without serious harm to either health or morals, the impact of an ERA on protective legislation was no longer relevant. In any event in view of the *Darby* decision, the future prospects for sex-neutral protective legislation were good. An ERA—in its proponents' minds— would not be at the expense of working-class women.[39]

Opponents continued to use much the same arguments they first used in the twenties. Their central concern was the issue of "the hard won protective legislation," made necessary because "sex was destiny." While acknowledging that the "importance of biological sex differences is being considerably diminished" and that more and more women were their own providers and protectors, a male writer for *Collier's* reaffirmed the conventional view that "nature stands pat on some legislating she did a long time ago." Out of concern for women's child-bearing capacities and earlier maturity, he concluded, differences in age-of-consent legislation were essential; "rules for feminine conduct" would always have to be stricter. The author reflected the ambivalence of society in defending the right of woman to have "a career that excludes marriage and motherhood," while insisting that "what most women are best prepared to offer, and do offer, are not tangible commodities or paychecks, but human services and qualities."[40]

When in 1943 the House Judiciary Committee killed the ERA in committee, Alice Manning, writing for the National Business and Professional Women's Clubs, characterized the vote as "a sort of Pearl Harbor of the Equal Rights Amendment." Dismayed, she challenged her readers: "We Buckle on Our Armour and Return to the Fray." Although favorably reported by the Senate in 1944, the ERA was buried once more in the House Judiciary Committee, but by this time the ERA had ceased to be the exclusive property of the National Woman's Party.[41]

Neither the equal-pay principle nor the ERA would go away. In 1946 the issues became joined over whether equal-pay legislation and an ERA were mutually exclusive or were compatible. The Pepper–Morse Equal Pay Bill enjoyed the support of a broad spectrum of women's organizations. In the ensuing debate, the divided feminists did not revise their arguments in the light of the *Darby* case. Alma Lutz continued to argue that protective legislation that barred women from overtime and nightwork precluded women from competing with men on a basis of equality. She objected to the imputation of female frailty and inferiority on which such legislation rested. On the other side, Mary Anderson insisted that while special protective laws had narrowed the differences between the sexes in the labor force, they were still necessary. Anderson and her colleagues endorsed the Pepper–Morse legislation but organized the National Committee to Defeat the Unequal Rights Amendment. Much of the support for the equal-pay bill came from old-line social-feminist groups; support for the National Committee to Defeat the Unequal Rights Amendment, from labor unions.[42]

In the public arena the ERA was less threatening than when first proposed in the 1920s. The Republican Party endorsed the ERA principle in 1940; the Democrats, in 1944. During the war, some congressmen talked of approving the ERA as a vote of thanks to women for their "magnificent wartime performance." Congress, however, chose to reject both the equal-pay bill and the ERA in favor of the Full Employment Act of 1946. The latter reflected deep-seated fears that the nation might slide back into a depression. As the Full Employment Bill came before Congress, women's leaders expressed hope that the concept "full employment" would "include all women now at work." The War Manpower Commission seconded the point, emphasizing that every citizen, regardless of race or sex, enjoyed a "fundamental right to choose whether to work or not." The Full Employment Act facilitated the maintenance of relatively high employment levels following the war, enabling women to retain their place in the labor force. In turn, the expanding proportion of middle-class women in the labor force served to strengthen the groups urging equality for women. Furthermore, a number of state legislatures enacted equal-pay legislation during or at the end of the war.[43]

Supported by many women members of Congress, the Taft–Wadsworth Legal Status Bill (1947) purported to offer an alternative to the ERA. The bill provided "that in law and its administration no distinctions on the basis of sex shall be made except such as are reasonably justified by differences in physical structure, biological, or social function." The equalitarians were livid. Lutz denounced the bill: "[This puts women] in a class apart as not quite human beings." She was uncompromising; there was "no bridge" between protection of special status and equality. She agreed with the United Nations Commission on the Status of Women that "woman is as much a human being as a man."[44]

Once more in 1950, an ERA surfaced, only to be torpedoed. The debate in the Senate displayed as little sophistication or comprehension of the issues as any to date. Paul Douglas, Estes Kefauver, and Herbert Lehman arrayed themselves in opposition to the ERA, dredging up fears as to the effect such a measure might have on maternity leaves, the "homestead rights" of a surviving spouse, and the protections against divorce on grounds of insanity. Kefauver, in particular, conjured up the specter of an army with more women than men, of children left homeless as both parents were drafted, of the destruction of dower rights, and of the abolition of the crime of rape. Carl Hayden, an opponent, offered a rider emasculating the measure. Hayden's language provided that nothing in the ERA would impair any "rights, benefits or exemptions now or hereafter conferred by law on persons of the female sex." In short, he proposed an ERA that would let stand the single-sex protective legislation that ERA advocates were trying to purge from the statutes and would provide a loophole by which additional single-sex protective laws might be added.[45]

The media joined in the levity of the occasion. *Life* portrayed one young advocate of the ERA as "displaying woman's most invincible argument"—a comely pair of legs. In the same vein, *Time* helped its readers to an understanding of the issues by quoting actress Shelly Winters: "I don't want to smoke cigars, or go to stag parties, wear jockey shorts or pick up the check." *Newsweek* took delight in announcing that the women had been "outsmarted by mere men" on the Hayden amendment. Certainly the woman's case was fatally hurt by the continued division of ranks. While Alice Paul had Bess Truman in her camp along with various groups of business and professional women, the opponents counted Eleanor Roosevelt, Frances Perkins, and the leadership of the CIO and AFL, as well as of the National League of Women Voters and the American Association of University Women.[46]

Although the influx of women into the labor force—especially into blue-collar jobs—forced a discussion of protective legislation, child care, equal-pay legislation, and an ERA, Congress did not allow itself to be panicked into major legislative reforms. Congressional leaders concentrated their energies first on the war effort, then on tidying up the New Deal reforms at home and countering the Russians in foreign affairs. While the war necessitated the employment of women in unusual roles, it was not allowed to provide an excuse for long-term changes in the role of women.

Protective legislation became operative once more at the war's end. Ultimately Congress accorded a full-employment policy affecting all workers a higher national priority than either an equal-pay bill or an ERA.[47]

While equal pay, an ERA, and full employment engaged the interest of women's leaders and the Congress, the war years sensitized American blacks to their second-class status and strengthened their resolve to improve their lot. Blacks, males in particular, increasingly participated in the activities of major labor unions such as the UAW, the United Steel Workers, the National Maritime Union, and the United Rubber Workers. Such blacks gained the means of supporting their families in dignity.[48]

But the large-scale migration of blacks into new communities also generated tensions. In Los Angeles County, the black population doubled in five years (1940–1945), while San Francisco, Portland, and Seattle experienced similar growth. Of midwest cities, Detroit experienced the greatest stress. Whites acquired blacks as fellow workers. The lack of housing, the presence of race baiters and demagogues, the problem of organizing newly arrived workers, and the impotence of government created an environment in which the most serious race riot of the war occurred. When it ended, 25 blacks and 9 whites were dead.[49]

The black response to discrimination was epitomized in the "Double-V" campaign of the *Pittsburgh Courier*: victory at home as well as victory abroad. In the postwar years, blacks were determined not only to hold on to the wartime gains, but to press ahead vigorously for full equality. The NAACP began to campaign more actively for equal treatment; President Truman appointed a committee of distinguished blacks and whites to explore the condition of civil rights and to make recommendations for their improvements. The committee's report, *To Secure These Rights,* called for "the elimination of segregation based on race, color, creed or national origin." A second presidential commission called for the elimination of inequalities in educational opportunities. And in 1949 the president pressed the military to open all jobs to qualified persons without regard to race or color. The black community had come a long way since 1900, and black women had gained much thereby, but by law and custom black women were still second-class citizens. Most of their energies were focused on improving their status as blacks.[50]

EDUCATION

The forties saw the differences between the educational experiences of men and women continue to narrow at some levels, broaden in others. The proportion of children in elementary schools continued to inch upward.

More importantly the secondary schools reached almost as large a proportion of the young people as did the elementary schools. For the first time, more than half of the whites in the 25- to 29-year-old cohort had completed high school. In this achievement females lagged males slightly.[51]

More important for the national well-being, the differences in the proportions of white and nonwhite youth enrolled in school continued to narrow, and by 1950, for the first time, a majority of the nonwhite population in the 25- and 29-year-old cohort had completed at least eight years of schooling. Older women—whites as well as blacks—had distinctly less schooling than women in their early 20s. In 1940, white women over 40 had a median level of schooling of 8 to 9 years, whereas in the nonwhite population the median varied from 4.2 years for women in their early 60s to not quite 7 years for those in their late 30s. Even so, nonwhite women of all ages had higher levels of schooling than nonwhite males. Reflecting the limited educational opportunities available to nonwhites earlier in the century, one nonwhite in ten was illiterate in 1950. The proportion of nonwhites with sufficient schooling to compete for white-collar employments was small and limited to younger people. Many would have difficulty competing even for blue-collar jobs.[52]

The coming of World War II seriously disrupted enrollments in the nation's colleges and universities. First, the number of males enrolled dropped precipitously, then, with the war over, enrollments swelled to unprecedented levels. For women students the war was less traumatic. Although not subject to the draft, some chose work rather than college, so that in the midst of the war—1944—the number of women receiving baccalaureates dropped below the 1940 number by 10 percent. Thereafter female enrollments picked up, but in the late 1940s women had to share overcrowded classrooms, libraries, and laboratories with returning veterans. The proportion of women earning baccalaureates increased from 66.1 per 1,000 to 86.3 during the decade, steadily increasing the pool of women who could enter demanding white-collar jobs or pursue graduate or professional training. Even so, this pool of women was decidedly smaller than that of males with similar training.[53]

Women inched ahead in pursuit of a master's degree; its utility in the teaching and library professions stimulated many women with baccalaureate degrees to secure a master's degree. And in 1940, women were earning their master's at about the same rate as men did. During the midst of the war, women constituted a majority of the master's-level students, but in the postwar years, returning males, assisted by the GI Bill, outnumbered women by margins exceeding two to one. While the proportion of males who earned master's degrees would continue to exceed the proportion of females, the differences in future years would never be as great as in 1950.[54]

In the pursuit of doctoral degrees women lagged men by a wide and growing margin. During the forties the rate at which women with baccalaureates subsequently earned doctorates regressed slightly from 8.7 to 8.4. Males, by contrast, had rates of 38.8 in 1940 and 54.7 in 1950. The growing differentials in the completion of doctorates would have a long-term impact on the proportion of women to men in the elite professions, academia, and the specialized positions in business, as well as in the relative size of the pool of women who would be available in later years for leadership roles. The completion of a doctorate typically took eight to ten years, half of which time was devoted to study that precluded more than part-time employment and often required deferral of marriage. Males, in far greater proportions than females, were encouraged and enabled to make the commitments of time and money to secure the degree. The rising demand for college teachers centered on males; the GI Bill subsidized part or all of the costs for many veterans. These conditions, which continued from the end of the war to the late fifties, contributed to the increased disparity in educational attainment of young men and women at the graduate and professional level.[55]

Although women did not expand their educational horizons as rapidly as men, they nonetheless moved ahead. During the war years, women were less inclined to limit themselves to teaching and nursing, and the number of women taking degrees in medicine and law doubled. With the men away, women began to outnumber men in academic fields that had been male-dominated, and some men's schools, including Rensselaer Polytechnic Institute, the nation's oldest engineering school, admitted women. Pennsylvania State University's Department of Industrial Engineering joined the rest of the institution in becoming coed. Colleges supported the war effort with special programs to train women for industrial employment.[56]

Arguments over curriculum reform centered on the nature of the wife–mother–homemaker sex role. Noting that this was *the* role most women filled, many educators assumed it was the one women *ought* to pursue. This point of view drew encouragement, if not an imperative command, from sociologists such as Margaret Mead, Henry A. Bowman, and Talcott Parsons. Mead reached her audience through a series of books exploring and comparing sex roles in a variety of societies: *Sex and Temperament, Male and Female,* and *And Keep Your Powder Dry.* Although she noted that the behavior one society defined as male another might well label feminine, she cautioned that in every society the individual who failed to abide by the prescribed sex roles faced severe problems. Bowman, in his widely read *Marriage for Moderns* (1942), advised that "the sexes are complementary ... Neither is superior, neither is inferior. Each must be judged in terms of its own functions.... When men and women engage in the same occupations or perform common functions, the complementary relationship may break down."[57]

Talcott Parsons, the preeminent theorist of the family, added his authority, asserting that dire social consequences would follow unless "a clear separation of sex roles such as to insure that they (husband and wife) do not come into competition with each other" were observed. Lest anyone misinterpret the differentiated roles of men and women, Parsons spelled it out: "only in very exceptional cases can an adult man be genuinely self-respecting and enjoy a respected status in the eyes of others if he does not 'earn a living' in an approved occupational role." By contrast, "the woman's fundamental status is that of her husband's wife, the mother of his children, and traditionally the person responsible for a complex of activities in connection with the management of the household, care of the children, etc." Clearly any conflict in roles had to be resolved in terms of what was good for the male; the status quo had to be the pattern of the future.[58]

Several different approaches to curriculum reform surfaced. Least discussed was the norm—coeducation in which women pursued curriculums that had been designed without thought as to whether women and men had different needs. Although these curriculums were presumably sex-neutral, the elective system permitted women to choose majors and courses that males might avoid. While some educators argued for curriculums that prepared women primarily for roles as wife, mother, and homemaker, others championed curriculums that prepared women for careers to the exclusion of other roles. In the middle were those that would equip women for social-service activities, that might complement the wife–mother–homemaker role, or that might provide a base for a career before and after the child-rearing years.

Lynn White, Jr.—president of Mills College, a woman's college—dissatisfied with the focus of higher education generally, declared that the "narrowness" of its concerns "impoverishes all of us." Further, "the masculine bias of our education cheats men as well as women." It would be a grievous error to put women into a curriculum designed for men, which tacitly sought to make her a man. White would have women educated so that they could support themselves if they did not marry, so that they could manage a family, if they did. He would have coeds understand the "ambiguous and transitional status" that women occupied in America in 1950. But most important he sought an environment in which "it is taken for granted that women are as worthy of respect as men and that the things they tend to do best are as significant and honorable as the things men tend to do best." In elaborating his position, White saw women as clearly differentiated from men. Women were preoccupied with "conserving and cherishing." He enthusiastically supported a "family-minded" curriculum. Home economics would be given a family, as opposed to an institutional, empha-sis; courses in the family, cooking, clothing, interior decoration, and child development would be explored for their importance to the individual family. White's enthusiasm for a course in gourmet cooking subsequently led Mirra Komarovsky and Betty Friedan to charge that he favored substi-tuting cooking for college-level chemistry.[59]

George D. Stoddard, president of the coed University of Illinois, agreed substantially with White. He tacitly assumed that the wife–mother–homemaker role was the natural order of affairs and that the curricu-lum for women should reflect this. Yet his position was tempered by an ambivalence that led him to acknowledge that "the differences between individuals of a single sex are of a greater order than anything related to the class as a whole." The struggle to provide a proper education for women was not "a battle for equal rights, if by equal we mean identical, but for equivalent rights in which some things of small interest to men will develop into excellent programs for women." Stoddard's solution was moderate. Like White, Stoddard would have women devote a part of their collegiate program to courses relating to the home and family—courses in health and hygiene and child development. In addition, women would choose a major that offered career possibilities. Some of these majors prepared them for a traditional "woman's career"—teaching, home eco-nomics, applied arts, physical education, social welfare, nursing, occupa-tional therapy, and secretarial services; but the entire range of career majors pursued by men was equally available. Stoddard also thought that "home education" was as needful for men as for women. Taken in context, White and Stoddard wanted to incorporate into the collegiate programs studies that had specific content relating to the wife–mother–homemaker role, a role they assumed that most of their women students would occupy. Nei-ther of them, however, proposed to restrict women to a home-and-family curriculum.[60]

Leaning in the opposite direction, Katharine McBride, president of Bryn Mawr College, rebutted Freudian-minded educators, arguing that there was no evidence to support a claim that "all energies directed toward a goal other than the family and home . . . actually impoverish these." Nor was it possible for a modern woman to "actually devote full energies to her family and her home . . . without all the widely accepted but casual outside activities. . . ." "When women go beyond the home at all, their education can no more follow a single pattern than can education for men." She rejected the need for "such a thing as *women's* educations," because "women's abilities and interests . . . extend over much or all of the range of men's and . . . [because] the fields of human knowledge and the prob-lems of society remain the same whichever sex attacks them."[61]

That the educators of the late 1940s and 1950s were more "sex-directed" than the general populace is questionable. In surveying public opinion in 1949, *Fortune* reported that while nearly half (46 percent) of its sample thought a collegiate education should prepare women for marriage and family life, only 10 percent thought this was a proper function in educating men. The same poll indicated a much stronger consensus that college should prepare men for an occupation (57 percent) than women (33 percent). To the public it seemed far more appropriate that a college education give women an appreciation of literature, art, and music (26 percent) than men (7 percent). A survey of some 30,000 members of the American Association of University Women—a third of the total membership—revealed that women who were best-informed as to the nature of collegiate education opted for an education that was "broad enough to cover every important aspect of each woman's life," yet would enable her to develop "specific skills" with career value.[62]

Rather clearly academe accommodated and reinforced popular views of the "educational needs" of women. The proportion of women who entered colleges and universities seemed destined to grow, the choices of curriculums wide open—at least to undergraduates. Yet the weight of convention and social conditioning continued to steer most young women away from math and science or professional curriculums and toward literature, languages, sociology, psychology, nursing, home economics, or teaching. Society conditioned women to subordinate education to marriage.

REDEFINING WOMAN'S PLACE

As the United States entered the war, American officials anticipated that the nation faced a "labor vacuum" of such magnitude that several million women would have to be recruited for technically demanding work or for physically taxing, dirty, even dangerous jobs that men found odious. In the crisis of war, the national interest required that public policy redefine woman's place so as to make such employment acceptable.

In doing so, planners expressly counseled employers to recruit women in terms of the attributes traditionally regarded as uniquely feminine: women were pliant, had unusual manual dexterity, were exceptionally accurate, were well-adapted to the monotonous and repetitive tasks, and were especially sensitive to color and texture. Initially, then, planners hoped to ease the entry of women into male work roles by capitalizing on their stereotypical female qualities. They also evidenced an awareness of the adverse effects on women of lifting heavy weights and of inhaling toxic fumes—concerns that had prompted generations of social feminists to lobby for protective legislation for women. In this case, however, the planners minimized the degree of innate female delicacy. Major Howard J. Lepper, an area director of the War Manpower Commission, insisted, on the basis of testing, that women over 16 years of age were capable of continuous lifting and carrying of loads far greater than were presumed safe by protective legislation. Women's special sensitivity to toxic substances was also downplayed. At the same time there was recognition that some industrial activities—the operation of pneumatic hammers—could be especially hazardous to women. And, indeed, perhaps 20 percent of the jobs in heavy defense industries were classified as unsuitable for women. The war, then, focused attention on stereotypical sexual differences. If expediency led policymakers to cite the virtues of the presumed feminine skills, the effort to make work more acceptable to women also resulted in a broadening of the areas in which men and women were held to share common abilities and limitations.[63]

In recruiting women for "male" jobs, employers recognized that they were asking women to undertake a role for which they had not been socialized as children through exposure to tools or by rough-and-tumble games. Management went out of its way to get "the right [women] workers . . . in the right places . . . at the right time," hoping thereby to optimize hiring and retention rates. A variety of training programs—some in schools, others in extension classes, and still others run by employers—were instituted so women could "get the feel of work" and to prepare them for a specific job. Where possible, job training was interpreted in terms of past domestic experiences. War Manpower Commission personnel sounded out and counseled managers and foremen on the anticipated problems of working with women. Personnel officers utilized testing programs to assist in job placement. If the initial job assignment did not work out, the assignment was shifted. Despite injunctions by the National Safety Council to treat women as individuals, employers often reacted to them as a class. To "protect" male workers from distraction, Vultee Aviation banned tight sweaters for female employees, while North American Aviation, to safeguard its women employees, posted signs: "No Profanity, Women Working Inside." Many of these efforts represented the enlightened self-interest of managements that were recruiting from a rapidly dwindling reserve labor force. But underlying these measures was a pervasive belief that women were different and required special treatment.[64]

A major concern related to child care. From the beginning, the War Manpower Commission affirmed that "the first responsibility of women with young children, in war as in peace, is to give suitable care in their own homes." The full statement, though bowing to traditional sex roles, was carefully phrased. It acknowledged that married women would have to be recruited, including mothers of young children. The commission advised employers against unilaterally barring mothers of young children from employment; rather it urged that the decision to work or not work be "an individual decision made by the woman herself in the light of the particular conditions prevailing in her home." Sensitive to the problems of such women, the commission urged employers to arrange working hours so as to cause "the least disruption" in family life and to explore job sharing. Communities were urged to develop child-care facilities.[65]

Management's experience with women workers was generally positive. A mix of patriotism and a sense of being pioneers gave women "a greater incentive to set records." Several million women acquired a familiarity with power tools with which they had no prior familiarity. Such women acquired a new self-respect and self-confidence in their abilities, even if they viewed their job as a wartime diversion. Family members, friends, and the general public—thanks to the spotlight cast on them by the press—also altered their perceptions of what women could do. The records dispelled the conventional wisdom that "women made poorer supervisors than men," or that they had "very little mechanical adeptness, aptitude or skill." While some employers remained convinced of women's limitations as workers and others hailed women as superior to men, a more balanced view held that there was no real proof that "women were generally more patient than men in their jobs, nor that they could generally 'excell men in close accurate work.' " Many employers and supervisors came to acknowledge that the range of jobs that women could do as well as men proved far wider than employers and supervisors had anticipated. But throughout the war years it was equally apparent that society assumed women would supervise the home—cleaning, food preparation, and child care—whether they worked or not, and that while husbands might help out, few genuinely shared those tasks with working wives. If anything, women proved more versatile than men in assuming "a double role with noticeable skill and finesse." The war experience, then, did not eradicate all the old stereotypes, but it gave many women a variety of experiences and roles that approximated those of men; it provided evidence that men and women were far more alike than society had hitherto acknowledged.[66]

The role of the movies in shaping and reshaping the image of women was less focused. The loss of overseas markets in 1939 and 1940 and the ending of block- and blind-booking at home forced movie makers to start revising their mode of operations before the United States became a belligerent. The responses of the major studios reflected their leadership and the mix of stars that each had under contract rather than any generally held view about women. Metro-Goldwyn-Mayer built its "stories of nice people involved in heartbreak, finding their happiness at last in each others arms" around Mickey Rooney, Clark Gable, and Spencer Tracy. Warner's had the laconic, dry-voiced Humphrey Bogart; the sultry, sexy Lauren Bacall; the tough, energetic Barbara Stanwyck; the dominating Joan Crawford; and the queen of the lot, Bette Davis. At Paramount, the influence of Ernst Lubitsch, Preston Sturges, Billy Wilder, Charles Brackett, and Buddy de Sylva was geared to "high-key comedies and skilled farce." Columbia concentrated its efforts on "its only major female star and sex symbol," Rita Hayworth; at Twentieth Century Fox, Betty Grable, "The G.I.'s favourite pin-up girl" was the leading female attraction; and Universal concentrated on Deanna Durbin musicals. As a business selling entertainment to the masses, the movie industry produced for all tastes—from light comedy and musicals to melodrama, problem films, and literary adaptations. Women could be exploited and trivialized; they could be conventionally feminine and submissive; or they might be assertive and independent.[67]

The war, of course, affected the subject matter. Many war movies—*Wake Island, Destination Tokyo,* and *Thirty Seconds over Tokyo*—were male pictures, but others focused on women in wartime: on Rosie the Riveter, on the working girl doing her part on the home front, on Wacs and Waves and nurses serving the military, and on the wives and sweethearts waiting at home. In these women-centered pictures the heroines "came to grips with their manless existence." "Bitchiness and frivolity on the screen gave place to female strength; strength and love and support between mother and daughter, woman and woman." Greer Garson in *Mrs. Miniver* defended her bombed-out house from a Nazi intruder. In *Tender Comrade,* Ginger Rogers set up house with three other women who comforted her and her newborn when she was notified of her husband's death. In *Watch on the Rhine,* Bette Davis watched her husband and sons risk their lives for the underground. The war also generated frothy, girl-centered pictures exploiting "the peaches-and-cream wholesome sexuality" of Rita Hayworth and Betty Grable. The GIs responded by plastering barracks' walls with pinups of Hayworth kneeling on an unmade bed and Grable in a skin-tight swimsuit.[68]

The forties continued the woman's film in which "*a* woman is at the center of the universe"—an antidote for the male-dominated world from which women were generally excluded. Such films confronted the circumscribed world that was the norm of the middle-class housewife and the "fulfillment" that required translating "woman" into "wife" and "mother," thereby ending her independent identity. The genre, however, permitted as many kinds of women's films as there were kinds of women. At one end of the continuum were the "extraordinary," emancipated women who transcended "the limitations of their sexual identities"; at the other, the "ordinary" woman who was "stuck and would rather be stuck than sorry"; in between was the woman who rose "through pain, obsession, or defiance, to be the mistress of her fate." Joan Crawford, Bette Davis, Rosalind Russell, and Katharine Hepburn, in particular, took roles of strong women who possessed a high level of intelligence, but instead of trading on their femininity, adopted "male characteristics in order to enjoy male prerogatives." Davis in *Beyond the Forest,* Russell in *His Girl Friday, My Sister Eileen,* and *Take a Letter Darling,* Crawford in *Mildred Pierce,* and Hepburn in *Christopher Strong* and *Adam's Rib* were able to achieve their ends in a man's world, to be intelligent and to insist on using their intelligence. The only films that allowed "dignity to working women were those based on historical figures, . . . the singularity of whose achievement would not make them a threat to men or to other women." Reaching its peak in the late forties, the woman's film was superseded by afternoon TV soap operas.[69]

In the postwar years other emphases surfaced. The wholesome sexuality of the wartime musicals gave way to overt sexuality as Rita Hayworth, in a black strapless sheath, sang "Put the Blame on Mame" in *Gilda.* Esther Williams, Jennifer Jones, and even Joan Crawford exuded sex appeal rather than independence. The tone of the postwar era, however, was set by *Mr. Blanding Builds His Dream House,* a reaffirmation of domesticity. Imitating society, the movie industry reaffirmed male dominance and female subservience as the norm in human relations.[70]

The bounds of women's roles were made especially clear by the advertising community. Most copy reminded women of the extraordinary requirements of wartime. It cautioned women to be sparing in the use of soap, to plant victory gardens, to buy war bonds, to take a defense job, or to enlist in the armed forces. "These are the days the 'Girl He Left Behind' must remember she is more than a wife," a Florida Grapefruit Juice ad proclaimed as it portrayed a young mother, her hair in a bandana and a lunchbox under one arm, waving to her child as she departed for work. But there might also be conventional rewards, for while Ipana reminded: "your country needs you in a vital job," it assured that "after hours hearts are drawn to a bright, sparkling smile." And the background of the copy illustrated women engaged as cadet nurse, tractor driver, teacher, pilot, welder, and postal clerk. Advertisers did not allow women, however, to forget the traditional roles. Tangee declared: "We're still the weaker sex. . . . It is still up to us to appear as alluring and lovely as possible." Producers of durable goods, currently not in production, looked ahead to the end of the war. Seth Thomas, the clock maker, praised Joan, "a Smart Little Girl." Her fellow was in the army; she had a war job. Joan was pictured clipping "items and ideas" from magazines, planning for their home-to-be when "the wonderful day" arrived. At the height of the war these advertisers explicitly prepared the ground for a return to the cult of domesticity at the war's end.[71]

By 1950, with domesticity the norm, advertisers tacitly assumed that women were preoccupied with being "Radiant! Lovely," with fulfilling the maternal role by wise choice of food and clothing for the children, and fulfilling the housekeeping role by intelligent selection of housewares. A proper woman owed it to her husband to make her own jellies and preserves, Certo averred, for that was "how to prove you're a wonderful wife." Dodge cultivated the female market by emphasizing that its cars were safer and roomier, but it implied that driving was more difficult for a wife than for her husband and that features such as "high compression" were beyond "her comprehension." In another explicit invocation of the differentiated sex roles, Listerine had Dora, clad in cap and gown alongside two jubilant girl friends, glumly ask herself "What was the diploma compared to those precious sparkling rings that Babs and Beth were wearing?" Somehow Babs and Beth had learned an extracurricular lesson that Dora had flunked. A diploma was, after all, a poor substitute for the prospect of marriage.[72]

The nation's mood at the end of the forties was incomparably better than at the start. Considering the scale of operations, the country had survived the war with relatively few casualties. Although Americans were concerned with inflation at home and the cold war abroad, there was a high level of employment. Women had enjoyed an unprecedented period of high public visibility. Employers had become accustomed to the use of married and postmenopausal women, while women had come to regard participation in the labor force as an increasingly acceptable concomitant of marriage and motherhood. However, rather than trigger a revolution in the character of the female labor force, the wartime use of female workers reinforced long-term trends. The questions relating to equal pay, protective legislation, child care, and equal rights remained unresolved. Women's acceptance of market work was well in advance of society's willingness to provide support in terms of equal pay, child care, or community services. Certainly in the course of the war, policymakers consciously reacted to sexual stereotypes, sometimes accommodating policy to the traditional, other times attempting to circumvent the stereotypes. While advertisers encouraged women to adopt male roles in support of the war effort, they held out the promise of an idyllic postwar world in which the traditional wife–mother–housekeeper role would be the norm. Despite a postwar rush to the altar and maternity ward, by 1950 an unprecedented proportion of the female population was seeking to balance traditional homemaking and child-care roles with nontraditional roles at work.

NOTES

[1] Frederick Lewis Allen, *Since Yesterday* (New York: Bantam, 1961[1939]), 261.

[2] "Women and the War Effort," *Commonweal,* 36(May 29, 1942): 125.

[3] Mary Gilson, "Why Not Equal Pay?" *Independent Woman,* 22(Sept. 1943): 257–73. Laura Nelson Baker, *Wanted: Women in War Industry* (New York: Dutton, 1943). Helen Baker, *Women in War Industries* (Princeton: Princeton University Industrial Relations Section, Research Report no. 66, 1942). Leila Rupp, *Mobilizing for War: German and American Propaganda, 1939–1945* (Princeton: Princeton University Press, 1978).

[4] Women's Bureau, "Women's Work in the War," *Bulletin* no. 193 (Washington: GPO, 1942). Women's Bureau, "Changes in Women's Employment During the War," *Special Bulletin* no. 20 (Washington: GPO, 1944).

[5] Chester W. Gregory, *Women in Defense Work During World War II* (New York: Exposition, 1974). See "Women in Steel," *Life,* 15(Aug. 9, 1943): 75–80. William Henry Chafe, *The American Woman* (New York: Oxford, 1972), chaps. 6–8. Susan M. Hartmann, *The Home Front and Beyond: American Women in the 1940s* (Boston: Twayne, 1982).

[6] Chafe, *American Woman,* 142.

[7] John Hope Franklin, *From Slavery to Freedom,* 3rd ed. (New York: Knopf, 1967), 577–80. Harvard Sitkoff, *A New Deal for Blacks: The Emergence of Civil Rights as a National Issue* (New York: Oxford, 1978), 314.

[8] Chafe, *American Woman,* 142–143. Alice Kessler-Harris, *Out to Work* (New York: Oxford, 1982), 279, terms the wartime gains of black women "especially dramatic."

[9] Franklin, *From Slavery to Freedom,* 581, 584, 589.

[10] Karen Tucker Anderson, "Last Hired, First Fired: Black Woman Workers during World War II," *JAH,* 69(1982): 81, 84, 88, 89. See also Karen Anderson, *Wartime Women: Sex Roles, Family Relations, and the Status of Women during World War II* (Westport: Greenwood, 1981). Jacqueline Jones, *Labor of Love, Labor of Sorrow* (New York: Basic, 1985), 234.

[11] Annual employment figures for the war years are most easily accessible in Bureau of the Census, *Statistical Abstract of the United States: 1946* (Washington: GPO, 1946), 174–75.

[12] Gertrude Bancroft, *The American Labor Force* (New York: Wiley, 1958).

[13] *Fortune,* 28(Feb. 1943): 94.

[14] Margaret Hickey quoted in Chafe, *American Woman,* 145. "Postwar Horizons," *Newsweek,* 22(Aug. 23, 1943): 54.

[15] Bancroft, *American Labor Force,* 28–29. John D. Durand, *The Labor Force in the United States, 1890–1960* (New York: SSRC, 1948), 26, 70–72.

[16] Frances Perkins, "Women's Work in Wartime," *MLR,* 56(April 1943): 665. "Postwar Horizons," 54. Mary Anderson, "The Post War Role of American Women," *AER, Supplement,* 34(March 1944): 237–44. "Labor Safeguards after War Sought," *NYT,* 13 Feb. 1945. See also, Alan Clive, "Women Workers in World War II, Michigan as a Test Case," *Labor History,* 20(1979): 44–72.

[17] Eric F. Goldman, *The Crucial Decade—And After: America, 1945–1960* (New York: Vintage, 1961), 6–7.

[18] Bureau of the Census, *Statistical Abstract of the United States: 1953* (Washington: GPO, 1953), tab. 226.

[19] Chafe, *American Woman,* 180 ff.

[20] Bureau of the Census, "A Statistical Portrait of Women in the United States," *CPR,* Special Studies P-23, no. 58 (Washington: GPO, 1976), 16. Bureau of the Census, *Historical Statistics of the United States, Colonial Times to 1970,* Bicentennial Edition, pt. 2 (Washington: GPO, 1975), 49, 64, 131.

[21] Bancroft, *American Labor Force,* tab. D-2.

[22] Ibid. See also tab. D-6.

[23] Frieda Miller, "What's Become of Rosie, the Riveter?" *NYT Magazine,* 5 May 1946, 21 ff. See also, Sheila Tobias and Lisa Anderson, "Whatever Happened to Rosie the Riveter?" *MS,* 1(June 1973), 94 ff; "Rosie Is Back," *New Republic,* 118(May 10, 1948), 7–8.

[24] Bancroft, *American Labor Force,* tab. D-6.

[25] Ibid., tab. D-7 provides figures for specific occupations.

[26] Ibid., tab. D-6. Declines occurred in the following occupations: dancing and dancing teachers, librarians, nurses, teachers, library attendants, physicians' and dentists' attendants, office-machine operatives, dressmakers and seamstresses, milliners, tobacco manufacturers, housekeepers (private), laundresses (private), and boardinghouse and lodging housekeepers.

[27] Ibid., tab. D-1, pp. 202–6.

[28] Bureau of Labor Statistics, *Labor Force Statistics Derived from the Current Population Survey. A Data Book.* vol. 1, Bulletin 2096 (Washington: GPO, 1982), C-6, C-11.

[29] Durand, *Labor Force in the United States,* 27. James A. Sweet, *Women in the Labor Force* (New York: Seminar, 1973), 23. Robert W. Smuts, *Women and Work in America* (New York: Columbia University Press, 1959), 147 ff.

[30] Anderson, "Last Hired, First Fired," 95, 96, 97.

[31] Franklin D. Roosevelt, *The Public Papers and Addresses of Franklin D. Roosevelt,* ed. Samuel I. Rosenman, 13 vols. (New York: Random House, 1938–1950), vol. 9, 672.

[32] "Policy of War Manpower Commission on Woman Workers," *MLR,* 56(April 1943): 669–71.

[33] Katherine Glover, *Women at Work in Wartime* (New York: Public Affairs Committee, 1943), 10. Baker, *Women in War Industries,* 51–58. Constance Green, *The Role of Women as Production Workers in War Plants in the Connecticut Valley* (Northampton: Smith College, 1946), 40.

[34] Chafe, *American Woman,* 160–71. Henry L. Zucker, "Working Parents and Latchkey Children," in *The Annals,* 236(Nov. 1944): 43–50. Howard Dratch, "The Politics of Child Care in the 1940's," *Science and Society,* 38(1974): 167–204.

[35] Chafe, *American Woman,* 163, 165, 166–70. See also Children's Bureau, "Understanding Juvenile Delinquency," *Bulletin,* no. 300 (Washington: GPO, 1943). Alfred Toombs, "War Babies," *WHC,* 71(April 1944): 32 ff.

[36] NWLB, General Order 16, Nov. 1942. Chafe, *American Woman,* 154–56. Dorothy S. Brady, "Equal Pay for Workers," *The Annals,* 217(May 1947): 53. Frieda S. Miller, "Equal Pay—Its Importance to the Nation," *Independent Woman,* 25(Nov. 1946): 325–26. Caryl Reeve Grantham, "Why Equal Pay Now," *Independent Woman,* 22(Nov. 1943): 319, 331.

[37] Gregory, *Women in Defense Work,* 168–69. *Cong. Rec.,* 79th Cong., 1st sess., 27, for Norton's bill. *Cong. Rec.,* 79th Cong., 1st sess., 6411, for Pepper–Morse bill, S. 1178. H.R. 5221, introduced by Woodhouse, replaced the Norton bill; it was reported with amendments, *Cong. Rec.,* 79th Cong., 2nd sess., 313, 10328. See H. Rept. 2687. Mary Anderson, "Letter," *Christian Science Monitor,* 13 April 1946.

[38] *NYT,* 24 July 1937, p. 17, col. 1. Susan D. Becker, *The Origins of The Equal Rights Amendment* (Westport: Greenwood, 1981). The ERA appeared as Senate Joint Resolution 25 and House Joint Resolutions 1, 18, 20, and 137. *Cong. Rec.,* 78th Cong., 1st sess., 25.

[39] Alma Lutz, "Why Bar Equality?" *Christian Science Monitor Magazine,* 22 July 1944. See also *Cong. Rec.,* 78th Cong., 2nd sess., 7663–69. U.S. Senate, *Hearings, Amend the Constitution Relative to Equal Rights for Men and Women,* 79th Cong., 1st sess., 1945. U.S. Senate Committee on the Judiciary, *Hearings, Equal Rights Amendment,* 79th Cong., 1st sess., 1945.

[40] Amram Scheinfeld, "How 'Equal' Are Women?" *Colliers,* 112(Sept. 18, 1943): 15, 73–74. See also *Cong. Rec.,* 78th Cong., 2nd sess., 1037, 7905.

[41] Alice Manning, "We Buckle on Our Armour and Return to the Fray," *Independent Woman,* 22(Nov. 1943): 338 ff.

[42] Alma Lutz, "Only One Choice," *Independent Woman,* 26(July 1947): 199, 205. *Christian Science Monitor Magazine,* 13 April 1946. See also Elizabeth S. Magee, "What Are Equal Rights for Women?" *New Republic,* 112(Jan. 29, 1945): 149. Debate on the Pepper–Morse bill was blocked by a parliamentary maneuver of Senator R. A. Taft, *Cong. Rec.,* 79th Cong., 2nd sess., 10547.

[43] Gregory, *Women in Defense Work,* 178–81. Chafe, *American Woman,* 175.

[44] Lutz, "Only One Choice," 199, 205. Cong. Rec., 80th Cong., 1st sess., 1067, 1124. See also Editorial, *Washington Post,* 19 Apr. 1948, reprinted *Cong. Rec.,* 80th Cong., 1st sess. A2434–2435.

[45] "Senate's Ladies Day," *Life,* 28(Feb. 13, 1950): 16 ff. *Cong. Rec.,* 81st Cong., 2nd sess., 738–44, 759, 809–13, 828–34, 872–79. Kefauver introduced a list of state laws "jeopardized" by the ERA, *Cong. Rec.,* 81st Cong., 2nd sess., 828–34.

[46] *Life,* 28(Feb. 13, 1950): 16 ff. "Women," *Time,* 55(Feb. 6, 1950): 12–13. "Outsmarting the Ladies," *Newsweek,* 35(Feb. 6, 1950): 20–21.

[47] Public Law 304, 79th Congress.

[48] Franklin, *From Slavery to Freedom,* 593–94. Jones, *Labor of Love, Labor of Sorrow,* 235–56.

[49] Franklin, *From Slavery to Freedom,* 597–98.

[50] Ibid., 598. Jones, *Labor of Love, Labor of Sorrow,* 261–62, charges that rather than take decisive action, the president "preferred to try to appease black leaders with symbolic gestures."

[51] Bureau of the Census, *Historical Statistics of the United States, Colonial Times to 1957* (Washington: GPO, 1960), ser. H 374–82.

[52] Ibid., 395–406.

[53] The rate is the number of women receiving bachelor's and first professional degrees per 1,000 women age 23; Bureau of the Census, *Statistical Abstract of the United States: 1981* (Washington: GPO, 1981), tab. 283.

[54] Ibid. The rate for master's is the number of women (men) earning master's degrees per 1,000 women (men) who earned baccalaureates two years earlier.

[55] Ibid. The rate for doctorates is the number of women (men) earning doctorates per 1,000 women (men) who earned baccalaureates ten years earlier.

[56] Chafe, *American Woman,* 141.

[57] Margaret Mead, *Male and Female* (New York: Dell, 1968[1949]), 38–39, 347–56. Henry A. Bowman, *Marriage for Moderns* (New York: Whittlesey House, 1942), 21.

[58] Talcott Parsons, "An Analytical Approach to the Theory of Social Stratification" (1940), in *Essays in Sociological Theory,* ed. Talcott Parsons, rev. ed. (New York: Free Press, 1954), 79–80. Talcott Parsons, "Age and Sex in the Social Structure of the United States" (1942), in *Essays in Sociological Theory,* 94–95.

[59] Lynn White, Jr., *Educating Our Daughters* (New York: Harper, 1950), 13, 15, 34–35, 63, 64, 77–78.

[60] George D. Stoddard, *On the Education of Women* (New York: Macmillan, 1950), 4, 10, 65–66, 89.

[61] Katherine Elizabeth McBride, "What Is Women's Education?" *The Annals,* 251(May 1947): 147–48, 150–52.

[62] Elmo Roper, "The Public Looks at Higher Education," *Fortune,* Supplement, 40(Sept. 1949).

[63] Gregory, *Women in Defense Work,* 13, 290–91.

[64] National Manpower Council, *Womanpower* (New York: Columbia University Press, 1957), 147. Gregory, *Women in Defense Work,* 43. Peter Gabriel Filene, *Him/Her/Self: Sex Roles in Modern America* (New York: Harcourt Brace Jovanovich, 1974), 187.

[65] "Employment in War Work of Women with Young Children," *MLR,* 55(Dec. 1942): 1184. National Manpower Council, *Womanpower,* 147.

[66] Gregory, *Women in Defense Work,* 164, 79, 140.

[67] Charles Higham and Joel Greenberg, *Hollywood in the Forties* (New York: Barnes, 1968), 9–11.

[68] Marjorie Rosen, *Popcorn Venus: Women, Movies and the American Dream* (New York: Coward, McCann and Geoghegan, 1973), 24–26.

[69] Molly Haskell, *From Reverence to Rape: The Treatment of Women in the Movies* (New York: Rinehart and Winston, 1973), 155, 160, 161, 181.

[70] Rosen, *Popcorn Venus,* 26.

[71] Quotations from advertisements in *Ladies' Home Journal,* 1940–1950.

[72] Ibid.

5

Minority Women to 1950

Although the values of white middle-class women set the norms of American society, American womanhood included women from numerous minority groups that lived outside the mainstream. White Americans were conscious of blacks, but generally they overlooked other minority women except in times of crisis. The Jews were characterized by a distinctive religion; Asian Americans, American Indians, Hispanic Americans, and blacks, by racial and ethnic differences. All of these minorities came from traditional societies with cultural norms and value systems, with roots as deep and durable as those that undergirded Anglo-American society. Racial, ethnic, and cultural differences separated the minorities from the Anglo-Americans and from one another. Between the Anglo-Americans' reluctance to assimilate their minorities and the minorities' unwillingness to give up their identity, the latter formed separate subcultures. Women in each group had unique experiences as they were pushed and pulled by their own cultural traditions and those of the mainstream.

A common denominator in the lives of minority women was the discrimination they encountered. Racism, embraced by the white middle-class, was rampant in 1900 and would get worse before it was disavowed. Minority women were members of groups lacking in political, economic, and social status. Those who were white had fathers or husbands who could qualify for citizenship and the vote; blacks were citizens, but as of 1900 many states had adopted legislation that deprived them of the suffrage. Indians, though the original Americans, generally were not yet citizens; Asian-born persons were not even eligible for citizenship. These minority women ordinarily lacked fathers or husbands who could command employment that would provide the family with a stable, year-round income. The white majority—both through public policy and informal action—had separate policies for each minority group. Women of the various minorities were kept at arm's length from social and cultural contacts with Anglo-American women; and, separated from one another by geography, cultural traditions, and language, they could not make common cause to rectify their position. Indeed, they were torn between the need to gain status for their own ethnic community and their needs as women. Because the value systems of their cultures curbed their freedom as women to have public roles, these women generally had to search for solutions alone.

THE JEWISH COMMUNITY

The nation's 1.5 million Jews did not share the values of the Christian majority, nor did they form a homogeneous community of their own in 1900. The Jewish community consisted of a handful of Sephardic Jews, descendants of Jews who had arrived during the colonial era; a much larger number of predominantly middle-class western-European Jews, whose forebears began arriving in the 1840s and 1850s, most of whom came from Germany and were of the Reform faith; and an even larger number of predominantly working-class eastern-European Jews, whose forebearers began arriving in the 1880s, most of whom came from Russia and Poland and were of the Orthodox faith.[1]

The Judaic Heritage

The heritage of European Jewry prescribed a narrow, domestic role for women. Parents ordinarily arranged the marriage of a daughter through a marriage contract providing for her financial security. The husband was obligated to support his wife financially and to provide sexual satisfaction. The wife was his servant: she washed his hands and face, filled his cup, made his bed, and accepted his "natural dominion." The traditional Jewish wife was subservient and deferential beyond anything required of the nineteenth-century True Woman.[2]

Jewish tradition recognized female sexuality; there was no "madonna syndrome." Sexuality was thought difficult to contain, and women were regarded as temptresses who might entrap even the most pious male. Marriage, in fact, was a social necessity in order to regulate sexual desire and afford fulfillment. While strict chastity was enjoined on the Jewish woman, Jewish males were not forbidden sexually to other unmarried women. Fear and repugnance for woman's biological functions reinforced male distrust of women. A menstruating woman must have no physical contact with a man and must not touch him or hand him anything directly, nor could she do so until seven days had passed and she had undergone purification in a *mikvah* (a ritual bath). Thus, while acknowledging woman's sexuality, tradition contributed to a rigid segregation of the sexes. Pious males could not speak to or look directly at women; it was immoral for a man to listen to a woman sing, to look at her hair, or to walk behind her on the street. To conceal their bodies, married women covered their heads and wore long sleeves and long skirts. When male guests were present in the house, women ate in the kitchen. Tradition reminded the Orthodox: "Many daughters, many troubles; many sons, many honors." The Talmud added its caution: "Woe to the father whose children are girls."[3]

Judaism encouraged women to be pious but in ways that differed from male piety. As a girl she was constrained to observe the forms of Jewish worship, but she was not systematically instructed in the faith. As a woman she was exempted from religious duties; she could not be counted in the *minyan* (the quorum required for public prayer); she could not lead religious services; she had to pray in a curtained-off balcony. Even so she was responsible for the moral quality of family life. By contrast, Judaism imposed on males a demanding list of religious obligations. The male expressed his masculinity in the synagogue and in religious scholarship, not on the battlefield or in business. Men could be gentle and emotionally expressive; women were expected to be strong, capable, and shrewd. To enable her husband to fulfill his religious obligations, the Jewish wife assumed heavy economic responsibilities, such as acting as a partner in her husband's business, selling home-produced wares, or working in shops and factories.[4]

The Reform Community

By 1900 the Jewish community in America was led not by the followers of Judaic tradition but by members of the Reform community. Chiefly of German background, approximately 250,000 Jews arrived in America between 1850 and 1880. Many were the younger sons or the unmarried daughters to whom Germany offered a limited future. Coming from cities and towns, they scattered, settling in the towns of the Midwest, the South, and the Far West.[5]

By the time this migration began, the German-Jewish community was in the process of revising the roles prescribed for women. In imitation of affluent Christians, daughters learned to read and speak French and Italian and to play charming tunes on the piano. Some women attended school. A few advanced synagogues ended the segregation of women, developed a confirmation ceremony for girls, *bat mitzvah,* and created choirs that included women. The male prayer of thanks for not having been born a woman was discarded. Abraham Geiger, one of the reformers, insisted that only by granting women equal rights "will the Jewish girl and woman . . . [become] conscious of the significance of our faith and . . . fervently attached to it." Joining in the reform, Jewish women pressed for a double-ring ceremony in the wedding and abandonment of the dowry.[6]

Reforms begun in Germany proliferated in America as the German Jewish community accepted the "aesthetic standards and cultural patterns of Protestantism." Given the pattern of scattered settlements, Jews could not observe the Sabbath strictly; they abandoned traditional dress, shaved their beards, and neglected the dietary laws and study of the Torah. Issac Mayer Wise, a leading reformer and founder of the Hebrew Union College (1875) and the Union of American Hebrew Congregations, urged reforms to keep young women faithful to Judaism. He supported woman suffrage, the establishment of an academy for girls, and the appointment of women to temple school boards. His congregation in Albany, New York seated females on the main floor, adopted family pews, and instituted a *bat mitzvah.* In 1869 the Philadelphia Rabbinical Conference altered the marriage ceremony to provide an exchange of vows and an exchange of rings, and it abolished the *get* (religious divorce). By 1880 the Reform community constituted the vast majority of the Jewish population.[7]

The Reform community was well established by 1900 with a broad range of philanthropic, educational, and benevolent societies. One of the first to serve women, the Young Woman's Hebrew Association (YWHA), operated an educational and social center for German-Jewish women and girls. A second organization of importance was the National Council of Jewish Women founded by Hannah Greenbaum Solomon in 1893, the same time at which Anglo-American women were organizing their first women's clubs. While not denigrating the home, the council urged women "to personal and active interest in philanthropic and religious educational work." It directed special attention to scientific social work, to promoting sex education, and to combatting juvenile delinquency. While the leadership flirted with feminism, the rank and file declined to support the suffrage amendment. By 1920 the council counted 20,000 members in a Jewish population of 3,500,000. While retaining its Judaism, the Reform community assimilated much of "the mores, attitudes, and ideological patterns" of the rising Anglo-American middle class.[8]

The Orthodox Community

As the Reform community established itself, narrowing the differences between itself and the Anglo-American middle class, Orthodox Jews began pouring into the United States. Throughout the nineteenth century, Orthodox Jewish women in Eastern Europe remained steeped in tradition. Their husbands—often "gentle, dreamy and soft-spoken"—appeared "feminine," while the "forthright and aggressive" women seemed "masculine" to outsiders. Following the pogroms of 1881 to 1882 instigated by Czar Alexander II, the Orthodox fled Russia. Additional pogroms, overpopulation, and lack of economic opportunities drove others to follow; by 1920, 2,250,000 had come. The great majority settled in New York City; smaller settlements developed in Philadelphia, Chicago, Cleveland, and Boston. Along with the Orthodox came a significant minority of Jews whose values had been shaped by socialism or Zionism.[9]

Still steeped in the values and practices of the older Judaic heritage, the Orthodox woman was as isolated from women of the Reform faith as she was from those of the Anglo-American community. Orthodoxy imposed an especially restrictive domesticity. She was likely to speak only Yiddish; she had little formal education. Yet acculturation worked its slow course. In America, Jewishness was irrelevant in the public sphere. The male shed his skullcap except for home or synagogue; his wife abandoned her wig. Many became slack in observing the talmudic dietary regulations. Secular Jews attended socialist meetings and read free-thinking Yiddish papers. Poverty forced men to become the principal breadwinners; wives and daughters shared in the family support. Of the married women, 7 percent worked; of the unmarried, nearly 75 percent. Married women with young children ordinarily worked at home—taking in laundry, doing hand sewing, caring for the children of others, producing goods at home, or taking in boarders and lodgers. While such work added to family income, it did not contribute to the woman's understanding of the new society. On the other hand, the "moms" of "mom and pop" shops had as good a chance as their husbands to expand their intellectual and social horizons. The women who went into the sweatshops and factories had still greater opportunities to develop an understanding of the new society as well as a degree of personal autonomy. As of 1900 the Jews were the most industrialized ethnic group in New York City.[10]

The American-born second generation, the oldest of whom were coming of age by 1900, fared better than their parents. To educate their sons, immigrant parents often exploited their daughters as "money-earning machines." Even though parents ignored compulsory-attendance laws by sending their daughters to work, the latter usually received more education

In an age when to work was still an act of derring-do for middle-class Anglo-American women, large numbers of Jewish women worked in sweatshops such as this one in 1910.

than their mothers had. Some entered vocational courses in dressmaking, sewing, and hat trimming. Others pursued typing, stenography, and book-keeping—"middle-class" occupations.[11]

The women of the second generation embraced a different set of values than their mothers. "Desperately anxious to become unequivocably American," second-generation women abandoned the immigrant culture and sought to project an "American" look, responding to an assumed preference of Jewish men for women who "looked American." Whereas their mothers viewed marriage "primarily as an economic and social arrangement," the daughters "espoused romantic notions," seeking "fulfillment through companionship with their mates." The arranged marriage became passé; the second generation expected to choose their own mates without need for a dowry. The criteria for marriages changed. Family reputation, scholarly achievements, and wealth—so important in Europe—yielded to more flexible standards. A young man with more talent than capital might seek a wife with a wealthy father; a woman without wealth might marry a professional in training, supporting him until he was able to support her.

In the process of acculturation the Orthodox male abandoned the ideal-ized role of scholar and pontificator of wisdom and talmudic law to become the family breadwinner. As he succeeded in business or the professions, he took delight in withdrawing his wife from the labor force so she might become the "mistress of the house and educator of her children." Increas-ingly the wife's status derived from the economic and social success of her husband. Wives of business and professional men often became "preoc-cupied with their looks, fashion, and possessions, areas in which they competed with other women." They passed much time "shopping, playing cards, and doing some club work." This sudden alteration in roles caused some women to become the "foolish, overdecorated wife of the parvenu."[12]

Mothering changed, too. The realities of the *shtetl* (small Jewish village) abroad and the ghetto in America necessitated a close protectiveness by the Jewish mother toward her children that stood in marked contrast to the efforts of other immigrant mothers to foster early self-reliance in chil-dren. Jewish mothering encouraged children to be physically and emo-tionally dependent, but it also freed them from slavish dependence on peer groups and hence made them less conforming and allowed them to be more original in intellectual matters. To this sustained protectiveness, Zena Smith Blau attributes the "unquestionable success of the Jewish mother in educating her children and immunizing them from severe emotional disorders." Whereas the mother of the immigrant generation had lived for her children, the Jewish woman of the second generation thought she "owed it to herself" to receive an education, to develop personal grooming, and to build outside social relationships to facilitate her family's upward mobility. As a consequence, these women emerged ambitious and pos-sessive. Her children, relatively free of anti-Semitic harassment, often found her protectiveness irksome rather than functional.[13]

The coming of World War I brought a halt to the migration of Jews from the Old World. While generally excluded from the highest public offices, some Jews, chiefly those of western European origin, achieved recognition and status in the business community, but most of the Ortho-dox were employed in the crafts or the less-prestigious white-collar jobs. Jewish women had a limited but growing opportunity for public roles. If some, like Rebekah Bettelheim Kohut, had to curb their ambitions, some, like Lillian Wald, freely pursued active roles in public affairs. In fact much of the energy of the Reform leadership was directed toward establishing ties with the Orthodox. One step entailed the redefining of the mission of the YWHA; by adopting programs patterned after the settlement houses, the YWHA enabled the established Reform community to reach out to those of the Orthodox group who were in distress. A second step was the found-ing in 1912 of Hadassah, the woman's Zionist organization, by Henrietta

Szold. Within the United States, Hadassah operated educational programs in Jewish history and culture, but its principal mission was to raise funds to maintain a network of hospitals, clinics, vocational schools, welfare agencies, land-reclamation services, and youth centers in Palestine. In doing so, Szold sought to enlist the support of both the Reform and Orthodox communities. In the years after World War I the YWHA again redefined its mission, now focusing on the Jewish middle class, while Hadassah stepped up its programs in Palestine. Thus Jewish women developed a social life apart from home and family.[14]

In the period following World War I the Jewish community once again became the targets of organized anti-Semitism that exposed it to insults and occasional acts of violence and limited vocational mobility as well as access to particular colleges. The campaign was conducted by the resurrected Ku Klux Klan, which also made Roman Catholics and blacks the targets of its perverted Americanism, and by Henry Ford's *Dearborn Independent.* But important elements of the Anglo community, while dissociating themselves from the Klan, quietly practiced discrimination. At the same time, the halting of large-scale immigration in 1924 gave the Jewish community time to acculturate. Led by Solomon Schecter, Judaism developed a third stream, Conservative Judaism, that pursued a middle course between Orthodoxy and Reform. Appealing especially to the third generation of the Orthodox, Conservative Judaism represented an abandonment of ethnic (for example, Russian) identification for a return to "Jewishness." For others, beginning in the early 1900s, Judaism became more a cultural than a religious concern. Equally important, the Protestant community ceased to wield the influence it had hitherto possessed. As more and more Americans identified themselves as Protestant, Catholic, or Jew, members of each faith increasingly acknowledged the legitimacy of the other two faiths: live and let live. The upsurge of anti-Semitism in the thirties in Nazi Germany led Americans generally to repudiate anti-Semitism at home and to become more accepting of the Jewish population now numbering over 4,600,000. In these circumstances the Jewish communities, religion aside, slipped more and more into the mainstream of American life, the Reform Jews in the vanguard; the Orthodox trailing behind.[15]

ASIAN AMERICANS

In 1900 the United States had a tiny Asian American population concentrated almost exclusively in California. Though sharing some common characteristics, the Chinese American and the Japanese American communities were separated from each other by language and by historic traditions and antipathies.

The Chinese American Community

First among the Asian peoples to migrate to the United States, the Chinese community had made little adjustment to America by 1900 and was in bad repute. The demand for cheap labor, created first by the California gold rush and then by the railroads, led "'district companies" to recruit Chinese men and send them to California. These sojourners had expected to return after a few years to the wives and children they had left in China. "Mutual peculiarities of dress, language, habits, customs, and diet, not to mention the physical distinctiveness of racial identities" kept Chinese and Anglos apart. The "district companies" that recruited these laborers in China also imported a handful of Chinese women as prostitutes. By 1900 the Chinatowns of America were "honeycombed" with brothels. The girls were brought to America, having been kidnapped, sold by impoverished parents, or lured by a false promise of a proxy marriage, and "placed under contract to individual Chinese, or, more often, to brothels in the Chinese quarter." Some escaped, seeking asylum with missionaries who served Chinatown; some became concubines of men with wives in China; a few married one of their patrons; the majority, however, lived a life that was "as brutish as it was short." At least to the 1930s, "prostitution and its attendant opportunities for affluence and community power" continued unabated.[16]

The Chinatowns, replete with prostitution and opium dens, alienated Anglo-Americans as did the tendency of the Chinese to work for substandard wages. As a result, in 1882 Congress halted the further migration of Chinese coolies, so that the Chinese population, which had reached 107,000 in 1890, was on the decline by 1900. Thus, the Chinese community was characterized by an extreme imbalance in the sex ratio. In 1900 there were 1,887 Chinese males per 100 Chinese women; by 1920 the ratio had dropped to 695 to 100, and as late as 1960 the ratio was 135 to 100.[17]

Within the Chinese American community, completed families—husband, wife, and children living together—remained uncommon. In 1900 approximately one Chinese husband in ten had his wife with him in America. When family members came to join him, sons came first, and when his wife came, she was often beyond child-bearing age. Not only were there few American-born children, but many parents took their American-born children to China to be educated and to marry. By 1900 the American-born Chinese population numbered only 9,000, or about 9 percent of the total Chinese American group; by 1920 there were but 18,500, of whom only 5200 were females.[18]

Chinese values respecting the family differed greatly from those of Anglo-Americans. As the Chinese family worshiped its ancestors, continuance of the family was all important, the responsibility falling on the eldest male. Women occupied an inferior, supporting role. Marriages were arranged by third parties; affection followed rather than preceded marriage. The sexes were strictly separated; from the age of seven boys and girls took meals at different tables or at different times at the same table. Man and woman, even brother-in-law and sister-in-law, were not to touch each other's hands. In the extended family, the young husband remained subject to his father; the wife was subordinate not only to her husband but to his father and mother. As marriage was designed to perpetuate the family, not to promote sexual or personal fulfillment, concubinage coexisted with marriage without threatening the marriage tie. Children were "raised for the parents." Male children were highly regarded; female children, likened to "maggots in the rice," were not counted as heirs, nor could they offer sacrifices to ancestors; their education was neglected. Paternal authority was supreme, the father having the right to sell a child or even to put it to death, though few fathers ever did so.[19]

Life in America precluded replication of the traditional Chinese family. When a Chinese did bring his wife to America, the result was de facto a nuclear family but without the conviction that it was a proper relationship. The Chinese wife in America bore the conventional obligations of wife, mother, and housekeeper but without the supporting apparatus that the extended family provided in China. While she was compelled to shoulder more responsibility, she also enjoyed more autonomy than she would have enjoyed in China. She might assist her husband as an unpaid laborer in his laundry, store, or noodle parlor. But only rarely did she work outside the home as did wives of European immigrants or of black Americans. Sometimes she earned money by repairing, tailoring, or laundering clothes for single men, but this work she did at home. Such earnings she might retain, buying gold jewelry, which represented a kind of savings account to be drawn upon in times of family need or in her widowhood.[20]

Married or single, a Chinese woman lived a far more restricted life than the most-sheltered urban middle-class Anglo-American wife. Married by proxy in China, the young bride might see her husband for the first time at dockside in the United States. Raised in the Chinese fashion, her feet were bound, hence crippled. One such woman, taken to Butte, Montana, where her husband was a merchant, reported that she visited outside her home once a year—New Year's Day. Not until her children were grown and they could take her did she first see downtown Butte, though she had lived there for ten years. On hearing of the Chinese Revolution (1911), she unbound her feet, a painful experience, but a "symbolic act of personal emancipation." She subsequently discarded her Chinese wardrobe for American-style dress.[21]

The American environment affected the life-style of the American-born children, especially the girls. The children attended public schools, mastered English, and acquired the "ideas, sentiments and attitudes" of the Anglo-Americans. Though they went to a Chinese school at night or on Saturday and learned some of the language, they did not learn the customs, history, or traditions of China. Having learned English and adopted American dress, they seemed most worldly and undesirable as a mate to other Chinese Americans. One older Chinese pointed up the differences: "Chinese girl I think very much better than American-born Chinese. No spend so much money. No like to go shows. All they think about stay home help husband, save money. American-born Chinese girl, my god, spend lots of money, buy all the time pretty clothes, fancy shoes. American girl no know Chinese custom, no like big family, little family. Yes, I think China boy much better marry girl in China."[22]

Changes in American immigration laws in the 1920s substantially altered the status of Chinese-Americans. As a result of the Cable Act, a China-born woman could not acquire citizenship by marrying an American citizen, while the Immigration Act of 1924 made foreign-born Chinese wives inadmissible to the United States. The result enforced a separation of thousands of couples for years at a time unless the husband returned permanently to China. Yielding to Chinese values, daughters eligible to migrate to America remained in China to provide companionship for their mothers. The ratio of males to females among Chinese in America remained unbalanced.[23]

From 1924 to 1945 the Chinese community in the United States was isolated from continuing cultural and personal contacts with China. During this interval, the number of American-born males doubled, that of females tripled. As the number of American-born Chinese began to equal the foreign-born, bride-hunting males developed a new regard for American-born Chinese women.

By caring for their needy during the depression, the Chinese community won the admiration of the Anglo-American middle class, while the Japanese attacks on China in the 1930s won them sympathy. In December 1941 the Chinese became allies. Subsequently Congress repealed the demeaning Chinese Exclusion Act, established a token quota of immigrants, and, early in 1944, permitted the Chinese-born to become citizens. American labor unions, too, began to abandon exclusionary rules that barred Chinese from employment in skilled jobs. After nearly a century, the Chinese succeeded in establishing communities based on stable, nuclear families. At the same time, the Anglo community kept the Chinese-Americans at arm's length. Many of the children attended segregated schools, churches, and youth associations; furthermore, antimiscegenation laws in about one fourth to one third of the states barred marriages between Chinese and Anglo Americans.[24]

Japanese Americans: Issei and Nisei

The second Asian group to migrate, the Japanese began arriving in the mid-1880s, just as the Chinese Exclusion Act halted the influx of Chinese. Displaced by the modernization of Japan, these Japanese peasants had gone to Hawaii, then an independent nation, to work on American-owned sugar plantations, but a few ventured to the Pacific coast. After the United States annexed Hawaii in 1898, the Japanese came in numbers to the mainland where they found employment as railway-construction laborers or as migratory workers in sugar-beet and hop fields. Drawing on the anti-Chinese sentiment, Californians raised the specter of the "Yellow Peril," damning the Japanese as amoral and subversive. Labor unions, seeking to avoid competition with them, led the opposition. Efforts of the San Francisco school board to assign a handful of Japanese children to separate schools provoked an international controversy that was resolved in 1907 by the Gentlemen's Agreement by which the Japanese government deterred unskilled workers from migrating to the United States.[25]

Though they came as sojourners, the Japanese settled down in ghettos, "comforted by the similarity of language, custom, and culture." In a remarkably short time the Japanese became imbued with "the Protestant ethic." Indeed, about one third of them adopted Christianity. Excluded from trade unions, the Japanese drew on their skills as farmers. Quickly they emerged as share tenants and cash renters; a few became owners. Others founded small enterprises that served the ethnic community; still others engaged in contract gardening, domestic service, or fishing. But truck farming was the most important and it provoked the greatest hostility. In 1913 California enacted an Alien Land Act that sought to restrict Japanese Americans to employment as farm laborers. As persevering as they were expert, the Japanese Americans reclaimed desert, swamp, and cut-over timberlands. They pioneered the raising of cotton and cantaloupes in the Imperial Valley; they founded vineyards and orchards on the west slope of the Sierras. Despite obstacles, they established a solid economic base for their community. By 1941 the Japanese Americans were producing between 30 and 35 percent of all commercial-truck crops grown in California. They also secured a dominant position in the distribution of fruits and vegetables.[26]

In the miniscule Japanese American community—numbering just over 50,000 in 1907—males outnumbered females three or four to one. During the years 1907 to 1924, this imbalance was eradicated and a Japanese community took root. As the Gentlemen's Agreement permitted those living in the United States to send for relatives, Japanese men sent for their wives—many of them "picture brides," women married by proxy in Japan to men in America whom they had never met. Such marriages allowed the women no say in the choice of mates. Patriarchal in the extreme, the

Japanese family displayed strong solidarity. As male superiority was assumed, the father was the object of respect and awe. The mother, by contrast, was identified with warmth and affection. While she was submissive to her husband, the children deferred to her. The eldest son and his family ordinarily lived with his parents after marriage, in time taking over the family farm as well as the responsibility for the parents in their old age. The younger sons, as well as the daughters, expected to move off on their own after marriage.[27]

In America the Japanese woman had a far different experience than the Caucasian woman. As an Asian she was an object of hostility; she lacked the language facility to function outside her ethnic community; her culture confined her to the family circle. On the other hand, at a time when the cult of domesticity limited the Anglo-American woman's economic functions, Japanese American women, like black women in the South, worked in the fields along with their husbands. In contrast to the Chinese community, which was still predominately male and shrinking, the Japanese community moved toward a balance in the sexes and grew steadily.[28]

During the twenties, thirties, and forties, the Japanese American community experienced growing pains that centered about the differences in the life-styles of the Issei (first generation) and the Nisei (second generation), who by 1930 were reaching adulthood. For the Issei, "ethnic cohesion was an advantage" that helped them "gain a foothold in American society"; for the Nisei, affiliation with the ethnic community was a disadvantage. Throughout this period, the Issei were thwarted from fully enjoying the status and respect traditionally due parents by their children. Unfamiliar with English, the Issei had to rely on the Nisei to interpret for them. Although federal law barred the Issei from citizenship and California's Alien Property Act barred them from owning land, the Nisei were citizens and could own property. The late marriages entered into by the Issei resulted in wide age differences between fathers and children, while the cultural distance between Japan and the United States further exacerbated the generation gap. While most Issei remained Buddhist, by 1930 half of the Nisei were Christian. The major differences centered on courtship and marriage, the Nisei resisting the arranged marriage.[29]

The generational conflict smoldered until World War II. As the Nisei came of age, many found the traditional family-centered culture unduly restrictive. In rural areas, where families worked as a unit, daughters and sons had little choice but to work for their fathers. In urban areas, where the young pursued a variety of social and economic relationships independent of paternal supervision, generational conflicts were magnified. The depression, though, compelled many Nisei to seek employment within their ethnic community, subjecting them to economic control by Issei. This also inhibited the pace of acculturation, since it restricted contacts with non-Japanese. On the other hand, the limited employment opportunities prompted large numbers of Nisei to continue their education at the college level. Given traditional Japanese values, this was acceptable as it conferred added honor upon the parents, but it also equipped the Nisei for a wider range of employment outside the ethnic community once prosperity returned.[30]

Issei dominance collapsed during World War II. As all Issei were enemy aliens, the government impounded their funds, restricted their travel, and suspended the Japanese-language press. Immediately the ethnic institutions—the language schools and the Buddhist temples—that supported Issei control of the Japanese American community vanished. The confinement of 110,000 Japanese Americans in relocation centers completed the destruction of Issei influence. Camp authorities excluded the Issei from

The lives of Japanese Americans were disrupted during World War II as the U.S. Government ordered them confined to internment camps.

membership on camp councils. Crowded into one-room apartments, families had little privacy. Camp mess halls did not provide for family dining; the lavatories, showers, and washrooms were community affairs. Recreation was organized not by family but by age and sex groups. The patriarchal family ceased to function as a unit. By 1945 the males of the Issei generation were typically 60 years old or more, their wives, 50. Their numbers were declining.[31]

As the Japanese Americans were released from internment camps at the end of the war, they faced an uncertain future. They had long borne the Californian's hatred and fear of Asians. Whereas the Chinese Americans had withdrawn into self-contained communities, the Japanese Americans had challenged whites in a variety of businesses and professions. In addition, the United States had just concluded a bloody war with Japan and anti-Japanese feelings still ran high. On the positive side, the Issei had made an effort to acculturate and to prepare their children for an active role in Anglo-American society. Thus, Nisei women, unlike their mothers, were literate in English, moderately well educated, and familiar with Anglo-American practices. Finally, by 1945 the Nisei were of age and free to pursue their own interests.

AMERICAN INDIANS

In the first two decades of the twentieth century, the various American Indian societies reached their nadir. With a death rate that exceeded their birthrate, the Indians were "vanishing Americans." The place of Indian women in American society reflected traditions and experiences that set them apart from other women. First, while the Anglo population thought of them as homogeneous, in reality American Indians were heterogeneous, belonging to one or another of a dozen linguistic–cultural groups. In 1900 more than a hundred different languages were still in use, the differences between the major languages being as great as those between English and Russian. Some American Indians, like the Pueblos, had traditionally been village-dwelling gardeners; others, such as the Sioux, as late as the 1870s, nomadic hunters; still others, like the Ute, nomadic hunters and gatherers. Although the extended family was the norm, some families were matrilineal; others, patrilineal. Most Indian cultures had permitted polygynous marriage, and polygyny was still practiced on some reservations.

For a few Indians, contact with the white majority had begun in the 1500s; for others it had been deferred until the 1840s. The Cherokee, Creek, and Choctaw had experienced a long period of contact with white traders that permitted them to acculturate at their own pace; by 1900— relocated in Oklahoma—they were on the point of being incorporated into the mainstream of Oklahoma society. By contrast, the Hopi and Navajo had remained free of close white contact, had retained most of their traditional culture, and were largely autonomous. Still others, notably the Comanche and Sioux, were sullen, dispirited, and divided, virtual prisoners on their reservations. While the dominant white population was unaware, Indian groups realized that dozens of tribal cultures—including the Calusa, Yamasee, Pequot, and Mandan—had disappeared, victims of disease, enslavement, or warfare. For the various Indian cultures in 1900, the present was grim; the future, uncertain.[32]

Most Indian peoples were subject to the Dawes Severalty Act (1887). This act intended to end the Indian "problem" by turning the male Indian into a farmer–citizen. The hope was that in becoming a landowner, he would develop a set of skills and a sense of responsibility that would enable him to become become self-supporting and would prepare him to be a responsible citizen.[33]

The impact of the Dawes Act on the Indians proved devastating. Unscrupulous whites conned Indians—who had neither the competence nor an interest in farming—into leasing their lands at scandalously low prices; they stripped timberlands and abandoned them. Judges, agency officials, and Indian Bureau executives shared in looting the Indians. Even when the Indian kept his land, the impact was disastrous. Farming did not provide the Indian male with a sense of fulfillment. Ironically the Dawes Act was introduced at a time when many white farmers were fleeing the land to seek their fortunes in the cities. "Severalty may not have civilized the Indian," one historian has concluded, "but it definitely corrupted most of the white men who had any contact with it."[34]

As a conquered people, the life-styles of Indian women were shaped more by their identities as Indians than as women so far as the Anglo community was concerned. The Dawes Act implicitly sought to make them farm wives, imposing on them the alien sex roles of rural white women. When Indian husbands failed to become successful farmers, their families, including wives and children, were condemned to poverty. If the husbands in desperation sought solace in alcohol, so much the worse. The boarding schools tended to alienate the children from parents. If the youngsters survived their school years—and many did not—their schooling unfitted them for reservation life, while white society rejected them.[35]

In the 1920s, as the white community recognized that the Dawes Act had failed, Lewis Meriam, a specialist in public administration, undertook an exhaustive study of Indian affairs. His report provided an in-depth picture of the degradation experienced by most of the diverse Indian societies. Confined to reservations, Indians were compelled to abandon the traditional means of supporting themselves—seed gathering, dibble-stick gardening, or hunting. In spite of the fact that few Indians had succeeded in mastering agriculture or grazing, the government slashed food and clothing rations. Invoking their traditional sense of community responsibility, the Indians shared the little food they had as well as their hunger.[36]

The physical conditions of Indian existence threatened life itself. Thousands still lived in primitive wickiups, dark hogans, or canvas tepees. The bare earth floors, cold and damp in winter, were a source of dust and dirt the rest of the year. Open fires used in cooking produced much smoke, contributing directly to a high incidence of trachoma and tuberculosis. During the early years of the century the death rate exceeded the birthrate. And although the federal government created an Indian health service before 1910, the death rate did not decline until the 1930s.[37]

The Meriam Report prompted major reforms. The Hoover administration initiated changes in Indian education, shifting from reliance on boarding schools for the few to day schools for everyone. General reform, however, was the work of John Collier, commissioner of Indian affairs in the Roosevelt administration. Long familiar with Indian problems, Collier assumed that the "clan instinct," was inherent in the Indian. "The tribal Indian," he argued, "remains the self-reliant and self-supporting Indian." He accepted, too, the ideal of "cultural pluralism"—that a democratic society could and should facilitate a variety of life-styles. This meant nurturing those aspects of traditional culture that gave meaning and satisfaction to the Indian. The Wheeler–Howard Act (1934) allowed Indians to pursue private-land ownership if they chose, but traditional tribal ownership was again permitted. Unsold reservation lands were returned to the tribes, and provisions were made for adding new lands. To make the Indian Service more responsive to Indian needs, Indians were employed by the Bureau of Indian Affairs; administration of Indian affairs was decentralized. Tribal self-government was encouraged; tribal business ventures, promoted. Instruction was given in modern land-use practices; tribal crafts were revived; adult education and student loan programs were instituted.[38]

The results were uneven. Some Oklahoma Indians—largely acculturated and assimilated—denounced the Collier reforms as perpetuating an inferior status for Indians. The Navajo were especially outraged when the Collier administration ordered the reduction of their sheep and goat herds in order that the remaining animals would be larger, healthier, and more valuable. Most tribes went along. Some 100 tribes drafted constitutions and some 200 tribal businesses incorporated. In consequence of these reforms, native religious practices, ceremonials, and crafts were revived. Because the disruption of the Indian cultures in the nineteenth century made wholesale revival of the old cultures impossible, the tribes borrowed from one another. The result was a blurring of tribal distinctions. On balance, most tribes benefitted modestly from the new policies. By 1954, beef production had increased 23-fold; farm production, 4-fold. The combination of economic, educational, and social reforms reversed the decline in Indian population. Paradoxically the improved financial prospects of the individual Indian generated a sense of self-interest that weakened clan and family ties.[39]

The respect for the diverse Indian cultures that underlay the Collier reforms removed pressure on Indian women to abandon traditional sex roles, but the reforms introduced modern health practices and increased access to education. A minimum level of education was required to enable the Indian woman to appreciate and practice the principles of cleanliness, good diet, and child care, which would reduce the incidence of disease and premature death. Formal education also gave Indian women access to jobs off the reservation. However, the woman who lived or worked in the off-reservation society found herself expected to conform to the values of the white middle class.

Before the Collier reforms were fully implemented, World War II intruded. Some 25,000 Indians served in the armed forces, and nearly 50,000 others left the reservations for jobs in industry. The travel and observations of wartime resulted in greater fluency in English and familiarity with the white culture, broadened the veterans' perspectives, and encouraged many to cast their lot with modernization. Dependency allowances to families of servicemen underscored the value of a monogamous marriage solemnized by official rites. The war over, Indians in New Mexico and Arizona successfully sued to secure the suffrage, expanding the political rights of Indian women as well. They also demanded better access to education, more effective health care, increased job opportunities, and an end to discriminatory legislation and regulations.[40]

At midcentury, Indian women ranked at the bottom of all major population groups in terms of well-being. Many still lived and died within the framework of traditional societies and had no desire to emulate the culture of the white middle class. Others were in varying stages of acculturation in terms of education, religion, and mode of living. To the extent that survival offered a crude measure of well-being, Indian women fared far better in 1950 than at the start of the century.

HISPANIC AMERICANS

Least well-known of America's ethnic minorities, the Hispanic Americans prior to World War II were located primarily in the Southwest. A Hispanic culture began to flourish at Santa Fe in 1609, and Anglo-Americans encountered Hispanics on entering Texas in the 1820s, at the end of the

Santa Fe Trail in the 1830s, and in California in the 1840s. Genetically these Hispanics consisted of diverse Indian peoples with some admixture of Spanish, united by common ties of language and religion. Although some 73,500 Hispanics became American citizens as a result of the Mexican War, they remained largely isolated from the mainstream of American society in 1900.

Up until 1912, in New Mexico a handful of Spanish American families dominated the territorial government; together with a few Anglo-Americans they controlled the ranching, railroading, banking, and mining. As Anglo-Americans enclosed the grazing lands and developed the railroads, the mass of Hispanics slid backwards. In Texas, too, Anglo-Americans, helped by barbed wire, enclosed the grazing lands, freezing out the few Mexican American ranchers. When cotton culture was introduced after the Civil War, the Mexican Americans were employed as field hands. Similarly, the small Mexican population in California was overwhelmed. By 1900 the Mexicans—reduced to landless laborers—had become politically and economically impotent, targets of ethnic discrimination.[41]

After 1900 the Southwest turned to intensive agriculture. "Factory farms" appeared in the valleys of the Messila, Gila, Salt, Imperial, and San Joaquin rivers. Production of lettuce, strawberries, melons, grapes, citrus fruits, sugar beets, cotton, and vegetables employed enormous numbers of Hispanic laborers—men, women, and children—drawing some away from the older settlements and luring others from old Mexico. The work was seasonal, and these migratory workers settled into "a pattern of low earnings, miserable health and housing conditions, child labor, and virtually no contact with the Anglo world beyond the labor agent (or smuggler) and the grower, together with a squalid 'Mextown' somewhere near the fields." The railroads, too, employed cheap Hispanic labor. However poverty-ridden, the Mexican American community grew in numbers.[42]

Shaped both by Hispanic ideals and the realities of poverty, the role of the Mexican American woman was tradition-bound. Although the Mexican American male occupied a place in the economic structure akin to that of black males in the South, the Hispanic tradition established highly differentiated sex roles that restricted women to the household as dependent daughters, wives, or mothers. In the extended Hispanic family, several generations either shared common quarters or lived in close proximity and restricted most of their social life to the family, while regarding with great suspicion those outside the family circle. Hence the range of contacts of the Mexican American woman was more proscribed than that of the black or the Anglo-American woman of the same time period. The extended family, however, provided Hispanic woman a degree of social life that was denied Asian American wives. Marriage—the one "career" open to an adult woman—was arranged, usually by a third party. The Mexican American culture cast the woman in the role of the Virgin Mother and charged her menfolk with protecting her. Paradoxically, the male set great store on his own masculinity—*machismo*—which found expression in being powerful, assertive, and dominant. By contrast, the female was weak, docile, and submissive.[43]

Despite the pervasive influence of traditional roles, Mexican American culture developed a feminist tradition with roots of its own that dated to the Mexican War for Independence; this tradition was reinforced during the Carranza era in the early years of the twentieth century. Although the Carranza regime legalized divorce and granted women marital equality on paper, women gained few benefits in practice. Instead, a handful of anonymous Chicanas—working sometimes in Mexico, sometimes in the United States—organized workers, protested legal abuses, established mutual-aid societies, and lobbied for better educational opportunities. Thus Tucson in 1894 had its Alianza Hispano-Americano; Crystal City, Texas, its Sociedad Funeraria Miguel Hidalgo. Prior to 1920, Chicana activists were concerned with lynchings, corporate takeover of lands, and exclusion of Chicano youth from schools. Faced with poll taxes, subjected to literacy tests, and challenged to prove their citizenship, Chicanas did not gain access to the suffrage in 1920.[44]

Prior to 1900 neither the Hispanic culture nor the economy allowed a wage-earning role to women. At most they worked as unpaid farm laborers for fathers or husbands. After the turn of the century, Mexican American women worked as migrant farm laborers but only in the company of their fathers or husbands. Her culture discouraged a girl from pursuing more than the minimum of formal education, further restricting her aspirations as well as her capacity to realize any but traditional goals. Unable to break out of the role prescribed for her by tradition, the Mexican American woman was unable to assist her children—male or female—to experience a broader range of opportunities.[45]

Slowly, often unnoticed, Mexican Americans enlarged their range of activities during the 1920s. Some found work in the canneries; employment as railroad section hands or as migrant farm workers carried many out of their native Southwest, and a few "dropped out" along the way to become builders of interurban lines or to become operatives in meat-packing or steel plants in Chicago, in auto factories in Detroit, or in the steel plants of Ohio and Pennsylvania. Mexican American communities took root outside the Southwest, and contact with Anglo-Americans resulted in emulation of Anglo-American ways. But simultaneously the Mexican American community in the Southwest grew substantially by immigration from old Mexico. During the 1910s, 11,000 to 22,000 Mexicans migrated to the United

States each year. During the twenties, migration averaged about 50,000 a year. Given the new restrictions on immigration from Europe and Asia, these Mexicans constituted a significant fraction of all migrants entering the United States during the 1920s. These new immigrants, of course, reinforced the tradition-ridden culture of the barrios.[46]

The depression of the 1930s brought further changes to the Mexican American community. First, Anglo-Americans, driven by necessity, competed with Mexican Americans for employment, forcing the latter to look elsewhere for work. Second, because numerous Mexicans had entered the United States illegally, deportation to Mexico became "a constant specter." Some left voluntarily, others were deported. During the depression decade the Mexican population in the United States dropped from 639,000 to 377,000. Third, labor unions, encouraged by the Wagner Act, began to organize Mexican American workers, a move that in the long run gave them a new level of security and dignity. Several Chicanas, especially Emma Tenayuca, came to public attention as union leaders.[47]

The 1940s brought a slight improvement in the status of the Mexican Americans. In the booming wartime economy, fears of competition from the Mexicans were forgotten, and as labor shortages appeared, employers recruited Mexican Americans. Numerous Chicanas found employment as the garment industry migrated to the Southwest, opening an alternative that would grow in importance after World War II. Some 300,000 to 500,000 Mexican American youth served in the armed forces, getting a view of the Anglo world hitherto unknown to them and ending their cultural and physical isolation. Most significant was the shift that sent Mexican Americans from Texas to California, from rural areas to urban centers. Anglo resentment at the rapidly growing Mexican communities in Los Angeles and San Diego resulted in the "zoot suit" riots of 1943. In the long run, migration not only broadened the range of economic and cultural opportunities, but it gave the Mexican Americans visibility and forced Anglo-Americans to view them as a permanent part of the scene; educators ceased to ignore Mexican youth and sought methods to promote their acculturation. Mexican Americans, too, began to develop a self-consciousness, the first manifestation of an aggressive political style that produced the Chicano movement.[48]

Up until 1945, the migration of Mexican Americans to the cities created greater potential for change than change itself. In the unfamiliar urban environment, the Chicano had to deal with time and punctuality, transportation schedules, machines, office buildings, crowds of people, unions, and bureaucracies. In disrupting the extended family, migration forced husband and wife to rely on each other. The male sought—often in vain— to maintain his position as undisputed head of *his* family while he faced "the uncertitudes and hazards of the outside world." As his wife's protector, he resisted letting her "Americanize" herself or the home. As wives seldom spoke English, they remained "subordinate, home-centered creatures." He vigilantly protected his daughters from personal contacts with men. Nevertheless, male and female roles gradually changed, for the husband found it difficult to fulfill his obligation as the family provider in the face of seasonal unemployment. His children acculturated. Wherever Mexican Americans met Anglo-Americans head-on, the role of parent and child might be reversed. Educated in an Anglo-American school, the oldest boy, by virtue of his mastery of American ways, became a quasi foster parent to his brothers and sisters. While a girl might accept the subordinate role as the norm for women, she had an opportunity to see alternative roles before she committed herself to any particular pattern as an adult woman.[49]

In communities like Detroit, Chicano families in the mid-1940s retained a working-class orientation. Their aspirations did not include the conventional middle-class ones of a better home, travel, and education for their children. And the evidence indicated that the children did not blindly follow the traditions of their parents. Mexican holidays ceased to be celebrated; Mexican artifacts were absent from the home. While husbands continued to expect their wives to be subordinate, the wives enjoyed more freedom than had their mothers.[50]

The exclusion of Mexicans from the mainstream of Anglo-American life permitted the development of a small middle-class group serving the Mexican community—much as a black middle class emerged in Harlem. To the extent that Mexican Americans participated in the larger political life of the nation, it was the middle class that did so. Yet this Mexican middle class had restricted contacts with those outside the ethnic community.[51]

Large numbers of Chicanas continued to pursue tradition-ridden lifestyles, their education too limited to enable them to follow any but the well-beaten paths. Many Chicanos, in the barrios of the upper Rio Grande valley, lived "in an isolation and bitterness" that had "enveloped them for a century." Among the poorest ethnic enclaves in the United States, these barrios remained bastions of tradition. And as the ambitious moved away, the ways of the barrio remained unchallenged. Here the Chicana continued to be protected by father or husband. The wife remained "submissive, unworldly, and chaste," interested primarily in the welfare of her husband and children. Her social relationships and recreation consisted chiefly of visits to cousins and other relatives. Emotional ties between mother and daughters and between sisters often were stronger than those between wives and husbands.[52]

* * *

The various minority peoples were far better equipped to act in their own behalf in 1950 than in 1900. At midcentury, Judaism was widely accepted on a plane with Protestantism and Catholicism. The Chinese Americans, American Indians, and Hispanic Americans were still invisible to most Anglo-Americans. Japanese Americans were faced with creating a place for themselves. Generally these minority groups were sufficiently isolated that the Anglo-American middle class saw them chiefly in stereotypical terms and reacted to them as a group rather than as individuals. In these circumstances the status of minority women continued to be shaped by their group identification rather than their sex. Women, however, who sought to function outside their ethnic or racial group found themselves expected to abide by Anglo-American views of woman's place.

NOTES

[1]   Marshall Sklare, *American Jews* (New York: Random House, 1971), 5 ff.

[2]   Charlotte Baum, Paula Hyman, and Sonya Michael, *The Jewish Woman in America* (New York: New American Library, 1975), 6–7.

[3]   Ibid., 8, 10, 11.

[4]   Ibid., 5, 14.

[5]   Ibid., 24–25. Will Herberg, *Protestant, Catholic, Jew* (New York: Anchor, 1960), 174.

[6]   Baum et al., *Jewish Woman in America*, 23.

[7]   Oscar Handlin, *Adventure in Freedom* (New York: McGraw-Hill, 1954), 6.

[8]   Nathan Glazer, *American Judaism* (Chicago: University of Chicago Press, 1957), 87–90. "Hannah Greenbaum Solomon," *NAW*, vol. 3, 324–25. [Monroe Campbell] *The First Fifty Years: The History of the National Council of Jewish Women* (New York: no pub., 1943).

[9]   Baum et al., *Jewish Woman in America*, 56–57.

[10]   Ibid., 204 ff. Herberg, *Protestant, Catholic, Jew*, 178.

[11]   Baum et al., *Jewish Woman in America*, 123.

[12]   Ibid., 218–19, 240. Herberg, *Protestant, Catholic, Jew*, 183. Rudolf Glanz, *The Jewish Woman in America*, vol. 2. *The German-Jewish Woman* (no place, KTVA Publishing House and National Council of Jewish Women, 1976), 18, 199. Alexander Grinstein, "Profile of a Doll," in *The Psychodynamics of American Jewish Life*, ed. Norman Kiell (New York: Twayne, 1967), 87–88.

[13]   Grinstein, "Profile of a Doll," 87–88. Martha Wolfstein, "Two Types of Jewish Mothers," in *Childhood in Contemporary Cultures*, ed. Margaret Mead and Martha Wolfstein (Chicago: University of Chicago Press, 1955), 438. Pauline Bart, "Depression in Middle-Aged Women," in *Woman in Sexist Society*, ed. Vivian Gornick and Barbara K. Moran (New York: Basic, 1971), 99–117. Zena Smith Blau, "In Defense of the Jewish Mother," *Midstream*, 13(1967): 42–49.

[14]   Glazer, *American Judaism*, 90–91. "Henrietta Szold," *NAW*, III, 417–20. See also Irving Fineman, *Woman of Valor: The Life of Henrietta Szold* (New York: Simon & Schuster, 1961).

[15]   Handlin, *Adventure in Freedom*, 6.

[16]   Rose Hum Lee, *The Chinese in the United States of America* (Hong Kong: Hong Kong University Press, 1960), 1, 12. Norman S. Hayner and Charles J. Reynolds, "Chinese Family

Life in America," *ASR,* 2(1937): 630–31. Most of the Chinese immigrants came from Kwantung province.

[17] Bureau of the Census, *Abstract of the Fifteenth Census of the United States* (Washington: GPO, 1933), tab. 11.

[18] Lee, *Chinese in the United States,* 19, 39.

[19] Hayner and Reynolds, "Chinese Family Life in America," 630–37.

[20] Lee, *Chinese in the United States,* 198–99.

[21] Ibid., 192–93.

[22] Hayner and Reynolds, "Chinese Family Life in America," 630–37.

[23] Lee, *Chinese in the United States,* 12–19.

[24] Ibid., 47–48, 121 ff.

[25] Harry H. L. Kitano, *Japanese-Americans: The Evolution of a Sub Culture* (Englewood Cliffs: Prentice-Hall, 1969). Masakazu Iwata, "The Japanese Immigrants in California Agriculture," *Agricultural History* 36(1962): 25–37. Roger Daniels, *The Politics of Prejudice* (New York: Atheneum, 1968), chaps. 2, 5.

[26] Daniels, *Politics of Prejudice,* 106, chap. 4. Iwata, "Japanese Immigrants in California Agriculture," 33.

[27] Iwata, "Japanese Immigrants in California Agriculture," 41–45. Thomas A. Bailey, *A Diplomatic History of the American People,* 3rd ed. (New York: Crofts, 1946), 571. Kitano. *Japanese-Americans,* 61. William Petersen, *Japanese-Americans Oppression and Success* (New York: Random House, 1971), 191.

[28] Darrel Montero, "The Japanese Americans; Changing Patterns of Assimilation Over Three Generations," *ASR,* 46(1981): 836.

[29] Leonard Broom and John I. Kitsuse, *The Managed Casualty, The Japanese-American Family in World War II* (Berkeley: University of California Press, 1956), 7 ff. Petersen, *Japanese-Americans, Oppression and Success,* 206–7.

[30] Broom and Kitsuse, *Managed Casualty,* 9–11.

[31] Ibid. James K. Morishima, "The Evacuation: Impact on the Family," in *Asian-Americans: Psychological Perspectives,* ed. Stanley Sue and Nathaniel N. Wagner (Ben Lomond, CA: Science and Behavior Books, 1973), 13–19.

[32] Clark Wissler, *Indians of the United States,* rev. ed. (Garden City: Anchor, 1966[1940]).

[33] Angie Debo, *A History of the Indians of the United States* (Norman: University of Oklahoma Press, 1970), 299–315.

[34] William T. Hagan, *American Indians* (Chicago: University of Chicago Press, 1961), 146. Loring Benson Priest, *Uncle Sam's Step Children* (New Brunswick: Rutgers University Press, 1942), 217–52.

[35] See for example David Wallace Adams, "Schooling the Hopi: Federal Indian Policy Writ Small, 1887–1917," *Pacific Historical Review,* 48(1979): 335–56.

[36] Institute for Government Research, *The Problem of Indian Administration,* Lewis Meriam, dir. (Baltimore: Johns Hopkins Press, 1928).

[37] Ibid.

[38] John Collier, *Indians of the Americas* (New York: Mentor, 1947), 154–71.

[39] Donald L. Parman, *The Navajos and the New Deal* (New Haven: Yale University Press, 1976).

[40] Hagan, *American Indians,* 158–59.

[41] Joan W. Moore, *Mexican Americans* (Englewood Cliffs: Prentice-Hall, 1970), 12–19. See also Matt S. Meier and Feliciano Rivera, *The Chicanos: A History of Mexican Americans* (New York: Hill and Wang, 1972).

[42] Moore, *Mexican Americans,* 20–21.

[43] Ibid., 100–106.

[44] Alfredo Mirande and Evangelina Enriquez, *La Chicana, The Mexican-American Woman* (Chicago: University of Chicago Press, 1979), 215–24.

[45] R. Griswold del Castillo, "La Familia Chicana: Social Changes in the Chicano Family of Los Angeles, 1850–1880," *Journal of Ethnic Studies,* 3(1975): 41–58.

[46] Ibid. Moore, *Mexican Americans,* 22, 41.

[47] Meier and Rivera, *The Chicanos,* 150–67 ff. Moore, *Mexican Americans,* 42.

[48] Moore, *Mexican Americans,* 28–29. Meier and Rivera, *The Chicanos,* 197–201. Robin F. Scott, "The Zoot-Suit Riots," in *The Mexican-Americans: An Awakening Minority,* ed. Manuel P. Servin (Beverly Hills: Glencoe, 1970), 116–24.

[49] Norman Daymond Humphrey, "The Changing Structure of the Detroit Mexican Family: An Index of Acculturation," *ASR,* 9(1944): 622–23. Arthur J. Rubel, *Across the Tracks* (Austin: University of Texas Press, 1966), chap. 3. Emory S. Bogardus, *The Mexican in the United States.* (New York: Arno, 1970[1934]), 24–29. Moore, *Mexican Americans,* 104, 105, 107.

[50] Moore, *Mexican Americans,* 99. Rubel, *Across the Tracks,* chap. 3.

[51] Manuel P. Servin, "The Post-World War II Mexican-American, 1945–1965: A Non-Achieving Minority," in *The Mexican-Americans: An Awakening Minority,* 156–60.

[52] Meier and Rivera, *The Chicanos,* 203–9, chap. 13, and pp. 197–200.

6

Encountering the Mystique: The 1950s

World War II marked a watershed for Americans. Whereas after the Great War of 1914–1918 the United States had been able to disengage itself from world affairs, the ending of World War II afforded no such opportunity. Nor did it seem that the United States would recover the sense of security it had known prior to the war. The cold war was in full sway, and by mid-1950 the United States was engaged in the Korean War. At home fears of a renewed depression dissipated as the nation headed into what would prove to be a prolonged period of prosperity. For women, the postwar decade promised to be tranquil enough. On the surface they seemed to slip comfortably into traditional roles as dutiful daughters or else as wives and mothers. The prevailing value system, later characterized as the "feminine mystique," was an updated version of the Cult of Womanhood. But in fact, without any major debate, women ventured into nondomestic roles on an unprecedented scale.

AN ACCELERATED DEMAND

The prosperity that had marked the American economy in the late 1940s continued through the fifties, adding 8,760,000 persons to the labor force. In keeping with the postindustrial character of the economy, the primary sector (farming and mining) continued its downward plunge, resulting in the displacement during the decade of two farmers or farm laborers in every five. The secondary sector, which grew at a rate slower than did the total economy, added roughly one million jobs each in the craft and operative occupations while losing nearly a quarter of a million unskilled labor jobs. Once more the tertiary sector fueled the expansion of the national economy, generating nearly 6 million new jobs of which nearly 2.5 million were clerical and another 2.3 million, professional (see Figure 6-1). Driven by the expansive force of the tertiary sector, the economy afforded women 5.8 million new jobs, two out of three of all new jobs. The female labor force, which numbered 16,500,000 in 1950, stood

Figure 6-1
Female Labor Force by Occupation, 1950 and 1960

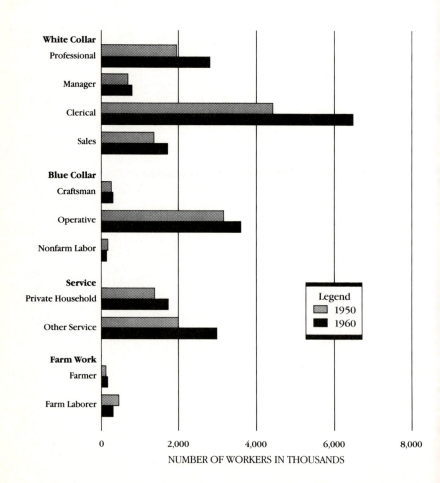

NUMBER OF WORKERS IN THOUSANDS

at 22,300,000 a decade hence. And the LFPR for adult women, 30.04 in 1950, jumped to 37.32 by the end of the decade, the decade of the "feminine mystique."[1]

The revolution in the scale of agricultural operations required ever-larger commitments of capital and higher levels of training. As it became more difficult to enter agriculture, the number of men engaged as owners or managers dropped precipitously. But as women continued to become owners by inheriting a working farm from a husband or other relative and since ownership provided a modicum of economic security, the number of women farmers held up. On the other hand, as the revolution in agriculture reduced the demand for farm workers, two thirds of whom were unpaid family workers, women abandoned the occupation in larger proportions than did men. Changes in women's share of the major occupational groups are indicated in Figure 6-2.[2]

Figure 6-2
Changes in Demand for Female Workers, 1950–1960

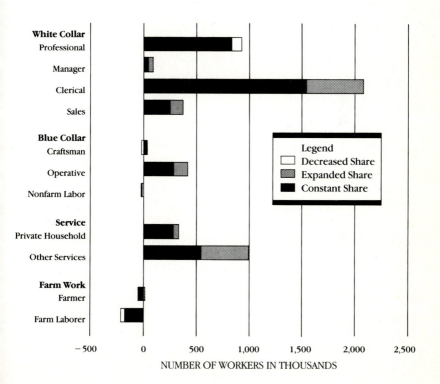

NUMBER OF WORKERS IN THOUSANDS

Blue-collar employments generated some 430,000 new jobs for women. However, both the number and proportion of women who worked in the unskilled occupations declined during the fifties. As with farm laborers, the decline in women's share of unskilled labor jobs was facilitated by the greater tendency of girls to complete their high-school education and by the wider range of attractive jobs that became accessible as a result. At the other end of the blue-collar spectrum—skilled crafts—women slightly improved their miniscule share of these occupations. However, despite the wartime experience of women in a broad range of skilled employments, the crafts remained "male turf." In the middle area—usually as semiskilled factory operatives—women gained in numbers as well as in their share of such employments.[3]

The expansive element of the economy centered in various service and professional jobs of the tertiary sector. At the bottom of the scale, six of every seven new workers in the personal-service area were women. Whereas during the war years women had deserted domestic service for better-paid, less-onerous work, in the fifties the number of women domestics increased sharply and women's share of private-household service increased. Much of this increase reflected the obstacles that blocked black women from securing better-paying work—especially factory jobs—as well as the increased demand for cleaning ladies generated by white women, who, if they were to work themselves, required housekeeping help and could afford it. Increased employment opportunities in service work other than in private households generated another 1,000,000 additional jobs, as an affluent society could afford to expand the staffs of hospitals and required more cooks, waitresses, hairdressers, and cosmetologists. An unusually high proportion—47 percent—of these additional jobs resulted from the increase in women's share of this category of work. Such service occupations created a demand for women who had not finished high school.[4]

The major increase in the demand for women in the tertiary sector was for white-collar workers, 3,375,000 additional jobs. Clerical employments—which included a number of "female" jobs—provided women with over 2,000,000 additional jobs of which 500,000 can be attributed to women's increased share of clerical work. Women also increased their share of sales jobs as well as of managerial and administrative work. They did not, however, increase their share of professional jobs. Although women gained an impressive 817,000 professional and technical jobs, this number was at least 280,000 fewer than would have occurred if they had kept a constant share of the field. The gains women made in professional employments—41.3 percent for the decade—ranged over the spectrum of the professions, but men gained more—50.2 percent. As males successfully competed for employment as elementary and secondary teachers, the proportion of women employed in this major "female" profession declined. Men also gained nearly 200,000 engineering jobs, a field from which women remained largely excluded.[5]

The demand for "female" labor remained a key factor in the growth of the female labor force. Of the 4 "female" occupations that had been so important in creating white-collar employments in the first years of the century—elementary teacher, nurse, telephone operator, and secretary— only the demand for secretarial workers increased more rapidly than the demand for women in the labor force as a whole. The demand for elementary teachers and nurses held steady, while the demand for telephone operators lagged. The 26 "female" occupations that in 1950 had employed 40.0 percent of the female labor force, by 1960 employed but 41.6 percent of it. However, during the fifties, 12 new "female" occupations emerged, all but one in the service area, so that in the aggregate, 54.3 percent of the female labor force in 1960 was employed in "female" occupations. There was an interesting paradox at work: women who challenged traditional feminine roles by entering the labor force did so by entering socially approved "female" occupations. Indeed, of the 38 "female" occupations of 1960, all but 5 were in the tertiary sector, 18 in the white-collar areas, and the rest in the personal-service area (see Figure 6-3).[6]

The content of "female" occupations was often a matter of happenstance and tradition rather than of the intrinsic character of the job. In the Midwest, for example, cornhuskers were traditionally women, while trimmers were almost always men. In the Far West, cornhuskers were men and trimmers were women. In the same vein, a majority of clerical workers in the manufacturing, transportation, and communications industries were male, while the preponderance of clerical workers in wholesale and retail trade, various service enterprises, and public administration were women. Similarly in sales work, few women worked as sales representatives of manufacturing or wholesale firms, but they were the dominant group in retail sales, especially in general-merchandise and variety stores that sold to the general public. Wholesale selling frequently entailed travel, which men found easier to accommodate than women, while retail selling often involved part-time work, which proved more acceptable to women than to men.[7]

The evidence of the 1950s confirmed a broad commitment to sex differentiation in work assignments. Employer conferences held by the National Manpower Council continued to affirm the belief that if even one or two women were introduced into an all-male work group, "the necessary adaptations to her presence appear excessive to every one concerned, including immediate changes in verbal habits, dress and comportment, and potential changes in the organization of the groups." Further, the

Figure 6-3
Major "Female" Occupations, 1950 and 1960

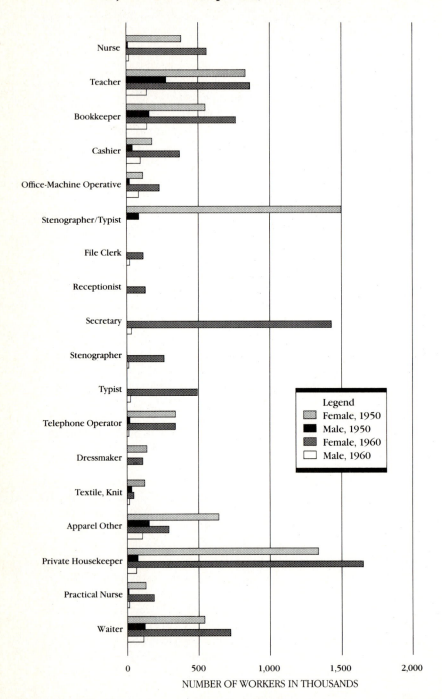

NUMBER OF WORKERS IN THOUSANDS

council reported that most employers "maintained that women as well as men generally prefer male supervisors." Employers who sought white-collar workers with a fairly high level of general education along with some specialized training had access to a rapidly growing pool of younger women whose training in high school or college cost the employer nothing. By the same token, the intermittent character of women's employment deterred employers from hiring women for jobs requiring extensive on-the-job training, from employing them in professions and crafts where continuity of employment was important to maintaining skills, and from considering women employees for promotion. Reaffirmation of conventional views disposed employers, then, to hire women in less demanding sales and clerical jobs and to avoid employing them in professional positions. But whatever employers said about women's managerial skills, in fact the proportion of women in managerial posts increased during the decade.[8]

A TRANSFORMED SUPPLY

The accelerated demand for women transformed the supply of female labor. During the 1950s the total number of women age 15 and over increased by 7,920,000, but the ongoing changes in birth and mortality rates produced an uneven distribution. Reflecting the short-term dip in birthrates in the early 1930s and their subsequent recovery in the early 1940s, the pool of young women in 1960 had an "extra" 529,000 persons relative to 1950. Given the larger percentage of young women completing their secondary education, the proportion of teenagers who were available to the labor force declined. The long-term trend in declining birthrates was responsible for reducing the proportion of women age 20 to 39, causing a shortfall of 2,819,000 women in their 20s and a smaller shortfall of 723,000 in the number of women in the 30- to 39-year age range. By contrast, the falling mortality rates contributed to an increase of 1,142,000 women 40 to 64 years of age. The net effect of these shifts in the age distribution of the female population was an increase in the proportion of women in the age ranges that had relatively low labor-participation rates and a sharp decrease in the proportion of women in age ranges with a high propensity to work (see Figure 6-4).[9]

The shift in the age mix interacted with changes in the marriage rate, the divorce rate, and the death rate to affect the mix of women by marital status. Although the number of single women in the total population increased during the fifties, the proportion who were single—especially women in their 20s—declined slightly. Reflecting the emphasis on marriage, family, and togetherness, the proportion of married women moved upward in

Figure 6-4
Female Population by Age Groups, 1950 and 1960

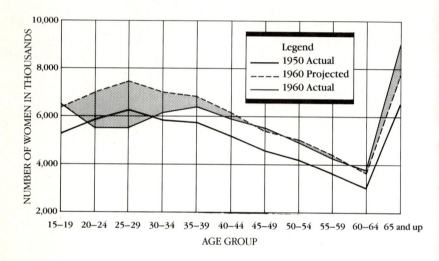

every age group from 20 and over. A declining death rate for males com-bined with a growing tendency for widows to remarry caused the propor-tion of widows in every age group to drop. The increased tendency of divorcées to remarry, however, was offset by an escalating divorce rate, so that the proportion of divorced women continued its upward climb. Thus as the nation moved through the 1950s, the pool of young women—both single and married—declined. The increases in the pool of married women occurred among women age 30 and over—women whose children, if any, were likely to be of school age and, thus, less of a bar to employment (see Figure 6-5).[10]

How was the expanding demand for females in the labor force affected by the changing structure of the female labor supply? In 1950 the pool of women without husbands—single, widowed, and divorced—was 19,525,000, barely sufficient to fill the demand for female labor if all of them had worked. By 1960 the total labor-force demand for females exceeded the total population of single, widowed, and divorced women age 14 and over. Indeed, the increase in the demand for female workers during the dec-ade—5,457,000 women—exceeded the net increase in the female popu-lation in the age range 20 to 64 years. This demand for female labor was accentuated in the early fifties as the United States fought a war in Korea while maintaining the Seventh Army in Western Europe, thus removing

Figure 6-5
Marital Status of the Female Population, 1950 and 1960

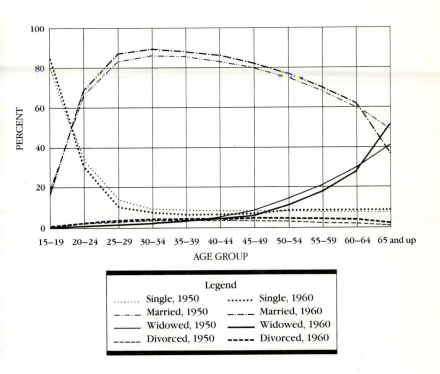

Legend	
.... Single, 1950	.... Single, 1960
_.._.._ Married, 1950	_.._.._ Married, 1960
_____ Widowed, 1950	_____ Widowed, 1960
_ _ _ _ Divorced, 1950	- - - - Divorced, 1960

1,500,000 men from the civilian labor force. The "feminine mystique" not-withstanding, married women became the main source of additional personnel for the female labor force.[11]

The operation of traditional values about woman's place was apparent in the effect that the presence of children in the home had on women's labor-force activity. Of the married women, husband present, who were in the labor force in 1950, 57.8 percent had no children under age 18, and only 16.4 percent had children under 6 years of age. During the decade, attitudes about woman's place were changing such that married women generally and mothers in particular found paid work more acceptable. The labor-force rates for married women with no children under 18 rose by 4.4 percentage points, but 10.7 points for those with children 6 to 17 years of age, and 6.7 points for those with children under 6 years. As Figure 6-6 illustrates, the labor-force rates for separated, divorced, and widowed women with children were markedly higher than the rates for women with a

Figure 6-6
LFPR for Women by Marital Status and Age of Children, 1950–1980

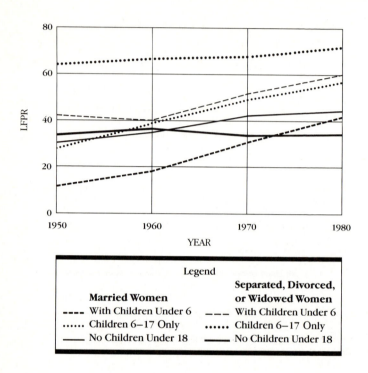

husband present. Despite the "feminine mystique," the labor-force rates for these women, generally, were rising. The changes in the proportion of divorced women and of widowed women were too small to affect the supply of women in the labor force significantly.[12]

The expanding demand for female labor drove the labor-force rates for adult women of all ages and marital conditions upward. By age groups, labor-participation rates which in 1950 ranged from a high of 42.9 points to a low of 23.5 points, shifted upward, running between 46.7 points and 35.0 a decade later. For adult single women under age 55 the labor-force rates in 1950 ranged between 70.7 and 79.8, and by 1960 these rates ranged from 73.2 to 79.4. For adult married women under age 50, the rates ran between 22.1 and 26.5 in 1950, between 26.8 and 39.3 in 1960. While the rates for the single, widowed, or divorced in their 20s declined slightly, the rates for their married peers increased. For all marital groups, the largest gains in labor rates were scored by older women (see Figure 6-7).[13]

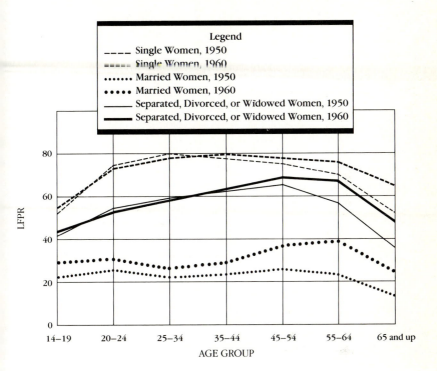

Figure 6-7
LFPR for Women by Marital Status and Age, 1950–1960

These figures, in fact, understate the participation of women in the labor market. The conventional measure of labor-force participation—the proportion of the population that is employed or seeking work during the survey week—seriously undercounts the number of persons with labor-force experience by skipping those who, though not working during the survey week, worked sometime during the year. In 1950, for example, the conventional method reported a female labor force of 17,490,000, yet 23,350,000 women worked during some part of the year, an understatement of the females with work experience of 5,860,000. Women with work experience in 1960 numbered 30,585,000, yet the Census Bureau put the female labor force at 22,196,000, an undercount of nearly 8,400,000 persons.[14]

The movement of women into the labor force was greatly facilitated by the availability of intermittent and part-time work. An examination of the work experience of women in 1950 reveals that less than four women in ten worked full-time for 50 or more weeks, while another 8.2 percent worked part-time (less than 35 hours a week) for 50 or more weeks. In fact, a large segment of the female labor force worked less than half the year. These included persons either just entering the labor force or retiring from it, as well as seasonal workers and students working after school, weekends, or during vacations. One woman in four worked part-time, whether year-round or part of the year. The growth of the female labor force in the fifties came about primarily through the expansion of part-time work. While the proportion of women who worked full-time year-round held constant during the decade, the proportion who worked full-time for part of the year dropped by 6 percentage points. The data, illustrated in Figure 6-8, discloses what happened, rather than the cause. One may hypothesize that the proportion of women free to take full-time year-round employment remained relatively fixed. As the demand for labor escalated, women responded by entering the labor force at points in the life cycle in which work outside the home had not been the norm. Such women, many of them mothers of young children, may have felt themselves unable to undertake more than part-time employment until their children entered school or to make work commitments except for strictly limited periods. It is also likely that employers, regarding women as a reserve labor force, earmarked the full-time year-round jobs for men, the extra part-time part-year work for women.[15]

Figure 6-8
Women with Work Experience by Extent of Employment, 1950–1983

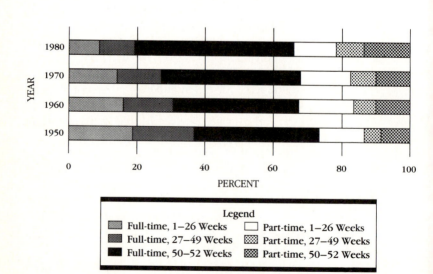

Several generalizations emerge as one looks at the interplay of demand and supply forces on the female labor force. First, during the fifties, women's propensity to seek employment outside the home increased by a larger amount than in any previous decade. The addition of 5.8 million women to the labor force exceeded the net increase during the forties and approached the maximum number added during the war emergency. Second, the influx of women into the peacetime labor force in the late forties and fifties occurred in the absence of an organized feminist movement. Third, the decline in the proportion of women in two of the low-status occupational categories—farm labor and nonfarm labor—coincided with the opening of better opportunities in jobs suited to women with less than a high-school education. Fourth, the decline in the proportion of women in two elite occupational categories—skilled crafts and professional and technical employments—reflected the power of traditional views that made employers reluctant to invest time and money in the formal training requisite to employment in these areas. Ideas about the suitability of specific jobs for women may have encouraged some women to escape the drudgery of farm labor and unskilled labor for more genteel work and deflected others from crafts and professions regarded as "male" occupations. Fifth, while the middle-class women who entered the labor force in the late forties and fifties were not driven to seek work in order to survive, many may have done so in response to the economic pressure that postwar inflation exerted on the family's level of living. Furthermore, as the proportion of two-income families increased, their standard of living became the norm, putting the single-income family at a disadvantage and exerting a subtle, but powerful, pressure that undercut the opposition of the husband and the reluctance of the wife to break with tradition that kept wives at home. Finally, as one compares the changes in the female labor force during World War II with those of the fifties, it is apparent that the wartime push of women into blue-collar jobs was ephemeral; the movement into the white-collar employments was not. Blue-collar jobs remained "male" jobs with few exceptions; white-collar jobs were often "female." The postwar increases in the female labor force were rooted in structural changes in the economy that were independent of the existence, or nonexistence, of a feminist ideology and were irreversible.

RISE OF THE "FEMININE MYSTIQUE"

The movement of unprecedented numbers of women—especially married women—into the labor force during the war years evoked both praise and criticism. Women's response to the emergency was hailed as "noble, impeccable, and shining." Yet there was an undercurrent of dis-

The young wife of the fifties made her home, her husband, and her children the center of her life as she embraced the ideals of the "feminine mystique."

approval. One line of attack came from social workers who, protesting against working mothers who left their children unattended at home, forecast a rising tide of juvenile delinquency. A second attack, with Philip Wylie in the forefront, laid many of the ills of society at the feet of "mom." Writing in 1942, Wylie argued that while Americans venerated motherhood, even establishing an annual day in her honor, all was not well. American women experienced "a pathological emptiness" in their lives that led them to smother their children with affection so as to preclude their maturing as well-adjusted adults and to become tyrants in the household, thereby emasculating their husbands. From Wylie's perspective, women had become a race of parasites—"an idle class, a spending class, a candy-craving class" that consumed all the money, affection, and virility their husbands could offer.[16]

Seemingly corroborating Wylie's categorization of women as "a generation of vipers," army psychologists and doctors identified a disturbingly large number of inductees with nervous disorders. By the war's end, 3,000,000 men had been excused from or rejected for military service because of emotional instability. Though less flamboyant than Wylie, Dr. Edward Strecker, a psychiatric consultant to the secretary of war, charged "mom" with overprotecting her sons and cultivating such emotional dependency that they were unable to mature and assume the responsibilities of manhood. Still another damning critique came from Amram Scheinfeld. In *Women and Men* (1943), Scheinfeld charged that "of all the fallacies that have led to difficulty and confusion among modern women" one of the biggest was "the belief that the path of equality with men lies in the direction of sameness.... Instead of striving for the fullest expression of their own special capacities and attributes, all too many women," he argued, "have thought that what was most masculine was therefore most desirable for them, too." A common denominator of these critiques that accompanied the flooding of the labor market with women was the assumption that woman's place was in the home and the conclusion that women were not performing their role acceptably.[17]

As the nation settled back into peacetime, social criticism of woman's place continued apace. Two fundamentally different approaches were utilized: one, psychological-biological; the other, cultural. In the psychological-biological analysis "to be born a woman," meant "to inhabit from early infancy to the last day of life, a psychological world which differs from the world of the man." The latter-day work of Sigmund Freud and that of followers, such as Helene Deutsch and Marynia Farnham, asserted that "anatomy is destiny." In the twenties, Freud's doctrines seemed to be liberating, to provide scientific approval for "doing one's thing." But as Freud continued into the 1930s to explore and explicate the role of sexuality—developing the theory of the Oedipus and Electra complexes, of the castration complex, and of penis envy to explain the differentiated routes by which boys and girls arrived at sexual maturity—his theories suggested, at least to the general public, that males were inherently superior to females. In his later essays he betrayed a condescending attitude toward female patients, and in "The Psychology of Women" (1933) he suggested that biophysiologically, women were intellectually less able than men, that they ought to leave things of the mind alone. He expressed his fear that "intellectual training" for women might cause some to "deprecate the feminine role" for which he thought they were intended. He argued that women often experienced "psychological rigidity." Thus the task of the analyst was to aid males to develop their capacities, to aid females to resign themselves to their destiny.[18]

In the post–World War II era, Freudian views, as interpreted by Helene Deutsch, prevailed among psychiatrists. Shifting the emphasis from penis envy to genital trauma, Deutsch identified passivity, masochism, eroticism, and narcissism as peculiarly female traits. She then went on to delineate a variety of female types depending on the relative strength of the various female traits. These ranged from the passive "feminine" woman to the active "masculine" woman. Women achieved eminence on their own only at the expense of feminine fulfillment, Deutsch argued. Such active, intellectual women she regarded as neurotic, even pathological.[19]

Unlike Deutsch, who addressed an audience of specialists, Ferdinand Lundberg, a writer, and Marynia Farnham, a psychiatrist, employed Freudian views as they addressed their attack on contemporary society to a general audience in *The Modern Woman: The Lost Sex* (1947). Women, they insisted, were endowed with "a complicated reproductive system, . . . a more elaborate nervous system, and an infinitely complex psychology revolving about the reproductive function." As a consequence of the conflicting demands on her, modern woman was "a bundle of anxieties." The result for society was frightful: the rising tide of juvenile delinquency, divorce, homicide, crime, and alcoholism, along with a decline in the birthrate, they attributed to the fact that women had left home, rejecting their natural role, to compete with men. Women's problems, as well as society's, came about because women—married women especially—had abandoned the home for male roles. This psychological-biological analysis of woman's place afforded women no escape; anatomy was everything.[20]

Not all psychiatrists accepted this interpretation of Freud, however. Karen Horney and Clara Thompson rejected penis envy and genital trauma as inevitable. As each sex has unique biological qualities, Horney asked, why assume that women experienced envy of men and not men of women? She suggested that men might well envy the woman's capacity to bear children and find compensation in the drive to create. Challenging the prevalence of penis envy in women, she suggested that women might be less envious of the male anatomy than of the male's social advantages. Thompson, in particular, pointed to the curtailment of freedom, the obstacles in the way of play, education, and social life, and the inhibitions on her sexual expression that could lead a girl to doubt her self-worth. Horney also questioned whether it was legitimate to conclude that if masochism was common among neurotic women, it was characteristic of all women. Horney and Thompson, while admitting that biological factors were operative in molding the female character, concluded that cultural factors played an important part; anatomy was not everything.[21]

The major alternative analysis of women's nature came from social scientists who argued that women were the product of their culture. Whether one compared men and women in terms of intelligence, personality traits, or aptitude, the tests disclosed greater differences between members of the same sex than between the sexes, which is to say that most females are like most males. Throughout the twenties, thirties, and forties behavioral psychologists built up an impressive body of knowledge that illustrated the degree to which the human personality was shaped by cultural and social conditioning. Of special importance was Margaret Mead, a cultural anthropologist, whose studies of sex roles in a variety of societies indicated that there were no universal "female" or "male" qualities. In her studies of South Sea islanders, Mead found that qualities such as aggressiveness, independence, gentleness, and passivity were not sex-linked but rather were the products of social conditioning. However, Mead cautioned that behavior that trespassed the accepted sphere of the opposite sex posed a grave danger to the individual. "It is of doubtful value," she warned, "to enlist the gifts of women if bringing women into fields that have been defined as male frightens the men, unsexes the women, muffles, and distorts the contribution the women could make. . . ."[22]

Mirra Komarovsky, a Barnard College specialist in family and marriage, and Viola Klein and Alva Myrdal, sociologists, explored the operation of female roles thoroughly. Rejecting the Freudians, Komarovsky argued that women had become "a social problem" because of cumulative technological and social changes over the previous century. She noted that parents pressured daughters to play with "girl's toys and to be more restrained, sedentary, quiet and neat" than their brothers. Social pressures conditioned girls to be gentler and more emotionally demonstrative than males. Parents accorded girls fewer opportunities for independent action: a bicycle hike in the company of a girl friend to her grandmother's home a dozen miles distant could be the daring adventure in an adolescent girl's life. Finally a more exacting code of filial and kinship obligations was imposed on a young woman. Beyond this her family was likely to confront the young woman with "compelling but contradictory pressures." Her father expected her "to get an 'A' in every subject, while her mother cautioned her that an 'A' in Philosophy is very nice dear. But please don't become so deep that no man will be good enough for you." Uncle John urged her not to be a "grind," while Aunt Mary advised, "Prepare yourself for some profession." The young woman's confusion was further compounded by male friends who sought "an intelligent companion, a 'good sport,' a mother-image and a Venus de Milo" all in one. In Komarovsky's analysis, the woman was the product of the cultural conditioning of the girl. The risks came in attempting to transcend the bounds set by her own culture's stereotype of feminine roles.[23]

Whether women were the captives of their biology or the products of their cultural environment continued unresolved throughout the fifties. To the Freudians, the world was a mess because women had ignored their natural roles—housewife and mother—to enter the labor force; to the sociologists and anthropologists, women experienced personal disaster because they ignored cultural traditions. Accordingly one would expect the woman who accepted the traditional role of homemaker to be content with her lot; the working woman, to be dissatisfied. Contemporary studies, however, suggested that the reverse was often the case.[24]

Paradoxically as the "feminine mystique" flowered, critics of all persuasions agreed that a great many women were distressed with their lot. Mirra Komarovsky argued that of college-trained women, "many, perhaps a majority, lead more or less contented and useful lives." For such young women, marriage "makes up in opportunities for versatility what it lacks in specialization. It affords a balance between sedentary and active work, manual and intellectual work, a flexibility which is true of few occupations." Nonetheless, at least a sizable minority of women were discontented. Housewives in urban communities often experienced "isolation and loneliness." They complained of overwork, drudgery, and fatigue. The "strain of being constantly with the children for twelve hours a day, day in day out" left them "tied down." Any leisure time they had was broken up; they experienced "mental stagnation"—a major gripe. There were too few occasions to be "persons and sweethearts." In exploring the "American Woman's Dilemma" in 1947, *Life* portrayed a housewife with "a nice husband" and "three fine children" whose better-than-average circumstances permitted her to employ a diaper service and afford a cleaning woman once a week. Nonetheless, she put in a 100-hour week. She reported no problem, but she had given little thought to the future—"to satisfactory ways of spending the important years after her children have grown up and left home."[25]

But not all women had "a nice husband" and "three fine children"; nearly half of all adult female Americans, *Life* reported, were "essentially idle." They had no children under 18, were not members of the labor force, did not work on farms, nor were they aged or infirm. They were "bored stiff." Many of these women were over 40 and belonged to a generation that disapproved of market labor for any women but the poverty-stricken. Their husbands worked hard to provide them such leisure, yet they existed in a "desert of wasted time." Such women Farnham and Lundberg characterized as "little more than wastrels . . . seething into afternoon movies, teashops, cocktail lounges, [and] expensive shopping centers." What was wrong was that though these women were not pursuing male roles in the labor force, neither were they performing the nurturing roles traditionally associated with the wife and homemaker. As the home had long since ceased to be the center of social and economic activities that formed the "center of woman's scheme of values and ego support," these women were as much the victims of the prevailing culture as they were its villains.[26]

While the Freudians could not condone market work as consistent with woman's place, the non-Freudian critics noted that the "employment of women has become a lasting and important feature of the social structure in industrial countries." The economic realities of the time were not in harmony with the view that "woman's place is in the home." The position of working women varied from satisfactory to unsatisfactory. Young women, *Life* explained, continued working at full-time jobs after marriage because they found "offices and factories more satisfying than housework and child care." But, *Life* cautioned, this was "a good plan" only if the woman was very successful and earned enough money to afford ample housekeeping and child-care services. For the full-time factory employee, "things" were "not so simple." In such cases the combined incomes of the husband and wife were not sufficient to afford housekeeping services, and the wife carried a double burden of work and homemaking.[27]

Problems remained. Full-time housewives tended "to envy the employed women their financial independence, the greater variety of their social contacts, and their sense of purpose." In turn, working women seemed to "begrudge housewives their freedom to do things in their own time and in their own way, and possibly also the prestige that tends to go with greater leisure." As many women moved back and forth between work and homemaking, some of the dissatisfaction was related to the change in status. Komarovsky reported that when career-minded women resumed homemaking, they experienced a loss of economic independence and difficulty in reviving old habits of self-discipline that guided them when on the job. Work provided a focal point for daily activities, while the resumption of full-time houseckeeping brought a "sense of disorganization and emptiness." It also led to a break in group identification, a loss in self-esteem— a sense that those without an occupation "don't amount to much" and a "sense of injustice" at having to give up a career.[28]

The indicated solution "for the bored housewife or an idle woman" was a part-time career, once the children were off at school. Komarovsky argued the need to raise the prestige of homemaking among educated women. It was not right that "in glorifying careers, we have robbed some women of self respect." A woman ought not "yearn for a job" because her peer group deprecates housewifery; neither should she spurn a job because of the attitude of her peer group or husband. In endorsing work as a solution, Komarovsky emphasized that prior to the industrial revolution, women had performed a major economic function in connection with homemaking. In taking employment in the twentieth century, they were resuming a traditional function. The increase in the life span, the reduction in time devoted to maternal duties, and the uncertainty relating to later and "possible lonely" years when their children had left home warranted a redefinition of women's roles. Furthermore, neither the economy nor a democratic ideology could afford a dependent leisure class. What she envisioned was a dual-career pattern in which the young woman worked, probably full-time, prior to marriage or perhaps until she became pregnant, then a period of full-time homemaking, followed by a return to work in her late 30s when her children no longer required full-time care. Myrdal and Klein cautioned that modern mothers who made no plans outside the family for their future will "play havoc with their own lives" and "make nervous wrecks of their over-protected children and of their husbands."[29]

As the critics explored the solution, they outlined a wide variety of steps. Women would have to do a better job of planning for "a long full life," giving hard thought to the choice of work consistent with their interests and talents. Men, too, needed to make some adjustments in their "minds and habits." Specifically there needed to be a recognition that the patriarchal family with a protective father and submissive mother was passé and that "bread-winning is no longer a monopoly of men and home-making should no longer be the monopoly of women." The husband's attitude toward a wife's job was a "crucial factor" in the employed homemaker's sense of success or failure. Recognizing that some young mothers would be in the labor force out of economic necessity, if not choice, provisions for extended maternity leaves and public day care for children were in order. Other Gilman-type reforms were also endorsed: housing for working women so designed that it afforded group-eating facilities, laundry services, and child care. Retraining for women over 40 to update old skills or to acquire new ones and changed attitudes toward the employment of older women were specified. For its part, *Life* advised that part-time jobs were not always easy to come by, not invariably glamorous, but it was certain that when a woman finds "really satisfying work to do she will discover that she is more interesting to her friends, to her husband and to herself."[30]

The critics aside, the "feminine mystique" derived much of its vitality from the peculiar circumstances of the postwar decade. By 1950 the groundwork for the "feminine mystique" was in place. Couples who had deferred completing their families during the last years of the depression or the war years had helped swell the birthrate in the late forties, as had younger married couples who had been separated during the war. Couples who had deferred marriage to the war's end were the major factor in the nation's rising marriage and birthrates. This preoccupation with family formation in the late forties set the tone for the family-centeredness of the fifties.[31]

Despite its reputation for dedication to family and children, the fifties did not sustain the intensity of the late forties. The postwar rush to the altar was over by 1950. As Figure 6-9 illustrates, the rate of first marriages,

Figure 6-9
Rate of First Marriages and Divorces for Women Age 14 to 44 Years,
1921–1977

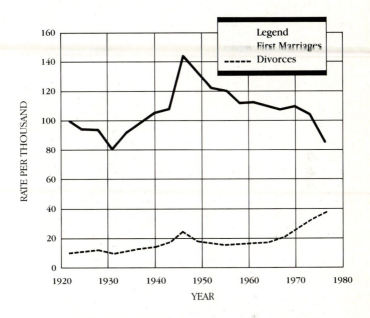

having dropped 21 points between the peak years, 1945–1947, and the first years of the fifties, 1951–1953, eased downward another 10 points by 1957–1959. This occurred in a context in which the median age at first marriage for women had been declining since the start of the century. On reaching a low in 1955, the age began to rise, a factor that would slow the rate of new-family formation. During the fifties, new-family formation was higher than in prewar years but lower than for the years 1945–1950. The fertility rate, shown in Figure 6-10, followed an analogous pattern. From a postwar peak in 1947, the fertility rate for white women dropped until 1950, then began a steady rise, passing the postwar peak in 1952 and reaching a new peak in 1957 before beginning a prolonged slump that carried into the 1970s. For blacks, a wartime peak in 1943 was followed by a decline for two years, then a steady rise until 1957. Thereafter the fertility rate for blacks, always higher than that for whites, subsided into the 1970s. As a consequence, women in every age group from 15 to 44 had substantially more children in 1960 than women in the same age group a decade earlier. In reality the 1950s marked the end of the postwar trend of a rising level of family formation and of increasing fertility rates.[32]

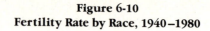

Figure 6-10
Fertility Rate by Race, 1940–1980

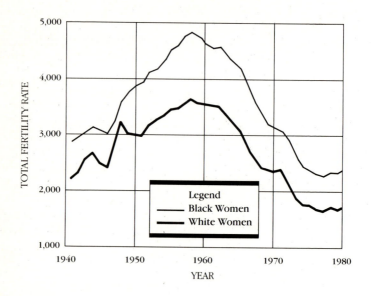

During the war years advertisers urged couples to look ahead to the end of the war when they might realize their desire for a fine clock, sterling-silver service, or bone china. In the fifties, advertisers, advice columns, and service features in women's magazines capitalized on this. The "togetherness" campaign mounted by *McCall's* in 1954 focused wide public attention on the centrality of home and family and served to reinforce traditional views of women's roles. Fashioned as a promotional theme, the concept was quickly reworked as "the tie that binds American families to their mothers," or in the words of the Reverend Norman Vincent Peale, as the "creative mechanism which fuses the man and woman into a team." It not only affirmed that woman's place was in the home but heightened the role of the father–husband in family affairs. "Families That Play Together, Stay Together," one author advised readers of *Parent's Magazine*. The concept was consistent with the do-it-yourself craze that had white-collar males expressing themselves at home by acting as their own carpenters, plumbers, and electricians, while fading into anonymity as "the organization man" at work. The concept served as a unifying theme for merchandising household goods among the affluent middle class. But it also served the suburban housewife, who spent long hours homebound with her children, with a rationale that called on husbands to devote their leisure time to sharing domestic responsibilities. So too, it served the interests of antifeminists who were disturbed by the increasing proportion of working mothers. The campaign ended quickly enough, as perceptive critics noted that the editorial content of *McCall's* fell far short of illustrating togetherness and that "the real secret of family life is a little separateness." Although *McCall's* quickly abandoned its "togetherness" campaign, throughout the decade the home and family continued to receive homage.[33]

POLITICAL ROLES

Changes in the political roles of women were less visible than their expanding economic roles. Most apparent was the attention office seekers accorded women voters. In the 1952 presidential contest between Adlai Stevenson and Dwight Eisenhower, leaders such as Estes Kefauver, Eleanor Roosevelt, and Harry Truman repeatedly lauded women's past participation in politics. Margaret Hickey, who had shepherded women into the labor force during the war, was certain their participation was "vital," while Dean Millicent McIntosh, assuming the air of an educator, urged active involvement in politics as an act of responsible citizenship. Inevitably women party leaders—India Edwards and Gladys H. Knowles—used the forums of the Republican and Democratic conventions to urge women to greater activity. As for the candidates themselves, Stevenson was content to recall the suffrage campaign of the past, while Eisenhower hailed women as "guardians of Government morality."[34]

The effort to enlist women as voters was no less organized in 1956 or 1960, but it drew less attention from the press than in 1952. Women's magazines, such as *Cosmopolitan* and *Woman's Home Companion,* as well as general-circulation magazines, such as *Collier's, Harper's,* and *Newsweek,* felt impelled to explore the role of the woman voter in presidential politics. Both parties aimed appeals at special-interest groups, including women. When Senator Kennedy enlisted his mother, his sisters, and his wife to campaign in his behalf, Hubert Humphrey appealed to women by passing out one of his wife's recipes. The 1960 campaign differed from the 1952 campaign in one telling respect. The pious injunctions of 1952 regarding the civic responsibility of women to participate in the election process were replaced by expressions of awareness from both the Nixon and Kennedy camps that the women's vote would decide the election. Both sides, of course, had women's committees such as Celebrities for Nixon, cochaired by Helen Hayes, the distinguished actress. Both candidates arranged their tours to attract women voters. Yet a review of both campaigns underscores the fact that women were conspicuously absent from the inner councils of both parties and of both candidates. Only one woman had a significant political role—Eleanor Roosevelt.[35]

Campaign strategists were well advised to court the woman's vote. By 1952 only those women in their 50s or older had reached adulthood prior to the ratification of the suffrage amendment; those who were 32 or under had never known a time when women could not vote. If some of the older women still regarded the suffrage as "men's business," the younger ones had been indoctrinated in school to regard it as a civic duty. The differences in voter-participation rates of men and women all but disappeared during the fifties. Younger educated women voted in the same proportions as men, foreshadowing the day when women would outnumber men at the polls. As educated women were more inclined to vote than the less well educated ones, so working women had a higher propensity to vote than full-time homemakers. Thus the expansion of the female labor force had a positive impact on broadening the political roles of women. As the civil rights movement gained strength, black women—only 13 percent of whom had ever voted prior to 1952—began to register and vote. By 1960, despite the difficulties and risks in challenging custom and ingrained habits, the proportion of black women who voted reached 37 percent.[36]

While women had to be courted at the polls, they had far less access to public office. Despite the example of Jeannette Rankin a third of a century before, a woman in high office, whether legislative, executive, or judicial, was still a rarity in 1950. Whereas 11 of the 23 women who served in the U.S. House of Representatives during the forties remained a single term or less, only one woman did so in the fifties, a measure of increased professionalism. Increasingly women entered Congress with legislative experience at the state level rather than as widows temporarily holding the seat of their deceased spouse. In 1950, two congresswomen, Mary Norton and Edith Nourse Rogers, had behind them a quarter century each of congressional service, while Frances Bolton was a ten-year veteran. Although Norton left the House in 1951, Rogers and Bolton served throughout the decade as did 5 other women. In the company of Helen Gahagan Douglas, Katharine St. George, Edith Green, and Martha Griffiths, they added distinction to the House. And Margaret Chase Smith, having made a creditable record in the House, moved to the Senate where she immediately distinguished herself as one of the first to challenge the demagoguery of Senator Joseph McCarthy.[37]

Although the lower civil-service ranks were filled with women clerks, most higher policymaking positions in the federal government remained beyond their reach. Women might be appointed to those few posts that might benefit from the special insight their sex presumably gave them: the Children's Bureau, the Women's Bureau, and the Bureau of Home Economics. Because of the number of women clerical workers in the federal service, one of the three positions on the U.S. Civil Service Commission was usually given to a woman, as was a seat on the U.S. Employee's Compensation Commission. The principle of appointing women to positions that dealt with women had justified the appointments of Jane M. Hoey, a social worker, to the Bureau of Public Assistance and of Mary Dewson to the Social Security Board. It also underlay the appointment of Josephine Roche to be assistant secretary of the Treasury, thereby placing her in charge of the U.S. Public Health Service.[38]

The late forties and fifties brought no revolution, but the circle of offices to which women were appointed expanded, as successive presidents increasingly ignored the question of whether an office dealt primarily with women's affairs. President Truman appointed Georgia Neese Clark to be treasurer of the United States and Anna Rosenberg as assistant secretary of defense in charge of personnel. Subsequently, President Eisenhower made Mrs. Cecil Harden special assistant in the Post Office Department with responsibility for personnel. Although Truman did not bring a woman into his cabinet following the retirement of Frances Perkins from the Labor Department, he did appoint Frieda Hennock to the Federal Communications Commission, the first woman to serve as a commissioner of an independent regulatory agency. President Eisenhower appointed Oveta Culp Hobby, wartime head of the WAC, to head the Federal Security Administration, and when Congress created the Department of Health, Education and Welfare, Hobby became its first secretary.[39]

As women trickled into administrative posts that were not exclusively concerned with women, the first women began to appear in diplomatic and judicial posts. Truman followed the lead of Franklin Roosevelt in assigning a woman to head an overseas legation by posting Eugenie Anderson to Denmark and Pearl Mesta to Luxembourg. In his turn, Eisenhower sent Clare Booth Luce to Italy, the first major embassy to be directed by a woman, and Frances E. Willis, a career foreign-service officer, to Switzerland. Subsequently she represented the United States in Norway and Ceylon. Following the footsteps of Mary Woolley, president of Mount Holyoke, who was a member of the U.S. delegation at the Geneva Disarmament Conference in 1932, Virginia Gildersleeve, dean of Barnard College, joined the U.S. delegation at the San Francisco conference in 1945. Building on those precedents, President Truman appointed Eleanor Roosevelt to represent the United States in the United Nations General Assembly and in the United Nations Economic and Social Organization (UNESCO). Subsequently, Truman appointed a number of women to other United Nations commissions, including Ruth Bryan Owen Rhode, Helen Gahagan Douglas, Anna Lord Strauss, and Dorothy Kenyon.[40]

In similar fashion, the appointment of Florence Allen, a justice of the Ohio Supreme Court, to the federal appeals bench in 1934 set a precedent for the appointment of other qualified women to the federal judiciary. Truman appointed Burnita S. Matthews, one-time attorney for the National Woman's Party, to be the first woman to sit as a justice of a U.S. district court. While these were token appointments, it was the case that the pool of women possessing either the administrative or legal experience was miniscule. It was also the case that once a post had been filled by a woman, that post might be regarded as a woman's post thereafter.[41]

Although the number of women occupying major federal posts remained small, women gained much experience in local politics. The nation's state legislatures included over 230 women in the early fifties. But the chief training grounds were county and state offices. The 10,000 women serving as county officers in 1952—as clerks, tax collectors and assessors, treasurers, recorders, auditors, registers of deeds, clerks of court, superintendents of schools, and judges of probate or orphan's courts—doubled by 1959. Herein lay a partial explanation for the change in the character of the women entering Congress during the fifties.[42]

Overall the political climate of the fifties did not impel women to mount the barricades. The causes that roused women at the start of the century had run their course. The NWTUL, so important before World War I, disbanded in the wake of World War II. The National Consumers' League, which had provided a platform for Florence Kelley, was seldom heard from. And the Women's Joint Congressional Committee—an aggressive agent of the social feminists in the 1920s—had become an information clearinghouse. In reviewing the status of women in the early sixties, Alice Rossi concluded there was "practically no feminist spark left among American women." Implicit in her assessment was the view of feminists as women organizing to correct a wrong. To a degree, the social feminists had worked themselves out of a job by the fifties. Protective legislation and the threat of protective legislation had eradicated or curbed the worst abuses of female labor. The NRA codes and the Fair Labor Standards Act had further reduced the exploitation of women and all but eliminated child labor. Finally the *Parrish* case had opened the way for effective sex-neutral protective legislation. Though all problems were not solved, the working conditions of most blue-collar workers were of an order the general public would tolerate.[43]

Furthermore, the general economic milieu was healthy. As Congress responded to the recommendations of the Council of Economic Advisors, created by the Full Employment Act of 1946, the economy acquired a degree of stability that benefitted all conditions and classes of men and women. Following Truman's election in 1948, Congress raised the minimum wage to 75 cents an hour and overhauled the Social Security program by raising the benefits to retired workers and by extending the coverage to an additional ten million workers. When the economy began to slump following the end of the Korean War, the new Eisenhower administration invoked a variety of countervailing measures that quickly righted the economy, creating the "Eisenhower Prosperity." With the president's support, Congress moved to affirm and tidy up the old New Deal social-welfare programs, while declining to venture into new areas. In particular, in 1954, Congress once more extended the Social Security system to yet another ten million workers and unemployment compensation to an additional four million persons. Despite the fact that the regulation of wages and hours and mother's pensions had initially been key concerns of social feminists, these reforms—all sex-neutral—were not regarded by women or society generally as feminist measures. The middle-class women moving into the labor force had yet to publicly identify problems that their new roles created.[44]

Women did, of course, express political concerns. The major issue at the federal level remained the ERA. On one side, Alice Paul promoted the amendment; on the other, Eleanor Roosevelt urged a campaign against discriminatory state laws. Although Congress rejected the ERA in 1950, the ERA did not go away. During the fifties, Katharine St. George became its chief advocate in Congress. In 1953 the amendment was again before Congress, supported enthusiastically by the National Federation of Business and Professional Women's Clubs, but once more the Hayden rider, ostensibly safeguarding protective legislation for women but in reality negating the basic principle of the ERA, was attached to it. The amendment surfaced in 1954, 1956, and 1957. Although President Eisenhower endorsed the proposal in 1957, as before, the ERA failed to muster the requisite congressional support.[45]

Women's political energies were diverted into other channels. As the seriousness of American involvement in Korea became apparent, a variety of writers urged a more activist role for women in defense matters. Other political issues included eligibility for jury duty and equal pay for equal work. Throughout the decade there were major expressions of concern about the quality of the nation's schools. Some echoed Arthur Bestor's devastating attack on the pervasive anti-intellectualism of the public schools; some focused more narrowly on the need to upgrade the teaching of mathematics and science following the launching of the first Soviet satellite. Rachel Carson's *Silent Spring* set in motion a movement to protect the environment. Most of all, the nation's attention was drawn to the gap between its ideals and practices as the Supreme Court in *Brown* v. *Topeka* (1954) repudiated the separate-but-equal principle and called for a racially desegregated society. These "big" issues claimed the attention of women as citizens but not as feminists.[46]

The major women's organizations, the National Business and Professional Women's Clubs and the League of Women Voters, operated at a distinct disadvantage relative to the pressure groups dominated by men. The political activity of men's organizations generally grew out of their vested interests as veterans, professionals, businessmen, industrialists, farmers, or laborers, and these interests were expressed through such organizations as the American Legion, the American Medical Association, the U.S. Chamber of Commerce, the National Association of Manufacturers, the American Farm Bureau Federation, the AFL, and the CIO. That each of these groups had an axe to grind gave their political activity a degree of intensity that led their constituencies to contribute large sums of money to support lobbying activities and to subsidize election campaigns.

The National Business and Professional Women's Clubs, with a relatively homogeneous membership, focused on job-oriented issues in which members had a vital stake. But because its membership tended to be salaried employees rather than owners or managers, it lacked the funds and prestige of the men's organizations. Further, it often had to operate by itself. For its part the League of Women Voters, with a heterogeneous membership of affluent educated women, was avowedly nonpartisan and committed to studying an issue and arriving at a consensus that would serve the general public interest. The national agenda of the league in the midfifties, for example, concerned individual liberty and foreign trade policy. This rational civic-interest approach of the league differentiated it not only from the National Business and Professional Women's Clubs and the various men's pressure groups but also from the social feminists of the Progressive era, who, having encountered a problem that roused them to anger—generally a woman-oriented problem—banded together to seek a remedy. Many of the social-feminist groups focused on a single interest; the league tackled a series of diverse problems. When the social feminists embraced general civic reform, they argued the principle that management of local civic affairs represented an extension of household management, an area of female expertise. Many of the problems they addressed were close at hand, confronted women in hundreds of communities, and lent themselves to local solutions. The reform agenda of the league in the 1950s, while no less significant, dealt with problems that were often more abstract, national or international in scope, and often lacking in the moral or ethical dimension of the concerns that reformers such as Jane Addams, Florence Kelley, Grace Abbott, Julia Lathrop, or Alice Hamilton had addressed. The strength of the league's lobbying rested not on its numbers or on the economic resources at its command but the thoughtfulness and intelligence of its positions.[47]

Ultimately the limits on women's political status during the fifties resulted from their lack of experience as administrators qualified to assume major policymaking posts in the political sector and from their lack of control over resources of the business sector.

A DIFFERENTIATED EDUCATION

Although American youth shared equally in access to the secondary schools—at least white youth did—the patterns of attendance and graduation and the curriculum and subject-matter choices of males and females remained substantially different; equal access did not assure equal educations. The student clientele of the fifties included the sons and daughters of the working class as well as of the middle class; curriculum changes gradually shifted the primary concern from college preparation to vocational training. Courses in social living, group guidance, personal problems, human relations, social adjustment, consumer buying, safety education, driver education, and home management were introduced to accommodate the needs of the non-college-bound student. The new curriculum provoked charges that the nation's high schools had become an educational wasteland.[48]

Despite the attention focused on the quality of secondary education, there was a growing realization that young men and women received markedly different educational experiences. An extensive survey in 1954 by the Educational Testing Service (ETS) indicated that males were more inclined to pursue academic curriculums than females by a ratio of four boys to three girls; boys outnumbered girls by a ratio of three to two in the general curriculum. Whereas boys had a two to one lead in vocational curriculums, young women led males by nearly four to one in commercial programs. Even among those deemed qualified to undertake college work (the top 30 percent of all senior students), boys had a greater propensity to choose the college-preparatory curriculum by a margin of 12 percentage points. Thus "about two out of five girls in the senior year of high school, in contrast to approximately one out of four boys," were enrolled in courses in which the primary emphasis was on the development of skills qualifying them for employment immediately after graduation.[49]

Comprehensive data on the subject-matter choices of girls enrolled in the various curriculums are lacking, but data for those students in the federal-aided vocational programs provide suggestive insights. For the most part only girls enrolled in home-economics programs—programs that prepared them for homemaking rather than paid employment. Of those girls who enrolled in trade and industry courses, most studied practical nursing, cosmetology, dressmaking, the operation of sewing machines, and food preparation or food handling; that is, they were training for employment in "female" jobs. Similarly, of students enrolled in the commercial curriculums, girls congregated in typing, shorthand, and general business courses, whereas boys tended to take bookkeeping, commercial law, and selling.[50]

The differences in preparation for college were especially apparent in mathematics and science. Of senior students, an ETS survey revealed, nearly half the boys but less than a tenth of the girls would complete more than six semesters of mathematics by the time they graduated. One fourth of the girls would have had two semesters or less. Similarly, substantial differences occurred in the amount of training in the sciences. Three fourths of the boys but only one half of the girls completed even three semesters of work in science. While girls outnumbered boys in biology courses, boys outnumbered girls 60 to 40 in chemistry and 80 to 20 in physics. In another critical area, foreign languages, the schools shortchanged both sexes, but boys were less encouraged to pursue the subject than girls. Inevitably the proportion of girls graduating from high school who were academically prepared for college was markedly smaller than the proportion of males.[51]

Although by the early 1950s working wives and mothers were "familiar and accepted figures," most teenage girls, nonetheless, took for granted that their future lives would be "centered chiefly, if not exclusively, around homemaking responsibilities." Their choice of curriculums in high school as well as their occupational leanings reflected the existing distribution of women in the labor market. Indeed their occupational preferences seemed "to be reinforced rather than altered by the vocational guidance and counseling available at the high school level." The ETS survey indicated that boys had a far higher expectation of attending college than girls. Of those youth in the top 30 percent in mental ability, only 62 percent of the girls, in contrast to 78 percent of the boys, expected to attend college. Of those in the top 10 percent of ability, one girl in ten had neither an interest in nor plans to attend college, whereas only one boy in twenty displayed such disinterest. For many young women the anticipation of marriage, motherhood, and homemaking was strong enough to deter them from investing more time, and money, in education beyond high school. The career preferences of young women who expected to enter the labor force immediately after high school focused heavily on office or clerical work, but even for those women who expected to attend college, interest focused on teaching, office or clerical work, and nursing or medical-technician's work. In evaluating the nation's schools, Bruno Bettelheim commented: "our educational system has ostensibly prepared them [women] for a kind of liberated marital and occupational life that in fact rarely exists in our society; at the same time it celebrates the values of an antiquated form of marriage inherited from a time when wives were prepared for little else." A girl is educated the same way as a boy, he noted, "but a girl is made to feel that she must undergo precisely the same training only because she may need it if she is a failure—an unfortunate who somehow cannot gain admission to the haven of marriage and motherhood where she properly belongs."[52]

From the perspective of the awakening feminist movement, the fifties was a disaster for women in higher education. According to this scenario, the proportion of women among college students declined from 47 percent in 1920 to 35.3 percent in 1960. Of the women's colleges of an earlier day, 5 had closed, 21 had become coeducational, and 2 had become junior colleges. Whereas in 1920 one doctorate in six was earned by a woman, by 1959 women received but one doctorate in ten. Critics argued that during a period in which women in Sweden, Britain, and France had expanded their role in higher education, American women had regressed. Indeed, the shock Betty Friedan experienced while interviewing women college students in the late fifties did much to shape her attack on the "feminine mystique."[53]

In reality women fared substantially better in the quest for baccalaureate degrees than feminists of a later period supposed. College enrollments from 1947 to 1955 were grossly distorted by the "veteran's bulge." Nevertheless, the proportion of women receiving first degrees as a percent of all women age 23 years climbed steadily from 6.2 in 1946 to 8.9 in 1950 and reached 10.0 in 1955. These figures reflect a changing labor market in which women as well as men found a baccalaureate a prerequisite to suitable employment. Yet one must recognize the fact that the number of women taking first degrees in the mid-fifties was but 17 percent of the number of girls who had graduated from high school four years earlier; the comparable figure for boys was 33 percent.[54]

The collegiate experience of women differed even more sharply from that of men than did their high-school experience. In the first instance, women differed from men in the type of school they preferred to attend. Women attended teacher's colleges in much larger proportions than did men. While women were underrepresented in the ranks of university graduates, they were overrepresented in liberal arts colleges. Although a majority of women attended coeducational institutions, the proportion of women securing an A.B. from women's colleges was far greater than the proportion of men securing an A.B. at men's colleges.[55]

The differences in the types of colleges women attended reflected the fields of study pursued by women. For many young women the postcollege employment possibilities shaped their fields of study. Thus, teaching attracted nearly two of every five women, and another one woman in seven qualified herself to teach although majoring in some other academic field. Home economics and the health sciences each attracted one woman in fourteen. In fact, women students almost completely dominated enrollments in home economics, library science, and education. Reflecting their traditional roles as bearers of culture, a disproportionate number of women majored in "cultural" subjects, such as foreign languages, literature, and fine arts. By the same token, women almost completely ignored engineering, the single most important field for men interested in the natural sciences. These enrollment patterns indicate that undergraduate women in the fifties were nearly as tradition-driven as their high-school peers who entered the job market directly.[56]

Approximately the same proportion of women holding baccalaureates went on to earn master's degrees as men with baccalaureates. But there the similarity ended. While a few women might be found in most areas of study, two thirds of all master's degrees awarded them were earned in education; four fifths, in one or another of five fields: education, English, home economics, nursing, and fine arts. This concentration, far more intense than that at the undergraduate level, seriously restricted the areas in which these talented women students might pursue doctorates or enter professional careers.[57]

While it is the case that the percentage of doctorates awarded to women had fluctuated since the start of the century, the percentage of women earning baccalaureates who subsequently earned doctorates had climbed slowly but steadily, and it continued to do so during the fifties. The fluctuations in the proportion of all doctorates awarded to women reflected chiefly the increasing attraction of the doctorate to males. Indeed, as important as the structural changes in the American economy were in creating a large number of white-collar employments for women, those same changes generated a flood of managerial and professional positions for which baccalaureate and graduate degrees provided an entrée for men.[58]

Women's pursuit of doctoral degrees in the fifties was shaped by three factors. First, marriage served as a potent deterrent to women. Of women who received baccalaureate degrees in June 1955, the proportion of single women enrolled full-time in school six months later was 12 percent; of married women, 4 percent; of those with children, 2 percent. Women aspiring to marry and raise a family were loath to invest time and money in pursuit of graduate degrees. Second, the knowledge that men were preferred in top positions, "even in occupations in which women predominate," also inhibited women, married or single, from investing in an advanced degree. Put another way, males in general secured greater rewards from advanced degrees than did women in general. *Who Should Go to College?*, a study directed by Byron Hollinshead, documented that among those youth with intellectual potential for earning a doctorate, one of 30 men did so but only one of 300 women. This differential greatly affected the pool of women available for leadership roles in public and private sectors of society.[59]

The debate over the kind of education that best equipped a young woman for her role as an adult continued through the fifties. One line of analysis championed women's liberal-arts colleges on the grounds that such colleges freed young women from competition with males, enabling the women to concentrate on preparing themselves for responsible leadership in adult life. Others followed Lynn White in insisting that the differences between men and women required a college curriculum geared to distinctively feminine abilities, interests, and functions. Still others, Louis William Norris, for example, argued that collegiate education should encourage those women who sought paid employment "to choose work as a means of self-expression and personal enrichment" for themselves rather than for material gains alone.[60]

The fifties did not produce a revolution in women's education; there was no quantum leap forward, but neither was there regression. By 1960 there was an awareness of the differences between the educational experiences of men and women that had not existed earlier and a growing awareness of the implications those differences held for women and for society.

BLACK WOMEN

While white women confronted the milieu of the "feminine mystique," black women were gripped by the struggle over civil rights. Already sensitized to their second-class citizenship, black Americans were determined not only to hang on to the modest gains they had scored during the war but to press for a fuller measure of equality. The white middle class, too, was aware of what Gunnar Myrdal, the Swedish social economist, termed "The American Dilemma." Published in 1944, Myrdal's study noted that the "Negro problem" assumed "varying forms and intensity in the different regions of the country and among diverse groups of the American people." The "Negro problem" could not be shunted aside in the aftermath of the war. President Truman's special Committee on Civil Rights noted that the American "promise of freedom and equality" still awaited "complete realization." It was clear, moreover, that "the gulf" between America's "principles" and "practices" affected a significant population.[61]

Because white Americans begrudged admitting minority people to a full share in mainstream society, blacks were compelled to make a life of their own. Racial, cultural, economic, and social differences as well as geography separated the two communities. In these circumstances black women tended to subordinate their interests as women to their concern for the welfare of the black community. Their lives were defined in part by the values of Anglo-American society. Their status in the mainstream society continued to be less a function of their sex than of their race. Challenging the Anglo-American establishment to extend the principles of equal protection of the law to black Americans, the black community sensitized the entire nation to the issues of civil rights.

A variety of measures underscored the disabilities under which black Americans—men and women alike—operated in 1950. Whites used a variety of stratagems to deny blacks the right to vote. In many states, statute law excluded them from public facilities, while custom expanded the areas in which segregation restricted their freedom. A pattern of segregated housing in northern cities resulted in de facto segregation in neighborhood schools, while statute law mandated segregated schools in most southern and border states. North or South, blacks were restricted to a narrow range of relatively unskilled and semiskilled employments. At the end of World War II, in Washington, D.C., which prided itself as the center of the free world, a black could not secure a room in a downtown hotel, could not be served a meal in a first-class restaurant, could not attend a downtown movie or theater. A black who chose to locate in Washington faced a choice of homes in an overcrowded, substandard, and segregated neighborhood; his children would attend overcrowded, inferior, segregated schools; his family's health would depend on medical agencies, which, if they treated blacks at all, did so on a segregated basis. Much of this was irrational. For example, the Daughters of the American Revolution seated audiences at Constitution Hall without distinctions of color but excluded black performers from their stage; the commercial theater, on the other hand, permitted blacks to perform on stage but refused to seat them as patrons.[62]

By 1950 the nation was sensitive to the problems of the blacks. Several factors were at work. The churches—Protestant and Catholic—had begun to extend the doctrines of the "social gospel" to the black and his problems. So, too, southern liberals were speaking out, notably the Southern Regional Council and the Southern Council for Human Welfare. Other impersonal forces transformed "the peculiar problem" of the South into a national problem. First was the northern migration of blacks, so that by 1950 nearly half lived outside the South. Second, the cold war made racial discrimination "grist for the Communist propaganda mills." In these terms the

United States could no longer ignore discrimination as "the South's problem," nor, in terms of the cold war, could it afford to tolerate racial discrimination while claiming to lead the free world.[63]

As early as 1946, President Truman's Commission on Higher Education
warned with respect to the status of blacks: "There will be no fundamental
correction of the total condition until segregation legislation is repealed."
From then to 1955 the executive and judicial branches took the lead in
promoting reform. Among the major milestones was the Report of the
President's Committee on Civil Rights (1947), which sketched the dimensions of the minority problem and proposed a variety of solutions. In
response, President Truman in his inaugural address called for fair-employ-
ment-practices legislation, the outlawing of lynching and the poll tax, fairness in elections, and a permanent civil-rights commission. Unable to persuade Congress to adopt his proposals, Truman used his authority as president
to issue two far-reaching executive orders, one ending discrimination in
federal employment, the other directing an end to segregation in the armed
forces.[64]

By contrast, President Eisenhower, who had little use for those who
"believed that legislation alone could institute instant morality," nevertheless believed that every citizen had a right to vote. Accordingly, he proposed a civil-rights act aimed at "securing and protecting" the right to vote.
Although extremely modest in scope, the Civil Rights Act of 1957 was the
first such law to be enacted by Congress since Reconstruction. A second
act in 1960 provided for the appointment of "voter-referees" to assure that
qualified individuals were permitted to register, to receive a ballot, and to
have it counted. In addition, the president used his considerable personal
influence to terminate much informal segregation in the District of
Columbia.[65]

The judiciary was even more aggressive in promoting civil rights. As
early as 1940 the U.S. Supreme Court held that blacks could not be excluded
from juries because of their color. In *Smith* v. *Allwright,* the Court, reversing
earlier rulings, prohibited further use of white primaries, the most for-
midable of all the disfranchising devices. Although between 1940 and 1947
the percentage of blacks who qualified to vote rose by 2 to 12 percentage
points, the Deep South "by one means or another including intimidation
and terror" continued to prevent blacks from registering and voting. Other
judicial actions declared restrictive covenants—which limited the housing
available to blacks—invalid and barred segregated dining cars on interstate
trains. While the Court's decisions were widely ignored, the law was beginning to shift from the promotion of segregation to the prohibition of it.[66]

The area that caused the Court to reassess the meaning of "equal
protection of the laws" was education. In *Plessy* v. *Ferguson,* the Court,
while permitting segregation, expressly made equality a necessary condi-

tion of that separateness. Beginning in the late 1930s, in a series of cases involving graduate and professional education, the Court confronted the issue of inequality—cases in which specific benefits enjoyed by white students were denied to black students with the same qualifications. Thus, in 1938 the Court held it impermissible for a state to pay the tuition costs of black students at out-of-state schools in order to maintain lily-white colleges within the state. In *Sweatt* v. *Painter* (1950), the Court declared that separate graduate and professional schools for blacks in and of themselves failed to offer an education "substantially equal" to that available to white students; later in *McLaurin* v. *Oklahoma,* the Court ruled there was no equality when students were segregated in the classrooms, the cafeterias, and the libraries. Such situations "impair and inhibit his ability to study, engage in discussion and exchange views with other students, and, in general, to learn his profession." In consequence of these decisions, 23 public graduate and professional schools began to accept black as well as white students.[67]

Next the Court began to confront "the effect of segregation itself on public education" in asking whether "segregation of children in public schools solely on the basis of race, even though the physical facilities and other 'intangible' factors may be equal," deprives the children of the minority group of equal educational opportunities. On reviewing the arguments in *Brown* v. *Board of Education of Topeka* (1954), the Court concluded unanimously that "in the field of public education," at least, "separate but equal" had no place. Segregated schools were "inherently unequal." Implicit in its statement was that any *publicly authorized* or *publicly permitted* racial segregation would be unconstitutional. The decision, "the most momentous and far-reaching of the century" thus far, was not self-executing. For a year the nation awaited the implementation order, which was issued in May 1955. Although a number of school districts in border states integrated their schools without awaiting the implementation order, conservative southerners began to resist compliance with the 1955 order.[68]

Over the course of the next decade, Harry Byrd of Virginia, Orval Faubus of Arkansas, Ross Barnett of Mississippi, and George Wallace of Alabama, among others, directed campaigns of "massive resistance." Senator Byrd revived the pre–Civil War doctrine of "interposition" of state authority to prevent implementation of the Court's order, while 96 southern congressmen, nearly the whole of the southern contingent, joined in a "Declaration of Constitutional Principles" denouncing the Court's usurpation of the powers of the state and urged the use of "every lawful means" to resist its implementation. Southern state legislatures joined in the attack. The Louisiana legislature moved to withhold funds from integrated schools; Georgia made it a felony offense for a school official to spend tax money on an integrated school; while Mississippi made it unlawful for students to attend integrated schools. Other measures involved the dismantling of public schools or at least the organization of private schools for white children. White Citizens' Councils directed economic reprisals against blacks who actively campaigned to desegregate the schools and against whites who urged compliance with the *Brown* decision. By September 1956, defiance of the Supreme Court was general. The Court was further isolated as President Eisenhower withheld his support and failed to speak out for compliance.[69]

Attempts to integrate schools in the Deep South occasioned violence, much of it on college campuses. The first major riot accompanied the effort of Autherine Lucy, a black woman, to enter the University of Alabama at Tuscaloosa as a graduate student. Backed by a federal court order, she enrolled only to be expelled by the regents. Under similar conditions, Charlayne Hunter and Hamilton Holmes integrated the University of Georgia and Vivian Malone, the University of Alabama. Hunter and Malone became the first black students to receive degrees from those schools. The critical test came in Little Rock, Arkansas, where Daisy Bates, president of the local NAACP, led the effort to enroll nine black youngsters in Central High School. After a "hysterical, shrieking, and belligerent" white mob forced removal of the children, President Eisenhower ordered 1,000 paratroopers to reestablish order and to carry out the Court's order. Governor Faubus responded by closing Little Rock's public schools for the following school year. During the period, 1956 to 1959, further school integration virtually halted.[70]

Despite the campaign of "massive resistance," the NAACP kept up an unremitting pressure on school officials to abandon de jure segregation, and in the fall of 1959 Little Rock reopened its schools, while Houston, Raleigh, Knoxville, Richmond, and Roanoke admitted blacks to schools with white students. But by and large the only systems that integrated were those in which the black population was tiny. In the autumn of 1962, eight years after the *Brown* decision, of 2,800,000 black school children in the 11 states of the former Confederacy, only 13,000 attended classes with white students.[71]

OTHER AMERICANS

While President Truman's special Committee on Civil Rights focused on the black community, it also reported that one in five Americans spoke a language other than English at home, and it reminded the nation of its oldest minorities—the American Indians and the Hispanics of the Southwest—of its Asian Americans, and of its newest group, the Puerto Ricans.

Sensitized by the black civil-rights movement, these other Americans began to insist that America's principles and practices be brought into greater congruence. Inevitably these minority women also began to examine their status as women.

Hispanic Americans

The Hispanic population became larger and more diverse in the fifties. The Mexican Americans, increasingly termed Chicanos, grew in numbers and became more widely dispersed. In addition, a small Puerto Rican population mushroomed to become a major element of New York City's population.

Mexican Americans   During the fifties the composition of the Mexican American population changed. An increasing proportion were born in the United States—a circumstance that promoted Anglo-American influences. Mexican traditions, however, were reinforced by the addition of legal immigrants who averaged 30,000 a year or more during the 1950s; by illegal immigrants whose numbers were imprecise but certainly exceeded the number of legal migrants; and, from 1942 to 1964, by temporary workers called *braceros.*[72]

The legal migrants came in family groups, the number of males and females in balance. Of the family heads, 80 percent were laborers, private-household workers, or service workers; only 10 percent were white-collar employees. While the Chicano community in Los Angeles was the principal destination, they also sought out the Chicano enclaves in Illinois, Michigan, Nebraska, Kansas, and Ohio. The illegal migrants, termed variously *mojados* or wetbacks, had a solid impact, too. During the years 1947 to 1955 some 4,300,000 *mojados* were apprehended and deported; in the mid-1950s the number reached 1,000,000 a year. Despite the deportations, hundreds of thousands eluded apprehension. Bearers of traditional culture, they sought refuge among the Chicanos to escape detection.[73]

For over two decades the *braceros* provided a large part of the migrant labor force. First entering the United States in 1942, the number of *braceros* ranged from a low of 30,000 in the 1940s to an average of 430,000 in the late 1950s. Coming chiefly from isolated villages of central Mexico, they were bearers of the traditional culture; on the other hand their influence was restricted, for generally the males came alone, worked in gangs, and returned to Mexico. Many of them subsequently returned to the United States with their families to become permanent residents.[74]

The status of Chicano women continued to be defined more by the socioeconomic circumstances of their community than by their sex. Although the Chicano farm worker captured public attention, in 1970 less than 10 percent of the males and less than 3 percent of the women engaged in such work. For those who did, life was grim. Requiring vast quantities of low-paid hand labor, farm owners of the Southwest recruited workers in excess of their needs to ensure that the job got done on time; the wages barely permitted a subsistence living even when husband, wife, and children worked together in the fields. In Colorado beet fields, for example, half the migrant families made do in one- and two-room shacks, 5 to 11 persons sharing a room. Public-health authorities noted high rates of infant mortality, high incidence of tuberculosis, active malaria, rickets, arthritis, and rheumatism. One group of 140 families in the Arkansas River valley of Colorado lost 308 children; in Saginaw County, Michigan, Chicanos, who constituted but 1.5 percent of the population, contributed 25 percent of the hospitalized tuberculosis patients. Ordinarily children worked in the fields during the fall months, entered school after Christmas, and withdrew two months early in spring as their families headed north once more. Few northern communities provided educational programs for these children. Welfare officials often refused assistance to Chicanos. At best Chicanos enjoyed limited access to schools, libraries, doctors, and hospitals. Underpaid, overcharged, cheated, and discriminated against, the Chicano farm laborer and his family, if not "the most thoroughly underprivileged group in American life," had few rivals.[75]

Nor did the Mexican American community share fully in the benefits of the civil-rights movement. Living in ethnic enclaves in which traditional values were continuously reinforced by new arrivals from old Mexico, the Chicanos were less acculturated than black Americans and so were less equipped to participate in the mainstream society. Kept restricted to a narrow range of social contacts with other Hispanic women, Chicanas had little opportunity to develop ties with Anglo-American women.

Puerto Ricans   A second Hispanic American minority, the Puerto Ricans, made a token appearance before 1945. First attracted to the United States during World War I by the availability of jobs, nearly 70,000 had moved to the mainland by 1940, the overwhelming majority to New York City. Following World War II the Puerto Rican community mushroomed, reaching 300,000 in 1950 and approaching 1,000,000 by 1960. The Puerto Ricans uniformly secured poor housing in New York; landlords failed to make repairs. While the "alley ways and streets [were] filthy," living conditions usually were better than those left behind. Refrigeration was generally available in New York, and electricity, running water, and toilets were universally available.[76]

The Puerto Rican "immigrant" woman had a unique position, since by the terms of the Jones Act of 1917 she was an American citizen. Yet in terms of her culture she was also foreign. Class differences combined with racial differences precluded close ties between Puerto Ricans and other Roman Catholics. Although located chiefly on the fringes of Harlem, the Puerto Ricans and blacks viewed one another with suspicion. In brief, the Puerto Rican was isolated in New York City and became the new mudsill of New York's economic life.[77]

A peculiar problem of the Puerto Ricans centered on race. If white, the Puerto Rican had to identify with Anglo-American culture; if black, to identify with the black community and to accept the status thereof. Particularly troublesome was the problem of the *grif* or *indio* (an individual of mixed-blood), who in Puerto Rico had held an intermediate position, regarding herself as a notch above the Puerto Rican black. On the mainland, however, Anglo-Americans regarded her as black and classified all Puerto Ricans—white, black, or mixed—as different from other Americans.[78]

In many ways the values and practices of the Puerto Ricans, with respect to family matters, were like those of the Mexicans. The extended family was the norm, kinship providing the "social hub" of Puerto Rican society. Ostensibly, power rested with the male—the despotic father–husband. Family obligations weighed heavily; older people and the ritual kin (*compadre* and *comadre*) were taken seriously; nepotism was both expected and approved. While boys had much freedom, girls in the upper class were protected by chaperonage, but those in the lower class received little supervision. Although in many parts of Puerto Rico consensual marriage was the norm, in the rural areas such relationships ordinarily were as stable as legal ones; in the urban areas, they were unstable.[79]

In sharp contrast to most immigrant groups, Puerto Rican women migrated in larger proportions than men by a ratio of 100 women to 63 men. The women migrants tended more often to be white than black; most were in the age range 18 to 29. Of those over 18 years of age, two thirds were legally married, another 6 percent had entered consensual marriages, 8 percent were widowed or divorced, and 11 percent were unmarried. Only half of the women had as much as six and one-half years of schooling. Most of these women had come from urban areas—San Juan or Ponce. Older women were often skilled operatives; the younger women, white-collar or semiskilled workers. Thus, even before they left for the mainland, Puerto Rico women were far more assertive and sophisticated than were the Chicanas in the barrios of southern Texas. Women—especially those who came alone—found New York to be "a place of new freedom," free of the restrictions of Latin culture.[80]

Inevitably Hispanic traditions were challenged and weakened. Whereas in San Juan or Ponce a husband lost status if his wife worked for wages, in New York he learned to live off her income when he could not find a job of his own. In Puerto Rico a wife might escape the home only to make a necessary purchase or to attend church, however in New York she enjoyed a greater degree of freedom. As one woman put it: "Whether I have a husband or not I work. So I do what I want, and if my husband dare to complain, I throw him out. That is the difference; in Puerto Rico I should have to stand for anything a man asks me to do because he pays the rent. Here I belong to myself." Males acquiesced, but not without complaint: "Women get lost with liberty they have up here and many, not all, become bitches." Old ways, though, were not forgotten. Where the husband earned enough, the wife often stopped working, losing opportunities for contacts with people outside her own apartment. Soon she felt closed in. Compared to Mexican women, the studies of Oscar Lewis indicated, Puerto Rican women were more aggressive, outspoken, and even more violent. Compared to Anglo-American women, Puerto Rican women lived restricted lives.[81]

Generational conflicts followed the usual pattern of immigrant communities. The American-born son or daughter often developed a self-reliant, aggressive, competitive attitude and became estranged from his or her parents and culture. In responding to peer, rather than family, values, the mainland-born son or daughter seemed disrespectful to the parents. Relatively, a substantial number of Puerto Rican youth married outside their ethnic community, an indication of a high degree of cultural assimilation. Family ties weakened.[82]

Living "on the cultural margins of two worlds," the Puerto Rican in New York gained greater personal freedom while losing emotional security. Men and women became less bound to rigid moral standards and entered a world in which people neither knew nor cared much about one another. Relations between husband and wife tended to be distorted as wives found readier access to jobs than did husbands, altering the dependency relationship. Parents felt upstaged by sons and daughters who gained access to jobs closed to themselves.[83]

Asian Americans

America's Asian American communities—separated from one another by language, cultural traditions, and historical development—followed separate paths. The Chinese American community acquired significant accretions while developing a stability it had seldom enjoyed prior to the war. The Japanese American group emerged from the "relocation camps" under the leadership of its American-born members and faced an uncertain future.

Chinese Americans   By the end of World War II, the future of the Chinese American community lay with the American-born. While the latter were not integrated into the mainstream of American society, they were far more American in their life-style than the foreign-born Chinese. The young people of both sexes were relatively well educated. The younger children participated in Boy Scouts and Girl Scouts; the parents, in PTA. More and more the home was separated from the family business. A majority of the young women worked prior to marriage. Mixed dancing and dating were no longer condemned. Except on social occasions, women ordinarily wore American dress; likewise, they got permanent waves. The youth resisted arranged marriages; American standards of childrearing were followed. Older traditional Chinese shook their heads, but they acquiesced in the new social norms.[84]

Between 1945 and 1950, the Chinese American community was augmented by three new groups: some 6,000 Chinese war brides and their babies; several thousand separated wives along with their teenage children; and Chinese students stranded in the United States when the Communists drove Chiang Kai-shek from the mainland to Taiwan. The three groups possessed quite different backgrounds. The war brides were young; few had much formal education. While the husband, often China-born, had served in the American army and had lived for a time in the United States, the war bride possessed a limited understanding of Anglo-American practices and values. In removing to the United States the family relationships altered sharply. In the process of acculturation, the wives relied on their husband's knowledge, often imperfect, of home furnishings, child care, and even feminine fashions. While the women bobbed their hair and got permanents, they did not style it. They carried handbags but did not wear gloves or hats. Husbands, who in China would have thought it improper, regularly did the family shopping. Economic necessity forced many of these women to work outside the home in their husband's business or in factories or canneries.[85]

The separated families experienced sharp reversals in sex roles and serious problems of adjustment. Women who had been separated from their husbands for as long as 18 to 25 years and who had managed their families alone, were uprooted from friends and family to begin a new life in America with husbands whom they knew chiefly through correspondence. Coming from the relatively westernized cities of southern China, these women had to adjust to the socially conservative Chinatowns of the United States. Husbands who had lived for years in the all-male environment of the sojourners suddenly became heads of families with teenage children they scarcely knew and who had experiences and views utterly strange to the fathers.[86]

The stranded students brought still another element to the Chinese community. Mostly in their late 20s or early 30s, they had not yet entered on careers. With no relatives at hand, they chose mates from among the other stranded Chinese, their courtships following the American style. The young women, westernized in views, enjoyed higher status in America than in China; many took jobs and insisted on a large measure of personal freedom; their husbands ended by sharing in the housework. Of necessity the new families were nuclear, not extended.[87]

The dominant group, however, consisted of the established families of American-born Chinese. By 1950, developments in China made it clear that there could be no "going home" to the mainland. Ties with Taiwan, however, permitted a limited reinforcement of Chinese cultural values. For the time being, then, many established families stood with one foot in American culture and the other in the Chinese. The use of Chinese food— especially rice and seasonings—continued at the main meal, while American-style breakfasts and lunches were adopted. Special efforts were made to retain a command of Chinese, particularly since it enhanced one's occupational mobility. So, too, older Chinese took pains to maintain memberships in all-Chinese associations, although younger Chinese also took part in nonethnic organizations. Reflecting old-country values, Chinese-American families sent their sons to school, even to college, in ever-larger proportions; reflecting American values, they also sent their daughters. When the Chinese Americans married, they did so within the Chinese community. Relatively unconcerned with family lineage, they married for companionship and affection; acquainted with birth control, they limited the size of their families. While the Chinese Americans became highly acculturated, they did not allow themselves to be assimilated by the mainstream society.[88]

Japanese Americans   As they were released from internment in the last months of the war, the Japanese Americans encountered bumper stickers declaring "No Japs Wanted in California"; and some American Legion posts refused membership to Nisei veterans. In resuming civilian life, most Japanese-Americans had to start over. Nearly two thirds returned to the West Coast, while one fifth moved east of the Rocky Mountains, Chicago becoming the chief center.[89]

The achievement of the Nisei in rebuilding their lives was hailed by the press in captions such as "Success Story" and "Outwhiting the Whites." As the Issei had sent their sons to college in far greater proportions than their daughters, Nisei women found the adjustments challenging. As children, most had lived in predominantly Japanese American neighborhoods where their socialization had been supported by a community that shared a common language, customs, and culture. Their parents had raised them in accord with Japanese values: "duty and obligation" guided the young woman's behavior and life-style. Even so, many Issei parents had acquiesced in letting their children forsake the Buddhist faith for Christianity. When the Nisei married, the spouse was usually another Nisei of long acquaintance. The Nisei family reflected much of the old tradition: the husband was the decision maker; the wife's chief concern was her family. Yet here, too, they accommodated new values and practices that carried them still further from Japanese tradition. Typically the family had two children. Nisei mothers lived vicariously through their children; to have a public role was enervating, for to be effective she must be aggressive, assertive, and visible, whereas her girlhood training had stressed passivity, submission, and modesty.[90]

In the postwar environment, Nisei culture underwent significant changes. While as children many had lived in rural areas—their parents engaged in horticulture—as middle-aged adults they lived in urban communities where they built new lives in business and industry, pursuing economic opportunities wherever they might be found. In these circumstances the Sansei, the third generation, grew up in an Anglo-American milieu and gained a far greater acquaintance with the values and practices of Anglo-America than their parents had possessed at the same stage in life.[91]

American Indians

American Indians emerged from the war years with a familiarity with white culture and a degree of self-confidence they had never previously possessed. They began by demanding the right to vote, up-to-date health-care facilities, increased job opportunities, better schools, and an end to discriminatory legislation.[92]

For its part, the federal government, in a reversal of policy, embraced "termination," an effort to end federal responsibility for Indian affairs. While the Indian Reorganization Act was not repealed, the Bureau of Indian Affairs ceased making student loans; it began transferring responsibility for health and education programs to the states. During the mid-fifties the Eisenhower administration ended federal responsibility for several tribes, including the Menominees in Wisconsin and the Klamaths in Oregon. Termination proved disastrous. Tribal governments complained that they had not been consulted; some states were unprepared, and perhaps unwilling, to assume the additional burdens. Both the Menominees and the Klamaths, two of the most acculturated tribes, were thrown into disorganization by termination. By 1958 enthusiasm for termination eased, the Interior Secretary Fred Seaton promised that thereafter termination would be initiated only where tribal leadership thoroughly understood and consented to the policy.[93]

The postwar years brought greatly increased access to education. Returning veterans pressed their younger siblings to attend school and called on the government to provide the facilities. In responding, the government emphasized vocational training, utilizing off-reservation boarding schools. Students who attended the Sherman Institute in Riverside, California, or the Intermountain Indian School in Brigham City, Utah, usually entered the urban labor market. Among the least well educated women in America, Indian women made dramatic progress. Of Indian women born in 1905 or earlier, the median level of education was 7.5 years and scarcely one in seven completed high school. The cohort born between 1946 and 1950 were destined to become the first generation of Indian women in which a majority completed high school.[94]

The Jewish Community

Post–World War II society pulled Jewish women in several, sometimes opposite, directions. Memories of the Holocaust and the formation of Israel strengthened Orthodoxy. The tiny Hasidic group, located chiefly in Brooklyn, hewed to their traditional Orthodoxy, the woman subordinated to her father or husband as in an Eastern European *shtetl* of two centuries earlier. Matchmakers arranged marriages; educational opportunities remained limited; Yiddish was the vernacular language; dress was distinctive; dietary laws were rigorously observed. Some American-born Jews turned to Orthodoxy. While comfortable with middle-class society, in religious matters, they embraced tradition: they observed the *mitzvahs,* revived the use of Hebrew in the service, consulted a matchmaker (chiefly youths seeking mates), and barred women from the rabbinate. As in earlier days, the Orthodox woman was supreme within her home and had a role in the Jewish educational structure.[95]

At the other extreme, the prevailing secularism of the age drew many Jews into the mainstream of Gentile America. Some changed their names to eradicate evidence of their Jewish antecedents, and often they married outside the Jewish faith. They adopted the life-style of the predominant American middle class. In the middle were those who acknowledged their Judaism. Reform and Conservative Judaism drew closer. Reform Jews revived the use of Hebrew in the service and the wearing of *yarmulkas* by congregants and a prayer shawl by the rabbi; Conservative Jews expanded the use of English in the service and placed more emphasis on social concerns in the sermon.[96]

By 1960 the values that society invoked in socializing women and in shaping their roles were in sharp variance with the realities of their lives. A "feminine mystique," while not expressly enjoining piety, purity, and submissiveness, did assume that the major focus of most women's lives should be their home and family. This entailed sharply differentiated sex roles and a sexual division of labor. This was reflected in the more-restricted public roles of women whether as voter or officeholder. It was reflected in the reluctance of public officials—even of many women's groups—to actively embrace an ERA. It was affirmed in the disproportionate number of women concentrated in the predominantly female occupations, as well as the markedly lower labor-force rates of married women compared to single or divorced women, and in the inverse relationship between labor-market participation and the presence of children in the household. It was reflected in the sexually differentiated curricular and enrollment patterns of women at both the high-school and college level.

But if women seemed immersed in homemaking and childrearing roles in the fifties, there was a strong undercurrent that challenged these roles as being the undisputed center of the lives of the great majority of women. By 1960, structural changes in the nation's economy necessitated the employment of married women to meet the demand for female work-ers. Although a majority of the married women were not in the labor force, a majority of the female labor force consisted of married women. Although women lagged men in access to the kinds of academic programs that prepared them for positions of leadership, the proportion of women com-pleting undergraduate and graduate degrees continued to climb. Although "togetherness" frequently shaped family social life, the testimony of Clara Thompson, Mirra Komarovsky, and *Life's* reporting staff indicated that many women did not find the traditional roles invariably fulfilling. Indeed, the "thoughtful young woman" of 1960—freed from "the tyranny of her body," from "the tyranny of ignorance," and from "the tyranny of poverty"—was dissatisfied with "a lot that women of other lands can only dream of." But her discontent, nonetheless, was "deep" and "pervasive."[97]

The experiences of the minority women varied substantially from those of Anglo-American women. Minority women acquired a visibility in the wake of the black civil-rights movement, and many legal barriers to polit-ical, economic, and social opportunities were removed. Among the Amer-ican Jewish, Chinese, and Japanese populations that traditionally had accorded high value to formal education, the young were able to secure as much education as their natural talent permitted. Among some Indians, such as the Navajo, whose wartime experiences underscored the value of literacy and formal education, traditional values were replaced by new ones. For others—the blacks and the Chicanos—de jure discrimination fell by the wayside, but public officials—federal, state, and local—were often slow to implement or enforce the civil-rights laws. Yet overall minority groups remained frustrated, less because the status quo continued than because progress came at a slower pace than desired. In terms of political rights and access to education, jobs, and public amenities—transportation, restaurants, hotels, theaters, and parks—minority women benefitted along with other members of their group. Even within a traditional setting, women as daughters, wives, and mothers benefitted as their fathers, brothers, and husbands gained new opportunities. In the course of working to promote expanded opportunities for their group, minority women, too, began to question their status as women.

By 1960 there was a broad undercurrent of discontent with women's status and a growing gap between the wife–mother roles assigned to women and the away-from-home roles that occupied an increasing proportion of women. At the same time, the discontents of the black community—over race not sex—were approaching the boiling point and becoming a national issue.

NOTES

[1] Bureau of the Census, *Statistical Abstract of the United States: 1964* (Washington: GPO, 1964), tab. 308.

[2] Ibid.

[3] Ibid. Susan Estabrook Kennedy, *If All We Did Was to Weep at Home: A History of White Working-Class Women in America* (Bloomington: Indiana University Press, 1979).

[4] The data is from the Bureau of the Census, *Statistical Abstract: 1964,* tab. 308. The calculations are mine.

[5] Ibid. Louise Kapp Howe, *Pink Collar Workers: Inside the World of Women's Work* (New York: Putnam, 1977). Cynthia F. Epstein, *Woman's Place: Options and Limits in Professional Careers* (Berkeley: University of California Press, 1970).

[6] Bureau of the Census, *Statistical Abstract: 1964,* tab. 308.

[7] National Manpower Council, *Womanpower* (New York: Columbia University Press, 1957), 9. Valerie Kincade Oppenheimer, *The Female Labor Force in the United States* (Westport: Greenwood, 1970), chap. 3. Bureau of the Census, *Statistical Abstract: 1964,* tab. 308.

[8] National Manpower Council, *Womanpower,* 108. Theodore Caplow, *The Sociology of Work* (New York: McGraw-Hill, 1964), 242. Oppenheimer, *Female Labor Force,* 109–11.

[9] Bureau of the Census, *Statistical Abstract of the United States: 1953* (Washington: GPO, 1953), tab. 220. Bureau of the Census, *Statistical Abstract of the United States: 1961* (Washington: GPO, 1961), tab. 27.

[10] Ibid.

[11] Bureau of the Census, *U.S. Census of Population, 1950,* vol. 2, *Characteristics of the Population, Part I, U.S. Summary* (Washington: GPO, 1953), tab. 102. Victor R. Fuchs, *How We Live: An Economic Perspective on Americans from Birth to Death* (Cambridge: Harvard University Press, 1983), chap. 5. Lois Wladis Hoffman and F. Ivan Nye, *Working Mothers* (San Francisco: Jossey-Bass, 1974). Robert Blood, "Employment of Married Women," *Journal of Marriage and the Family,* 27 (Feb. 1965): 43–47.

[12] Bureau of the Census, "A Statistical Portrait of Women in the United States," *CPR,* Special Studies P-23, no. 58 (Washington: GPO, 1976), tab. 7-5. Bureau of the Census, *Statistical Abstract: 1961* tab. 28.

[13] Bureau of the Census, *Census of Population: 1960, Subject Reports. Marital Status,* PC(2)-4E (Washington: GPO, 1966), tab. 6, p. 52.

[14] Bureau of Labor Statistics, *Handbook of Labor Statistics* (Washington: GPO, 1979), tab. 33.

[15] Ibid.

[16] Florence R. Kluckhohn, "American Women and American Values," *The Annals of America* (Chicago: Encyclopedia Britannica, 1952), 159–62. Philip Wylie, *Generation of Vipers* (New York: Holt, Rinehart & Winston, 1964[1942]), 194–217.

[17] Edward A. Strecker, *Their Mother's Sons* (Philadelphia: Lippincott, 1946). Amram Scheinfeld, *Women and Men* (New York: Harcourt Brace, 1944), 377.

[18] Sigmund Freud, "The Psychology of Women," in Sigmund Freud, *New Introductory Lectures on Psycho-Analysis,* trans. W. J. H. Sprott (New York: Norton, 1933), chap. 5. Mirra Komarovsky, *Women in the Modern World: Their Education and Their Dilemmas* (Boston: Little, Brown, 1953), 18.

[19] Helene Deutsch, *The Psychology of Women,* 2 vols. (New York: Grune & Stratton, 1944–1945), vol. 1, chaps. 5 and 8. See also Brenda S. Webster, "Helene Deutsch: A New Look," *Signs,* 10(1985): 553–71, for a more positive view of Deutsch.

[20] Ferdinand Lundberg and Marynia Farnham, *Modern Woman: The Lost Sex* (New York: Harper, 1947), 3, 10, 47.

[21] Karen Horney, "The Flight from Womanhood," *International Journal of Psycho-analysis* (1926) and "The Demise of the Vagina," International Journal of Psychoanalysis (1933). Karen Horney, *New Ways in Psychoanalysis* (New York: Norton, 1939), chap. 3. Clara M. Thompson, *On Women,* ed. Maurice R. Green (New York: New American Library, 1971).

[22] Margaret Mead, *Male and Female: A Study of the Sexes in a Changing World* (New York: Dell, 1968[1949]), 16–18, 278 ff.

[23] Komarovsky, *Women in the Modern World,* 48, 55, 67. Viola Klein and Alva Myrdal, *Women's Two Roles, Home and Work* (London: Routledge & Kegan Paul, 1956), 140.

[24] Thompson, *On Women,* 113 ff.

[25] Komarovsky, *Women in the Modern World,* 102, 104, 109, 112, 118. "American Woman's Dilemma," *Life,* 22(June 16, 1947): 105. "Changing Roles" *Life,* (Holiday Issue, Dec. 24, 1956): 111 ff. "Young Wives" *Newsweek,* 55(March 7, 1960): 57 ff. "Americana, The Roots of Home," *Time* (June 20, 1960): 14 ff. Other postwar assessments include Agnes Meyers, "Women Aren't Men," *Atlantic,* 186(Aug. 1950): 32–36. Reuben Hill, "The American Family: Problem or Solution," *AJS,* 53(Sept. 1947), 125–30.

[26] "American Woman's Dilemma," 109. Lundberg and Farnham, *Modern Women,* 210, 89.

[27] "American Woman's Dilemma," 102.

[28] Myrdal and Klein, *Women's Two Roles,* 10. Komarovsky, *Women in the Modern World,* 139, 61.

[29] Komarovsky, *Women in the Modern World,* 298. Myrdal and Klein, *Women's Two Roles,* 1, 24.

[30] Komarovsky, *Women in the Modern World,* 185. Myrdal and Klein, *Women's Two Roles,* 162–84. "American Woman's Dilemma," 110.

[31] Bureau of the Census, *Historical Statistics of the United States: Colonial Times to 1970,* Bicentennial ed., pt. 1 (Washington: GPO, 1975), ser. B 11–19, p. 50.

[32] Ibid., *CPR,* ser. P-23, no. 58, tab. 4-1. Bureau of the Census, *Historical Statistics: Colonial Times to 1970,* ser. B 11–19, p. 50.

[33] William E. Leuchtenberg, *A Troubled Feast* (Boston: Little, Brown, 1973), 73. Charles Frankel, "The Trouble with 'Togetherness,'" *NYT Magazine,* 27 Apr. 1958, sec. 6, p. 26. Margaret L. Lane, "Too Much Together," *Parent's Magazine,* 34(Feb. 1959): 36–37. Mabel M. Hagen, "Families that Play Together, Stay Together," *Parent's Magazine,* 29(Feb. 1954): 119. Elizabeth Pope, "Is a Working Mother a Threat to the Home?" *McCall's,* 82(July 1955): 29 ff.

[34] *NYT,* 30 Jan. 1962, p. 14, col. 8; 4 Oct. 1952, p. 9, col. 1; 28 Sept. 1952, p. 52, col. 4; 3 May 1952, p. 24, col. 8; and 4 Oct. 1950, p. 10, col. 5.

[35] Louise M. Young, "Why Do Women Vote the Way They Do?" *WHC,* 83(Nov. 1956): 46–47. Ruth Montgomery, "Will Women Elect a President Again?" *Cosmopolitan,* 140(May 1956): 90–93. "Women in National Politics," *Newsweek,* 45(May 9, 1955): 30–32. "Women and the Result?" *Newsweek,* 48(Nov. 5, 1956): 29–30. Marion K. Sanders, "Women in Politics," *Harper's,* 211(Aug. 1955): 56–64. *NYT,* 13 Oct. 1960, p. 26, col. 3; 13 March 1960, p. 51, cols. 1, 2; 16 Aug. 1960, p. 15, col. 1; 8 Sept. 1960, p. 21, col. 4; 14 Sept. 1960, p. 39, col. 1; 11 Sept. 1960, p. 1, col. 14; 16 Sept. 1960, p. 17, col. 1; and 25 Sept. 1960, p. 57, cols. 1, 2. Theodore H. White, *The Making of the President 1960* (New York: Atheneum, 1961). Ithiel de Sola Pool, Robert P. Abelson and Samuel L. Popkin, *Candidates, Issues, and Strategies* (Cambridge: MIT Press, 1964), 18.

[36] Jane S. Jaquette, ed., *Women in Politics* (New York: Wiley, 1974), 36.

[37] Martin Gruberg, *Women in American Politics: An Assessment and Source Book* (Oshkosh: Academia, 1968), 125–26, 160–62, 165.

[38] Ibid., 134–39.

[39] Ibid., 141–44.

[40] Ibid., 144–47.

[41] *NYT,* 7 March 1934, p. 9, col. 3 and 18 Oct. 1949, p. 55, col. 2.

[42] Gruberg, *Women in American Politics,* 201. See also "Progress Report on Women in Government Policy-Making Posts," *Independent Woman,* 33(Jan. 1954): 4.

[43] Alice Rossi, "Equality Between the Sexes: An Immodest Proposal," *Daedalus,* 93(1964): 608.

[44] Harold G. Vatter, *The U.S. Economy in the 1950's An Economic History* (New York: Norton, 1963), especially chaps. 3 and 4.

[45] *NYT,* 26 Jan. 1950, p. 19, col. 2; 17 July 1953, p. 10, col. 4; and 17 Jan. 1957, p. 16, col. 4 and p. 17, col. 7.

[46] *NYT,* 8 July 1950, p. 16, col. 7; 2 Feb. 1951, p. 17, col. 6; and 12 July 1951, p. 28, col. 1. N. Palmer, "Ten Most Pressing Problems," *National Business Woman,* 36(Nov. 1957): 6. *NYT,* 7 May 1950, sec. 6, p. 22. A. Troth, "How We Won Jury Service in Georgia," *Independent Woman,* 33(Feb. 1952): 37–8. James C. Nix, "Equal pay for equal work," *MLR,* 74(Jan. 1952): 41–45. Dorothy P. Buck, "Colorado Women Go After Equal Pay," *Independent Woman,* 33(Sept. 1954): 330–32. Arthur Eugene Bestor, *Educational Wastelands* (Urbana: University of Illinois Press, 1953). Rachel Louise Carson, *Silent Spring* (Boston: Houghton Mifflin, 1962). Brown v. Board of Education of Topeka, 347 U.S. 483 (1954).

[47] *NYT,* 30 April 1954, p. 14, col. 4.

[48] See, for example, Mirra Komarovsky, "What Should Colleges Teach Women?" *Harper's,* 199(Nov. 1949): 33–37. M. J. Fisher, "Educating Women for What?" *Independent Woman,* 29(Aug. 1950): 231–32. Charles G. Spiegler, "Are Our Girls Getting a Boys' Education?" *NYT Magazine,* 14 May 1950, 29 ff. See also Komarovsky, *Women in the Modern World.*

[49] National Manpower Council, *Womanpower,* 176. Compare "Education for Women Surveyed by AAUW," *Journal of Home Economics,* 42(Feb. 1950): 119 ff.

[50] National Manpower Council, *Womanpower,* 175–77.

[51] Ibid., 178. James B. Conant, *The American High School Today* (New York: McGraw-Hill, 1959), 22–23, 120. Kenneth E. Brown, "National Enrollments in High School Science," *The Science Teacher* 23(March 1956): 89.

[52] National Manpower Council, *Womanpower,* 179–82. Conant, *American High School,* 180, 181–82. Bruno Bettelheim, "Growing up Female," *Harper's,* 225(Oct. 1962): 121.

[53] Bureau of the Census, *Historical Statistics, Colonial Times to 1970,* ser. H 751–65.

[54] National Manpower Council, *Womanpower,* 197–98.

[55] Ibid., 199–201.

[56] Department of HEW, *Earned Degrees Conferred 1960–61* (Washington: GPO, 1963), tab. 1.

[57] Ibid. Dael Lee Wolfle, *America's Resources of Specialized Talent* (New York: Harper, 1954), 229. National Manpower Council, *Womanpower,* 204.

[58] Bureau of the Census, *Historical Statistics, Colonial Times to 1970,* ser. H 751–65.

[59] Wolfle, *America's Resources of Specialized Talent,* 187. Byron Hollinshead, *Who Should Go to College?* (New York: Columbia University Press, 1952), 208.

[60] National Manpower Commission, *Womanpower,* 215. Louis William Norris, "How to Educate a Woman," *Saturday Review,* 37(Nov. 27, 1954): 9–10, 38–40. Norris was president of MacMurray College (for women).

[61] Gunnar Myrdal, *An American Dilemma,* 3rd ed. (New York: Harper, 1944). Report of the President's Committee on Civil Rights, *To Secure These Rights* (Washington: GPO, 1947), 3, 14, 15.

[62] Report of the President's Committee on Civil Rights, *To Secure These Rights,* 88–89.

[63] C. Vann Woodward, *The Strange Career of Jim Crow,* 3rd rev. ed. (New York: Oxford, 1974), 125–32.

[64] Ibid., 135. Executive Order 9980, *Federal Register,* 13(1948), 4311. Executive Order 9981, *Federal Register,* 13(1948), 4313.

[65] Charles C. Alexander, *Holding the Line: The Eisenhower Era, 1952–1961* (Bloomington: Indiana University Press, 1975), 194–97.

[66] Smith v. Texas, 311 U.S. 128 (1940). Smith v. Allwright, 321 U.S. 649 (1944). U.S. Commission on Civil Rights, *Political Participation* (Washington: GPO, May 1968), 8. Shelly v. Kraemer, 334 U.S. 1 (1948). Hurd v. Hodge, 334 U.S. 24 (1948). Henderson v. United States, 339 U.S. 816 (1950).

[67] Plessy v. Ferguson, 163 U.S. 537 (1896). Missouri ex rel Gaines v. Canada, 305 U.S. 337 (1938). Sweatt v. Painter, 339 U.S. 629 (1950). McLaurin v. Oklahoma State Regents, 339 U.S. 6 (1950).

[68] Brown v. Board of Education of Topeka, 347 U.S. 483 (1954), at 495. Brown v. Board of Education of Topeka, 349 U.S. 294 (1955).

[69] *NYT,* 12 March 1956. Arthur Larson, *Eisenhower, The President Nobody Knew* (New York: Scribner's, 1968), quotes the President as saying in 1957: "As a matter of fact, I personally think that the decision was wrong." In his memoirs, *The White House Years: Mandate for Change, 1953–56* (Garden City: Doubleday, 1963), 230, Eisenhower wrote: "There can be no question that the judgment of the Court was right."

[70] Woodward, *Strange Career of Jim Crow,* 163, 166. Alexander, *Holding the Line,* 197–200.

[71] Woodward, *Strange Career of Jim Crow,* 172–73.

[72] Vernon M. Briggs, Jr., Walter Fogel and Fred H. Schmidt, *The Chicano Worker* (Austin: University of Texas Press, 1977), 484.

[73] Matt S. Meier and Feliciano Rivera, *The Chicanos: A History of Mexican Americans* (New York: Hill and Wang, 1972), 203–209, chap. 13. Alejandro Portes, "Labor Functions of Illegal Aliens," *Society,* 14(Sept./Oct. 1977), 31–37, argues that only one third of the "illegals" are involved in agriculture, one third in goods-producing industries, and one third in service jobs.

[74] Meier and Rivera, *The Chicanos,* 150–67.

[75] Bureau of the Census, *Census of Population: 1970, Subject Reports, Persons of Spanish Origin,* PC(2)-1-C (Washington: GPO, 1973), tab. 32. Carey McWilliams, *Ill Fares the Land* (Boston: Little, Brown, 1942), 117–18, 354. The figures for Chicano farm workers are low; much farm work continues to be done by undocumented workers who fail to be enumerated by the Census Bureau and by contract laborers who are not subject to enumeration; the mechanization of agriculture since 1960 has also reduced the demand for farm labor.

[76] Bureau of the Census, *Census of Population: 1970, Subject Reports, Puerto Ricans in the U.S.,* PC(2) 1-E (Washington: GPO, 1973).

[77] C. Wright Mills, Clarence Senior, and Rose Kohn Goldsen, *The Puerto Rican Journey* (New York: Harper, 1950), 129–36.

[78] Ibid., 133. Patricia Cayo Sexton, *Spanish Harlem: An Anatomy of Poverty* (New York: Harper & Row, 1965), provides a view of life in the Puerto Rican section of New York City.

[79] Mills et al., *Puerto Rican Journey,* 8–10.

[80] Ibid., 37, 88.

[81] Ibid., 97.

[82] Joseph P. Fitzpatrick, *Puerto Rican Americans* (Englewood Cliffs: Prentice-Hall, 1971), 95. Piri Thomas, *Down These Mean Streets* (New York: Knopf, 1967), treats the generation conflicts.

[83] Mills et al., *Puerto Rican Journey,* 123. Fitzpatrick, *Puerto Rican Americans,* 95.

[84] Rose Hum Lee, *The Chinese in the United States of America* (Hong Kong: Hong Kong University Press, 1960). "Flower Drum Song" (1958), based on the novel of C. Y. Lee, captures the traumas of social change.

[85] Lee, *Chinese in the United States,* 219–25.

[86] Ibid., 203.

[87] Ibid., 235.

[88] Ibid.

[89] Leonard Dinnerstein and David M. Riemer, *Ethnic Americans, A History of Immigration and Assimilation* (New York: Dodd, Mead, 1975), 142, 148. Bureau of the Census, *Census of Population: 1970, Subject Reports. Japanese, Chinese, and Filipinos in the U.S.,* PC (2)-1G (Washington: GPO, 1973).

[90] "Success Story: Outwhiting the Whites," in *Newsweek,* 77(June 21, 1971): 24–25. Darrel Montero, "The Japanese-Americans: Changing Patterns of Assimilation Over Three Generations," *ASR,* 46(Dec. 1981): 829–39. Irene Fujitomi and Diane Wong, "The New Asian-American Woman," in *Asian-Americans: Psychological Perspectives,* ed. Stanley Sue and Nathaniel N. Wagner (Ben Lomond, CA: Science and Behavior Books, 1973), 258.

[91] Montero, "The Japanese-Americans," 836.

[92] William T. Hagan, *American Indians* (Chicago: University of Chicago Press, 1961), 158–59.

[93] Angie Debo, *A History of the Indians of the United States* (Norman: University of Oklahoma Press, 1970), 349, 382. Kirke Kickingbird and Karen Ducheneaux, *One Hundred Million Acres* (New York: Macmillan, 1973), present an Indian view of Menominee and Klamath termination.

[94] Bureau of the Census, *Census of Population: 1970, Subject Reports, American Indians,* PC(2)-1F (Washington: GPO, 1973), tab. 5, p. 36.

[95] *NYT,* 6 Mar. 1977, p. 54.

[96] Ibid., 31 Jan. 1977, p. 23.

[97] "Young Wives," *Newsweek,* 55(March 7, 1960): 57.

7

A New Frontier for Women: The 1960s

The 1960s, which began with the excitement and high hopes of John F. Kennedy's New Frontier, was marked by trauma and tragedy as first John Kennedy, then Martin Luther King, Jr., and finally Robert Kennedy were assassinated; American cities were ravaged by race riots; and Lyndon Johnson's Great Society withered as the United States lost its sense of direction in the morass of Vietnam. At the start of the decade there were intimations of malaise among middle-class women; by the decade's end a feminist movement—more correctly movements—had blossomed. Whether one examines the role of the schools in the socialization of women, the role of government in delineating the legal and political status of women, or the role of the economy in affording women a place in the labor force, one finds women being pushed and pulled by a complex of forces into a wider variety of public roles. To the extent that feminism shaped the political and economic roles of women in the sixties, it was the moderate feminism of *The Feminine Mystique* and the National Organization of Women (NOW) that did so. Late in the decade a grass-roots radical feminism provoked a reexamination of the role of the schools—elementary, secondary, and collegiate—in the shaping of sex roles. But throughout the sixties, it was the civil-rights campaign of black Americans that set the pace for the redefinition of women's rights.

BLACK REVOLUTION

The resistance of whites to school desegregation provoked blacks to act more aggressively; the campaign to end segregated schools became linked to efforts to end all de jure segregation. In 1956, after Rosa Parks—a long-term member and secretary of the Montgomery, Alabama, NAACP—was arrested for refusing to yield her seat to a white man, a yearlong bus boycott was conducted to halt segregated seating. The boycott forced Martin Luther King, Jr., to refine his views on peaceful resistance and brought into existence the Southern Christian Leadership Conference (SCLC), a loose alliance of clergy who assumed the civil-rights leadership in their communities. While King headed the SCLC, Ella Baker—a Virginia-born activist—was its organizer and coordinator.[1]

A full-scale campaign for civil rights began with a sit-in at the all-black North Carolina Agricultural and Technical College, started by four students who had been refused service at a local lunch counter. Within a week, the tactic was being employed in six other North Carolina communities, and within a month, it had spread to seven other states. Sometimes the sit-ins were sponsored by the Congress of Racial Equality (CORE), which had operated chiefly in the North for two decades, but usually they were initiated by local black youth. At this point, with the help of the SCLC and Ella Baker, the Student Nonviolent Coordinating Committee (SNCC) emerged in April 1960. "Small, militant, very youthful, largely Negro and Negro-led," the SNCC broadened the attack on segregation to include desegregation of theaters, hotels, public parks, swimming pools and beaches, churches, court rooms, libraries, and art galleries. Black women played "an integral part" in making the SNCC "the most dynamic" organization in the civil-rights crusade. One of their tactics was "jail, no bail," an inherently dramatic tactic that conserved scarce funds, while catching the public eye. Among the leaders were Diane Nash, who—though pregnant at the time—refused bail, hoping that while her child might be born in prison, her act would "hasten the day when my child and all children will be free." Ruby Doris Smith, a Spelman College student, along with Nash and several other women from the SNCC joined the Freedom Riders—challenging the continued segregation of interstate transportation facilities. For their participation in the rides, some were suspended by their colleges; some lost their jobs; some were beaten by the police. The most notable woman, though, was Fannie Lou Hamer—44 years old when she first heard about an SNCC voter-registration drive. For registering to vote, she and her husband were evicted from the land they had worked for 18 years; the house in which they took refuge was shot at; and she was beaten with leaded leather straps.[2]

Black Americans, like this Birmingham couple pictured here, demonstrated for their civil rights as Americans, even at the risk of being arrested.

The blacks' efforts to exercise their constitutional rights continued to be met with violence. In 1963, when James Meredith attempted to enroll at the University of Mississippi, Governor Ross Barnett ordered all federal officials acting in support of Meredith "summarily arrested and jailed." After 320 federal marshals installed Meredith in a dormitory, an all-night battle— waged with "stones, bricks, clubs, bottles, iron bars, gasoline bombs, and fire arms"—left 2 dead and 375 injured, 166 of them marshals. At his inauguration as governor of Alabama, George Wallace pledged himself to "segregation now, segregation tomorrow, segregation forever," thus encouraging resistance to integration. In April 1963, when blacks demonstrated to have Birmingham's city parks, playgrounds, and golf courses reopened, they were met with fire hoses and police dogs. When Governor Wallace defied a federal court order admitting Vivian Malone and James Hood to the University of Alabama, President Kennedy federalized the Alabama National Guard and forced the integration. Subsequently 4 young girls were killed and 14 other persons were injured by a dynamite blast that rocked Montgomery's Sixteenth Street Baptist Church during Sunday school; when the black community vented its outrage at this bombing, still others were killed. Then in June, Medgar Evars, Secretary of the Mississippi

NAACP, was assassinated from ambush. Finally, when black leaders called for a march on the national capital, over 200,000 persons gathered at the Lincoln Memorial.[3]

The explosive character of the racial crisis drove President Kennedy, who as a senator had been a moderate on civil-rights issues, to become a leader. On entering the White House in January 1961, he endorsed the *Brown* decision as "both legally and morally right." His first concrete action was to join congressional liberals in moving against the poll tax. In August 1962 Congress approved a constitutional amendment abolishing the poll tax in national elections. Ratification was completed in February 1964. Second, the president focused national attention on the disabilities faced by black Americans. Speaking to the American people on television in June 1963, the president took the high ground that "the rights of every man are diminished when the rights of one man are threatened." He pointed out that "The Negro baby born in America today . . . has about one-half as much chance of completing high school as a white baby born in the same place on the same day, one-third as much chance of completing college, one-third as much chance of becoming a professional man, twice as much chance of becoming unemployed, about one-seventh as much chance of earning $10,000 a year, a life expectancy which is seven years shorter, and the prospects of earning half as much." As Kennedy spoke to the problem, his focus was on the disabilities of being black; as he defined the issue, he argued that "all Americans are to be afforded equal rights and equal opportunities." Here was the reassertion of the natural-rights principle with implications, unexplored at the time, for other minorities or for women. For the moment, the president was content to send Congress a tough Civil Rights Bill intended to ensure equal access to all public accommodations; to prohibit discrimination in state programs receiving federal monies; to outlaw racial barriers in employment, in labor-union membership, and in voting; and to authorize the Justice Department to bring suits. The bill was still stalled in Congress when Kennedy was assassinated.[4]

President Johnson, one of two southern senators to refuse to sign the Declaration of Constitutional Principles, promptly made the cause of civil rights his own, devoting all his "passionate energy" to securing its enactment in 1964. Title II assured all persons "the full and equal enjoyment" of the facilities of inns, hotels, motels, restaurants, motion-picture houses, theaters, concert halls, sports arenas, and the like "without discrimination or segregation" because of "race, color, religion or national origin." Title VII banned discrimination in employment and created an Equal Employment Opportunity Commission (EEOC). As it was now apparent that neither the Civil Rights Act of 1957 nor that of 1960 had proved effective, Roy

Wilkins of the NAACP, James Farmer of CORE, and Martin Luther King, Jr., of the SCLC demanded a stronger federal statute respecting voting. To dramatize the situation, King mounted a series of "marches" on Selma, an Alabama community in which blacks had made almost no advances in registering or voting, and on Montgomery, the state capital. Alabama officials countered with state police using clubs, dogs, and tear gas. At the height of the demonstrations hoodlums murdered two persons, including Viola Liuzzo, a Detroit housewife. When 25,000 civil-rights supporters flooded Selma for a massive "march" on Montgomery, President Johnson ordered military protection for the marchers, then went to Congress to demand a new, tough Voting Rights Act. That Act, signed in August 1965, set aside literacy tests and authorized federal examiners to register black voters. Finally, Johnson urged Congress to enact a national fair-housing law. Although Congress delayed acting for two years, in the wake of the Martin Luther King assassination it enacted a compromise measure that banned racial and religious discrimination in the sale and rental of housing.[5]

By the mid-sixties, de jure segregation was largely ended in the South. Yet the struggle for equality was far from over. The slow pace and ill-grace with which the civil-rights legislation was secured and enforced was profoundly disheartening to southern blacks. The *Brown* case had given blacks "the first seemingly real sense of equal citizenship." But by 1963, it was apparent that the desegregation process was in trouble. Of the South's black children, only 1 percent were in classes with white children. Substantial integration had occurred in towns and in small- and medium-sized cities in which blacks numbered no more than one in five persons. In the larger cities, integrated schools were more available to middle-class than to working-class black students, but in the Deep South scarcely any desegregation had occurred. Only in the border states were black children likely to attend integrated schools. Outside the South, school integration was thwarted as white families fled the cities with their multiracial populations for all-white suburbs. As early as 1960 Kenneth Clark, a psychologist, observed that effective desegregation would come to pass only when desegregation was regarded as advantageous by the dominant white power group. This was all the more frustrating in the light of the Coleman Report of 1966, which concluded that black students achieved better in integrated schools simply because their classmates were white.[6]

Northern blacks, who had thus far empathized with southern blacks, now became equally disenchanted. Though the civil-rights campaign had destroyed the legal basis for segregation and discrimination, it had had little effect on "the extra legal pattern of discrimination in jobs, housing, educational opportunities, and law enforcement plaguing black Americans throughout the nation." In the North, de facto segregation of housing resulted in segregated schools and segregated facilities, all very informal but very real. Furthermore, the advance of automation, which displaced unskilled and skilled workers, hit hard at blacks. Suddenly northern blacks reacted to the "striking incongruities" between the "needs and moods of the black ghetto and the goals and strategies of the civil rights crusade." A new emerging black leadership spoke less of "civil rights and more about economic demands."[7]

At the same time, "the dream of racial harmony" was "cracking around the edges." The turning point came in the failure of the Mississippi Freedom Democratic Party (MFDP) to be seated at the Democratic National Convention in 1964. Many of the MFDP leaders were black women, including Fannie Lou Hamer, Ella Baker, Jean Smith, and Eleanor Holmes Norton. While the president was willing to nudge the South toward the mid–twentieth century, he was not about to alter its political structure. Black leaders—some of whom had put their lives in jeopardy by joining the MFDP, moved away from interracialism toward black separatism. Ruby Doris Smith concluded that civil rights was a dead issue, since it meant nothing to blacks concerned with the "basic necessities of life." Jean Smith echoed her view, declaring that she had come to understand "there wasn't room enough in the society for the mass of Black people." Nor were the new leaders eager to share leadership with whites. Black power and black nationalism came to the fore. CORE, interracial since its founding in 1942, adopted a "blacks only" membership policy under Floyd McKissick and Roy Innis. The SNCC—all-black from the start—had fought segregation and aimed at a vaguely defined, racially integrated society. Under Stokely Carmichael, the SNCC endorsed Black Power, then under H. Rap Brown, it flirted with guerrilla warfare. Harking back to Marcus Garvey, these black nationalists made black separatism their goal. Added to these were small groups of extremists such as the Black Panthers. Far more numerous were those who turned to the black separatism espoused by the Black Muslims under Elijah Muhammed and Malcolm X. The black nationalists spoke for a minority; the NAACP, which had carried the burden in the legal fight for civil rights, remained the largest of the civil-rights organizations. But by the mid-sixties, the black community was in despair and deeply divided.[8]

In this context, the civil-rights movement became a national, rather than a southern, concern. The turmoil, thus far concentrated in the South, boiled over into the urban areas of the North and West. An especially violent riot ravaged the Watts district of Los Angeles in the summer of 1965. Then, for the following three summers, riots rocked other major cities outside the South—New York, Cincinnati, Des Moines, Chicago, Milwaukee, Erie, Buffalo, New Haven, Washington, Newark, and Detroit. The riot in Detroit—the worst and bloodiest—left 43 dead, over 1,000 injured, and 2,700 businesses sacked. The violence was directed less at whites as individuals than as symbols of white authority—policemen, firemen, and national guardsmen and white property.[9]

By 1970 the nation was face-to-face with "the appalling gap between the ideal of an integrated society and the cold reality of *de facto* racial segregation." In an effort to resolve the problem of de facto segregation that resulted from residential segregation, Judge J. Skelly Wright suggested as early as 1965 that a program of busing youngsters between white suburban districts and black inner-city districts would have to be undertaken. While the Supreme Court supported busing within established school districts, it balked at ordering the merger of inner-city and suburban districts into a single metropolitan district. Nor would the Court support compulsory busing of students across district lines. In these circumstances many blacks concluded that school integration in many places had turned into "a grand hoax." As they did so, an increasing number of black leaders asked whether the interests of the black community would be better served by striving for a higher quality of education than by continuing the campaign for integrated schools, in effect acquiescing to a separate-but-equal policy for education.[10]

By 1970 there was also a widespread white backlash, by no means confined to the South. Whites, especially the affluent, had abandoned the larger cities for the suburbs to avoid integrated schools; Californians had amended their state constitution to negate fair-housing legislation. This backlash got a quasi-official stamp of approval in the "Moynihan Memorandum" of 1970. Written for President Nixon, the report hailed "the extraordinary progress" made by the black community during the 1960s. Although he cautioned that serious problems remained, Moynihan recommended to the president a policy of "benign neglect," a policy quite compatible with the president's "southern strategy" for building a political power base in the South. Subsequently President Nixon spoke of securing a "better balance" on the Supreme Court in civil-rights cases. He also warned federal officials to stop pressing for desegregation of schools through "forced busing" and expressed the view that efforts to force integration in the suburbs were "counterproductive, and not in the interest of better race relations." The unanimity that the Supreme Court had exhibited on the segregation issue in 1954 disappeared as the Court grappled with the complex issues raised by de facto segregation. Finally, the growth of "a radical and alienated black 'left'" undermined support within the black community for a strong national policy on racial integration. Indeed, at the end of the sixties, the National Advisory Commission on Civil Disorders reported: "Our nation is moving toward two societies, one black, one white—separate and unequal."[11]

The growth of the civil-rights movement in the sixties had far-reaching implications for black women and for women in general. Blacks scored significant advances in their political status. As legal barriers to the suffrage fell, blacks generally acquired the means of participating in the political process, and black women could now vote and hold office. Blacks acquired political visibility and status. During the decade, Thurgood Marshall—who had directed the NAACP's attack on school segregation—served successively on the court of appeals, as solicitor general, and on the Supreme Court, while Robert Weaver, as secretary of the Department of Housing and Urban Development, became the first black cabinet officer. President Johnson appointed Mrs. Franklin Freeman to the U.S. Civil Rights Commission, Marjorie Lawson to UNESCO, Patricia Harris as ambassador to Luxembourg, and Constance Baker to the federal bench. Blacks also became increasingly visible in elective posts. Forty blacks—all in the North and West—sat in state legislatures in 1956 and 172 in 1970. The number of blacks in Congress stood at three in 1954, six in 1964, and ten in 1970, including Shirley Chisholm.

Alongside these gains were major disappointments. Blacks felt that while they had given Harry Truman and John Kennedy vitally needed votes in closely contested elections, they had received fewer rewards than their aid merited. Despite the *Brown* decision, segregated schools still remained the norm for most black youngsters. Worse yet, the new Nixon administration seemed more concerned with courting southern white support than with seeking solutions to blacks' problems.[12]

This black "revolution" had important consequences for black women. It successfully challenged legal support of segregation, which had condemned the whole black community to second-class citizenship, had limited the black man's ability to support his family, had thwarted the black woman's efforts as a mother to create a wholesome environment for her children, and had frustrated her own efforts at self-realization. The struggle stimulated blacks—male and female—to assert economic, social, and political roles they had often eschewed in the past. Black women not only gained vicariously as their fathers, husbands, sons, and daughters were able to participate more fully in the mainstream of American society, but they were moved to examine their own position as women. Last but not least, in challenging the white community to extend the principles of equal protection of the laws to black Americans, the black community sensitized the entire nation to the issues of civil rights and became role models to the other minority Americans.

BLACK FAMILY

As the struggle for civil rights expanded the opportunities for black women, it also focused attention on the character of black family life. The studies of Charles S. Johnson, Hortense Powdermaker, E. Franklin Frazier, and especially the widely circulated work of Gunnar Myrdal shaped America's image of the black family. Drawing on the work of other scholars, Myrdal emphasized that "the average Negro family is more disorganized than the white family." But he offered the caveat that in the rural South, a class of "Black Puritans" adhered to the ideals of "the monogamous patriarchal Christian family." In addition there were the ultrapuritanical upper-class Negro families in the towns and cities, more straight-laced than their white counterparts. But the mass of black families—whether measured in terms of divorce, separation, desertion, female family-head, children in broken homes, or illegitimacy—was disorganized, dysfunctional, and pathological. These families provided neither a stable base for the husband and wife nor a supportive emotional milieu for the children. Because of the incidence of divorce, desertion, and widowhood, between one fifth and one fourth of ever-married black women had no husband in the household, a proportion two to three times higher than in the white community.[13]

A variety of other indices were cited to delineate the extent and character of family disorganization among the blacks. Single black women with children frequently described themselves as "widows." The proportion of "widows" among blacks who were in their 20s and 30s was three times as high as among white women in the same age range. "One-person" families—a reflection of the status of adults whose legal or common-law marriage had broken up (if they had no children or had abandoned them)—and "single-parent" families (if they stayed with their children) were more numerous among blacks by a margin of three to two. Lodgers—often a disruptive factor—appeared in 30 percent of the black families in the North, as opposed to 10 percent of the white families. Again the "doubling-up" of families in a single household was far more prevalent among blacks.[14]

The debate over the character of the black family continued throughout the sixties. Oscar Lewis argued that blacks shared "a culture of poverty" with other impoverished Americans. This point of view received wide dissemination in Michael Harrington's *The Other America* (1962). Hylan Lewis, on the other hand, contended that Afro-Americans were indistinguishable from white Americans in terms of values but differed in situational adaptations. But it was Daniel Moynihan's *The Negro Family: The Case for National Action* (1965) that had the greatest impact on public policy. An assistant secretary of labor, Moynihan characterized the black family as "pathological," and conditions were getting "*worse not better,*" he warned. The "fundamental problem was that the Negro family in the urban ghettoes was crumbling. . . . The fabric of conventional social relationships has all but disintegrated." At the heart of this "tangle of pathology" was the matriarchal family in which so many blacks lived. Husbands had "unusually low power," since 44 percent of black wives were dominant, as compared with 20 percent of white wives. Worse yet, the pathology was self-perpetuating because of the absence of "a warm, supportive home" that might otherwise "effectively compensate for many of the restrictions the Negro child faces outside of the ghetto." Without this supportive environment, the black child did less well in school, was more likely to be below grade level for his or her age, performed less well than might be expected on IQ tests, and was underenrolled in college. In turn, blacks fared less well in the competition for employment. Although black women fared better than black males, in Moynihan's analysis this simply compounded the difficulties the black male faced in attempting to fulfill the traditional male role. The "combined impact of poverty, failure, and isolation among Negro youth" resulted in "a disastrous delinquency and crime rate." Blacks were overrepresented in institutions for juvenile delinquents; they constituted a majority of those arrested for murder and nonnegligent homicide, forcible rape, and aggravated assault. In his conclusion Moynihan argued that if the United States were to bring the black American "to full and equal sharing in the responsibilities and rewards of citizenship," the Federal Government must not rest until every able-bodied black man was working, even if this meant that some women's jobs had to be redesigned to enable men to fulfill them.[15]

At the start of the seventies, Moynihan's was again the major voice on the black family. As counselor to President Nixon, he authored a "Memorandum on the Status of Negroes." He rejoiced that in terms of jobs and income, the 1960s had seen a "great breakthrough" for blacks. Outside the South, the income of young black husband–wife families stood at 99 percent of that for analogous white families. Blacks had increased their share of professional and technical employments. They were attending high school at almost the same rate as whites. Black enrollment in college had increased 85 percent between 1964 and 1968. On the other hand, the proportion of husband–wife families among blacks had declined; the illegitimacy ratio had risen to nearly 30 percent. The number of "poor Negro children in female-headed families" exceeded the number of children in male-headed families. Moynihan expressed alarm that a great deal of "the crime, the fire-setting, the rampant school violence" in the black community have become "quasi-politicized," that is, had come to be regarded as a legitimate form of protest. Furthermore, this "social alienation among the black lower classes is matched, and probably enhanced, by a virulent form of anti-white feeling among portions of the large and prospering black middle class." Convinced that the material progress blacks had made in the sixties was solid and would continue, Moynihan sought "a period in which Negro progress continues and racial rhetoric fades." The "time may have come," he counseled, when "the issue of race could benefit from a period of 'benign neglect.' " For the present, he suggested that the President address the problem of crime.[16]

Moynihan's studies, coinciding with a developing feminist ideology, assumed the desirability of traditional family roles for husband and wife. To be an effective individual, the male must be able to support his family and provide the headship of the family; the female must play the traditional wife–mother–homemaker role and furnish emotional support to the family. While Frazier, Myrdal, and Moynihan described the black family as matriarchal, the fact was, as Moynihan's figures abundantly showed, that at any time between 1949 and 1962, at least 72.0 percent of the nonwhite families were husband–wife families compared to 87.8 percent for white families. Most black children, like most white children, lived in families with two parents present.[17]

Moynihan's "pathological" diagnosis judged black family life by white family values. Within black society, common-law marriages and out-of-wedlock births were not "seriously condemned"; they were not the social disasters that they would have been in white society. In her "Georgiatown" study, Virginia Heyer Young found that the illegitimate child was often cared for in the household of an older, stable couple, often that of a grandparent or aunt or uncle. Negro families provided "secure groups" for child raising. Furthermore, the occurrence of illegitimate births did not relate to male- or female-headed families. Young also documented a progression from "extraresidential mating, to consensual union, to stable marriage." Most black women, in fact, established stable marriages by their mid-20s.[18]

The "Georgiatown" study revealed that in the black family, male–female roles differed markedly from the stereotypes attributed to the black family. Industrial employment enabled males to earn far more than women could from domestic service, the main occupation available to them, permitting the male to be the principal breadwinner. The "Georgiatown" interviewees recalled growing up in families in which "a strict authoritarian father . . . supervised the whole family in their farm chores, punished the children, read aloud from the Bible daily, and said he could spell better than the school teacher." In the present time, women acted as though their husbands had authority and were deferential to them. Black lower-class husbands were not "powerless in either their conjugal or parental roles," but a remarkable degree of overlap existed in the behavior considered appropriate for men and women. Behavior that the Anglo community associated with male roles Young found in both male and female roles in black families. In the black value system, females and males could be individualistic and nonconforming; both were responsible for the economic support of the family; both had authority in the home; she was expected to take "an active role in the male's attempt to establish a sexual encounter." By the same token, behavior that the Anglo society designated as feminine was characteristic of both men and women in black families. Husbands and wives were nurturing and highly interactive physically with children; both valued interpersonal relationships and were expressive emotionally. The black family delineated by Virginia Young and Hylan Lewis exhibited the androgynous values that many whites would endorse as the feminist movement matured.[19]

OTHER MINORITY WOMEN

The black revolution and the debate over the character of the black family made women in other minority groups self-conscious about their own status, while sensitizing the Anglo-American majority to their presence. While many minority women acquired the education necessary to perform effectively in mainstream society, they were often inhibited by the drive to put the needs of their ethnic or racial group ahead of their interests as women.

Hispanic Americans

Mexican Americans   During the sixties the character of the Mexican American population continued to change. By 1970, 15 percent of the Chicanos were Mexican-born; 30 percent were U.S.-born offspring of Mexican-born parents; while the remaining 55 percent were U.S.-born children of U.S.-born parents with Mexican antecedents. Mexican influences diminished; Anglo-American influences flourished.[20]

Fundamental changes in agriculture caused the demand for farm labor to slacken in the 1960s. Although the importation of *braceros* ended, the plight of the Chicano farm worker gave the Mexican Americans a high degree of visibility. Yet in actuality the U.S.-born Chicanos increasingly secured employment as blue-collar and service workers; this switch was facilitated by the relocation to the Southwest of the men's and women's clothing industries, which sought to profit from the ample supply of non-union, low-wage laborers. The magnitude of illegal Mexican immigrants forced to take whatever work they could find served to depress the wages of all Mexican-origin workers. When in trouble, the *mojados* could not call on the government for assistance, nor were they eligible for welfare benefits. Their children, even if U.S.-born, were frequently denied the right to attend public schools; their family life was often disrupted, as well as impoverished. The social and economic problems they created helped intensify feelings against all Mexican Americans. With a common border extending 1,800 miles from Brownsville, on the Gulf of Mexico, to Tijuana, on the Pacific, large numbers of *mojados* continued to cross the border.[21]

The well-being of Chicano women still depended greatly on the quality of jobs to which their menfolk had access. In the 1960s the Chicano male was more likely to be a factory operative than a farm laborer, to be a craftsman than a service worker. Compared to Anglo-Americans, few secured white-collar employments. Typically they worked "in low wage or marginal firms—in the less profitable, non-unionized fringes of the high wage industries." Acculturation, however, had proceeded to the degree that a Chicana, responding to economic necessity, might work outside the home away from the rest of her family. Of 438,000 Chicanas who were employed in 1970, over half were in unskilled occupations—domestic workers, service employees, and operatives—another 30 percent were in sales and clerical work; and less than 10 percent were managers or professionals.[22]

In reality the Chicano community was fragmented. Some Chicanas, even though born in the United States, thought of themselves as Mexicans, others as Americans. Some spoke only Spanish; others, only English; still others spoke both. Generational differences as well as educational, economic, and urban–rural differences separated them. In this context the acculturation and assimilation of the Chicana was selective, adding to the heterogeneity of the Mexican American society.[23]

Puerto Ricans   The status of poorer Puerto Rican women underwent especially sharp changes in New York as they became involved in far wider social, community, and political activities than in Puerto Rico. Although Puerto Rican women lagged behind Mexican-American women in completing high school, a small but growing number entered college, a development facilitated by the open-admissions, tuition-free City University of New York. The first Puerto Rican women secured substantial roles in public affairs. The appearance of Puerto Rican communities in Chicago, Milwaukee, Cleveland, Philadelphia, and northern New Jersey assured that they would play an ever-wider role in American society.[24]

Cuban Americans   Rather than accept the "massive restructuring of the social and political order" triggered by Fidel Castro's victory, a massive migration of Cubans began in January 1959. This first wave brought members of the Batista regime, landowners, industrialists, and former Cuban managers of American-owned firms. Following the Bay of Pigs disaster in April 1961, the flow of refugees increased and its composition diversified, reaching into the middle classes and elements of the working classes. By the end of 1962, 215,000 Cubans had arrived. Thereafter, this influx continued at a somewhat slower pace, so that by 1970 the Cuban-American population numbered 545,000.[25]

In several respects these Cuban Americans differed from other Hispanic Americans. Whereas the latter had been "pulled" to the United States by hopes of economic betterment, the Cubans had been "pushed" by political developments at home. The first wave included a disproportionately large number of professional and white-collar workers. Compared to the general population of Cuba, these early refugees were wealthier, better educated, and largely urban middle class. Less than six percent were either black or partly black. When they arrived in Miami, the Cuban women were far less tradition-bound than other Hispanic women in the United States.[26]

Although their decision to leave Cuba entailed losses in material possessions, within five years Miami had become a "Cuban" city. Many of the Cubans were caught up in the "enclave economy"—that is they found employment in immigrant-owned and operated enterprises. The enclave firms concentrated on textiles, leather, furniture, cigar making, construction, and finance, as well as restaurants, supermarkets, private clinics, legal firms, funeral parlors, and private schools. Initially enclave workers had to settle for unskilled jobs at minimum wages and with little job security, but in the long run their past investments of time and money in training and education enabled them to secure employment comparable to that which they had held in Cuba.[27]

Overall Cuban women fared well. Reflecting their relatively high educational attainment and the need to start over, their labor-force rate in 1970 was 51.0, far and away the highest of any Hispanic women. In the course of a decade, Cuban women of the first wave managed to establish a lifestyle at least as favorable as that of the Puerto Ricans, a community well into its second generation, and far better than that of the Mexican Americans, the majority of whom were U.S.-born.[28]

Asian Americans

Within the Asian American communities, the Chinese Americans were preoccupied with acculturating; the Japanese Americans were moving ahead in carving out new lives for themselves. The major development was the arrival of a new group, the Filipinos.

Chinese Americans   Most Chinese Americans continued to live in largely self-sufficient ethnic enclaves in large cities. The university-trained holders of graduate and professional degrees found employment in the primary labor force. Many of these joined college or university faculties or the staffs of research organizations. Far more typical were those who found employment in enclave enterprises, where their knowledge of the Chinese language and customs added to their employability and where a wide spectrum of employments was open. Freed from the restraints of the extended Chinese family, Chinese American women took employment outside the family, an unusually large proportion in professional work.[29]

Japanese Americans   By 1970, the Sansei—now in their late 20s and 30s—were making their mark. Tradition still operated, but differentially. Generally the females were less traditional than the males. Sansei males tended to endorse the "classical male-dominant 'Japanese' marriage"; Sansei females preferred the more egalitarian husband–wife roles of the Anglo family. The arranged marriages of the Issei had been replaced by Anglo patterns of dating and marrying for "love based on mutual interests and compatibility." Exposed day in and day out to Anglo culture, Sansei often adopted Anglo views of physical attractiveness. The stereotype of the Japanese male as "short and unmasculine," placed Sansei men in an unfavorable light compared to the Anglo ideal; on the other hand, the "tiny, exotic" Sansei female was viewed as attractive in Anglo terms. In fact the rate of intermarriage for Sansei was high—40 percent compared with 10 percent for the Nisei generation. Sansei women were more likely to marry outside their ethnic group than Sansei men. As a result, one group of Sansei women—the majority—lived with their Sansei husbands and their children; another—a large minority—had Anglo mates. But in both groups the children grew up apart from Nisei grandparents, who might pass on elements of the traditional culture, as well as from other Japanese American children, who might also serve to reinforce elements of Japanese culture.[30]

The Sansei were generally well educated and, in view of their acculturation, able to compete for jobs in the primary labor market, three fifths in white-collar occupations. As a result, a large part of the Nisei and Sansei enjoyed a middle-class standard of living. Sansei, typically, were active in non-Japanese organizations, lived in non-Japanese neighborhoods, and had close friends who were non-Japanese. In most respects they lived by the same values and ways as the Anglo-American middle class.[31]

Filipino Americans   The rapidly growing Filipino population shared little in common with the other Asian Americans. Ethnically related to the Indonesians and the Malaysians, the Filipino, despite three centuries of Spanish rule, was most likely to speak a regional language at home, although

English, learned at school, was widely used. A great majority, at least nominally, were Roman Catholic.[32]

The Filipino migration was stimulated by a demand for cheap labor that arose when the Immigration Act of 1924 expressly cut off further Chinese and Japanese migration. Recruited for agricultural work, these Filipinos, chiefly males, arrived with "low educational and occupational credentials." They brought a "traditional, rural-based" Philippine culture. Like the Chinese and Japanese who preceded them, they became the focal point of prejudice and discrimination, denounced as "a menace" from both a "moral and sanitary" standpoint. Joining the secondary labor force, they moved from job to job and hence did not establish an ethnic enclave. The group had little cohesiveness as they remained divided by "tribal linguistics and attitudes." This first wave of migration was essentially halted by the terms of the Philippine Independence Act in 1936.[33]

In the post–World War II era, the Filipino population was reinforced by a small group of war victims and veterans and their families who brought "forgotten Philippine amenities." The major source of the Filipino American population, however, began arriving after the adoption of a new immigration law in 1965. This act, giving preference to those with skills in short supply in the United States, produced a major shift in the character of the Filipino American population. During the period of American rule, the Philippines developed an extensive school system. When this system was revived after World War II, the Philippines enrolled the second-highest number of students per capita in the world. The system succeeded in producing more college graduates and professionals than the economy could absorb. Unable to find suitable employment at home, Filipino scientists, engineers, and physicians took advantage of the new American immigration law to migrate to the United States. Similarly, large numbers of women in the nursing, medical, and other professions who found themselves excluded from employment at home also migrated. The addition of single professional women to the wives of the male migrants resulted in women constituting the majority of the adult immigrants.[34]

This second wave located chiefly in California, but they did not settle in ethnic neighborhoods. Given their education, many moved directly into the primary labor force where they shared more in common with Anglo colleagues than with their less well educated, tradition-rooted countrymen of the first wave.[35]

American Indians

During the sixties the status and roles of Indian women varied widely. A few like the isolated Hopi and Zuni remained relatively unaffected by

*American Indian mothers faced raising their families
without the aid of amenities such as electricity, which
the Anglo-American majority took for granted.*

white culture, but the Navajo, now the largest single Indian society, experienced major changes as they acculturated. At the same time, Indians in
Oklahoma and a growing minority elsewhere lived and worked in a white-
dominated urban society. At most one can illustrate some of the changes
that Indian women experienced.

The proportion of Indian youngsters completing high school skyrock-
etted, greatly enlarging the range of employment opportunities for young
Indian women. Reservations offered employment as teachers, nurses, secretaries, and office clerks. Employment opportunities off the reservations
were wider, but the educational background of most Indian women chan-
neled them into three broad occupational categories: service, clerical, and
operative. Because so few had earned college degrees, few Indian women
held professional or managerial positions. Efforts to expand employment
opportunities by relocating Indians in urban centers away from tribal res-

ervations provoked hostility as many Indians associated it with the termination policy. Overall Indian women generally lagged most other women
in sharing the bounty of America's resources.[36]

Navajo   The largest, most-unified Indian nation, the Navajo, numbered
nearly 100,000 in 1970, a tenfold increase since 1870. Their reservation
occupied nearly 25,000 square miles of land in New Mexico, Arizona, and
Utah. Prior to World War II the Navajos had remained aloof from the Anglo-
American culture. As late as 1940, 88 percent of the males between 18 and
35 were illiterate, and no more than 500 Navajo youth could read their
own language. Inasmuch as before the war only 1 child in 3 ever attended
school and then irregularly for 2 or perhaps 3 years, the lack of literacy
was understandable. In 1944 to 1945, only 100 Navajo youth were enrolled
in high school. Once Navajo servicemen urged their parents to send their
younger brothers and sisters to school, the transformation was dramatic.
Most Navajo youth entered school. High-school enrollments swelled; tribal
scholarships enabled a few to enter college, and by 1966, 600 youth were
so enrolled. Navajo girls especially entered nursing training.[37]

The war also gave many Navajo a taste for elements of white culture—
homes with wooden floors, wood- or kerosene-burning stoves, dishes and
glasses, battery-operated radios, and second-hand automobiles. A tribal
council—first formed in the 1920s—developed an effective, responsible
organization. Operating from their capital at Window Rock, Arizona, an
elected chairman, a vice-chairman, four judges, and 74 councilmen directed
the Navajo government. The council sought to attract industrial firms to
locate nearby. Royalties from oil discovered on the reservation paid for
programs of improved land management, road construction, irrigation,
public health, housing, and education. Profoundly conservative, most of
the population continued to use Navajo as their primary language.[38]

The extended family, though rarer than in earlier days, had not completely disappeared, and matrilocal living arrangements survived. As in
earlier days, plural marriage continued among 1 family in 14. Livestock
raising continued as a joint family enterprise. Farmland and rangeland
remained in the family with "inherited-use ownership." The land passed
from mother to daughter with the husband acting as trustee for his wife.
While he worked the land, he could not alienate it from the family. To a
degree, inherited-use ownership applied to the livestock as well. A husband
could "own" animals, but he was obliged to share in the support of the
family. He could not sell his animals to satisfy a personal whim. The only
indisputable private property consisted of one's personal clothing, orna-
ments, saddles, and ceremonial equipment.[39]

Even as younger Navajo adopted the nuclear family, family lineage continued to be traced through the female line. Wives owned property independently of their husbands, but the husband represented the family in its business relationships with outsiders and was de facto head of the family. Change was evidenced in other ways, too. Youth flocked to jazz sessions in off-reservation towns; in imitation of the white teen culture, the Navajo elected their own candidate for the Miss Indian America contest. Younger children joined the Boy Scouts, Girl Scouts, and 4-H. Garbed in blue jeans, the Navajo became almost indistinguishable from the tourists who came to gawk. Slowly Navajo women edged closer to the life-styles of Anglo women.[40]

Urban Indians   In the wake of World War II, many Indians drifted to the cities, a move promoted by the Bureau of Indian Affairs. To facilitate this movement, the Bureau established placement offices in Los Angeles, Phoenix, Denver, and Salt Lake City. During the 1950s some 30,000 Indians relocated in urban areas; in the 1960s, over 40,000. By 1970, communities of 2,500 or more Indians could be found in 30 cities scattered from Seattle to New York, from Minneapolis to Houston. Only the Deep South and New England lacked Indian communities. Los Angeles-Long Beach, the largest Indian community, had 23,908. Altogether, in 1970 approximately 30 percent of the nation's 800,000 Indians lived in urban areas.[41]

Urban-dwelling Indians fared relatively well, compared to reservation-dwelling Indians, though they generally lived in circumstances deemed unattractive by white middle-class standards. Urban life offered them an escape from the contaminated water supplies and lack of sanitary facilities that produced high levels of gastrointestinal diseases among reservation dwellers. Urban Indians had readier access both to health facilities and to schools. Economic opportunities were better in the cities. The mean family income of all Indians was low, $6,838 in 1969, yet in only five communities did urban Indian families fall below that level. Indian women especially benefitted from the wider range of employments available in the cities. Thus, whereas only 30 percent of the total Indian population lived in urban areas, 50 percent of those women who were employed were urban dwellers. The urban areas afforded employment in sales, clerical, and craft work, as well as in professional and technical jobs. Although many Indian women had to settle for the ragtag jobs of the secondary labor market, in Washington, D.C., and a half dozen other cities, a modest number of Indians broke into the primary labor force, enabling those who did so to provide financial stability to their families. This also threw them in contact with non-Indians as fellow employees and promoted acculturation and assimilation.[42]

Indian family life and sex roles changed sharply in the cities. Migration to the cities by single individuals and couples precluded preservation of the extended family. Temporarily a "composite" family resulted—a combination of kin and nonkin, sharing common quarters. It reflected a pragmatic effort to secure housing and companionship during a period of migration that led some family members to the city, while others remained behind on the reservation. Sex roles were often altered. When husbands failed to find work, their working wives often left them at home to care for the house and children. Frustrated, "emasculated" males on occasion resorted to physical abuse of the children or wife, which could be further exacerbated when the wife, having earned money that she regarded as hers to spend, exhibited a degree of independence that further deflated her husband's self-regard. Even when the husband was regularly employed, he was likely to go home, eat, change clothes, and go out alone. She became a domestic convenience that kept house, cleaned, cooked, cared for the children, and was a sex partner. While his wife might not be his only sex partner, the husband insisted that she be scrupulously faithful to him.[43]

Urban Indians tended to be standoffish. Those Navajo, for example, who migrated to Denver did not form tribal-based voluntary organizations, much less join non-Indian groups. Harboring "a great animosity toward the whites" who had taken his ancestor's land and who blocked his progress at the moment, the Navajo steered a solitary course. In spite of themselves, Indians were thrown in contact with other minorities. In Denver they were often confused with Mexican Americans; in Chicago they had contact with Mexican Americans, Puerto Ricans, Appalachian whites, and blacks, and toward none of these did they manifest respect or interest. Many of the Indians' problems of adjustment to urban life reflected the anxieties of a minority group seeking to carve out a place for itself in a strange environment and were typical of those that rural folk experienced in moving to urban communities. Non-Indian neighbors perceived them not as Navajo or Sioux or Chippewa but as just plain Indians. And indeed as differences between tribes blurred and English became the first language of many, the Indians made common cause, giving rise to a pan-Indian movement.[44]

The Indian woman remained ambivalent. For some a sense of Indianness persisted, expressing itself in close family ties, periodic participation in tribal ceremonies, and a propensity for endogamous marriage; yet in other respects she was as gripped by television and style magazines as any white woman of comparable education and income. For other Indian women, the way of the future was acculturation and assimilation. Historically, Indian cultures had borrowed appealing elements of one another's cultures. Indians had been quick to adopt the metal tools, wool blankets, mirrors, and beads of European traders. So, too, many Indian cultures had found no problem in adapting elements of Christianity to their native religious practices. And they allowed their daughters, in particular, to inter-marry with whites. Thus, in the 1970s the Indian societies had the highest rate of intermarriage of any ethnic group—39 percent of the Indian women marrying a non-Indian.[45]

Clearly the status of women in the diverse Indian cultures varied widely. Those who lived in urban communities had better prospects for economic success than those who stayed behind on reservations. If reservation life remained bleak, urban life exacted a toll from the confrontation with alien values. While there were evidences of a pan-Indian spirit bringing persons of the diverse cultures together, divisions remained. The effect of migration was that the better-educated mixed bloods might drift into the Anglo com-munity, leaving the Indian community to those who adhered to traditional values and practices and retarding the acculturation of those who contin-ued to think of themselves as Indians.

The various minority women of the United States experienced a wide variety of changes in the sixties. They acquired a public visibility in the wake of the black civil-rights movement, and many legal barriers to polit-ical, economic, and social opportunities were removed. Among the Amer-ican Jewish, Chinese, and Japanese populations, which traditionally had accorded high value to formal education, the young were able to secure as much education as their natural talent permitted. Among many Indians whose wartime experiences had underscored the value of literacy and formal education, traditional values were replaced by new ones. For others—the blacks and the Chicanos—de jure discrimination fell by the wayside, but federal, state, and local officials were often slow to implement or enforce the civil-rights laws. Yet overall minority groups remained frus-trated, less because the status quo continued than because progress came at a slower pace than desired. In expanding their political rights and access to education, jobs, and public amenities—transportation, restaurants, hotels, theaters, and parks—minority women benefitted directly. Even within a traditional family setting, women as daughters, wives, and mothers bene-fitted indirectly as their fathers, brothers, and husbands gained new oppor-tunities. In the course of working to promote expanded opportunities for their group, a few women would begin to question their status as women.

EQUALITY ENTICES

Though not intended, the Kennedy administration focused national attention on questions of women's rights and the need for an ERA. Politically troublesome, the ERA issue seemed as likely to embarrass the new administration as to aid it. Congressman Emanuel Cellar, a long-standing foe of an ERA, proposed a Presidential Commission on the Legal Status of Women, hoping it would prove an ERA unnecessary and unwise. Esther Peterson, head of the Women's Bureau, having worked with women in the Kennedy campaign, felt that a presidential commission would discharge Kennedy's "debt" to women and help ensure reelection support for him. It could also get the new president "off the hook" by sidetracking an ERA that his labor constituency did not want. Although designed to block an ERA, the presidential commission had a bona fide charge "to make women's rights a reality." It was to explore two areas: (1) private employment policies and practices and (2) federal government employment practices. Eleanor Roosevelt was named chairperson.[46]

The commission's report, *American Women,* burst on the scene in 1963 just as Friedan published *The Feminine Mystique.* The report kept a deliberately moderate tone to make it widely acceptable, but the supporting committee reports spelled out the facts: most women who worked did so to earn a living; the status of women in the labor market was low; the educational level of women was low; the law discriminated against women at many points. While the details were spelled out, the commission played down discrimination against women as a class and emphasized the underutilization of women as a resource. Society was the loser. The report argued that the principle of equality was already embodied in the equal-protection clause of the Fourteenth Amendment. Accordingly, the commission called for an "early and definitive court pronouncement . . . to the end that the principle of equality become firmly established in constitutional doctrine." Clearly if the Supreme Court would so oblige, an ERA would not be required.[47]

Equal Pay

The first concrete by-product of the report was the Equal Pay Act of 1963, which amended the Fair Labor Standards Act. In acting, the Congress took notice that the wage structure in American society had all too often been based "on an ancient but outmoded belief that a man, because of his role in society, should be paid more than a woman even though his duties are the same." A simple piece of legislation, the Equal Pay Act barred an employer from discriminating in the payment of wages for "equal work on jobs, the performance of which requires equal skill, effort, and responsibility, and which are performed under similar working conditions. . . ." Wage differentials based on factors other than sex were permitted. The act further prohibited an employer from reducing any employee's wages in order to comply with the law. In the administration of the law, the Department of Labor directed that where state laws mandated a higher minimum wage to either sex than that required by federal law, the higher wage must be offered to employees of the opposite sex for equal work. Thus the query raised in the 1920s as to how one resolved differences in standards to achieve equality between the sexes was answered: invoke the higher standard. The Equal Pay Act had special significance, for it was the first piece of federal legislation banning discrimination on the basis of sex alone.[48]

Civil Rights: Title VII

A second, farther-reaching measure was the Civil Rights Act of 1964. A broad-based effort to ensure the civil rights of blacks, the measure had been before Congress for four months when Representative Howard Smith, seeking to defeat it by making it unpalatable, moved to prohibit sex discrimination in the job market. Smith's tactic confronted the women members of the Congress with a choice not unlike that which feminists a century earlier had faced in deciding whether to support the Fifteenth Amendment—which granted the suffrage to black males but not women—or whether to oppose it because it did not ensure woman suffrage. Edith Green, author of the Equal Pay Act, while expressing hope that "the day will come when discrimination will be ended against women," thought that Smith's amendment would only "clutter up the bill" and it might be used to defeat it. Congresswoman Martha Griffiths, on the other hand, argued it would be disastrous to women to let Congress go on record as having rejected a measure that would enlarge their civil rights. Accepting Smith's challenge, she worked against great odds to see that the Civil Rights Act passed with language applicable to women as well as to blacks. Griffiths succeeded.[49]

As adopted, Title VII—the Equal Employment Opportunity section of the Civil Rights Act—expressly prohibited discrimination based on race, color, religion, national origin, or sex by private employers, employment agencies, and unions. The public sector, including educational institutions, was exempted. The law established an Equal Employment Opportunity Commission (EEOC) to investigate complaints. While the EEOC might conciliate or recommend intervention by the Justice Department, it had no enforcement powers of its own. So far as women were concerned the act was schizoid; for in order to provide flexibility, the Congress allowed the commission to grant employers exemptions for "bona fide occupational qualifications" (BFOQ). Further, the EEOC was thrust into a head-on confrontation with the protective legislation and regulations of the states that treated women differently than men.[50]

Initially the EEOC directed its enforcement energies toward the problems of blacks and ignored those of women. In fact, Herman Edelsberg, director of the EEOC, termed the sex provisions of the act "a fluke . . . conceived out of wedlock." Taking the path of least resistance, the EEOC guidelines of December 1965 accepted state laws as BFOQ exceptions if the laws effectively protected women and if employers acted in good faith. The equalitarians objected, for the EEOC seemed bent on approving automatically state laws that some feminists regarded more as a source of discrimination than of protection. Equivocation by the EEOC continued. In the guidelines issued in 1966, the EEOC disclaimed responsibility for deciding whether Title VII superseded state laws and left the issue to the courts. This reluctance of the EEOC to employ the act in behalf of women prompted Betty Friedan and others to found the National Organization of Women (NOW) in 1966. Two years later the EEOC, responding to pressure from NOW and other women's organizations, reversed itself and began a case-by-case review of conflicts between Title VII and the states' protective legislation. Finally, in 1969 it held that "state laws and regulations, although originally promulgated for the purpose of protecting females, have ceased to be relevant to technology or to the expanding role of the female worker in our economy." Accordingly, it held that Title VII superseded state laws and regulations. In fact some state attorneys general had already issued opinions to that effect; others had ruled that state laws would remain effective until a federal court ruled to the contrary.[51]

Ultimately the courts refined the meaning of Title VII. Generally they invalidated state protective legislation that treated women differently from men. In the *Weeks* case, which revolved about a state law and company regulations that limited the weight women might lift on the job, the court laid out a principle for BFOQ exceptions: ". . . the employer has the burden of proving that he has . . . a factual basis for believing that all or substantially all women would be unable to perform safely and efficiently the duties of the job involved." In an analogous case, a federal appeals court held that weight-lifting restrictions were invalid if applied only to women. Equally important was the attitude with which the court in the *Weeks* case viewed protective legislation: "Title VII rejects just this type of romantic paternalism as unduly Victorian and instead vests individual women with the power to decide whether or not to take on unromantic tasks. Men have always had the right to determine whether the increase in remuneration for strenuous, dangerous, obnoxious, boring or unromantic tasks is worth the candle. The promise of Title VII is that women are now to be on equal footing."[52]

In successive decisions federal courts gave effect to Title VII. In *Phillips* v. *Martin-Marietta Corporation,* the Supreme Court held that a firm could not have "one hiring policy for women and another for men." The Court did suggest that parenthood, "if demonstrably more relevant to job performance for a woman than for a man," could be the basis for excluding women from jobs. In another case the federal court directed Libbey-Owens and its union to stop the practice by which they assigned all women employees to a single plant in which they were given only the less-desirable, lower-paid jobs.[53]

Similarly, a multiplicity of suits had been required to end the use of "male only" and "female only" help-wanted advertisements. Initially the EEOC allowed single-sex ads, insisting that such sex-designated ads simply indicated "that some occupations are considered more attractive to persons of one sex than the other," in short, a convenience to assist the advertiser to "obtain the maximum reader response." Women's-rights groups protested vociferously that "the repetition of Help Wanted Male; Help Wanted Female" played "a role-conditioning part in continuing myths" that relied on "false assumptions about sex in relation to work." Yielding to the pressure from NOW, the EEOC prohibited separate help-wanted columns for men and women. After the Pittsburgh City Council prohibited help-wanted ads in sex-designated columns, the *Pittsburgh Press* challenged the ordinance as violating First Amendment freedoms. The Supreme Court rejected the paper's defense, stating that "the advertisements, as embroidered by their placement, signaled that the advertisers were more likely to show an illegal sex preference in their hiring decisions." At the beginning of the controversy, Martha Griffiths protested: "I have never entered a door labeled 'men' and I doubt that [a man] has frequently entered the women's room. . . . The same principle operates in the job-seeking process." The Court's action, then, undercut employers who sought to recruit in terms of sex stereotypes, while it removed a psychological barrier that restrained women from exploring the full range of job openings. A half-dozen years were consumed in securing the redress; and the solution at most enlarged the potential range of jobs a woman might explore.[54]

The problems of achieving equality between the sexes by relying on judicial review made equalitarians fretful with anything short of an ERA. Several separate suits had been required to deal with weight-lifting regulations. Such suits were expensive in time, energy, and money, lacked assurance of success, and at best solved only a small segment of the total problem of discrimination.

While the Equal Pay Act and Title VII aimed at reducing job discrimination in the private sector, the federal government acted to tidy up its own house. First, John Kennedy issued an executive order opening all civil-service ranks to women. Beyond this promising start, efforts to end discrimination against women were frustrated by the higher national priority given to curbing racial discrimination. Repeatedly women's leaders pressed federal officials to expand policies and regulations, initially designed to prohibit racial discrimination, to prohibit sex discrimination as well. Thus, in 1965 President Johnson, by executive order, sought to prohibit racial discrimination either in federal employment or by federal contractors and subcontractors. To that end, the Department of Labor created an Office of Federal Contract Compliance (OFCC). Women's groups lobbied 2 years to get President Johnson to issue the necessary order to prohibit sex discrimination as well. This order charged the Civil Service Commission with its enforcement and with developing plans to actively recruit and promote women to top-level jobs. Even so, the OFCC apparatus was more assiduous in combatting racial discrimination than sex discrimination. Not until 1969 did the OFCC release proposed guidelines on sex discrimination, and another 17 months passed before it published its official guidelines. Even then these guidelines were far less rigorous than those for racial discrimination; in particular there was no mention of specific goals and timetables applicable to women. After NOW protested vehemently, Labor Secretary James D. Hodgson stated candidly that he had "no intention of applying literally exactly the same approach" for women as had been developed to eliminate discrimination against other minority groups. Renewed outcries by women's groups forced Hodgson to revise his position and promise "some kinds of goals and timetables applying to some kinds of federal contractors. . . ." Women's groups did not wait for the guidelines. On June 25, 1970, NOW filed a blanket complaint against more than 1,300 corporations receiving federal funds, charging them with sex discrimination. Formal charges were also filed against more than 300 colleges and universities—recipients of more than $3 billion in federal funds each year.[55]

When Richard Nixon became president in January 1969, he immediately came under strong pressure to create new machinery to deal expressly with sex discrimination. When he failed to respond, Congresswomen Florence Dwyer, Catherine May, Charlotte Reid, and Margaret Heckler subjected him to intense lobbying. Finally in August 1969, the president appointed the new members to the Citizen's Advisory Council on the Status of Women, a group established by President Kennedy; and in September he appointed a Task Force on Women's Rights and Responsibilities, one of 14 groups that was to generate ideas for his State of the Union message. In reality the task force was created more to silence his critics than to provide ideas, for while its report, *A Matter of Simple Justice,* went to the White House in mid-December, he ignored the subject of women in his address. Although the *Miami Herald* printed in full a leaked copy of the document in April 1971, the administration did not release the report officially to the public until two months later.[56]

A Matter of Simple Justice, though it took no new positions, stated the case for reform in stronger, more-urgent terms than any earlier document. It noted that the United States "lags behind other enlightened, and indeed some newly emerging, countries in the role ascribed to women." Discriminatory practices against women were "so widespread and pervasive," the report declared, that "they have come to be regarded, more often than not, as normal." The report disclaimed "special privileges" for women; rather it sought "equal rights." To secure these it recommended:

1. The establishment of an Office of Women's Rights and Responsibilities, whose director would report directly to the president
2. A White House Conference on Women's Rights and Responsibilities to be called by the president in 1970
3. A presidential message to Congress proposing legislation to curb discrimination against women and the passage of the ERA
4. The appointment of more women to high-level positions within the administration
5. Immediate issuance by the secretary of labor of guidelines to implement Executive Order 11375[57]

Presidential response was minimal. The sought-for sex-discrimination guidelines to implement Executive Order 11375 were issued; but the Women's Bureau, not the White House, hosted a conference. Congressional response, however, was considerable. Proposals were introduced to give the EEOC enforcement powers, to broaden the coverage of the Equal Pay Act, and to set up a nationwide program of child-care centers. The most comprehensive proposal, H.R. 916, introduced by Abner Mikva, embodied most of the task force's recommendations. Congress faced a broad agenda of women's issues in the seventies.[58]

While the White House remained cool to women's issues, the leadership of the Women's Bureau was warming up to them. A longtime proponent of protective legislation for working women, the bureau shifted its stance sharply when Elizabeth Koontz became director in January 1969. A black and a former teacher and president of the National Education Association (NEA), Koontz abandoned the Bureau's preoccupation with protective legislation and committed it to support an ERA. A conference commemorating the bureau's 50th anniversary warmly endorsed the task force's recommendations, including the ERA. Koontz also persuaded the Department of Labor to endorse the ERA, while Patricia Nixon reaffirmed the president's support of an amendment.[59]

WORK PROLIFERATES

At the onset of the sixties the American economy was booming. In the course of the decade the labor force increased by 13,187,000 persons, a 19.5 percent gain. Although the nation's growing population required more production and service workers, the major occupational groups grew unevenly, as is illustrated in Figure 7-1. The farm sector declined in absolute numbers of workers. While demand for nonfarm laborers increased modestly in numbers, the growth rate was only three-fourths that for the

Figure 7-1
Change in Employment by Occupational Group,
1960–1970 and 1970–1980

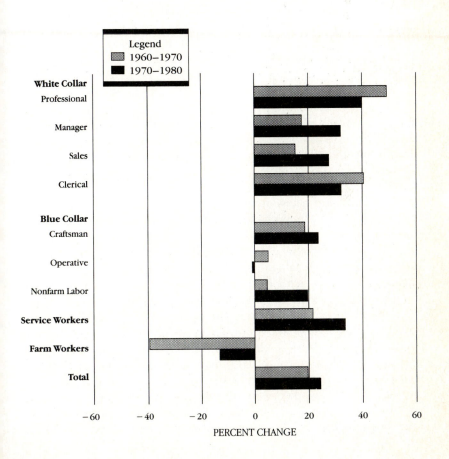

total economy. Four other occupational groups—managers, sales workers, operatives, and craft and kindred workers—fell short of keeping pace with the total economy. Service employment fared slightly better, but only two occupational groups—clerical and professional workers—grew at rates markedly faster than the whole economy. The growth of corporate enterprise generated a "tidal wave of paper work," requiring increasing numbers of secretaries, business-machine operatives, and clerks. A rising level of affluence combined with the spread of group health insurance, medicare, and medicaid strengthened the demand for health workers. The baby boom of the late forties and early fifties increased the demand for teachers in the sixties.[60]

The Rising Demand

With the great majority of working-age males already in the labor force, continued economic growth required the recruitment of an increasing proportion of women into the labor market. Indeed, women provided three fifths of the incremental labor force. Three factors shaped the demand for these additional female workers. First, the highest growth rates occurred in the service sector. Thus, clerical and professional employments, which grew by 40.5 percent and 49.1 percent respectively during the sixties, absorbed 5.2 million of the 7.8 million women who joined the labor force. Blue-collar service work added another 1.2 million women to the ranks. Even within these broad occupational groups, women's gains were centered in selected occupations. Internal shifts in the professional groups that began in the forties continued through the sixties, so that men tended to concentrate even more in the classic professions as doctors, lawyers, engineers, and college professors. Women, however, continued to dominate the ranks of elementary and secondary teachers, nurses, and librarians. With the rise of new professions, the classic male professions lost some of their special patina. There was modest growth in factory employments, and women increased their presence in such employments, especially in enterprises that were female-intensive.[61]

Second, the old female-dominated occupations provided the principal vehicle for expanding women's roles in the labor force. Thus, clerical work—in which two of three workers in 1960 were female—was also a major growth area; 3.6 of the 3.9 million persons added to the clerical occupations were women. In the blue-collar service area in which nearly two of every three workers were women, women's share increased a modest 1.6 percentage points, but because of the magnitude of this area, 1,248,000 jobs were added to the work force. Demand for operatives grew sluggishly, yet nearly 1 million additional women found employment in this sector, almost matching worker-for-worker the males who entered this area (see Figure 7-2; compare with Figure 6-1).[62]

Third, women scored modest inroads in occupations that had long been male-dominated. The demand for women as nonfarm laborers increased from 82,000 in 1960 to 136,000 in 1970, a 65 percent increase. Crafts, which employed a scant 250,000 women in 1960, employed 332,000 a decade later, a 49.5 percent increase. So too, women increased their

Figure 7-2
Female Labor Force by Occupation, 1960 and 1970

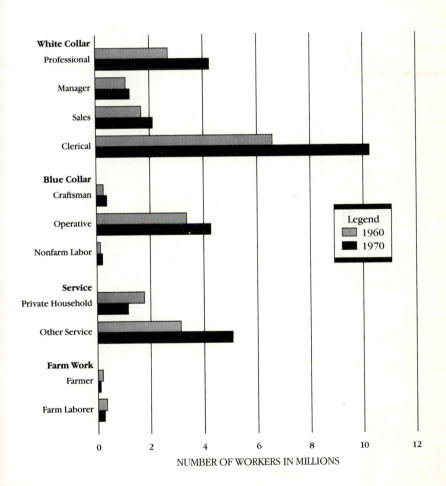

NUMBER OF WORKERS IN MILLIONS

presence as construction workers, mechanics, and repairers, as well as blue-collar supervisors. Signal gains were scored in such nontraditional employments as transport. As in earlier decades, the number of women engaged as farm laborers declined by over 400,000.[63]

A final question respecting the changing demand for female labor has to do with how much of the total increment in the female labor force was attributable to the growth of the occupations—a constant share vis-à-vis male workers—and how much was attributable to an expanded employment share for women. Of the women who poured into the labor force in the sixties, 74 percent, or 5.8 million, were accounted for by the growth in various occupations. Inevitably those occupations that already had large concentrations of women absorbed large numbers of them. More telling is the occupational distribution of the 2,027,000 women who constituted the expanded share. As is evident in Figure 7-3 (compare with Figures 2-2, 3-7, 4-2, and 6-2), the largest numbers were recruited into clerical work, a "predominantly female" occupation, with employment as professionals and operatives a distant second and third, respectively. Proportionately, however, the three blue-collar occupations outdrew all others, the expanded employment share accounting for as much as 93 percent of the increments to the ranks of nonfarm laborers to as little as 43 percent for operatives. At a time when a feminist ideology was being actively debated, employers were offering and women were accepting employment in jobs previously regarded as "male" positions.[64]

The Escalating Supply

In evaluating the changing supply of female labor, two considerations are relevant—demographic and attitudinal factors. As labor economists began studying the female labor force in the 1960s, a number of scholars—John D. Durand, Robert Smuts, Gertrude Bancroft, and Clarence Long among them—concluded that prior to 1960, at least, demographic changes had operated to depress the aggregate labor force rate for women or, at most, accounted for only a small part of the increases.[65]

Demographic Factors   As noted earlier, the expanding demand for female workers in the 1940s coincided with a decline in the proportion of young single women in the population. Indeed, between 1940 and 1965 the shifting mix of single and married women produced a shortfall of 9.7 million single women and a bonus of 7.1 million married women. Of necessity, employers recruited married women or did without. In the second half of the sixties the "aging baby-boom" children (those born 1945 to 1950) came of age, reversing the earlier trend and swelling the pool of

Figure 7-3
Changes in Demand for Female Workers, 1960–1970

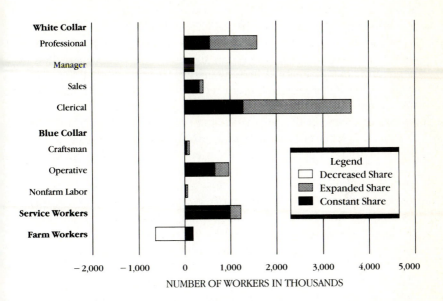

young single women who joined the enlarged pool of older married women.[66]

Working hand in hand with this shift in the mix of single and married women was a sharp rise in the age at first marriage, a declining marriage rate, and a falling birthrate. The rise in age at first marriage and the declining marriage rate worked to enhance the proportion of single women at the expense of the number of young married women. Of the cohort of women who reached age 20 in the late 1950s, 30 percent had married by age 18 in contrast to 17 percent of the cohort that reached age 20 in the early seventies. Even without a change in their attitude toward the acceptability of employment, either an increase in the proportion of young women in the total female population or a decision of young women to delay marriage or a combination thereof was capable of boosting the aggregate labor rate of women.[67]

A concomitant of the introduction of oral contraceptives in the early sixties was a drop in the fertility levels. Between 1960 and 1976 the birthrate plummeted by 24.2 percent, reaching the lowest rate thus far recorded in the United States (see Figure 6-10). The causes for this remain debatable. Richard Easterlin attributes the decline "chiefly to a reduction in fertility intentions." Larry Bumpass goes further, suggesting that improved fertility control triggered a shift in values toward motherhood, encouraging couples "to weigh more objectively the costs and benefits of having children" and permitting the wife to make "a fuller commitment to non-familial roles, including employment." But others such as Norman B. Ryder and Charles Westoff accord greater emphasis to the reduction of "accidental pregnancies" as a result of the pill. Certainly the delay first in marriage then in beginning a family enabled these young women to get a solid start in a career. The smaller families in turn reduced the quantity and duration of the mother's child-care responsibilities. Given the still diminished supply of single women in the late sixties, the pressure to meet the increased demand for female labor impinged most directly on younger, married women with preschool children. Their entrance into the labor force was facilitated by their relatively high level of education and its recency. The pressure of inflation in the late sixties, which added to the difficulty of supporting a family on a single income, acted as another goad to push women into the labor force and to keep them there.[68]

Finally, a soaring divorce rate, illustrated in Figure 6-9, augmented the supply of women likely to enter the work force. During the fifties the divorce rate had run along at 15 to 16 divorces per 1,000 married women (14 to 44 years of age), but in the late sixties, the rate suddenly shot upward, reaching a level of 32 during the period 1972 to 1974. The effect was to increase the percentage of divorced women in the population and to add an extra 500,000 divorced women to the labor force. These women shifted statistically from a group with a labor-force rate in the range of 30.5 to 47.6 to one in the range of 71.2 to 74.0. The net impact here too was to nudge upward the aggregate labor-participation rate of women.[69]

There seems to be ample reason to conclude, then, that during the late sixties changes in the demographic mix of women gave employers a more ample pool of young single women from which to recruit female workers—women with a high propensity to enter the labor market. The changes also enhanced the supply of older married women. Although the labor-force rate for these older women ought to have declined, in fact, it rose as women's attitudes toward market labor changed. In deciding whether or not to seek market work, a woman was subject to "a complex combination of social, psychological, and economic factors in her current and past (and even future) environments." These factors impacted differently on women according to their marital status, age, and ethnicity.[70]

MARITAL STATUS   Marital status was the most important determinant of the escalating supply of female labor. In 1960, single women constituted almost one fourth of the female labor force, and they were the predominant element among working women under 25. Entering the labor force part-time or temporarily while still in school, they moved to full-time work as they completed their education. By their mid-20s, four fifths or more were employed, and their employment rates remained high, though the number of single women dwindled. A second block of women, numbering about one fifth of the female labor force, consisted of the separated, the divorced, and the widowed. Separated and divorced women were distributed rather evenly throughout the population over age 25. Their employment rates were relatively high—60 percent for separated women, 80 percent for divorced women. Widows in their late 50s and early 60s, the age when this group formed a significant part of the labor force, had an employment rate of 50 percent.[71]

Married women, who comprised 60 percent of the total female work-ing population in 1960, formed its central core. Even within this group the propensity to secure market work varied widely according to the number and ages of the woman's own children. For example, women living with their husbands and who had children under 3 years old had labor rates at the 15 percent level compared to 39 percent for women whose youngest child was at least 6 years old.[72]

Between 1960 and 1970 the propensity of women to substitute market labor for home work rose by 5.6 points and expanded women's partici-pation in the labor force by 5.25 million persons. Of first importance, married women accounted for seven tenths of this expanded participation in the labor force. Those with preschool children made an impressive showing. Their labor-participation rate climbed nearly 12 points, and they provided 16 percent of the expanded participation increment; women with school-age children accounted for another 25 percent as their labor-force rates increased 10 points; and those with no children under 18, whose rates rose but 7.5 points, contributed 28 percent. At the same time, the labor-force rates of single women rose nearly 9 points, and they contrib-uted not quite one fifth of the expanded participation (compare with Fig-ure 4-3). The other marital-status groups failed even to maintain a constant share of the female labor force.[73]

The growing female labor force recruited selectively by age group as well as by marital status. The increased participation of women in the labor force, which had begun with older women during the 1940s and 1950s, became general among all women age 25 to 54 during the sixties. Figure 7-4 illustrates the point (compare with Figures 1-3, 2-4, and 3-5). Of women beyond age 65, however, a declining proportion were in the work force. The immunity of these older women to the blandishments of the labor market reflected the increasing efficacy of the Social Security system in blunting the need to work after age 65 in order to survive; at the other

Figure 7-4
LFPR of All Women by Age, 1940–1980

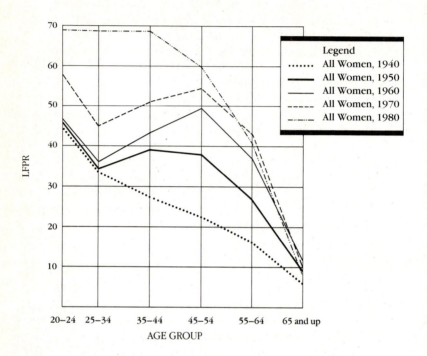

end of the age continuum, teenagers contributed only a token number of additional workers in the sixties. Most of those under 18 were preoccupied with school. In fact their labor-force rates declined between 1960 and 1965, then shot ahead in the late sixties. The 25- to 34-year-old group—the age range of married women with young children—contributed most heavily to the expansion of the female labor force and generated 26 percent of the increment during the sixties.[74]

MINORITY WORKERS   Women in the nonwhite, non-Anglo cultures responded in varying degrees to the pushes and pulls that moved Anglo women into the labor force. Comprising 83.4 percent of the female labor force, the Anglo population set the norms. The blacks, the largest minority, contributed 11.7 percent to the female labor force; Hispanics, 3.6 percent. The other minorities—the Asian Americans and Indians—contributed the balance, less than 2 percent.[75]

The labor-participation rates of the minority women varied widely in 1960. The aggregate rate for white women was 36 percent, 38.5 percent

for black women. Chinese American and Japanese American women surpassed the rate for white women by a margin of 6 points, while American
Indian women had a rate 14 points lower.[76]

During the sixties, minority women increased their participation in
the labor force by wider margins than did white women. Blacks, for example, advanced their labor-force rate by 9 percentage points compared to 6
for white women. Japanese American and Chinese American women fared
even better, advancing by 14 to 15 points, while the labor rate for Indian
women ostensibly jumped 23 points. Among the various Hispanics, whose
rates were first measured in 1970, the Puerto Ricans had the lowest rates,
followed closely by the Mexican Americans. By contrast, only Filipino women
had a higher rate than did Cuban women.[77]

These aggregate labor force participation rates are often deceptive,
for severely skewed age distributions tended to distort the aggregate labor
rate. When the age distributions are standardized, differences in the labor-
force rates between Japanese and Chinese women with respect to white
women are cut by one half. Although substantial differences marked their
aggregate labor-force rates, the age-specific rates for black, white, and
Chinese women age 20 to 24 were almost identical; at the same time,
though Chinese and Japanese women had similar aggregate rates, their
age-specific rates differed by as much as 7 points. The participation rates
for blacks inflate their labor effort as compared with whites, because the
blacks were so much more extensively involved in the labor force as part-
time and part-year workers. As the minority women stood outside the
mainstream of American society, the rising tide of feminism can scarcely
be credited with stimulating them to adopt more favorable views of market
work. On the other hand the operation of the Civil Rights Act of 1964 made
employers more receptive to applications from minority women, which
emboldened some minority women to seek employment who otherwise
would have stayed home.[78]

The occupational distribution of minority women differed significantly
from that of Anglo-American women, as Figure 7-5 indicates. Among the
Anglos in 1970, 64 percent were in white-collar employments, 17 percent
in blue-collar work, and 16 percent in service work. Only the Japanese
American and Chinese American women approximated Anglo women's
involvement in white-collar work, a reflection of the high level of education
they attained. No more than 35 to 40 percent of the black, Indian, Mexican,
and Puerto Rican women obtained white-collar work. A disproportionate
43 percent of the black women were in low-paying, low-status service
work, many as domestics. Indian women, too, were likely to be employed
as service workers, while Puerto Rican women stood out because of the
high proportion employed as operatives.[79]

Figure 7-5
Occupational Distribution by Race and Ethnic Group, 1960 and 1970

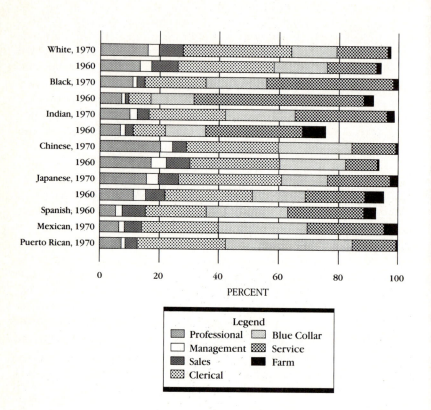

During the sixties, minority women generally expanded their employment in white-collar work and reduced the differences between white and minority employment patterns. As blacks continued to shed their position as private-household workers, they made substantial advances in securing clerical and professional employment. As compared with white women, blacks remained underrepresented in professional fields and overrepresented in service occupations. Although remaining at the bottom of the socioeconomic scale, Indian women increased their position in clerical work by 70 percent. As they extricated themselves from private-household work, they expanded their activity in comparatively more secure service work. Japanese American women increased their already strong position in white-collar work.[80]

With the exception of black women, the minority groups made little impact on the female labor force. Clearly the largest minority, during the sixties black women increased their numbers in the labor force by 1,136,000, of whom 680,000 represented the increment due to higher labor-force rates. Indians, Japanese Americans, and Chinese Americans also entered the labor force in unprecedented numbers. The magnitude of the expanded shares for them—110,000 in all—had little effect on the size or character of the female labor force. But because entrance into the labor market provided access to a higher level of living, better medical care, and expanded educational opportunities for their children, the gains were critically important to the long-term well-being of the minority worker and her family.[81]

ELASTICITY OF LABOR　An important aspect of the supply of female labor was its elasticity. The availability of work ranging from full-time year-round to part-time part-year offered women wide choices in trading off home work and leisure for market work. It eased the burden of women who were ambivalent about the propriety and feasibility of committing themselves to the labor force. Certainly the massive influx of married women with young children, which did so much to swell the aggregate female labor rate, was facilitated by part-year and part-time employment. It also inflated the labor-force rate of females as compared with men, for whom the labor-force rate more nearly represented full-time year-round work.[82]

In 1960, 46.9 percent of all working women were employed at least 50 weeks a year, but as Figure 7-6 indicates, the proportions varied widely according to marital status. Among single and divorced women in the age range 25 to 54, 50 to 55 percent worked year-round in contrast to 20 to 40 percent of married women with preschool children. But by far the largest number of working women either in 1959 or 1969 worked either part-year or part-time.[83]

During the sixties the proportion of part-time workers held constant at one third of the female labor force. But the number of weeks per year of employment increased significantly. So, too, numbers of full-time part-year workers began working year-round, the proportion climbing to 42 percent. Altogether the rise in the mean number of weeks women devoted to market labor accounted for 34 percent of the gain in the total female labor effort (see Figure 6-8). An unresolved question remained—the impact of this expanded work commitment on the number of women in the labor force.[84]

EDUCATIONAL ATTAINMENT　The supply—both in quantity and quality—of the female labor force was affected by educational attainment. Women who

Figure 7-6
Percent of Working Women Employed 50–52 Weeks Per Year
by Marital Status and Age, 1959 and 1969

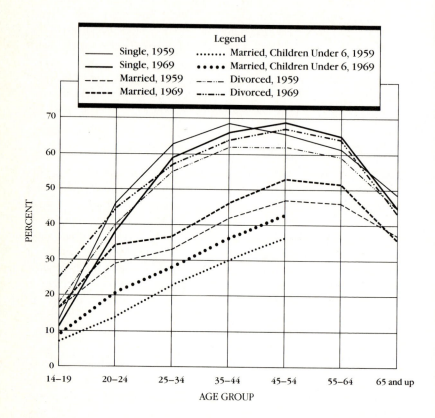

did not complete high school were markedly less likely to work than those with four or more years of college by a margin of nearly 22 points in 1959 and 33 points in 1978 (see Figure 7-7). Changes in school- and college-enrollment patterns of the sixties in effect reduced the size of the population least likely to enter the labor force by two thirds while doubling the group with the highest propensity to work. But those women who had not completed high school were increasingly at a disadvantage in competing for employment.[85]

Acquisition of an education enhanced employability and earning potential. It both reinforced and reflected an individual's motivation for a career. The potential wages from market labor increased the opportunity

Figure 7-7
LFPR for Women 18 Years and Over by Years of School Completed

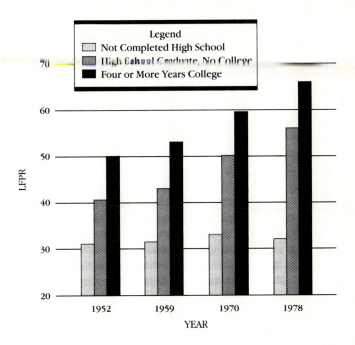

costs of restricting oneself to home work. But it did more. The more education a woman acquired, the longer she was likely to remain single and the less likely she would ever marry. Well-educated women bore fewer children, reducing the impediments to substituting market work for home work. The level of education substantially affected "access to the cleaner, more pleasant, more interesting jobs." Women with no more than an elementary education were concentrated in service and factory work. Scarcely one in ten such women got any kind of white-collar job. By contrast nearly two thirds of the high school graduates and 95 percent of the college graduates were in white-collar jobs, the former in sales and clerical work, the latter in professional and technical employments. The relationship between access to education and access to employment commensurate with one's abilities was crystal clear.[86]

During the sixties the largest single factor in accounting for the numerical growth in the female labor force was the growth in the total population—the constant-share increment. The changing demography of the female population explains some of the growth—the expanded share—of which the woman's education and expected family size were the most important variables. The age of the mothers of preschool children, the age of the youngest child, and the number of hours worked most adequately explain the rising labor-force participation of married women with preschool children.[87]

Attitudinal Factors   Attitudinal factors operated in tandem with the forgoing demographic factors. Researchers using data from the Census Bureau or the Bureau of Labor Statistics have generally ignored the question of attitude, but as the research of Jean Dowdall reveals, attitudes cannot be ignored. Furthermore, the importance of the attitudinal variable depended on the economic position of the woman. High-income married women tended to hold paid jobs "in accord with their own attitudes of approval or disapproval," while the employment status of low-income women was "more closely associated with their familial responsibilities." It seems clear that if the numerical growth of the labor force reflected the growth of the total population, the chief dynamic ingredient was attitudinal: a change in the acceptability of work that induced a larger proportion of women in all categories—marital groups, age groups, educational levels, ethnic groups—to view market work more favorably. It is also clear from the statistics that in the sixties women moved into the labor force in advance of the emergence of a full-blown feminist movement.[88]

EDUCATION IN THE SIXTIES

The outstanding development in women's education in the sixties was the unprecedented increase in the number and proportion of women securing high-school diplomas and completing undergraduate, graduate, and professional degrees. Although ever since the Seneca Falls convention access to education had been a major tenet of feminist faith, the reemergence of organized feminism was a concomitant rather than a principal cause of this development. First, there was a marked increase in the magnitude of the high-school- and college-age population, which was responsible for record numbers of women completing high school, receiving baccalaureate degrees, and earning advanced graduate degrees. More important, however, was the increasing propensity of women to secure a collegiate education. At the baccalaureate level the proportion of college-age women earning degrees rose from 15 percent in 1960 to 21 percent in 1970. The disparities in rates at which men and women earned baccalaureates narrowed. The proportion of women with baccalaureates who secured master's degrees increased sharply from 21 percent in 1960 to 30 percent in 1970, while the proportion who earned doctorates jumped from 10 in 1,000 to 26 in 1,000 in the same time period. Although men continued to have a greater propensity to earn doctorates than women, here too the disparities between the rates for men and women narrowed.[89]

A second phenomenon, the change in the fields of study in which women took their degrees, was more important for the direction of change than for its magnitude. Two thirds of the women baccalaureates of 1960 had majored in education, English and journalism, or the social sciences. Women were conspicuously absent in such major areas as business and commerce and engineering. They were also underrepresented in such areas as architecture, agriculture, philosophy, and the physical sciences. On the other hand, they were much overrepresented in home economics, library science, health professions, education, foreign languages, literature, English, and journalism. In the course of the decade, women increased their share of baccalaureates in nearly every field, which meant that women were reaching out into areas in which they had been underrepresented, especially in architecture, mathematics, and psychology. At the professional level women secured a miniscule share of the degrees in all fields, obtaining 9.2 percent of the medical degrees in 1970 and 7.3 percent of the law degrees. In most other fields they earned fewer than three percent of the degrees. The advances, then, were concentrated in the undergraduate areas.[90]

During the sixties, American schools were severely criticized as inadequate. Russian schools, William Benton reported from personal observation, were "bursting with new energy, new ingenuity." In the same vein, Vice Admiral Hyman Rickover argued that by comparison with English youngsters, American school children were behind "almost from the first day at school." Having studied the American system extensively, James B. Conant singled out specific areas of weakness. He pointed to a shortage of qualified teachers and the need for higher salaries to attract competent ones. He also argued for the need for "pushing our bright students harder." Other critics focused on community control, ghetto schools, the participation of blacks, teacher power, and tax reform. Taken as a whole, the major focus was on the nationwide character of school problems and the need for national solutions. A major program of federal aid was proposed in January 1963 by President Kennedy, a program that was reshaped as part of Lyndon Johnson's Great Society program. To the extent that the discussion focused on educational quality, females would be beneficiaries of the reforms, but as students not as females. A perceived need for continuing education did, however, recognize that older women had special educational needs in their character as women.[91]

During the late sixties, feminists became increasingly sensitive to flaws in the educational programs of the nation's schools that had hitherto escaped attention. Much of their energy was directed at exploring the mechanisms by which the schools inculcated traditional differentiated sex roles. One target was the teaching materials, especially books used in elementary schools, that invariably portrayed "women as mothers—nurses, mothers, teachers, mothers, mothers, mothers, mothers—mothers in an endless round of baking, dusting, ironing, and waving goodby." By contrast, fathers were doers—they drove trucks, flew airplanes, fixed broken wagons, ran businesses, and were important, decision-making, power-wielding persons. Boys played exciting games; girls watched. Feminists first surveyed school textbooks as well as children's trade books and picture books. Feminists on Children's Media—a group of New York and New Jersey teachers, children's book editors, and mothers—sent their report to the state committees responsible for the selection of school readers. In April 1970, in a move reminiscent of the "white label" campaign of the National Consumers' League, they compiled and distributed a list of 200 "good" children's books. Similar lists were prepared by the New York Task Force on the Status of Women in the Church and by numerous state commissions on the status of women. Yet another approach resulted in the formation of feminist presses to produce "nonsexist" children's books and educational materials. Concern with sex-role conditioning also led to deemphasizing at home and school both play and toys that directed girls toward dolls and stoves and boys toward building blocks and toy cars and trucks.[92]

Feminist concern with high schools took a different tack. In a number of institutions, students, supported by parents, pressed school authorities to open shop classes to girls and home-economics courses to boys. In New York, a junior-high-school girl sued to be admitted to a shop course; in Seattle a suit alleged that girls were discriminated against by being required to take home economics as a graduation requirement whereas boys were not. In a number of districts, girls pressed for equity in school athletic programs—for the right to participate in noncontact sports, such as tennis, if they could make the team, for equitable financial support of girls' sports, for equal pay for coaches of girls' teams. Still another area of concern was high-school dress codes. Although the length of boys' hair was the major issue, the right of female students to wear slacks to school was also at issue. Subsequent to a favorable ruling by the New York State commissioner of education, a Westchester County girl declared that in wearing slacks she felt "more equal with boys" and less worried as "to how my legs are placed" and that she was no longer "fighting other girls for the attention of boys." As at the elementary level, the problem of sex-biased texts cropped up. Conventional history texts presented a world populated chiefly by men, according token attention to queens and an occasional woman reformer or writer. Taking note of this state of affairs, the American Federation of Teachers in August 1970 called for a major investigation of school texts. Corrective action was left for the seventies.[93]

The principal target of feminists was higher education because the potential for harm or help was more immediate than at the elementary or secondary level. Without access to undergraduate, graduate, or professional training, women were excluded from many social, economic, and political paths to equality. Indeed, they were blocked from realizing their personal potential. The recognition of the negative impact of sex-stereotyped education led many older middle-class college-educated women to respond positively to Betty Friedan's attack on the "sex-directed educators." As early as 1953, Mirra Komarovsky challenged the "neo-anti feminism" of Lynn White, Amram Scheinfeld, and the functionalists. Reviewing psychological test data, Komarovsky concluded that the differences between members of the same sex far exceed the differences between the sexes. From this she inferred "the need for a rich and flexible curriculum within which both the common and unique talents of individuals, irrespective of sex, will be recognized and fostered." If women were ever to contribute fully to American society, they would have to gain positions of leadership where their talents could count. That women were not attaining such leadership roles was evident by the conspicuous absence of women in public office and on the medical and surgical staffs of the nation's hospitals, the rosters of the bar associations, the ranks of corporate directors, and the faculties of the country's colleges.[94]

The heart of the problem remained society's perception of the proper sphere of woman. Catholic women's colleges, numbering about half of all the nation's women's schools, were generally "ideological bastions of resistance" to the feminist cause. Founded "to educate girls while protecting their chastity," such schools offered little support for a major shift in sex roles. Neither did the "finishing schools," which were designed primarily to prepare girls for marriage and motherhood or, failing a suitable match, a "feminine" job. Even the elite Seven Sisters had succumbed to traditional views of womanhood. To the 1930s these colleges had offered women "the most exacting" education women could obtain; to that time they had been "dominated by social reformers, dedicated to androgyny or minimizing sex differences, and hopelessly upper class." After World War II these colleges, led by proestablishment administrators "concerned with making college a place where daughters of self-made fathers could learn how to meet and marry desirable husbands," adopted traditional views of the female role. The coed colleges remained male-dominated and career-oriented. The coeds were surrounded by males who regarded them as "date bait" or—if the relationship became serious—a possible source of support, the young woman dropping out of college to work so her student-husband might complete his degree. Most coeds might see firsthand that the few women employed by their colleges occupied the low-prestige, low-paid "women's jobs."[95]

A student feminist movement first blossomed in coed schools in the late 1960s, as women who had been active in the civil-rights movement, the New Left and the Students for a Democratic Society (SDS), and the peace movement began to examine their status as women. Some of their demands reflected radical student interests, others those of sexual liberation, and still others a feminist ideology. The issues surfaced in no particular order, although a cause célèbre at one school often stimulated similar demands at other institutions.[96]

During the late sixties, women students pressed a variety of concerns relating to sexuality. The Pill, introduced in the early sixties, and the sexual revolution resulted in more casual male–female relations and less concern with marriage. Women students pressed campus health services for birth-control information and access to contraception, demands that college administrators resisted until after the Supreme Court held that the unmarried had a right to access to contraception.[97]

More troublesome—because of the emotional reactions and legal issues—were questions relating to pregnancy counseling and abortion referral. College health services were not equipped to perform abortions, and most declined to refer students seeking abortions to clinics that were. To the extent that anyone took responsibility for abortion counseling, it was the campus pastors who did so.[98]

Feminist attacks on institutional efforts to exercise the *in loco parentis* role rocked hundreds of campuses. From the inception of higher education for women, residential schools asserted a degree of personal control over women students never imposed on men. Typically until the late 1960s or early 1970s, college authorities required women students to sign out whenever leaving their dormitories after supper; required them to return to their dormitories by 10:00 or 10:30 on weeknights and by midnight on Saturdays; and prohibited men and women students from visiting each other in their dormitory rooms. Most schools proscribed slacks or shorts in the classrooms or at the principal meal of the day in the dining halls. By the late 1960s women students claimed the right to be as free of such paternalistic rules as men students. One prescription for terminating such regulations was a mass walk-out of women students after-hours, which was repeated nightly until college authorities nullified the regulations. Hours' regulations and dress codes fell first; in time a wide variety of plans permitting visitation in rooms were introduced. While some students demanded coed dormitories, others opted to live off-campus, making their living arrangements to suit themselves. By the mid-seventies, coed dormitories were commonplace, and many colleges abandoned all efforts to restrict students to "approved housing."[99]

As radical students organized "free universities" that offered courses on peace and war, Marxism, Leninism, and Maoism (along with instruction in macrame and organic gardening), feminists demanded courses in women's studies. An informal colloquium on the nature of the female personality at Cornell University in spring 1969 was transformed a year later into a formal course, "Evolution of the Female Personality." In the early seventies, dozens of institutions, including Harvard and MIT, introduced one or more credit courses on women; by 1972 the number had passed 700. Such courses ranged broadly: literature, history, psychology, economics, law, and government.[100]

As the sixties came to an end, three points merit special emphasis. First, the considerable strides that women made in gaining equal access not only to college generally but to particular academic programs got much of its thrust from the same long-term secular trends that accounted for the rising LFPR for women and for the reemergence of organized feminism. Second, the reemergence of feminism, spurred by Betty Friedan, focused attention on the general problems of sexual discrimination in education. However, the concerted efforts to effect change began toward the end of the decade at the hands of militant feminists who sought not just to remove discriminatory barriers but to effect reforms that would facilitate the realization of an androgynous society. Whereas in earlier decades the leading critics of education usually came from the ranks of college administrators, in the sixties much of the leadership came from student activists and women faculty. Third, expressions of student feminism in the sixties had an ad hoc flavor. Organized student feminism was still very new, not widespread, and lacked a comprehensive program. The women's leaders were generally those who had been activists in the civil-rights movement, the New Left, or the peace movement. These activists were able to enlist mass followings for resolving a specific issue, such as *in loco parentis* regulations, when the rank and file of supporters were required to do little more than exhibit the enthusiasm of a homecoming pep rally. Student feminists, however, were on the threshold of having a major impact on women's education.

The nation was also deeply troubled by its unfulfilled promises. It was acutely aware of the pervasive poverty in which many of its people lived, of the second-class status of its blacks and other minorities, and of the economic problems engendered by its efforts to pursue both "butter and guns" and by its involvement in Vietnam. In the course of the decade unprecedented numbers of women had entered the labor force; the proportion of women earning college degrees had increased dramatically; and the Equal Pay Act and Title VII of the Civil Rights Act ostensibly had accorded women equality in the labor force. If the moderate statement of *The Feminine Mystique* had brought the issue of woman's place into the public realm, the emergence of radical feminist groups at the end of the sixties made solutions to those issues an urgent national concern.

NOTES

[1] C. Vann Woodward, *The Strange Career of Jim Crow,* 3rd rev. ed. (New York: Oxford, 1974), 169, 172. Lerone Bennett, Jr., *What Manner of Man, Martin Luther King, Jr.* (Chicago: Johnson, 1964), 71–76. Howard Zinn, *SNCC, The New Abolitionists* (Boston, Beacon, 1964). Clayborne Carson, *In Struggle SNCC and the Black Awakening of the 1960s* (Cambridge: Harvard University Press, 1981). Sara Evans, *Personal Politics: The Roots of Women's Liberation in the Civil Rights Movement and the New Left* (New York: Knopf, 1979). Mary Aicken Rothschild, "White Volunteers in the Freedom Summers," *FS,* 5(1979): 466–95. Paula Giddings, *When and Where I Enter* (New York: Morrow, 1984), 268–69.

[2] Giddings, *When and Where I Enter,* 277–92. Woodward, *Strange Career of Jim Crow,* 169.

[3] Woodward, *Strange Career of Jim Crow,* 174–79.

[4] Theodore C. Sorensen, *Kennedy* (New York: Harper & Row, 1965), 472. *NYT,* 12 June 1963, p. 20, col. 7. Woodward, *Strange Career of Jim Crow,* 172.

[5] Woodward, *Strange Career of Jim Crow,* 182–85.

[6] Leon Jones, "Brown Revisited: From Topeka, Kansas to Boston, Massachusetts," *Phylon,* 37(1976): 343. Robert J. Havighurst, "These Integration Approaches Work—Sometimes," *The Nation's Schools,* 80(Sept. 1967): 73–75. Kenneth B. Clark, "Desegregation: The Role of the Social Sciences," *Teachers College Record,* 62(Oct. 1960): 1–17. U.S. Commission on Civil Rights, *Isolation in the Public Schools* (Washington: GPO, 1967), vol. 1.

[7] Charles C. Alexander, *Holding the Line* (Bloomington: Indiana University Press, 1975), 121. Woodward, *Strange Career of Jim Crow,* 193, 194, 198.

[8] Giddings, *When and Where I Enter,* 296.

[9] *Report of the National Advisory Commission on Civil Disorders* (New York: Bantam, 1968), 42–107, reports on Cincinnati, Newark, and Detroit among other cities.

[10] Alfred H. Kelly and Winfred A. Harbison, *The American Constitution,* 4th ed. (New York: Norton, 1970), 973. Swann v. Charlotte-Mecklenburg Board of Education, 402 U.S. 1 (1971). Milliken v. Bradley, 41 L.Ed.2d 1069 (1974).

[11] "Moynihan Report," *NYT,* 1 March 1970. Kelly and Harbison, *American Constitution,* 972–73. John Hope Franklin, *From Slavery to Freedom,* 5th ed. (New York: Knopf, 1980), 482–84.

[12] Franklin, *From Slavery to Freedom,* 479.

[13] Charles S. Johnson, *The Negro in American Civilization* (New York: Holt, 1930). Johnson was editor of *Opportunity,* the journal of the National Urban League. Hortense Powdermaker, *After Freedom* (New York: Viking, 1939). E. Franklin Frazier, *The Negro Family in the United States* (Chicago: University of Chicago Press, 1939). Gunnar Myrdal, *An American Dilemma* (New York: Harper, 1944), 930–35.

[14] Myrdal, *An American Dilemma,* 933–35.

[15] Oscar Lewis, "The Culture of Poverty," *Scientific American,* 215(Oct. 1966): 19–25. Hylan Lewis, *Blackways of Kent* (Chapel Hill: University of North Carolina Press, 1955). Daniel Patrick Moynihan, *The Negro Family: The Case for National Action* (Washington: Dept. of Labor, March 1965), introduction, 29, 39, 48.

[16] Daniel P. Moynihan, "Moynihan Memorandum on the Status of Negroes," *NYT,* 1 Mar. 1970.

[17] Ibid.

[18] Virginia Heyer Young, "Family and Childhood in a Southern Negro Community," *American Anthropologist,* 72(April 1970): 272–74.

[19] Ibid., 271. Warren D. TenHouten, "The Black Family: Myth and Reality," *Psychiatry,* 33(May 1970): 170. Diane K. Lewis, "The Black Family: Socialization and Sex Roles," *Phylon,* 36(1975): 229 ff.

[20] The growth of the Mexican American population can only be estimated. The Census Bureau first used the label "Mexican-origin" in 1970. For earlier census tabulations it reported the number of Spanish-surname people and also of Spanish-language people for five states in the Southwest. The problem is further complicated by a serious undercount of undetermined magnitude of the Chicanos. A revised 1973 figure placed the Mexican-origin population at 6.3 million compared to 4.5 million in 1970. Bureau of the Census, "Persons of Spanish Origin in the United States: March 1973," *CPR,* P-20, no. 264 (Washington: GPO, 1973), 7–9.

[21] Matt S. Meier and Feliciano Rivera, *The Chicanos: A History of Mexican Americans* (New York: Hill and Wang, 1972), 203–209, chap. 13. Alejandro Portes, "Labor Functions of Illegal Aliens," *Society,* 14(Sept./Oct., 1977): 31–37, argues that only one third of the "illegals" are involved in agriculture, one third in goods-producing industries, and one third in service jobs.

[22] Carey McWilliams, *Ill Fares the Land* (Boston: Little, Brown, 1942), 23.

[23] Alfredo Mirande and Evangelina Enriquez, *La Chicana, The Mexican-American Woman* (Chicago: University of Chicago Press, 1979), 11–12.

[24] C. Wright Mills, Clarence Senior, and Rose Kohn Goldsen, *Puerto Rican Journey* (New York: Harper, 1950), 123. Joseph P. Fitzpatrick, *Puerto Rican Americans* (Englewood Cliffs: Prentice-Hall, 1971), 95.

[25] Kenneth L. Wilson and Alejandro Portes, "Immigrant Enclaves: An Analysis of the Labor Market Experiences of Cubans in Miami," *AJS,* 86(1980): 303.

[26] Richard R. Fagen, Richard A. Broady, and Thomas J. O'Leary, *Cubans in Exile* (Stanford: Stanford University Press, 1968). Wilson and Portes, "Immigrant Enclaves," 303.

[27] Wilson and Portes, "Immigrant Enclaves," 298, 303–304, 315. Bureau of the Census, *Census of Population: 1970, Subject Reports. Persons of Spanish Origin,* tabs. 7 and 8.

[28] Bureau of the Census, *Census, 1970, Persons of Spanish Origin,* tabs. 7–8.

[29] Bureau of the Census, *1980 Census of Population. Vol. 1, Characteristics of the Population,* PC 80-1 (Washington: GPO, 1981), tab. 163.

[30] Irene Fujitomi and Diane Wong, "The New Asian-American Woman," in *Asian-Americans: Psychological Perspectives,* ed. Stanley Sue and Nathaniel N. Wagner (Ben Lomond, CA: Science and Behavior Books, 1973), 259–60.

[31] Darrel Montero, "The Japanese-Americans: Changing Patterns of Assimilation Over Three Generations," *ASR,* 46(Dec. 1981): 829–39.

[32] Nathaniel N. Wagner, "Filipinos: A Minority within a Minority," in Sue and Wagner, *Asian-Americans,* 295.

[33] Antonio J. A. Pido, "Brain Drain Philippinos," *Society,* 14(Sept./Oct. 1977): 51. Wagner, "Filipinos," in Sue and Wagner, *Asian-Americans,* 296. Fred Cordova, "The Filipino-American: There's Always an Identity Crisis," in Sue and Wagner, *Asian-Americans,* 137.

[34] Cordova, "The Filipino-American," in Sue and Wagner, *Asian-Americans,* 137. Pido, "Brain Drain Philippinos," 50–51.

[35] Pido, "Brain Drain Philippinos," 53.

[36] Bureau of the Census, *Census of Population: 1970, Subject Reports, American Indians* PC(2)-1F (Washington: GPO, 1973), tab. 7, p. 86.

[37] D'Arcy McNickle, *Native American Tribalism* (London: Oxford University Press, 1973), 171. Clyde Kluckhohn and Dorothea Leighton, *The Navaho* (Cambridge: Harvard University Press, 1947), 92.

[38] Evon Z. Vogt, "Navajo," in *Perspectives in Indian Culture,* ed. Edward H. Spicer (Chicago: University of Chicago Press, 1961), 318.

[39] *NYT,* 12 Dec. 1976. Kluckhohn and Leighton, *The Navaho,* 59. Gary Witherspoon, "A New Look at Navajo Social Organization," *American Anthropologist,* 72(1970): 62–64.

[40] Ruth Underhill, *The Navajos* (Norman: University of Oklahoma Press, 1956), 268–69.

[41] James E. Officer, "The American Indian and Federal Policy," in *The American Indian in Urban Society,* ed. Jack O. Waddell and O. Michael Watson (Boston: Little, Brown, 1971), 46. Bureau of the Census, *Census, 1970, American Indians,* tab. 14.

[42] Bureau of the Census, *Census, 1970, American Indians,* tab. 14.

[43] Joseph G. Jorgensen, "Indians and the Metropolis," in Waddell and Watson, *American Indian in Urban Society,* 78–79. Merwyn S. Garbino, "Life in the City," in Waddell and Watson, *American Indian in Urban Society,* 169–205.

[44] Peter S. Snyder, "The Social Environment of the Urban Indian," in Waddell and Watson, *American Indian in Urban Society,* 207–243. William N. Fenton, "The Iroquois Confederacy in the Twentieth Century: A Case Study of the Theory of Lewis H. Morgan in 'Ancient Society,' " *Ethnology,* 4(1965): 259.

[45] Bureau of the Census, *Census of Population, 1970, Subject Reports, Marital Status,* PC(2)-4C (Washington: GPO, 1973), tab. 12.

[46] Judith Hole and Ellen Levine, *Rebirth of Feminism* (New York: Quadrangle, 1971), 18–28. Executive Order 10980, 14 Dec. 1961, established the commission. See also Cynthia E. Harrison, "A 'New Frontier' for Women: The Public Policy of the Kennedy Administration," *JAH,* 67(1980): 630–46.

[47] President's Commission on the Status of Women, *American Women* (Washington: GPO, 1963).

[48] Leo Kanowitz, *Women and the Law: The Unfinished Revolution* (Albuquerque: University of New Mexico Press, 1969), 121 ff. S. Rep. 176, 88th Cong., 1st sess., 1963.

[49] Caroline Bird, *Born Female* (New York: Pocket Books, 1969), 1–12. *Cong. Rec.,* 88th Cong., 2nd sess., 2577.

[50] Pub. L. No. 88-352.

[51] Bird, *Born Female,* 13.

[52] Weeks v. Southern Telephone and Telegraph Co., 408 F.2d, Rev. and rem, S.D. Ga. 277 F.Supp. 117 (1969).

[53] Phillips v. Martin-Marietta, 400 U.S. 542 (1971). U.S. v. Libbey-Owens-Ford, United Glass and Ceramic Workers of North America, AFL-CIO, Local 9; this suit, the first filed by the Justice Department under Title VII, was settled by a consent decree Dec. 7, 1970. *NYT,* 8 Dec. 1970, p. 53, col. 2.

[54] Quoted in Hole and Levine, *Rebirth of Feminism,* 42. Pittsburgh Press Co. v. Pittsburgh Commission on Human Relations, 413 U.S. 376 (1973); Griffiths quoted in *Cong. Rec.,* 89th Cong., 2nd sess., June 20, 1966, 13691.

[55] Hole and Levine, *Rebirth of Feminism,* 99. *NYT,* 26 July 1970 and 31 July 1970.

[56] President's Task Force on Women's Rights and Responsibilities, *A Matter of Simple Justice* (Washington: GPO, 1970).

[57] Ibid.

[58] U.S. Congress, House, *Hearings before Subcommittee No. 4 of the Committee on the Judiciary, 92 Cong., 1 sess., H.J. Res. 35, 208, and Related Bills and H.R. 916 and Related Bills, "Equal Rights for Men and Women 1971."*

[59] Department of Labor, Wage and Labor Standards Administration, *To Benefit Women at Work* (Washington: GPO, April 1969), 5–6, 54.

[60] Elizabeth Waldman and Beverly J. McEaddy, "Where women work—an analysis by industry and occupation," *MLR,* 97(May 1974): 3–13. Jean A. Dowdall, "Structural and Attitudinal Factors Associated with Female Labor Force Participation," *SSQ,* 55(June 1974): 122.

[61] Rudolph C. Blitz, "Women in the professions, 1870–1970," *MLR,* 97(May 1974): 34–39. Waldman and McEaddy, "Where women work," 3.

[62] Bureau of the Census, *Statistical Abstract of the United States: 1979* (Washington: GPO, 1979), tab. 685. Bureau of the Census, *Statistical Abstract of the United States: 1974* (Washington: GPO, 1974), tab. 571.

[63] Bureau of the Census, *Statistical Abstract, 1974* tab. 571.

[64] Bureau of the Census, *Statistical Abstract, 1979,* tabs. 660, 661, 662. Bureau of Labor Statistics, *Employment and Earnings,* 27(Dec. 1980), tab. A21, p. 34.

[65] John D. Durand, *The Labor Force in the United States 1890–1960* (New York: SSRC, 1948). Gertrude Bancroft, *American Labor Force* (New York: Wiley, 1958). Robert W. Smuts, *Women and Work in America* (New York: Columbia University Press, 1959). Clarence Long, *The Labor Force Under Changing Income and Employment* (Princeton: Princeton University Press, 1958). A. J. Jaffe and S. L. Wolfbein, "Demographic Factors in Labor Force Growth," *ASR,* 11(Aug. 1946): 393–96. Stanley Lebergott, "Population Change and the Supply of Labor," in National Bureau of Economic Research, *Demographic and Economic Change in Developed Countries* (Princeton: Princeton University Press, 1958), 377–422. Jacob Mincer, "Labor Force Participation of Married Women: A Study of Labor Supply," in National Bureau of Economic Research, *Aspects of Labor Economics* (Princeton: Princeton University Press, 1962), 63–105.

[66] Beverly L. Johnson, "Changes in marital and family characteristics of workers, 1970–78," *MLR,* 102(April 1979): 51–52.

[67] Bureau of the Census, "A Statistical Portrait of Women in the United States," *CPR,* Special Studies P-23, no. 58 (Washington: GPO, 1976), tab. 5–3, p. 20. Valerie Kincade Oppenheimer, "Demographic Influence on Female Employment and the Status of Women," *AJS,* 78(Jan. 1973): 946–61.

[68] Bureau of the Census, *Statistical Abstract, 1979,* tab. 48. Richard Easterlin, *Population, Labor Force and Long Swings in Economic Growth: The American Experience* (New York: National Bureau of Economic Research, 1968): 123–28. Charles Westoff et al., *Toward the End of Growth* (Englewood Cliffs: Prentice-Hall, 1973), 70. Larry Bumpass, "Is Low Fertility Here to Stay?" *Family Planning Perspectives,* 5(Spring, 1973): 78.

[69] Bureau of the Census, "A Statistical Portrait of Women," tab. 4-1, p. 16.

[70] Dowdall, "Structural and Attitudinal Factors Associated with Female Labor Force Participation," 121. Bancroft, *American Labor Force,* 41, observes that the unmarried, some widows and divorcees have the same need to work as men, but they don't grow up facing the need as inevitable as do their brothers.

[71] Allyson Sherman Grossman, "Labor force patterns of single women," *MLR,* 102(Aug. 1979): 46–49.

[72] Bureau of the Census, "A Statistical Portrait of Women," 15–20.

[73] Bureau of Labor Statistics, *Handbook of Labor Statistics* (Washington: GPO, 1979), tab. 5, 14.

[74] Janet L. Norwood and Elizabeth Waldman, "Women in the Labor Force: Some New Data Series," Bureau of Labor Statistics, 1979, Report 575, p. 2. Allyson Sherman Grossman, "Women in the labor force: the early years," *MLR,* 98(Nov. 1975): 3–9, treats women 16 to 24

years old. Deborah Pisetzner Klein, "Women in the labor force: the middle years," *MLR* 98(Nov. 1975): 10. Robert W. Bednarzik and Deborah P. Klein, "Labor force trends: a synthesis and analysis," *MLR,* 100(Oct. 1977): 8.

[75] Bureau of the Census, *U.S. Census of Population: 1960 Subject Reports, Occupational Characteristics,* PC(2)-7A (Washington: GPO, 1963), tabs. 3, 6, 33, 34, 35. Dale L. Hiestand, *Economic Growth and Employment Opportunities for Minorities* (New York: Columbia University Press, 1964).

[76] Bureau of the Census, *Census of Population, 1960, Occupational Characteristics,* tabs. 3, 6, 33, 34, 35.

[77] Ibid., tab. 2, p. 12–27. Bureau of the Census, *Census, of Population: 1970, Persons of Spanish Origin,* PC(2)-1C (Washington: GPO, 1973), tab. 7, pp. 75, 81, 84.

[78] Daniel E. Jaco and George L. Wilber, "Asian-Americans in the labor market," *MLR,* 98(1975): 33–38. William G. Bowen and T. Aldrich Finegan, *The Economics of Labor Force Participation* (Princeton: Princeton University Press, 1969), 91–94. Sally R. Sherman, "Labor Force Status of Women on the Threshold of Retirement," *SSB,* 37(Sept. 1974): 7–9, concludes that "the health of white and nonwhite women had a substantial bearing on the LFPR of women. When health limitations are controlled, the racial differences in participation virtually disappear. Her study treated women 58 to 63 years of age.

[79] See note 77.

[80] Mary Ellen Ayres, "Federal Indian policy and labor statistics—a review essay," *MLR,* 101(April 1978): 22–27.

[81] These calculations used the data cited in notes 75 and 77.

[82] Jean C. Darian, "Factors Influencing the Rising Labor Force Participation Rates of Married Women with Pre-school Children," *SSQ,* 56(1976): 618–19, rejects the hypothesis that part-time work was "more important to mothers of young children than to other women." So far as 1960 is concerned, her argument is that such women resorted to part-time work at the same rates as other women.

[83] Bureau of the Census, *Census of Population: 1970. Employment Status and Work Experience,* PC(2)-6A (Washington: GPO, 1973), tab. 21.

[84] Bureau of Labor Statistics, *Handbook of Labor Statistics* (1979), tab. 33.

[85] Bureau of the Census, "A Statistical Portrait of Women," tab. 7-3.

[86] Glen Cain, *Married Women in the Labor Force* (Chicago: University of Chicago Press, 1966), 117. Darian "Factors Influencing the Rising Labor Force Participation Rates of Married Women with Pre-school Children," 623–24, disputes the impact of education. Marion Gross Sobol, "A Dynamic Analysis of Labor Force Participation of Married Women of Child Bearing Age," *JHR,* 8(Fall 1973): 503–504. Bowen and Finegan, *Economics of Labor Force Participation,* 114–27. James A. Sweet, *Women in the Labor Force* (New York: Seminar, 1973), 107 ff., accords education "a slight, but irregular positive influence."

[87] Sobol, "A Dynamic Analysis of Labor Force Participation of Married Women of Child Bearing Age," 504. Darian, "Factors Influencing the Rising Labor Force Participation Rates of Married Women with Pre-school Children," 629.

[88] Dowdall, "Structural and Attitudinal Factors Associated with Female Labor Force Participation," 128. Sweet, *Women in the Labor Force,* 132, emphasizes that wives of high-income husbands are often deterred from participation in the labor force by the "status work" they perform—entertaining in behalf of their husbands or assuming unpaid community leadership roles. See William H. Whyte, Jr., "The Wives of Management," *Fortune,* 44(Oct. 1951): 86 ff; and Rosabeth Moss Kanter, *Men and Women of the Corporation* (New York, Basic, 1977), chap. 5.

[89] Bureau of the Census, *Historical Statistics of the United States, Colonial Times to 1970,* Bicentennial ed., pt. 1 (Washington: GPO, 1975), ser. H 751–65.

[90] Department of Health, Education and Welfare, *Earned Degrees Conferred 1960–61* (Washington: GPO, 1963), 10–11. *CHE,* 17(Oct. 23, 1978): 11.

[91] Benton and Rickover quoted in "Editorial: Low Marks for U.S. Education," *Saturday Evening Post,* 235(Oct. 20, 1962): 96. James B. Conant, *Slums and Suburbs* (New York: McGraw-Hill, 1961). See also "Top of the Agenda," *Newsweek,* 65(Jan. 25, 1965): 56–57. "Critical Issues in Education," *School and Society,* 97(Summer 1965): 297–98. "The President's Program for Education," *Saturday Review,* 46(March 23, 1963): 68–69. Virginia L. Senders, "The Minnesota Plan for Women's Continuing Education: A Progress Report," *Educational Record,* 42(Oct. 1961): 270–78.

[92] *NYT,* 16 Oct. 1970. Feminists on Children's Media, *Little Miss Muffet Fights Back: Recommended Non-Sexist Books About Girls for Young Readers* (New York: Feminists on Children's Media, 1971). Hole and Levine, *Rebirth of Feminism,* 333–37.

[93] Hole and Levine, *Rebirth of Feminism,* 331–33. Connie Dvorkin, "The Suburban Scene," in *Sisterhood is Powerful,* ed. Robin Morgan (New York: Vintage, 1970), 363–64.

[94] Mirra Komarovsky, *Women in the Modern World* (Boston: Little, Brown, 1953), 20, 24, 268.

[95] Caroline Bird, "Women's Colleges and Women's Lib," *Change,* 4(April 1972): 60, 61, 62.

[96] Hole and Levine, *Rebirth of Feminism,* 108 ff. Jo Freeman, "The Origins of the Women's Liberation Movement," *AJS,* 78(1973): 792–811; this also was published as "The Women's Liberation Movement: Its Origins, Structures, Impact, and Ideas," in *Women: A Feminist Perspective,* ed. Jo Freeman (Palo Alto: Mayfield, 1975), 448–60.

[97] Lucinda Cisler, "Unfinished Business: Birth Control and Women's Liberation," in *Sisterhood is Powerful,* ed. Robin Morgan (New York: Vintage, 1970), 258–81, treats abortion. Susan Griffin, "Rape: The All-American Crime," *Ramparts,* 10(Sept. 1971): 26–35. Susan Pascale, Rachel Moon, and Leslie B. Tanner, "Self-Defense for Women," in Morgan, *Sisterhood is Powerful,* 469–77.

[98] See, for example, *Time,* 94(Nov. 28, 1969): 82. *Redbook,* 125(Oct. 1965): 70. *Life,* 58(June 4, 1965): 3, 24–31. *Atlantic,* 216(Aug. 1965), 66–68. *Parent's Magazine,* 40(June 1965), 50–51. This discussion preceded the organization of NOW.

[99] Some colleges refused to permit undergraduates to keep an automobile on campus; male students might be required to wear a coat and tie to the evening meal. A survey of 339 colleges in 1976 indicated that 73 percent operated at least one coed dormitory. *CHE,* 13(Oct. 18, 1976): 2.

[100] Hole and Levine, *Rebirth of Feminism,* 324–28. Beverly T. Watkins, "Feminist Educators Seek to Improve Status of Women's Studies," *CHE,* 13(Jan. 31, 1977): 8. Carnegie Commission on Higher Education, *Opportunities for Women in Higher Education* (New York: McGraw-Hill, 1973), 79–80.

8

The Reformulation of Feminism: The 1960s

The reformulation of a feminist ideology in the 1960s dates to Betty Friedan and her book, *The Feminine Mystique*. Although much in her analysis was in the tradition of the Seneca Falls Declaration, she struck a tender spot, triggering a flood of reactions to the problems of women: civil and political rights, the job market—access to it and discrimination within it— and educational opportunities. The reemergent feminism drew on many sources, including federal policies and legislation, existentialism, socialism, the new openness in matters of sex, and the general spirit of protest and reform that marked the decade. The new feminism wore many faces. First to proclaim it were the women rallied by Friedan—essentially mature white middle-class women, the intellectual heirs of the suffragists. At the end of the sixties, a second, younger group of women's liberationists, at odds with the establishment, struggled to formulate a feminist ideology of their own. By 1970 "two separate movements" drawn from "two different strata of society, with two different styles, orientations, values, and forms of organization" had emerged.[1]

FRIEDAN AND THE MODERATES

Friedan probed a "problem with no name," the "strange discrepancy between the reality of our lives as women and the image to which we were trying to conform." Society talked of equality of opportunity for women as well as for men in education at undergraduate, graduate, and professional levels, which tantalized with the possibilities of challenging careers. The reality society offered women was the "feminine mystique"—a pattern of social conditioning that restricted feminine development to the traditionally sanctioned role of housewife and mother. "Their only dream was to be perfect wives and mothers; their only fight, to get and keep their husbands. They had no thought for the unfeminine problems of the world outside the home; they wanted the men to make the major decisions. They gloried in their role as women, and wrote proudly on the census form: 'Occupation: housewife.'" While the "feminine mystique" regarded "femininity" as "in no way inferior to the nature of man," it conditioned women to find fulfillment only in "sexual passivity, male domination, and nurturing

Betty Friedan's The Feminine Mystique *stirred middle-class women to examine their second-class status. Here, Billie Jean King looks on as Bella Abzug and Betty Friedan greet each other in a women's march for the ERA.*

maternal love." Condemning women to a vicarious existence, it denied them an opportunity for self-fulfillment independent of the wife–mother role. By limiting her existence to dependency on her husband and children, the wife compromised her own individual growth. Inevitably such women became dissatisfied with themselves. As one confided to Friedan, "I want something more than my husband and my children and my home."[2]

Diagnosis and Prescription

As analyzed by Friedan, the "feminine mystique" was a twentieth-century version of the Cult of Womanhood. In common with the Cult, it directed women to find their identity in the domesticity of wifehood and motherhood. A woman's aspirations must always be subordinated to the welfare of her husband and family. But there were differences, too. In a secular age, piety had lost the importance it possessed in the Cult. Nor was sexual purity a central issue of the mystique. As Friedan appraised this reformulation of woman's sphere, her conclusion was unequivocal; the mystique was demeaning to women.

An experienced clinical psychologist, Friedan probed the causes of the malaise. The anatomy-is-destiny hypothesis of Sigmund Freud she dismissed as untenable. Except in "sheer muscular strength," women were the equal of men in every way. Yet she noted that following World War II, Freudian thought had become the bulwark of the "feminine mystique." Helene Deutsch, in her definitive two-volume *The Psychology of Women* (1944), equated "'femininity' with 'passivity,' and 'masculinity' with 'activity,' not only in the sexual sphere, but in all spheres of life." Women achieved eminence on their own only at the expense of feminine fulfillment, Deutsch asserted. While Friedan rejected this biological determinism, she recognized that the arguments formed part of the social conditioning of women.[3]

Conditioning, not inherent qualities, she argued, limited the roles occupied by women. Among the most important promoters of the mystique was Margaret Mead, whose functionalism insisted that behavior that trespassed the accepted sphere of the opposite sex posed a grave danger to one's personality. "It is of very doubtful value," Mead warned, "to enlist the gifts of women if bringing women into fields that have been defined as male frightens the men, unsexes the women, muffles, and distorts the contribution the women could make. . . ." Sex-directed educators, too, had narrowed the growing girl's perspective of what she might become, while advertising campaigns of the late 1940s and 1950s told women they could find fulfillment as homemakers through the use of new washers, dryers, blenders, refrigerators, and irons. New standards of whiteness for laundry, sparkle for floors, and shine for furniture were proclaimed. Personal acceptability to one's friends and husband required knowledgeability with respect to creams, rinses, soaps, shampoos, and deodorants.[4]

No romantic, Friedan shared Margaret Fuller's concern with self-realization and Simone de Beauvoir's ideal of the independent woman. Friedan framed her concerns in terms of A. H. Maslow's self-actualized personality. Rejecting the "feminine mystique," she insisted that "there is something less than fully human in those who have never known a commitment to an idea, who have never risked an exploration of the unknown, who have never attempted the kind of creativity of which men and women are potentially capable." Friedan's solution was personal. It required no special enabling legislation. Women, in the pursuit of self-fulfillment, would "test and evaluate" who they were in the work world, just as men did. While she would have women and men competing as equals in the job market, she did not posit any shift in male–female roles. Her assumption was that by careful use of time, women could successfully combine marriage with a career. A woman, no less than a man, had a "basic need to grow and fulfill her potentialities as a human being." Moreover such realization, while unfeminine in a traditional sense, permitted women to fully experience "sexual fulfillment and the peak experience of human love."[5]

By any reasonable standard of values Friedan was a moderate. A white college-educated middle-class woman, she prescribed for others like herself that housekeeping and motherhood were not enough. But she did not renounce either. Housework was to be done as quickly and efficiently as possible in order "to save time that can be used in more creative ways. . . . The only way for a woman . . . to find herself . . . is by creative work of her own." But just any job would not do; it had to be a job that challenged her talents, "a job that she can take seriously as part of a life plan, work in which she can grow as part of society." Such a job was not to supplant marriage and motherhood, but to enable the wife–mother to function more effectively. Younger women with little children might find short-term opportunities in community work. A few women might find opportunities for self-expression in the arts, but the key, Friedan insisted, was "commitment," the sort of professional commitment that resulted in being paid for one's work or for teaching it to others. To prepare women to pursue a life plan, Friedan urged that they be educated "to the limit of their ability. . . . They must study science—to discover in science; study the thought of the past—to create new thought; study society—to pioneer in society." For young women with such a life plan and so educated, marriage would not be "an escape but a commitment shared by two people that becomes a part of their commitment to themselves and society." The pursuit had an existential quality; there was no certainty as to where the search for identity would lead; it involved struggle and conflict; it meant loneliness; it required courage. But it would enable women to realize their humanity.[6]

Friedan articulated the sentiments of a generation of college-trained married women with school-age children. Her book came at a time when the roles assigned women and the roles occupied by them had been diverging for nearly two decades. The culture pressed women to marry and conform to the ideal of the homemaker; in fact, since World War II, a rapidly growing proportion of married women—many with young children—had entered the labor force. Postwar "inflation, a rising standard of living, and the desire to share the benefits of consumerism" had promoted the growth of two-income families. Ironically, in entering and remaining in the labor market, women had not sought to compete with men, only to help the family, "so that children could go to college, a new addition could be built on the house, or the family could have a longer and better vacation." Women had also been sensitized by the decade-old civil-rights movement to a concern with rights in general. Friedan's diagnosis and prescription drew together the varied expressions of the American woman's dilemma that had been voiced in the preceding 15 years.[7]

Some women, sensitized by *The Feminine Mystique,* further expanded their understanding of the female dilemma by reading Simone de Beauvoir's *The Second Sex.* Published in France in 1949 and first available in English in 1953, Beauvoir's work was the most comprehensive analysis of woman's condition in print. The American Academy of Arts and Sciences added to the discussion with its spring 1964 issue of *Daedalus,* subtitled *The Woman in America.* Alice Rossi, in particular, added the voice of the concerned scholar to the issue. A sociologist, Rossi's arguments supported those of Friedan. Full-time motherhood, Rossi asserted, was neither sufficiently absorbing to the woman nor beneficial to the child to justify a contemporary woman devoting 15 or more years to it as an exclusive occupation. Rossi made explicit, as Friedan did not, that if women were to pursue careers seriously, a redefinition of sex roles was in order. She called for "a socially androgynous conception of the roles of men and women." Men and women should be "equal and similar in such spheres as intellectual, artistic, political and occupational interests and participation, complementary only in those spheres dictated by the physiological differences between the sexes." To permit the "full and equal involvement of women in the occupational world," she urged (1) development of child-care facilities to enable women with children to pursue careers with a minimum of disruption; (2) a halt to urban sprawl, which had tended to isolate young women with children and to minimize job opportunities; and (3) a more equitable distribution of men and women in all occupations.[8]

The National Organization of Women

Although *The Feminine Mystique* caught the public eye, the reassertion of feminist views had other independent origins as well. While Friedan was researching and writing, the Kennedy administration—caught between advocates of an ERA and defenders of protective legislation for working-class women—had appointed a Commission on the Status of Women. Its report, *American Women,* appearing at the same time as Friedan's book, spelled out in stark terms the status of women politically, economically, educationally. Like Friedan, the commission argued that women might combine roles as wives and mothers with that of wage earner. Again, independent of the feminists, Congress enacted an Equal Pay Act in 1963 and a major Civil Rights Act in 1964. Although both measures had far-reaching implications for women, federal authorities made little effort to enforce the provisions of the Civil Rights Act relating to women. Outraged, Betty Friedan and Aileen Hernandez organized the National Organization of Women (NOW) in 1966. The founders envisioned NOW as a forum for feminist ideas and as a political lobby for women's rights. NOW aimed "to bring women into the mainstream of American society now, exercising all the privileges and responsibilities thereof in truly *equal partnership with men.*" Recognizing that the realization of equality required adjustment of the statutes, in 1967 NOW drafted a comprehensive program. Foremost was a demand for an ERA, but along with it a number of other planks were shaped: enforcement of laws banning sex discrimination in employment; maternity-leave rights; tax deductions for the home and child-care expenses of working parents; and the establishment of child-care centers, equal and unsegregated education, and job-training opportunities for women in poverty. The most controversial plank—the right of women to control their reproductive lives—raised the question of access to abortion.[9]

To those unaccustomed to women asserting themselves in the political arena, *The Feminine Mystique* and NOW seemed radical. In fact, excepting the plank relating to reproduction, most of Friedan's analysis and program evolved out of the earlier woman's movement. Whereas the suffragists had sought equality by giving women the same right to vote enjoyed by men, Friedan sought equality by giving women the same access to jobs enjoyed by men. In updating the woman's rights program, NOW elected to pursue both the course of piecemeal reform and of across-the-board prohibition of sex discrimination by a constitutional amendment, thus ending the decades-long split between the protectionists and the equalitarians. Those who shared in organizing NOW were generally white middle-class college-educated women. Many were also members of state commissions on the status of women and part of the establishment. As such, NOW's leadership from the start was in a position to press its objectives at both the state and federal levels.[10]

Alongside NOW stood a number of organizations supportive of a broader public role for women. First, of course, was the small but venerable National Woman's Party of Alice Paul, which had been promoting an ERA since 1923. Far more influential, the National Federation of Business and Professional Women's Clubs, which first endorsed the ERA in 1937, enjoyed a good rapport with congressmen and state legislators as well as state and federal officials. Federation leaders such as Marguerite Rawalt and Virginia Allan had contributed importantly to efforts to secure women's equality, but its rank and file declined to identify the federation as a feminist organization. Similarly the nonpartisan League of Women Voters, the most active public-interest organization of women, refused to embrace the reemerging woman's movement lest it be labeled "feminist" and "militant."[11]

Several new organizations emerged to actively champion the feminist cause. The Women's Equity Action League (WEAL), founded in 1969, recruited professional women—lawyers, educational administrators, professors, counselors, judges, and legislators. An activist organization, WEAL focused on sex discrimination in employment, education, and taxes. Using Title VII of the Civil Rights Act as a lever, WEAL initiated suits to force compliance with the law. Among its more notable activities were some 350 complaints filed with the Department of Health, Education and Welfare against some of the nation's leading institutions, charging discrimination in hiring and promotion. In October 1970, WEAL instituted a class-action suit against all the nation's medical schools for their discriminatory admissions policies.[12]

Also allied with NOW, the National Women's Political Caucus (NWPC), a bipartisan political organization, sought to support women for public office, to raise the level of women's participation in government, and to lobby for women's issues: child care, abortion reform, birth control, guaranteed annual income, and equal-employment and educational opportunities. The organization's National Public Council included such diverse persons as Bella Abzug, Shana Alexander, Liz Carpenter, Shirley Chisholm, Betty Friedan, Fannie Lou Hamer, La Donna Harris, Wilma Scott Heide, and Gloria Steinem. The NWPC's principal interests lay in the areas of civil rights, human rights, economic rights, and a national commitment to women.[13]

As the 1960s drew to a close, a new presidential commission, the Citizens Advisory Committee on the Status of Women, incorporated many of the planks of NOW into its reports. Because its Family Law Task Force— led by Marguerite Rawalt, Mary Eastwood, and Alice Rossi—consisted of women not on the federal payroll, the task force was free to take a strong position. It began by affirming the right of a woman to control her own reproductive life as a basic civil right. Accordingly it called for repeal of all laws that made abortion a criminal offense and for repeal of laws that restricted access to contraceptive devices and information. Viewing marriage as an economic partnership, the task force recommended that child support and alimony laws be revised to reflect the ability of the former partners to pay and the level of need for support. Married women should have the same property rights as husbands, while out-of-wedlock children should be accorded the same legal rights as those born in wedlock. Finally in 1970, President Nixon's Task Force on Women's Rights and Responsibilities, chaired by Virginia Allan, urged the administration to endorse the ERA.[14]

RADICAL FEMINISM

While the moderate feminism of Betty Friedan found expression in the program of NOW, a radical feminism evolved out of the discontents of the sixties. Many of the radical women leaders had been socialists before they became feminists. As the New Left came into being in the early 1960s, it was largely amorphous, "a mood in search of a movement." "Born in deed, not in doctrine," the New Left recruited from the antisegregation protestors in the South, the Free Speech Movement at Berkeley, and the burgeoning antiwar movement. Its principal organization initially was the SDS (Students for a Democratic Society), and its membership, drawn from "secure, upper-middle-class white families," included a mix of "gifted graduate students and sophomore dropouts, Christian pacifists and militant confrontationists, weekend potheads and midnight mystics." Its Port Huron Statement (1962) focused primarily on the problem of "ethical existence," denouncing the "cold war, the welfare state, and the military–industrial complex." Departing from orthodox Marxism, the SDS rejected the idea of a worker-led revolution for a "democracy of individual participation." The SDS ideology blended socialism with a "vague, existential humanism."[15]

The New Left Connections

As the 1960s wore on, other tough-minded socialist groups challenged the preeminence of the SDS in the New Left. The Progressive Labor Party, having broken with the old Communist Party, was Maoist in inspiration and Leninist in organization; the Young Socialist Alliance represented Trotskyite youth of the Socialist Worker's Party, while the DuBois Clubs of America recruited from the children of old-line communists. On the fringes of the New Left were separatists—Black Panthers and Yippies. The SDS sensitized the college community to the escalating war in Vietnam through bull sessions, teach-ins, happenings, and demonstrations. The continuing escalation of the war, however, undermined the SDS's assumption that it could influence national policy by working within the system. As the SDS went down, the Progressive Labor Party rose.[16]

Within the New Left, women occupied subordinate roles—making coffee, rolling the bandages, and providing sex. In the hierarchy of values of the SDS leadership, women's issues were inconsequential compared to the issues of civil rights, poverty, and the Vietnam War. But following the publication of *The Feminine Mystique,* SDS women began to examine their own subordinate status. Initial efforts to raise the issue at national SDS meetings brought hoots and catcalls. Following workshops held in conjunction with the SDS meeting at Ann Arbor in June 1967, Naomi Weisstein, Heather Booth, and Sue Munaker organized an autonomous radical women's group. Fearing fragmentation of their own movement, SDS leaders sought accommodation, and *New Left Notes,* their publication, featured articles by radical feminists. Cleavages within New Left ranks soon became unbridgeable. Women in the national office of the SDS insisted that women were oppressed as women; members of the Progressive Labor faction were equally positive that women's oppression was but another form of class oppression that would end with the overthrow of capitalism. Even within the ranks of the national SDS leadership tactical differences emerged. One group opted to pursue feminist objectives within the framework of SDS; a second group, including Shulamith Firestone, Robin Morgan, Jo Freeman, and Roxanne Dunbar, opted for an autonomous woman's movement. At this point the radical feminists agreed chiefly that only women could liberate women, that all males, not just capitalist ones, oppressed women. These women from the New Left brought to radical feminism concerns framed in terms of socialist and existential rhetoric, though they had yet to formulate a comprehensive feminist theory.[17]

In their search for a radical-feminist ideology, they turned to socialist doctrine, reshaping and expanding it. The great socialist thinkers of the nineteenth century had noted the subordinate status of women. Charles Fourier, a utopian socialist, as well as an "ardent and voluminous advocate of women's liberation and of sexual freedom," had argued that "the progress of women towards freedom," provided a measure of social progress. While Fourier's formulations were at the "level of utopian moral injunction," Karl Marx reshaped them, "integrating them into a philosophical critique of human history." Ultimately he submerged the problem of women in an analysis of the family. In the end it was Friedrich Engels who developed a systematic statement. In *The Origin of the Family, Private Property and the State,* Engels asserted that one of the first class struggles to emerge among humans was that "between man and woman in the monogamous marriage, and the first class oppression was that of the female sex by the male." Although initially society was matrilineal, woman's independence was checked when inheritance became patrilineal. With the establishment of private property, the wife's fidelity became essential and monogamy became irrevocable. In the process the woman became a private servant, performing menial household labor. "The emancipation of women," Engels concluded, "becomes possible only when women are enabled to take part in production on a large, social scale, and when domestic duties require their attention only to a minor degree...." Fundamentally the Marxist testimony was that women were subordinated by capitalism.[18]

Juliet Mitchell: Woman's Estate

Feminist theorists were both attracted to and repelled by the historic socialist analysis. Even as radical women became restive with their SDS relationships, Juliet Mitchell, the New Zealand-born English-educated feminist, argued that woman's liberation was not structurally integrated into classic socialist theory. She contended that woman's condition was the product of a "complex unity" of four key structures: production, reproduction, socialization, and sexuality. Woman's liberation required a coordinated transformation of all four structures, lest partial reform render continued exploitation palatable. Borrowing from classical Marxism, Mitchell argued: "The main thrust of any emancipation movement must still concentrate on the economic element—the entry of women fully into public industry." Historically woman's work—the housekeeping chores—while enormous in the aggregate, had been undervalued because it commanded no market price. Automation offered a solution, since it promised to open all levels of production to women.[19]

Mitchell's analysis was not a conventional socialist one resting on the primacy of economic determinism. Rather she placed fundamental emphasis on sexual oppression. Traditional marriage was "the weak link in the chain." Changes in the composition of the work force, the size of the family, and in the structure of education had diminished the function and significance of the family. Furthermore, "to focus women's existence exclusively on bringing up children is manifestly harmful to children." There was "absolutely no reason," she declared, "why there should be only one legitimatized form" of personal relationships. Rather than abolish the family, Mitchell favored "a plural range of institutions ... couples living together or not living together, long-term unions with children, single parents bringing up children, children socialized by conventional rather than biological parents, extended kin groups, etc. . . ." To bring reproduction under rational human control, she proposed free state provision of contraception, legalization of homosexuality (viewed as a form of nonreproductive sexuality), and the abolition of illegitimacy as a legal concept. Sexual liberation was a key element in Mitchell's solution to the exploitation of women.[20]

No American woman explored woman's liberation as comprehensively as Mitchell, but collectively Americans expanded her inquiry. In discussing the role of production in liberating women, Margaret Benston emphasized "the problem is not simply one of getting women into existing industrial production but the more complex one of converting private production of household work into public production." This industrialization of housework would afford women "an active place in the market," without which she would have "little control over the conditions that govern her life." In the tradition of Charlotte Gilman, Benston advocated communal eating places and laundries. This industrialization of housework would result in "better food, more comfortable surroundings, more intelligent and loving child care, etc., than in the present nuclear family." Child rearing, too, would become a community enterprise.[21]

A recurrent theme among radical feminists was that "the family unit is a decadent, energy-absorbing, destructive, wasteful institution. . . ." After all, "the same upper class of men who created private property and founded nation–states also created the family," Roxanne Dunbar reminded feminists. Thus, socialists transferred their hostility toward capitalism to the nuclear family. Capitalists, not satisfied with simply dominating property, had dominated human beings as well. With respect to women, she argued that the male was not content with just the satisfaction of his "private, individual sexual urge," which he fantasized he would get from a woman he sees; more central to his view of women, he visualized himself "taking her, dominating her through the sexual act."[22]

From the perspective of the New Left, "the most original and creative politics" of the woman's movement came from "a direct confrontation with the issue of marriage and sexuality. The cultural revolution—experimentation with lifestyles, communal living, collective child-rearing—have all come from the rebellion against dehumanized sexual relationships, against the notion of women as sexual commodities, against the constriction and spiritual strangulation inherent in the role of wife." Convinced that women were oppressed as a class, the radicals took a dim view of monogamy and of traditional marriage. Likewise, they exuded hostility toward men. Though convinced that the primary struggle should be against sexism at home, they remained mindful that "women's liberation is serious about fighting racism and capitalism and is not just concerned with 'liberating' white middle-class women." Ultimately white radical women could become a link to "third worlders" by seeking to understand the position of black, Asian, and Latin women.[23]

Radical Feminists Organize

Radical feminists developed their own organizational style and form. They abjured conventional political techniques, which they believed would limit their impact on society. Hostile to men, or at least wary of them, they excluded men from their groups. As most of the radical women had college backgrounds, they suffered a plenitude of articulate leaders. By way of organizing, they adopted leaderless structures that accorded a maximum of equality to all—participatory democracy. The diverse, decentralized committees made extensive use of street theater. One of the first demonstrations, in September 1968, had the Miss America pageant as its target, by way of asserting that such contests degraded women. To dramatize this point, a live sheep was crowned Miss America and a "freedom trash can" was set up in which women discarded items symbolic of traditional femininity: "old bras, girdles, high-heeled shoes, women's magazines, curlers, and other instruments of torture to women." Reflecting the radical heritage, the demonstrations did not always have a direct connection with feminism. Thus at Halloween 1968 a group of women, calling themselves WITCH (Women's International Terrorist Conspiracy from Hell) and costumed as witches, hexed and spooked the New York Stock Exchange, a demonstration aimed at capitalism rather than at sexism. Inspired by the "witches," women's groups across the country adopted the acronym WITCH, modifying it to suit particular targets. A group protesting high prices termed itself Women's Independent Taxpayers, Consumers and Homemakers; a demonstration aimed at various telephone companies became Women Incensed at Telephone Company Harassment. Such tactics secured media attention and incurred the wrath of the establishment. However much fun these demonstrations afforded the participants, the flippancy of the protests often obscured the intended message. The tactics used by radical feminists were mild compared to those of other protest groups of the day, some of which turned to violence and terror. By 1969, feminist leaders had recognized that "arty, gimmicky, game-playing" techniques often alienated those whose support they needed.[24]

Beginning in 1968 the radical feminists explored "consciousness raising" as a means of more sharply defining their perceptions. At its best, this technique proved a means of establishing that "what was considered a personal problem has a social cause and probably a political solution." It was to "clean out our heads—uncork and redirect our anger politically—learn to understand other women—learn that our 'personal' problems are not ours alone." As the Redstockings—a New York feminist group—phrased it, "we do not need to change ourselves, but to change men." For some women, consciousness raising became an end in itself; for others it led to a clearer perception of long-term action and was momentarily an effective recruiting device.[25]

In 1967 radical feminists met as part of a National Conference for the New Politics, that is as part of the New Left; a year later, Thanksgiving weekend 1968, they met alone in Chicago, bringing together over 200 women. The varied interests of the radical women were indicated by the discussions. Kathie Sarachild presented a paper, "A Program for Feminist Consciousness Raising," while Anne Koedt offered her statement, "The Myth of the Vaginal Orgasm." The conference was marked by earnest discussion and sharp divisions. The end result, however, was the rapid proliferation of local feminist organizations.[26]

A spate of radical-feminist groups appeared from Seattle and San Francisco to Boston, New York, and Washington. Likewise, women on college campuses organized, while professional women formed women's caucuses. Most of the women were under 30. The organizations were usually small—consciousness raising called for groups of 5 to 15 persons—and often ephemeral. Factions seceded to form new groups; groups reorganized under new names to reflect refined tactics or objectives.

Because of their visibility, the evolution of feminist organizations in New York City set the pattern for the rest of the nation. And with the formation of these local groups the transition period ended; an independent radical-feminist movement began. The Redstockings, founded by Ellen Willis and Shulamith Firestone, was a militant, activist, feminist organization. It became the first group to clearly articulate the function, purpose, process, and use of consciousness raising. It denied that a woman could work out her relationship individually with a man so as to avoid her subordination. "In reality, every such relationship," the Redstockings' Manifesto of July 1969 maintained, "is a *class* relationship, and the conflicts between individual men and women are *political* conflicts that can only be solved collectively." The Redstockings further argued that women were in no way responsible for their own oppression. The point was fundamental, for they were denying that women were subordinate by design, but they also rejected the notion that women had become subjugated through sex stereotyping—"brainwashing." Rather women had been subjugated as a result of "continual, daily pressure from men." Ultimately the Redstockings succumbed to their own rhetoric. Consciousness raising, rather than leading to political action as anticipated, ended as a form of therapy. It destroyed the group.[27]

Alongside the Redstockings appeared The Feminists, led by Ti-Grace Atkinson. "A theory-action group," The Feminists first drew public attention when they demonstrated in support of Nathan Rappaport, a Boston doctor charged with homicide in connection with an abortion case. The Feminists demanded the repeal of abortion laws. Under Atkinson's leadership, the organization attempted a vigorous theoretical analysis of woman's social role and experimented with an egalitarian structure of organization. Rejecting consciousness raising, The Feminists undertook an analysis of the nature and source of woman's oppression. They declared that the sex-role system "distorts the humanity of the Oppressor and denies the humanity of the Oppressed." (Thomas Jefferson had noted that slavery exploited the black man while it debauched his master.) As their analysis proceeded, they concluded that marriage, love, motherhood, and heterosexual sex reflected and reinforced subjugation. The division of roles by sex thwarted woman's capacity to fulfill herself as a person. Their solution was the annihilation of sex roles. Using the term "radical feminism" to describe their viewpoint, The Feminists took care to insist that the enemy was the male role, not males per se. But the group faltered on its organizational principles. The group was faced with the paradox of a strong leader who urged a system of administration that accorded leadership by lot. And while disclaiming an antimale outlook, they restricted membership so that no more than one third were married women or women living with men.[28]

At the end of 1969 the New York Radical Feminists (NYRF) attempted to provide radical feminists with a workable organization and a broad ideology. Of the leadership, Anne Koedt came from The Feminists and Shulamith Firestone from the Redstockings. Drawing on past experiences, the NYRF reformulated feminist ideology. Breaking completely with traditional socialist doctrine, they rejected the notion that women were victims of capitalism or any other economic system. They turned away from the Redstockings' doctrine to aver that society conditioned women to feel inferior to men and that in the process women's egos were destroyed. Similarly they steered away from an extreme antimale position. They condemned "love" as a dominant–submissive relationship, but they affirmed the possibility of a "healthy love" expressed in nonoppressive relationships that promoted the growth of the other party. Organizationally the group foundered on the issues of elitism and leadership. The membership consisted of angry, articulate individuals whose radical experiences had introduced them to participatory democracy; hence they tended to regard any leader as an elitist and thus objectionable.[29]

Germaine Greer

The radical-feminist viewpoint reached its broadest public, not through the various New York groups or the hundreds of anonymous groups in other cities, on campuses, or in women's caucuses across the country, but through the books of Germaine Greer and Shulamith Firestone. The Australian-born English-trained Germaine Greer found a wide audience in her *Female Eunuch* (1970). Greer was at one with Henrik Ibsen's Nora, who considered her "most sacred duty" to be "my duty to myself. . . . I believe that before everything else I'm a human being." Greer insisted that women's subordinate position in England and the United States was not the product of biological deficiencies but rather the product of persistent cultural conditioning. "The castration of women," she contended, "has been carried out in terms of a masculine–feminine polarity, in which men have commandeered all the energy and streamlined it into an aggressive conquistadorial power, reducing all heterosexual contact to a sadomaso-chistic pattern."[30]

Although a socialist, Greer joined other radical feminists in rejecting "the factory [as] the real heart of civilization or the reentry of women into industry as the necessary condition of liberation." Nor did she have con-fidence that the principle of equal pay for equal work would rescue women from exploitation in the marketplace. The difficulty lay in that "the pattern of female employment follows the course of the role that women play outside industry: they are almost always ancillary, handmaids in the more important work of men." Greer approached female liberation from the vantage point of an existentialist. "Security," she affirmed, "is the denial of life." Her concern was that women, in the pursuit of security—emotional as well as economic—had plunged into marriage and lost their person-hood thereby. She warned: "Liberty is terrifying but it is also exhilarating. Life is not easier or more pleasant for the Noras who have set off on their journey to awareness, but is more interesting, nobler even." The conven-tional course, to achieve status by attracting and snaring a man, corrupts and destroys. "To abdicate one's own moral understanding, to tolerate crimes against humanity, to leave everything to someone else, the father–ruler–king–computer, is the only irresponsibility." No less than Betty Friedan, Greer sought the self-actuated personality.[31]

As with other feminists, much of Greer's analysis focused on the rela-tionships of men and women and the implications of female sexuality. Greer contended that contemporary concepts of femininity perpetuated an asexuality that thwarted a woman's development as a person. "The acts of sex are themselves forms of inquiry" she argued, and as a woman curbed "the element of quest in her sexuality," the inhibitions carried over to all aspects of life. Sexual liberation—in the sense of developing the female libido—was prerequisite to full realization of woman's human potentialities. Self-assertion as a female person required the abandonment of monogamy and the nuclear family. The woman not yet married, ought not marry. As "no worker can be required to sign on for life," so no woman should make a lifetime commitment to a husband. Forgoing marriage, however, need not mean forgoing love. Marriage most assuredly did not guarantee security; to marry either to avoid taking a job or in order to have children and a home were poor reasons. Love, she assured, could exist outside marriage. She took her text from Victoria Woodhull: "I have an inalienable constitutional and natural right to love whom I may, to love as long or as short a period as I can, to change that love every day if I please." The woman who was already married ought to stand up for her rights; men, after all, were almost as fearful of abandonment as women. Yet the woman with children caught in an exploitive marriage ought not shrink from leaving both husband and children. The children, she pointed out, "are not *hers,* they are not her property." The father, in many cases, would be able to support the children better than she. Greer's counsel was earnest. It was not the advocacy of hedonism, but rather of the pursuit of "purpose, achievement and dignity." Only thus would women become fully realized persons.[32]

Shulamith Firestone

The most comprehensive analysis of radical feminism by an American came from Shulamith Firestone. Her dual concerns, socialism and sexual liberation, were explicitly reflected in the title of her work, *The Dialectic of Sex* (1970). Like Mitchell and Greer, Firestone regarded Marxist analysis as deficient. Nor did the "rigidly existentialist interpretation of feminism" of Simone de Beauvoir satisfy her. Firestone argued that "throughout history, in all stages and types of culture, women have been oppressed due to their biological functions. . . . The *patriarchal family* was only the most recent in a string of 'primary' social organizations, all of which defined woman as a different species due to her unique child-bearing capacity." In place of Engel's economic determinism, Firestone posited a sexual one. Employing a Marxist analogy, she argued that just as to eliminate economic classes required the revolt of the proletariat and their seizure of the means of production, so "to assure the elimination of sexual classes requires the revolt of the underclass [women] and the seizure of control of *reproduction.*" This entailed "the full restoration to women of ownership of their own bodies" and "control of human fertility," as well as "all the social institutions of childbearing and childrearing." The "end goal of the feminist revolution," she concluded, was "not just the elimination of male *privilege* but of the sex *distinction* itself."[33]

Unlike most feminists, Firestone assumed that "sex is destiny," but she subjected Freud's biological determinism to searching criticism and revision. "Freud," she agreed, "grasped the crucial problem of modern life: Sexuality." But Freud and feminism were both reactions to smug Victorianism—"Its familycenteredness, and thus its exaggerated sexual oppression and repression." Freud was merely "a diagnostician for what Feminism purports to cure." Freudianism, which began as a theory, was transformed into clinical practice in which the key word was "adjustment." In the process it was "subverted for a reactionary end—socialization of men and women to an artificial sex-role system." She reexamined basic Freudian concepts— the Oedipus complex, its inverse, the Electra complex, and penis envy— from a radical-feminist point of view "in terms of power." In these terms the Oedipus complex explained the boy's shifting attachments as he came to realize that it was his father who showed him *"the road into the world."* The Electra complex, similarly, illuminated the dilemma of the girl, who, as she reached puberty, came face-to-face with her sex. Power was not hers; she could enjoy it only vicariously through a male: father, brother, husband, or son. Drawing on the analysis of Ruth Hirshberger in *Adam's Rib,* Firestone argued that contemporary views and practices made "a totally fulfilled sexuality impossible for anyone, and a well-functioning sexuality for only a few."[34]

Firestone's solution eradicated the family. Specifically, she would free women from "the tyranny of their reproductive biology by every means available" and diffuse "the childbearing and childrearing role to the society as a whole, men as well as women." She called, too, for "the full self-determination, including economic independence, of both women and children." In turn, "the total integration of women and children into all aspects of the larger society" would follow. Finally, she demanded "the freedom of all women and children to do whatever they wish to do sexually." Only sexual liberation would permit a human being to "realize oneself fully, simply in the process of being and acting."[35]

By way of illustration she outlined multiple options for alternative life-styles. A woman dedicated to a career might well pursue "single professions," organizing her life "around the demands of a chosen profession," and forgo marriage. For others, she suggested "living together"—two or more partners of whatever sex—"a nonlegal sex/companionate arrangement." The duration of these relationships would be variable. She envisioned living-together becoming, in time, the standard unit in which most people would live for most of their lives. A third possibility—"households"—offered an arrangement for those adults who wished to live in an environment with children. These adults might, or might not, be the parents of the children in the household. She proposed that the adults contract for a period of seven to ten years to live within the household—the minimal time required to permit children to grow up in a stable structure. At the end of the contractual period, the individuals would be free to depart; new members might join. In essence the "household" would form an extended family.[36]

BLACK FEMINISM

Black women pursued their own course to feminism, their viewpoints shaped by their experiences in the civil-rights movement. The SNCC (Student Nonviolent Coordinating Committee), organized in 1960, recruited thousands of southern black college students who sought to end segregation in the South through sit-ins, marches, and voter-registration drives. Although Congress subsequently enacted the Civil Rights Act, change came too slowly. As major cities from Newark to Los Angeles experienced destructive riots, black militants proclaimed "black power." Interracial cooperation began to deteriorate, and even some black moderates concluded that blacks must pursue their goals alone.[37]

Black Liberation

Black women had special problems in defining their future course. Although they had worked alongside men in the civil-rights movement, they found themselves excluded from policymaking and relegated to kitchen work, mimeographing, typing, and "as a sexual supply" for their male comrades after hours. They took special offense as northern white women paired off with black males, a factor that proved divisive both to the SNCC and to interracial cooperation in the woman's movement. When Ruby Doris Smith Robinson wrote a paper, "The Position of Women in SNCC," Stokely Carmichael reputedly responded: "the only position for women in SNCC is prone." Though resentful of the chauvinism of many civil-rights leaders, black women generally agreed that eradication of racism had first priority. They further argued that the reemerging feminist movement of the sixties, largely white, afforded no place for black participation. They were conscious that black women had been exploited economically by white women and sexually by white men. They were sensitive that "some of those women's lib girls are asking for jobs that black men haven't been able to get." Black mothers all too often were forced to rear their children in crime-ridden neighborhoods; they had to struggle to see that their children received "a decent basic education." For most black women, race and class, not anatomy, were destiny.[38]

Black women, then, continued during the sixties to work within the framework of the black liberation movement. As they discussed their predicament as women, they focused on economic issues, control of sexuality, and family relationships. Militant black women saw all blacks, men and women alike, engaged in "a life-and-death struggle . . . to combat the capitalist, racist exploitation of black people." From the perspective of a female SNCC leader, "any white woman's group that does not have an antiimperialist and antiracist ideology has absolutely nothing in common with the black woman's struggle." Linking capitalism to male exploitation of women, Patricia Robinson insisted that, "Capitalism is a male supremacist society," for women and their children were "ever pressed into service and labor for the maintenance of a male-dominated class society."[39]

Campaigns "to promote sterilization of non-white women" especially enraged militant black feminists. They averred that the white establishment intended "to maintain the population and power imbalance between the white 'haves' and the non-white 'have-nots.'" They denounced programs in Puerto Rico and in third-world countries to curb population growth by sterilization—whether by vasectomies or by salpingectomies—as "outright surgical genocide." At home some public authorities pressured welfare mothers to be sterilized as a condition for continued eligibility for relief funds. Blacks viewed the use of Puerto Rican and black women to test the efficacy and safety of the Pill prior to its general introduction in the United States as further evidence of white contempt for persons of color.[40]

Black Feminists

When black women examined their predicament in terms of the black family, their views differed substantially from those of male proponents of black power. While rejecting the stereotype of the matriarchal black family, these black women were acutely aware that, far more often than white women, they had been forced to provide family leadership. A principal concern of black women was to "stabilize their families" and to establish "a decent way of life in America as it exists today." Black children seldom had "the same sense of security that white children have when they see their father accepted as a successful member of the community." To some this meant giving "sustenance to the black man," even if it meant continued second-class status for black women. Increasing the number of jobs available to black men so that they could more adequately support their families took precedence over jobs for black women.[41]

Eventually older, articulate black women—with ties to the white power structure but no less devoted to the betterment of blacks than the SNCC leadership—began to insist that black women should participate in the broad feminist movement that had emerged. The positions of black militants on the family and on birth control and abortion were subjected to penetrating criticism. Pauli Murray entered a vigorous dissent to the argument of *Ebony* magazine that "the immediate goal of the Negro woman today should be the establishment of a strong family unit in which the father is the dominant person," that she should emulate the stereotypical Jewish mother in self-effacement and supportiveness. A less restrained black feminist commented: "Hell, the white woman is already oppressed in that set up." To Murray, improvement of the condition of the black woman meant improving the condition of black males. Supportiveness in this sense, however, did not justify subservience. While commending William H. Grier and Price M. Cobbs, the joint authors of *Black Rage,* for their sensitive description of the traumatic experiences of growing up black and female in a society that defined beauty in terms of "the blond, blue-eyed, white-skinned girl with regular features," Murray expressed disappointment that nowhere were black women urged to achieve as persons.[42]

Shirley Chisholm, a congresswoman, addressed herself to the questions of birth control and abortion. She dismissed as "male rhetoric, for male ears," the "deep and angry suspicion among many blacks" that birth control and abortion were "a plot" by the white power structure to keep down the number of blacks. From another perspective, the oppression of black women resulted from poor black men who "won't support their families, won't stick by their women—all they think about is the street, dope and liquor, women, a piece of ass, and their cars." The well-being of the black family—and black woman—Chisholm argued, would be served far better by "two or three children who are wanted, prepared for, reared amid love and stability, and educated to the limit of their ability . . . than any number of neglected, hungry, ill-housed and ill-clothed youngsters." To achieve a healthier family, she endorsed contraception as the first means to this end; but she noted that women, desperate at the prospects of an unwanted pregnancy, regularly broke the law, risking injury and death to secure abortions. "Abortions," she concluded, "will not be stopped. . . . The question becomes simply that of the kind of abortions society wants women to have—clean, competent ones, performed by licensed physicians or septic, dangerous ones done by incompetent practitioners." As to genocide? Destruction came from the socioeconomic effects of children who could not be adequately cared for. Birth control was "freedom to fight genocide of black women and children."[43]

Into the early 1970s black women expressed their feminism through the various black liberation movements. As a black, a feminist, and a moderate, Pauli Murray insisted that black women had an "equal stake in women's liberation and black liberation." Black women, she argued, shared with white feminists common interests in "adequate income maintenance and the elimination of poverty, repeal or reform of abortion laws, a national system of child-care centers, extension of labor standards to workers now excluded, cash maternity benefits as part of a system of social insurance, and the removal of all sex barriers to educational and employment opportunities at all levels." Indeed, Murray insisted that the black revolution itself could be jeopardized by the failure to adhere to the principle that "all human rights are indivisible." Ultimately, in fall 1973 the National Black Feminist Organization emerged with headquarters in New York City. Within a year it reported ten chapters. A second group, Black Women Organized for Action, served women on the West Coast. Black feminists remained wary of the major white feminist organizations.[44]

CHICANA FEMINISM

The Chicanos, no less than the blacks, developed a liberation movement in the mid-1960s that aggressively promoted a better life for its constituents. The movement—male centered—had as its principal focus the enhancement of the political and economic power of the Mexican American community, which had been systematically exploited and oppressed by the Anglo-American community. The Chicana feminist regarded "her oppression as a woman" as "usually overshadowed by the common oppression of both male and female." In her value system, Chicanos had a right to—indeed "must"—preserve their "cultural distinctness." The main efforts at reform, then, were directed at improvement of La Raza—the race. In so doing, Chicana feminists sought to resist assimilation by Anglo-Americans. As a means to this end they emphasized the use of Spanish and loyalty to family and friends, while they deprecated individualism. Conditioned by their own culture to a submissive role, Chicanas generally agreed that "some semblance of equality had to be achieved for their people as a whole before feminine concerns could be voiced."[45]

Convinced that the Mexican American community generally was exploited by Anglo-Americans, Chicanas found little in common with the Anglo-led woman's movement. The knowledgeable Chicana was aware that suffragists such as Stanton and Catt had urged an "educated" vote and that in the postsuffrage years, the woman's movement had ignored them because of "the low opinion" Anglo women had of Chicanas as being "too passive and too submissive to their men and families." To an articulate Chicana such as Marta Cotera, the Anglo woman's movement of the 1960s seemed preoccupied with "employment and power, not human rights." Too many Anglo feminists depicted the traditional female role in negative terms. Often marriage and the traditional family were held responsible for woman's oppression. Male roles were viewed as the "enemy" responsible for the limitations placed on women. For the Anglo feminists, the ultimate identity was with women; for the Chicanas, it was with the Chicano community. For Anglos, the movement was for women; for Chicanas, feminism was integrated into the larger movement to enhance the power and status of their ethnic community. The Chicana sought "a new female ideal—a woman who respected men, the family, and home, but who combined this with wider opportunities for work outside the home and active political commitment to the Chicano community."[46]

Transformation of the Chicano sex roles proceeded from two directions. Chicana militants, though placing La Raza first, argued that the movement, itself, required the modification of both male and female traditional roles. Specifically, each woman had to develop an "assertiveness and independence" that would enable her to function as an equal of her male colleagues. In discovering her own "powers, strengths, and talents," politicized reformers were moved to challenge male domination within the family. As industrialization, urbanization, and modernization modified the environment within which the Mexican American community operated, the extended kinship units with "rigid sex role divisions" would give way to the "nuclear, autonomous, egalitarian family units." In this view, Chicano cultural transformations represented an evolutionary adaptation to new modes of social and economic organization. Traditional values of "conformity, strict child rearing, and authoritarian submission" were challenged. Familism and patriarchy would cease to characterize Chicano family structures. The emerging life-style was characterized by higher rates of intermarriage with non-Chicanos and increased geographical, social, and occupational mobility.[47]

SEXUAL LIBERATION

The feminist renaissance coincided with the changing attitudes and behavior in the realm of human sexuality. The sexual revolution at the start of the century had been marked by a significant increase in premarital intercourse, a wider awareness of contraceptive practices, and an increased recognition of female sexuality. Whereas most feminists of the 1920s had been repelled by the "revolution in manners and morals," the feminists of the sixties appreciated the importance of female sexuality. The impetus for sexual liberation came from several sources, some within, others without the woman's movement.

By the time feminists of the 1960s refined their ideology, society's attitudes toward sexuality were more permissive than ever before. The causes varied. The work of Havelock Ellis and Sigmund Freud provided scientific authority for the naturalness of sexuality, female as well as male. Efforts to curb prostitution had led men to make increased sexual demands on "nice" girls. The wider participation of women in the economy provided them with more frequent, continuing contacts with men outside their own families. While the anonymity of urban centers permitted sexual indulgence without discovery, the accessibility of contraception permitted sexual indulgence with minimum risk of pregnancy.[48]

Although no part of her intention, Margaret Sanger's campaign in behalf of birth control had contributed to the sexual revolution. In abandoning radical causes, Sanger effectively diverted the birth-control movement away from the working classes toward the middle classes. As her cause gained respectability, a small group of monied men—Noah Slee, John D. Rockefeller, Jr., Alvin R. Kaufman, and Clarence J. Gamble—funded the production and distribution of contraceptive devices. Condoms, diaphragms, foams, and jellies, along with information on birth control, became widely available. Others, notably Robert Latou Dickinson, became increasingly important as leaders in family planning. During World War II, in the interest of limiting venereal disease, the armed forces instructed millions of service personnel in contraception. Oral contraceptives, first marketed in 1960, completed the revolution in birth control. Easy to use, the Pill gave women highly effective control over reproduction and contributed to spontaneity in sexual relationships. For those experiencing unpleasant side effects from the Pill, other alternatives were available, including the new intrauterine device—the IUD.[49]

However much individual women welcomed birth control, the birth-control movement progressed at its own speed, divorced from the woman's movement. Planned-parenthood groups justified their existence in terms of aiding family stability. The clinics advocated "child spacing" but made no attempt to alter the power relationships within the family, nor did they look behind sexual problems to the underlying causes—money worries, lack of privacy, inaccessibility of child care, inability to leave the house, and lack of equality for women in status, wealth, and power. Furthermore, many of the new leaders—enlightened doctors, professors, scientists, social workers, lawyers, clergy, and philanthropists—viewed birth control as "a means of lowering the birth rate selectively among those less likely to produce babies of merit." At this level, the birth-control movement had abandoned its feminist content, as well as its working-class orientation, to emphasize population control with a hint of racism. As birth control gained wider popular acceptance among the middle class, Congress in 1937 repealed prohibitions on the dissemination of birth-control information and devices. Many, but not all, of the states followed suit. The issue was still before the courts in 1983.[50]

Still another force contributing to the sexual revolution was existentialism. Although existentialism had roots going back to the mid-nineteenth century, it first found popular expression after World War II. Christian existentialism, drawing on the writings of Sören Kierkegaard, the moody Dane, was interpreted and disseminated to the twentieth century by theologians including Karl Barth and Reinhold Niebuhr. An even more influential secular existentialism, implicit in the writings of Ernest Hemingway and F. Scott Fitzgerald, was expounded explicitly by Jean-Paul Sartre, husband of Simone de Beauvoir, beginning in the mid-1940s.[51]

Neoromantic in character, existentialism placed heavy emphasis on feeling, on experiencing. To the existentialist life was a never-ending quest for "authentic existence." While life was "an adventure," the quest was not to be undertaken lightly. To the existential philosopher, man was alone in the world, exercising his freedom with a sense of forlornness, anxiety, and despair. Yet every decision was vital, offering the possibility of self-realization. To many youth of the 1960s, however, existentialism offered primarily a rationale for the hedonistic pursuit of excitement and sensation. According high value to the individual, it deprecated the rules and traditions of the past and encouraged its devotees to "do their thing," suggesting that the only valid values were those the individual made for himself or herself. The religious dimension of existentialism bestowed a mantle of respectability, but the bulk of its adherents drew on the secular version that emphasized that each decision in life tested one's character, enabling the individual to more completely realize one's full potential as a human being. The vicariousness of conventional female life was anathema. This popular version encouraged an unrestrained individualism along with a compulsive urge to override barriers to full self-realization. Questioning Christian ethics and traditional marriage alike, the secular existentialist enthusiastically rejected conventional sexual mores and joined the sexual revolution.[52]

Marriage manuals of the day catered to, if not promoted, the pursuit of sexual pleasure. Some such as Dr. David Reuben's *Everything You Always Wanted to Know About Sex, But Were Afraid to Ask* (1969), his *Any Woman Can* (1971), and Alex Comfort's *The Joy of Sex* (1972) and *More Joy of Sex* (1974) became best sellers. In the early seventies, Nena and George O'Neill's

Open Marriage (1972) matter-of-factly reported a current belief that traditional marriage denied the partners the "needed room to grow." While exploring ways to make monogamous marriages fulfilling, the O'Neill's argued that "outside sexual experiences when they are in the context of a meaningful relationship may be rewarding and beneficial to an open marriage." Columnists, such as Ann Landers, who in the 1950s counseled that "every girl must hang on to her virginity until marriage or death—whichever came first," were by the mid-1970s unwilling to "call her a tramp if she failed to do so." For Abigail Van Buren, the criterion by which to judge premarital sex was: "If you feel sufficiently mature and competent to set your own standards for your own reasons, do it." *Human Sexuality: New Directions in American Catholic Thought,* a work by five Catholic scholars, expounded an existential view as it asserted that sexual relations outside marriage are moral if they contribute to "creative growth" and "integration of human personality" and are "honest, faithful, self-liberating, other-enriching, socially responsible, life-serving, and joyous."[53]

During the 1960s, sexual permissiveness became increasingly more pervasive and open. Some persons refused to marry at all or delayed marriage. Others joined communes "in all shapes and sizes, utopian and utilitarian, some permitting free sex, others attempting to preserve monogamy even if not marriage." Married couples swapped partners for the evening; a few, with a nod to convention, through repeated divorce and remarriage, practiced serial monogamy.[54]

In the search for "room to grow" Americans explored a variety of alternative life-styles. As late as 1968, Columbia University made national headlines when it expelled a coed for living with a young man to whom she was not married. But by the mid-seventies many campuses offered coed housing as an option, and uncounted thousands of unmarried couples lived together in off-campus housing. For such couples, living-together was more nearly a form of courtship than of trial marriage, less than ten percent of the couples intending to marry each other. Nor was living-together limited to college students. Encouraged by the mass circulation journals, numerous "liberated" women mixed careers with living-together. Helen Gurley Brown, *Cosmopolitan's* editor, extolled the L-T-A (living-together arrangement) with her handbook, *Sex and the Single Girl* (1962). At the upper end of the age continuum, retired widows and widowers lived together in order to avoid loneliness, reduce living expenses, and preserve their separate Social Security benefits. By the mid-seventies some 1,320,000 unmarried Americans lived with a member of the opposite sex, more than double the number at the start of the decade. Although some feminists embraced sexual liberation, the new sexual views had independent origins.[55]

Anatomy and Destiny

Despite the greater sexual freedom, feminists still had to confront Freud's dictum that "anatomy is destiny." The work of psychologists and psychiatrists such as Marie Bonaparte and Helene Deutsch reinforced if not confirmed Freud's views. Erik H. Erikson added his authority, arguing that some of woman's psychological characteristics derived solely from her anatomical structure. Women, he argued, are more prone to be concerned with "inner space"—the home and domesticity—while men have a greater preoccupation with "outer space"—the world beyond the home. More pointedly, Terese Benedek and B. B. Rubenstein in exploring the relationships between ovarian activity and psychodynamic processes concluded that there was "a definite relation between mood swings of aggressivity and passivity, dependency attitudes and independence, and the differing hormone production of various phases of the menstrual cycle." Before women could be liberated, the sex-is-destiny doctrine had to be laid to rest.[56]

Long before the new feminism flowered, cracks in the Freudian view of women surfaced. In the 1940s Clara Thompson, drawing on 20 years of clinical and teaching experience, concluded: "The basic nature of woman is still unknown." The biologic effect of anatomic differences and the hormone secretions remained difficult to evaluate. The "characteristics and inferiority feelings which Freud considered to be specifically female and biologically determined can be explained as developments arising in and growing out of Western woman's historic situation of underprivilege, restriction of development, insincere attitude toward the sexual nature, and social and economic dependency." The record of women in behalf of social justice and human brotherhood amply refuted the charge that women displayed a deficient superego. Anticipating Betty Friedan and Germaine Greer by two decades, Thompson insisted that woman's need was "a feeling of the importance of her own organs," to accept "her own sexuality in its own right."[57]

Sex researchers probing the nation's changing mores gained an understanding of female sexuality that often contradicted Freud. A strongly held tenet of Freud had been that in maturing, a woman shifted her erotic focus from the clitoris to the vagina; failure to do so was a mark of infantilism and frigidity. By implication, the female was rendered dependent on the male for sexual gratification. Marriage manuals placed great emphasis on sexual performance. The male ego suffered if he failed to bring his partner to orgasm; the woman felt pressure to reach orgasm as a means of enhancing her lover's self-regard. Failing this, she was sexually inadequate, frigid.

As Anne Koedt evaluated the Freudian interpretation: "women have thus been defined sexually in terms of what pleases men." William Masters and Virginia Johnson, in documenting that women were capable of repeated orgasms, refuted the notion that women were sexually inferior to men. That normal women were naturally submissive and masochistic while normal men were naturally dominant and aggressive came to be regarded as "another myth that the changing patterns of relationship between the sexes has begun to dispel." After Alfred Kinsey and then Masters and Johnson established that the clitoris, rather than the vagina, was responsible for orgasm, some feminists argued that males were "sexually expendable." As Shere Hite expressed it, female sexuality in the past had been regarded as a response to male sexuality and intercourse. Now female sexuality acquired "a complex nature of its own." Radical feminists insisted that a woman must be permitted "to define and enjoy the forms of her own sexuality." No longer cowed by the sex-is-destiny argument, feminists of the sixties shed any sense of inherent sexual inferiority to men.[58]

The Lesbian Connection

A collateral, controversial issue that would trouble the feminists of the seventies concerned lesbians. The interest in sexual liberation, along with the existential emphasis on "doing one's thing," and the concern for civil rights encouraged lesbians to go public. Since 1955 the Daughters of Bilitis had attempted to promote a sympathetic understanding of lesbianism. By 1970 it had chapters in San Francisco, San Diego, Los Angeles, and New York, with other chapters forming in cities from Portland, Oregon, to Boston and Miami. Within the gay community, lesbians encountered the same sexual denigration from male homosexuals that women experienced from male heterosexuals: mixed groups were "'chaired' by the men and 'charred' by the women."[59]

Lesbian feminists insisted on a hearing from the woman's movement on two grounds: civil rights and sexual liberation. Having been condemned by church and society, lesbian activity in many jurisdictions was subject to civil sanctions; a lesbian also risked loss of her job and social ostracism if her sexual orientation were publicized. Lesbian couples insisted on the "simple rights granted the heterosexual society—the right to marriage, divorce, protection of property, self-declaration without job loss or social discrimination." Lesbians likewise viewed their life-style as "one road to freedom—freedom from oppression from men." The rigid sex roles of a male-dominated society, they argued, "dehumanize women" by defining them as "a supportive service caste in relation to the master caste of man. . . ." In this regard they averred that the lesbian mode of living was "neither

Lesbian feminists insisted that even though they challenged convention in terms of sexual preference, they were entitled to the same civil rights that heterosexual women enjoyed.

better nor worse than others." For lesbian feminists, homosexuality was more than a matter of personal sexual preference; it was a political act against the institutional source of all women's oppression—men. In this view, all males oppressed all women and the primary means of control was the heterosexual relationship. Thus, the "nice girl next door, virginal until her marriage," traded her individuality and her freedom for community respect by marrying; the career woman gained independence and a large margin of freedom at the cost of having to work twice as hard as a man for less pay; the "starlet, call girl, or bunny" paid for her temporary financial independence and freedom from housework through her psychological degradation as a sex object. On one hand the lesbian found satisfaction in being "freed of dependence on men for love, sex and money."

She found her most satisfying emotional ties with another woman rather than with a man. The lesbian identity was primarily a positive and passionate orientation toward women. Sexual behavior was only a relatively small part of lesbian social identity. Lesbian feminism tended to regard the patrilineal system, not men, as the enemy. On the other hand she was denied the rewards of child-rearing, faced the same job and salary discriminations as heterosexual women, and encountered "the most severe contempt and ridicule that society can heap on a woman," the epithet, lesbian. Contending that "our kind of love is as valid as anyone else's," lesbians insisted: "The revolution must be fought for us, too." The anger of lesbians, at least in part, resulted from the experience of encountering ignorance and prejudice on the part of the heterosexual majority.[60]

As the woman's movement matured in the 1970s, some feminists discovered they were lesbians as well, and unwilling to conceal their sexual orientation, they demanded public support from the woman's movement. NOW leaders were in a quandary. To the general public, lesbianism was an intolerable form of sexual perversion. If NOW supported lesbian rights or accepted lesbian support, it risked loss of public acceptance. Friedan, who regarded conventional heterosexual relationships within marriage as the norm, termed the lesbian issue "the lavender herring." NOW had to reckon with the views of radical feminists, who tended to support all women as a *class* and to oppose all men as a *class* and were often sympathetic to lesbians. Committed to securing women's rights, the NOW leadership recognized that they could not be consistent if they demanded civil rights for themselves but declined to support the civil rights of others. Invoking the natural-rights ideology that had undergirded the woman's movement at its founding, Aileen Hernandez, Friedan's successor as NOW's president, told the lesbians that NOW did not "prescribe a sexual preference test for applicants," adding, "we ask only that those who join NOW commit themselves to work for full equality for women and that they do so in the context that the struggle in which we are engaged is part of the total struggle to free *all* persons to develop their full humanity." Indeed, some feminists insisted "if women were rebelling against social roles predetermined by sex, sexual preference should be equally irrelevant." Most feminists argued that lesbianism was not and should not be "a central issue of the women's movement," that the primary attack must be on the sex-role system. Militant lesbians, like militant leftists, joined the feminist movement.[61]

EVOLVING SEX ROLES

Of critical importance in assessing the impact of the emerging woman's movement are the changing societal attitudes toward sex roles. Given that the movement addressed itself to a broad spectrum of issues, some relating to roles within the home and others to social, economic, and political roles outside the home, one must compare and contrast changes in sex-role attitudes in each of these various areas; because the population itself was heterogeneous, one needs to identify which segments clung to traditional sex roles and which embraced feminist views; finally one needs to assess the degree of change in attitudes that occurred.

There is a dearth of systematic data on sex-role attitudes prior to the appearance of Friedan's *The Feminine Mystique*. The only two questions asked by the national opinion surveys with any regularity were first, "If your party nominated a woman for president, would you vote for her if she were qualified for the job?" and second, "Do you approve or disapprove of a married woman earning money in business or industry if she has a husband capable of supporting her?" The proportions saying they would vote for a woman for president increased gradually from 1937, the first time the question was asked, to the late 1950s; then during the 1960s while the feminist movement was reemerging, attitudes remained steady. Initially women were far more supportive of voting for a woman presidential candidate than were men by a margin of 40 to 27 percent, respectively. During the next quarter century these differences narrowed. The proportion of women favorably disposed to a woman president increased to 57 percent, before dropping back to 51 percent in 1963. The proportion of men so disposed increased even faster, so that by 1963 men were more favorable to a woman presidential candidate than were women.[62]

The percentage of persons approving a married woman earning money in business or industry declined between 1938 and 1945, but it shot upward between 1945 and 1969. By 1969, 55 percent of the respondents approved. Where the sex of the respondents was tallied, women were invariably more approving of market labor for married women than were men. The responses to these two questions suggest that during the quarter century prior to the publication of Friedan's book, public attitudes were increasingly supportive of broader participation by women in the mainstream of American political and economic life.[63]

This trend continued in the years immediately following the appearance of Friedan's book, but there were marked differences between various segments of the female population. In both 1964 and 1970, first-year women college students were as tradition-oriented as any segment of the population. And among married women with baccalaureate degrees, fewer than one third questioned the traditional male–breadwinner role. But these women graduates underwent "sizable" attitude shifts. Between 1964 and 1970 the proportion of such women who disagreed with the statement that "a man can make long-range plans for his life, but a woman has to take things as they come," increased by one third. The proportion who agreed that a working mother could establish "just as warm and secure a relationship" with her children as a nonworking mother increased by 15 percentage points, while the proportion who rejected the statement "it is more important for a wife to help her husband than to have a career herself," increased 7 percentage points. During the middle and late sixties these recent college graduates shed many traditional sex-role beliefs respecting the family as well as those relating to the sexual division of labor.[64]

Older women generally were less tradition-minded in the early 1960s than younger women. The well-educated and those with the most recent labor-market experience were "less supportive of traditional norms and beliefs than other women." Women married to better-educated husbands were more supportive of equalitarian views than women with less well educated spouses. This suggests that white-collar women were more "liberated" than blue-collar women. Differences between the currently married and the divorced, separated, and widowed were small. Divorced and separated women tended to be more tradition-oriented than the currently married, however, they were more likely to support equal rights for women in the labor market.[65]

As of 1970, the time "women's lib" became a recognized term, a reasonably cohesive sex-role ideology could be delineated, an ideology that was "neither strictly traditional nor equalitarian." Women generally accepted a traditional sex-based division of responsibilities in family matters, and they agreed that maternal employment harmed preschool age children. At the same time, this ideology endorsed egalitarian views of women's roles in the labor force. An especially strong consensus supported equal pay and job opportunities for women. On other issues—whether working mothers can have "emotionally secure relationships" with their children or whether husbands should "share the work around the house" with wives—opinion was split. What existed, then, was "a 'core' gender-role ideology" built around the traditional sex-based division of domestic responsibilities and a second, independent cluster of nontraditional attitudes with respect to labor-market rights—attitudes that women either regarded as logically unrelated to the core or else felt did not need to be consistent with the core. In this regard, women in the general population did not share the "analysis" of the leaders of the woman's movement, who saw "familial sex roles, women's labor-market rights, and non-familial institutions" as "intimately interrelated."[66]

By 1970 the woman's movement began to coalesce. Working through autonomous organizations, radical feminists increasingly focused on feminist issues to the exclusion of the political, economic, and social questions that had attracted them to the New Left. Dropping their New Left rhetoric, they began examining with more care the positions of NOW and other moderate organizations. Simultaneously women in NOW, the National Federation of Business and Professional Women's Clubs, and the League of Women Voters began to respond to the consciousness-raising promoted by radical feminists. Thus moderates and radicals began moving toward a common ground of shared concerns, though both kept their own special emphases.

The woman's movement was in fact many movements. At its center stood NOW, supported by other moderate groups: the National Federation of Business and Professional Women's Clubs, WEAL (the Women's Equity Action League), Federally Employed Women, and the League of Women Voters. Women in various academic specialties and professional fields organized caucuses loosely affiliated in the Professional Women's Caucus. Radical women, lacking any comparable national organizations, operated through scores of local groups. A myriad of organizations, not feminist in origin, included women's issues on their agendas. As a case in point the Women's Department of the UAW lobbied state and federal legislators in support of equal-pay laws, strict enforcement of Title VII, abortion-law reform, child-care centers, and an ERA. Many others, though, limited themselves to a single issue or several related issues, rather than addressing the entire spectrum of women's issues. As of 1970, organized feminism drew its following from older established women in the white middle class and from younger women with an activist or radical orientation. Blacks, Chicanas, and lesbians were struggling to balance their unique concerns with those of feminism.

NOTES

[1] Betty Friedan, *The Feminine Mystique* (New York: Dell, 1964[1963]). Jo Freeman, "The Women's Liberation Movement: Its Origins, Structures, Impact, and Ideas," in *Women: A Perspective,* ed. Jo Freeman (Palo Alto: Mayfield, 1975), 448–60.

[2] Friedan, *Feminine Mystique,* 7, 14, 27, 37. Clara M. Thompson, *On Women* (New York: Mentor, 1971[1941]), commented on the restlessness of women in 1941, p. 112ff.

[3] Friedan, *Feminine Mystique,* 96, 112, 113. Juliet Mitchell, *Psychoanalysis and Feminism* (New York: Vintage, 1975), believes Friedan's argument faulty, pp. 319–27. Helene Deutsch, *The Psychology of Women A Psychoanalytic Interpretation* (New York: Bantam, 1973[1944]).

[4] Margaret Mead, quoted in Friedan, *Feminine Mystique,* 136.

[5] A. H. Maslow, *Motivation and Personality* (New York: Harper, 1954). Friedan, *Feminine Mystique,* 305, 306, 314. Gayle Graham Yates, *What Women Want* (Cambridge: Harvard University Press, 1975), 40.

[6] Friedan, *Feminine Mystique,* 329–30, 332–33, 336, 353.

[7] Mary Ryan, *Womanhood in America* (New York: New Viewpoints, 1975), 329–32. William Henry Chafe, *The American Woman* (New York: Oxford University Press, 1972), 190–91.

[8] Simone de Beauvoir, *The Second Sex* (New York: Bantam, 1961[1953]). Alice S. Rossi,

"Equality Between the Sexes: An Immodest Proposal," *Daedalus,* 93(Spring, 1964); 607–652; the entire issue has been reprinted as *The Woman in America,* ed. Robert J. Lifton (Boston: Beacon, 1967), 98–143; see especially 99, 115, and 119ff.

[9] President's Commission on the Status of Women, *American Women* (Washington: GPO, 1963). NOW's Statement of Purpose appears in *Up From the Pedestal,* ed. Aileen S. Kraditor (Chicago: Quadrangle, 1970), 363–69. NOW Bill of Rights (1967), in *Sisterhood is Powerful,* ed. Robin Morgan (New York: Vintage, 1970), 512–14.

[10] Chafe, *American Woman,* 237–38.

[11] Judith Hole and Ellen Levine, *Rebirth of Feminism* (New York: Quadrangle, 1971), 82.

[12] Ibid., 95–98.

[13] Yates, *What Women Want,* 48–50.

[14] Women's Bureau, *Reports of the Task Forces to Citizen's Advisory Council* (Washington: GPO, 1968). President's Task Force on Women's Rights and Responsibilities, *A Matter of Simple Justice* (Washington: GPO, 1970).

[15] John P. Diggins, *The American Left in the Twentieth Century* (New York: Harcourt Brace Jovanovich, 1973), 156, 169, 171, 176. See also Anne Koedt, Ellen Levine, and Anita Rapone, eds. *Radical Feminism* (New York: Quadrangle, 1973).

[16] Diggins, *The American Left,* 168–176. Sara Evans, *Personal Politics: The Roots of Women's Liberation in the Civil Rights Movement and the New Left* (New York: Knopf, 1979).

[17] Irwin Unger, *The Movement: A History of the American New Left* (New York: Dodd, Mead, 1974), 153, 155. For the origins of the feminist movement see Roberta Salper, "The Development of the Women's Liberation Movement," 1967–1971," in *Female Liberation,* ed. Roberta Salper (New York: Knopf, 1972). Jo Freeman, "The Origins of the Women's Liberation Movement," *AJS,* 78(1973): 792–811. Hole and Levine, *Rebirth of Feminism,* 15–166. Beverly Jones and Judith Brown, "Toward a Female Liberation Movement," in *Voices From Women's Liberation,* ed. Leslie B. Tanner (New York: Mentor, 1970), 362–415. Donald Allen Robinson, "Two Movements in Pursuit of Equal Employment Opportunity," *Signs,* 4(1979), 413–33.

[18] Juliet Mitchell, "Women: The Longest Revolution," *New Left Review,* 40(Nov./Dec. 1966): 11–37. Charles Fourier, *Theorie des Quatres Mouvements,* in *Ouvres Completes* (Paris: Editions Anthropes, 1966[1846]). Karl Marx, *The Holy Family,* trans. R. Dixon (Moscow: Foreign Language Publishing House, 1956[1845]) and *Private Property and Communism* in *Early Writings,* trans. T. B. Bottomore (London: Watts, 1963[1844]). Friedrich Engels, *The Origin of the Family, Private Property and the State* (New York: International, 1942[1892]).

[19] Mitchell, "Women: The Longest Revolution," 171. Juliet Mitchell, *Woman's Estate* (New York: Vintage, 1973[1971]).

[20] Mitchell, "Women: The Longest Revolution," 172, 173.

[21] Margaret Benson, "The Political Economy of Women's Liberation," *Monthly Review,* 21(Sept. 1969): 13–25; the piece is reprinted widely.

[22] Roxanne Dunbar, "Female Liberation as the Basis for Social Revolution," in *The New Feminism in Twentieth-Century America,* ed. June Sochen (Lexington: Heath, 1971), 187, 188–89.

[23] Marlene Dixon, "The Rise of Women's Liberation," *Ramparts,* 8(Dec. 1969): 57–63. Salper, *Female Liberation,* 183–84.

[24] Hole and Levine, *Rebirth of Feminism,* 123–30. Carol Hanish, "A Critique of the Miss America Protest," in *Notes from the Second Year* (Boston: n.p., 1970), 87.

[25] Yates, *What Women Want,* 103. Freeman, "The Women's Liberation Movement," 451–52. Hole and Levine, *Rebirth of Feminism,* 138.

[26] Kathie Sarachild, "A Program for Feminist 'Consciousness Raising,'" in *Notes from the Second Year* (Boston: n.p., 1970). Anne Koedt, "The Myth of Vaginal Orgasm," in *Notes from the Second Year;* it also appears in Sochen, *The New Feminism,* 140–49.

[27] Hole and Levine, *Rebirth of Feminism,* 135–36. "The Redstockings Manifesto," in Morgan, *Sisterhood is Powerful,* 533–36.

[28] "The Feminists: A Political Organization to Annihilate Sex Roles," quoted in Hole and Levine, *Rebirth of Feminism,* 142–52.

[29] Ibid., 152–57, 440–43.

[30] Germaine Greer, *The Female Eunuch* (New York: Bantam, 1972[1970]).

[31] Ibid., 19, 13, 120–21, 255.

[32] Ibid., 11, 65–66, 340, 343, 345.

[33] Shulamith Firestone, *The Dialectic of Sex* (New York: Bantam, 1971[1970]), 7, 10–11, 74.

[34] Ibid., 46–47, 51, 64, 70.

[35] Ibid., 206–209.

[36] Ibid., 227–31.

[37] Unger, *The Movement,* 93–94.

[38] Anne Koedt quoted in Hole and Levine, *Rebirth of Feminism,* 110. Cellestine Ware, *Woman Power: The Movement for Women's Liberation* (New York: Tower, 1970), chap. 2. Toni Cade, ed., *The Black Woman: An Anthology* (New York: New American Library, 1970), 9. Patricia Robinson, "Poor Black Women," in *Black Women in White America,* ed. Gerda Lerner (New York: Vintage, 1973), 599–602. Renee Ferguson, "Women's Liberation Has a Different Meaning for Blacks," in Lerner, *Black Women in White America,* 589.

[39] Frances M. Beal, "Double Jeopardy: To Be Black and Female," in Morgan, *Sisterhood is Powerful,* 350. Robinson, "Poor Black Women," in Lerner, *Black Women in White America,* 601.

[40] Beal, "Double Jeopardy," in Morgan, *Sisterhood is Powerful,* 347, 348–49.

[41] Ferguson, "Women's Liberation," in Lerner, *Black Women in White America,* 587, 589, 591. Dara Abubakari (Virginia E. Y. Collins), "The Black Woman is Liberated in Her Own Mind," in Lerner, *Black Women in White America,* 585. Joyce A. Ladner, *Tomorrow's Tomorrow: The Black Woman* (Garden City: Doubleday, 1971). Bonnie Thornton Dill, "The Dialectics of Black Womanhood," *Signs,* 4(1979): 543–55. See especially Paula Giddings, *When and Where I Enter* (New York: Morrow, 1984), 299–324.

[42] Editorial, "For a Better Future," *Ebony,* 21(Aug. 1966): 150. Pauli Murray, "The Liberation of Black Women," in *Women: A Feminist Perspective,* ed. Jo Freeman (Palo Alto: Mayfield, 1975), 355. Ryan, *Womanhood in America,* 392. William H. Grier and Price M. Cobbs, *Black Rage* (New York: Bantam, 1968). Special issues of *Ebony,* 21(Aug. 1966), and *The Black Scholar,* 6(March 1975), focus on the concerns of black women.

[43] Shirley Chisholm, *Unbought and Unbossed* (Boston: Houghton Mifflin, 1970), 113–22. "Black Sisters," in *Masculine/Feminine,* ed. Betty Roszak and Theodore Roszak (New York: Harper & Row, 1969), 212–13.

[44] Murray, "The Liberation of Black Women," in Freeman, *Women: A Feminist Perspective,* 362.

[45] Maxine Baca Zinn, "Political Familism: Toward Sex Role Equality in Chicano Families," *Aztlan,* 6(1975): 13–26.

[46] Marta Cotera, "Feminism: the Chicano and Anglo Versions," in *Twice a Minority: Mexican-American Women,* ed. Margarita B. Melville (St. Louis: Mosby, 1980), 217–34.

[47] Zinn, "Political Familism," 19, 20. Leo Grebler, Joan W. Moore, and Ralph Guzman, *The Mexican-American People* (New York: Free Press, 1970), 9. Ellwyn R. Stoddard, *Mexican Americans* (New York: Random House, 1973), 103–104.

[48] Alfred Kinsey et al., *Sexual Behavior in the Human Female* (Philadelphia: Saunders, 1953), 299. See also "Sex and the Contemporary American Scene," *The Annals,* 376(March 1968) and "Women—Sex and Sexuality," *Signs,* 5(Summer 1980) and 6(Autumn 1980).

[49] Lucinda Cisler, "Unfinished Business: Birth Control and Women's Liberation," in Morgan, *Sisterhood is Powerful,* 245–89, gives a feminist perspective.

[50] Elizabeth Fee and Michael Wallace, "The History and Politics of Birth Control: A Review Essay," in *FS,* 5(1979): 205. *NYT,* 9 July 1983, sec. 1, p. 5, col. 1, 15 March 1983, sec. 1, p. 16, col. 6, and 25 June 1983, sec. 1, p. 8, col. 1.

[51] Ernst Breisach, *Introduction to Modern Existentialism* (New York: Grove, 1962), 1–9, 94–106.

[52] Compare Greer, *Female Eunuch,* 340–43, 345 ff. Firestone, *Dialectic of Sex,* 11–14.

[53] Nena O'Neill and George O'Neill, *Open Marriage* (New York: Avon, 1973), 9, 254. Abigail Van Buren, column of 7 July 1974. *Human Sexuality: New Directions in American Catholic Thought,* Anthony Kosnik, chair (New York: Paulist Press, 1977), 168.

[54] Mary Ryan, *Womanhood in America,* 2nd ed., (New York: New Viewpoints, 1979), 235–39.

[55] James W. Croake, James F. Keller, and Nancy Catlin, "Unmarrieds Living Together: It's Not all Gravy," *NYT,* 23 Sept. 1975. Helen Gurley Brown, *Sex and the Single Girl* (New York: Pocket Books, 1962). *NYT,* 9 Feb. 1977. O'Neill and O'Neill, *Open Marriage,* 14.

[56] Marie Bonaparte, *Female Sexuality* (New York: International Universities Press, 1953). Helene Deutsch, *Psychology of Women.* Erik Erikson, "Inner and Outer Space: Reflections on Womanhood," in *The Woman in America,* ed. Robert J. Lifton (Boston: Beacon, 1967), 1–26. Terese Benedek and B. B. Rubenstein, "The Sexual Cycle in Women," cited in Thompson, *On Women,* 19.

[57] Thompson, *On Women,* 141, 149, 152.

[58] Judd Marmor, "Changing Patterns of Femininity, Psychoanalytic Implications," in *The Marriage Relationship,* ed. Salo Rosenbaum and Ian Alger (New York: Basic, 1968), chap. 3. William H. Masters and Virginia E. Johnson, *Human Sexual Response* (Boston: Little, Brown, 1966), 66–67. Anne Koedt, "Myth of Vaginal Orgasm," in Sochen, *New Feminism,* 141, 148. Susan Lydon, "The Politics of Orgasm," in Morgan, *Sisterhood is Powerful,* 205. Shere Hite, *The Hite Report* (New York: Dell, 1976), 11.

[59] Gene Damon, "The Least of These: The Minority Whose Screams Haven't Yet Been Heard," in Morgan, *Sisterhood is Powerful,* 305. See also John D'Emilio, *Sexual Politics, Sexual Communities: The Making of a Homosexual Minority in the United States,* 1940–1970 (Chicago: University of Chicago Press, 1983), chap. 6, and Adrienne Rich, "Compulsory Heterosexuality and Lesbian Existence," *Signs,* 5(1980): 631–60.

[60] Damon, "The Least of These," in Morgan, *Sisterhood is Powerful,* 304. Martha Shelley, "Notes of a Radical Lesbian," in Morgan, *Sisterhood is Powerful,* 306, 307, 310. "The Woman-Identified Woman," quoted in Salper, *Female Liberation,* 181–82.

[61] Betty Friedan, *It Changed My Life* (New York: Dell, 1977), 210–13, first used the term "sexual red herring" in December 1979. Hole and Levine, *Rebirth of Feminism,* 94, 240–42.

[62] Hazel Erskine, "The Polls: Women's Role," *Public Opinion Quarterly,* 35(1971): 277–79.

[63] Ibid., 282–86.

[64] Ibid.

[65] Karen Oppenheim Mason, John L. Czajka, and Sara Arber, "Changes in U.S. Women's Sex-Role Attitudes, 1964–1974," *ASR,* 4(Aug. 1976): 582–84.

[66] Karen Oppenheim Mason and Larry L. Bumpass, "U.S. Women's Sex-Role Ideology, 1970," *AJS,* 80(1975): 1213, 1215.

9

The Pursuit of Equality: The 1970s

By 1970, "woman's hour" had arrived, or so it seemed. NOW was nationally known. "Women's lib" had entered the vocabulary. The civil-rights movement had sensitized Congress and the public to the need to make American practices accord with American ideals. Women sought to bend this new sensitivity to equality, or the lack of it, to their own case. As the demands of women were far less threatening to the establishment than those of the New Left or the antiwar movement, the prospects seemed bright. In the pursuit of equality, women pressed not only for the ERA but for a wide range of corrective legislation touching on family law, employment, criminal law, political status, and education to end differential treatment of men and women.

REFORM BY AMENDMENT: THE ERA

Support of an ERA was widespread among organized women in 1970. After a half century the idea of assuring women equality by constitutional amendment was no longer strange. In May 1970, when Senator Birch Bayh conducted the first hearings on an ERA since 1956, leaders of nearly every woman's rights organization in the nation testified in support of the amendment. In midsummer Martha Griffiths, long an advocate of woman's rights, shepherded the amendment through the House of Representatives, which adopted it 350 to 15. Aroused, opponents of the ERA rallied. Led by Sam Ervin, Jr., the Senate adopted a rider designed to keep intact all state protective legislation and to exempt women from the draft. Although the measure died, feminists would not be denied.[1]

Griffiths Proposes

In the next session, Representative Martha Griffiths reintroduced an ERA, the operative language declaring: "Equality of rights under the law shall not be denied or abridged by the United States or by any State on account of sex." In testifying for the amendment, Griffiths ticked off the varieties of legal discriminations imposed on women by action of national and state statutes, city and township ordinances, school-board regulations, and by the administrative regulations of multitudinous government agencies. She pointed to inequalities in family law, exclusion from jury service, unequal Social Security benefits, discrimination in credit, and exclusion from employment. She emphasized that "the right to be free of sex discrimination would have to harmonize with other constitutional rights such as the right to privacy" and that where considerations of health and safety were paramount, sex-neutral legislation would protect men and women alike. Anticipating the argument that women's interests could be protected under the equal-protection clause of the Fourteenth Amendment, she asserted: "The 14th Amendment has been with us since 1868 and in all those years the Supreme Court has never once held unconstitutional a law which discriminated on the basis of sex." Nor could women rely on "piecemeal statutory attempts to curb sex discrimination." Citing *Phillips* v. *Martin-Marietta,* she argued that the BFOQ (bona fide occupational qualification) clause of Title VII had allowed an unsympathetic court to thwart the intention of statute law. Protective legislation had become restrictive. "The only real protection there is for any woman is to be able to make her own living," and an ERA was needed to maximize that opportunity.[2]

Ervin Opposes

Senator Ervin led the attack against the ERA. While admitting to the multiplicity of discriminations encountered by women, the senator insisted that "they ought to be abolished by law in every case where they are created by law." But, he added, many of women's "just grievances are founded upon discriminations not created by law, and, for this reason the equal rights amendment will have no effect whatsoever in respect to them." Equally basic to his attack on the ERA was Ervin's "abiding conviction that the law should make such distinctions between them [the sexes] as are reasonably necessary for the protection of women and the existence and development of the race." As surely as Sigmund Freud, Ervin affirmed that sex is destiny: "When He created them, God made physiological and functional differences between men and women. These differences confer upon men a greater capacity to perform arduous and hazardous physical tasks. Some wise people even profess the belief that there may be psychological differences between men and women. To justify their belief, they assert that women possess an intuitive power to distinguish between wisdom and folly, good and evil." In saying this, the senator disclaimed that either sex was superior to the other. "The all important truth" was that "men and women complement each other. . . ." A sexual division of labor was of God. "From time whereof the memory of mankind runneth not to the contrary, custom and law have imposed upon men the primary responsibility for providing a habitation and a livelihood for their wives and children to enable their wives to make the habitations homes, and to furnish nurture, care and training to their children during their early years. . . . Any country which ignores these differences when it fashions its institutions and makes its laws is woefully lacking in rationality." Thus spake Senator Ervin.[3]

Generally opposed to the ERA, the legal community focused on constitutional aspects of sex-based discrimination in American law. Legal scholars such as Bernard Schwartz, Paul Freund, Leo Kanowitz, and Phillip Kurland argued that an ERA was neither "necessary nor appropriate to alleviate the very real discriminations suffered today by women in American society." The equal-protection clause and the commerce powers, they insisted, were sufficiently broad to protect women against discrimination, and they argued that had "the energy and dedication" poured into the ERA campaigns been "devoted to the selection and sponsorship of test cases" in the courts, then "a great deal more accomplishment could be shown with respect to the advancement of equal rights. . . ." To these legal scholars the ERA possessed "a certain beguiling panacea-like quality." They also found the ERA ambiguous, on the one hand commanding "the treatment of men and women as if there were no differences between them. . . ," while on the other insisting only on "the elimination of discrimination against women, a ban on treating females as a disabled class." In the first instance they saw the ERA as demanding a unisex standard for all, depriving women of benefits while relieving them of discriminatory burdens; in the second, it would protect them from invidious discriminations while leaving them with special benefits. The confusions about the purposes of the ERA needed to be cleared up. Clearly the lawyers preferred a policy of "specific pills for specific ills." The ERA, they thought, offered "a potentially destructive and self-defeating blunderbuss approach" to reform.[4]

By 1971 Leo Kanowitz, who had written extensively on women and the law, had shifted his position from "mild opposition" to the ERA to a conviction of the necessity for the amendment. His conversion resulted from the repeated failure of the Supreme Court "to apply existing constitutional provisions, especially the Fourteenth Amendment, to the sex discrimination areas." He was particularly distressed that the Court in *Phillips* v. *Martin-Marietta* had suggested that certain "conflicting family obligations" might justify separate treatment for women under the BFOQ provisions of Title VII. His discomfort was increased by Justice Marshall's criticism that the Court was thinking in terms of "ancient canards about the proper roles of women." Kanowitz urged strongly that the legislative record of the ERA proceedings indicate clearly to the Court that it ought to utilize the due-process clauses of the Fifth and Fourteenth amendments and the equal-protection clause of the Fourteenth Amendment to strike down sex-based discrimination even if an ERA were ratified. The legislative history should also show a clear intent on the part of Congress to see that the Court extend the benefits of protective legislation to men and women alike. Kanowitz joined other lawyers in arguing that to achieve equality, much existing legislation would need to be rewritten. The range of such legislative reform would be broad: marriage and family relationships, children, employment, insurance, pension and taxes, criminal law, political status, and education.[5]

The ERA debate indicated that supporters embraced a wide spectrum from "the most conservative Republican women, some of whom find 'feminism a dirty word,' to the most radical feminists who challenge the institutions of marriage, the family, and in fact define sexual relationships as a political institution to be restructured." Opponents, who included conservative male politicians, much of organized labor, and some radical women of the New Left, once more attempted to nullify the ERA by a crippling amendment; but feminists, at high tide, kept Congress in line. In October 1971 the House approved the ERA 354 to 23, and on March 22, 1972, the Senate did likewise, 84 to 8. Within a few hours Hawaii ratified the ERA; other ratifications followed quickly. By the end of 1973, 30 states had approved the amendment.[6]

FEMINISM AND THE FAMILY

As the ERA went to the states for ratification or rejection, feminist groups—local, state, and national—continued to refine their goals. While giving the ERA first priority, feminists did not limit themselves to a single goal as the suffragists and National Woman's Party had done. NOW's succinct eight-point program of 1967 became increasingly detailed and comprehensive. The 1973 statement contained 12 sections starting with "Equality Under the Law" and concluding with "Human Sexuality." In between were sections on economic, educational, and political equality, legislative goals, child care, reproduction, family relations, war and violence, criminal violence, and feminine and masculine mystiques. At the same time, a multitude of women's organizations—some local, others national—addressed a broad range of concerns of women. The NWPC (National Women's Political Caucus), founded by Shirley Chisholm, Bella Abzug, and others, became an "umbrella organization" to provide "the weight and muscle for those issues which the majority of women in this country see as concerns." As women explored and expanded the concept of feminism, they gave special attention to ways of reconciling the responsibilities of child care and the control of reproduction with achieving full equality. No subjects in the whole range of feminist concerns were so sensitive, for no other issues so directly affected husband–wife relationships.[7]

Child Care

At the start of the century, Charlotte Perkins Gilman had insisted that a system of child care was needed if women were to enjoy the same opportunities as men to pursue careers. By the seventies, Sweden and France had established government-supported child-care centers, both emphasizing the educational and developmental potentials of child care. The NOW platform addressed these issues. A national child-care program became increasingly urgent as the proportion of working women with young children grew. The growing proportion of two-income families made it increasingly difficult to maintain a family on the husband's income alone. The need for a national child-care program increased as more and more women entered jobs with long-term career possibilities. President Johnson gave child care a boost in 1964 when, as part of his War on Poverty, he launched the Head Start Program for preschool children. In 1970, at the urging of women's groups, the President's Task Force on Women's Rights and Responsibilities declared: "Our national goal" should include "a system of well-run child-care centers available to all preschool children." The emphasis, however, was on the potential for "reducing the welfare burden" by enabling low-income mothers to enter the labor force."[8]

Although Congress promptly responded with the Child and Family Services Act of 1971, President Nixon vetoed the measure as "deeply flawed." The expenditure of $2 billion on a program whose effectiveness had not been demonstrated, he termed "fiscal irresponsibility." "Neither the immediate need nor the desirability of a national child development program of this character has been demonstrated," the president declared. Child-care centers for children of welfare parents, he averred, were adequately provided for in other legislation. His major objection was with its "family-weakening implications." Good public policy required that "we enhance rather than diminish both parental authority and parental involvement with children—particularly in those decisive early years when social attitudes and a conscience are formed and religious and moral principles are first inculcated." Nixon refused to commit the moral authority of the federal government to the side of "communal approaches to child-rearing over against the family-centered approach."[9]

The president's defense of traditional family ties ignored realities. In March 1974, 6,100,000 children under age five had working mothers. The mothers of three fourths of these children were single, separated, divorced, or widowed heads of families. Clearly the child-care problem arose not out of the efforts of women to escape parental responsibilities but rather out of the pressing economic realities of mothers striving to meet them. Support for the child-care bill had come from labor, church, and public-interest groups, as well as from the woman's movement. Dispirited, these advocates bided their time. Once Gerald Ford succeeded to the presidency, Congress enacted the Comprehensive Child and Family Services Act of 1975. Taking a cue from the Nixon veto, the act acknowledged the family as exerting the "primary and most fundamental influence on children," and it funded child care primarily as a means of shifting mothers off public assistance. Congress was not yet prepared to treat child care as "an educational investment in the future." The liberating effect for mothers and the educational benefits for children that feminists sought were not realized. Even this modest child-care program encountered an uneasy path as Congress periodically threatened to reduce funding levels or to terminate the support altogether.[10]

Reproductive Control

During the sixties the woman's movement asserted "the right of women to control their own reproductive lives." One aspect of this called for "access to contraceptive information and devices." Birth control was valued for itself, enabling the individual to determine whether or when she would become pregnant. It permitted keeping family size within the bounds that family income could support and facilitated long-term careers. Although by the sixties birth control was in common use among the affluent, the educated, and the young, it was not universally available. As late as the mid-sixties, nearly 40 percent of low- and moderate-income women lacked access to any kind of family-planning services. Several states still forbade dissemination of birth-control information and devices. By endorsing birth control, the woman's movement incurred the wrath of several groups. Although surveys indicated Roman Catholics utilized birth control to about the same degree as non-Catholics, the Church leadership reaffirmed its long-standing opposition to contraception. Feminists also ran into conflict with those blacks who regarded birth control as a means by which the white majority sought to retard the growth of black and other nonwhite populations. Many married persons who themselves used birth control had misgivings about making contraceptive materials readily available to the unmarried and especially to minors.[11]

In view of the widespread acceptance of birth control by the dominant middle class, these opponents were unable to block the remaining legal restraints on access to birth control. In 1973 the U.S. Supreme Court struck down as an invasion of privacy those state statutes barring access to contraceptive devices. The Court held that "if the right of privacy means anything, it is the right of the individual, married or single, to be free of unwarranted government intrusion into matters so fundamentally affecting a person as the decision whether to bear or beget a child."[12]

Gaining complete control over reproduction remained a troublesome issue. Although in the early sixties women had hailed the introduction of the pill and the IUD, in the seventies feminists expressed increasing concern with the safety of some contraceptive methods. The Dalkon Shield, an IUD, was withdrawn from the market as evidence accumulated that it posed a risk to the woman's health and life. Oral contraception also came under a shadow as research linked long-term use of the pill to an increased risk of tumors, blood clots, strokes, and heart attacks. Many women came to feel that male doctors had been much too casual in prescribing birth-control methods that placed the woman user at risk. After 1973, contraceptive sterilization for males as well as females increased greatly in popularity, especially among couples who had completed formation of their families. The Public Health Service Act of 1975 funded family-planning services to low-income patients. Such services—virtually the only source of preventive health care available to low-income women—included blood-pressure-testing services, cancer screening, and venereal-disease detection. On balance, by the mid-seventies a broad spectrum of American women enjoyed effective control over their fertility.[13]

Abortion

Conviction that each woman should have the right to choose whether or not she gave birth triggered a raging dispute over the legalization of abortion. While some feminists argued for abortion on demand, others wanted to prohibit abortion altogether. Most states, operating under laws adopted in the late nineteenth century, prohibited abortion except to save the life of the mother, but abortion had not disappeared. In 1940 the number of illegal abortions was estimated to be between 318,000 and 415,000; in 1970, between 200,000 and 1,200,000.[14]

Reform of American abortion law began prior to and independently of the revived feminist movement. In 1959 the American Law Institute (ALI) drafted a model abortion law designed to broaden the grounds to permit abortion (1) if there were a "substantial risk" that a continued pregnancy would "gravely impair the physical or mental health of the mother," (2) if the child would be born "with grave physical or mental defects," or (3) if the pregnancy had "resulted from rape or incest." In 1962 the effort of Sherri Finkbine to secure a therapeutic abortion, because she seemed likely to bear a deformed child, drew national attention. The rubella epidemic of 1964, just as the new feminism was spreading, reinforced interest in access to legal abortion. In 1967 Colorado, followed by 11 other states, adopted new laws based on the ALI model. Four other states amended their laws to provide for abortion on the request of the woman and her doctor. It was in this climate that NOW urged repeal of "penal laws governing abortion." Lengthy, emotional argument ensued. Some feminists objected that abortion reform had nothing to do with civil rights; a larger group, while personally supporting abortion reform, opposed public endorsement of abortion reform, lest it adversely affect the woman's movement. But a majority supported reform. An important factor in this decision was that a separate abortion-reform movement already existed and had assumed the principal burden of securing change. In 1968 the Citizens' Advisory Council forwarded to President Johnson its report recommending repeal of abortion laws.[15]

The most sweeping reform of abortion law came at the hands of the U.S. Supreme Court. In January 1973 in *Roe* v. *Wade,* the Court ruled that the abortion decision (1) was protected by the Constitutional right of privacy and the exercise of that right, (2) was a matter only for the pregnant woman and her physician, (3) could not be prohibited by the State during the first three months of pregnancy, although the State might thereafter regulate abortion in ways reasonably related to the mother's health, and (4) must be protected whenever the woman's life or health was at stake. What the Court upheld was not a *woman's* right to "determine whether to bear a child," but a *doctor's* right to "administer medical treatment according to *his* professional judgment. . . ." In 1976 the Court refined its position, asserting that a state could not interfere with abortions in the first trimester of a pregnancy; the state might impose regulations in the second trimester to protect the woman's health; and in the third trimester, after viability, it could forbid abortions. The Court expressly declined to permit a husband unilaterally to block an abortion sought by his wife or to require a minor girl to secure parental consent for an abortion.[16]

The abortion issue polarized Americans. Antiabortion groups—supported by the Catholic hierarchy and by Protestant fundamentalists—opposed the limited proposals of the ALI and grew rapidly after the 1973 Supreme Court decisions. Terming the 1973 decision "an unspeakable tragedy," Cardinal Krol insisted that "the child in the womb has the right to the life he already possesses." An angered Cardinal Cooke spurred a movement "to reverse this injustice to the rights of the unborn child." As feminists had endorsed the principle of abortion on demand, the antiabortion campaign was directed against the woman's movement as well. The San Diego diocese refused the Eucharist to members of proabortion groups, including members of NOW. In November 1975 the National Conference of Catholic Bishops drafted a "pastoral plan for pro-life activities." And by early 1976 Ellen McCormack, as the presidential candidate of the Pro-Life Action Committee, drew national attention to the antiabortion campaign. A Roman Catholic, McCormack was supported by Dr. Mildred Jefferson, head of the National Right to Life Committee. A black, a Methodist, and a surgeon, Jefferson argued that "life begins at conception" and denounced abortion as the "very ultimate in sex perversion, because it's like pretending sex didn't happen, and throwing away the evidence that it did." She insisted, too, that abortion is genocidal to black people—"a class war against the poor." The Pro-Life group sought a constitutional amendment to reverse the thrust of the Supreme Court's position on abortion.[17]

On the other side, the National Abortion Rights Action League and the Religious Coalition for Abortion Rights sought to preserve the freedom of choice that the Supreme Court had given women. Rabbi Balfour Brickner of the Union of American Hebrew Congregations insisted that the issue was "abortion and the human right to choose that option, not Catholic, not Protestant, and not Jew." In the same vein, Meta Mucahy, vice-president of Catholics for a Free Choice, declared that "in conscience, concerned Catholics must deem reproductive decisions to be a person's most basic civil liberty." While most feminists rejected abortion as "an acceptable method of family planning," they opposed any constitutional amendment to prohibit abortion; but they proved unable to block state and federal legislation that severely curbed the use of public (usually medicaid) funds for elective abortions, and in June 1977 the Supreme Court allowed such curbs to stand.[18]

As a result, even women able to pay for abortions had difficulty in securing them. Officials in a few states, ignoring the Court's 1973 decision, threatened women seeking elective abortions with criminal prosecution. Catholic hospitals uniformly refused to perform abortions, and during

1975 less than one fifth of the public ones did so. In ten states no public hospital provided such services. In the largest cities women might find safe, relatively inexpensive care; in many small towns and in rural areas neither doctors nor health-care facilities were available. Nonetheless the demand for abortions climbed sharply in the early seventies, reaching 1,554,000 in 1980; nationwide there were 428 legal abortions for every 1,000 live births. During these same years the number of deaths resulting from abortion dropped sharply, as did serious complications from illegal abortions.[19]

FEMINISM CHALLENGED

Feminist efforts in behalf of child care, family planning, and abortion reform carried feminism into areas that earlier generations of reformers had avoided. NOW's refusal to exclude lesbians from membership and its defense of the right of individuals to be free of legal harassment for pursuing unorthodox sexual preferences attracted more attention than the wide range of political, economic, and educational reforms that were central to the movement. The concreteness of the proposals with respect to child care, family planning, and abortion reform provided a focus for opponents to the ERA.

Opposition came from traditionalists, who regarded the role of woman as homemaker and childbearer as sacrosanct, and from protectionists, who continued to insist that legislation that protected or favored women was the better way. The organized opposition included labor unions, church organizations, and right-wing conservatives. This is not to say that all unions, churches, or conservatives were in opposition. AFL-CIO opponents objected that "the amendment could destroy more rights than it creates by attempting to create equality through 'sameness,'" though acknowledging that some protective legislation seemed "anachronistic." Most such statutes remained "necessary and appropriate to assure women safe and healthful conditions on the job." So, too, the Amalgamated Clothing Workers of America—a union of 390,000 members, 75 percent of whom were women—endorsed the Women's Equity Bill in 1971 and dismissed the ERA approach as "false" and "dangerous." The representative of the Hotel and Restaurant Employees and Bartenders International Union (AFL-CIO) concurred. A recurrent theme was that because women in the bottom ranks of the labor force remained unprotected by union contracts and were uncovered by Title VII, they would be defenseless if protective labor laws were to be wiped out by the ERA.[20]

Church groups opposed to the ERA emphasized the threat to family relationships. Protestant fundamentalists invoked a literal interpretation of the Bible to justify a subordinate role for women. Mormon spokesmen based their opposition both on theology and physiology. Recognizing men and women "as equally important before the Lord," Mormon leaders rejected the ERA as failing to recognize "the differences, biologically, emotionally and in other ways." The National Council of Catholic Women endorsed the view that "the husband should continue to have the primary responsibility for the support of his wife and minor children." It was prepared to go no further in support of the "partnership view of marriage" than to say that "the wife should be given some legal responsibility for sharing in the support of herself and the children to the extent she has sufficient means to do so." The council was skeptical of suggestions that women could assume "equal" responsibility for the support of the family.[21]

By far the most vocal opponent of the ERA was Phyllis Schlafly. A long-time propagandist and publicist of right-wing causes, she authored *A Choice, Not an Echo,* a campaign biography of Barry Goldwater, and *Kissinger on the Couch,* which deplored the loss of American missile superiority to the Soviet Union. In *None Dare Call It Treason,* she questioned the patriotism of Dwight David Eisenhower. Despite an extensive career of writing, public speaking, two unsuccessful campaigns for Congress, presidency of the Illinois Federation of Republican Women, and editorship of her own monthly newsletter, Schlafly represented herself as an ordinary housewife and mother of six children. Opposing the ERA, she insisted that "it won't do anything to help women and it will take away from women the rights they already have. . . ." She insisted that the ERA automatically would legalize homosexual marriages and coed bathrooms and end women's colleges—claims without foundation but which nonetheless stirred deep emotions. Organized feminism she attacked as "an anti-family movement that is trying to make perversion acceptable as an alternative life-style." Drawing on connections established during years of participation in the National Federation of Republican Women, she handpicked 40 women to be state chairpersons of STOP E.R.A. She reached a still-wider following through her monthly newsletter. By 1975 Schlafly and her allies had succeeded in halting the forward momentum of ERA ratification.[22]

Supporters of the ERA were stunned in November 1975 as voters in both New York and New Jersey defeated state ERA amendments. Postelection analyses indicated that women voters were the key to both defeats. Overall, men had been more supportive of a state ERA than women; older women, more supportive than younger women; and non-Catholic women, more supportive than Catholic women. Conservative political organizations actively organized opposition to the ERA. Annette Stern, leader of Operation Wakeup, the principal opposition group in New York, insisted that "people were fed up by all that radical nonsense and concerned about what has been happening to the family." The opposition literature insisted that "a vote for the ERA is a vote against the family" and "a vote for homosexual marriage." Special concern centered on unisex toilets, fear that women would be drafted, and dislike of "women libbers."[23]

Organized feminism and NOW in particular had their own internal problems that undercut their effectiveness at the time the ERA began encountering organized opposition. As the 1972 presidential election unfolded, women's leaders—including Gloria Steinem, Bella Abzug, and Betty Friedan—divided over which candidate to support. When Shirley Chisholm, the first black woman in Congress, made a bid for the presidential nomination, she encountered "coolness" on the part of other women, including the leadership of the NWPC (National Women's Political Caucus) and NOW. While the women's leaders were strong personalities, their clashing interests meant that NOW lacked the counterpart of Carrie Catt's leadership or her "winning plan" to push ratification of the ERA to a successful conclusion.[24]

International Women's Year

As a backlash to the ERA developed, the United Nations General Assembly proclaimed 1975 as International Women's Year. American women in turn secured the support of President Ford and the Congress to use the occasion "to focus attention throughout the country on the rights and responsibilities of women" and to explore "practical and constructive measures for the advancement of women in the United States." The National Commission on the Observance of International Women's Year, functioning through 13 committees produced "... *To Form a More Perfect Union* ... *Justice for American Women,*" an agenda of unfinished business for the nation on the occasion of its bicentennial.[25]

The International Women's Year was marked by a series of conferences, at least one in each state, capped by a national conference in Houston, Texas, in November 1977. Both advocates and opponents of the ERA used the state conventions to further refine positions, recruit support, and generate publicity. The factional composition of the woman's movements became apparent. Members of NOW attended in force. Less numerous but visible and vocal, black women, Indian women, lesbian women, welfare-rights women, union women, League of Women Voters, members of the National Federation of Business and Professional Women's Clubs, proabortion women, Right-to-Life women, and Protestant, Catholic, and Jewish women also attended. The democratic openness of the state meetings provided each of these groups with a forum. Groups hostile to the ERA often sought to take over the state meetings and discredit the ERA. In Ohio, for example,

The International Women's Year Conference in Houston in 1977 was the largest gathering of women devoted to women's issues in the nation's history.

Right-to-Life groups chartered buses to transport members en masse to pack the state convention; in Utah the Relief Society, the women's auxiliary of the Mormon Church, mobilized 12,000 women to ensure support of "correct principles," that is, to condemn the ERA. The New York State meeting, which drew upwards of 13,000 participants, was characterized as "chaotic" and "nightmarish"; the Florida parley "ended in disarray" with angry women spending much of the final meeting chanting slogans for and against the ERA.[26]

The state conventions, operating with an agenda of draft resolutions based on the report of the national commission, gave highest priority to those calling for ratification of the ERA, legalization of abortion on demand, and civil rights for lesbians. The resolutions were passionately debated; to win endorsement of the ERA, middle-of-the-road feminists formed coalitions with proabortion and lesbian-rights groups. In most states, those supportive of the ERA and abortion reform were in the majority; in a few, chiefly in the South and Southwest, they were not. In Ohio, for example, the state International Women's Year convention endorsed the ERA, but Right-to-Life groups blocked endorsement of abortion on demand. In Florida, the delaying tactics of contending groups prevented formal action on any resolutions. In Utah the Mormon-dominated convention voted to oppose the ERA as well as abortion reform. Encouraged by their success in Utah, the Relief Society hurriedly, but successfully, organized anti-ERA groups in Washington and Montana. Working hand in glove with Right-to-Life and Mormon opponents of the ERA was the Phyllis Schlafly organization.[27]

Houston Conference   The Houston conference gave feminism in the mid-seventies a concreteness and a sense of direction as it formulated a National Plan of Action. The 2,000 delegates represented a sampling of American womanhood. Two thirds were white; the remaining third were black and Hispanic, Asian, and Indian Americans. They varied in age from 16 to past 80, in occupation from waitress to priest; one fourth came from low-income families, while a modest number came from the ranks of the affluent. The great majority were from middle-income families. If most of the women had only local reputations, a few were nationally known: Billie Jean King, Jean Stapleton, and Coretta Scott King; Barbara Jordan, Bella Abzug, and Gloria Schaffer; Betty Friedan and Eleanor Smeal; Rosalyn Carter, Betty Ford, and Lady Bird Johnson. Never had such a broad cross section of American women gathered to discuss women's problems.[28]

While a majority of the delegates came committed to support the ERA, a minority were equally determined to block it and the companion measures. In fact, opponents of the ERA, led by Phyllis Schlafly, held a separate "pro-family" rally simultaneously in Houston. In many ways the character of the national conference was delineated by the coalition that opposed it: STOP ERA, an avowedly antifeminist group; the National Right-to-Life and the March for Life, antiabortionist organizations; the Conservative Caucus, the Eagle Forum, and the John Birch Society, right-wing political groups; the National Council of Catholic Women and the Mormon church; and the Daughters of the American Revolution and the Ku Klux Klan.[29]

Central to the conference was support for the ERA. Betty Friedan exhorted the conference: "There is only one issue for women this year and that's the Equal Rights Amendment. . . . Everything else is subsidiary." Certainly a decade and a half of debate had made clear the need for an explicit constitutional guarantee that the equal protection of the laws could not be denied women because of their sex. To the opposition however, the ERA remained open-ended. As a Montana delegate explained: "We're not really sure where the ERA is going to take us, you see." Preferring to encounter the uncertain future with an ERA, a majority of the delegates overwhelmingly called for the speedy ratification of the amendment. While to most delegates the ERA had top priority, past experience had demonstrated an equally clear need for a broad spectrum of specific legislative reforms to assure women equality in specific areas of their political, economic, social, and family life. Feminists of the seventies declined to subordinate everything for an ERA.[30]

Many elements of the National Plan of Action aimed at increasing equality in the economic sphere. It identified specific areas in which access to employment was sought: upper-level positions in federally financed libraries, museums, universities, and public radio and television; greater access to management-training programs and managerial positions in the private sector. Tighter enforcement of antidiscrimination laws and more conscientious application of nondiscriminatory hiring practices were of major import. To assist women generally, the group asked for stricter enforcement of the Federal Equal Credit Opportunity Act of 1974 and sought legislation forbidding health-care insurers from excluding pregnancy-related expenses or the newborn from coverage.[31]

In keeping with feminist tradition that began with Mary Wollstonecraft, the National Plan of Action sought to increase effective access to education. It supported development of programs to enable the disabled to pursue an education. So, too, it supported bilingual instruction for those whose first language was not English. The education plank aimed at ending practices in schools at all levels that pointed women toward some types of academic work and away from others. An end to sex discrimination in sports programs was demanded. The "sex-directed" educators, as Friedan termed them, were pressured to remove racial and sexual stereotypes from textbooks. Such sex stereotypes had long been regarded as a principal means of conditioning women to depreciate their innate capabilities and to accept a subordinate status quiescently.

In the political arena the National Plan of Action sought to increase women's participation in the processes of governance. It called for the inclusion of women in the formulation and execution of foreign policy and an increase in the number of women in the judiciary. A proposal to create a department of women's affairs, regarded by some delegates as a ploy to create a cabinet position for Bella Abzug, was defeated. Others objected that the proposal, far from integrating women into the mainstream, would isolate concern for their interests in a single executive department.

The conference endorsed a wide-ranging plan for the Rights of Minority Women, a group that historically had never occupied a central position in the woman's movement. A comprehensive statement was drafted to explore the means of achieving equal employment and educational opportunities for black, Indian, Alaskan native, and Hispanic American and Asian American women, who faced "double-discrimination" as members of a minority group as well as women.

The conference tackled its two most controversial issues—lesbian rights and abortion—forthrightly. The positions, couched in terms of each woman's right to control her own body, invoked the long-accepted principles of natural rights that formed the framework of American political and social thought, rather than the existential rationale of radical feminists. Betty Friedan, who had initially denounced "the lavender menace," told the convention: "The issue has been used to divide us too much." But, she added, "we have all been mistaken in our focus on this issue. . . . I believe we must protect women who are lesbians in their own civil rights." The convention did not endorse lesbianism, rather it defended each individual's inherent right to one's own sexual preferences and to equal treatment before the law. The abortion statement supported the 1973 Supreme Court decision, falling far short of radical feminist demands for repeal of all abortion legislation. Nor did it yield to the demands of the right wing that abortion be proscribed.

Policies to enhance the position of women as mothers, wives, and homemakers received major attention. Feminists of all varieties had been preoccupied during the 1960s with expanding women's roles outside the home, and Phyllis Schlafly, focusing on this, alleged that the ERA and the national conference were "anti-family." By way of counteracting this charge, the conference identified a number of specific problem areas involving women in the home. For women generally, it proposed a national health-security program, taking note of research documenting the hazards of oral contraceptives and the high incidence of unnecessary mastectomies and hysterectomies. In dealing with the homemaker, the conference proceeded on the premise that marriage was a partnership between equals. Where marriages failed, the conference endorsed no-fault divorce and a sharing of responsibilities by the ex-partners in the continuing care of their children. It endorsed programs to enable widowed and divorced homemakers to attain self-sufficiency. For older women this meant provision for the special medical and social services required by the elderly. It favored covering homemakers in their own right by Social Security to ensure income maintenance during old age and disability. Battered women required shelter and assistance. Likewise the National Plan of Action requested special programs to treat and to prevent, where possible, child abuse. It endorsed low-cost child care underwritten by the federal government and private industry to assist both the children and their working mothers. By these measures the conference hoped to reassure the mainstream of American society that feminism was supportive of wives and mothers and of family well-being. The positions on divorce, shared family responsibilities, and child care did not, however, dispel the objections of Schlafly and her followers.[32]

The national conference on the International Women's Year disclosed the spectrum of views within society—an angry, vocal, tradition-oriented group at one pole pitted against essentially pragmatic groups committed to moderate reform of existing social, economic, and political arrangements. While many delegates represented special interests—welfare rights, lesbian rights, or Indian rights, for example—Lenore McNeer, head of the Vermont delegation, reflected the mood of the majority: "Many of us are going to have to sacrifice our personal agendas to give a plan of action to the Government which we may never have the opportunity to do again." For the most part the conference succeeded in subordinating special concerns to the general welfare. The most controversial planks—the ERA, abortion, lesbian rights, and child care—tackled problems hitherto ignored. The proposed solutions, although they offended the traditionalists, dealt humanely and constructively with the problems. Despite the temptation to subordinate all issues to the ERA, the conference conceived of feminism as embodying a multiplicity of issues. Its definition and refinement would be an ongoing task, and the success of the movement would not hang on the achievement or the delay or the defeat of any one element of the program. Overall the tone of the conference and the National Plan of Action was positive.[33]

Schlafly's Positive Woman

Unable to control the Houston conference, Phyllis Schlafly conducted her own anti-ERA conference. Subsequently she submitted her views to the general public as *The Power of the Positive Woman*. Her opposition to the ERA and to NOW was unmeasured. She presented ERA as "basically an attack on the legal and financial rights of the homemaker." Women's libcrationists, she alleged, portrayed marriage as "an institution of dirty dishes and dirty diapers." Supporters of the ERA included "the unkempt, the lesbians, the radicals, the socialists, and the government employees." "Obscene language and foul four-letter words" constituted the "everyday language of the women's lib movement." She attacked NOW's program, especially its positions on abortion, "taxpayer-financed state kiddy-care centers," and "prolesbian legislation." She charged that NOW sought "to force the churches to ordain women" and "to deprive the churches of their tax exemption." Furthermore, it hated veterans and was "working actively to eliminate all veteran's preferences. To Schlafly, NOW was against God and country, as well as motherhood.[34]

In Schlafly's "Vision for America," the proper starting point for the Positive Woman was "the knowledge that America is the greatest country in the world and that it is her task to do her part to keep it that way." Schlafly saw her country under assault by a Supreme Court that had "banned God from the public schools," by the prospect of a welfare state and its concomitants—industrial inefficiency, public housing and socialized med-

Phyllis Schlafly, the sweetheart of the silent majority, organized the opposition to the ERA.

icine—and by the "tremendous buildup of military power by the Soviet Union." The Positive Woman "must be a patriot and a defender of our Judeo-Christian civilization."[35]

To restore the nation to its proper course, she offered her own 12-point checklist of goals. On the surface it was family-oriented, while looking to local and state governments to safeguard the family. First and foremost among her goals was "the right of a woman to be a full-time wife and mother and to have this right recognized by laws that obligate her husband to provide the primary financial support and a home for her and their children." She placed the primary responsibility for the care of pre-school children with the parents. Job preference ought to be accorded to the wage earner, male or female, with dependents. Women employed in physical labor ought to be protected by "laws and regulations that respect the physical differences and different family obligations of men and women." Society should protect itself by "designating different roles for men and women in the armed forces and police and fire departments." To safeguard the family, husbands and wives should be accorded certain rights "not given to those choosing immoral lifestyles."[36]

She had other concerns as well, many irrelevant to feminism. With respect to the public schools, she would restore voluntary prayer; teach the "fourth R," right and wrong according to the prescripts of the Holy Scriptures; use textbooks that do not offend the religious and moral values of the parents and that honor the family, monogamous marriage, woman's role as wife and man's role as provider and protector; teach reading and writing rather than spend time and money on "frills"; rely on neighborhood schools; and separate the sexes in gym, academic and vocational classes, if so desired. She would give local governments the right to ban "printed or pictorial materials that degrade women in a pornographic, perverted, or sadistic manner." She asserted "the right to life of all innocent persons from conception to natural death." Other planks called for "swift and certain" justice by state and local government and for the federal government to "adequately provide for the common defense against aggression by any other nation." Threaded through Schlafly's program was the conservative's distrust of the federal government and opposition to the Supreme Court's position on the use of prayer in the public school, as well as its efforts to overcome racial segregation in schools by busing. While endorsing "equal opportunity in employment and education for all persons regardless of race, creed, sex, or national origin," she expressly supported the sex-role differentiation that in the past had precluded the realization of equal opportunity for women. Schlafly and her allies succeeded in blocking ratification of the ERA and in placing elective abortions beyond the reach of many working-class women.[37]

REFORM BY STATUTE

Debate over the ERA and feminism prompted the massive piecemeal reform of statutes that Alice Paul had eschewed. Many lawyer-opponents of the ERA urged such reform as more useful than an ERA, while Leo Kanowitz concluded it must accompany adoption of the ERA. Congress, of course, had a role to play, but most of the action fell to state legislatures.

Reform by Congress

Congress had taken two giant strides in the 1960s with the Equal Pay Act and Title VII of the Civil Rights Act. Having sent the ERA to the states for their approval or rejection, Congress began to close loopholes in existing federal legislation. In 1972 the Equal Pay Act was made applicable to executive, administrative, professional, and travelling sales employees and in 1974 to federal, state, and local government employees. The 1968 Civil Rights Act prohibited sex discrimination in the selling and renting of housing. In 1972 Congress extended the protections of Title VII of the Civil Rights Act to employees of state and local governments and of educational institutions. It did so through Title IX of the Education Amendments of 1972, which sought to prohibit sex discrimination in admissions, financial aid, rules governing behavior, access to courses, and training programs. It also struck at sex discrimination in wages, recruitment, hiring, job classification, and most fringe benefits. Schools in the health-services area and affiliated hospitals that received federal support were forbidden to discriminate on the basis of sex in admissions and research or in training programs. The Equal Credit Opportunity Act (1974) broke new ground by prohibiting creditors from discriminating against applicants on the basis of sex or marital status.[38]

State legislatures worked to bring state laws into harmony with ERA principles, preferring to keep the initiative in their own hands rather than to leave reform to the judiciary. While the intention was to eliminate conflict between statute law and the ERA, these reforms stood on their own and became operational as they were adopted. States that ratified the ERA necessarily adopted the most comprehensive reforms, but even states that did not were often caught up in the winds of change. Most often legislators rendered statutes sex-neutral. Where an existing law provided a benefit to one sex, the tendency was to extend it to both sexes; where an existing statute imposed a burden on one sex, the tendency was to remove it. As the states began from widely different bases, the sweep and specifics of reform varied from state to state. In the best pragmatic tradition, the reformers recognized that the realization of equality rested not on general principles but in the detail of the statutes.[39]

Marriage and Family Law

A variety of changes relating to marriage and family relationships provided a legal underpinning for a democratic family in which husband and wife shared responsibilities and leadership. Remnants of the old doctrine of *feme covert* fell by the wayside. Spurred by the Twenty-sixth Amendment, which enabled 18-year-olds to vote, states hastened to establish a uniform age of majority, permitting persons of both sexes 18 years of age or over to marry without parental consent and to set a uniform age—typically 16—at which both boys and girls might marry with parental consent. In ongoing marriages, husbands and wives received the right to establish separate legal residences, enabling a wife to claim a separate domicile for purposes of voting, holding office, or paying taxes.[40]

A major area of reform dealt with married women's property law. Despite reforms of the mid and late nineteenth century, married women still fell far short of equality in property rights. As late as 1969, five states still prohibited a wife from making a valid conveyance of real property unless joined by her husband. To remedy this the Committee on Civil and Political Rights of the President's Commission on the Status of Women recommended that "during marriage each spouse should have a legally defined and substantial right in the earnings of the other spouse and in the real and personal property acquired as a result of such earnings, as well as in the management of such earnings and property." Community-property states granted wives a share in control of the community property during marriage; common-law states removed lingering restrictions on the wife's capacity to contract in her own name or to convey real property without the concurrence of her husband, so that the wife's property rights became identical to his.[41]

Widows had long enjoyed special benefits with respect to property: the "widow's allowance," the "homestead exemption," and property exemptions from attachment, liens, and repayment of debts. Designed to offset the disadvantaged economic position of the homemaker left bereft of her husband's support, these laws offered no similar protections to surviving dependent widowers. ERA compliance moved in the direction of conferring these benefits on the surviving spouse of either sex. Thus, Ohio granted the surviving spouse the right to remain in the mansion house of the deceased partner free of charge for one year, and it assured the surviving spouse a life estate of one third of the real property to which the deceased spouse had held title at any time during the marriage. These reforms rendered marriage a partnership of equals in death as well as in life.[42]

Some women activists in the 1960s and 1970s took offense that convention expected them to take the name of their spouse on marriage. Although statute law did not require this change of name, administrative regulations and creditors often prevented women from retaining their birth names after marriage. Reform permitted a choice of names to both parties of a marriage, so long as there was no intent to defraud. Likewise, parents might give their child any name they chose.[43]

Divorce and dissolution of marriage brought many problems. In a few states the grounds for divorce differed according to sex. While Kentucky, for example, allowed a husband to divorce his wife on proof of a single act of adultery, a wife lacked the reciprocal right. Likewise in Kentucky a woman could divorce an alcoholic husband only if he had wasted his money and not provided for the family; the husband, however, could divorce his wife on the grounds of drunkenness alone. More common were statutes that permitted a divorce "in favor of the husband, when the wife was pregnant at the time of marriage, without his knowledge or agency." No state, however, permitted a wife to divorce her husband if, prior to marriage, he had caused another woman, not his wife, to become pregnant. ERA reforms called for ending the differences in the grounds for divorce. Adoption of dissolution or no-fault divorce greatly broadened the grounds for divorce and simplified the procedures in uncontested actions.[44]

Assuming that marriage was "an equal economic partnership," the reformers rewrote legislation respecting alimony, child support, and child custody. The reformers recognized that hitherto when marriages dissolved, the husband had seldom honored his legal responsibility for supporting his former wife or their children. The reformers also recognized that oftentimes the wife was capable of bearing part or even all of the burden of supporting herself and her children. A model Uniform Marriage and Divorce Act assumed the principle of "mutual obligation of each spouse in a marriage to support the other spouse to the extent possible" and that "both spouses bear the responsibility for their children." In divorce, this principle made the ex-wife as liable to support her ex-husband in circumstances where she was self-supporting and he was the dependent as he would be to support her if their circumstances were reversed. The changes enjoined the court to consider factors of age, education, job skills and experience, the contributions of the homemaking spouse, any physical or emotional disability, and the financial resources of both parties in making property settlements and alimony awards and in deciding child custody and support. The reforms specifically rejected the assumption that responsibility for child support automatically belonged to the father or that child custody should be accorded routinely to the mother. While there was no single formula, ERA reforms made child support a mutual responsibility of the parents; child custody became a matter of sharing or of according responsibility to the parent best able to provide care.[45]

Both courts and legislators addressed the problems related to illegitimacy. Traditionally the rights and duties running between a father and the child were substantially less than those between the mother and the child. A child born out of wedlock had no right of inheritance against the father's estate (though it had a claim against the mother's), nor had it a right to support from its father unless paternity was acknowledged or established in court; in contrast, the mother had an automatic duty of support. At the same time, however, the father had minimal custodial rights, and the child might be placed for adoption without his consent. To reduce the unequal operation of the law, some states abolished legal distinctions between legitimate and illegitimate parent–child relationships. The indicated legislative reform was embodied in the Uniform Parentage Act—draft legislation treating adoption, inheritance, custody, and child support. All biological parents who could be reasonably identified would have potential rights in their children regardless of sex or the marital status of the parents until such time as the child was adopted with parental consent or until the rights were forfeited by neglect of parental obligations.[46]

Terms of Work

The "major, most important effect of ERA," was in sparking reforms in legislation respecting the employment of women. State laws affected tens of thousands of women not covered by Title VII or the Equal Pay Act. Several states followed the lead of President Kennedy by eliminating sex-based classifications in civil-service employment. In doing so the states took notice of the EEOC judgment that there were few jobs that could legally be classified as unisex jobs and that the "bona fide occupational qualification [BFOQ] exception as to sex shall be interpreted narrowly." Regulations of school boards requiring a pregnant teacher to take an unpaid leave of absence fell as courts held the timing of such leaves was for the woman and her doctor to decide case-by-case. Nepotism rules—used in the 1920s and 1930s to bar employment of married women—were repealed. Height and weight regulations, whether set by state agencies or by private employers, were successfully challenged in courts, and employers were required to demonstrate a reasonable relationship between such regulations and the job.[47]

State-made regulations affected many private-sector employees. Federal courts pressed the states to repeal regulations that created male-only and female-only occupations in businesses licensed by the state. Regulations, for example, that restricted barbering to men and cosmetology to women were especially vulnerable. In Ohio, Louisiana, Maryland, and Texas, such regulations were challenged successfully on grounds that they denied the equal protection of the laws; the courts also held that licensed cosmetologists must be permitted to practice their professions on persons of either sex. Another area of concern was employment agencies. Despite the Civil Rights Act of 1964, many employment agencies continued to use sexually discriminatory corporate names, for example, "Girl Place." More importantly, agencies accepted job orders from employers who indicated preferences based on sex, and they failed to refer women for interviews for jobs traditionally considered male. In the case of licensing laws, corrective legislation called for opening the occupations to qualified persons of either sex. In the case of discriminatory employment agencies, corrective legislation was in order in those states whose statutes did not yet prohibit sex-discriminatory practices; in other jurisdictions enforcement of the law was indicated.[48]

A major area of reform dealt with reshaping protective labor legislation in order to open all occupations to persons of both sexes. Health and safety regulations were redrafted to operate equally on both male and female employees, even regulations requiring that both men and women who prepare food for canning must wear "clean washable caps covering the hair." State laws that in the name of protection exclude women from occupations as varied as crossing attendants and freight-elevator operators came under attack, and repeal was in order. Regulations establishing weight-lifting maximums for women fell in state and federal courts. The U.S. Department of Labor recommended that if states or employers deemed weight-lifting maximums necessary, then these ought to be based on the physical capabilities and physiological makeup of the individual.[49]

When protective legislation took the form of hours' limitations, reformers insisted that neither sex ought to be required to work more than 8 hours a day or 40 hours a week without premium pay in line with the Fair Labor Standards Act but also that refusal to work overtime should not constitute grounds for dismissal. Regulations requiring work breaks and lunch breaks should apply to males as well as females. Indeed, as challenges to protective legislation came forward in the 1970s, the federal courts mandated that benefits be extended to both sexes in order to conform with the nondiscrimination provisions of Title VII.[50]

State-regulated employment benefits—workmen's compensation and unemployment compensation—which historically had been discriminatory, were subject to revision. In the case of workmen's compensation the assumptions had been that the worker was male and the beneficiaries were widows. While surviving widows had automatically qualified for disability benefits, surviving widowers had to prove their dependency in order to receive benefit payments. Reform—in this instance designed to end discrimination against males—called for rendering the legislation sex-neutral. Legislation respecting unemployment compensation that denied benefits to persons who "quit work to marry or because of marital, parental, filial, or other domestic obligations or became unemployed because of pregnancy," discriminated against women. Critics maintained that society imposed an unequal burden on women, for it expected a wife to quit her job to follow a husband who was transferred by his employer, and it expected the wife to stay home to care for a sick child. Reform called for repeal of statutes that denied benefits to persons unemployed because of marital, parental, filial, or domestic obligations, as well as pregnancy. Further, in the case of unemployment resulting from pregnancy, it sought abolition of special conditions for reinstatement to eligibility status. In establishing her eligibility for aid to dependent children, a working mother confronted special requirements when she claimed that she was the primary wage earner and was supporting a child. Ohio reformers recommended that the spouse who had the greater income should be considered the chief supporter of the children.[51]

Insurance, Pensions, and Taxes

Both private and public sectors came under pressure to end sex-linked qualifications in insurance, pensions, and taxes. Insurance firms ordinarily restricted the types of insurance available to women, withheld from them options available to men, charged women higher rates, and imposed special standards of insurability on women. In group health policies, insurers generally withheld maternity coverage from single women; they offered lesser maternity benefits to female employees than to wives of male employees; frequently they declined to include husbands of female employees as dependents, although wives of male employees were included; maternity benefits were limited to fixed maximums, whereas other conditions were indemnified in proportion to actual costs; and major medical policies ordinarily declined to pay expenses related to normal pregnancy. Realization of equality required statutory and administrative changes that prohibited differential coverage and benefits based upon sex-linked classifications. In 1979 Congress resolved part of the problem by forbidding the exclusion of pregnancy coverage in group health-insurance policies.[52]

Differentials in the longevity of men and women posed problems in formulating equitable pension policies. In view of the greater longevity of women, private pension plans required women to pay higher premiums than men to secure the same annual retirement benefits or, if women paid the same premiums as men, to receive smaller annual benefits. The Social Security program posed other problems. The original act had provided family protection in terms of a society in which fewer than 15 percent of the married women were in the labor force and in which, because most women ultimately married, they would qualify for benefits as dependent wives or widows. By 1970 the situation had changed: the proportion of married women in the labor force approached 40 percent and was climbing. Although family living standards for nearly half the nation's families were based on two incomes, Social Security pensions ordinarily were based on the husband's income alone, ignoring the wife's record. The rising incidence of divorce required reassessment of provisions for divorced women. Yet another issue concerned pension benefits for homemakers. The multiplicity of retirement systems for state employees, as well as for federal employees—civil service, foreign service, and military—raised issues of providing benefits on a sex-neutral basis to dependent and surviving spouses, some with claims against a single pension system and others against several. Efforts at reform were complicated by the general questions about the philosophical basis for the Social Security system. The International Women's Year Commission recommended that the homemaker be covered "in her own right . . . to provide income security for the risks of old age, disability, and death." It also urged revisions in the method of computing retirement income and looked favorably on the principle of "indexing" income, that is, adjusting the income record to take note of changes in the average earnings of workers. Other recommendations urged exploration of formulas that would calculate benefits based on the combined earnings of a married couple. Implicit in these proposals was recognition of the economic contribution to the family by the homemaker.[53]

Tax equity for the married also posed incredibly complex issues, the magnitude of which grew as the proportion of two-income families increased. The problem existed with federal income-tax laws, as well as some state tax laws, which required married couples filing joint returns to pay higher taxes than they would be required to pay if unmarried. Another problem concerned the costs of a housekeeper and of child care. Many of the insurance, pension, and tax-equity issues remained unresolved at the beginning of the 1980s in anticipation of a general revision of the Social Security system.[54]

Criminal Law

Substantial changes were required in order to render criminal law sex-neutral, particularly with respect to rape, prostitution, and punishment. Feminists objected that existing rape laws reflected an outmoded viewpoint. A male-dominated legal establishment had long cautioned lawyers and judges that all too often "errant young girls and women" come before the courts "contriving false charges of sexual offenses by men" as a consequence of which "many innocent men have gone to prison." In times past, men had punished rape "not as sexual assault per se, but as an act of unlawful possession, a trespass against his tribal right to control vaginal access to all women who belonged to him and his kin." Other factors being equal, a virgin had commanded a higher dowry than a nonvirgin. Thus the father sustained an economic loss when his daughter was despoiled. But in the twentieth century, feminists pointed out, rape had nothing to do with wife capture or access to an inheritance, but rather was "a brief expression of physical power, a conscious effort of intimidation, a blunt, ugly sexual invasion. . . ." This sexual invasion could be oral or anal as well as vaginal; nor was the penis the only "instrument of vengeance." Males, as well as females, could be victims of sexual attack. Furthermore, feminists argued, "if women are to be what we believe we are—equal partners—then intercourse must be construed as an act of mutual desire and not as a wifely 'duty' enforced by the permissible threat of bodily harm or of economic sanctions." Feminists deemed the husband who forced his wife into sexual relations a rapist. The horror of rape, then, lay in the sexual exploitation of one person by another. Feminists objected to rape laws that made prosecution nearly as traumatic for the victim as the offense itself. Unlike the victim of assault, the rape victim was subject to public questioning about her reputation for chastity and the degree to which she resisted her attacker, as well as to requirements for corroborative testimony that the offense had occurred.[55]

By way of reform, statutes were redrafted to eliminate gender-linked language, to bring all sexual assaults against either sex under the same rules. To protect the victim's privacy, restrictions were placed on the introduction of evidence of past sexual conduct or reputation for chastity. So, too, requirements for corroborative testimony or evidence of physical resistance were dropped. Proposals were made to permit prosecution of a male who sexually abused his wife or forced her to engage in intercourse after their marriage had deteriorated to the point that they no longer lived together. The reformers also initiated programs to retrain police to accord victims of rape humane and serious consideration, with special emphasis on psychological and emotional considerations. Finally, reform moved toward shifting the costs of medical tests and forensic evidence from the victim to the state, as with other offenses.[56]

Prostitution, though clearly a sex-linked activity, sparked at least three alternative proposals for ending one-sided enforcement of legislation punishing it. While an act of prostitution required two parties, public authorities prosecuted the female prostitute far more often than her male customer. One approach was to render the laws sex-neutral, such that sexual activity for hire is prohibited. Accordingly the law might specify that both the prostitute and the customer must be arrested and prosecuted and that no prostitute shall receive a punishment different from that imposed on the customer. This solution struck at one-sided law enforcement. A second approach recommended decriminalization of prostitution on the grounds that "consensual behavior of adults that is not harmful to others should be regarded as falling within the scope of the right of privacy." With this approach, the state would license prostitution or otherwise establish standards for health inspection. It might also prohibit public solicitation. NOW endorsed decriminalization as an interim measure, regarding the existing criminal laws as unenforceable and ineffective. However, it rejected licensing, since that would force the prostitute to publicly proclaim herself as such in order to obey the law while placing governmental bodies in the business of profiting from the sale of women's sexual services. At the same time, NOW supported full prosecution of any person, public agency, or groups that coerced women to become prostitutes.[57]

Feminists also sought to end the discrimination women experienced when sentenced for violation of criminal laws. Pennsylvania law, for example, specified that all "women sentenced for offenses punishable by imprisonment for more than one year *must* be sentenced to the maximum permissible term. Men, on the other hand, *may* be sentenced to lesser terms." The Pennsylvania Supreme Court struck down this language, holding that "an arbitrary and invidious discrimination exists in the sentencing of men to prison and women to Muncy [the women's reformatory], with resulting injury to women." Connecticut legislation that imposed longer sentences on women than on men for commission of the same offense was rationalized on the grounds that because the state was seeking to provide women "a special protection and every reformative and rehabilitative opportunity," a longer term of confinement was justified. A federal court struck down this legislation as violative of the equal-protection clause. Although the courts provided relief to specific appellants, legislative reform rendered sentencing laws sex neutral.[58]

Analogous to the uneven treatment of women sentenced to prison was the treatment accorded the "unruly child" and the PINS—persons in need of supervision. The term "unruly child" is vague, and officials commonly incarcerated girls for noncriminal acts—acts for which boys were not incarcerated. A girl who became pregnant out of wedlock could be placed under the control of the juvenile court; the boy responsible for the pregnancy could not. New York subjected girls to the restrictive PINS legislation until age 18, boys until age 16. A New York appeals court in July 1972 negated the law. As in many other problem areas, redrafting of such legislation seemed in order, preserving those portions of the juvenile law that addressed antisocial and criminal behavior while correcting the inequities in the application of the law and providing appropriate juvenile facilities.[59]

The application of ERA principles to the correctional system is further illustrated by the Ohio experience. Whereas in Ohio male offenders were sentenced to one of five large institutions according to their age, offense, character, and previous record, all female offenders shared a single institution. Systems of housing for males varied from cell block to dormitory, security ranged from maximum to medium; women were housed in cottages in a minimum security environment. Disparities existed in the availability of vocational, industrial, and educational programs, the men having a far wider choice of programs than the women. In untangling its problems, an Ohio task force urged "the immediate equalization of male and female treatment facilities to the greatest extent feasible. . . ." It further recommended that educational, vocational, and industrial opportunities be equalized.[60]

Political Status

Consideration of the ERA also prompted a review of the political status of women. A half century after ratification of the Nineteenth Amendment, women were still not fully integrated into the political structure. Discriminatory language often lingered in provisions for jury duty; women in 22 states enjoyed a broader basis for avoiding jury service than men. Reform standardized the basis for exemption and deleted those references that assumed that all jurors were male and that the spouses of jurors were wives. Up until 1967, 3 states—Florida, New Hampshire, and Louisiana—required that women register in order to be considered for jury service. In January 1975 the Supreme Court, noting the shifting economic and social roles of women, struck down the Louisiana statute.[61]

In a variety of ways, many peculiar to a single state, old statutes embodied assumptions that public affairs was a man's world in which women had limited interests. Legislation providing for state militias commonly referred to "enlisted men" and specified different enlistment requirements for men and women. Military conduct codes presumed that sexual abuse was always directed by men against women; veterans' benefits presumed that male relatives were economically independent and female relatives dependent. Ohio law assumed that benevolent associations with women trustees required fiscal trustees and that only males might fill such an office. Statutes provided for "widow's homes" or "asylums for aged and indigent women," assuming that males never reached a state of dependency or indigency. Other statutes, for example, authorized fire wardens to summon male residents to duty in an emergency. Municipal library boards were to consist of six members, "not more than three of whom shall be women"; County Children's Service Boards were to consist of at least one woman. To resolve its problems, Ohio's task force urged legislation that would specify that "the number of members of a board that are of one sex shall never exceed the number of members of the opposite sex by more than one." Its rationale was that "if women are ever to be taken seriously as full citizens, they must have equal representation on regulatory commissions." Thus far this recommendation has not been implemented.[62]

In the mid-seventies, the pro-ERA forces encountered increasing difficulties in securing the necessary ratifications for the ERA. Thirty states had ratified within two years of its submission by Congress. Then the pace slackened, and after Indiana became the 35th in 1977, no other state could be persuaded. The pro-ERA forces experienced increasing frustration. Although the ERA did not engender as much enthusiasm in 1975 as in 1972, it still enjoyed solid popular support. As the deadline for ratification approached in 1979, the ERA leadership secured a three-year extension of time from Congress.[63]

As the leadership considered ways of securing the last three ratifications, their prospects of success were mixed. On the positive side was the general support of the amendment. Nonetheless, the leadership proved unable to mobilize the support the measure enjoyed in the 35 states that had already ratified the ERA to overcome the opposition to ratification in any of the remaining 15 states. Second, by the late seventies, public attention was increasingly diverted from the ERA to the problems of inflation, a sagging economy, rising unemployment, and dissatisfaction with foreign affairs. Third, the ratification campaign had been followed by a wide variety of reforms at the state and federal levels that were making the legal environment in which women lived sex-neutral. Many of these reforms, if not earthshaking individually, when taken in the aggregate represented substantial progress. And many reforms were still in the process of adoption. The effect was to generate an attitude of euphoria.

On the negative side, the ERA leadership had two major problems. First, it never succeeded in establishing close ties with minority women. NOW's endorsement of abortion and sterilization was disquieting to Hispanic women, and it failed to address the issues of major concern to black feminists. A Virginia Slims–Louis Harris Poll in 1972 confirmed that black women were more committed than white women to "efforts to strengthen or change women's status in society." And in 1973 several thousand black feminists organized their own National Black Feminist Organization. But close ties between it and NOW never materialized. Recommendations of a minority task force respecting specific concerns of minority women were largely ignored by the NOW leadership. Led by white middle-class women, NOW single-mindedly focused on "the inequality of being female"; minority women stressed "the inequality of society." NOW's leadership tried to bridge the differences by sponsoring NOW chapters in minority communities and by sidestepping minority issues. When in 1979, with time running out for the ratification of the ERA, it elected an all-white slate of officers, Aileen Hernandez, a founder of NOW and its second president, remonstrated, accusing NOW of being "too white and middle class" and recommended that black women should quit NOW or refrain from joining until it confronted its own racism."[64]

Second, the ERA leadership had to reckon with the emergence of a well-organized, well-financed opposition. While Phyllis Schlafly's STOP ERA was in the forefront, there were other forces at work. The hostility that radical feminists directed toward the nuclear family and the homemaking role alienated many moderates who had been attracted to the ERA-linked reforms that would ease their way in the labor force. The abortion issue especially undercut support of the ERA, as it spurred the Catholic hierarchy, fundamentalist Protestants, Mormons, and Orthodox Jews to lend their leadership, organizations, and resources to securing legislation, even a constitutional amendment, to prohibit abortion on demand. These groups also turned on the ERA itself and on elements of the National Plan of Action that were designed to support women in their expanding out-of-household roles.

NOTES

[1] Judith Hole and Ellen Levine, *Rebirth of Feminism* (New York: Quadrangle, 1971), 54–57. U.S. Congress, House, *Hearings before Subcommittee No. 4 of the Committee on the Judiciary,* 92nd Cong., 1st sess., H.J. Res. 35, 208, and Related Bills and H.R. 916 and Related Bills, "Equal Rights for Men and Women 1971" (hereafter cited as *Hearings,* 92nd Cong., 1st sess., "Equal Rights for Men and Women 1971.")

[2] *Hearings,* 92nd Cong., 1st sess. "Equal Rights for Men and Women 1971," 40, 41, 47.

[3] Ibid., 65.

[4] Kurland quoted, ibid., 580, 581, 582, Freund quoted, *Hearings,* 92nd Cong., 1st sess. "Equal Rights for Men and Women 1971," 64, 608. Leo Kanowitz, *Women and the Law* (Albuquerque: University of New Mexico Press, 1969), 196.

[5] Kanowitz, *Women and the Law,* 357.

[6] Hole and Levine, *Rebirth of Feminism,* 57.

[7] Chisholm quoted in Barbara Sinclair Deckard, *The Women's Movement* (New York: Harper & Row, 1975), 352.

[8] President's Task Force on Women's Rights and Responsibilities, *A Matter of Simple Justice* (Washington: GPO, 1970), 13.

[9] *NYT,* 10 Dec. 1971, 1, 20.

[10] Women's Bureau, *Handbook on Women Workers,* Bulletin 297 (Washington: GPO, 1975), 4. Editorial, *NYT,* 11 Dec. 1971. National Commission on the Observance of the International Women's Year, *". . . To Form a More Perfect Union . . ." Justice for American Women* (Washington: GPO, 1976), 149. Louise Gross and Phyllis MacEwan, "On Day Care," *Women: A Journal of Liberation,* 2(1970): 199, in an avowedly radical view urged child care as "an important means for liberating women from the traditional tasks of child rearing."

[11] Linda Gordon, *Woman's Body, Woman's Right* (New York: Grossman, 1976). Black Women's Liberation Group (Mt. Vernon, NY), "Statement on Birth Control," in *Sisterhood is Powerful,"* ed. Robin Morgan (New York: Vintage, 1970), 360–61.

[12] Eisenstadt v. Baird, 405 U.S. 438 at 453 (1972). *NYT,* 30 May 1974 and 15 Feb. 1976.

[13] *"To Form a More Perfect Union,"* 268–69.

[14] Lawrence Lader, *Abortion* (Indianapolis: Bobbs-Merrill, 1966). James C. Mohr, *Abortion in America* (New York: Oxford, 1978). Edwin M. Schur, "Abortion," *The Annals.* 376(March 1968): 136–47.

[15] Hole and Levine, *Rebirth of Feminism,* 278 ff.

[16] Roe v. Wade, 410 U.S. 113 (1973). Doe v. Bolton, 410 U.S. 179 (1973). Kristin Booth Glen, "Abortion In the Courts: A Laywoman's Historical Guide to the New Disaster Area," *FS,*

4(Feb. 1978): 9. Planned Parenthood of Missouri v. Danforth; Danforth v. Planned Parenthood, 428 U.S. 52 (1976).

[17] *NYT,* 23 Jan 1973; 14 April 1975; 9 Feb. 1976; 1 March 1976; 17 Aug. 1977.

[18] *NYT,* 18 Jan. 1976.

[19] *NYT,* 3 Feb. 1975; 27 May 1978. *"To Form a More Perfect Union,"* 273.

[20] *Hearings,* 92nd Cong., 1st sess., "Equal Rights for Men and Women 1971," 233, 332, 333. "Statement of the International Union of Electrical Workers, AFL-CIO," *Hearings,* 92nd Cong., 1st sess. "Equal Rights for Men and Women, 1971," 597.

[21] *NYT,* 25 July 1977, *Hearings,* 92nd Cong., 1st sess., "Equal Rights for Men and Women 1971," 476.

[22] *NYT,* 15 Dec. 1975. Carol Felsenthal, *The Sweetheart of the Silent Majority: The Biography of Phyllis Schlafly* (Garden City: Doubleday, 1981).

[23] *NYT,* 28 March 1976; 8 Nov. 1975; 6 Nov. 1975.

[24] Paula Giddings, *When and Where I Enter* (New York: Morrow, 1984), 337–40.

[25] See Executive Order 11832, 9 Jan. 1975. *"To Form a More Perfect Union,"* 118.

[26] *NYT,* 18 July 1977 and 25 July 1977. *Columbus* (Ohio) *Dispatch,* 13 July 1977.

[27] *NYT,* 25 July 1977 and 17 July 1977.

[28] *NYT,* 19 Nov. 1977; 23 Nov. 1977, p. 14, col. 4; 27 Nov. 1977, sec. 4, p. 4. National Commission on the Observance of the International Women's Year, *The Spirit of Houston* (Washington: GPO, 1978).

[29] *NYT,* 20 Nov. 1977.

[30] *NYT,* 21 Nov. 1977.

[31] Associated Press, *Athens,* (Ohio) *Messenger,* 21 Nov. 1977. "National Plan of Action," in National Commission on the Observance of the International Women's Year, *The Spirit of Houston,* 13–97.

[32] *NYT,* 21 Nov. 1977.

[33] *NYT,* 20 Nov. 1977.

[34] Phyllis Schlafly, *The Power of the Positive Woman* (New York: Jove, 1977), 227–228. In April 1971 NOW proposed to challenge the tax-exempt status of the Catholic church since "it is lobbying against abortion law repeal."

[35] Ibid., 213, 215, 216–18, 219.

[36] Ibid., 224–25, presents Schlafly's 12-point program.

[37] Ibid.

[38] Karen DeCrow, *Sexist Justice* (New York: Vintage, 1975), 118–90. Ordinarily a woman automatically acquired the legal residence of her husband. If he moved to a separate domicile or deserted her, his unilateral change of residence could affect her right to vote, to hold public office, to serve on juries. If he moved and she did not follow, he might charge her with desertion. As of 1969, five states permitted women to establish a separate domicile for any purpose; 13 states, for the purpose of voting; three, for holding public office; nine, for paying taxes.

[39] Ohio Task Force for the Implementation of the Equal Rights Amendment, *Ohio ERA* (Columbus: July 1975), viii (hereafter cited as *Ohio ERA.*.

[40] DeCrow, *Sexist Justice,* 171–72. In 1980, the U.S. Supreme Court set aside the common-law rule that husbands and wives could not testify against one another, *Time,* 115(March 10, 1980): 49. See also Henry H. Foster, Jr., "The Future of Family Law," *The Annals,* 383(May 1969): 129–44.

[41] Committee on Civil and Political Rights quoted in Kanowitz, *Women and the Law,* 60. DeCrow, *Sexist Justice,* chap. 7. A Louisiana court declared unconstitutional provisions of the state's community-property law that gave the husband "absolute dominion" over jointly owned property, *NYT,* 18 Feb. 1978.

[42] *Ohio ERA,* 5.

[43] De Crow, *Sexist Justice,* 280. Kanowitz, *Women and the Law,* 96. *Ohio ERA,* 6.

[44] Citizens' Advisory Council on the Status of Women, *Women in 1971* (Washington, GPO, Jan. 1972), 51. Kanowitz, *Women and the Law,* 96. See also Doris Jonas Freed and Henry H. Foster, Jr., "Divorce American Style," *The Annals,* 383(May 1969): 71–88.

[45] Levy v. Louisiana, 391 U.S. 68 (1968) and Stanley v. Illinois, 405 U.S. 645 (1972). *Ohio ERA,* 16. See also W. J. Brockelbank, "The Family Desertion Problem Across State Lines," *The Annals,* 383(May 1969), 23–33, and Thomas A. Coyne, "Who Will Speak for the Child?" *The Annals,* 383(May 1969), 34–47.

[46] DeCrow, *Sexist Justice,* 298. "Guidelines on Discrimination Because of Sex. Title 29 Labor, Chapter XIV, Part 1604," in *Federal Register,* 37(Apr. 5, 1972), p. 6835–37. See also Harry D. Krause, "Why Bastard, Wherefore Base?" *The Annals,* 383(May 1969): 58–70.

[47] Jones Metal Products v. Walker, 29 Ohio St.2d 173 (1972), held Ohio's protective laws could not be enforced against employers covered by Title VII. These laws were repealed in 1983.

[48] *Ohio ERA,* 24.

[49] Bowe v. Colgate-Palmolive Co., 416 F.2d 711, Rev. S.D. Ind., 272 F.Supp. 332 (1969) and Jones Metal Products v. Walker, 29 Ohio State 2d 173 (1972). U.S. Department of Labor, *Teach Them to Lift,* Bulletin no. 110 rev. (Washington: GPO, 1965).

[50] Hays v. Potlach Forests, 465 F.2d 1081 (8 Cir. 1972) and Manning v. General Motors Corp., F. Supp.3d EPD Sect 8325 (N.D. Ohio, 1971) aff'd 466 F.2d 812 (6th Cir. 1972), Cert. Denied, 410 U.S. 946 (1973).

[51] Ohio Code 4141.29 (D) (2). Lasko v. Garnes, C 72–1350 (N.D. Ohio, Aug. 14, 1973). *Ohio ERA,* 29, 31.

[52] *The Spirit of Houston,* 54, 60–62. *NYT,* 1 Nov. 1978.

[53] *"To Form a More Perfect Union,"* 16, 282.

[54] Ibid., 284–286.

[55] John Henry Wigmore, *Evidence in Trials at Common Law* (1940) rev. by James. H. Chadbourn (Boston: Little, Brown, 1970), vol. 3A, 736, sec. 924a. Susan Brownmiller, *Against Our Will, Men, Women and Rape* (New York: Simon & Schuster, 1975), 376–78; see also Susan Griffin, "Rape: The All-American Crime," *Ramparts,* 10(Sept. 1971): 26–35. Ruth Herschberger, *Adam's Rib* (New York: Harper & Row, 1970[1948]), 15–27.

[56] *Ohio ERA,* 40–42.

[57] Mary G. Haft, "Hustling for Rights," *Civil Liberties Review,* 1(Winter/Spring, 1974): 14–15. *Ohio ERA,* 43. DeCrow, *Sexist Justice,* 228–29. See also T. C. Esselstyn, "Prostitution in the United States," *The Annals,* 376(March 1968): 123–35.

[58] Kanowitz, *Women and the Law,* 167–72. Commonwealth v. Daniels, 430 Pa. 642 A.2d 400 (1968). United States ex rel. Robinson v. York, 281 F. Supp. 8 (1968).

[59] *Ohio ERA,* 13–15. "Status Offenders," in National Commission on the Observance of the International Women's Year, *"To Form a More Perfect Union,"* 158–60.

[60] *Ohio ERA,* 44.

[61] Ibid., 48–51.

[62] DeCrow, *Sexist Justice,* 218. *NYT,* 22 Jan. 1975.

[63] *Ohio ERA,* 49–52. *NYT,* 6 Nov. 1982, p. 51, col. 5.

[64] Giddings, *When and Where I Enter,* 340–48.

10

The Winds of Change: The 1970s

The defeat of the ERA in 1982 evoked expressions of dismay from its advocates with pledges to try again, yet it called forth expressions of satisfaction from its opponents. In fact, as noted in Chapter 9, the campaign for ratification had prodded governments—both state and federal—to begin the process of making administrative regulations and statutes sex-neutral. Throughout the seventies, American schools from elementary to university underwent major changes that would narrow the differences between the educational experiences of men and women and would enhance the ability of young women to compete with men in the economic and political sectors. So, too, attitudes of women toward work underwent marked changes, as measured by their response to the growing demand for workers.

THE COLLEGIATE MAJORITY

Student feminism developed an organized, increasingly cohesive quality in the seventies. Most of the activities begun in the sixties continued into the new decade, reaching a wider variety of campuses and often evolving into coordinated programs.

As black students had demanded programs in black studies, so women insisted on comprehensive programs in women's studies. San Diego State University, the first institution to create such a program, in fall 1970 offered a choice of ten elective courses. The effort to fashion women's studies into degree programs encountered far more resistance than did the introduction of individual courses. The main issue was whether material relating to women should be presented in separate courses or whether it ought to be integrated into the framework of existing courses. Alice Rossi, a sociologist, speculated that women's-studies courses would prove "transitional," receiving "special attention for a few years and then be incorporated into a basic curriculum that will be revised to fit students' needs." In 1973 the Carnegie Commission recommended that women's-studies programs "should be encouraged" with the caveat that they be "organized within existing disciplines and not under separate departments of women's studies. During the seventies some 300 colleges developed women's-studies programs. Most offered a certificate, but 50 awarded a baccalaureate in women's studies. Although the women's studies degree remained somewhat suspect, individual courses and certificate programs were well received.[1]

As the number of women's courses and programs soared, academic professional societies felt the impact, usually in the form of pressure to schedule programs on women's issues at annual professional meetings. In turn, the output of scholarly papers and articles relating to women increased. To provide an outlet for scholarly studies, *SIGNS* began publishing in 1975, rapidly establishing itself as the leading academic journal. Alongside it was *Feminist Studies,* a journal that mixed scholarship with advocacy. Feminist educators were encouraged and, in the mid-seventies, they organized the National Women's Studies Association, giving first priority to "feminizing" traditional curriculums in colleges and universities and to developing women's studies in institutions where they did not yet exist.[2]

To nurture collegiate feminism, women called for institutional support of women's centers. These took a wide variety of forms. At Barnard, women secured establishment of a special library on women's subjects, career-planning facilities, and a women's-studies curriculum of a dozen courses. As a minimum, a women's center got space, staff, and a modest budget. Such a center became a meeting place for campus feminists and served as a resource center for information on women's issues; it also provided support to students lobbying for birth-control and pregnancy-counseling services or for an abortion-referral center, a Women-Against-Rape organization, or day-care facilities for the children of student couples. Again it sponsored visiting speakers: Betty Friedan, Caroline Bird, Gloria Steinem, or Susan Brownmiller. The women's center became the instrumentality for exchanging information and ideas with women at other schools. Many centers enhanced their outreach by publishing a newsletter.[3]

As women students refined their feminist perceptions, they pressed college leadership to correct a variety of discriminatory practices. Exclusion of women from the marching band, provision of a sauna for men but not for women, single-sex classes in activities such as tennis, swimming, and bowling, and the inequitable distribution of student jobs and scholarships became bones of contention. Institutional inertia, reinforced by masculine obtuseness, delayed redress and escalated the stridency of demands.[4]

Growing feminist awareness led many women's colleges to institute special programs for older women. The first such program, instituted at the University of Minnesota in 1960, found many emulators in the 1970s. Some were highly specialized such as the Ford Foundation Program at Rutgers for the Re-Training in Mathematics of College Graduate Women. Others downplayed high-school records as a basis for admission. Many granted "life experience credits." Radcliffe, whose Schlesinger Library made it a major center for women's studies, established an Institute for Independent Study for older women. Sarah Lawrence, aided by the Carnegie Corporation, opened a Center for Continuing Education for Women in fall 1962 with special emphasis on career counseling along with special programs, internships, and independent studies.[5]

The feminist debates of the 1960s and 1970s caused women's colleges to reevaluate their roles. As androgynous life-styles came to the fore, some women's colleges began to view coeducation as offering women the best preparatory experience. Economic pressures also made this an attractive policy, as it permitted many single-sex institutions to increase enrollments (and income) without adding commensurately to expenses. After exploring and rejecting a possible merger with Yale, Vassar opened its classrooms to males. On the West Coast the Immaculate Heart of Mary, caught up in the ferment of Catholic reform as well as feminism, became "a slightly swinging" coed college. Other women's schools, including Mount Holyoke, Smith, Wellesley, and Bryn Mawr, adopted arrangements by which men from nearby institutions might enroll in their classes, though they declined to admit them as degree students. Radcliffe and Barnard revised their institutional ties to Harvard and Columbia, respectively, but retained a degree of autonomy. During the sixties, feminist-minded students began enrolling in coed colleges. Of some 300 women's colleges in 1960, fewer than half still operated as such in 1972.[6]

In the course of the seventies, leaders of some of the women's colleges had second thoughts about the education of women. Some of this reflected self-interest, but the arguments went beyond self-serving rhetoric. Women students at coed Vassar reported that the presence of males had changed the academic climate. Though men were in a minority, they tended to take over, as the women were too uncertain of their values to assert themselves. Wellesley's president, Barbara Newell, argued: "Coeducation has failed. Women coeds receive conflicting signals on the 'femininity' of intellectual vigor and do not take full advantage of the college." That "educational equity for women" could come out of male-dominated coed colleges and universities she termed "naive." Under her leadership, Wellesley chose to resist the trend toward coeducation and to seek a $70,000,000 addition to its endowment.[7]

The shortcoming of coeducation lay in the domination of most such colleges by male professors and administrators. The "climate" for male students was "more cordial" than for female students. Male faculty were less aware of or sensitive to issues affecting female students and colleagues; they were less concerned with discrimination. By contrast the women's colleges offered the means of encouraging women "both within the class-room and without, to exercise a capacity for independent thinking, critical judgment, and especially leadership without feeling that such attributes make them less attractive to men." The presence of female instructors as role models for female students was "a critical ingredient of a college environment that turns out talented women." Furthermore, female teachers were "more concerned with the emotional development of their students and with helping them attain a deeper level of self-understanding" than male professors. The studies of M. Elizabeth Tidball indicated that graduates of women's colleges were twice as likely to be cited for career achievements as were female graduates of coeducational institutions. Yet another study indicated that even when male and female students of equal abilities were compared, the women possessed lower self-esteem and, in the course of four years of college, lost much of their ambition. The coeducational campus seemed to place women at a disadvantage. But for better or worse, coeducation increasingly dominated the scene.[8]

The measure of educational progress that women made in the seventies was not limited to that directly promoted by feminist groups. Certainly one of the most significant gains was in enrollments, in which women approached parity with men to a greater degree than ever before. Throughout the decade the numbers of male and female high school graduates were roughly equal, the women holding a slight edge. In the climate of egalitarianism, women of all ages were more inclined than previously to enroll in college. At the start of the decade women constituted 46 percent of the enrollments in the four-year institutions; by the fall of 1980, women outnumbered men. Although historically women were less inclined to complete degree work than men, this differential, too, was diminishing.[9]

During a decade in which many young people expressed disillusionment with the established values and institutions by "dropping out," the
proportion of women completing a baccalaureate increased impressively
from 19.7 per 100 23-year-olds in 1970 to 29.9 in 1980. Women with baccalaureates continued to pursue masters degrees in ever-larger proportions, the rate increasing from 299.3 to 325.9 during the decade. Indeed,
in 1980 nearly as many women earned masters degrees as did men, and
the proportion of women baccalaureates who earned masters exceeded
the proportion of men who did so. In the face of a faltering demand for
newly minted doctoral degrees, the number of males pursuing such a
degree dropped during the seventies; by contrast the number of women
grew year by year. Thus, while in 1970 males outnumbered females six to
one in the receipt of doctorates, a decade later the ratio stood at 2.5 to
one, an impressive narrowing of the gap.[10]

In the effort to extend the reach of higher education, several developments affected women. First was the expansion of the readily accessible
two-year college, which accounted for nearly half of the growth in college
enrollments. A second development was the increase in part-time enrollments, a pattern especially suited to older women seeking to update old
skills or to acquire new ones but who were unable to become full-time
students. Third was the rapid increase in the number of these nontraditional students, persons 35 and over, of whom 1.2 million were enrolled
in 1980, two thirds of them women. The vast majority attended part-time;
two fifths enrolled as graduate students, most often in education.[11]

The seventies saw significant changes in the academic programs that
women pursued. The two most crucial shifts were in the fields of education
and business. The field of education—long dominated by women—offered
easy access and could be left for a short time while starting a family and
easily reentered if one chose. A teaching career did not entail assumption
of successively heavier levels of responsibility that might impinge on the
traditional homemaking responsibilities of the married woman. In response
to the declining birthrate in the 1960s and the resulting decrease in demand
for teachers, the number of women majoring in education declined in the
mid-1970s. The reduction in employment opportunities as teachers, reinforced by the rising tide of student feminism, pushed a growing number
of women into the more lucrative male-dominated fields such as business
and the sciences—fields in which success required long-term commitments, which women had not made in the past. To many young women,
business school seemed "like a good place to be." At the prestigious Columbia University, women constituted 42 percent of the graduate business
enrollments in 1976. Business degrees became even more attractive to
women as schools developed combined curriculums that linked business

administration with social work and public health, areas in which women had long functioned. By 1978 business was the largest major field of study for women, the proportion majoring in business rising from 9 to 13 percent since 1970; in the same interval the proportion of women majoring in education dropped from 21 to 13 percent. In some undergraduate areas long dominated by men—agriculture, the biological sciences, mathematics, and physical sciences—women made substantial gains, evidence of the lessening hold of sex stereotypes.[12]

This invasion of male-dominated fields cut across ethnic lines, though not across class lines. Abandoning their proclivity to major in education or social science, black students shifted their interests to business, biology, and the health fields. Hispanic students, too, were caught up in the rush to business, demoting education to second place. Although at least a few women from each status group entered each field of study, women from low-status families tended to choose occupation-oriented majors such as nursing; those from higher-status families tended to choose more general education fields such as English and the liberal arts.[13]

Overall, women scored impressive gains at the graduate and professional level. At the first professional level (dentistry, law, medicine, theology, veterinary medicine, chiropody or podiatry, optometry, and osteopathy) women's gains were dramatically striking—19,164 degrees in 1981 compared with 1,425 in 1966. Even so, women earned but 26.6 percent of all such degrees in 1981.[14]

As bars to the admission of women to the medical profession crumbled in the 1960s, the percentage of women among first-year medical students inched upward, reaching 9 percent in 1967; thereafter it escalated, and by fall 1976 women students comprised almost one fourth of the nation's first-year medical students. At some schools women constituted one third or more of the entering classes. A woman at Columbia University assessed the new milieu: "I don't feel like part of a minority group at all—there are just too many of us." Her father had reported that in his days as a medical student 25 years earlier "most of the girls were 'dogs' and kept to themselves most of the time. Things have changed completely," she concluded. This influx of women in medical schools ended their isolation and reduced the level of discrimination they encountered in admissions interviews, in lecture-hall humor, and in classroom and laboratory participation. Nonetheless, the United States continued to lag behind European countries such as Great Britain, France, and West Germany in training women as doctors.[15]

Even the theological schools were not immune to the winds of change. The willingness of such schools to admit women was related to the attitudes of the sponsoring organizations toward the ordination of women. Protestant churches had long steered women toward degrees in religious

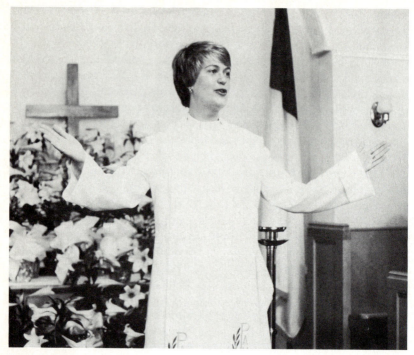

During the 1970s, women clergy increased significantly in mainline Protestant churches.

education. But increasing numbers of women sought a divinity degree. Between 1972 and 1975 alone, the number of women pursuing a masters or a doctorate in divinity studies nearly doubled, and by 1975, 16 percent of the students enrolled in Protestant seminaries were women. Although barring women from the priesthood, the Roman Catholic church permitted nuns to study in seminaries. Among the nation's Jews, the Orthodox continued to exclude women from their rabbinical seminaries; Conservative Jews admitted women as students but would not ordain them. Only Reform Judaism accepted women on an equal basis with men.[16]

Yet old practices did not die easily. The seventies were replete with complaints that colleges denied female students an equitable share of financial aid, fellowships, and teaching assistantships. Female applicants to graduate and professional schools faced queries about their marital status, intention to raise a family, and arrangements for care of children—questions seldom, if ever, asked of male applicants. An occasional female student complained of being pressured to engage in sexual activities with an instructor in return for academic favors. Even in coed schools such as Cornell University, female students reported being intimidated by their male colleagues or feeling that they must guard against appearing to compete with the males academically. Female students entering previously all-male colleges encountered hostility and harassment from male students as well as from administrators and faculty. Female students at Princeton complained of being excluded from the eating clubs that had long provided a center for social life and the camaraderie essential to a congenial college experience. At Dartmouth some "unabashedly raucous" fraternities subjected women to sexual harassment.[17]

Adoption of the Education Amendments Act of 1972 prodded university officials to unprecedented levels of self-examination. Title IX, which prohibited sex discrimination in institutions receiving federal funds, placed the weight of statute law on the side of equal treatment and provided a stick with which to prod balky institutions to a greater degree of compliance with the spirit of the law. Federal authorities pressed colleges and universities to end restrictive quotas, to admit women on the same basis as men, and to offer financial aid on similar terms. Many colleges promptly appointed affirmative-action officers and committed themselves to equal opportunity for all. Programs were launched to recruit female students, especially in graduate and professional programs. And these new procedures often reduced the barriers to equal treatment.[18]

One of the thornier problems involved equal opportunities in athletics at all grade levels, in school and out of school. Little League baseball and high-school athletics came under pressure to permit girls to compete on equal terms with boys. At the college level women experienced a variety of discriminations. Many colleges accorded the male varsity athlete free tuition, free room and board, free books, and hinted at attractive employment after graduation—aid extended to no other students. Female athletes, by contrast, had limited grants-in-aid, few coaches or trainers, and restricted access to gymnasiums for practice. They might have to buy their own equipment, whereas the men's teams were equipped at school expense. Women's teams had to arrange their own transportation to away contests, sleep in dormitories, and eat at fast-food restaurants, while the men traveled by chartered bus or plane, stayed in first-class motels, and ate in first-class restaurants. Obtuse administrators avoided correcting these discriminations until directed to do so by federal court orders. The National Collegiate Athletic Association, an organization of university presidents and athletic directors, took the lead in urging the Department of Health, Education and Welfare to exempt athletic programs from compliance with the terms of Title IX, claiming that the price might be the dismantling of intercollegiate football programs, clearly a national disaster. The Department of Health, Education and Welfare listened to the arguments, but it continued to press for compliance and women's sports received increasing financial support. However, organized intercollegiate athletics remained a potent lobby against equal opportunities for women.[19]

Women faculty bore the brunt of discriminatory practices. Prodded by the Education Amendments Act, most schools instituted procedures that ensured that women would be recruited for vacancies; reviews of time in rank and of salary structures were common and some adjustments in rank and salary made. Yet in too many cases these procedures did not ensure that the substance of equal treatment was realized. The women's athletic director who insisted too strenuously on a more equitable budget could be judged a "poor administrator" and dismissed for cause. Administrators could downgrade the professional achievements of women faculty and delay promotions, hold down salary increments, or deny tenure, again for what was termed "cause." Redress was nearly impossible when department chairmen and deans who had acquiesced in the original discrimination supervised the appeal process. The Department of Health, Education and Welfare evinced little enthusiasm for reviewing complaints filed under the provisions of Title IX, allowing an enormous backlog of complaints to pile up. Thus encouraged, some diffident administrators deferred redress of grievances until directed to take action by a Health, Education and Welfare hearing board, hoping that complainants, weary of delay, would move off and drop their charges. At the same time the American Council on Education—an organization of college administrators—filed a friend-of-the-court brief with the Supreme Court, arguing that Title IX did not permit individuals to seek redress of complaints through federal courts. The council ingenuously insisted that intra-institutional procedures sufficed to assure fairness. The Supreme Court, however, held that individuals, indeed, had the right to bring suit under the statute.[20]

AN UNPRECEDENTED DEMAND

The American economy continued to boom in the seventies, and as in the sixties, much of the additional labor was supplied by women. Of the 24 million workers added to the labor force, 14 million were women, an unprecedented number; indeed, more women joined the labor force during the seventies than had belonged to it in 1940. Much of this increase resulted from an expanding population, but it also reflected the growing acceptability of market labor for women. The most striking fact is that in 1979, for the first time, the LFPR for women reached the 50 percent level, and by 1980 it stood at 51.5 percent.[21]

Figure 10-1
Labor Force by Industry, 1970 and 1980

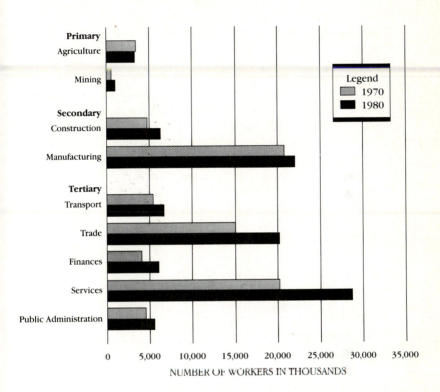

This economic growth permeated all major segments of the labor market except for farm work, which experienced a reduction of 386,000 workers, and for operatives, which had a very nominal increase. As Figure 10-1 illustrates, the chief area of growth was in the tertiary sector, and within that sector, professional and technical employment increased by 4.8 million jobs, clerical work by 4.7 million, and service work by 3.2 million; by comparison, the demand for blue-collar workers rose by 3.0 million. While the addition of 10.3 million men to the labor force cannot be dismissed as insignificant, the male share in the national work force, nonetheless, declined; the addition of 14.0 million women provided the expansive force to the nation's economy.[22]

Of the 12.4 million women added to the ranks of the gainfully employed, 9.68 million acquired white-collar jobs compared to 1.04 million in blue-collar work and 1.76 million in service jobs. During the interval, 33,000 women dropped out of agriculture. Overall the number of employed women increased by 42.0 percent in the seventies. To understand what was transpiring it is necessary to examine the changes in the major occupational sectors of the labor force as well as the shifts within those sectors.[23]

White-collar Occupations

Within the white-collar sector, the clerical occupations afforded women the largest number of jobs. In 1970 one in every three women in the labor force held a clerical job. Reflecting the growth of administrative bureaucracies and the proliferation of paperwork, the demand for women clerks increased by 44 percent, generating 4.55 million new jobs for women in the decade. These were jobs that suited the training of high-school grad-

Figure 10-2
Occupational Distribution of Women, 1970 and 1980

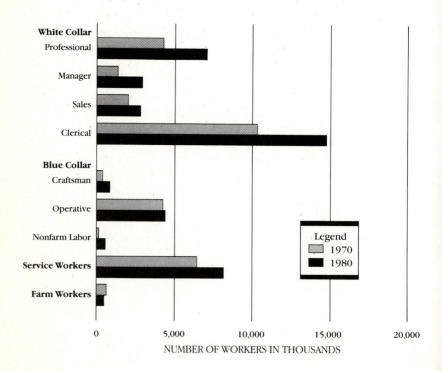

NUMBER OF WORKERS IN THOUSANDS

uates. Nevertheless a woman college graduate, though overqualified, might seek such work because it could be combined with lingering child-care and homemaking responsibilities without creating unacceptable levels of stress. But numerous women also pushed into clerical positions that previously had been male preserves: mail carriers, postal clerks, computer operators, shipping and receiving clerks, stock clerks and storekeepers (see Figure 10-2).[24]

Professional and technical employment, the second major consumer of white-collar women, increased its demand by 64.3 percent. As the demand for teachers and nurses—the traditional professional occupations for women—was relatively weak, much of the increase in professional employment resulted from women entering nontraditional occupations. In the elite, male-dominated professions, from which women had been excluded, women increased their occupational share: in law, by 9 percentage points; as physicians, by 3.6 points. A woman engineer was still a rarity in 1980, but women's share of engineering jobs had increased by a factor of five. Their share of college and university teaching posts increased by nearly 6 percentage points, and they found significant new opportunities for employment as managers and administrators. The expanded demand for women in professional and managerial posts gave women with college and university degrees opportunities for employment commensurate with their level of education.[25]

Blue-collar Occupations

Reflecting the structural changes in the American economy, blue-collar occupations lagged the rest of the economy in growth. Although the level of factory employments generally remained stationary, there were some occupations in which the demand for labor declined. Some of these like dressmakers and sewers and stitchers were overwhelmingly dominated by women; others like garage workers and gas-station attendants, meat cutters, and precision-machine operators were largely dominated by men. Yet in both kinds of labor markets women succeeded in expanding their share of the occupation, and in a few occupations such as delivery and route workers women displaced male workers. Women also increased their presence as bus drivers, forklift operators, and taxi drivers.[26]

The push into "men's jobs" was most evident in the ranks of the unskilled laborer, as some women, backed by Title VII and NOW, secured jobs as construction laborers, freight handlers, and livestock handlers. While a great majority of the women employed in the blue-collar sector were operatives, most of the incremental jobs were either in the skilled crafts at the top or in unskilled labor at the bottom. Relatively well educated white women defied tradition by making a bid for skilled craft jobs, while the removal of racial barriers permitted minority women to bid for unskilled work.[27]

Service Workers

The tug between traditional views of "women's work" and the egalitarian views of radical feminists was played out most clearly in the service-work sector. As many service jobs utilized the traditional homemaking skills of women, such work required a minimum of formal training. Employment as private-household workers had been restricted almost exclusively to women. During the seventies, child care—the most maternal of any occupation—remained attractive to women, and women's share of the occupation increased; on the other hand, their share of jobs as cleaners and servants dropped a fraction of a percentage point. Service work, not in private households, however, with its aura of professionalism and range of fringe benefits proved enticing, and women enlarged their share of this work as they undertook the full range of custodial duties previously limited to men. Although women still occupied nine of every ten jobs as waiters and over half of the jobs as cooks, their share of food-service work declined. The health-care field, which not only was expanding but increasingly demanded higher levels of training, proved attractive, and women increased their share of such jobs at every skill level—health aide, nurses aide, and practical nurse.[28]

The ramifications of the changing views of what was proper was well illustrated in the area of personal service—barbers and hairdressers and cosmetologists. The clientele had been sex-segregated by law and custom—barbers served men; hairdressers and cosmetologists, women. The response of state governments to the ERA and Title VII prompted the removal of these legal barriers. The movement toward unisex fashion created a two-sex clientele for both barbers and hairdressers, with the result that women greatly enhanced their share of the barbering trade, while their share of employment as hairdressers declined slightly. The efforts of a few women to become fire fighters, guards, and police occasioned as much controversy as any occupational change. Phyllis Schlafly rejected such employment for her Positive Woman as "incompatible with community morals." Wives of firemen and policemen objected vociferously to having their husbands working alongside women. Nevertheless a handful of women did succeed in becoming fire fighters, still more became police, and an even larger number became guards.[29]

Black Women

The operation of the Civil Rights Act of 1964, in placing the power of the federal government in support of equal employment opportunity in the labor market, lowered the double barriers that black women encountered as blacks and as women. During the seventies, approximately 1,000,000 black women were added to the labor force. The substantial shift in demand for black women during the decade is illustrated by Figure 10-3. The significantly higher level of education possessed by the young blacks entering the labor force, combined with the pressure on employers to hire minority women, enabled black women to take advantage of the structural changes in the economy that had created so many new white-collar jobs. The proportion of black women workers with white-collar jobs jumped from 37.9 percent to 49.3 percent between 1972 and 1980. By contrast, the proportion of blacks in blue-collar work remained relatively constant, while the proportion of black women in personal service and farm labor declined.[30]

The changing participation of black women in specific occupations resulted in uneven gains. In 1972 in the area of professional employment, black women were especially visible in social and recreation work, voca-

Figure 10-3
Occupational Distribution of Women by Race, 1972 and 1980

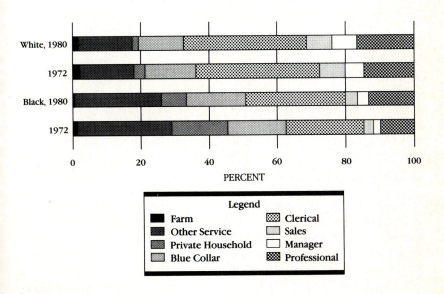

tional and educational counseling, and personnel and labor relations work. They were still concentrated in these occupations in 1980, but they had succeeded in expanding their participation in several other occupations. The most notable gains occurred in the computer field, but "noteworthy gains" were also scored as accountants, nurses, dieticians and therapists, engineers, and science technicians. While their gains in managerial jobs were slight, they substantially increased their participation as school administrators, insurance agents, and bank officials. In the clerical occupations the gains of black women were widespread, with strong gains as claims estimators and investigators, mail handlers, postal clerks, statistical clerks, and telephone operators.[31]

Despite the decline of blue-collar employment generally, black women continued to hold a disproportionate number of blue-collar jobs. Indeed, during the seventies the number of occupations in which they held 18 percent or more of the jobs doubled. Although this reflected the continuing operation of racial and sexual segregation, in terms of the historic concentration of black women in private-household work, the expansion of their share of blue-collar employments represented an advance. Certainly the most significant change in the labor-market role of black women was the decline in the percentage of black women who engaged in private-household work, the proportion dropping from 16 percent to 7 percent during this interval.[32]

Overall, the occupational structure of black women more nearly approached that of white women in 1980 than it had a decade earlier. The proportion of black women in white-collar jobs had increased, but they were concentrated in jobs at the lower end of the professional pay scale— jobs such as nurse, health technologist, social or recreational worker, and teacher. But within those occupations they received almost the same pay as their white counterparts. The clerical field was the one white-collar area in which black women were well dispersed and advancing into some of the better-paying positions. Black women in the 1980s were still underrepresented in the more prestigious white-collar occupations and overrepresented in the lesser-skilled, lower-paying jobs.[33]

Hispanic Women

Despite their common language, women of the Mexican, Puerto Rican, and Cuban communities functioned autonomously, and their labor-market experiences differed substantially. About 2.2 million women of Spanish origin were in the civilian labor force in 1980 as compared with 1,096,000 reported ten years earlier. This growth reflected not only the increases due to the high fertility rate and to the accretions owing to legal and illegal immigration but to improved techniques for accurately tabulating the Hispanic population. As of 1980, 1,189,000 women of Mexican origin, 235,000 women of Puerto Rican origin, and 181,000 women of Cuban origin were in the labor force. Because young adult women have higher LFPRs than older women, the disproportionate numbers of young women in the Hispanic population inflated the labor-force rate for all Hispanics as compared with the rate for Anglo women. It is especially necessary to examine labor-force participation for each of the major Hispanic groups (see Figure 10-4).[34]

The LFPR for Puerto Rican women rose by nearly 8 points during the seventies, yet it trailed the rates for Mexican and Cuban women by 9 to 15 points throughout the decade. Three factors were operative. First, the Puerto Ricans came from an island culture in which the labor rates of women from 1960 to 1976 had never exceeded 27 percent, meaning that nearly three fourths had little or no labor-force experience. Second, they had a relatively limited amount of formal education, severely restricting the range of jobs for which they might compete. Third, half of the Puerto Rican population lived in New York City, a community that experienced a 12.6 percent decline in jobs between 1969 and 1976. Three fourths of this loss was sustained in clerical and operative jobs, the job areas in which Puerto

Figure 10-4
LFPR for Women by Ethnic Origin, 1980

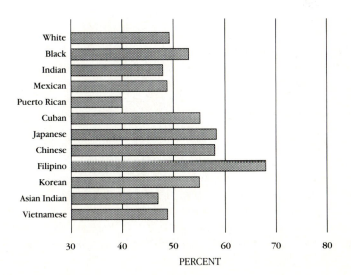

PERCENT

Rican women were heavily represented. Many of the jobs held by Puerto Ricans in the late forties and fifties were abolished as machines were introduced that produced the goods at lower cost. Unfortunately Puerto Rican women lacked the skill and training to operate the new equipment. Their difficulties were compounded by the flight of many factory jobs to other parts of the country. Relative to other Hispanic women, Puerto Rican women were overrepresented in clerical occupations, a fact that reflected their presence in New York City and the availability of clerical employment there. But generally, regardless of age group, Puerto Rican women had lower labor-force rates than other Hispanic women.[35]

Although their decision to leave Cuba entailed losses in material possessions, within five years Miami had become a "Cuban" city. Many of the Cubans were caught up in the "enclave economy"—that is, they found employment in immigrant-owned-and-operated enterprises, of which there were some 8,000 in 1976. The enclave firms concentrated on textiles, leather, furniture, cigar making, construction, and finance, as well as restaurants, supermarkets, private clinics, legal firms, funeral parlors, and private schools. Enclave workers initially had to settle for unskilled jobs at minimum wages and with little job security, but in the long run their past investments of time and money in training and education enabled them to secure employment comparable to that which they had held in Cuba.[36]

Overall the Cuban women fared well. Reflecting their relatively high educational attainment and the length of time they had had to establish themselves, their labor-force rate in 1980 was 55.4. Forty-one percent were in white-collar positions—though chiefly as clerical workers—another 43 percent were operatives, and a scant 13 percent were service workers. Relative to other Hispanic women, Cuban women were better able to secure professional employments and were the least dependent on service work. In the course of little more than a decade Cuban women of the first wave managed to establish a life-style at least as favorable as that of the Puerto Ricans, a community well into its second generation, or that of the Mexican Americans, the majority of whom were American-born.[37]

Mexican women, whose numbers more than doubled during the seventies, raised their LFPR by one third, to 49.0. In 1980 they stood well ahead of Puerto Rican women and only six points behind Cuban women. The surge in the number of Mexican women in the labor force resulted more from an increase in the working-age population than from the rise in their labor-force rates. The population was highly heterogeneous, including as it did American-born educated urban women as well as Mexican-born uneducated peasant women. Relative to other Hispanic-origin women, Mexican women had a low level of white-collar employments but a high level of service employments. Only a token 1.5 percent were farm workers, though many such workers—especially the "undocumented"—may have eluded enumeration.[38]

Other Americans

American Indian women, though still seriously disadvantaged as compared with women of most other minority groups in terms of economic well-being, gained remarkably in making a place for themselves in the labor force. Their labor-force rate in 1980, 48.3, was but one percentage point below that for white women not of Spanish origin; their numbers, some 214,000, placed them ahead of any single Asian American group and were outnumbered only by black, Mexican American, and Puerto Rican women. As a less well educated minority who had experienced far-ranging discrimination and whose isolation on reservations had limited employment opportunities, Indian women fared less well than white women in competing for the more demanding managerial, professional, and technical employments by a margin of 5 to 9 percentage points. By the same token Indian women were more likely than white women to be found in service employments—notably food service and cleaning- and building-service work. Likewise, Indian women were far more likely to be engaged as machine operatives, fabricators, or handlers. However, in comparison to black women, Indian women were somewhat more likely to secure managerial, professional, or technical employment and were less likely to work in service occupations or as operatives, fabricators, or laborers.[39]

By 1980 nearly 750,000 Asian American women were employed. Filipino women were most numerous, followed closely by Japanese and Chinese women, but there were also growing numbers of Korean, Asian Indian, and Vietnamese women. The labor-force rates of these Asian Americans, the Vietnamese excepted, exceeded those for white, black, Mexican American, or Puerto Rican women. Highest of all was the rate for Filipino women, 68.1. The rate for Vietnamese women, 48.9, approximated the rates for white, Mexican American, and American Indian women.[40]

As compared with white women, the Asian Indian, the Filipino, and the Chinese were more likely to hold managerial and professional employment and somewhat less likely to be found in technical, sales, and administrative-support occupations. Japanese women—who were the most acculturated of the Asian Americans—had approximately the same mix of employments as white women. As newcomers, Korean and Vietnamese women lagged behind other Asian American women, as well as white women, in access to the prestigious managerial, professional, technical, sales, and administrative-support occupations. The service occupations—which employed 1 in 6 white women—employed nearly 1 in 4 Korean women but less than 1 in 7 Chinese. Such work employed Filipino, Japanese, and Vietnamese women in the same proportions as it did white women. Proportionately, Asian women were more attracted to the crafts than white women. That Vietnamese and Korean women experienced little success in securing employment in prestigious white-collar areas (managerial, professional, technical, and sales work) but fared very well in competing for jobs in precision crafts suggests that the lack of language skills may have steered them away from white-collar and toward skilled blue-collar work. The proportion of Asian women employed as operatives, fabricators, and laborers varied from a low of 1 in 12 for Japanese to a high of 1 in 3 for Vietnamese women. While Japanese women were less likely to be employed as operatives than white women, Chinese, Korean, and Vietnamese women were far more likely to have such work. And indeed they were far more likely to be so employed than were black women. Precise measures of changes in the occupational patterns of Indian, Hispanic, and Asian American women during the seventies is not possible because of the changes in occupational classifications introduced by the Census Bureau in 1980. However, the 1980 data suggests that while 7 in 10 white working women were in the elite white-collar occupations, just over 5 out of 10 black or Hispanic women were so employed. By comparison, roughly two thirds of the Japanese, Chinese, and Filipino women, but less than half of Korean and Vietnamese women, were so employed. Ethnic background still shaped women's economic roles.[41]

Occupational Shares

During the seventies, the gains women scored in the labor force reflected not just the growing economy but an increase in the share of employment in various occupations held by women. Thus of the 11,616,000 additional jobs women acquired during the decade, 7,033,000 were attributable to maintaining a constant share of the jobs in an expanding economy, but 4,583,000 jobs—39.5 percent of the increment—resulted from increases in women's propensity to engage in market labor. Because of the increase in their occupational share, the number of women added to the labor force in the seventies was double that of the sixties—evidence of changes in women's attitudes toward work, the impact of the feminist movement, the economic pressures generated by inflation, and the increasing effectiveness of Title VII and Title IX in pressuring employers to adopt sex-neutral employment policies. Even so, the increments attributable to rising occupational shares varied widely from occupational group to occupational group (see Figure 10-5).[42]

Among the white-collar occupations, women gained access to clerical, sales, and professional employment primarily on the basis of the growth of the occupations, for only one fifth to one third of the increments represented an increase in women's share in those occupations. Two thirds of the increased share was concentrated in professional services, finance, and insurance and real estate. Women also made significant gains in engineering and architectural services. But in the set of managerial jobs, nearly three fourths of the increment resulted from an expansion in women's share of the jobs.[43]

Among the blue-collar occupations, most of the increments resulted from the increase in occupational shares. Although the nation employed 95,000 fewer operatives in 1980 than in 1970, women actually held 2.8 percent more jobs at the end of the period. Often the demand for women in a particular occupation depended on the demand generated by a particular industry for persons with that occupational specialty. Thus, women gained significantly in their share of jobs as operatives through increased

Figure 10-5
Changes in Demand for Female Workers, 1970–1980

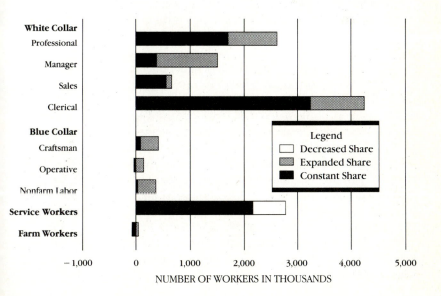

NUMBER OF WORKERS IN THOUSANDS

demands by manufacturers of furniture and fixtures and of instruments and related products. On the other hand, the production of electric and electronic equipment—a major employer of female labor—experienced little growth, yet women increased their share of jobs. In nondurable industries, although total employment declined during the decade, women increased their share of jobs in textiles, apparel, and food products—industries that accounted for 61 percent of all women employed in nondurables. Women also scored important gains in the chemical-, rubber-, and plastic-products industries, as well as in local and interurban transportation. With respect to the service-work sector, while women added 1,600,000 jobs, this increment fell short by over 500,000 jobs of maintaining a constant share.[44]

Employment opportunities as farm workers continued to decline. In reality, this job category included three quite different types of workers: farmers, paid laborers, and unpaid family laborers. Several significant developments greatly affected the position of women farm workers. One was the substitution of machinery designed to reduce the producer's dependence on migrant farm labor. In the transition, men became equipment operators; women, jobless. Second, at the start of the decade two thirds of the farm workers had less than four years of high school; by 1980 this proportion had declined to 36 percent, greatly increasing their job mobility. Third, the demand for unpaid family laborers dropped sharply. In the course of the decade the number of women farmers increased by two thirds; the number of paid farm workers, by one eighth; but the number of unpaid workers dropped nearly 50 percent. Altogether, the internal changes in the composition of farm workers left those who remained markedly better off.[45]

Overall, these various measures of economic change during the seventies provide a picture in which (1) two thirds of the growth in the national labor force was made possible by recruiting women into the work force; (2) most of the incremental jobs occurred in white-collar occupations that had long been deemed suitable to women—easing the way for both employer and prospective employee; and (3) women succeeded in increasing their share of employment in nearly every major occupational category. By inference, the degree of sexual segregation in the labor force declined during the decade; the results suggest that the assertions of feminist ideology and the thrust of the Equal Pay Act and of Title VII of the Civil Rights Act along with the debate over the ERA created a climate of opinion that encouraged an increasing percentage of women to enter the labor market and to venture into occupations not ordinarily associated with women.

A PLENTEOUS SUPPLY

To meet the unprecedented rise in the demand for women, employers recruited outside the traditional sources of the female labor supply. The process was already under way as the decade began. The female labor force in 1970 had numbered 31,233,000 women. To enlarge it to 44,934,000 within the decade required a plenteous supply. The increment of 13,701,000 women consisted of 6.5 million married women, 4.3 million single women, and 3.0 million divorced or separated women. In the same interval, the number of widowed women in the labor force dropped by 121,000. An analysis of this increment to the female labor force underscores the degree to which its composition continued to reflect the ever-changing mix of single, married, separated, divorced, and widowed women.[46]

Marital Status

The increase in the number of married women in the labor force reflected primarily the stepped-up pace of their LFPR; for single women the increase was equally divided between population growth and the rise in the labor-force rate.[47]

The proportion of single women in the total population grew as girls of the postwar baby boom came of age and the mood of the seventies encouraged them to defer marriage. As the younger women put off marriage, the pool of married women with spouses present declined, and sharply escalating divorce rates further cut into the ranks of the married. Indeed, the proportion of divorced women nearly doubled while the pool of widowed women declined, reflecting the greater acceptability of remarriage by older women. As divorced and single women had relatively high labor-force rates, the cumulative effect of these demographic shifts was to increase significantly the pool of women likely to seek and accept paid labor. The net effect of these demographic changes added 1,100,000 women to the labor force during the decade.[48]

More importantly, the propensity of women to seek market labor escalated markedly for women in nearly every marital-status group. The LFPR for single women rose 8.5 percentage points, reaching 61.5 in 1980. Allowing for the growing population, the increased propensity of single women to work added 1.5 million women to the labor force (see Figure 10-6).[49]

For the small but growing class of separated women, the LFPR rose 7.3 points, reaching 59.4 in 1980. Inasmuch as many of these women had children to support, the rise in their labor-force rates reflected the pressure of economic need overcoming the conventional reluctance of mothers to

Figure 10-6
LFPR of Women by Marital Status and Age, 1970 and 1980

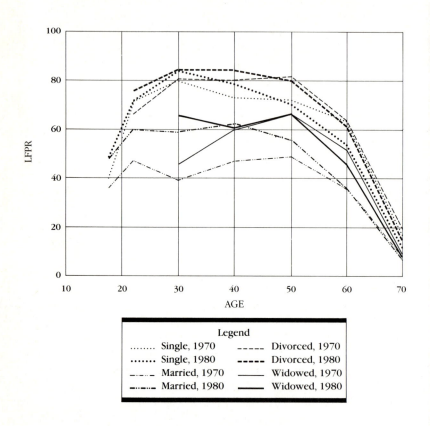

Legend

.... Single, 1970   _ _ _ _ _ Divorced, 1970

••••••• Single, 1980   _ _ _ _ Divorced, 1980

_.._.._ Married, 1970   _____ Widowed, 1970

_..___.._ Married, 1980   ████ Widowed, 1980

absent themselves from home to pursue market labor. The net result was
the addition of 238,000 women workers.[50]

Among divorced women, of whom seven out of ten were already in
the labor force, the labor-force rates jiggled up and down during the decade, but in 1980 the rate stood 3 points higher than at the start of the
decade. Among the younger divorced women—persons the courts were
likely to feel should contribute to their own support if practicable—the
labor rates rose by 10 points for women under 25, by 3 to 4 points for
those 25 to 44. Among women in their late 40s and early 50s—women
more likely to enjoy the court's sympathy and hence to be awarded alimony—the rates dropped slightly. Nonetheless the labor rates for these
women surpassed those for all other women except young single women.
Overall the labor force gained 2,500,000 divorced women.[51]

The economic pressure on widows to enter the labor force continued to decline as the Social Security system and private pension systems increasingly provided meaningful help. Accordingly the labor-force rates for widows 55 and older declined during the decade, reaching 46.7 in 1980, while the rates for widows between 35 and 55, for whom Social Security and private pensions were less adequate, remained virtually unchanged. The rates for the handful of young widows, those in their 20s and early 30s, escalated by more than 20 points. The combined effect was a net reduction of 121,000 women workers.[52]

The increment in the female labor force, then, rested heavily on the growing propensity of married women, with spouses present, to enter the work force. Their labor rates rose 6.7 points in the fifties—the era of the "feminine mystique"—pushed upward another 10.3 points in the sixties as a feminist ideology took form, and rose yet another 9.3 points during the seventies. By 1980 just over half of all such married women were in the labor force.[53]

This increased propensity of married women to engage in market labor reflected changing views about the compatibility of work with responsibility for the care of children. Between 1950 and 1970 the gap between the labor-market rates of single women and married women had narrowed appreciably because of the increased propensity of married women to seek market labor. Nonetheless, the spread between the labor-force rates of women with preschool children and those with school-age children grew appreciably.[54]

During the seventies this pattern changed dramatically. Whereas the LFPR of single women increased by 8.5 points, that for married women with preschool children jumped upward by nearly 15 points and that for women with school-age children, by 12.5 points. Indeed, by 1980 the labor-force rate for women with school-age children was fractionally higher than that for single women. A combination of the children's greater degree of maturity, the presence of an older son or daughter who could relieve the mother of some child-care and housekeeping duties, and rising family expenses pushed mothers of school-age children into the labor market. The presence of children under 6 continued to pose problems of balancing maternal responsibilities with the economic or psychological need to work.[55]

At first glance the labor-force rates for women with no children under 18 seem to contradict expectations. Although free of child-care responsibilities, these women ostensibly had lower labor-force rates than did women with children. The fact is that this group consisted of brides who had yet to bear their first child, childless wives in their 30s and 40s, and a large number of older women with grown families. The labor-force rates for the small group of childless wives under age 45 ranged from 64.5 percent for those 35 to 44 years old to 81.5 percent for those 25 to 34 years. The very large group of women 55 years and over had a rate of 24.1 percent, depressing the rate for the total group.[56]

Age

As the propensity of women to enter the labor force varied by marital status, so it varied by age group. Several features stand out. Young women were in the labor force in considerably larger proportions in 1980 than in 1970, reflecting the force of feminism. The differential between the labor-force rates of teenage girls and boys lessened. Beginning in the mid-1960s, the labor-force rates for women under 45, especially those in the 25- to 34-year-old cohort, rose dramatically. "Constrained by marriage and child responsibilities," the 25- to 34-year-old cohorts had not entered the labor force in numbers until "changing attitudes toward women's role in society" became evident in the mid-1960s and early 1970s. The steep decline in fertility during the sixties "probably had the greatest effect" on the labor-force participation of this group, though rising separation and divorce rates also contributed. Beyond age 45 the labor-force rates declined slightly. It is clear, however, that the ranks of the female labor force were augmented chiefly by women under age 45.[57]

Educational Attainment

The supply—both in quantity and quality—of female workers varied directly with their educational attainment. Women who had not completed high school were far less likely to work than those with four or more years of college by a margin of nearly 22 points in 1959 and 33 points in 1975. The changes in school and college enrollment patterns during this time in effect reduced the population least likely to enter the labor force by two thirds while doubling the group with the highest propensity to work.[58]

Acquisition of an education enhanced employability and earning potential. It both reinforced and reflected the taste for a career. The woman with a high-school diploma who gave up a minimum-wage job to be a homemaker "lost" $7,000 in income; the college woman who gave up a professional job to be a homemaker "forfeited" twice as much in income. But education did more. The more education a woman acquired, the longer she was likely to remain single and the less likely she would ever marry. Well-educated women bore fewer children, making it easier to substitute market work for child care. The level of education substantially affected "access to the cleaner, more pleasant, more interesting jobs." Women with no more than an elementary education were concentrated in service and factory jobs. Such work was not only poorly paid but often intermittent or part-time. Scarcely one in ten such women held any kind of white-collar job. By contrast, nearly two thirds of the women high-school graduates and 95 percent of the women college graduates held white-collar jobs, the former in sales and clerical work, the latter in professional and technical employments. The higher general level of education of women, especially the push into programs in business administration, math, the sciences, medicine, and law, was responsible for the substantial increases in women's share in the more demanding professions and managerial and administrative jobs. As a result, the differences in the kinds of jobs held by men and those held by women narrowed perceptibly during the seventies.[59]

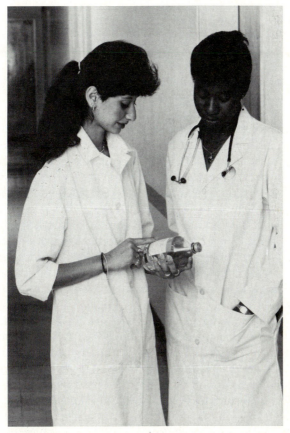

The civil-rights movement and the women's movement combined to enable minority women to enter the medical profession.

Labor Elasticity

An important aspect of the supply of female labor was its elasticity. The availability of full-time year-round as well as part-time and part-year employment offered women wide choices in trading off housework and leisure for market work. These choices eased the burden of women who were ambivalent about the propriety and feasibility of combining market labor and homemaking. Certainly the massive influx into the labor force of married women with young children, which did so much to swell the aggregate female labor rate, was facilitated by part-year and part-time employment. It also inflated the labor-force rates of females as compared with men for whom the rates typically represented full-time year-round work.[60]

In 1960, 37 percent of all working women were employed full-time at least 50 weeks a year, but the proportions varied widely according to marital status. Among single women age 25 to 54 and among divorced women age 35 to 54, 50 to 55 percent worked full-time year-round in contrast to 6 to 7 percent of married women with preschool children. But by far the largest number of working women, whether in 1959, 1969, or 1981, did so only part-year or part-time.[61]

During the sixties and seventies the proportion of part-time workers held constant at one third of the female labor force. But for part-time workers the number of weeks-per-year of employment increased significantly. So, too, numbers of full-time part-year workers began working year-round, the proportion climbing to 42 percent. Altogether the rise in the mean number of weeks that women devoted to market labor accounted for 34 percent of the gain in the total female labor effort. At this point we do not know whether this expanded work commitment of women reduced the demand for part-time labor and so minimized the number of women in the labor force or whether the greater economic rewards of year-round work acted as a magnet, drawing women into the labor force who would not otherwise have been there.[62]

The growing involvement of women in market work had far-reaching implications for husband–wife roles. The conventional view had the husband as the family provider, the wife as the mother–housekeeper. The reality by 1981 was that whereas 67 percent of the husbands worked year-round, the husband was the family's *sole* earner in only 26 percent of the married-couple families. In 36 percent of the families, however, the husband and wife shared in family support. In 4 percent of the families, the wife was the sole earner. These two-earner families, as compared with all families, tended to have significantly higher family incomes; the spouses

Figure 10-7
Work Experience of Wives and Husbands, 1981

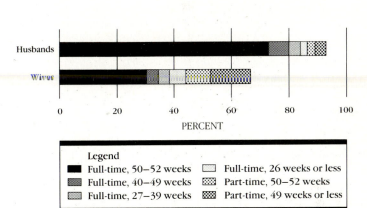

Legend	
■ Full-time, 50–52 weeks	▢ Full-time, 26 weeks or less
▨ Full-time, 40–49 weeks	▨ Part-time, 50–52 weeks
▨ Full-time, 27–39 weeks	▨ Part-time, 49 weeks or less

tended to be younger and were more likely to have completed at least one year of college than spouses in one-earner families (see Figure 10-7).[63]

By 1980 the organized woman's movement and the ERA were becalmed. Nonetheless, in two areas crucial to the character of women's lives, both within and without the family, the winds of change continued to propel women further and further into the main currents of human activity. First, although differences continued—often significant ones—women pursued undergraduate, graduate, and professional education in ways that reduced the gap in educational attainment between the sexes both quantitatively and qualitatively. Young women reaching adulthood in 1980 trained at about the same level as their brothers with much the same potential for a lifetime of political, social, intellectual, and economic activities. Second, by 1980 for the first time, market labor was the norm rather than the exception for women. While they were less likely than men to hold jobs that exercised great power or that conveyed the greatest rewards either in money or prestige, women had moved much closer. Whether one embraced a feminist ideology or not, the reality was that support of the family was more commonly shared by the husband and wife together rather than carried by the husband alone.

NOTES

[1] Judith Hole and Ellen Levine, *Rebirth of Feminism* (New York: Quadrangle, 1971), 324–28. Beverly T. Watkins, "Feminist Educators Seek to Improve Status of Women's Studies,"

CHE, 13(Jan. 31, 1977): 8. Carnegie Commission on Higher Education, *Opportunities for Women in Higher Education* (New York: McGraw-Hill, 1973), 8.

[2] Watkins, "Feminist Educators," 8.

[3] Elizabeth Stone, "Women's Programs Grow Up," *Change,* 7(Nov. 1975): 16–20.

[4] U.S. Congress, House, *Hearings before the Special Subcommittee on Education of the Committee on Education and Labor on Sec. 805 of HR 16098,* 2 parts, March 1971, "Discrimination Against Women," see especially pp. 435–50, 491–95, and 791–819.

[5] Hole and Levine, *Rebirth of Feminism,* 322–29. *NYT,* 11 Jan. 1969 and 31 May 1963.

[6] James Real, "Immaculate Heart of Hollywood," *Change,* 3(May/June, 1971): 48–53. *CHE,* 11(Feb. 9, 1976): 10.

[7] "Wellesley Says It Won't Go Coed," *NYT,* 9 March 1973, 43.

[8] Gael M. O'Brien in *CHE,* 12(April 5, 1976): 8. Betty Littleton, "The Special Validity of Women's Colleges," *CHE,* 11(Nov. 24, 1975): 24. M. Elizabeth Tidball, "The Search for Talented Women," *Change,* 6(May 1974): 51–52, 64. Noreen McGrath, "Coeducation May Place Women at a Disadvantage, Study Finds," *CHE,* 17(Jan. 8, 1979): 20.

[9] Bureau of the Census, *Statistical Abstract of the United States: 1984* (Washington: GPO, 1983), tabs. 255, 256, 257.

[10] Ibid., tab. 275.

[11] Ibid., tabs. 257, 258. Census Bureau, "School Enrollment—Social and Economic Characteristics of Students," *CPR,* ser. P-20, no. 362, 1–3.

[12] *CHE,* 19(Sept. 17, 1979): 12. *NYT,* 3 March 1976, 33. Bureau of the Census, "Major Field of Study of College Students: October 1978," *CPR,* ser. P-20, no. 351, 1–2.

[13] *CHE,* 19(Sept. 17, 1979): 12.

[14] Department of HEW, *Digest of Educational Statistics 1968* (Washington: GPO, 1968), tab. 108, p. 87. Department of HEW, *Digest of Educational Statistics 1983–84* (Washington: GPO, 1983), tab. 105, p. 127.

[15] *NYT,* 16 March 1977, sec. B, p. 4. See also *NYT,* 17 July 1974, 1, 44, and *Athens* (Ohio) *Messenger,* 27 Sept. 1970.

[16] *CHE,* 13(Oct. 18, 1977): 6.

[17] *CHE,* 18(June 18, 1979): 7. *CHE,* 18(July 16, 1979): 2. *CHE,* 19(Sept. 17, 1979): 1, 10.

[18] National Commission on the Observance of International Women's Year, *The Spirit of Houston* (Washington: GPO, 1978), 36–37, insists that the Department of Health, Education and Welfare did little to enforce Title IX.

[19] *NYT,* 13 June 1974, 26, and 12 Jan. 1976, 22. *CHE,* 17(Feb. 20, 1979): 2, reports on a case at Michigan State University. *CHE,* 19(Sept. 17, 1979): 15.

[20] *CHE,* 18(May 21, 1979), 1, 8–10. *NYT,* 15 May 1979. Cheryl M. Fields, "Women's Groups Sue to Compel HEW to Probe Charges of Sex Bias in Sports," *CHE,* 18(July 16, 1979): 7, 10.

[21] Bureau of the Census, *Statistical Abstract of the United States: 1982–83* (Washington: GPO, 1982), tab. 626.

[22] Ibid. See also Bureau of the Census, "Population Profile of the United States: 1979," *CPR,* ser. P-20, no. 350 (Washington: GPO, 1980), 29–31. Howard Davis, "Employment gains of women by industry, 1968–78," *MLR,* 103(June 1980): 3–9.

[23] Bureau of the Census, *Statistical Abstract: 1982–83,* tab. 626.

[24] The measures for specific occupations are for 1972 and 1980. The Census Bureau reclassified occupations in 1975 so that 1980 data are not strictly comparable with 1970 data; the 1972 and 1980 data are comparable. Bureau of the Census, *Statistical Abstract of the United States: 1981* (Washington: GPO, 1981), tab. 675. See Bureau of the Census, *Statistical Abstract: 1982–83,* tab. 649 for occupation by level of education.

[25] See note 24.

[26] Ibid.

[27] Ibid.

[28] Ibid.

[29] Ibid.

[30] Diane Nilsen Westcott, "Blacks in the 1970's: Did they scale the ladder?" *MLR,* 105(June 1982): 30.

[31] Ibid.

[32] Ibid., 30.

[33] Ibid., 30, 34–35.

[34] Bureau of the Census, *Census of Population: 1970. Occupational Characteristics.* PC(2)-4C (Washington: GPO, 1972), tab. 2. There were also 563,000 women of "other" Hispanic origins, chiefly from Central and South America. See also, Bureau of Labor Statistics, *Employment and Earnings,* 28(Jan. 1981), tab. 45.

[35] Morris J. Newman, "A profile of Hispanics in the U.S. workforce," *MLR,* 101(Dec. 1978): 3–13. See also Lois Gray, "The jobs Puerto Ricans hold in New York City," *MLR,* 98(Oct. 1975): 12–16.

[36] Kenneth L. Wilson and Alejandro Portes, "Immigrant Enclaves: An Analysis of the Labor Market Experiences of Cubans in Miami," *AJS,* 86(1980): 296–313. Robert L. Bach, "The new Cuban immigrants: their background and prospects," *MLR,* 103(Oct. 1980): 39–46. Eleanor M. Rogg, *The Assimilation of Cuban Exiles: The Role of Community and Class* (New York: Aberdeen, 1974).

[37] Bach, "The new Cuban immigrants," 39, 44–45. Bureau of the Census, *1980. Census of Population. Vol. 1. Characteristics of the Population,* PC-80-1 (Washington: GPO, 1981), tab. 169.

[38] Newman, "A profile of Hispanics," 12.

[39] Bureau of the Census, *1980. Census of Population. Vol. 1,* PC-80-1, tab. 163.

[40] Ibid.

[41] Ibid.

[42] Bureau of the Census, *Statistical Abstract: 1981,* tab. 673.

[43] Ibid.

[44] Ibid.

[45] Ibid., tab. 675. Bureau of the Census, *Statistical Abstract: 1982–83,* tab. 649.

[46] Bureau of the Census, *Statistical Abstract: 1982–83,* tab. 639.

[47] Bureau of Labor Statistics, *Labor Force Statistics Derived from CPS: A Databook,* vol. 1, *Bulletin* 2096 (Washington: GPO, 1982), tab. C6, C7, C9. Allyson Sherman Grossman, "Labor force patterns of single women," *MLR,* 102(Aug. 1979): 46–49.

[48] Bureau of Labor Statistics, *Labor Force Statistics Derived from CPS,* vol. 1, tab. C6, C7, C9. In fact, the proportion of the labor force comprised of single and divorced women increased during the seventies; the proportion of women in the labor force who were married with spouse present declined. The computations are mine.

[49] Ibid., tab. C-6. Grossman, "Labor force patterns of single women," 46–49.

[50] Bureau of Labor Statistics, *Labor Force Statistics Derived from CPS,* vol. 1, tab. C-7.

[51] Ibid., tabs. C-7, C-9.

[52] Ibid.

[53] Ibid., tab. C-6.

[54] Ibid., tabs. C-6, C-11.

[55] Ibid.

[56] Elizabeth Waldman, Allyson Sherman Grossman, Robert Hayghe, and Beverly L. Johnson, "Working mothers in the 1970's: a look at the statistics," *MLR,* 102(Oct. 1979): 39–49.

[57] Allyson Sherman Grossman, "Women in the labor force: the early years," *MLR*, 98(Nov. 1975): 3–9. Deborah Pisetzner Klein, "Women in the labor force: the middle years," *MLR*, 98(Nov. 1975): 10–16. Beverly Johnson McEaddy, "Women in the labor force: the later years," *MLR*, 98(Nov. 1975): 17–24. See also Carol Leon, "Young adults: a transitional group with changing labor force patterns," *MLR*, 101(May 1978): 3–5.

[58] Bureau of the Census, "A Statistical Portrait of Women of the United States," *CPR*, ser. P-23, no. 58 (Washington: GPO, 1976), tab. 7-3.

[59] Bureau of the Census, *Statistical Abstract: 1982–83,* tab. 649 provides an alternative view of the relationship between education and occupation.

[60] Ibid., tab. 632. In this data the full-time worker is one who worked 35 hours or more in the week for which the data was collected. Many such persons, however, worked only part of a year. Some part-time workers worked year-round; many in the secondary labor force worked only part-year. Data based on *work experience* gives a more accurate picture of full-time full-year and part-year or part-time workers.

[61] Bureau of Labor Statistics, *Handbook of Labor Statistics,* tab. 33.

[62] Ibid.

[63] Bureau of the Census, "Perspectives on American Husbands and Wives," by Stephen Rawlings, *CPR*, ser. P-23, no. 77 (Washington: GPO, 1977), 25.

11

The Present Hour: Retrospect and Prospect

The experience of American women since the start of the century has brought both triumphs and disappointments. In 1900 the agenda of organized women was still framed largely in terms of the Seneca Falls Declaration of 1848 as modified by the interests of the social feminists of the 1890s. In the mid-1960s NOW updated the women's program with its Bill of Rights. The varied concerns provide a useful checklist for assessing the changes in women's status since 1900.

THE CHARACTER OF WOMANHOOD

American society in 1900 was decidedly race conscious. Power was exercised by the native white middle class; blacks and other minorities were powerless. While most Americans had a rural heritage, urban life and urban values set the norms. A modified version of the Cult of Womanhood prescribed women's lives. The conventional woman identified herself as religious; she attended church and perhaps participated in the women's society. She was chaste. Society expected her to be a virgin until her marriage and to scrupulously avoid romantic encounters with other men after marriage. She deferred to her husband as the unquestioned head of the family. She subordinated her individual interests to those of her children and husband.[1]

The chief point of departure from this older view of woman's role appeared in the reshaping of the domestic role. If bookish, she could attend high school, and if exceptional, she might go on to normal school or even college. If unusually independent, she might work before marriage, but the norm for the adult woman was marriage and motherhood. After marriage she lived vicariously through the achievements of her husband and her children. Yet she was permitted a restricted role outside the home. She might join other women in the Women's Christian Temperance Union. If she had attended college, she could join the American Association of University Women. As a concerned mother, she might belong to the local parent–teacher's organization. If a gregarious soul, she might participate in a garden club or literary society affiliated with the General Federation of Women's Clubs. In some jurisdictions she could vote in school elections; though only in four states—Colorado, Idaho, Wyoming, and Utah—could she vote in statewide or national elections. If especially interested in political affairs, she might join the NAWSA (National American Woman Suffrage Association).[2]

The prescriptions for American women in 1900 were formulated for white Anglo-Saxon Protestant women of the urban middle class. There was no thought that these values should define the lives of working-class women, many of whom were immigrants or daughters of immigrants, or the lives of black or other minority women. Nor did minority women participate in the organizational life of the majority woman. Most black women lived in the rural South, the younger adults being only a generation removed from slavery and most of those over 35 having been born slaves. Although culturally, socially, and politically isolated from white Americans, black women were socialized to be pious, pure, submissive, and domestic. Yet the circumstances of their lives were such that in political matters their husbands were as deprived of the suffrage and other political rights because of race as they were because of race and sex. Because of the difficulties their fathers or husbands had in supporting their families, black women came of age expecting to enter the labor force and contribute to the family income. Indian, Mexican American, and Asian American women were even more isolated than black women, their values shaped by their own ethnic or racial heritage rather than that of the white majority.[3]

The young woman of the mainstream coming of age in the 1980s responded to many of the same ideals her great-grandmother embraced in 1900. Nevertheless, there was less consensus, and more alternatives were available. Conventional society still honored the pious but imposed few sanctions on those who were not. Purity was no longer *de rigueur,* but open promiscuity won no distinction. An unmarried woman who lived discreetly with a man not her husband was tolerated, but only marriage unequivocally legitimatized the sexual union for women. As she sought to develop her own value system, the conventional middle-class woman was confronted with a radical-feminist minority, which rejected traditional marriage and advocated living-together arrangements and communal homes, and with a conservative minority, which reaffirmed traditional marriage. Many of these conventional women accepted, even expected, male leadership in family matters, but they expected, even demanded, a share in decision making. Blind submission was passé, but followers of Phyllis Schlafly, devout Mormons, and Christian fundamentalists still continued to invoke scriptural authority in support of undisputed male leadership in the family. Domesticity, too, survived but in transvalued terms. Most young women, especially those from middle-class homes, expected a period of autonomy in which they lived on their own, supporting themselves by a job. Most expected to marry and raise a family, though they anticipated bearing fewer children than the bride of 1900. Marriage permitted an active social, cultural, intellectual, economic, and political life. As male roles had not changed in step with female roles, married women still carried the major responsibility for home and child care, a double burden if she pursued nondomestic interests as freely as she had as a single woman.[4]

Among the white working class, the values of the urban middle class were likely to be honored in the breach. Piety was pursued through their own evangelical and fundamentalist groups. Purity was more likely to proscribe extramarital than premarital encounters, though members of tightknit religious groups valued chastity as highly as women of the nineteenth century. The reality that a husband alone could not support his family made market labor for his wife and daughters a necessity and prompted pragmatic adjustments in notions about feminine submissiveness and domesticity.[5]

Older women of the white middle class were often more comfortable with the somewhat restrictive but familiar values that had been the norm during their youth than with the more permissive values of their daughters and granddaughters. Piety was likely to be more highly valued and expressed in church attendance. Purity was defined in terms of traditional values tempered perhaps by tolerance born of experience. Some who had spent their lives chiefly as homemakers were defensive about their economic dependence on their spouses and annoyed with suggestions by radical feminists that they had failed to fully realize themselves. Some others, however, who may have alternated homemaking and market labor might see no conflict between the domestic role and working outside the home.

Such women may have had a long history of sharing in the support of the family and enjoying a measure of economic and psychological autonomy.[6]

Women in the various ethnic and racial minorities lived segregated from urban middle-class whites, though the minority groups had their own urban middle class. While the schools, radio and television, and the press acquainted them with the values of the mainstream, minority women often found the traditions and needs of their own ethnic community more prescriptive. There was no single norm for minority women. Piety did not invariably enjoin Protestant values or even those of Catholicism. If they endorsed the ideal of purity, they might do so in terms other than those of Christianity. All groups proscribed extramarital affairs, but some American Indian societies still permitted polygynous marriages. Hispanic American and Asian American wives were likely to be more submissive to husbands than Anglo-American women. The domestic roles might permit a black woman or a Chicana to work in the fields alongside her father or husband and allow other minority women into private homes, factories, shops, and offices to perform menial jobs that Anglo women eschewed. If Hispanic views of a male-dominated family derived from the Spanish heritage, those of Asian Americans and American Indians had their own unique roots. Only those minority women who worked in close proximity to the Anglo middle class or who aspired to be socially and economically mobile in Anglo society had to embrace the values and practices of the mainstream.[7]

THE CHARACTER OF THE FAMILY

Much as ideas about the character of womanhood have been modified since the start of the century, so ideas about the character of the family changed. In 1900 the family was sacrosanct. Rich or poor, educated or uneducated, young or old, white or nonwhite, all women lived out the basic functions of womanhood within the family. In 1900 social critics of the family were scarce. But even Charlotte Perkins Gilman, the most perceptive feminist critic, focused on ways to expedite housekeeping and child-care tasks in order to permit the married woman and mother to have a life of her own outside the home. Other turn-of-the-century critics—Theodore Roosevelt was typical—decried the falling birthrate and the rising divorce rate as evidence of a weakening of the family. A monogamous nuclear family remained the ideal.[8]

Not all women found the traditional roles within the family emotionally satisfying. A minority of young urban women—the New Woman and the flapper—kicked up their heels just before and after World War I and succeeded in expanding the public roles of the young unmarried woman. Young mothers—motivated by patriotism and abetted by an acute labor shortage—raised the eyebrows of traditionalists as they entered the labor force rather than stay at home with their children. From 1940 onward the reports of Clara Thompson, Ferdinand Lundberg and Marynia Farnham, *Life* and *Newsweek,* and Mirra Komarovsky documented that numerous white middle-class women found traditional roles within the family emotionally unsatisfying. Betty Friedan's *Feminine Mystique* elevated this "problem with no name" to a national issue. But her solution explored ways and means of enabling a woman to find fulfillment as a person within the husband–wife family. Only the lesbian and radical feminists who had surfaced in the late 1960s rejected the monogamous nuclear family for a variety of other relationships. During the late 1970s, sparked by Phyllis Schlafly, antifeminists courted public support by tagging the woman's movement as antifamily. As the organized woman's movement lost its forward thrust, Friedan in *The Second Stage* announced "if not the beginning of the end," the "end of the beginning" of the woman's movement. From the radical end of the spectrum, Barbara Ehrenreich agreed: "The women's movement has peaked."[9]

The mood of the 1980s was different; the woman's movement lacked focus. As Friedan looked over her shoulder, she recalled the frustrated housewives whom she had addressed in *The Feminine Mystique* and the tough-minded women professionals who had been her allies in NOW as "women with our roots in the middle American mainstream. . . ." Especially sensitive to the attack on feminism as antifamily, Friedan chastised the woman's movement for having denied "the importance of the family." She professed to be "shocked and outraged" by the "antics" of "anti-man, anti-family, bra-burning" feminist "extremists." Recanting her earlier endorsement of lesbian rights and abortion at the Houston conference, she denounced radical feminists for "[making] it easy for the so-called Moral Majority to lump the ERA with homosexual rights and abortion into one explosive package of licentious, family-threatening sex." She further indicted the radicals for their "distorted priorities" and for their preoccupation with "sexual battles" that "took energy away from the fight for the equal rights amendment. . . ." Having presumably gained a measure of equality with men, women could look forward to a "second stage" in which harmony would characterize relationships between men and women, between "women-as-individuals" and women as "servers-of-the-family." Friedan's analysis insisted that women, no less than men, should be free to develop and express their talents within the framework of marriage. Implicit in her analysis was the view that self-realization for the wife was no more threatening to the family than was self-realization for the husband.[10]

Radical feminists did not accept Friedan's reformulations. From a radical perspective, Friedan was a bourgeois reformer whose "Bill of Rights" in 1967 was "a landmark in . . . contemporary feminism," but whose *Second Stage* was "feminism's Atlanta Compromise." For her revised views she was dubbed "Aunt Betty." Sarah Stage, a historian, characterized *The Second Stage* as "perhaps as dangerous as it is specious." Friedan's failure, the radicals averred, was that she saw feminism as a reform program rather than as "a wholesale critique of the power relationship between men and women." Whereas Friedan and the moderates aimed at separate but equal roles of the marriage partners, the radicals eschewed sex roles altogether. By 1980 the tenuous alliance of the diverse women's movements at Houston had dissolved.[11]

The diversity of their ideologies stood in sharp relief. The small lesbian-feminist movement focused on all-female families and a "woman-centered culture." Socialist feminism located "the source of women's oppression in the 'larger' problems of capitalist society," while radical feminism saw "women's oppression as stemming from the nature and implications of gender itself." For radical and socialist feminists, the ERA alone was inadequate; the liberation of women required "major structural changes in the home and workplace." Although operating with differing analyses of the causes of women's "oppression," radical and socialist feminists shared a common belief in the necessity of addressing women's need for social and economic independence. Their analyses insisted that "women's economic position is a function of their social position." Conventional society presumed that a woman's job took second place either to her husband's job or to her family responsibilities. These views that reduced women to secondary-earner status were clearly dysfunctional for the woman head of a household. But even for the family that required two incomes, the disabilities under which women worked took their toll by condemning many women to working in a job for which they were overqualified, by forcing them to work longer hours than men to earn a given income, or by pressing their husbands to take a second job in order to make up the income the family needed but which women could not earn. Radical feminism took exception to the assumption that what was good for the husband was good for the family. Its solutions insisted that the well-being of the family flowed from the well-being of the wife. Radical feminists insisted that a woman ought not—as in the traditional family—be dependent on her husband for economic and psychological support; she ought to be self-sufficient.[12]

Off on the right, antifeminists represented themselves as the defenders of the traditional family. Basic to their ideology was the view that a stable family required the limitation of women's choices—especially to be sexually or economically autonomous. Family harmony required that satisfaction of the wife's sexuality take second place to her husband's. She could not terminate an unwanted pregnancy or an unrewarding marriage. Family harmony, they insisted, required a single leader—the husband—whose views must prevail should the couple disagree. By the same token he must bear the responsibility for support of the family. Family harmony required that the wife's involvement in the labor force supplement the work of her husband. This limited her to jobs that left her free to meet ongoing home-making and child-care responsibilities and barred her from demanding professional and managerial responsibilities.

One problem with the ERA, in Phyllis Schlafly's judgment, was that it threatened marriages by throwing men and women together in the work force, a situation made worse to the extent that feminism broke down the segregated labor market. A second problem was that it would drive women who were content with their "nice, comfortable kitchen," to accept work as a cook or waitress. Schlafly emphasized that the reality for at least half the nation's women was that marriage, rather than market labor, provided the principal source of their economic security. In urging women to find jobs, feminism made it easier for husbands to evade their financial obli-gations and their marriages. Furthermore, as the courts enforced equal-rights legislation, women lost their customary rights to child custody, ali-mony, and child support.[13]

By 1980 the principal center of antifeminism was the New Right. The profamily politics of the New Right neatly combined social and economic conservatism. It pulled together into a positive, profamily political alliance single-issue groups opposed to gun control, liberal divorce laws, busing, higher taxes, abortion, and welfare. "Feminists, youth culture and drugs, black music, homosexuals, abortion, pornography, liberal educators, lib-eral divorce laws, contraception, and a melange of other phenomena," Paul Weyrich argued, were "all assimilated to a common feature"; they were "destructive of the family, and along with it the society." In general, the New Right interpreted the family not as an institution evolving over time but rather as "a God-given, immutable part of a 'National order.'" Jean Bethke Elshtain, a social critic, argued that "in the absence of any workable alternative," the family was the only institution that fulfilled "the human need for intimacy, love, continuity, and security." Her argument viewed the family as a positive force, indispensible to the psychic well-being of society as compared with the radical feminists' view of the traditional family as exploitive, oppressive, and destructive to women.[14]

The debate over the character of the family was more than a matter of rhetoric; the family was in flux. During the first half of this century, the proportion of single women 14 years old and over dropped gradually from 33.3 percent in 1900 to 27.6 percent in 1940, then plummeted to 19.6 percent by 1950. In part, the increase in the proportion of women who married reflected the aging of the American population and the resulting increase in the proportion of women of marriageable age. Not all marriages endured, even in 1900; some ended in divorce, others in the death of a spouse. A tiny .5 percent were divorced in 1900, 1.66 percent in 1940. The proportion of widows remained stable during most of these years.[15]

Since 1960 the propensity of women to marry has slackened. In 1960, of the female population 18 and over, 11.9 percent had never married; by 1982 the proportion was 17.6 percent. This shift, of course, reflected chiefly the behavior of women who in 1980 were under 35 years of age—that is, women who reached adulthood in the mid-1960s and later. Between 1960 and 1982 the proportion of women married at any given time declined by nearly 10 percentage points, while that of divorced women rose by nearly 7 percentage points; the proportion of widowed women increased only 1 percentage point. Inasmuch as the number of women 20 to 35 years of age who had never married doubled between 1960 and 1982, the prospects were that the number and percentage of never-married women would continue to rise during the eighties and nineties. Yet even among those women in their early 30s, seven of every eight had married.[16]

Marriage was far from dead, but American behavior with respect to the proper age for marriage, nontraditional family groupings, the desired family size, and the acceptability of divorce were changing. This became apparent after World War II as nonfamily households and single-parent households proliferated far more rapidly than married-couple households. Thus, while the number of married-couple households—the ideal that made traditionalists misty-eyed—grew from 34 million in 1950 to 49.5 million in 1982, an increase of 44.1 percent, in the same time period, nonfamily households increased from 4.7 million to 22.5 million—a five-fold increase—and the number of female householders increased two and one-half times, reaching 9.4 million in 1982. Although the family in which Dad goes out to earn a living while Mom stays home with the kids remained the ideal, the reality was that of 51.5 million family households in 1970, only one half consisted of married couples with children under 18, and by 1982 the proportion had dropped to 40.1 percent. And the family was changing in other ways, too.[17]

A changed view of marriage was expressed in an upward shift in the age at which women married for the first time. In 1963 when Friedan published her *Feminine Mystique,* the median age at first marriage for women was 20.5 years. By 1970 when Firestone's *Dialectic of Sex* appeared, the median age had risen to 20.8. During the intense atmosphere of the seventies, the median age continued to rise, and in 1980 it was 22.0—the highest in this century—and still rising. The propensity to marry later affected the whole spectrum of women. Whereas of the women who married in 1963 one fourth were 18.6 or under, in 1982 one fourth were 19.6

or under. While in 1963 one fourth of the first-time brides were 22.5 or older, in 1982 one fourth were 26.6 or older. During the same interval, the median age at first marriage for males rose even more sharply than for women, rising from 22.8 to 25.2 years. These rates for women (and for men) in the 1980s approximated those last seen in the 1890s and 1900s.[18]

The delay in marriage had its own raison d'être. As the median age at first marriage was rising prior to the publication of Friedan's book, it is evident that it was not a by-product of the feminist movement. Paul Glick, a demographer, has suggested that when the first cohort of women in the baby-boom generation came of age in the mid-1960s, there was a "marriage squeeze" because of the smaller number of males in the cohorts from which they would ordinarily find a husband. But here, too, the deferral of marriage preceded the "marriage squeeze." Like reemergent feminism, it reinforced the delay in marriage. Certainly the availability of jobs tempted some women to delay marriage, while the growing mood of disenchantment with traditional values led others to forgo marriage for the time being.[19]

This delay in marriage had important implications both for the woman and for society. First, it enabled most women to complete high school and permitted many time to pursue a higher education before assuming the responsibilities of homemaking and child care. During the 1970s alone, the proportion of women who put off marriage to age 23 doubled. Second, it afforded a woman an extra year or two or even three to establish her identity as an autonomous person through a job. Indeed, the increase in the proportion of single women was greatest among women who did not attend college, and at every age level delay added to the proportion of women most available to the labor force. Finally, the delay in marriage had long-term implications for the number of children a woman would ever bear.[20]

The postponing of marriage was accompanied by a drop in the birthrate. In the family-centered climate of the fifties, the birthrate for women 20 to 24 years old reached a peak of 260.6 in 1957 and held steady to the end of the decade. In the milieu of student unrest, the civil-rights movement, and the antiwar movement, the birthrate dropped, so that in 1969 at 166.0 it was at the lowest level since the end of World War II; and it continued to decline, bottoming out in 1978 at 109.9. By 1980 the rate was on the rise, having reached 115.1. This reluctance of women to bear children was not, of course, restricted to women 20 to 24 years old, and indeed the fertility rate (the number of children per 1,000 women of childbearing age) dropped from a high of 3,767 children per 1,000 women in 1957 to a low of 1,760 in 1978. In fact, after 1972 the rate was below the level needed to maintain a constant population.[21]

A corollary of the drop in fertility rates was an increase in childlessness. Changes in attitudes toward childbearing were almost immediately reflected in the proportion of childless wives in their early 20s. Among ever-married women 20 to 24 years old, the proportion who were childless increased from 35.7 percent in 1970 to 42.9 percent in 1982. Of the baby-boom cohort born 1946 to 1950, women who were nearing the end of their prime childbearing years in 1980, 13.7 percent were childless compared to 8.3 percent for women in the 1935-to-1939 cohort at the same stage in life. This statistic suggests that the inclination to forgo bearing children was rooted in attitudes that became operative in the mid-sixties. The declining birthrates of the seventies were reflected promptly in a smaller average-family size, the median number of children for married-couple families dropping from 2.3 to 1.9 in just eight years from 1970 to 1978. Clearly, the postponing of marriage, the lower birthrates, the increase in the proportion of childless wives, and the smaller families facilitated the entrance of married women into the labor force.[22]

But the causal relationships between changing fertility rates and LFPRs were not simple. Whether they were in the labor force or not, mothers from married-couple families had virtually the same number of children, but of mothers who did not live with their spouses, those in the labor force had fewer children than those who were not in the labor force. Among childless wives, 76 percent of those age 16 to 24 were in the labor force as were 81 percent of those age 25 to 34, compared with 40 and 49 percent, respectively, of the mothers. Whether couples restricted family size in order to permit the wife to work outside the home or whether working mothers restricted their fertility to remain on the job has been the subject of much research. Richard Easterlin has suggested an inverse relationship between cohort size and fertility; that is, women in the small birth cohorts of the 1930s experienced favorable labor-market conditions in the 1950s in part because of their "smallness," and, enjoying a comfortable level of living, they increased their fertility. William Butz and Michael Ward, using microeconomic theory of utility maximization, related the postwar upswing in fertility to rising male income; the decline in fertility of the 1960s and 1970s, to rising female wages and female employment ratios. More recently Barbara Devaney has argued that female wage rates are "the dominant factor in explaining recent variations in fertility and female labor force participation." The opportunity costs of child care and housekeeping became so high that wives chose to limit fertility and to work outside the home.[23]

In economic terms, these opportunity costs were directly proportional to the level of education: the more time, energy, and money a woman invested in her education, the greater the incentive to limit her fertility and seek a job. Between 1960 and 1970 the fertility rate of women 20 to 24 years of age with four years of high school dropped 22 percent, but for those with four years of college, it dropped over twice as much. Black women—whose commitment to the civil-rights movement tended to keep them out of the woman's movement—reduced their fertility levels by lesser amounts, 12 percent for those with high-school diplomas and 20 percent for those with four years of college. That college women experienced the largest reductions in fertility rates confirms that they were more responsive to the social ferment of the sixties than less-educated women. Data for the seventies affirms that the higher the level of education women attained, the lower the level of fertility.[24]

One indication of a weakening attachment to traditional values respecting the family was the increase in out-of-wedlock childbearing. Illegitimacy, of course, was not a twentieth-century innovation. But birth-registration data documents major increases in the rate of illegitimacy between 1940 and 1980. Whereas in 1940 there were 7.1 out-of-wedlock births per 1,000 unmarried women 15 to 44 years old, in 1980 the rate was 29.4. In 1940 4.0 percent of all births were out-of-wedlock; in 1980, 18.4 percent. Out-of-wedlock children accounted for less than 2 percent of white babies in 1950, under 6 percent in 1970, and 11 percent in 1980. By contrast, out-of-wedlock children accounted for one sixth of the nonwhite babies in 1950, one third in 1970, and almost one half in 1980. Out-of-wedlock childbearing was more prevalent among women from very low income families than among those from higher income families; it occurred far more commonly among those who had not completed high school than among those who had completed at least one year of college. The pattern of changes in out-of-wedlock birthrates was complex. During the fifties the rate for teenagers increased by one third; that for women 20 through 34 more than doubled. During the sixties, the rate for teenagers increased by one half; the rates for older women remained constant or even declined slightly. During the seventies, the rate for teenagers increased by one fifth; for women in their early 20s, by less than 10 percent; and for those 25 through 34, the rate continued to drop.[25]

The connections between reemergent feminism and the escalating rate of out-of-wedlock births was tenuous. The incidence of out-of-wedlock childbearing in the 1980s reflected much the same pattern as the incidence of premarital sexual activity reported by Alfred Kinsey a third of a century before, suggesting that it was a cultural rather than an ideological phenomenon. It was likewise significant that out-of-wedlock childbearing was concentrated in the population that had the highest unemployment rates and, hence, the greatest difficulty in establishing a stable economic basis for marriage. Although the radical feminists often rejected monogamous marriage and extolled single motherhood as a legitimate option, the out-of-wedlock birthrate had been rising for two decades before the radical doctrine began to be articulated. Furthermore, the women under 20 years old and black women in general were among the least receptive to the radical doctrines. At the same time, in arguing that sexuality could be legitimately expressed outside the marriage relationship, radicals put at risk those women who accepted that part of their doctrine.[26]

More reflective of the radical-feminist critique of the family was the rise of the living-together arrangement. Although unmarried-couple households existed prior to 1970 when Shulamith Firestone outlined various modes of living-together, relatively few unmarried-couple households—1 in 20—was maintained by a householder under 25 years of age, and another 1 in 9 was headed by a householder between 25 and 34 years. In the decade that followed, the number of households composed of unmarried couples increased threefold. By 1982, however, of the 1.86 million such households, 1 in 5 was headed by a householder under 25, and another 3 in 10 had a householder between 25 and 34. Four fifths of the growth of these unmarried-coupled households involved householders without children. Despite the great publicity that the living-together arrangement occasioned, such households represented but 3 households in 100 in 1980.[27]

Divorce, which in 1900 was tolerated at best, progressively lost its onus. And while feminists had an existential view of marriage and divorce, their support of divorce-on-demand reinforced a secular trend that had pushed the divorce rate up generation by generation. The conventional explanations for the rise in divorce rates in the 1960s and 1970s cited the liberalization of divorce laws, the impact of the Vietnam War, and the rise in women's labor-force rates. These explanations were questionable, for the rise in divorce rates in the seventies was not unique to the United States. The rate—the annual number of divorces per 1,000 married women, age 15 and over—was 10.3 in 1950, reflecting the termination of many wartime and postwar marriages. Subsequently the rate dipped to 9.2, still a higher rate than for any year before World War II. Thereafter it bounced upward to 10.6 in 1965, then shot upward to 14.9 in 1970, 20.3 in 1975, and 22.6 in 1980.[28]

An examination of the age-specific divorce rates indicates that the rise was stimulated by different age groups from one time period to another. During the early sixties, the annual divorce rate for women in their late 40s increased more rapidly than the rate for women of any other age group except those in their late 20s. During the period of its most rapid growth, 1965 to 1975, over 60 percent of the increase in divorce was attributable to women in their 20s, although they represented but one fifth of the married population.[29]

As the divorce rate advanced, receded, then soared, the ratio of divorced persons grew. This ratio—the number of divorced persons per 1,000 persons in intact marriages—reflected the rates of divorce in earlier years as well as the remarriage of divorced persons. In 1960, there were 35 divorced persons for every 1,000 married persons; the figure advanced to 47 in 1970, then jumped to 100 in 1980, and was still hurtling upward in 1982. Reflecting the greater propensity of males to remarry, the ratios were higher for females than for males by about 50 percent; the stresses on black marriages resulted in ratios double those for white persons. Here again the secular trend had produced a slowly climbing divorce ratio that the feminist movement of the sixties and seventies reinforced. The freer access to jobs and the higher educational attainment of younger women further eased the way of the woman who sought marital freedom.[30]

The lessening dependence of women on marriage for economic and psychological support had a major impact on the living arrangements of children. The number living with both parents dropped by one fifth during the seventies, so that in 1980 only 75 of every 100 children lived in a two-parent family. The rising incidence of divorce added over 1,000,000 youngsters a year to single-parent homes. Another notable source of single-parent families was the unmarried mother and her offspring, of whom two thirds of a million were born in 1982. Between 1970 and 1982 the number of children living with an unmarried mother increased from 527,000 to 2.8 million. Female-headed families increasingly provoked national attention because a large proportion lived below the poverty line and, hence, were welfare clients.[31]

The black family in particular became a "problem" family. The proportion of black women choosing to remain single increased by two thirds during the seventies; the number who were divorced nearly doubled. Relative to white women, the divorce rate for black women was twice as high. By 1980 only 42 percent of the children in the black community lived in two-parent families; 47 percent lived with their mother; 2 percent, with their father; and 9 percent, with someone other than a parent. This was not a matter of minority status, for in the Hispanic communities 69 percent of the children lived in two-parent families; only 27 percent lived with a single parent, typically a divorced or separated mother. Particularly distressing was the rise in the proportion of births to unwed black women. The rate, which had been one in six in 1950, exceeded one in three in 1970, was over one in two by 1976, and was still climbing. Many of these women were less than 20 years old. In the 1980s, black leaders who had challenged the Moynihan reports began to explore ways of coping with the troubled black family.[32]

As America entered the eighties, the family was far from dead, but Americans regarded it differently than they had at the start of the century or even at the end of World War II. Marriage, though important, was less sacrosanct. Young women—especially the college-educated—would enter marriage in their late 20s or 30s, having first acquired considerable experience in a career. A minority might live with a male more or less openly without the formality of marriage, and a few of these couples might have children. Yet the prospects were that most women would marry, but in marrying later in life, they would have fewer children than their counterparts of 1900. Most brides of the eighties expected to share in the support of the family. If the marriage proved unsatisfying, they were not averse to terminating it. And the prospects were that many more of the brides of the eighties would divorce and become female heads of households. Many of the children born to these women would live part of their childhood in a home with both parents, part of their lives with a single parent, and perhaps part of their lives with a stepparent.[33]

EQUALITY IN THE CLASSROOM

While Stanton had charged in 1848 that man denied woman "the facilities for obtaining a thorough education," in 1969 NOW still found it needful to assert "the right of women to be educated to their full potential." In 1900 girls enjoyed about the same access to elementary education as boys; the proportion of young women who graduated from high school was well ahead of the proportion of males doing so; and at the collegiate level, women lagged males in taking baccalaureate degrees by a margin of one to four. While a majority of youngsters attended elementary school, only a tiny minority went to high school and a still smaller group to college. By 1920, evolving technology necessitated the extension of secondary education to the native white population; during the late 1940s the demand for college-trained youth burgeoned, and in the 1950s blacks demanded that they be given equal educational opportunities at all levels. As NOW focused on women's rights, it pointed to the elimination of "all discrimination and segregation by sex, written and unwritten, at all levels of education, including colleges, graduate and professional schools, loans and fellowships, and federal and state training programs such as the Job Corps."[34]

Women of the 1980s could count many blessings. School enrollment rates for children of elementary-school age had passed the 90 percent level in the mid-1940s; the proportion of 18-year-old women completing high school had risen from 7.4 percent in 1900 to 74.3 percent in 1980. Equally impressive was the quantum advance from the less than 6 women per 1,000 23-year-olds who earned a baccalaureate in 1900 to the nearly 300 in 1980.[35]

The question arises: how much equality of educational opportunity had women achieved? Specifically, how had minority women fared in the classroom relative to majority women? How had the various groups of minority women fared with respect to their own past experiences? How had women fared relative to males of their own ethnic group?

The experiences of majority women, that is, white women not of Hispanic origin, provide a benchmark for women's educational attainment. By most standards they had done well, and their lot was improving. During the 1960s and 1970s, the proportion who were two or more years behind the most common grade level for their age declined; the proportion who dropped out without completing high school fell by one half; the proportion who completed high school rose by more than one fifth; and the proportion who completed college more than doubled. A young woman in America in the 1980s enjoyed broader educational opportunities than any cohort before her.[36]

Minority women, in general, raised their level of educational attainment during the sixties and seventies. As the proportion of young women who were behind in grade level or who dropped out of school fell, the proportion who completed high school rose. For black women, the proportion who completed high school rose from 42 percent in 1960 to 74 percent in 1976; for Mexican American women, the proportion of graduates rose from 35 to 58 percent in the same interval. These gains were especially important both because of the magnitude of the advance and the size of the minority. All groups of minority women increased their college-completion rates, but the rates for Indian, black, Mexican American, and Puerto Rican women were no higher than 5 percent in 1976.[37]

While minority women consistently improved their educational attainment, their performance as compared with majority women varied. In most respects the educational attainments of women of Japanese, Chinese, and Filipino origin or parentage surpassed those of majority women. Women of all three groups were more likely to be at the grade level appropriate for their age; Japanese American students had a lower dropout rate; both Chinese Americans and Japanese Americans completed high school and college in larger proportions than majority women. Black women, however, fared less well. Although their dropout rate fell to the same level as that of majority women, they were twice as likely to lag in grade level and were well behind in terms of completing high school and college. But in every respect, the gap between the educational attainments of black women and majority women narrowed during these years. Most disadvantaged were Indian and Hispanic women, especially Puerto Ricans. The proportion of these women who at age 15 through 17 were two or more years behind the grade level appropriate for their age level was three to four times that for majority women; the proportion of dropouts was at least twice as high; and the proportion of college graduates, one fifth to one fourth as large.[38]

When the attainments of women are measured against those of males, the picture is mixed. Both majority and minority women were less likely to be behind in school than the males of their own group. Both majority women and black women had high-school dropout rates comparable to their male peers, but the proportion of Indian, Mexican American, Filipino American, and Puerto Rican women completing high school was 6 to 12 percentage points lower than for males of their own group. College-completion rates for women were generally lower than for males of their own group by a margin of 22 to 34 points for majority women, 5 to 11 points for Mexican Americans. Among black males and females, however, the college-completion rates were the same by 1976. While women still lagged males in high-school and college completion, their gains over the years were impressive.[39]

By the end of the seventies, women had won the struggle for access to the full range of undergraduate programs, and for the first time they constituted a majority of the undergraduate body. Women were also expanding their share of degrees in male-dominated fields such as business and management, the physical sciences, engineering, and the professions. For the woman seeking a career, the opportunity to pursue collegiate studies of her choice was as vital to her as to any male; for the woman who accorded family interests higher priority than a lifelong career, a free choice of educational programs greatly enhanced opportunities for her to develop interests and skills that would enrich her life as homemaker and add to her employability if she chose to work on occasion.[40]

Access to undergraduate-, graduate-, and professional-school classrooms promised expanded public roles for women. As the Lynds discovered in Muncie in the 1920s, the more formal education a woman had, the greater her participation in the public life of her community would be. Whereas working-class women experienced "social isolation," college-educated women felt fewer qualms about registering, voting, campaigning, or even seeking public office. As a disproportionate number of officeholders were lawyers or businessmen, policies that excluded women from these occupations had the side effect of excluding them from public office as well. In the 1970s the pool of women with baccalaureate degrees who were in their 50s and 60s—the age at which men commonly attained major state and national offices—was one-half to two-thirds that of men; women in that age group with law degrees were outnumbered by men 20 to 1. Considering the reduction in the differentials in educational attainment during the 1970s, one would expect younger women in the 1980s to register and vote in proportions similar to younger men; likewise, one might expect that, by the late 1990s, given the projected pool of women in their early 40s with career experience, there should be equal numbers of qualified women and men to choose from in the selection of local party candidates. But to the extent that a law degree remains an asset for major public offices, the projected pool of potential candidates at the start of the next century should contain but one woman for every four men. At this level the realization of equality lies far in the future.[41]

Equal access to collegiate education promised to have its greatest impact on women's perception of themselves and on society's attitudes toward them. Women have long had the reputation of being inhibited in mixed company—less able to share fully in conversation, more likely to be interrupted—and of being regarded as superficial when they were not ignored. So long as the pool of educated men far exceeded that of educated women, large numbers of college-educated males married women less well educated than themselves, a circumstance that encouraged the husband to put the wife down and inhibited her from challenging the views of her husband and his male associates.[42]

In the aggregate, a college education had "profound effects" on traditional sex roles, marital relationships, divorce, family planning, rearing of children, and other family relationships. In assessing "The Effects of Going to College," Howard R. Bowen concluded that a college education was associated with "a perceptible narrowing of traditional differences between the sexes in interests, attitudes, and behavior patterns." College-educated couples, he reported, tended to share roles. College-educated men shared more fully in housework and the care of children than did noncollege men; at the same time, college-trained women were less likely to expect "masculine" behavior of men. Thus, college education promoted the androgynous personality.[43]

But college education did more; it had a potential for enriching the quality of women's lives and of their families as well. Among both sexes, college seniors viewed the woman's movement with more favor than did freshmen, suggesting that the college experience broadened viewpoints. Unplanned, unwanted, and actual births were inversely related to education, indicating that college-educated individuals exercised a higher level of control over their sexuality than others. In their family life, college-educated parents expended more "thought, time, and money" on behalf of their children than their non-college-educated peers. Likewise, the college-educated couple spent more for books, magazines, and reading material. Among persons with equal incomes, the college-educated spent a smaller proportion of their income on food, tobacco, alcohol, and automobiles. Education per se, Bowen argued, "enhances the life chances— the opportunities and personal happiness" of the offspring of the college-educated. These advantages in turn affected succeeding generations, which he termed perhaps "the most important single consequence of higher education." At the very least, the growing equality of access to collegiate, graduate, and professional education opened to women broader roles in public affairs and the job market, as well as the prospect of a greater degree of self-respect, a greater sense of achievement and self-fulfillment.[44]

CIVIL RIGHTS AND PRIVILEGES

At the beginning of the 1980s the central issues concerning the political and legal status of women were focused in the ERA, which was still awaiting ratification. Women were not of a single mind about the ERA. Some, comfortable with their roles as wives and mothers and with a mix of volunteer and paid work, remained apprehensive about the changes an ERA might mean in their lives; others, aware of discrimination against women, believed that specific inequities should be resolved by specific reforms. Yet others— a majority according to the public opinion polls—supported ratification of the ERA. Most of those who had taken part in or followed the ERA debate in the seventies recognized that glaring differences continued to exist between the civil, contractual, and property rights of women and men. While in 1980 the debate over the ERA preempted the headlines and absorbed much of the energy of the feminists, the abortion issue increasingly attracted attention. As the ERA failed to be ratified, the Houston coalition disintegrated; moderate feminists and radical feminists, as well as antifeminists, articulated diverse approaches to women's issues.[45]

By the start of the eighties the woman's movement was mired down. Although the ERA had received 35 ratifications and enjoyed broad support, no state had ratified it since Indiana early in 1977, and several states had rescinded their ratifications. As the rise of the New Right gave respectability to traditional practices, conservatives grabbed the lead in critiquing public policy. James Kilpatrick, a widely syndicated columnist, took the tack that the defeat of the ERA would be no tragedy, since the U.S. Supreme Court "little by little" with "some help from Congress" was "granting ERA proponents almost everything they reasonably might ask from the amendment itself." Women were losing the battle but winning the war. In Kilpatrick's opinion, the ERA was a "blunderbuss." The use of law suits and statutory amendments were far more preferable as "rifles, capable of hitting precise targets and no others." Kilpatrick also reflected the conservative's fear of the assertion of authority by the federal government. In this view the ERA was "virtually a blank check" authorizing the Supreme Court "to rewrite all the laws that in any way distinguish between male and female. For the states to cede this power to the national government would be to renounce the right to govern themselves in significant respects." Phyllis Schlafly continued to reach a broad audience with her oft-reiterated claim that the ERA threatened women in traditional family roles. "We do not want to be coerced and conscripted into a world in which women will be treated exactly like men," she declared.[46]

Despite action by Congress that extended the deadline for ratification of the ERA to June 30, 1982, the pro-ERA forces were unable to regain the initiative. NOW focused its efforts on seven states—Georgia, Florida, Illinois, Missouri, North Carolina, Oklahoma, and Virginia—in which approval hinged on a few votes in the legislature. But to no avail. Preoccupied with budget cuts and legislative reapportionment, state legislators were leery of embracing a position that might provoke a voter backlash against them. Further, in 1980 the Republican National Convention, at the behest of the Reagan faction, endorsed a plank that called for "equal rights and equal opportunities for women" while leaving the fate of the ERA to the states "without federal interference or pressure." In the midst of campaigns to get the needed ratifications, U.S. District Judge Marion Callister—a onetime Mormon Church official—held that Congress had acted unconstitutionally in extending the deadline to ratify the ERA. He further ruled that Idaho, Tennessee, Kentucky, South Dakota, and Nebraska were within their rights in rescinding their acts of ratification of the ERA. The pro-ERA forces were stunned, and while they did not abandon the fight, for the most part they grasped for straws. NOW pressed the U.S. Department of Justice to appeal Judge Callister's decision, but the Reagan leadership declined to do so. As time ran out in June 1982, Mariwyn Heath for the National Federation of Business and Professional Women's Clubs recognized the realities of the moment: "I do not think a reintroduced ERA can pass the [U.S.] Senate as it is presently constituted." An ecstatic Phyllis Schlafly announced, the ERA "is dead for now and forever in this century."[47]

In the aftermath there were a variety of postmortems. Some like that of Joan Beck, a Chicago *Tribune* columnist, blamed the defeat on "women who have yet to develop sufficient leadership, political savvy, lobbying skills and clout to elect candidates and get legislation passed with consistency." Militant feminists received special condemnation, especially those Illinois activists who, emulating Alice Paul, had chained themselves together outside the Illinois Senate chambers as well as those who had written in animal blood the names of anti-ERA legislators on the walks about the State House. Others argued that the initial "popularity of the ERA lulled its proponents into complacency." Thus, supporters had failed to establish a national head-quarters or to develop and fund state coalitions. Indeed, Gloria Steinem and her coeditors of *Ms.* magazine attributed the defeat to three reasons: (1) "too many people, both men and women," who "dislike women"; (2) "most of the majority" who, having expressed support in the polls, remained "at best, complacently expectant instead of becoming politically insistent"; and (3) an opposition that was "better organized." Still other critiques focused on the role of interest groups that felt threatened by the ERA or by one aspect or another of the women's movement. These ranged from the American Farm Bureau Federation and Amway to the Mormon Church and the Moral Majority. Not the least were the nation's banking and insurance communities. While there was some merit to these explanations, they tended to ignore the fact that the legislatures of 35 of the 50 states had ratified the ERA and that throughout the seventies and into the eighties public opinion polls confirmed that the ERA had the support of a majority of the American people.[48]

Undoubtedly proponents of the ERA had failed to recognize the degree to which opponents perceived feminism and the ERA as threatening "to destroy the American family and sap the strength of a society already crippled by moral permissiveness and political weakness and indecision." The opponents succeeded in politicizing "women whose personal and familial experience made them wary of changes that would transform their way of life." The proponents of ratification dismissed as "alarmist apocalyptism" claims that ratification of the ERA would bring the drafting of young mothers, sexual integration of public rest rooms, decriminalization of rape, legitimation of homosexuality, entrenchment of abortion, increased opportunities for federal intervention, the loss by women of legal privileges, and the destruction of the family. But underlying these extravagant allegations, were "patterns of behavior and shared ways of talking about self and community," which had provided coherence to the lives of these women and which the ERA threatened to destroy. The ERA became "the symbol of feminism, an ideology profoundly alien to their experience of what being a woman meant." Indeed, the opponents perceived the woman's movement as "part of the degeneracy" and "the confusion" of society.[49]

The checkmating of the ERA owed far more to the role of parliamentary tactics designed to thwart the popular will than to ineptitude on the part of the ERA leadership or the skills of the STOP ERA leadership. Ratification rested with 50 separate state legislatures, in each of which the legislative process allowed willful legislators to exercise exceptional influence exempt from popular pressure. Illinois opponents to the ERA, for example, were able to fend off ratification by the requirement of a three-fifths majority to ratify an amendment. In North Carolina a gentlemen's agreement of 13 key legislators kept the amendment from coming to the floor for debate and vote. In Virginia, where redistricting in accordance with the 1980 census was incomplete, legislators were unwilling to take on a controversial issue. In both Oklahoma and Virginia the ERA failed by a single vote in the state senates. Of special importance was the resistance of the southern states to the measure. Efforts to revive the ERA in 1983 failed in the House by a margin of six votes.[50]

Abortion Rights

A woman's right to decide whether to terminate her pregnancy generated far more controversy than the ERA. One line of attack on *Roe* v. *Wade* (1973) came in the form of local and state legislation to curb abortions; the other, in the form of a constitutional amendment to overturn *Roe* v. *Wade*. The most sweeping of the local ordinances, that of Akron, Ohio, placed a number of obstacles in the path of access to abortion, including a highly detailed "informed consent" provision, a 24-hour waiting period, and a requirement that all abortions beyond the first trimester be performed in hospitals. In striking down the Akron ordinance, the U.S. Supreme Court stood its ground by reaffirming that "the right of privacy . . . encompasses a woman's right to decide whether to terminate her pregnancy." The decision was important in several respects. It left the *Roe* decision intact. It rejected an argument advanced by the Reagan administration that the justices adopt a "deferential standard," that is, that the Court give the legislators the benefit of the doubt with respect to the constitutionality of the measure. The decision also had practical significance, since 21 states limited second trimester abortions to hospitals, and the validity of these statutes now became suspect. The court did not authorize abortion on demand; it remained a medical decision to be made by a patient and her doctor.

In a companion case the Court upheld portions of a Missouri statute, notably those requiring the presence of a second physician at third-trimester abortions and a provision for parental or judicial consent before an abortion might be performed on a teenager who was not considered "emancipated" or mature enough to make her own decision. This latter decision was consistent with a position the Court had taken in 1979 that "the State may not impose a blanket provision requiring the consent by a parent . . . as a condition for an abortion of an unmarried minor." A state could require parental consent, however, if it also provided a procedure by which a pregnant minor might demonstrate to the court that she was sufficiently mature to make an abortion decision herself or that, despite her immaturity, an abortion would be in her best interests. Although the

The controversy engendered by the abortion issue led pro-life and pro-choice demonstrators to engage in shouting matches.

woman's movement had come under bitter attack for endorsing a woman's right to abortion, the initiative in contesting the constitutionality of the Akron and Missouri laws was taken by the American Civil Liberties Union, and it was their attorney who hailed the decision as "an enormous victory for women's rights."[51]

While the Akron case wound its way through the courts, in 1982 Senators Jesse Helms and Orrin Hatch, the chief antiabortion leaders in Congress, moved to overturn the *Roe* decision. Helms introduced a human-life bill that would establish the legal personhood of a fetus. His measure included a declaration that Congress believed that "scientific evidence demonstrates that the life of each human being begins at conception." Senator Hatch proposed a constitutional amendment: "A right to abortion is not secured by this Constitution." Despite the intensity with which the antiabortionists denounced the "immorality" of abortion, they were widely split; some favored Helms' human-life bill, others were pledged to Hatch's amendment. As President Reagan endorsed the antiabortion position and welcomed March-for-Life leaders to the Oval Office, pro-choice organizations—Planned Parenthood, the National Abortion Rights Action League, the Religious Coalition for Abortion Rights, Catholics for Free Choice, and the American Civil Liberties Union—joined forces. Aligned with them were NOW, the Ms. Foundation for Women, the American Medical Association, and the American Bar Association. In the showdown Helms abandoned his human-life bill to support an alternative measure, which he tied to a school-prayer bill. The tactic, far from gaining support for his antiabortion measure, divided his followers, and the pro-choice coalition succeeded in sidelining his proposal. Subsequently, when the Hatch amendment came forward for a vote, it was defeated 50 to 49, a solid defeat since the amendment required a two-thirds majority to pass.[52]

The abortion issue raised a variety of nonlegal, nonconstitutional issues. First, women were highly ambivalent in their attitudes toward abortion. In the most comprehensive survey of opinion, Yankelovich, Skelley, and White reported in November 1981 that whereas 56 percent of their national sample thought having an abortion was morally wrong, 67 percent thought that any woman who wanted an abortion should be permitted to obtain it legally. Women's opinions varied "by region, income group, religion, race, and every other significant demographic factor." Yet the national consensus was clear, for not one major group believed a woman should be denied the right to choose an abortion if she determined that procedure was necessary. It was also the case that women were far less supportive of freedom of choice for an unmarried teenager than for an adult woman. A majority of women believed a teenager should be required to notify her parents if she chose an abortion. Furthermore, a large minority believed that the mother of a pregnant unmarried high-school girl should encourage her to have the baby.[53]

Second, the morality or immorality of abortion continued to provoke controversy. A resolution of the matter was not forthcoming, since the major religious bodies disagreed over the moment when human life began. To Catholics, abortion entailed the taking of human life, but Protestants and Jews were divided on the issue. The mainline Protestant churches and secular and liberal Jews tended to support abortion; Protestant fundamentalists and Orthodox Jews were likely to oppose it. In these circumstances both proponents and opponents of free choice clothed their arguments in terms of right and wrong. Furthermore, opponents could point an accusing finger at "immoral" single women and welfare mothers who, rather than curb their sexuality, sought to avoid the consequences by resorting to an abortion.[54]

To those who equated abortion with the taking of human life, *Roe* v. *Wade* was immoral in that it seemed to elevate abortion "to the status of a constitutional right throughout the nine months of pregnancy." Deeply offended, Catholic opponents drew an analogy between abortion and slavery, between *Roe* v. *Wade* and the *Dred Scott* decision. Abolitionists, they recalled, had condemned slavery as immoral. When the Supreme Court in the *Dred Scott* case affirmed the constitutionality of slavery, those opposed to slavery felt compelled to overturn the judgment of the Court by amending the Constitution—the Thirteenth Amendment. So now, the analogy ran, abortion is immoral; therefore, the Court's judgment must be overturned by constitutional amendment. In this context in November 1981 the National Conference of Catholic Bishops endorsed the Hatch amendment.[55]

Third, in many minds the ERA and abortion seemed interrelated. From the start, NOW endorsed both reproductive freedom and an ERA, though these two planks reflected NOW's concept of feminism rather than an intrinsic relationship between the two. Phyllis Schlafly did much to promote this identification by repeatedly asserting that an ERA would "repeal all and every kind of antiabortion laws we now have and prevent enactment of any antiabortion law in the future." Disregarding such claims, the National Conference of Catholic Charities endorsed both the ERA and the Human Life Bill. Similarly the Leadership Conference of Women Religious pointed out that "the issues around which the abortion debate rages are not the issues entailed in the Equal Rights Amendment. . . ." Those court decisions that affirmed freedom of choice, they argued, were grounded in the constitutionally guaranteed right of privacy—First and Fifth Amendment rights, while the ERA debate focused on the equal-protection clause of the Fourteenth Amendment.[56]

The abortion issue remained highly divisive in the eighties. A majority of women, many of them rejecting abortion as an option they would pursue for themselves, affirmed their support of freedom of choice for other women. Yet a determined minority was committed to prohibiting abortion. Because freedom of choice seemed linked to the ERA, opponents of the latter seemed likely to continue to exploit the abortion issue in order to discredit the ERA. The success of medical doctors in saving the lives of premature babies strengthened the hand of those who equated abortion with the taking of human life, but the proportion of abortions occurring beyond the first trimester dropped during the seventies and involved fewer than 9 abortions in every 100.[57]

The Shifting Debate

Expiration of the time limit for the ratification of the ERA, far from ending the controversy over women's civil status, only transformed it. On the left, radical feminists, predominantly younger college-educated women, were bent on creating "a new, androgynous version of the marital relationship." Of critical importance to realization of their goals was giving the individual woman control over her reproduction, including access to abortion, an end to the double standard in sex behavior, reform of rape laws, and adoption of child-care arrangements that increased a mother's competitiveness in the job market. They were clearly determined to reduce "the role of the family, of a husband and children, in defining a woman's life and identity." They had opposed the Hyde amendment, which had cut off Medicaid funds for abortions. In the center, moderate feminists, somewhat older and predominantly white and middle-class, shared common interests in equality with men, especially in the labor market. These women were particularly sensitive to practices that discriminated against them in private pension plans, life-insurance policies, and Social Security benefits. Both radicals and moderates felt threatened by the reluctance of the Reagan administration to enforce Title VII and Title IX.[58]

On the right, antifeminists sought to enlist the power of the state to establish the "moral mother" and a "moral society." As Phyllis Schlafly defined the issues, the "gender-free, rigid, absolute equality of treatment of men and women" that the ERA would create threatened "a radical loosening of the legal bonds that tend to keep the family together." With concerns far broader than antifeminism, the New Right made "the politics of the family, sexuality, and reproduction—and most directly of abortion"— a primary instrument of their rise to power. The New Right sought to shrink government and to shift some functions to state and local political agencies, but it also sought the "reprivatization" of society—to promote a social order in which benefits came from the private sector rather than from the state. The New Right was also militantly anticommunist and almost paranoid in its sense of urgency in enlarging the military apparatus of the United States.[59]

With its original constituency in the business world and concerned with limiting government regulation of business, the New Right was able to expand its constituency by becoming a vehicle for opposition to the ERA and abortion and by "galvanizing" additional voters, funds, and resources. Thus it linked an antifeminist backlash to an anti-social-welfare backlash. This linking of antifeminism to the New Right in turn expanded the outreach of antifeminists.[60]

Responding to the concerns of the New Right, the 1980 Republican party platform spoke of restraining the federal government from exercising "power over families." Posing as a defender of the traditional family—one in which the wife was primarily a homebody caring for her husband and children—the Reagan administration regarded the social programs of the sixties and seventies as unnecessary if not misguided. In practice it sought to limit the number of federal contractors subject to affirmative-action requirements; it rejected the use of numerical goals and timetables in the enforcement of Title VII of the Civil Rights Act. It was less assiduous in enforcing Title IX. While talking of reducing federal programs overall, the administration ended by seeking to reduce federally supported social programs for child care, food stamps, and Medicaid and Medicare—programs with a large clientele of women and children. The administration also opposed federal programs respecting domestic violence, family planning or birth control for teenagers, federal funds for gay, lesbian, or women's studies, and school busing for racially balanced schools. Despite its distaste for deficit spending and large federal budgets, the administration found little difficulty justifying greatly increased outlays on weapons systems.[61]

This marriage of antifeminism to the New Right in the service of preserving the American family was reflected in Paul Laxalt's Family Protection Act. Introduced in the 96th Congress, his measure was designed to make "the family" the final authority over all "moral" questions and the husband the "household head." Specific provisions were designed to reward those persons who embraced the traditional family. Among these were tax benefits for married couples filing joint federal income tax returns and tax deductions for nonworking married women engaged in "volunteer," "charity," or "religious" work. In addition Laxalt proposed to reauthorize "voluntary prayer" in the public schools, to authorize parents to review school textbooks, to reauthorize sex segregation in sports or other school-related activities, to withhold funds from school programs that "tend to denigrate, diminish or deny the role differences between the sexes as it has been historically understood," and to offer tax credits to parents of children enrolled in private or parochial schools. A miscellany of provisions aimed at withholding funds for any individual or group advocating homosexuality, at requiring parental notification for teenage birth or abortion services, and at granting immunity from federal supervision to all religious and other private welfare and educational programs, child-care centers, counseling programs, and drug-abuse treatment centers. This omnibus measure shared much in common with the program for the Positive Woman outlined by Phyllis Schlafly. It was consistent with her concern that women have a right "to be dependent, cared for, subordinate to men and defined by marriage and motherhood."[62]

If the New Right was unwilling to accept the ERA or *Roe* v. *Wade,* the mainstream of American society was unwilling to accept either the profamily program of the New Right or the ideology of the radical feminists. Perhaps the most common articulation of belief about women's status was prefaced with, "I'm not a feminist, but...." The statements that followed, however, were most likely to reflect the views of moderate feminists.[63]

The heat generated by the debate over the ERA, abortion, and profamily legislation obscured far-reaching changes in the civil status of married women. Although Stanton had remonstrated in 1848 that in law the married woman was "civilly dead," by 1900 most states had granted married women limited rights to make contracts, to sue and be sued, to hold property, and to claim their wages without the consent of the husband. Nonetheless the ERA debate, especially at the state level, disclosed the magnitude of discriminatory legislation that remained. While some states clung to the status quo, others moved ahead to accord men and women in similar circumstances sex-neutral treatment. In the eighties the covenant of marriage did not make the husband "to all intents and purposes, her master." Yet the woman of 1980 who wanted a career and marriage, faced far more problems than the male who pursued both, but the formal and informal social and legal barriers were far fewer in 1980 than in 1900.[64]

Stanton had complained bitterly that male legislators had framed the laws of divorce so that "the proper causes, and in the case of separation, to whom the guardianship of the children shall be given" were stacked in the male's favor. By 1900, the grounds for divorce had been broadened, and though social critics decried the rising incidence of divorce, divorce was still not easy. The legal process accentuated the differences between the couple; the divorcée was a social pariah; the labor market offered the woman limited opportunities to become self-supporting, while the wage structure did not invariably permit a working-class male to support his family from his income alone and certainly did not allow for alimony or child support. By the eighties a number of states had adopted no-fault divorce, which took some of the sting out of severing marital ties; to be divorced no longer was a social disgrace. Guidelines for awarding guardianship tended to focus on the relative ability of the father and mother to function as a parent; yet in practice few divorced women could count on the receipt of alimony or child-support payments, and many were reduced to poverty. Access to divorce, then, was eased, but property and financial settlements continued to impose hardships on the ex-wife far more often than on the ex-husband.[65]

The Expanding Presence

After 1920 women could no longer protest that they were denied the "inalienable right to the elective franchise," but they did not always exercise that right. Although during the seventies women of voting age outnumbered males by eight to nine million persons, they were less inclined to vote than males by a margin of 1 to 3 percentage points. By 1980 the difference between the sexes in the proportion who voted was negligible, but black women still voted in smaller proportions than white women, and Hispanic women voted in smaller proportions than either white or black women.[66]

Although women had not voted en bloc, in the eighties public opinion polls underscored that women did not mindlessly echo the political positions of fathers, husbands, or other males. The term "gender gap" came into political discussions in the eighties as it became apparent that women voters exhibited less enthusiasm for conservative candidates than men by a margin of five percent and were even less supportive of the Reagan policies regarding the economy, Social Security, inflation, unemployment, and military policy. Wage-earning women who worked at low-paying jobs that offered little long-term security were especially prone to contribute to this gender gap.[67]

If women had reached parity with men at the polls, they trailed far behind as officeholders. The Reagan administration developed a reputation for being indifferent to women, but it nominated women to roughly ten percent of the top 320 appointive offices. It made history in appointing Sandra Day O'Connor to the U.S. Supreme Court. While no women occupied a major post in the Executive Office, Jeanne Kirkpatrick became the U.S. ambassador to the United Nations, and in time two women became cabinet officers—Margaret Heckler at the Department of Health and Human Services and Elizabeth Dole at the Department of Transportation. In 3 departments—Treasury, Labor, and Health and Human Services—2 or more women held major sub-cabinet-level jobs, but in 6 departments no woman was among the departmental leaders. Of the 107 U.S. independent agencies, 13 were directed by women. Tokenism was still the order of the day in top-level positions. Yet the appointments to the United Nations, the Supreme Court, and the Department of Transportation were not ones that utilized women for their stereotypical feminine qualities.[68]

The ascendancy of the New Right to public office shook women's groups from their lethargy. In the first reaction, women hastened to join NOW, nearly tripling its membership. Prior to the November 1982 election, women's groups, civil-rights groups, and some labor unions initiated "a get-out-the-women's-vote drive." The League of Women Voters launched a nationwide campaign around the slogan: "It's a Man's World—Unless Women Vote." A variety of women's organizations with diverse approaches and constituencies also joined. NOW—the largest women's group with 230,000 members and more money than any other women's organization—targeted for defeat state legislators who had blocked ratification of ERA. The NWPC (National Women's Political Caucus) the second largest group, and Bella Abzug's Women USA joined in this effort to encourage women to register and vote and to support women candidates. The National Abortion Rights Action League and Friends of Family Planning endorsed candidates and contributed funds to those who supported the pro-choice position. Professional groups with primarily a female constituency—the American Association of University Women, 9 to 5, the American Nurses Association, and the Association of Social Workers, as well as the NEA (National Education Association)—worked with the others.[69]

The campaigns were generally successful. Exit polls in 1982 indicated that women voted in the same proportion as males, but as the adult female population was in a majority, women had a potential for determining the outcomes of elections as never before. And indeed, election analysts credited women's votes with electing Mario Cuomo, the pro-choice candidate, to be governor of New York; Mark White who defeated the incumbent governor of Texas; and James Blanchard, a proequality Democrat, who

Geraldine Ferraro made history when the Democratic National Convention chose her as its vice-presidential candidate. Here she speaks at a NOW meeting, against a backdrop of the ERA text.

captured the governor's office in Michigan. Equally important, the women's coalition forestalled efforts of the National Conservative Political Action Committee and the Moral Majority to purge pro-ERA and pro-choice senators and representatives. Instead, in both Florida and Illinois a number of anti-ERA legislators were defeated for reelection. Twenty-one women were elected to the U.S. House of Representatives, one more than in the previous Congress. Of the five new congresswomen, four were feminists endorsed and supported by NOW, the Women's Campaign Fund (WCF), or the NWPC. In statewide contests three women, including Martha Griffiths, became lieutenant governors; eleven women became secretaries of state; and nine were elected state treasurers. As the nation's state legislatures convened in 1983, 966 legislators were women; at the local level close to 15,000 women held elective office.[70]

As the national parties geared up for the 1984 presidential contest, the administration seemed more attentive to congresswomen, to the party's own female constituency, and to organized women's groups. Although this attention was self-serving and extended reluctantly, political realism in the eighties required that the effort be made. In July 1984 the Democrats grabbed the initiative by nominating Geraldine Ferraro, a New York congresswoman, as their vice-presidential candidate. Women still had a very limited, but growing, share in the processes of government.[71]

ALL PROFITABLE EMPLOYMENTS

In the economic sphere, women of the 1980s participated in the labor force on a broader scale than ever before, though as in the political sphere, they were grossly underrepresented in prestigious positions. Not the least among Elizabeth Stanton's charges against man was that he had "monopolized nearly all the profitable employments." He excluded women from "all the avenues to wealth and distinction" and in particular barred them from theology, medicine, and law. One hundred nineteen years later NOW condemned sex discrimination that excluded women from equal access to the labor market. To realize equality in the labor force, NOW sought maternity leaves without loss of seniority or other benefits, child-care facilities, and job-training programs.[72]

A retrospective glance at women's changing place in the labor force since 1900 reveals both progress and problems. Quantitatively women made much progress, as the female labor force expanded from 5,000,000 persons in 1900 to 45.5 million in 1980, and the aggregate LFPR rose from 20.0 to 51.5. Of the increase in the female labor force 12.7 million represented the growth in the female population; 27.8 million, the change in women's propensity to seek market labor. This increased presence affected women of all ages, marital statuses, and races, but unevenly. During this interval, the labor-force rate for women in their early 20s more than doubled; that for women in their late 50s, tripled. Whereas in 1900 two thirds of the female labor force were single women, by 1980 only one fourth were single. In 1900 less than 6 percent of the married women were employed; in 1980, just over 51 percent, an eightfold increase. In 1900 the labor-force rate of black women led that for white women 41.2 to 17.2; by 1980, the rates were almost the same, 53.6 and 51.2 respectively. Notwithstanding women's vastly expanded presence in the labor force, a great disparity continued to characterize the participation of men and women. In the aggregate, the rate for men led that for women 78.2 to 51.2, a ratio of 3 to 2. For persons in their teens, the ratio was 60 to 53, while for adults between age 25 and 54, 90 to 95 percent of the males were employed as compared with 60 to 65 percent of the women.[73]

Birth Cohorts

A comparison of two birth cohorts—those of 1896 to 1900 and of 1946 to 1950—underscores the change in the work experience of American women. When women of the birth cohort of 1896 to 1900 entered the labor force in 1920 as single women, they had a participation rate of 37.5. These young white middle-class women of the flapper generation worked for a short time, then many withdrew from the labor market to marry and raise families. During their late 20s and early 30s, their labor rate dropped to 23.6 percent. Responding to the labor shortage of World War II these women, now in their 40s, challenged tradition by reentering the labor force and remained there into the 1960s. They exemplified a pattern of two careers—first working while young and single and second as mature married women with grown-up families. Although a majority of this cohort worked for pay at some time in their lives, no more than two fifths were ever in the labor force at any one time.[74]

The birth cohort of 1946 to 1950, the baby-boom generation, highlighted the changes of a half century. First, their labor-force rate while in their early 20s was 57.8; by the time they reached age 30, it still stood at 57.0, "a dramatic shift in the life-cycle labor force patterns." Having entered the labor market in unprecedented proportions, these women hung on—in part-time part-year employments when family burdens pressed most heavily. As a result the baby-boom generation, unlike the flapper generation, did not experience a sharp decline in their labor-force rates as they entered their late 20s.[75]

Overall, the girl born in 1900 had a life expectancy of 48 years and a work-life expectancy of 6.3 years; by comparison a boy born the same year had a life expectancy of 46 years and a work-life expectancy of 32 years. The woman would expect to spend few of her adult years in the labor force; the man would expect to spend few of his adult years outside the labor force. The girl born in 1980 had a life expectancy of 77 years—29 more years than her counterpart in 1900—and a work expectancy of 27.5 years, more than four times that of her 1900 counterpart. A male born in the eighties faced a life expectancy of 69 years, with the prospect of spending 37 years in the labor force. While other measures indicated that women would typically enter and leave the labor market more often than men, in fact their labor-force expectations were converging.[76]

The increases in labor-force rates for women in the sixties and seventies resulted from an increase in the long-term commitment of working women, rather than from an increase in the number of marginal workers with high turnover rates. Put another way, a larger proportion of women worked full-time year-round year after year; a smaller proportion worked part-time for short intervals. The demand for labor had taken a turn such that it seemed unlikely that demographic changes would reduce the labor-force participation of women.[77]

Segmented Labor Market

While women scored impressive gains in the number of jobs they held, they fared less well in improving the quality of jobs. The dominant feature of the female labor force has been and continues to be a sexual division of labor that concentrates a large proportion of the female labor force into a limited range of "female" jobs. This sexual division of labor—rampant in 1900 when two women out of five in the labor force worked either as domestic servants or farm laborers—continues but somewhat less blatantly. The expansion of occupational shares recorded by women during the 1970s suggests that the degree of sexual segregation is dropping; the increased enrollment of women in high-prestige professional and managerial programs foreshadows a reduction of sexual segregation in medicine, law, and business. Yet the great increases in female employment in the seventies—over 60 percent—were achieved by women taking jobs in the conventional "female occupations."[78]

This pervasive sexual division of labor was an aspect of a broader phenomenon—a segmented labor market in which a primary market offered steady long-term employment, attractive wages, promotions, and a variety of fringe benefits, while a secondary market provided intermittent employment, minimum wages, little opportunity for advancement, and few, if any, fringe benefits. Far from creating male and female labor forces that were separate but equal, sexual segregation produced "dichotomized labor markets" in which a disproportionate number of the "female" jobs were in the secondary labor market.[79]

The aggregate labor-force rate of 20.0 for women in 1900, of course, represented a weighted average of the labor-force rates of a highly segmented labor force in which market labor was a necessity for many black women, both single and married, as well as for many immigrant women and their daughters, but a decidedly uncommon experience for women of the white middle class. The differences in labor-force rates for women in their teens and early 20s as opposed to women in their mid-20s and over indicates that the great bulk of women held jobs suited to young persons with a minimum of skills. That so few married women worked meant that few women secured career-oriented jobs in the primary labor market. For the daring single white woman who had completed high school, employment as a teacher for two or three years was permissible; for those who entered the first commercial programs, employment as a secretary, typist, or stenographer was possible. In either case, marriage and home-making responsibilities were the norm by their mid-20s unless financial reverses, a broken marriage, or widowhood forced them back into the labor force. The tiny minority who, having secured a college degree, embarked on a lifelong professional career did so at the price of forgoing marriage. For the immigrant woman and her daughters or for native-born Anglo-American women from working-class families, market work meant employment in the secondary labor force, usually as domestic servants or as sweated laborers. After marriage such women worked at home as seam-stresses or dressmakers or caring for lodgers and boarders. The black woman came of age expecting that she would have to work by way of supporting herself and her family. Her job choices, also in the secondary labor market, were restricted chiefly to field work—often as unpaid labor for her family—or as a domestic servant. Both black and immigrant women dropped out of the labor force for longer or shorter periods of time either in response to seasonal or cyclical market pressures or to bear children. Such women took special satisfaction in being able to withdraw from the labor force when their husband was able to support the family from his income alone.[80]

Within the range of jobs deemed appropriate to women, age, educational attainment, ethnic background, and race continued to affect the type of job available. Typically, in the eighties girls entered the secondary labor market while in their teens as babysitters, moved on to part-time work as sackers in supermarkets and as countergirls in fast-food emporiums, and graduated to file clerks, typists, and office-machine operators or factory operatives—jobs that might be full-time but paid minimum wages, offered no prospect for promotion, and were susceptible to seasonal and cyclical layoffs. In the absence of any recognized measures of the magnitude of the secondary labor force, one is left with subjective estimates of changes in the magnitude of women's involvement.[81]

Young women who entered the primary labor market often first worked as baby-sitters while teenagers, but their entrance into the primary labor force came via specialized training in high school and especially college, which prepared them for demanding work that commanded premium wages, fringe benefits, and long-term employment with prospects for promotion. The growing proportion of women in the professions, management, and skilled trades during the seventies reflected women's increasing penetration of the primary labor market.[82]

Sexual segregation continued in both the primary and secondary labor markets as employers practiced restrictive hiring based on "statistical discrimination," that is, employers excluded an individual from consideration for employment because he or she belonged to a group considered unsuitable for the job at hand. Thus, a man was not considered for employment as a typist; a woman was not considered for employment as a carpenter. Women professionals had analogous experiences. They could secure the requisite training, but they could not always enter the mainstream of professional employment. While Title VII opened many doors, it did not open all. For example, pursuant to Title VII major law firms in order to recruit male graduates of prestigious law schools had to recruit women graduates as well, but such women were seldom promoted to partnerships. Title VII, however, had less impact in the small county-seat towns where much law was practiced but the firms were small; men got bids from the private firms, but, with few exceptions, women were restricted to public-service law or to public employment.[83]

The Meaning of Work

In 1980, work still had different meanings for men and women, though certainly the differences were narrowing. Basic to these differences remained the assumption that work was the norm for males, an option for females.

A woman entering the labor market in 1980 had to reckon with the fact that historically employers perceived men as the core of the primary labor force—their year-round staff. The ablest blue-collar males might become foremen; the ablest, most ambitious white-collar males might enter the ranks of management. Employers perceived women as the core of the secondary labor force. Some women might remain on the job year after year, but their level of responsibility would remain unchanged and undemanding. Employers welcomed a moderate turnover in female personnel as a means of keeping wages close to the entry level. An increasing number of employers recruited women for temporary work during busy periods, avoiding thereby the costs of health insurance, vacation pay, and pension contributions. Even so, the operation of Title VII and Title IX forced employers to survey the roster of female employees for persons of leadership potential; it gave ambitious women encouragement to prepare themselves for more demanding jobs and lifetime careers in the primary labor force.[84]

Historically, "systematic differences" characterized "the quantity of human capital investment" of men and women. Regarding formal education as a first step toward a lifetime career with successive increases in responsibilities and rewards and expecting to derive their identity from their job, men invested more time and money in education and vocational training than did women. Anticipating short-term employment and expecting to derive their identity as much, or more, from their husbands as from their work, women invested sparingly in human capital. They tended to invest their time and energy in general programs that might find utility in a variety of employments rather than programs geared to a specific job or firm. By the same token employers, expecting higher turnover rates for women employees, especially married women, historically recruited males for those jobs requiring specific, in-service training. Until the 1960s, sex differences in job training were enormous; Jacob Mincer's estimate placed women's investment in job training at ten percent that of men. Cynthia Lloyd and Beth Niemi in their 1979 analysis of the economics of sex discrimination concluded that it is "unlikely that women's occupational distribution will ever approach that of men until the quality and type of training women receive changes."[85]

By the 1980s the balance was shifting. Women in their 20s seemed less willing than earlier generations to seek their identity primarily through marriage. Title IX had placed the law on the side of equal access to the full range of academic and career-oriented curriculums. The sex differentials in enrollments in traditional "male" curriculums narrowed markedly, encouraged by the decline in employment opportunities for women in teaching positions. If women still invested less in human capital than men, women of 1980 invested more of their time and funds in preparation for careers than any previous generation. The woman's movement of the seventies succeeded in creating a climate in which women ventured into programs in business administration and pursued graduate and professional degrees in unprecedented proportions. Again the enforcement of Title VII forced such major employers of women as Bank of America and American Telephone and Telegraph to include women employees in their in-house management training programs.[86]

Sexual segregation in the labor force continued. Yet on balance, the labor market of the 1980s was marked by greater similarity in work for men and women, as well as by significant dissimilarity between the sexes in labor-supply behavior. Historically, of course, whether in the hunting–gathering economies of pre-Columbian American Indian societies or the preindustrial economies of Europe or America, women had had major economic roles. The deprivation of economic functions of urban middle-class women in the effort to make ladies of them was an aberration of nineteenth-century society. In acquiring a role in the labor market in the twentieth century, American women regained an older, historic role.[87]

This massive influx of women into the labor force had major implications for women's future economic roles. First, as the proportion of women who entered the labor force rose, women became more firmly attached to the labor market, "unwilling to give up the income needed to maintain or increase consumption in the wake of rising prices or to leave promising careers to raise a family on a full-time basis." Second, the rapid rise of two-earner families and the concomitant increase in women's earnings had the effect of permitting greater flexibility among men (opting for early retirement, for example) while reducing women's labor-force sensitivity to changes in women's wage rates, the supply of women, the industrial mix, or their husbands' incomes. The prospect was that "older, more experienced work-oriented wives" would "behave more like male workers" in the future. Third, as two-earner families became the norm, pressure mounted on nonworking wives to enter the labor market in order that their families remain competitive. Fourth, the realization of equal employment opportunities, higher educational attainment, and lower fertility rates were making women's "worklife patterns more closely resemble those of men." At the same time, as long as the value of "home productivity"—the child-care and homemaking activities of women—approximated their "market productivity," women would continue to exhibit more responsiveness to economic upturns and downturns than men. Fifth, while statute law was pledged to ensure equal access to the labor force, neither state nor federal authorities assumed the initiative to organize child-care centers, ensure paid maternity leaves, or develop an adequate job-training program for women in poverty. Finally, the concept of comparable worth offered a prospect of reassessing the work performed by women and of setting pay scales in terms of the economic contribution of the worker.[88]

COMPARABLE WORTH

The eighties brought the issue of "comparable worth" to the fore. The concept aimed at ensuring that people in different jobs should be paid the same if the jobs entail effort, skills, and knowledge of a comparable level and are of equivalent value to the employer. The issue surfaced in the late

1970s as women recognized that in spite of the Equal Pay Act and Title VII, women workers earned but 59 cents for every dollar earned by males. Critics pointed, for example, to the $23,500 paid in Montgomery County, Maryland, to a starting male liquor-store clerk compared to the $11,000 paid to a beginning female librarian. Feminists charged that such pay differentials were as discriminatory as paying men and women different rates for the same job.[89]

In 1981 public attention focused on the issue as women employees in Washington County, Oregon, and San Jose, California, demanded that pay schedules be realigned in terms of comparable worth. In both cases, job studies by the employer documented that women employees were underpaid as compared with males in different but comparable jobs, but in both cases the employers refused to adjust the wage schedules. But the most important development occurred in 1983 when a federal district judge found the state of Washington guilty of massive discrimination because it paid women in "female" jobs less than it paid persons in comparable male-dominated jobs.[90]

While women's groups quickly embraced and promoted "comparable worth," business groups, political conservatives, and the Reagan administration opposed it. Established by business leaders in the mid-1970s to counter affirmative-action programs and guided by a board of directors that included officials of such firms as General Electric, Exxon, Sears, General Motors, and Prudential Insurance, the Equal Employment Advisory Board charged that comparable worth was ill-defined, that the wage gap had little to do with bias, and that upward mobility for women, not arbitrary realignment of pay, was the solution. Rather than evaluate the issues, the right-wing *National Review* invoked the authority of Bill Niskanen, the White House economist, to brand comparable worth as "a truly crazy idea." Also choosing the light-hearted approach, *Fortune* attributed the proposal to "professional complainers" in the woman's movement and characterized the concept of pay equity as "incomparable silliness." Not to be outdone, Clarence M. Pendleton, Jr., chairman of the U.S. Civil Rights Commission, termed pay equity as the "looniest idea since Looney Tunes came on the screen." Undergirding this light-hearted treatment was the argument that market forces should dictate wages. Drawing its rationale from classical economics, *Fortune* asked why, "in a situation where jobs were acknowledged to be dissimilar, should there be any 'right' relationship at all between compensation levels for men and women?" Supply and demand should alone determine wage rates. The U.S. Chamber of Commerce warned women that comparable worth would raise labor costs and that "women might simply find their employment opportunities vanishing rapidly as employers replaced them with men and machines" or alternatively contracted the work to overseas firms. The implication was that men might be paid the value of their work; women should not expect to be. Alternatively the business community insisted that staffing patterns (the differing mix of men and women in entry-level, middle-level, and senior-level jobs) along with range-of-pay schedules explained much of the differentials in the earnings of men and women.[91]

The debate brought no meeting of minds. Proponents of pay equity emphasized that supply and demand forces do not always set wages equitably in an environment where a "history of segregation" had closed certain jobs to women and blacks. The "heart of occupational segregation, wage discrimination, and future promotional opportunity" was the product of "initial assignment discrimination." This occurred when men and women with "equivalent education, training, and ability" initially entered the labor force and the employer assigned them on the basis of sex to predominantly female or male jobs. It was this process that regularly placed women in lower-paying jobs.[92]

The resurgence of political conservatism that brought Ronald Reagan's election in 1980 created a political climate that was unsympathetic toward comparable worth. Attorney General Edwin Meese set the tone in describing the concept as "bad doctrine." In 1985 the U.S. Civil Rights Commission rejected comparable worth in favor of the principle of equal pay for equal work and urged federal civil-rights agencies, the Justice Department, and the Congress to do likewise. The commission chairman, Clarence M. Pendelton, Jr., charged proponents with making "a disingenuous attempt to restructure our free enterprise system into a state-controlled economy under the false guise of fairness." Subsequently the Equal Employment Opportunity Commission ruled that "Congress never authorized the government to take on wholesale restructuring of wages that were set by non-sex-based decisions of employers—by collective bargaining—or by the marketplace."[93]

Despite the opposition of the Reagan administration, the comparable-worth concept made considerable headway. Buoyed first by *Washington County* v. *Gunther* and then *Washington State,* the American Federation of State, County, and Municipal Employees pursued comparable-worth wage scales in contracts with public employers and launched a dozen suits against recalcitrant employers. Cities such as Spokane, Washington, and Santa Clara, California, and states such as Minnesota restructured their wage schedules to reflect comparable worth. Major gains were scored when first New York State and then the city of Los Angeles negotiated union contracts that embodied comparable-worth adjustments. By the mid-1980s over 100 jurisdictions, including at least 22 states, had job evaluations underway.[94]

The private sector, too, responded to pressure. In the wake of the *Washington County* case, Westinghouse Electric, which was the subject of a union lawsuit, settled out of court, agreeing to revise its pay scales for women in line with comparable-worth principles. The American Telephone and Telegraph leadership—which had lost an equal-pay case under Title VII—set up joint union–management committees to develop a job-evaluation system. Furthermore, AT&T's leadership suggested abandoning the traditional approach to job evaluation, which favored men by placing a premium on jobs requiring physical skill, and adopting a system that took into account the "mental fatigue" generated by "work frustrations, boredom, [and] exacting output standards" that characterized the white-collar jobs of its female employees. With over half of the adult women in the labor force and with women constituting more than half of the nation's college students and a growing proportion of those in graduate and professional schools, the issue of comparable worth was not likely to go away.[95]

Women's roles continued to vary according to age, education, ethnicity, and marital status. The white middle-class woman continued to set the standard and generally to enjoy the widest options and to experience the fewest barriers. It remained the case that white working-class women had a different set of expectations and experiences. Although black, Indian, and Hispanic women still lagged in the realization of a full range of political, educational, and economic opportunities, the differences were narrowing. Ethnic, racial, and sometimes religious heritages continued to shape the ideals of proper womanly behavior and roles, so that American women did not uniformly share common perspectives or values, nor did they invariably seek the same goals. Yet as the Houston conference demonstrated, many of these women found it possible to form coalitions, to identify some common problems, and to work for broader public roles for women.

For decades American women had poured into what Margaret Dreier Robins termed "the festival of life." In the eighties, women moved relatively freely in the mainstream of America's political, social, and economic life. Their enlarged public roles were not problem-free. Women still encountered conflicts between traditional views of women's roles and the demands of life beyond the bounds of home and family. Minority women still faced barriers not encountered by white middle-class women. And women with a traditional orientation might well avoid the "festival." While the woman coming of age in the eighties enjoyed a range of opportunities and choices that Margaret Dreier Robins could only fantasize, much unfinished business remained.

NOTES

[1] Nancy Woloch, *Women and the American Experience* (New York: Knopf, 1984), 12. Sheila M. Rothman, *Woman's Proper Place: A History of Changing Ideals and Practices, 1870 to the Present* (New York: Basic, 1978), chaps. 1–3. Carl Degler, *At Odds: Women and the Family in America from the Revolution to the Present* (New York: Oxford, 1980), chaps. 7–13. Mary P. Ryan, *Womanhood in America* (New York: New Viewpoints, 1975), chap. 4. Lois W. Banner, *Women in Modern America: A Brief History,* 2nd ed. (San Diego: Harcourt Brace Jovanovich, 1984), chaps. 1–2.

[2] Patricia Albjerg Graham, "Expansion and Exclusion: A History of Women in American Higher Education," *Signs,* 3(1978): 759–73. Roberta Frankfort, *Collegiate Women: Domesticity and Career in Turn-of-the-Century America* (New York: New York University Press, 1977). Karen J. Blair, *The Clubwoman as Feminist: True Womanhood Redefined, 1868–1914* (New York: Holmes & Meier, 1980). Barbara Leslie Epstein, *The Politics of Domesticity* (Middletown: Wesleyan University Press, 1981), chaps. 4–5. Estelle Freedman, "Separatism as Strategy: Female Institution Building and American Feminism, 1870–1930," *FS,* 5(1979): 512–49.

[3] Gerda Lerner, "Black Women in the United States: A Problem in Historiography and Interpretation," in Gerda Lerner, *The Majority Finds Its Past* (New York: Oxford, 1979), 63–82. Sharon Harley and Rosalyn Terborg-Penn, eds., *The Afro-American Woman: Struggles and Images* (Port Washington: Kennikat, 1978). Gerda Lerner, "Early Community Work of Black Club Women," *JNH,* 59(1974): 158–67.

[4] See Susan Harding, "Family Reform Movements: Recent Feminism and Its Opposition," *FS,* 7(1981): 60–66. Judith M. Bardwick, *In Transition: How Feminism, Sexual Liberation and the Search for Self-Fulfillment Have Altered America* (New York: Holt, Rinehart & Winston, 1979). Janet Giele, *Women and the Future: Changing Sex Roles in Modern America* (New York: Free Press, 1978). Woloch, *Women and the American Experience,* 530–36. Adrienne Rich, *Of Woman Born* (New York: Norton, 1976) provides a full analysis of motherhood as an institution.

[5] See Louise Kapp Howe, *Pink Collar Workers: Inside the World of Women's Work* (New York: G. P. Putnam's Sons, 1977); Lillian Rubin, *Worlds of Pain: Life in the Working-Class Family* (New York: Basic, 1976); and Susan Estabrook Kennedy, *If All We Did Was to Weep at Home: A History of White Working-Class Women in America* (Bloomington: Indiana University Press, 1979). Nancy Seifer, *Nobody Speaks for Me: Self-Portraits of American Working-Class Women* (New York: Simon & Schuster, 1976). Alice Kessler-Harris, *Out to Work: A History of Wage-Earning Women in the United States* (New York: Oxford, 1982), 315–19.

[6] Helena Z. Lopata, *Occupation: Housewife* (New York: Oxford, 1971). Rae Andre, *Homemakers: The Forgotten Workers* (Chicago: University of Chicago Press, 1981). Woloch, *Women and the American Experience,* 535.

[7] Bonnie Thornton Dill, "The Dialectics of Black Womanhood," *Signs,* 4(1979): 543–55. Gloria T. Hull, Patricia Bell Scott, and Barbara Smith, *But Some of Us Are Brave: Black Women's Studies* (Old Westbury: Feminist, 1982). Pauli Murray, "The Liberation of Black Women," in *Voices of the New Feminism,* ed. Mary Lou Thompson (Boston: Beacon, 1970), 87–102. Maxine Baca Zinn, "Political Familism: Toward Sex Role Equality in Chicano Families," *Aztlan,* 6(1975): 26. Joe R. Feagin and Nancy Fujitaki, "On the Assimilation of Japanese Americans," *Amerasia Journal,* 1(1972): 13–30. Darrel Montero, "The Japanese Americans: Changing Patterns of Assimilation Over Three Generations," *ASR,* 46(1981): 829–39.

[8] Charlotte Perkins Gilman, *Women and Economics* (New York: Harper & Row, 1966[1898]). Theodore Roosevelt, "Race Decadence," *The Outlook,* 97(1911): 763–69.

[9] Clara M. Thompson, *On Women,* ed. Maurice R. Green (New York: New American Library, 1971), 153–61. Ferdinand Lundberg and Marynia Farnham, *Modern Woman: The Lost Sex* (New York: Harper, 1947). Mirra Komarovsky, *Women in the Modern World: Their Education and Their Dilemmas* (Boston: Little, Brown, 1953). Betty Friedan, *The Feminine Mystique* (New York: Norton, 1963). Phyllis Schlafly, *The Power of the Positive Woman* (New York: Jove, 1977). Betty Friedan, *The Second Stage* (New York: Summit Books, 1981), 27.

Barbara Ehrenreich, "The Women's Movements, Feminist and Anti Feminist," *Radical America,* 15(1981): 101.

[10] Betty Friedan, *It Changed My Life: Writings on the Women's Movement* (New York: Random House, 1976), 87–91. Friedan, *The Second Stage,* 206. Betty Friedan, "Feminism's Next Step," *NYT Magazine,* 5 July 1981, 14. Sarah J. Stage, "Women," in *AQ,* 35(1983): 174. Degler, *At Odds,* makes the assumption that the well-being of the family requires that the husband realize his full potential in the world outside the home; the well-being of the family, however, is threatened to the degree that the wife attempts to realize her potential outside the family circle.

[11] Stage, "Women," 170, 172, 174. See Anita Diamant, "Reactionary Feminism: Are You Ready for Aunt Betty?" in Stage, "Women," 174. Harding, "Family Reform Movements," 67.

[12] Stage, "Women," 169 n. 2, 173, 190; see Alison Jaggar and Paula R. Struhl, eds. *Feminist Frameworks* (New York: McGraw-Hill, 1978); Harding, "Family Reform Movements," 64. Brigitte Berger and Peter L. Berger, *The War Over the Family: Capturing the Middleground* (Garden City: Anchor, 1983). Christopher Lasch, *Haven in a Heartless World* (New York: Basic, 1977). Mary Jo Bane, *Here to Stay: American Families in the Twentieth Century* (New York: Basic, 1976). Linda Gordon and Allen Hunter, "Sex, Family, and the New Left: Anti-Feminism as a Political Force," *Radical America,* 11(Nov. 1977–Feb. 1978), 9–25.

[13] See Sarah Stage's critique of Schlafly, "Women," 181–82. Carol Felsenthal, *The Sweetheart of the Silent Majority: The Biography of Phyllis Schlafly* (Garden City: Doubleday, 1981). Frances Fitzgerald, "The Triumphs of the New Right," *NYRB,* 28(Nov. 19, 1981): 19–26. Andrea Dworkin, *Right-Wing Women* (New York: Perigee, 1983). See Andrew Hacker, "ERA-RIP," *Harper's,* 261(Sept. 1980): 10–11.

[14] Paul Weyrich quoted in Allen Hunter, "In the Wings: New Right Ideology and Organization," *Radical America,* 15(1981): 121. Stage, "Women," 179. Jean Bethke Elshtain, "Feminists Against the Family," *The Nation,* 229(Nov. 17, 1979): 500.

[15] Bureau of the Census, *U.S. Census of Population: 1950.* vol. 2. *Characteristics of the Population, Part I, U.S. Summary* (Washington: GPO, 1953), tab. 102. James A. Sweet, "Components of Change in the Number of Households: 1970–1980," *Demography* 21(May 1984): 129–40.

[16] Bureau of the Census, *Statistical Abstract of the United States: 1984* (Washington: GPO, 1983), tabs. 56 and 57 (hereafter cited as *Statistical Abstract: 1984*).

[17] Ibid., tab. 60.

[18] Bureau of the Census, "Marital Status and Living Arrangements: March 1982," *CPR,* ser. P-20, no. 380 (Washington: GPO, 1983), tabs. B and C.

[19] Paul C. Glick, "Some Recent Changes in American Families," in Bureau of the Census, *CPR,* ser. P-23, no. 52 (Washington: GPO, 1975), 4. Elizabeth Waldman, Allyson Sherman Grossman, Howard Hayghe, and Beverly L. Johnson, "Working mothers in the 1970's: a look at the statistics," *MLR,* 102(Oct. 1979): 44–45.

[20] Bureau of the Census, *CPR,* ser. P-20, no. 380, tab. A. The figures were 22.4 in 1970, 43.4 in 1982.

[21] Bureau of the Census, "A Statistical Portrait of Women in the U.S.," *CPR,* ser. P-23, no. 58 (Washington: GPO, 1976), tab. 5-1, p. 19. Bureau of the Census, *Statistical Abstract: 1984,* tab. 85. Bureau of the Census, "Population Profile of the United States: 1980, *CPR,* ser. P-20, no. 363 (Washington: GPO, 1981), 13 14.

[22] Bureau of the Census, *Statistical Abstract: 1984,* tab. 93. Bureau of the Census, *CPR,* ser. P-20, no. 363, 14. Waldman et al., "Working mothers in the 1970's," 41.

[23] Richard A. Easterlin, *Population, Labor Force, and Long Swings in Economic Growth* (New York: National Bureau of Economic Research, 1968) and "Relative Economic Status and the American Fertility Swing," in *Family Economic Behavior,* ed. Eleanor B. Sheldon (Philadelphia: Lippincott, 1973). William Butz and Michael Ward, "The Emergence of Countercyclical U.S. Fertility," *AER,* 69(1979): 318–27. Barbara Devaney, "An Analysis of Variations in U.S. Fertility and Female Labor Force Participation Trends," *Demography,* 20(May 1983): 148–61.

[24] Bureau of the Census, *Women by Number of Children Ever Born, Final Report,* PC(2)-3A (Washington: GPO, 1964), tab. 25. Bureau of the Census, *Women by Number of Children Ever Born, Subject Reports,* PC(2)-3A (Washington: GPO, 1973), tab. 36–37. Bureau of the Census, *Statistical Abstract of the United States: 1971* (Washington: GPO, 1971), tab. 65. The calculations are mine.

[25] Larry Freshnock and Phillips Cutright, "Models of Illegitimacy, United States, 1969," *Demography,* 16(Feb. 1979): 37–47. Bureau of the Census, *CPR,* ser. P-23, no. 58, p. 18. Bureau of the Census, "Fertility of American Women: June 1981," *CPR,* ser. P-20, no. 378 (Washington: GPO, 1983), p. 5. See Kristin A. Moore, Sandra L. Hofferth, Stephen B. Caldwell, and Linda J. Waite, *Teenage Motherhood, Social and Economic Consequences* (Washington: Urban Institute, 1979). Waldman et al., "Working mothers in the 1970's," 46.

[26] Bureau of the Census, *CPR,* ser. P-20, no. 378, p. 5. Waldman et al., "Working mothers in the 1970's," 46.

[27] Bureau of the Census, *CPR,* ser. P-20, no. 363, 14–15. Bureau of the Census, *CPR,* ser. P-20, no. 380, tab. F, p. 6.

[28] Robert T. Michael, "The Rise in Divorce Rates, 1960–1974, Age-Specific Components," *Demography,* 15(1978): 177. See also Paul C. Glick and Arthur J. Norton, "Perspectives on the Recent Upturn in Divorce and Remarriage," *Demography,* 10(1973): 310–14. Bureau of the Census, *Statistical Abstract: 1984,* tab. 120.

[29] Michael, "Rise in Divorce Rates, 1960–1974," 181.

[30] Bureau of the Census, *Statistical Abstract: 1984,* tab. 55. Bureau of the Census, *CPR,* ser. P-20, no. 380, 3–4, 53.

[31] Bureau of the Census, *Statistical Abstract: 1984,* tabs. 120 and 97.

[32] Bureau of the Census, *CPR,* ser. P-20, no. 380, 3–4.

[33] Compare Woloch, *Women and the American Experience,* 530–34.

[34] "The Seneca Falls Declaration of Sentiments and Resolutions," in *Documents of American History,* 7th ed., Henry Steele Commager (New York: Appleton-Century-Crofts, 1963), vol. 1, 316. "NOW Bill of Rights for 1969," in June Sochen, *Herstory: A Woman's View of American History* (New York: Alfred, 1974), 436.

[35] Bureau of the Census, *Historical Statistics of the United States, Colonial Times to 1957* (Washington: GPO, 1960), ser. H383-394.

[36] U.S. Commission on Civil Rights, *Social Indicators of Equality for Minorities and Women* (Washington: GPO, 1978), tab. 2-1, p. 6. The calculations are mine.

[37] Ibid., 10, 12.

[38] Ibid., 5–16.

[39] Ibid.

[40] Bureau of the Census, *Statistical Abstract: 1984,* tab. 260.

[41] Anne McDougall Young and Howard Hayghe, "More U.S. workers are college graduates," *MLR,* 107(March 1984): 46–48. Bureau of the Census, *Statistical Abstract: 1984,* tab. 277.

[42] In 1900 the proportion of males to females receiving baccalaureates was four to one; in 1940, four to three. The ratio was 5.3 to 4.7 in 1980. At the doctoral level the ratio was still two to one in 1980. Bureau of the Census, *Historical Statistics of the U.S., Colonial Times to 1970,* ser. H753–754. Bureau of the Census, *Statistical Abstract: 1984,* tab. 275.

[43] Howard R. Bowen, "The Effects of Going to College," *CHE,* 15(Oct. 31, 1977): 3–4. See also Howard R. Bowen, *Investment in Learning: The Individual and Social Value of American Higher Education* (San Francisco: Jossey-Bass, 1977).

[44] The Roper Organization, *The Virginia Slims American Women's Poll,* vol. III (1974). College-educated women identified more strongly with feminist positions than did less well educated women. Bowen, *CHE,* 15(Oct. 31, 1977): 3–4.

[45] Stage, "Women," 170–75.

[46] Kilpatrick, *Nation's Business,* 67(Oct. 1979): 15–16. Walter Berns, "Breaking the Rules: Congress and the ERA," *Atlantic,* 243(May 1979): 66–67. "Last Hurrah," *Newsweek,* 90(July, 13, 1981): 24.

[47] *USNWR,* 89(July 21, 1980): 8. Associated Press, 23 Dec. 1981. "What Killed Equal Rights?" *Time,* 120(July 12, 1982): 32.

[48] "Politics in a Post-ERA Era," *Newsweek,* 100(July 12, 1982): 33. *Newsweek,* 99(June 12, 1982): 32. Elizabeth Pleck, "The ERA Defeat, *OAH Newsletter* (Aug. 1983): 3. Gloria Steinem, with Joanne Edgar and Mary Thorn, "Post-ERA Politics Losing a Battle but Winning the War?" *Ms,* 11(Jan. 1903). 37, 38, 59 62. Donald G. Mathews and Jane DeHart Mathews, "The Cultural Politics of ERA's Defeat," *OAH Newsletter* (Nov. 1982): 13.

[49] Mathews and Mathews, "Cultural Politics of ERA's Defeat," 13, 14.

[50] *Newsweek,* 98(July 13, 1981): 24. "ERA Dies," *Time,* 120(July 5, 1982): 29.

[51] *NYT,* 16 June 1983, 1, 12.

[52] Helms' measure, S.2148, was "To Protect Unborn Human Beings"; the Hatch amendment was S. J. Res. 199. See also Sheila Caudle, "Abortion Rights Rescued: The Triumph of Coalition Politics," *Ms,* 11(Jan. 1983): 40–41, 62–64. *NYT,* 29 June 1983, 1.

[53] The Yankelovich survey asked: "When do you think a fetus becomes a human being?" The responses were: at conception, 39 percent; when the fetus's nervous system begins to function, 11 percent; when the fetus would be able to survive outside the mother's womb, 9 percent; when the baby is actually born, 5 percent; or, this is a question that can't really be determined one way or the other, 30 percent. "Abortion: Women Speak Out An Exclusive Poll," *Life,* 4(Nov. 1981): 45–54.

[54] James C. Mohr, *Abortion in America* (New York: Oxford, 1978).

[55] Edward Bryce, "Abortion and the Hatch Amendment," *America,* 146(March 6, 1982): 166–67. Martin W. Helgesen, "Abortion as a Local Option," *America,* 141(Dec. 29, 1979): 426.

[56] Elizabeth Alexander and Maureen Fiedler, "The Equal Rights Amendment and Abortion: Separate and Distinct," *America,* 142(April 12, 1980): 314.

[57] Bureau of the Census, *Statistical Abstract: 1984,* tab. 99. In 1981 the rate of abortion and the ratio of abortions to live births declined for the first time since 1973. *The Detroit News,* 12 July 1984, 1.

[58] Harding, "Family Reform Movements," 67, 68. *USNWR,* 92(June 28, 1982): 55.

[59] Zillah Eisenstein, "Antifeminism in the Politics and Election of 1980," *FS,* 7(1981): 200. By definition the moral woman "lives for others, for her child, or her country." Rosalind Pollack Petchesky, "Antiabortion, Antifeminism, and the Rise of the New Right," *FS,* 7(1981): 207.

[60] Petchesky, "Antiabortion, Antifeminism," 207, 208.

[61] In a landmark decision in June 1984, the Supreme Court held that affirmative-action goals had to yield precedence to seniority rights. See *NYT,* 13 June 1984.

[62] The Laxalt bill was S.1808, "A bill to strengthen the American Family and promote the virtues of family life through education, tax assistance, and related measures." A revised version of this measure, S.1378, was introduced in the 97th Congress by Senator Roger Jepsen with Senator Laxalt as cosponsor. See *Cong. Rec.,* 97th Cong., 1st sess., s6329–6344. Petchesky provides an analysis of the proposed "Family Protection Act," *FS* 7(1981): 224–27, 233.

[63] The Roper Organization, *The Virginia Slims American Women's Opinion Poll,* vol. III, is the most extensive exploration of views. See also Louis Harris, "Changing Views on the Role of Women," *The Harris Survey,* 11 Dec. 1975.

[64] "Seneca Falls Declaration," in Commager, *Documents of American History,* vol. 1, 315.

[65] Ibid., 316. Robert T. Michael, "The Rise in Divorce Rates, 1960–1974: Age-Specific Components," *Demography,* 15(1978): 177–82, points out that a very large proportion of the growth in divorce was attributable to changes in age-specific divorce rates, especially those of women in their 20s.

[66] "Seneca Falls Declaration," in Commager, *Documents of American History,* vol. 1, 315. Bureau of the Census, *Statistical Abstract: 1984,* tab. 828.

[67] See ABC News/Washington Post exit polls, 1982 election. Gloria Steinem, "Post-ERA Politics," 65.

[68] *The 1984 World Book Year Book* (Chicago: World Book, Inc., 1984), 512–13.

[69] Gloria Steinem, "Post-ERA Politics," 35–36.

[70] Ibid., 36, 65–66. Bureau of the Census, *Statistical Abstract: 1984,* tab. 823.

[71] *NYT,* 2 Aug. 1983, sec. 1, p. 1; 3 Aug. 1983, sec. 1, p. 14; 4 Aug. 1983, sec. 1, p. 13; 16 Aug. 1983, sec. 1, p. 20; 27 Aug. 1983, sec. 1, p. 5; 12 July 1984; and 20 July 1984.

[72] "Seneca Falls Declaration," in Commager, *Documents of American History,* vol. 1, 316. "NOW Bill of Rights for 1969," in Sochen, *Herstory,* 436–37.

[73] Gertrude Bancroft, *The American Labor Force* (New York: Wiley, 1958), tabs. D-1 and D-1a for data from 1900 to 1950. Bureau of the Census, *Statistical Abstract: 1984,* tab. 626. In the narrowing of the differentials between male and female labor-force rates, the rise in the LFPR for women accounted for two thirds of the change; the drop in the LFPR for males, for one third. Cynthia B. Lloyd and Beth T. Niemi, *The Economics of Sex Differentials* (New York: Columbia University Press, 1979), 17.

[74] Bancroft, *American Labor Force,* tab. D-1a.

[75] Bureau of the Census, *Statistical Abstract of the United States: 1982–83* (Washington: GPO, 1982): tab. 626.

[76] Shirley J. Smith, "New worklife estimates reflect changing profile in labor force," *MLR,* 105(1982): tab. 3, p. 17.

[77] Lloyd and Niemi, *Economics of Sex Differentials,* 80. See *Economic Report of the President, 1973,* chap. 4, p. 100.

[78] Nancy F. Rytina and Suzanne M. Bianchi, "Occupational reclassification and changes in distribution by gender," *MLR,* 107(March 1984): 14–16.

[79] Lloyd and Niemi, *Economics of Sex Differentials,* 185.

[80] Ibid., 2, emphasizes that no one statistical measure adequately captures all dimensions of the labor-force supply. While the LFPR measures the relative number of women workers at one point in time, it fails to report the extent and continuity over the year, over the business cycle, or over the life cycle.

[81] Ibid., 185 ff.

[82] Bureau of the Census, *Statistical Abstract of the United States: 1981* (Washington: GPO, 1981): tab. 675.

[83] Lloyd and Niemi, *Economics of Sex Differentials,* 187, 189. See Wirtz v. Mid West Manufacturing Corp. 58 LC para. 32070 (DC Ill. 1968).

[84] Bancroft, *The American Labor Force,* 102ff. Lloyd and Niemi, *Economics of Sex Differentials,* 185 ff.

[85] Lloyd and Niemi, *Economics of Sex Differentials,* 81, 126, 146. Gary S. Becker, *Human Capital* (New York: Columbia University Press, 1964), 101 ff. Jacob Mincer, "On-the-Job-Training: Costs, Returns and Some Implications," *Journal of Political Economy,* 70(Suppl., Oct. 1962): S50–S79. Lloyd and Niemi, *Economics of Sex Differentials,* 146.

[86] Gregory Williams, "The Changing U.S. Labor Force and Occupational Differentiation by Sex," *Demography,* 16(1979): 73–87. Paula England disputes human-capital theory as an explanation of occupational sex-segregation in "The Failure of Human Capital Theory to Explain Occupational Sex Segregation," *JHR,* 17(Summer 1982): 358–70. Andrea H. Beller, "Occupational Segregation by Sex: Determinants and Changes," *JHR,* 17(Summer 1982): 371–92.

[87] Lloyd and Niemi, *Economics of Sex Differentials,* 17.

[88] Department of Labor, *Dual Careers, A Longitudinal Study of the Labor Market Experience of Women,* vol. 1 (Washington: GPO, 1970); this longitudinal study of 5,000 women age 30 to 44 years old indicates "a fair amount of slippage in occupational status" between a

woman's first job and the job held as a mature woman, p. 152. As the proportion of women who remain continuously in the labor force increases, the amount of "slippage" should decline, narrowing the gap in the quality of jobs held by men and women.

[89] John R. Schnebly, "Comparable Worth: a Legal Overview," *Personnel Administrator* (April 1982): 43–48, 90. George L. Whaley, "Controversy Swirls Over Comparable Worth Issue," *Personnel Administrator* (April 1982): 51–61, 92. Evan J. Spelfogel, "Equal Pay for Work of Comparable Value: A New Concept," *Labor Law Review*, 32(Jan. 1981): 30–39. Raymond L. Hogler, "Equal Pay, Equal Work, And the United States Supreme Court," *Labor Law Journal*, 32(Nov. 1981): 737–44.

[90] "Upping the Ante," *Time*, 118(July 20, 1981). "Women's Issue of the '80s," *Newsweek*, 97(June 22, 1981): 58–59. James T. Brinks, "The Comparable Worth Issue: A Salary Administration Bombshell," *Personnel Administrator* (Nov. 1981): 37–40. Roger B. Jacobs, "Comparable Worth," *Case and Comment*, 90(March–April 1985): 12–18.

[91] "A Business Group Fights 'Comparable Worth,'" *Business Week* (Nov. 10, 1980): 100, 102. "Incomparable Silliness," *Fortune*, 106(Oct. 4, 1982): 55–56. "A Crazy Idea," *National Review*, 36(Nov. 16, 1984): 17. Daniel Seligman, "Supreme Foolishness," *Fortune*, 104(July 13, 1981): 31–32. *NYT*, 20 May 1985. Harry Bacas, "Measuring the Value of Work," *Nation's Business*, 72(June 1984): 30, 32. An unspoken concern of opponents of comparable worth may well be the hodgepodge wage and salary schedules among male employees—salary schedules that accorded a David Stockman (head of the Office of Budget and Management) $75,000, a state governor $85,000, and a state-college president (in the same state) $90,000 a year.

[92] Winn Newman, "Pay equity emerges as a top labor issue in the 1980s," *MLR*, 105(April 1982): 49–51.

[93] *Washington Post*, 18 June 1985. *NYT*, 12 April 1985. "Breakthrough in Wage War," *Time*, 117(June 22, 1981): 70.

[94] "Women Win One in Washington," *Newsweek*, 102(Dec. 12, 1983): 47–48. *NYT*, 9 May 1985 and 20 May 1985. The 9th U.S. Circuit Court of Appeals overturned the Washington State case on September 5, 1985. See Mary Ann Galante, "'Comparable Worth' Theory Rejected by Appeals Panel," *National Law Journal* (16 Sept. 1985): 7, 37.

[95] "Beyond 'Equal Pay for Equal Work,'" *Business Week* (July 18, 1983): 169–70.

Key to Abbreviations

Publications

AER	*American Economic Review*
AJS	*American Journal of Sociology*
ANNALS	*Annals of the American Academy of Political and Social Science*
ASR	*American Sociological Review*
CHE	*Chronicle of Higher Education*
Cong. Rec.	*Congressional Record*
CPR	*Current Population Reports*
FS	*Feminist Studies*
JAH	*Journal of American History*
JEH	*Journal of Economic History*
JHR	*Journal of Human Resources*
JIH	*Journal of Interdisciplinary History*
JNH	*Journal of Negro History*
MLR	*Monthly Labor Review*
MVHR	*Mississippi Valley Historical Review*
NAW	*Notable American Women*
NYRB	*New York Review of Books*
NYT	*New York Times*
SSB	*Social Security Bulletin*
SSQ	*Social Science Quarterly*
WHC	*Women's Home Companion*

Organizations

CPS	Current Population Survey
GPO	Government Printing Office
MIT	Massachusetts Institute of Technology
NAWSA	National American Woman Suffrage Association
NWLB	National War Labor Board
SSRC	Social Science Research Council

Bibliography

A profitable place to begin an inquiry into the history of American women is with *Notable American Women 1607–1950,* ed. Edward T. James, Janet Wilson James, and Paul S. Boyer (Cambridge: Belknap, 1971). This three-volume biographical dictionary features sketches of 1,359 women. The Introduction provides a succinct overview of women's history, each biography concludes with references to materials by and about the subject; while the third volume concludes with lists that classify the women according to the activity that brought them recognition. A companion volume, *Notable American Women: The Modern Period,* ed. Barbara Sicherman and Carol Hurd Green (Cambridge: Belknap, 1980), brings the work up to date with an additional 442 biographies.

With the outpouring of articles and books on women's history since the late 1960s, bibliographies become quickly dated. Of special value are Gerda Lerner's *A Bibliography in the History of American Women* (Bronxville: Sarah Lawrence College, 1978) and her *Teaching Women's History* (Washington: American Historical Association, 1981), which is a bibliographical essay with extensive notes. Also of note is Barbara Sicherman, E. William Monter, Joan Wallach Scott, and Kathryn Kish Sklar, *Recent United States Scholarships on the History of Women* (Washington: American Historical Association, 1980), a bibliographical essay organized around three topics—Women's Work, The Private Sphere, and The Public Sphere. Barbara Haber's *Women in America: A Guide to Books 1963–1975,* rev. ed. (Urbana: University of Illinois Press, 1981) is annotated and has an appendix on books published from 1976 to 1979. The section on "Recent Articles" in each issue of the *Journal of American History* includes a unit on women, listing the most recent articles. The *Harvard Guide to American History,* rev. ed., ed. Frank Freidel (Cambridge: Harvard University Press, 1974), while not specifically addressed to women's history, nonetheless provides bibliographies on the whole spectrum of activities that engaged the energies of women.

A number of specialized bibliographies treat minority women. Priscilla Oaks' *Minority Studies: A Selective, Annotated Bibliography of Works on Native Americans, Spanish Americans, Afro-Americans and Asian-Americans* (Boston: Hall, 1976) provides a starting point. Rayna Green's *Native American Women: A Contextual Bibliography* (Bloomington: Indiana University Press, 1983) and Beatrice Medicine's "The Role of Women in Native American Societies: A Bibliography," *The Indian Historian,* 8(Summer, 1975): 50–54, deal with American Indian women. Lenwood G. Davis' *The Black Woman in American Society* (Boston: Hall, 1975) is both selective and annotated. Phyllis Rauch Klotman and Wilmer H. Baatz's *The Black Family and the Black Woman* (New York: Arno, 1976) is broader in scope. The Mexican American women are covered by Roberto Cabello-Argandona, Juan Gomez-Quinones, and Patricia Herrera, *The Chicana, A Comprehensive Bibliographic Study* (Los Angeles: University of Southern California, 1975).

The question as to what women's history is has generated a number of essays. Gerda Lerner has had a major impact through her essays "New Approaches to the Study of Women in American History," *Journal of Social History,* 3(1970): 53–62; "Placing Women in History: Definitions and Challenges," *FS,* 3(Fall 1975): 5–14; and "The Necessity of History and the Professional Historian," *JAH,* 69(June 1982): 7–20. Lerner's views on the nature and purposes of women's history, including the forementioned essays, appear in her *The Majority Finds Its Past* (New York: Oxford, 1979). Nancy F. Cott and Elizabeth V. Pleck, *A Heritage of Her Own* (New York: Simon & Schuster, 1979): 9–22, and William H. Chafe, *Women and Equality* (New York: Oxford, 1977), chap. 1, offer further statements. The connections and distinctions between women's history and social history are explored by Carroll Smith-Rosenberg, "The New Woman and the New History," *FS,* 3(Fall 1975): 185–98. Joan Kelly-Gadol, "The Social Relation of the Sexes: Methodological Implications of Women's History," *Signs,* 1(Summer 1976): 809–23, explores the problems of periodization. Bernice A. Carroll, ed., brings together a number of pieces in *Liberating Women's History: Theoretical and Critical Essays* (Urbana: University of Illinois Press, 1976). Two older essays are still useful: Arthur M. Schlesinger, "The Role of Women in American History," *New Viewpoints in American History* (New York: Macmillan, 1922): 126–59 and David Potter, "American Women and the American Character," in *American History and The Social Sciences,* ed. Edward Saveth (New York: Free Press of Glencoe, 1964), 427–45).

Three journals are of special value. *Signs* addresses women in culture and society both in America and abroad. *Feminist Studies* combines academic scholarship with advocacy. *Women's Studies* has a literary cast. In addition, a number of scholarly journals feature articles on women: *American Quarterly, Journal of American History, Journal of Interdisciplinary History,* and *Journal of Social History.*

Because the labor market has been a major factor in providing women with roles beyond those of wife and mother, materials bearing on women's labor-force activities are of major importance. While the Bureau of the Census' annual *Statistical Abstract of the United States* provides valuable data on the magnitude and character of the female labor force, the data is not invariably comparable from one decade to the next. The bureau's *Historical Statistics of the United States: Colonial Times to 1970* (Washington: GPO, 1976) overcomes these problems in part. Gertrude Bancroft's

The American Labor Force (New York: Wiley, 1958) provides uniform data by age and major occupational groups for the period 1890 to 1955. The Bureau of the Census' *Sixteenth Census of the U.S.: 1940 Population Comparative Occupation Statistics for the U.S. 1870 to 1940* (Washington: GPO, 1943), provides comparable data for detailed occupations.

The decennial census provides a wealth of information on the female labor force. *Subject Reports: Occupational Characteristics* summarizes data on women by race, age, and occupation. Other volumes of *Subject Reports* treat marital status, nonwhite population by race, persons of Spanish surname, Puerto Ricans in the United States, black Americans, American Indians, and Asian Americans. The titles vary from decade to decade.

The Bureau of Labor Statistics' *Handbook of Labor Statistics* (Washington: GPO, 1983) offers a wealth of data. Series of uniform data for the female labor force by race and age begin in 1947 as does data for the labor-force participation by marital status and age. The Bureau of Labor Statistics' *Labor Force Statistics Derived from the Current Population Survey: A Databook* vol. 1, *Bulletin 2096* (Washington: GPO, 1982), for example, gives employment figures for persons of Mexican, Puerto Rican and Cuban origin starting in 1976 and the employment status of the female population by marital status starting in 1947. *Perspectives on Working Women: A Databook, Bulletin 2080* (Washington: GPO, 1980) is especially useful.

Still another valuable source of data for years between censuses is *Current Population Reports.* The P-20 Series has current data on the family, divorce, birthrates, and education. The P-23 Series focuses on women. Of special importance is *A Statistical Portrait of Women in the United States: 1978, No. 100* (Washington: GPO, 1980). Many of these titles are updated periodically.

The *Monthly Labor Review,* a publication of the Bureau of Labor Statistics, presents up-to-date interpretive articles on women in the labor force as well as important articles on the labor-force behavior of Black, Hispanic American, and Asian American women. From 1920 into the 1940s the Women's Bureau published *Bulletins* on topics related to working-class women.

I: 1900–1920

Heritage and Place

The religious heritage is staked out in the Old and New Testaments. See especially Genesis 1:26–27 and 2:7–25, Leviticus 12 and Exodus 20. Paul's views appear in I Corinthians; William O. Walker, Jr., discusses them in "First Corinthians 11:2–16 and Paul's Views Regarding Women," *Journal of Biblical Literature,* 94(March 1975), 94–116. *Human Sexuality: New Directions in American Catholic Thought,* Anthony Kosnik, Chair (New York: Pauline Press, 1977), 7–17, is from a liberal Catholic viewpoint. Woman's place in sixteenth-century England is discussed by Lawrence Stone, *The Family, Sex and Marriage in England 1500–1800* (New York: Harper & Row, 1977). Edmund Morgan's *The Puritan Family* (New York: Harper Torchbook, 1966) should be examined along with Lorena S. Walsh's " 'Till Death Do Us Part,' Marriage and Family in Seventeenth-Century Maryland," in *The Chesapeake in the Seventeenth Century,* ed. Thad W. Tate and David L. Ammerman (Chapel Hill: University of North Carolina Press, 1979), 126–52.

The Cult of Womanhood

The impact of urbanization and the emergence of the "modern family" in England and France is explored by Louise Tilly and Joan W. Scott, *Women, Work, and Family* (New York: Holt, Rinehart, & Winston, 1978), 2–88; Carl N. Degler, *At Odds* (New York: Oxford, 1980), examines its appearance in early nineteenth-century America and its subsequent evolution. The new value system is analyzed in Barbara Welter's "The Cult of True Womanhood: 1820–1860," *AQ,* 18(1966): 151–74. Sheila M. Rothman's *Woman's Proper Place: A History of Changing Ideals and Practices, 1870 to the Present* (New York: Basic, 1978), chaps. 1–3, begins with the Victorian era.

Charlotte Gilman

Gilman's major work is *Women and Economics* (New York: Harper & Row, 1966[1898]). *The Living of Charlotte Perkins Gilman* (New York: Harper, 1975[1935]) is her autobiography. Mary A. Hill, *Charlotte Perkins Gilman: The Making of a Radical Feminist, 1860–1896* (Philadelphia: Temple University Press, 1980), traces her early life. Other works of note are Carl Degler's "Charlotte Perkins Gilman on the Theory and Practice of Feminism," *AQ,* 8(1956): 21–39, and Carol Ruth Berkin's "Private Woman, Public Woman: The Contradictions of Charlotte Perkins Gilman," in *Women of America: A History,* ed. Carol Ruth Berkin and Mary Beth Norton (Boston: Houghton Mifflin, 1979), 150–73.

Freud

The literature on Freud is immense. Of special relevance is " 'Civilized' Sexual Morality and Modern Nervousness" (1908) in Sigmund Freud, *Col-*

lected Papers, ed. Joan Riviere, 5 vols. (London: Hogarth, 1953), vol. 2, 76–99; Freud's *Three Essays on the Theory of Sexuality,* trans. James Strachey (London: Hogarth, 1962), is his first major statement; and Freud's "The Psychology of Women," in *New Introductory Lectures on Psychoanalysis,* trans. W. J. H. Sprott (New York: Norton, 1933), chap. 5, is his last major statement on women. Juliet Mitchell's *Psychoanalysis and Feminism* (New York: Vintage, 1975), is a feminist critique by a socialist. Betty Friedan's *The Feminine Mystique* (New York: Norton, 1963), chap. 5, is a critique of Freud by a moderate feminist.

Birth Control and Margaret Sanger

The best work on the birth-control movement is David M. Kennedy's *Birth Control in America: The Career of Margaret Sanger* (New Haven: Yale University Press, 1970). Linda Gordon's *Woman's Body, Woman's Right* (New York: Grossman, 1976), subtitled *A Social History of Birth Control,* reflects the views of the left. Also of value is Joan M. Jepson's "The Evolution of Margaret Sanger's 'Family Limitation' Pamphlet, 1914–1921," *Signs,* 6(1981): 548–57, which includes the 1914 edition. Margaret Sanger's *The Woman Rebel* (New York: Archives of Social History, 1976) reprints vol. 1, nos. 1–7 of Sanger's 1914 periodical. The major work of her mentor, Havelock Ellis, is *Studies in the Psychology of Sex,* 4 vols. (New York: Random House, 1936[1903–1910]). Mary Ware Dennett from 1915 through the 1930s treated birth control as a basic civil-liberty issue; see her journal, *Birth Control Herald* (1922–1925), and her book, *Birth Control Laws* (New York: DeCapo, 1970[1926]).

The "New Woman"

June Sochen's *The New Woman* (New York: Quadrangle, 1972) focuses on women radicals in Greenwich Village from 1910 to 1920. Other scholarly treatments include James R. McGovern's "The American Woman's Pre-World War I Freedom in Manners and Morals," *JAH,* 55(1968): 315–33, and Henry F. May's *The End of American Innocence* (Chicago: Quadrangle, 1964[1959]). Period pieces include "Sex O'Clock in America," *Current Opinion,* 55(Aug. 1913): 113–14; Agnes Repplier, "The Repeal of Reticence," *Atlantic Monthly,* 113(March 1914), 297–304; and Margaret Deland, "The Change in the Feminine Ideal," *Atlantic Monthly,* 105(March 1910): 289–302. Owen Johnson's *The Salamander* (Indianapolis: Bobbs-Merrill, 1914) provides an impressionistic view of the New Woman.

Political and Legal

Still the best general account of the suffrage movement is Eleanor Flexner's *Century of Struggle,* rev. ed. (New York: Belknap, 1975[1959]), but it should be supplemented with Aileen Kraditor's analysis of the changing rationale of the suffrage movement in *The Ideas of the Woman Suffrage Movement 1890–1920* (New York: Columbia University Press, 1965) and David Morgan's *Suffragists and Democrats* (East Lansing: Michigan State University Press, 1972), which focuses on the last years of the suffrage movement. William O'Neill discusses "Feminism as a Radical Ideology," in *Dissent: Explorations in the History of American Radicalism,* ed. Alfred F. Young (DeKalb: Northern Illinois University Press, 1968), 273–300. Ross E. Paulson's *Women's Suffrage and Prohibition* (Glenview: Scott Foresman, 1973) compares the suffrage movement in America with those abroad and details the source of organized opposition to the suffrage.

The major source of materials on the suffrage movement is the six-volume *History of Woman Suffrage,* ed. Elizabeth Cady Stanton, Susan B. Anthony, et al. (Rochester, 1881–1902, vols. 1–4 and New York, 1922, vols. 5–6). Mari Jo Buhle and Paul Buhle, eds., present the highlights of the suffrage movement in *The Concise History of Woman Suffrage* (Urbana: University of Illinois Press, 1981). Carrie Chapman Catt and Nettie Rogers Shuler, *Woman Suffrage and Politics* (New York: C. Scribner's Sons, 1923), present the history of the NAWSA. Maud Wood Park, *Front Door Lobby* (Boston: Beacon, 1960), outlines Catt's "Winning Plan." Inez Hayes Irwin's *The Story of the Woman's Party* (New York: Kraus, 1971[1921]) gives the account of Alice Paul's work. The major suffrage publications are available on microforms: *Woman's Journal* (1870–1917); *Suffragist* (1914–1918); and *Woman Citizen* (1917–1919). Belle Kearney, "The South and Woman Suffrage," in Aileen S. Kraditor, *Up From the Pedestal* (Chicago: Quadrangle, 1970), 262–65, and Paul E. Fuller, *Laura Clay and the Woman's Rights Movement* (Lexington: University of Kentucky Press, 1975), present the case of southern advocates of state, not federal, suffrage. Biographies or autobiographies of suffrage leaders include Anna Howard Shaw, *Story of a Pioneer* (New York: Harper, 1915) and Mary Gray Peck, *Carrie Chapman Catt* (New York: Wilson, 1944), which is by a devoted friend. Harriot Stanton Blatch and Alma Lutz, *Challenging Years* (New York: G. P. Putnam's Sons, 1940), present the memoirs of Elizabeth Stanton's daughter, an active suffragist of the 1910s. James P. McGovern's "Anna Howard Shaw: New Approaches to Feminism," *Journal of Social History,* 3(1969): 135–53, is a controversial assessment.

For women's legal standing, Sue Shelton White's "Women and the Law," *The Nation,* 112(1921): 402, is a report on sex discrimination in state legal codes. A lawyer, White made the survey for the Woman's Party. Other surveys include Women's Bureau's "State Laws Affecting Working Women," *Bulletin 16* (Washington: GPO, 1921). See also J. L. Wilson's *Legal and Political Status of Women in the U.S.A.* (Cedar Rapids: Torch, 1912), and National League of Women Voters' *A Survey of the Legal Status of Women in the Forty-eight States* (Washington: National League of Women Voters, 1930).

Economic

The basic analyses of women in the labor force follow: Valerie Kincade Oppenheimer, *The Female Labor Force in the United States* (Westport: Greenwood, 1970), employs the analytical concepts of the labor economist, and Gertrude Bancroft, *The American Labor Force* (New York: Wiley, 1958), provides uniform data from 1890 through 1955. Also indispensible are John D. Durand's *The Labor Force in the United States* (New York: SSRC, 1948) and Robert W. Smuts' *Women and Work in America* (New York: Schocken, 1979[1959]). Julie A. Matthaei's *An Economic History of Women in America* (New York: Schocken, 1982), is especially thoughtful. Hazel Kyrk, "Who Works and Why?" *The Annals,* 251(May 1947): 44–52, sets forth the basic argument for approaching women's labor-force participation in terms of supply and demand analysis. S. L. Wolfbein and A. J. Jaffe discuss "Demographic Factors in Labor Force Growth," *ASR,* 11(Aug. 1946): 393–96. The concept of the primary, secondary, and tertiary sectors of the economy is developed in Stanley Lebergott's *Manpower in Economic Growth* (New York: McGraw-Hill, 1964), 100–114, and in Oppenheimer's *The Female Labor Force,* chap. 5.

Some important contemporaneous studies follow: Edith Abbott, *Women in Industry* (New York: Appleton, 1910); Elizabeth Beardsley Butler, *Women and the Trades* (Pittsburgh: Charities Publications Committee, 1909) and her *Saleswomen in Mercantile Stores, Baltimore 1909* (New York: Charities Publications Committee, 1912); and Sophonisba Breckinridge, *Women in the Twentieth Century* (New York: McGraw-Hill, 1933). Joseph A. Hill's *Women in Gainful Occupations, 1870–1920* (Washington: GPO, 1929), is by a Census Bureau analyst.

Recent historical studies of the female labor force include Leslie Woodcock Tentler's *Wage-earning Women: Industrial and Family Life in the United States, 1900–1930* (New York: Oxford, 1979); Alice Kessler-Harris' *Out to Work* (New York: Oxford, 1982), chaps. 4–8; and Barbara Meyer Wertheimer's *We Were There: The Story of Working Women in America* (New York: Pantheon, 1977). David M. Katzman, *Seven Days a Week* (New York: Oxford, 1978), and Susan Strasser, *Never Done* (New York: Pantheon,

1982), treat domestic work, while Margery W. Davies, *Woman's Place Is at the Typewriter* (Philadelphia: Temple University Press, 1983), treats office workers from 1870 to 1930.

The role of immigrant women in the labor force is discussed in Virginia Yans-McLaughlin's "Patterns of Work and Family Organization: Buffalo's Italians," *JIH,* 2(1971): 299–314; Laurence A. Glasco's "The Life Cycles and Household Structure of American Ethnic Groups: Irish, Germans and Native-born Whites in Buffalo, New York, 1855," in *Family and Kin in Urban Communities, 1700–1930,* ed. Tamara K. Hareven (New York: New Viewpoints, 1977), 122–43; and Elizabeth H. Pleck's "A Mother's Wages: Income Earning Among Married Italian and Black Women, 1896–1911," in *The American Family in Social-Historical Perspective,* 2d ed., ed. Michael Gordon (New York: St. Martin's, 1978), 490–510.

The principal analysis of the impact of World War I on the female labor force is Maurine Weiner Greenwald's *Women, War and Work* (Westport: Greenwood, 1980). Mary E. Jackson, "The Colored Woman in Industry," *The Crisis,* 17(Nov. 1918): 12–17, and William J. Breen, "Black Women and the Great War: Mobilization and Reform in the South," *Journal of Southern History,* 44(1978): 421–40 fill out the role black women played in the wartime labor force.

Family and Women's Culture

The concept of "two spheres" is discussed in Carl N. Degler's *At Odds* (New York: Oxford, 1980), 7–13, and in William H. Chafe's *The American Woman* (New York: Oxford, 1972). See also Sheila M. Rothman's *Woman's Proper Place* (New York: Basic, 1978), chaps. 1–3. Rosalind Rosenberg, *Beyond Separate Spheres: Intellectual Roots of Modern Feminism* (New Haven: Yale University Press, 1982), explores new biological and sociological views of women.

David J. Pivar's *Purity Crusade* (Westport: Greenwood, 1973) traces a wide variety of social-reform efforts by women who were precursors of the Progressive movement. For the development of the Women's Christian Temperance Union see Barbara Leslie Epstein's *The Politics of Domesticity* (Middletown: Wesleyan University Press, 1981). Karen J. Blair, in *The Clubwoman as Feminist* (New York: Holmes and Meier, 1980), argues that "true womanhood" was redefined. See also: Blanche Wiesen Cook, "Female Support Networks and Political Activism: Lillian Wald, Crystal Eastman, and Emma Goldman," *Chrysalis,* 1(1977): 43–61; Jill Conway, "Women Reformers and American Culture, 1870–1930," *Journal of Social History,* 5(1971–1972), 164–77; Estelle Freedman, "Separatism as Strategy: Female Institution Building and American Feminism, 1870–1930," *FS,* 5(1979):

512–49; and Mildred White Wells, *Unity in Diversity: The History of the General Federation of Women's Clubs* (Washington: GFWC, 1958). Elizabeth Wilson, *Fifty Years of Association Work Among Young Women, 1866–1916* (New York: National Board of the YWCA, 1916), treats the early years of the YWCA.

Social Feminists

Allen F. Davis, *Spearheads for Reform: The Social Settlements and the Progressive Movement, 1890–1914* (New York: Oxford, 1967), offers the best general treatment of social feminists during the Progressive era. There are numerous works by or about participants: Jane Addams, *Twenty Years at Hull House* (New York: Macmillan, 1910) and *The Second Twenty Years at Hull House* (New York: Macmillan, 1930); Allen F. Davis, *American Heroine* (New York, Oxford, 1973), explores the life and legend of Jane Addams; Lillian Wald, *The House on Henry Street* (New York: Holt, 1915); Lloyd C. Taylor, Jr., "Josephine Shaw Lowell and American Philanthropy," *New York History,* 44(Oct. 1943): 336–64; Nancy Schrom Dye, *As Equals and Sisters: The Labor Movement and the Women's Trade Union League of New York* (Columbia: University of Missouri Press, 1980); Robin Miller Jacoby, "The Trade Union League and American Feminism," *FS,* 3(1975): 126–40; Josephine Goldmark, *Impatient Crusader: Florence Kelley's Life Story* (Urbana: University of Illinois Press, 1953); [Edith Abbott,] "Grace Abbott at Hull House," *Social Service Review,* 24(Sept. and Dec. 1950): 374–94, 495—518; Jane Addams, *My Friend Julia Lathrop* (New York: Macmillan, 1935); Mary E. Dreier, *Margaret Dreier Robins* (New York: Island Press Cooperative, 1950); Alice Hamilton, *Exploring the Dangerous Trades* (Boston: Little, Brown, 1943); and Barbara Sicherman, *Alice Hamilton: A Life in Letters* (Cambridge: Harvard University Press, 1984).

II: 1920–1950

An overview of women's history from the ratification of the suffrage amendment to mid-century is provided by Nancy Woloch's *Women and the American Experience* (New York: Knopf, 1984), chaps. 15–18. William Henry Chafe's *The American Woman* (New York: Oxford; 1972), chaps. 1–8, draws its strength from its breadth and from Chafe's researches in sources, but the treatment is broader for the period before 1950 than thereafter. Lois Banner's *Women in Modern America,* 2nd ed. (San Diego: Harcourt Brace Jovanovich, 1984), chaps. 2–5, is succinct. Mary Ryan's *Womanhood in America,* 2nd ed. (New York: New Viewpoints, 1981), chaps. 5 and 6, treats women's experiences at home and at work. In *Everyone*

Was Brave (Chicago: Quadrangle, 1971), chaps. 7–9, William O'Neill focuses on the development of feminism. June Sochen's *Herstory* (New York: Alfred, 1974), chaps. 11 and 12, emphasizes a woman's view of American history. Peter Gabriel Filene, in *Him/Her/Self* (New York: Harcourt Brace Jovanovich, 1974), chaps. 5 and 6, is concerned with sex roles of both sexes. Sheila M. Rothman's *Woman's Proper Place* (New York: Basic, 1978), chaps. 4 and 5, evaluates ideals and practices, whereas Joe L. Dubbert treats the changing roles of men in *A Man's Place* (Englewood Cliffs: Prentice-Hall, 1979).

Women in the Twenties

Fredrick Lewis Allen's *Only Yesterday* (New York: Harper, 1931), chap. 5, speaks of "the revolution in manners and morals," while Paul A. Carter's *Another Part of the Twenties* (New York: Columbia University Press, 1977) cautions that many Americans were not caught up in the Jazz Age. Paula S. Fass, *The Damned and the Beautiful* (New York: Oxford, 1977), focuses on college youth. In *Middletown* (New York: Harcourt, Brace, 1929), chap. 10, Robert S. Lynd and Helen Merrell Lynd explore women's roles. Major contemporary assessments include the following: Katharine Anthony, "The Family," in *Civilization in the United States,* ed. Harold E. Stearns (New York: Harcourt, Brace, 1922), 319–36; Dorothy Dunbar Bromley, "Feminist—New Style," *Harper's,* 155(Oct. 1927): 552–60, and her "Women in the Modern World," *The Annals,* 142(May 1929); and Sophonisba P. Breckinridge, "The Activities of Women Outside the Home," in *Recent Social Trends in the United States,* 1 vol. ed. (New York: McGraw-Hill, 1933), 709–750, and her *Women in the Twentieth Century* (New York: McGraw-Hill, 1933). Of special value are Estelle Freedman's "The New Woman: Changing Views of Women in the 1920s," *JAH,* 61(1974): 372–93, and Kenneth Yellis' "Prosperity's Child: Some Thoughts on the Flapper," *AQ,* 21(Spring 1969): 44–64.

Women in the Thirties

The major work on women in the depression decade is Susan Ware's *Holding Their Own* (Boston: Twayne, 1982). Other important but more specialized studies include Robert S. Lynd and Helen Merrell Lynd's *Middletown in Transition* (New York: Harcourt, Brace and World, 1937), which examines Muncie. The studies of Ruth S. Cavan and Katherine H. Ranck, *The Family and the Depression* (Chicago: University of Chicago Press, 1938) and of Mirra Komarovsky, *The Unemployed Man and His Family* (New York: Arno, 1971[1940]) are case studies of families in Chicago and New York, respectively. Studs [Louis] Terkel's *Hard Times* (New York: Pantheon,

1970) is an oral history of depression experiences, while Jeanne Westin's *Making Do* (Chicago: Follett, 1976) is a collection of reminiscences and interviews.

Women in Wartime

Susan M. Hartmann's *The Home Front and Beyond* (Boston: Twayne, 1982), chaps. 2, 9, and 10, provides the best point of departure. The war provoked a plethora of essays on woman's place, many expressing traditional viewpoints: Philip Wylie, *Generation of Vipers* (New York: Farrar & Rinehart, 1942); Amram Scheinfeld, *Women and Men* (New York: Harcourt, Brace, 1944); Helene Deutsch, *The Psychology of Women,* 2 vols. (New York: Grune & Stratton, 1944); Edward A. Strecker, *Their Mother's Sons* (Philadelphia: Lippincott, 1946); Ferdinand Lundberg and Marynia Farnham, *Modern Woman, The Lost Sex* (New York: Harper, 1947); and Margaret Mead, *Male and Female* (New York: Dell, 1968[1949]). Henry A. Bowman's *Marriage for Moderns* (New York: Whittlesey House, 1942) was a widely used text in American colleges. The views of Talcott Parsons, the preeminent social theorist of the day, can be found in "An Analytical Approach to the Theory of Social Stratification" (1940) in his *Essays in Sociological Theory,* rev. ed. (Glencoe: Free Press, 1964). *The Annals* published a special issue on the family in September 1943 and on the status of women in May 1947.

Political Roles

The two fundamental works on women reformers of the twenties are J. Stanley Lemons' *The Woman Citizen* (Urbana: University of Illinois Press, 1973), which explores the reformers from a social-feminist perspective, and Clarke A. Chambers' *Seedtime of Reform* (Ann Arbor: University of Michigan Press, 1967[(1963)]), which is concerned with social-welfare reform per se. Susan D. Becker's *The Origins of the Equal Rights Amendment* (Westport: Greenwood, 1981) is comprehensive and first-rate. It can be supplemented by Peter Geidel's "The National Woman's Party and the Origins of the Equal Rights Amendment, 1920–23," *Historian,* 42(1980): 557–82, and by Lois Scharf and Joan M. Jensen's, eds., *Decades of Discontent* (Westport, Greenwood, 1983), an anthology of pieces on the woman's movement in the twenties and thirties.

Women's political roles are explored in Marguerite J. Fisher and Betty Whitehead's "Women and National Party Organization," *American Political Science Review,* 38(Oct. 1944): 895–912. Martin Gruberg, *Women in Amer-*

ican Politics (Oshkosh: Academia, 1968) and Jane S. Jacquette, ed., *Women in Politics* (New York: Wiley, 1974), provide a wealth of detail about women who entered the political arena. Rudolf Engelbarts provides sketches of congresswomen in *Women in the United States Congress, 1917–1972* (Littleton, Colorado: Libraries Unlimited, 1974). Willa Louise Morris, "Women in Congress, 1921–1933," M.A. Thesis, Ohio University, 1960, treats the pioneer congresswomen. The ERA debate of 1945 is recorded in U.S. Senate, *Hearings, Amend the Constitution Relative to Equal Rights for Men and Women,* 79th Cong., 1st sess., Feb. 21–March 31, 1945.

Education

Preston William Slosson, *The Great Crusade and After* (New York: Macmillan, 1930), offers a contemporaneous evaluation of the achievements of the American public-school system, while Charles H. Judd, "Education," in *Recent Social Trends in the United States,* 1 vol. ed. (New York: Whittlesey House, 1934), assesses the problems as well as the accomplishments. The Lynds, in *Middletown* (New York: Harcourt, Brace, 1929), afford a picture of the place of public schools in the minds of community leaders, parents, and students.

The basic work on collegiate education for women is Mabel Newcomer's *A Century of Higher Education for American Women* (New York: Harper, 1959), but Thomas Woody's *A History of Women's Education in the United States,* 2 vols. (New York: Science Press, 1929), is rewarding. For the war years, National Manpower Council's *Womanpower* (New York: Columbia University Press, 1957) is of major importance. See also Patricia Albjerg Graham's "Expansion and Exclusion: A History of Women in Higher Education," *Signs,* 3(1978): 759–73. The standard work on higher education, Frederick Rudolph's *The American College and University* (New York: Vintage, 1965), places women's education in the perspective of higher education generally.

The history of specific colleges and statements by college leaders provide useful insights into the problems of higher education for women. Constance Warren of Sarah Lawrence, in *A New Design for Women's Education* (New York: Stokes, 1940), and Barbara Jones, in *Bennington College* (New York: Harper, 1946), address the question of a curriculum appropriate for women in prewar America. Lynn White, Jr., *Educating Our Daughters* (New York: Harper, 1950), and George D. Stoddard, *On the Education of Women* (New York: Macmillan, 1950), propose curriculums tailored to prepare women for family roles in the postwar era. Katherine Elizabeth McBride, "What Is Women's Education?" *The Annals,* 251(May 1947), insists that women need the same training that men receive.

Work

Because of its breadth and recency Alice Kessler-Harris' *Out to Work* (New York: Oxford, 1982), chaps. 8–10, is a good beginning point. Woman's place in the labor force can be discussed in terms of economic analysis and in terms of occupations. Gertrude Bancroft's *The American Labor Force* (New York: Wiley, 1958) provides a good introduction to an economic analysis and can be read easily by a person without a background in economics. Valerie Kincade Oppenheimer's *The Female Labor Force in the United States* (Westport: Greenwood, 1976[1970]), while more technical, is readable and useful.

Somewhat more demanding but eminently worthwhile and important are William G. Bowen and T. Aldrich Finegan's *The Economics of Labor Force Participation* (Princeton: Princeton University Press, 1969); John D. Durand's *The Labor Force in the United States, 1890–1960* (New York: SSRC, 1948); and James A. Sweet's *Women in the Labor Force* (New York: Seminar, 1973). Julie A. Matthaei's *An Economic History of Women in America* (New York: Schocken, 1982), chaps. 10–12, is topical.

Occupations

Of the general works, Winifred D. Wandersee's *Women's Work and Family Values, 1920–1940* (Cambridge: Harvard University Press, 1981) is especially useful. Mary Anderson's *Woman at Work* (Minneapolis: University of Minnesota Press, 1951) is by the longtime head of the Women's Bureau. Mary V. Demsey, "The Occupational Progress of Women, 1910–1930," in Women's Bureau, *Bulletin 104* (Washington: GPO, 1933), and Janet M. Hooks, "Women's Occupations Through Seven Decades," in Women's Bureau, *Bulletin 218* (Washington: GPO, 1947), provide a perspective of the magnitudes of the various occupational groups as well as the changing nature of some of the occupations. Also useful is Lorine Pruette's *Women and Leisure* (New York: Dutton, 1924).

The following works focus on professional and other white-collar women: Barbara Harris, *Beyond Her Sphere: Women and the Professions in American History* (Westport: Greenwood, 1978), chap. 5; C. Wright Mills, *White Collar* (New York: Oxford, 1956); Elizabeth Kemper Adams, *Women Professional Workers* (New York: Macmillan, 1921); and Frank Stricker, "Cookbooks and Lawbooks: The Hidden History of Career Women in Twentieth-Century America," *Journal of Social History,* 10(Fall 1976): 1–19. Frances Donovan's *The Saleslady* (Chicago: University of Chicago Press, 1929) is by a participant observer. Margery Davies, "Woman's Place is at the Typewriter: The Feminization of the Clerical Labor Force," in Richard Edwards

et al., *Labor Market Segmentation* (Lexington: Heath, 1975), 274–96, treats
a major development.

Among the excellent studies of working-class women are Leslie Woodcock Tentler's *Wage-earning Women* (New York: Oxford, 1979), which
covers the period 1900–1930; David M. Katzman's *Seven Days a Week* (New
York: Oxford, 1978); Susan M. Strasser's *Never Done* (New York: Pantheon,
1982); and Susan Kennedy's *If All We Did Was to Weep at Home* (Bloomington: Indiana University Press, 1979).

The 1930s

A basic study of working women during the depression decade, Lois
Scharf's *To Work and to Wed* (Westport: Greenwood, 1980) gives special
attention to married working women. No less important is Winifred D.
Wandersee's *Women's Work and Family Values, 1920–1940* (Cambridge,
Harvard University Press, 1981). Among the important articles are Ruth M.
Milkman's "Women's Work and Economic Crisis: Some Lessons of the Great
Depression," in *A Heritage of Her Own,* ed. Nancy Cott and Elizabeth Pleck
(New York: Simon & Schuster, 1979), 507–541, which explores the effect
of sexual segregation on women's employment opportunities, while Win-
ifred D. Wandersee Bolin's "The Economics of Middle-Income Family Life:
Working Women During the Great Depression," *JAH,* 65(June 1978): 60–74
studies the increase of married women in the depression-time labor force.

The 1940s

Susan M. Hartmann's *The Home Front and Beyond* (Boston: Twayne,
1982) surveys the wide range of women's experiences during the 1940s,
whereas Karen Anderson's *Wartime Women* (Westport: Greenwood, 1981)
focuses on sex roles, family relations, and status of women during the war,
including the experiences of black women. Leila J. Rupp's *Mobilizing Women
for War* (Princeton: Princeton University Press, 1978) compares the efforts
of the German and American governments to persuade women to enter
the labor force while upholding traditional sex roles. All three emphasize
the limits of change. Specialized studies on women's war work include
Constance McLaughlin Green's *The Role of Women as Production Workers
in War Plants in the Connecticut Valley* (Northampton: Smith College
Studies in History, 1946) and Alan Clive's "Women Workers in World War
II: Michigan as a Test Case," *Labor History,* 20(Winter 1979): 44–72. Karen
Anderson's, "Last Hired, First Fired: Black Women Workers during World
War II," *JAH,* 69(June 1982): 82–97, refutes the suggestion of Chafe in *The
American Woman* (New York: Oxford, 1972) that war work brought a

"second emancipation." Other worthwhile studies of working women include Helen Baker's *Women in War Industries* (Princeton: Princeton University Industrial Relations Section Research Report No. 66, 1942); Katherine Glover's *Women at Work in Wartime* (New York: Public Affairs Committee, 1943); Chester W. Gregory's *Women in Defense Work During World War II* (New York: Exposition, 1974); and Mary Elizabeth Pidgeon's "Changes in Women's Employment during the War," in Women's Bureau, *Special Bulletin 20* (Washington: GPO, 1944). The tale of Rosie the Riveter is detailed in Frieda Miller's "What's Become of Rosie, the Riveter? *NYT Magazine,* 5 May 1946, 21ff.; Sheila Tobias and Lisa Anderson's "Whatever Happened to Rosie the Riveter? *MS,* 1(June 1973): 92–94; and "Rosie Is Back," *New Republic,* 118(May 10, 1948): 7–8.

III: MINORITY WOMEN

Indian Women

Carolyn Niethammer, *Daughters of the Earth* (New York: Collier, 1977), works through the life cycle of women, whereas John Upton Terrell and Donna M. Terrell, *Indian Women of the Western Morning* (Garden City: Anchor, 1976), are topical in their presentation. Murray L. Wax, *Indian Americans: Unity and Diversity* (Englewood Cliffs: Prentice-Hall, 1971) and Edward H. Spicer, ed., *Perspectives in Indian Culture* (Chicago: University of Chicago Press, 1961), sample a variety of Indian communities. Jack O. Waddell and O. Michael Watson, eds., *The American Indian in Urban Society* (Boston: Little, Brown, 1971), discuss Indians in several urban settings. In Institute for Government Research, *The Problem of Indian Administration* (Baltimore: Johns Hopkins University Press, 1928), Lewis Meriam provides a wealth of information about all facets of Indian life in the 1920s. John Collier's *Indians of the Americas* (New York: Mentor, 1947) provides a brief history as well as a personal statement of Collier's approach to Indian policy.

Asian American Women

Irene Fugitomi and Diane Wong, "The New Asian-American Woman," in *Asian-Americans,* ed. Stanley Sue and Nathaniel N. Wagner (Ben Lomond, CA: Science and Behavior Books, 1973), compare the various Asian American women.

Rose Hum Lee's *The Chinese in the United States of America* (Hong Kong: Hong Kong University Press, 1960) and Betty Lee Sung's *The Mountain of Gold* (New York: Macmillan, 1967) are general studies. Norman S.

Hayner and Charles N. Reynolds, "Chinese Family Life in America," *ASR,* 2(1937): 630–37; Stanford M. Lyman, "Marriage and the Family Among Chinese Immigrants to America, 1850–1960," *Phylon,* 29(1968): 321–30; and Betty Lee Sung, "Changing Chinese," *Society,* 14(Sept./Oct. 1977): 44–49, focus on Chinese family life in America.

Harry H. L. Kitano, *Japanese-Americans* (Englewood Cliffs: Prentice-Hall, 1969), examines the acculturation of the Japanese Americans, as does Darrel Montero in "The Japanese-Americans: Changing Patterns of Assimilation over Three Generations," *ASR,* 46(1981): 829–39. Also invaluable are William Petersen's *Japanese-Americans Oppression and Success* (New York: Random House, 1971) and Leonard Broom and John I. Kitsuse's *The Managed Casualty* (Berkeley: University of California Press, 1956), which deals with the Japanese family during World War II. Joe R. Feagin and Nancy Fujitaki, "On the Assimilation of Japanese Americans," *Amerasia Journal,* 1(1972): 13–30, deal with postwar adjustments. Roger Daniels, *The Politics of Prejudice* (New York: Atheneum, 1968), treats the internment of the Japanese Americans in World War II.

Hispanic Women

Good introductions to the Mexican American community are Joan W. Moore's *Mexican Americans* (Englewood Cliffs: Prentice-Hall, 1970); Matt S. Meier and Feliciano Rivera's *The Chicanos* (New York: Hill and Wang, 1972); and Emory S. Bogardus' *The Mexican in the United States* (New York: Arno, 1970[1934]). Alfredo Mirande and Evangelina Enriquez, *La Chicana* (Chicago: University of Chicago Press, 1979), focus on the Mexican American woman. Marta Cotera's "Feminism the Chicano and Anglo Versions," in *Twice a Minority: Mexican-American Women,* ed. Margarita B. Melville (St. Louis: Mosby, 1980) is pointed, as is Maxine Baca Zinn's "Political Familism: Toward Sex Role Equality in Chicano Families," *Aztlan,* 6 (1975): 13–26. Robert Staples' "The Mexican-American Family: Its Modification over Time and Space," *Phylon,* 32(1971): 179–92, is first-rate. For the more recent period see Manuel P. Servin's "The Post-World War II Mexican-American, 1925–1965: A Non-Achieving Minority," in *The Mexican-Americans,* ed. Manuel P. Servin (Beverly Hills: Glencoe, 1970), and Norman Daymond Humphrey's "The Changing Structure of the Detroit Mexican Family: An Index of Acculturation," *ASR,* 9(1944): 622–26. Carey McWilliams, *Ill Fares the Land* (Boston: Little, Brown, 1942), explores the problems of the migrant laborers.

An especially useful study of the Puerto Ricans in America is Joseph P. Fitzpatrick's *Puerto Rican Americans* (Englewood Cliffs: Prentice-Hall, 1971). In addition, C. Wright Mills, Clarence Senior, and Rose Kohn Goldsen's *The*

Puerto Rican Journey (New York: Harper, 1950) is historical and Patricia Cayo Sexton's *Spanish Harlem* (New York: Harper, 1965) gives a feel for what life is like for the Puerto Rican in New York City, as does Piri Thomas' *Down These Mean Streets* (New York: Knopf, 1967).

The most useful work on Cuban American women is Richard R. Fagen, Richard A. Broady, and Thomas J. O'Leary's *Cubans in Exile* (Stanford: Stanford University Press, 1968), but this should be supplemented by Robert L. Bach's "The new Cuban immigrants: their background and prospects," *MLR,* 103(Oct. 1980): 39–46; Kenneth L. Wilson and Alejandro Portes' "Immigrant Enclaves: An Analysis of Labor Market Experiences of Cubans in Miami," *AJS,* 86(1980): 296–319; and Eleanor M. Rogg's *The Assimilation of Cuban Exiles* (New York: Aberdeen, 1974).

Filipino Americans

The literature is limited, but Nathaniel N. Wagner's "Filipinos: A Minority within a Minority," and Fred Cordova's "The Filipino-American: There's Always an Identity Crisis"—both in *Asian Americans,* ed. Stanley Sue and Nathaniel N. Wagner (Ben Lomond, CA: Science and Behavior Books, 1973)—provide an overview. Antonio J. A. Pido, "Brain Drain Philippinos," *Society,* 14(Sept./Oct. 1977): 50–53, explains the one-sided migration of women. Marcelino A. Foronda, Jr., in "America Is in the Heart: Ilokano Immigration to the United States (1906–1930)," Occasional Paper no. 3, De La Salle University, Manila, Philippines, 1976, details the problems of the first Filipino migrants.

Jewish American Women

Charlotte Baum, Paula Hyman, and Sonya Michael's *The Jewish Woman in America* (New York: New American Library, 1975) is the basic work. Marshall Sklare, *America's Jews* (New York: Random House, 1971), and Nathan Glazer, *American Judaism,* 2nd ed. (Chicago: University of Chicago Press, 1972), provide the context for the growth of the Jewish community in America. Leonard Dinnerstein and David M. Riemer's *Ethnic Americans* (New York: Dodd, Mead, 1975) concentrates on problems of immigration and assimilation.

Several pieces address the role of the Jewish woman: Rudolf Glanz, *The Jewish Woman in America,* vol. 2, *The German-Jewish Woman* (n.l.: KTAV Publishing House and National Council of Jewish Women, 1976); Zena Smith Blau, "In Defense of the Jewish Mother," *Midstream,* 13(1967): 42–49; Alexander Grinstein, "Profile of a Doll," in *The Psychodynamics of American Jewish Life,* ed. Norman Kiell (New York: Twayne, 1967); Martha

Wolfstein, "Two Types of Jewish Mothers," in *Childhood in Contemporary Culture,* ed. Margaret Mead and Martha Wolfstein (Chicago: University of Chicago Press, 1955), 424–40; and Pauline Bart, "Depression in Middle-Aged Women," in *Woman in Sexist Society,* ed. Vivian Gornick and Barbara K. Moran (New York: Basic, 1971), 99–117.

Black Women

By far the best general introduction to the history of black Americans is John Hope Franklin's *From Slavery to Freedom,* 5th ed. (New York: Knopf, 1980). A basic survey of all aspects of the black experience in America is Gunnar Myrdal's *An American Dilemma* (New York: Harper, 1944). Paula Giddings, *When and Where I Enter* (New York: Morrow, 1984), traces "the impact of black women on race and sex in America," while Jacqueline Jones, *Labor of Love, Labor of Sorrow* (New York: Basic, 1985), focuses on the relationship between work and family life. Rosalyn Marian Terborg-Penn's *Afro-Americans in the Struggle for Woman Suffrage* (Ann Arbor: University Microfilms International, 1978) explores the "two-pronged fight" black women waged against sexism and racism. Gerda Lerner's *Black Women in White America* (New York: Vintage, 1973) is a documentary history.

Black Women to 1920

Booker T. Washington's *Up From Slavery* (New York: Bantam, 1956[1901]) states his approach to the education of his fellow blacks. August Meier, "Toward a Reinterpretation of Booker T. Washington," *Journal of Southern History,* 23(May 1957): 220–27, puts the Washington–DuBois controversy in context. Also necessary in assaying educational opportunities for black Americans is Charles William Dabney's *Universal Education and the South* (Chapel Hill: University of North Carolina Press, 1936); Jeanne L. Noble's *The Negro Woman's College Education* (New York: Teachers College Press, 1956); and Marion V. Cuthbert's *Education and Marginality: A Study of the Negro Woman College Graduate* (New York: n.p., 1942).

William E. B. DuBois' *The Philadelphia Negro* (Philadelphia: University of Pennsylvania Press, 1899) is a pioneer work. Frank F. Furstenberg, Jr., Theodore Hershberg, and John Modell's "The Origins of the Female-Headed Black Family: The Impact of the Urban Experience," in *The Black Family: Essays and Studies,* 2nd ed., ed. Robert Staples (Belmont: Wadsworth, 1978) is an important corrective to the black matriarchy views of E. Franklin Frazier's *The Negro Family in the United States* (Chicago: University of Chicago Press, 1939).

Several studies should be consulted for the migration of blacks to the North. Of major importance are Louise V. Kennedy's *The Negro Peasant Turns Cityward* (New York: Columbia University Press, 1930); Florette Henri's *Black Migration* (Garden City: Doubleday, 1976); Gilbert Osofsky's *Harlem: The Making of a Ghetto* (New York: Harper & Row, 1966); Seth M. Scheiner's *Negro Mecca* (New York: New York University Press, 1965); and Henderson H. Donald's "The Negro Migration, 1916–1918," *JNH,* 6(1921): 383–498.

For the black organizations, Paula Giddings' *When and Where I Enter* (New York: Morrow, 1984) details the rivalries of Ida Wells-Barnett and Mary Church Terrell and the growth of black women's clubs. See also Gerda Lerner's "Early Community Work of Black Club Women," *JNH,* 59(1974): 158–67; Elizabeth L. Davis' *Lifting as They Climb* (Washington: National Association of Colored Women, 1933); and Robert L. Jack's *History of the National Association for the Advancement of Colored People* (Boston: Meador, 1943). "The Niagara Movement" is explored by Elliott Rudwick in *JNH,* 42(1957): 177–220, while L. Hollingsworth Wood looks at "The Urban League Movement," *JNH,* 9(1924): 117–26.

The experience of black women in the labor force is the subject of several studies: Elizabeth Pleck, "A Mother's Wages: Income Earning Among Married Italian and Black Women, 1896–1911," in Michael Gordon, *The American Family in Social-Historical Perspective,* 2nd ed. (New York: St. Martin's, 1978), 490–510; Claudia Goldin, "Female Labor Force Participation: The Origin of Black and White Differences, 1870 and 1880," *JEH,* 37(March 1977): 87–108; William J. Breen, "Black Women and the Great War: Mobilization and Reform in the South," *Journal of Southern History,* 44(1978): 421–40.

Black Women, Post–World War I

The flowering of black culture in the twenties is treated in Alain Locke's, ed., *The New Negro* (New York: Boni, 1925); Margaret Just Butcher's *The Negro in American Culture* (New York: Mentor, 1957[1956]); and Nathan Irwin Huggins' *Harlem Renaissance* (New York: Oxford, 1971). The first assertion of black nationalism can be studied in E. David Cronon's *Black Moses: The Story of Marcus Garvey and the Universal Negro Improvement Association* (Madison: University of Wisconsin Press, 1955). The lives of ordinary blacks are discussed in Kenneth Clark's *Dark Ghetto* (New York: Harper & Row, 1965) and Allison Davis and John Dollard's *Children of Bondage* (Washington: American Council of Education, 1940).

Special studies of black women in the work force in the twenties include Elizabeth Ross Haynes' "Two Million Negro Women at Work," *The*

Southern Workman, 51(Feb. 1922): 64–72, and her "Negroes in Domestic Service in the United States," *JNH,* 8(Oct. 1923): 384–442; Women's Bureau's "Negro Women in Industry," *Bulletin 20* (Washington: GPO, 1922); and Jean Collier Brown's "The Negro Woman Worker," in Women's Bureau, *Bulletin 165* (Washington: GPO, 1938), which treats the depression years. For black women during World War II, see Karen Tucker Anderson's "Last Hired, First Fired: Black Women Workers during World War II," *JAH,* 69(1982): 82–97; Chester W. Gregory's *Women in Defense Work During World War II* (New York: Exposition, 1974); and Susan M. Hartmann's *The Home Front and Beyond American Women in the 1940s* (Boston: Twayne, 1982).

Black Women, Post–World War II

A starting point for exploring segregation and civil rights is C. Vann Woodward's *The Strange Career of Jim Crow,* 3rd rev. ed. (New York: Oxford, 1974). Paula Giddings' *When and Where I Enter* (New York: Morrow, 1984) discusses the involvement of black women in the desegregation and civil-rights campaigns. *The Long Shadow of Little Rock* (New York: McKay, 1982) is by Daisy Bates, who orchestrated the effort to desegregate Little Rock's Central High School. See also, Mary Aickin Rothschild's "White Women Volunteers in the Freedom Summers," *FS,* 5(1979): 466–95, and Sara Evans' *Personal Politics* (New York: Knopf, 1979), which explores the origins of women's liberation in the civil-rights movement and the New Left.

The two reports on the black family by Daniel Patrick Moynihan, *The Negro Family: The Case for National Action* (Washington: Department of Labor, 1965) and "Moynihan Memorandum on the Status of Negroes," *NYT,* 1 March 1970, provoked an immense body of material. Among the more useful items are Lee Rainwater and William L. Yancey's *The Moynihan Report and the Politics of Controversy* (Cambridge: MIT Press, 1967); Elizabeth Herzog's "Is There a 'Breakdown' of the Negro Family?" in *Family Life of the Black People,* ed. Charles V. Willie (Columbus: Merrill, 1970), 331–41; J. Richard Udry's "Marital Instability by Race, Sex, Education, Occupation and Income," in *Family Life of the Black People,* Willie, ed., 143–55; Charles V. Willie's "The Black Family and Social Class," in Robert Staples, *Black Family,* 2nd ed. (Belmont: Wadsworth, 1978), 236–43; Robert Staples' "The Myth of the Black Matriarchy," *Black Scholar,* 1(Jan.–Feb. 1970): 9–16; Warren D. TenHouten's "The Black Family: Myth and Reality," *Psychiatry,* 33(May 1970): 145–73; Diane K. Lewis' "The Black Family: Socialization and Sex Roles," *Phylon,* 36(1975): 221–37; Jessie Bernard's *Marriage and Family Among Negroes* (Englewood Cliffs: Prentice-Hall, 1966); and Andrew

Billingsley's *Black Families in White America* (Englewood Cliffs: Prentice-Hall, 1968). Hylan Lewis' *Blackways of Kent* (Chapel Hill: University of North Carolina Press, 1955) and Virginia Heyer Young's "Family and Childhood in a Southern Negro Community," *American Anthropologist,* 72(April 1970): 269–88, are case studies.

The problem of being black and female also provoked an outpouring of materials: Toni Cade, ed., *The Black Woman: An Anthology* (New York: Signet, 1970); Joyce A. Ladner, *Tomorrow's Tomorrow: The Black Woman* (Garden City: Doubleday, 1971); and Bonnie Thornton Dill, "The Dialectics of Black Womanhood," *Signs,* 4(1979): 543–55. A number of pieces relate to the black feminist movement: Pauli Murray, "The Liberation of Black Women," in *Voices of the New Feminism,* ed. Mary Lou Thompson (Boston: Beacon, 1970), 87–102; Patricia Robinson, "Poor Black Women," in *Black Women in White America,* ed. Gerda Lerner (New York: Vintage, 1973), 599–602; Frances M. Beal, "Double Jeopardy: To Be Black and Female," in *Sisterhood is Powerful,* ed. Robin Morgan (New York: Vintage, 1970), 340–53; Dara Abubakari [Virginia E. Y. Collins], "The Black Woman is Liberated in Her Own Mind," in Lerner, ed., *Black Women in White America,* 585–87; "Black Sisters," in *Masculine/Feminine,* ed. Betty Roszak and Theodore Roszak (New York: Harper & Row, 1969), 212–13; and Renee Ferguson, "Women's Liberation Has a Different Meaning for Blacks," in Lerner, ed., *Black Women in White America,* 587–92. The Black Women's Liberation Group's (Mt. Vernon, NY), "Statement on Birth Control" appears in Morgan, ed., *Sisterhood is Powerful,* 360–61. Shirley Chisholm's *Unbought and Unbossed* (Boston: Houghton Miflin, 1970) comments on a number of black women's issues. William H. Grier and Price M. Cobbs, psychiatrists, discuss the conflicts of being black and female in a white-dominated society in *Black Rage* (New York: Bantam, 1968). *Ebony* devoted its August 1966 issue to black women as did *The Black Scholar* in March 1975.

Phyllis Wallace's *Black Women in the Labor Force* (Cambridge: MIT Press, 1980) focuses on the 1960s and 1970s. Also of major importance are Cynthia Fuchs Epstein's "Positive Effects of the Multiple Negative: Explaining the Success of Black Professional Women," *AJS,* 78(1973): 912–35, and Walter R. Allen's "The Social and Economic Statuses of Black Women in the United States," *Phylon,* 42(1981): 26–40. Diane Nilsen Westcott explores the question, "Blacks in the 1970s: Did they scale the ladder?" *MLR,* 105(June 1982): 29–38. Three federal reports also provide useful insights as well as data: Women's Bureau, *Negro Women Workers* (Washington: GPO, 1960); Department of Labor, *Negro Women* (Washington: GPO, 1967); and, especially, Department of Labor, *The Social and Economic Statuses of Black Women in the United States* (Washington: GPO, 1969).

IV: 1950 TO THE PRESENT

Nancy Woloch's *Women and the American Experience* (New York: Knopf, 1984) provides the most complete coverage of this eventful period. It should be supplemented for the fifties and sixties by William Chafe's *The American Woman* (New York: Oxford, 1972), Mary Ryan's *Womanhood in America,* 2nd ed. (New York: New Viewpoints, 1981), and Sheila Rothman's *Woman's Proper Place* (New York: Basic, 1978). William L. O'Neill stops short of the modern feminist movement in his *Everyone Was Brave* (Chicago: Quadrangle, 1971), while Lois Banner devotes but a single chapter to the period in *Women in Modern America,* 2nd ed. (San Diego: Harcourt Brace Jovanovich, 1984).

Feminism

While Betty Friedan's *The Feminine Mystique* (New York: Dell, 1964 [1963]) sparked a revival of organized feminism, it was far from the only source. Simone de Beauvoir's *The Second Sex* (New York: Bantam, 1961[1953]) had been available in English for a decade. Mirra Komarovsky, though directing her inquiry toward the education of women, raised many of the relevant questions a decade before Friedan in *Women in the Modern World* (Boston: Little, Brown, 1953). Following the publication of *The Feminine Mystique,* the Spring 1964 issue of *Daedalus* was devoted to women's issues, and it was reprinted as *The Woman in America,* ed. Robert J. Lifton (Boston: Beacon, 1967). Caroline Bird's *Born Female* (New York: McKay, 1968) concentrated on economic discrimination. Major statements of radical feminism include Germaine Greer's *The Female Eunuch* (New York: Bantam, 1972[1970]); Shulamith Firestone's *The Dialectic of Sex* (New York: Bantam, 1971[1970]); and Juliet Mitchell's *Woman's Estate* (New York: Vintage, 1973[1971]). Robin Morgan's *Sisterhood Is Powerful* (New York: Vintage, 1970), an anthology, was widely read and decidedly influential. Anne Koedt, Ellen Levine, and Anita Rapone's, eds., *Radical Feminism* (New York: Quadrangle, 1973), also provided a potpourri of materials.

Participants have left a wealth of accounts of the origins of this outburst of feminism. Treatments of importance include Judith Hole and Ellen Levine's *Rebirth of Feminism* (New York: Quadrangle, 1971), chap. 2; Jo Freeman's "The Women's Liberation Movement: Its Origins and Structures, Impact, and Ideas," in *Women: A Perspective,* ed. Jo Freeman (Palo Alto: Mayfield, 1975), 448–60; Roberta Salper's "The Development of the American Women's Liberation Movement, 1967–1971," in *Female Liberation,* ed. Roberta Salper (New York: Knopf, 1972), 169–84; Beverly Jones and Judith Brown's

"Toward a Female Liberation Movement," in *Voices From Women's Liberation,* ed. Leslie B. Tanner (New York: Mentor, 1970), 362–415; and Marlene Dixon's "The Rise of Women's Liberation," *Ramparts,* 8(Dec. 1969): 57–63. Among the latterday accounts are Jean Friedman's "Contemporary Feminism: Theories and Practice," in *Our American Sisters,* ed. Jean E. Friedman and William G. Shade (Boston: Allyn & Bacon, 1973), 340–54; and Donald Allen Robinson's "Two Movements in Pursuit of Equal Employment Opportunity," *Signs,* 4(1979): 413–33. The major treatment is Sara Evans' *Personal Politics* (New York: Knopf, 1979), which traces the roots of the feminist movement in the civil-rights movement and the New Left.

The feminist movement produced a number of notable documents: President's Commission on the Status of Women, *American Women* (Washington: GPO, 1963); President's Task Force on Women's Rights and Responsibilities, *A Matter of Simple Justice* (Washington: GPO, 1970); National Commission on the Observance of the International Women's Year, "... To Form a More Perfect Union..." *Justice for American Women* (Washington: GPO, 1976); and National Commission on the Observance of the International Women's Year, *The Spirit of Houston* (Washington, GPO, 1978). Two documents of importance relating to the ERA follow: U.S. Congress, House, Committee on Education and Labor, Special Subcommittee on Education, "Discrimination Against Women," Hearings, 91st Cong. 2nd sess., on Section 805 of H.R. 16098, 2 vols. (Washington: GPO, 1970); and U.S. Congress, Senate, Committee on the Judiciary, Subcommittee on Constitutional Amendments, *The "Equal Rights" Amendment,* Hearings, 91st Cong., 2nd sess., on S.J. Res. 61 (Washington: GPO, 1970). NOW's "Statement of Purpose" appears in *Up From the Pedestal,* ed. Aileen S. Kraditor (Chicago: Quadrangle, 1970): 363–69. The "NOW Bill of Rights" (1967) appears in Morgan's *Sisterhood Is Powerful,* pp. 512–14, along with statements by a variety of other feminist groups.

Latterday assessments of feminism include Betty Friedan's *It Changed My Life* (New York: Random House, 1976) and her *Second Stage* (New York: Summit Books, 1981); Janet Giele's *Woman and the Future: Changing Sex Roles in Modern America* (New York: Free Press, 1978); Judith M. Bardwick's *In Transition: How Feminism, Sexual Liberation and the Search for Self Fulfillment Have Altered America* (New York: Holt, Rinehart & Winston, 1979); Mary Jo Bane's *Here to Stay: American Families in the Twentieth Century* (New York: Basic, 1976); Barbara Ehrenreich's "The Women's Movements, Feminist and Antifeminist," *Radical America,* 15(1981); and Sarah J. Stage's "Women," in *AQ,* 35(1983): 169–90. In "A Biosocial Perspective on Parenting," *Daedalus,* 106(Spring 1977): 1–31, Alice Rossi steps back from the position she advanced in her *Daedalus* article of 1964.

Antifeminism

The chief antifeminist of the seventies and eighties was Phyllis Schlafly, who laid out her views in *The Power of the Positive Woman* (New York: Jove, 1977). Carol Felsenthal's *The Sweetheart of the Silent Majority* (Garden City: Doubleday, 1981) is a biography of Schlafly. Other antifeminist expressions are Midge Decter's *The New Chastity and Other Arguments Against Women's Liberation* (New York: Coward, McCann and Geoghegan, 1972); George Gilder's *Sexual Suicide* (New York: Quadrangle, 1973); and Jean Bethke Elshtain's "Feminists Against the Family," *The Nation,* 229(Nov. 17, 1979): 481, 497–500. Assessments of the right-wing opposition include Frances Fitzgerald's "The Triumphs of the New Right," *NYRB,* 28(Nov. 19, 1981): 19–26; Andrea Dworkin's *Right-Wing Women* (New York: Perigee, 1983); Zillah Eisenstein's "Antifeminism in the Politics and Election of 1980," *FS,* 7(1981): 187–205; and Susan Harding's "Family Reform Movements: Recent Feminism and Its Opposition," *FS,* 7(Spring 1981): 57–75.

The first assessments of the demise of the ERA have been offered by Gloria Steinem, with Joanne Edgar and Mary Thom, in "Post-ERA Politics Losing a Battle But Winning the War?" *MS,* 11(Jan. 1983): 35–36, 65–66; Donald G. Mathews and Jane DeHart Mathews in "The Cultural Politics of ERA's Defeat," *OAH Newsletter,* Nov. 1982, 13ff; and Elizabeth Pleck in "The ERA Defeat," *OAH Newsletter,* Aug. 1982, 3ff.

Family Matters

The revival of organized feminism was preceded and accompanied by what contemporaneous observers termed the "sexual revolution." Key elements of this included Alfred Kinsey's et al., *Sexual Behavior in the Human Female* (Philadelphia: Saunders, 1953); William H. Masters and Virginia E. Johnson's *Human Sexual Response* (Boston: Little, Brown, 1966); Helen Gurley Brown's *Sex and the Single Girl* (New York: Pocket Books, 1962); "Sex and the Contemporary American Scene," *The Annals,* 376(March 1968); Nena O'Neill and George O'Neill's *Open Marriage* (New York: Avon, 1973); James W. Croake, James F. Keller and Nancy Catlin's "Unmarrieds Living Together: It's Not All Gravy," *NYT,* 23 Sept. 1975; and *Human Sexuality: New Directions in American Catholic Thought,* Anthony Kosnik, Chair (New York: Paulist Press, 1977). See also Daniel Scott Smith's "The Dating of the American Sexual Revolution: Evidence and Interpretation," in *The American Family in Social-Historical Perspective,* ed. Michael Gordon (New York: St. Martin's, 1973), 321–35. A broad survey of the issues appear in *Signs,* 5(Summer 1980) and *Signs,* 6(Autumn 1980) as "Women—Sex and Sexuality."

Barbara J. Harris' "Recent Work on the History of the Family: A Review Article," *FS,* 3(1976): 159–72, surveys the field. Changing sex roles were discussed by Karen Oppenheim Mason, John L. Czajka, and Sara Arber in "Change in U.S. Women's Sex-Role Attitudes, 1964–1974," *ASR,* 41(Aug. 1976): 573–96, and Karen Oppenheim Mason and Larry L. Bumpass in "U.S. Women's Sex-Role Ideology, 1970," *AJS,* 80(1975): 1212–19.

Divorce

The standard studies of divorce in America are William L. O'Neill's *Divorce in the Progressive Era* (New Haven: Yale University Press, 1967) and Nelson Manfred Blake's *The Road to Reno* (New York: Macmillan, 1962). Robert T. Michael, "The Rise in Divorce Rates, 1960–1974: Age-Specific Components," *Demography,* 15(1978): 177–82, identifies the segments of the population within which divorce rates were changing. Doris Jonas Freed and Henry H. Foster, Jr., "Divorce American Style," *The Annals,* 383(May 1969): 71–88, and W. J. Brockelbank, "The Family Desertion Problem Across State Lines," *The Annals,* 383(May 1969): 23–33, highlight the concerns with divorce.

Lesbian Women

As the feminist movement gained momentum in the sixties, lesbian women joined in the protest. Among the widely circulated statements of the time are Gene Damon's "The Least of These: The Minority Whose Screams Haven't Yet Been Heard," in *Sisterhood Is Powerful,* ed. Robin Morgan (New York: Vintage, 1970), 297–306, and Martha Shelley's "Notes of a Radical Lesbian," in Morgan, ed., *Sisterhood Is Powerful,* 306–311. Of the more recent treatments, Adrienne Rich's "Compulsory Heterosexuality and Lesbian Existence," *Signs,* 5(1980): 631–60; John D'Emilio's *Sexual Politics, Sexual Communities* (Chicago: University of Chicago Press, 1983), chap. 6; and Lillian Faderman's *Surpassing the Love of Men* (New York: Morrow, 1981), stand out.

Birth Control/Abortion

Aside from lesbian rights, no issue generated so much heat as abortion. Even the question of birth control seemed to be unfinished business, as Lucinda Cisler argued in "Unfinished Business: Birth Control and Women's Liberation," in *Sisterhood Is Powerful,* ed. Robin Morgan (New York: Vintage, 1970): 245–89. Elizabeth Fee and Michael Wallace's "The History and Politics of Birth Control: A Review Essay," *FS,* 5(1979): 201–215, provides a survey. For the Jewish view of birth control see David M. Feldman's *Birth Control in Jewish Law* (New York: New York University Press, 1968); for the Catholic view see John T. Noonan, Jr.'s *Conception* (Cambridge: Harvard University Press, 1965).

Feminists were also very concerned with rape. Susan Pascale, Rachel Moon, and Leslie B. Tanner's "Self-Defense for Women," in Morgan, ed., *Sisterhood Is Powerful,* 469–77, and Susan Griffin's "Rape: The All-American Crime," *Ramparts,* 10(Sept. 1971): 26–35, are representative of the activist statements. Susan Brownmiller, *Against Our Will: Men, Women and Rape* (New York: Simon & Schuster, 1975) is a broad, historical study.

Lawrence Lader, *Abortion* (Indianapolis: Bobbs-Merrill, 1966), and James C. Mohr, *Abortion in America* (New York: Oxford, 1978), place the regulation of abortion in historical perspective. A legal and historical view is offered by John T. Noonan, Jr., ed., *Morality of Abortion* (Cambridge: Harvard University Press, 1970). In *Rebirth of Feminism* (New York: Quadrangle, 1971), chap. 6, Judith Hole and Ellen Levine provide an overview of the abortion issue from a feminist perspective. Linda Gordon, *Woman's Body, Woman's Right* (New York: Grossman, 1976), outlines the case for reproductive freedom, while Edwin M. Schur, "Abortion," *The Annals,* 376(March 1968): 136–47, provides a view from a time before the issue heated up. Kristin Booth Glen, "Abortion in the Courts: A Laywoman's Historical Guide to the New Disaster Area," *FS,* 4(1978): 1–26, explicates the meaning of *Roe* v. *Wade.* Martin W. Helgesen, "Abortion as a Local Option," *America,* 141(Dec. 29, 1979): 426, and Elizabeth Alexander and Maureen Fiedler, "The Equal Rights Amendment and Abortion: Separate and Distinct," *America,* 142(April 12, 1980): 314, examine abortion and the ERA from a Catholic perspective.

Women and the Law

The standard work through the sixties is Leo Kanowitz's *Women and the Law* (Albuquerque: University of New Mexico Press, 1969). Karen DeCrow's *Sexist Justice* (New York: Vintage, 1975) is by a one-time president of NOW. Henry H. Foster, Jr., "The Future of Family Law," *The Annals,* 383(May 1969): 129–44, offers a prefeminist review; Mary G. Haft's "Hustling for Rights," *Civil Liberties Review,* 1(Winter/Spring 1974): 14–15, reflects the feminist movement.

Education

The adequacy of American schools at all levels was repeatedly challenged, particularly after the Russians launched the first satellite, Sputnik, in 1957. Of the works with special relevance for women, Mirra Komarovsky's *Women in the Modern World* (Boston: Little, Brown, 1953); Betty Friedan's *The Feminine Mystique* (New York: Norton, 1963), chap. 7; and Judith Hole and Ellen Levine's *Rebirth of Feminism* (New York: Quadrangle, 1971), chap. 9, are of major importance. In *The American High School Today* (New York: McGraw-Hill, 1959) and *Slums and Suburbs* (New York: McGraw-Hill, 1961), James B. Conant explores the nation's secondary schools, pinpointing de facto differences in the curriculums of boys and girls. Of special importance to women's education is Patricia Albjerg Graham's "Expansion and Exclusion: A History of Women in American Higher Education," *Signs,* 3(1978): 759–73. Charlotte Williams Conable's *Women at Cornell* (Ithaca: Cornell University Press, 1977) details the informal but substantial barriers to equal opportunity that women faced within a coed university. "Perspectives on the History of Women's Education in the United States," *History of Education Quarterly,* 14(Spring 1974): 1–12, is by Jill K. Conway, subsequently president of Smith College.

A list of some notable works that pointed to greater access to schools and a nonsexist curriculum follow: Virginia L. Senders, "The Minnesota Plan for Women's Continuing Education: A Progress Report," *Educational Record,* 42(Oct. 1961): 270–78; Caroline Bird, "Women's Colleges and Women's Lib," *Change,* 4(April 1972): 60–65; Beverly T. Watkins, "Feminist Educators Seek to Improve the Status of Women's Studies," *CHE,* 13(Jan. 31, 1977): 8; Carnegie Commission on Higher Education *Opportunities for Women in Higher Education* (New York: McGraw-Hill, 1973); U.S. Congress, House, Hearings before the Special Subcommittee on Education of the Committee on Education and Labor on Sec. 805 of HR 16098, 2 parts, March 1971, "Discrimination Against Women." Feminists on Children's Media, *Little Miss Muffet Fights Back: Recommended Non-Sexist Books About Girls for Young Readers* (New York: Feminists on Children's Media, 1971) is a bibliography of nonsexist books for children.

The value of separate women's colleges was affirmed in Betty Littleton's "The Special Validity of Women's Colleges," *CHE,* 11(Nov. 24, 1975): 24; M. Elizabeth Tidball's "The Search for Talented Women," *Change,* 6(May 1974): 51–52; Noreen McGrath's "Coeducation May Place Women at a Disadvantage, Study Finds," *CHE,* 17(Jan. 8, 1979): 20; and Howard R. Bowen's *Investment in Learning: The Individual and Social Value of American Higher Education* (San Francisco: Jossey-Bass, 1977).

Work

Many of the titles mentioned in the section on Work in the part covering the period 1920 to 1950 are also relevant for the postwar years, especially Alice Kessler-Harris' *Out to Work* (New York: Oxford, 1982), Valerie Kincade Oppenheimer's *The Female Labor Force in the United States* (Westport: Greenwood, 1976[1970]), James Sweet's *Women in the Labor Force* (New York: Seminar, 1973), and Julie Matthaei's *An Economic History of Women in America* (New York: Schocken, 1982). Susan Estabrook Kennedy's *If All We Did Was to Weep at Home* (Bloomington: Indiana University Press, 1979) is a study of white working-class women. Louise Kapp Howe, *Pink Collar Workers* (New York: Putnam's, 1977), and Cynthia F. Epstein, *Woman's Place: Options and Limits in Professional Careers* (Berkeley: University of California Press, 1970), treat middle-class women, while Lois Wladis Hoffman and F. Ivan Nye, *Working Mothers* (San Francisco: Jossey-Bass, 1974), focus on mothers in the work force.

Necessarily much of the material for interpreting the recent period consists of articles. One area of special interest was the changing demographic structure of the female population and its impact on female labor-force participation: A. J. Jaffe and S. L. Wolfbein, "Demographic Factors in Labor Force Growth," *ASR*, 11(Aug. 1946): 393–96; Stanley Lebergott, "Population Change and the Supply of Labor," in National Bureau of Economic Research, *Demographic and Economic Change in Developed Countries* (Princeton: Princeton University Press, 1958), 377–422; Jacob Mincer, "Labor Force Participation of Married Women: A Study of Labor Supply," in National Bureau of Economic Research, *Aspects of Labor Economics* (Princeton: Princeton University Press, 1962), 63–105; Richard Easterlin, *Population, Labor Force and Long Swings in Economic Growth: The American Experience* (New York: National Bureau of Economic Research, 1968), 123–28; Valerie Kincade Oppenheimer, "Demographic Influence on Female Employment and the Status of Women," *AJS*, 78(Jan. 1973): 946–61; Charles F. Westoff et al., *Toward the End of Growth* (Englewood Cliffs: Prentice-Hall, 1973); Larry Bumpass, "Is Low Fertility Here to Stay?" *Family Planning Perspectives*, 5(Spring 1973): 67–69; Richard A. Easterlin, "Relative Economic Status and the American Fertility Swing," in *Family Economic Behavior*, ed. Eleanor Bernert Sheldon (Philadelphia: Lippincott, 1973): 170–223; Paul C. Glick, "Some Recent Changes in American Families," in Bureau of the Census, *CPR*, Series P-23, no. 52 (Washington: GPO, 1975); William Butz and Michael Ward, "The Emergence of Countercyclical U.S. Fertility," *AER*, 69(1979): 318–27; Larry Freshnock and Phillips Cutright, "Models of Illegitimacy, United States, 1969," *Demography*, 16(Feb. 1979): 37–47; Kristin A. Moore, Sandra L. Hofferth, Stephen B. Caldwell, and Linda J. Waite, *Teenage Motherhood, Social and Economic Consequences* (Washington: Urban Institute, 1979); Beverly L. Johnson, "Changes in marital and family characteristics of workers, 1970–78," *MLR*, 102(April 1979): 49–52; Barbara Devaney, "An Analysis of Variation in U.S. Fertility and Female Labor Force

Participation Trends," *Demography,* 20(May 1983): 148–59; and Bureau of the Census, "Fertility of American Women: June 1981," *CPR,* Series P-20, no. 378 (Washington: GPO, 1983).

The emergence of married women into the labor force, which fueled the postwar expansion of the female labor force, drew much attention: The major studies are Glen Cain's *Married Women in the Labor Force* (Chicago: University of Chicago Press, 1966), and James A. Sweet's *Women in the Labor Force* (New York: Seminar, 1973). These must be supplemented by later materials such as Jean C. Darian's "Factors Influencing the Rising Labor Force Participation Rates of Married Women with Pre-school Children," *SSQ,* 56(1976): 614–30; Marion Gross Sobol's "A Dynamic Analysis of Labor Force Participation of Married Women of Childbearing Age," *JHR,* 8(Fall 1973): 497–505; and Elizabeth Waldman, Allyson Sherman Grossman, Robert Hayghe, and Beverly Johnson's "Working mothers in the 1970s: a look at the statistics," *MLR,* 102(Oct. 1979): 39–49.

The following articles examine the work force in terms of age or other factors: Allyson Sherman Grossman, "Women in the labor force: the early years," *MLR,* 98(Nov. 1975): 3–9; Deborah Pisetzner Klein, "Women in the labor force: the middle years," *MLR,* 98(Nov. 1975): 10–16; Beverly Johnson McEaddy, "Women in the labor force: the later years," *MLR,* 98(Nov. 1975): 17–24; Carol Leon, "Young adults: a traditional group with changing labor force patterns," *MLR,* 101(May 1978): 3–9; Allyson Sherman Grossman, "Labor force patterns of single women," *MLR,* 102(Aug. 1979): 46–49; Rudolph C. Blitz, "Women in the professions, 1870–1970," *MLR,* 97(May 1974): 34–39; Robert W. Bednarzik and Deborah P. Klein, "Labor force trends: a synthesis and analysis," in *MLR,* 100(Oct. 1977): 3–12; Janet L. Norwood and Elizabeth Waldman, "Women in the Labor Force: Some New Data Series," in Bureau of Labor Statistics, *Report 575* (Washington: GPO, 1975); Elizabeth Waldman and Beverly J. McEaddy, "Where women work—an analysis by industry and occupation," *MLR,* 97(May 1974): 3–13; Howard Davis, "Employment gains of women by industry, 1968–78," *MLR,* 103(June 1980): 3–9; and Anne McDougall Young and Howard Hayghe, "More U.S. workers are college graduates," *MLR,* 107(March 1984): 46–49.

A question that requires further study is the degree to which the structure of the labor force and attitudes of workers and employers affect female labor-force participation. William H. Whyte's "The Wives of Management," *Fortune,* 44(Oct. 1951): 86ff. casts some light. Jean A. Dowdall addresses the question more systematically in "Structural and Attitudinal Factors Associated with Female Labor Force Participation, *SSQ,* 55(June 1974): 121–30; Rossabeth Moss Kanter, *Men and Women of the Corporation* (New York: Basic, 1977), chap. 5, provides additional insights.

A major debate has centered on the economics of sex discrimination in the labor force. The best study is Cynthia B. Lloyd and Beth T. Niemi's *The Economics of Sex Differentials* (New York: Columbia University Press, 1979). But one should also examine Jacob Mincer's "On-the-job Training: Costs, Returns, and Some Implications," *Journal of Political Economy,* 70(Supplement, Oct. 1962): S50–S79, and Gary S. Becker's *Human Capital,* (New York: Columbia University Press, 1964). Paula England challenges Becker in "The Failure of Human Capital Theory to Explain Occupational Sex Segregation," *JHR,* 17(Summer 1982): 358–70. Other relevant articles are Gregory Williams' "The Changing U.S. Labor Force and Occupational Differentiation by Sex," *Demography* 16(1979): 73–87; Shirley J. Smith's "New worklife estimates reflect changing profile of labor force," *MLR,* 105(March 1982): 15–20; Nancy F. Rytina and Suzanne M. Bianchi's "Occupational reclassification and changes in distribution by gender," *MLR,* 107(March 1984): 11–17; and Andrea H. Beller's "Occupational Segregation by Sex: Determinants and Changes," *JHR,* 17(Summer 1982): 371–92.

Index

A

Abbott, Grace, 33, 51, 115
Abortion, 294, 301, 307, 329–32, 337–38, 407–410; access to, 293, 331–32; and colleges, 280; decriminalization of, 295; and ERA, 410; issue, 335; law, 308; referral, 357
Abzug, Bella, 289, 294, 334, 336, 337, 414
Acculturation: of American Indians, 176–77, 255–56; of Chinese Americans, 225–26, 227; of Japanese Americans, 171, 227–28, 250; of Jews, 163, 164, 229; of Mexican Americans, 181, 248; of Navajo, 253; of Puerto Rican Americans, 224–25
Ackerman, Nathan, 87
Addams, Jane, 33, 38, 39, 55–56, 64
Adkins v. *Children's Hospital,* 54, 117
Advertising, 90–91, 154–55, 206–207, 260, 290–91
Age: at first marriage, 267; impact on female labor force, 269–70
Agricultural employments. *See* Economy, primary sector; Occupations
Akron abortion ordinance, 407
Alexander, Shana, 294
Alianza Hispano-Americano, 179
Alien Land Act (California), 171
Alimony, 295, 344
Allan, Virginia, 294, 295
Allen, Florence, 115, 210
Allen, Frederick Lewis, 59, 63
Amalgamated Clothing Workers of America, 332
American Association of University Women (AAUW), 32, 48, 144, 150, 415
American Bar Association, 409
American Civil Liberties Union, 408–409
American Council on Education, 364
American Federation of Labor (AFL), 91, 106, 144
American Indian women, 24, 271, 272, 373, 401–402
American Indians, 174–77, 228–29, 251–56; education of, 78; federal policy toward, 228–29; and suffrage, 22; urban, 254–56
American Law Institute, 330
American Legion, 227
American Medical Association, 409
American Medical Women's Association, 142
American Nurses Association, 415
American Red Cross, 124, 127

American Telephone and Telegraph Co., 25, 421, 425
American Woman Suffrage Association, 32
American Women, Report of the Commission on the Status of Women, 257, 293
Ames, Jessie Daniel, 108–109
Anatomy is destiny, 17, 199, 200, 290, 313–14
And Keep Your Powder Dry (Mead), 147
Anderson, Eugenie, 209
Anderson, Ida, 62
Anderson, Marian, 110
Anderson, Mary, 48, 51, 52, 55, 64, 91, 131, 143
Anderson, Sherwood, 17
Androgyny, and sex roles, 292
Anglican church heritage, 5
Anthony, Susan, 32, 35, 36
Antiabortion movement, 331
Antifeminists, 392–93, 411
Anti-imperialism: and black feminism, 306
Anti-lynching movement, 109, 110. *See* Lynching
Anti-semitism, 167
Antiwar movement, 295
Army Nurse Corps: black women in, 127
Asian Americans, 22, 24, 167–74, 225–28, 249–51
Assimilation, and Mexican Americans, 308
Association of Social Workers, 415
Association of Southern Women for the Prevention of Lynching, 108
Athletes: women, 59, 90
Athletics: for women, 278, 363–64
Atkinson, Ti-Grace, 301

B

Bacall, Lauren, 153
Baker, Constance, 243
Baker, Ella, 237, 241
Baker, Helen, 124
Bancroft, Gertrude, 266
Bank of America, 421
Banner, Lois, 2, 60, 64, 90, 115
Bara, Theda, 57
Barnard College, 358
Barnett, Ross, 220, 238
Barth, Karl, 311
Bates, Daisy, 221
Bayh, Birch, 323
Beauvoir, Simone de, 291, 292, 303
Beck, Joan, 405

Bellamy, Edward, 15
Benedek, Terese, 313
"Benign neglect," 242, 246
Bennington College, 112
Benston, Margaret, 298
Benton, William, 277
Berkeley, Busby, 88
Bestor, Arthur, 211
Bethune, Mary McLeod, 108, 109
Bettelheim, Bruno, 214–15
Bird, Caroline, 357
Birth cohort: and work experience, 417–18
Birth control, 57–58, 294, 310–11; access to, 280, 328; and Margaret Sanger, 18, 19, 58; rationale for, 19, 58, 307, 328
Birth control movement, 58, 310–11
Birthrate, 93, 135, 191, 204, 267, 395
Black community, 9–15, 62–63
Black family, 244–47, 306–307, 399–400
Black feminism, 305–308
Black liberation, 305–306, 308
Black Muslims, 241
Black nationalism, 241
Black Panthers, 241, 295
Black Power, 241, 305
Black Rage (Grier & Cobbs), 307
Black revolution, 237–43, 308
Black women: achievers, 62; educational attainment of, 61, 401; fertility rate of, 397; and the Pill, 306; and suffrage, 36–37, 208; values of, 388; as workers, 24, 137, 138, 270–72, 369; in World War I, 25; 1920s, 61–63; 1930s, 102–103; in World War II, 125–27; in postwar years, 137; 1950s, 217–21; 1960s, 272–73; 1980s, 399–400
Black Women Organized for Action, 308
Blacks: migration of, 13, 15, 25, 61, 145
Blackwell, Alice Stone, 39, 52
Blackwell, Lucy Stone. *See* Stone, Lucy
Blatch, Harriot Stanton, 38
Blau, Zena Smith, 166
Blue collar employment, 134, 188, 370, 375–76. *See also* Economy, secondary sector
Bolton, Frances, 208
Bona fide occupational qualifications (BFOQ), 258–59, 324, 326, 345
Bonaparte, Marie, 313
Booth, Heather, 296
Bowen, Howard R., 403–404
Bowman, Henry A., 147
Bowman, Laura, 62
Boyliss, Lois, 88
Braceros, 222, 247
Bradwell v. *The State,* 53
Brickner, Balfour, 331
Brown, Charlotte Hawkins, 109

Brown, H. Rap, 241
Brown, Helen Gurley, 312
Brownmiller, Susan, 357
Brown v. *Topeka Board of Education,* 212, 220, 239, 240, 243
Bryn Mawr College, 358
Buck, Pearl, 88
Buddhism, 172, 173, 227
Bumpass, Larry, 268
Burns, Lucy, 38
Bush, Anita, 62
Butz, William, 396
Byrd, Harry, 220

C

Cable Act, 49, 170
Cagney, James, 87–88
Calhoun School, 12
Callister, Marion, 405
Campbell, Helen, 21
Capitalism: and exploitation of women, 306; and subordination of women, 296–97, 298
Caraway, Hattie, 116
Carmichael, Stokely, 241, 305
Carnegie Commission on Higher Education, 357
Carpenter, Liz, 294
Carson, Rachel, 211
Carter, Paul, 59
Carter, Rosalyn, 336
Castration complex, 199
Catholic church: opposition to abortion, 331
Catholics for Free Choice, 331, 409
Catt, Carrie Chapman, 35, 36, 38, 308, 334; assesses suffrage, 51; opposes ERA, 52; organizes "final drive," 39; rationale for woman suffrage, 39; on women athletes, 60
Cellar, Emanuel, 257
Century of Struggle (Flexner), 1
Chafe, William H., 2, 31; on economic changes, 64; "second emancipation" thesis, 125; on women's education, 111
Chicana, feminism, 308–309; status of, 222–23. *See also* Mexican American women
Child care, 15, 16, 144, 151–52, 294, 308, 310, 327–28, 396; debate over, in World War II, 140–41; and feminism, 327, 332; IWY Conference on, 338; need for, in 1970s, 328, 396; views of: Gilman, 16; NOW, 293; Schlafly, 340
Child custody, 344
Child and Family Service Act: vetoed, 327
Child labor, 27–28, 34, 35, 39, 49–50, 59, 95, 106, 116
Child rearing: collective, 298

Child support, 295–344
Child welfare legislation, 48
Children: living arrangements of, 399
Children's books: feminist critique of, 278
Children's Bureau, 51, 140
Chinese American women, 24, 168–70, 225–27, 250, 271, 373–74, 401
Chinese Exclusion Act, 170, 171
Chisholm, Shirley, 243, 294, 307, 327, 334
Christian heritage, 5
Citizens' Advisory Committee on the Status of Women, 294
Citizens' Advisory Council: on abortion, 330
Citizens' Advisory Council on the Status of Women, 261
Citizenship: for minority women, 160–61; for women, 49. *See also* Cable Act
Civil rights, 217, 404–416; and abortion, 330; for blacks, 145; and lesbians, 314; and Mexican Americans, 223; versus women's rights, 296
Civil Rights Act: of 1957, 219, 239; of 1960, 219, 239; of 1964, 239, 258–62, 293, 294, 369; of 1968, 341–42
Civil rights movement, 208, 237, 240, 241, 243, 280
Clark, Georgia Neese, 209
Clark, Kenneth, 240
Clark, Mae, 88
Clay, Laura, 38, 39, 40
Clerical work. *See* Occupations
Cobbs, Price M., 307
Cold War, 131, 218
Coleman Report, 240
Colleges: baccalaureate degrees, 146, 215, 276–77, 360; curriculum, 78, 80, 111, 148–49, 214; doctoral degrees, 147, 216–17, 277; fields of study in, 215, 216, 277; masters degrees, 146, 216, 277, 360; professional degrees, 277; women in, 215, 277–81; women faculty, 364
Colleges: and civil rights movement, 280; and feminism, 280–81; and New Left, 280; and peace movement, 280; and SDS, 280
Collier, John, 176
Collier's: on women's political roles, 207
Comfort, Alex, 311
Commission on Higher Education, Report of, 219
Commission on the Legal Status of Women, 257
Committee on Civil Rights, Report of, 219
Committee for Industrial Organization (CIO), 106
Commonweal, on employment of women, 123–24

Commonwealth v. *Daniels,* 350
Communal living, 298, 305, 312
Comparable worth, 422–25; defined, 422
Comprehensive Child and Family Services Act of 1975, 328
Comstock, Anthony, 8
Comstock law, 19
Conant, James B., 277
Congress of Racial Equality (CORE), 237, 241
Congressional Union, 38
Consciousness raising, 299–300, 301, 319
Conservative Caucus, The, 336
Consumer economy, 56–57
Contraception. *See* birth control
Cooke, Terence Cardinal, 331
Cornell University, 111, 362–63
Cosmopolitan magazine, 207
Costigan-Wagner Anti-lynching Bill, 109
Cotera, Marta, 309
Council on Interracial Cooperation, 108
Cox, James M., 47
Crawford, Joan, 89, 153, 154
Criminal law, and women, 348–51
Cuban American women, 248–49, 371–72
Cult of True Womanhood, 7–8; challenged by New Woman, 19; compared to feminine mystique, 290, 387
Curtis, Henry, 59–60

D

Danforth v. *Planned Parenthood,* 330–31
Darby case. See *United States* v. *Darby*
Dartmouth College, 363
Daughters of the American Revolution (DAR), 110, 218, 336
Daughters of Bilitis, 314
Davis, Bette, 89, 90, 153, 154
Davis, Katharine B., 58
Davis, Maxine, 88
Dawes Severalty Act, 175
Dean, Jerome "Dizzy," 87
Death rate, 192
Debs, Eugene, 18, 58
Declaration of Constitutional Principles, 220, 239
"Declaration of Sentiments," 8, 32
Degler, Carl, 7, 31, 33, 60
Delinquent girls: treatment of, 350
Dell, Floyd, 17
Democratic Party: endorses ERA, 143
Demographic factors. *See* Population, demography
Dennett, Mary Ware, 58
Department of Health, Education, and Welfare, 364

Depression: and education, 110, 112–13; fear of postwar, 131; impact on: black Americans, 102–105; Chinese Americans, 170; Japanese Americans, 172–73; Mexican Americans, 180; sex roles, 87; working women, 92

Desmond, Cleo, 62

Deutsch, Helene, 199, 200, 290, 313

Devaney, Barbara, 396

Dewson, Mary (Molly), 114, 209

Dialectic of Sex, The (Firestone), 303

Dickinson, Robert Latou, 310

Didrikson (Zaharias), Mildred "Babe," 90

Dietrich, Marlene, 88

Dillingham, Mabel, 12

Discrimination, 160; against Filipino Americans, 251; against Mexican Americans, 223; in colleges, 362–63. *See also* Racial discrimination; Sex discrimination

Divorce, 5, 23; among blacks, 10; IWY conference on, 338; Puritan view of, 6; in 1980s, 394, 398

Divorce rate: 1921–1977, Fig. 6-9, 205; 1950s, 192; 1960s, 268; age-specific rates of, 398–99

Divorce reform, 8, 32, 343, 413

Doe v. *Bolton,* 330

Dole, Elizabeth, 414

Domestic servants, 53, 68, 188; black women as, 24, 76, 105, 126

Domesticity: female, 7–8, 21, 388. *See also* Woman's place

Donovan, Frances, 71

"Double V" Campaign, 145

Douglas, Helen Gahagan, 208, 209

Douglas, Paul, 144

Douglass, Frederick, 36

Dowdall, Jean, 276

Dreiser, Theodore, 17

Dress: changes in women's, 57, 59; feminist critique of, 278–79

DuBois Clubs of America, 295

DuBois, William E. B., 14, 62, 109

Dunbar, Roxanne, 296, 298

Durand, John D., 131, 266

Durant, Will, 18

Durbin, Deanna, 153

Dwyer, Florence, 261

E

Eagle Forum, 336

Easterlin, Richard, 267–68, 396

Eastman, Max, 17, 18

Eastwood, Mary, 294

Ebony magazine, 307

Economic roles: attitudes toward, 317; changes in, 1900–1940, 107; future, 422; radical and lesbian critiques of, 392; in 1930s, 92–108

Economic status, of women: in 1900, 23–25; in 1920, 30–31; in 1980s, 416–17

Economy: post-industrial, 131, 185–87; primary sector, 65, 131, 185–86, 187; secondary sector, 65, 131, 186, 188; state of, 210–11, 364–65; structural changes in, 28–30, 65, 76–77, 99, 107–108, 132, 197; tertiary sector, 65, 131, 186, 188, 264, 365

Edelsberg, Herman, 259

Ederle, Gertrude, 60

Education: access to, 8, 11–13, 32, 77–81, 293, 337, 402–403; of American Indian women, 176, 229–30; critique of women's, 359; and impact on fertility, 396–97; Mexican American women, 179; of minority women, 146, 401–402; opportunity costs of, 396–97; two-year programs, 360; uses of women's, 111; 1920s, 77–80; 1930s, 110–13; 1940s, 145–50; 1950s, 213–17; 1960s, 276–82; 1970s, 356–64; 1980s, 400–404

Education Amendments Act, 342, 363, 364

Educational attainment, 401–402; impact on female labor force, 273–75; impact on supply of female workers, 380–81

Educational Testing Service, 213, 214

Edwards, India, 207

Ehrenreich, Barbara, 391

Eisenhower, Dwight D., 207, 209; and civil rights, 219; endorses ERA, 211; and Little Rock crisis, 221

Electra complex, 17, 199, 304

Elementary school. *See* Schools, elementary

Ellis, Havelock, 17, 19, 310

Elshtain, Jean Bethke, 393

Employment. *See* Labor force; Occupations; Work

Enclave cultures: Chinese American, 250; Cuban American, 249; Harlem, 62; Mexican American, 181–82, 223; Puerto Rican, 223

Engels, Friedrich, 296–97

Equal Credit Opportunity Act, 337, 342

Equal Employment Opportunity Commission (EEOC), 239, 258, 260, 424

Equal Pay Act, of 1963, 257, 293; 1972 amendments to, 341. *See also* Pepper-Morse Equal Pay Bill

Equal pay for equal work principle, 39, 48, 141, 143, 144, 211, 257–58, 302, 318, 424

Equal Rights Amendment (ERA): and abortion, 410; attitudes toward, 352, 404–405;

debate over: in 1930s, 117; in 1940s, 141–43, 144; in 1950s, 211; defeat of, 405–407; endorsed, 92, 143, 211; need for, in 1960s, 256–57; and NOW platform, 293; opposition to, 325, 326, 332, 339, 392, 406; proposed 1923, 52, 54; ratification struggle, 351–53, 405; revived, 323–26; support for, 326

Equal Rights for women, 51–55, 91–92, 256–62, 325, 326. *See also* ERA
Erikson, Erik H., 313
Erskine, John, 88
Ervin, Sam, Jr., 324–25
Evars, Medgar, 238–39
Eve, 5
Everything You Always Wanted to Know About Sex, But Were Afraid to Ask (Reuben), 311
Executive Order: 8802, 125; 11375, 261
Existentialism: and feminism 296; and Germaine Greer, 302; and lesbianism, 314; and Margaret Sanger, 58; and New Woman, 21; and sexual revolution, 311

F

Fair Employment Practices Commission, 125
Fair Labor Standards Act, 95, 106, 116, 117, 210. *See also* Equal Pay Act
Family planning and feminism, 332
Family Protection Act (proposed), 412
Family, 7, 31–33, 326–32, 390–400; American Indian, 174, 253–54; black, 10–11, 244–47; Chinese American, 168–70; Hispanic, 399; Japanese American, 171–72, 228; Mexican American, 309; Puerto Rican, 224–25
Family: female-headed, 11, 245, 246, 306; in flux, 393–94; generational conflict, 170, 172–74, 177, 181, 225; patriarchal, 5, 303, 316; single-parent, 244, 394, 399; two-parent, 399
Family, critique of: anti-feminist, 392–93; feminists, 332; Germaine Greer, 302–303; Juliet Mitchell, 297–98; New Right, 392–93; radical feminist, 298, 392; Shulamith Firestone, 304
Farm laborers. *See* Occupations
Farmer, James, 240
Farnham, Marynia, 199, 200, 202, 391
Faubus, Orval, 220, 221
Fauset, Jessie Redmond, 62
Federal Council on Negro Affairs, 109
Federally Employed Women, 319
Felton, Rebecca Latimer, 50
Female Eunuch, The (Greer), 302
Female labor force. *See* Labor force, female

"Female" occupations, 26, 68, 102–103, 134, 189, 418–20; role of schools in training women for, 214
Female roles. *See* Sex roles
Feme covert, 49, 342
Feme sole, 50
Feminine mystique, 197–207, 327; defined, 290
Feminine Mystique, The (Friedan), 236, 288
Feminism: and birth control movement, 310–11; black, 305–308; and black liberation movement, 308; challenged, 332–41; and Charlotte Gilman, 16–17; Chicana, 179, 308–309; concept of, expanded, 326–27; and the family, 326–32; and Friedrich Engels, 296–97; goals of, 32; and growth of labor force, 197; and illegitimacy, 397–98; impact of, on women's education, 356–64; and Juliet Mitchell, 297; moderate, 289–95; perceived as anti-family, 406; radical, 295–305; re-emerges, 281; reinforced, 91; student, 280–81, 356–58; and view of female sexuality, 309–310; and view of history, 2–3; and women's economic roles, 64
Feminist Studies, 357
Feminists, The, 301
Feminization of American culture, 88
Ferguson, Miriam, 50
Ferraro, Geraldine, 415, 416
Fertility rate, 205, 397; rate by race, 1940–1980, Fig. 6-10, 206; relationship to LFPR, 396
Fifth Amendment: and sex discrimination, 326
Filipino Americans, 250–51; educational attainment of, 401–402; in labor force, 373–74; LFPR of, 271
Finkbine, Sherri, 330
Firestone, Shulamith, 296, 300, 301, 303–305
Fitzgerald, F. Scott, 57
Flappers, 55–61
Flexner, Eleanor, 1, 2
Flynn, Elizabeth Gurley, 58
Ford, Betty, 336
Ford, Gerald, 328, 334
Ford, Henry, 167
Foreign-born women: and suffrage, 22; unemployment of, 102
Fortune, 120, 150, 423
Fourier, Charles, 296
Fourteenth Amendment, 142, 324, 325, 326, 410
Frazier, E. Franklin, 244, 246
Free Speech Movement, 295
Freedom Riders, 237
Freeman, Jo, 296
Freeman, Mrs. Franklin, 243

Freud, Sigmund, 17–18, 199, 310, 313; critique of, 290, 304; popularization of, 57–58
Freudians, 17, 199–202, 203
Freund, Paul, 325
Friedan, Betty, 215, 259, 279, 281, 289–95, 302, 334, 336, 338, 357, 391; critique of, 391–92
Friends of Family Planning, 415
Full Employment Act, 143, 210–11
Fuller, Margaret: and Betty Friedan, 291
Functionalism: and Margaret Mead, 290

G

Gallup Poll, 92, 140
Gamble, Clarence J., 310
Garson, Greer, 153
Garvey, Marcus, 61–62
Gaynor, Janet, 88
Geiger, Abraham, 163
Gellhorn, Martha, 90
Gender-gap, 414
General Federation of Women's Clubs (GFWC), 32, 37, 48, 142
Genocide: of black society, 307–308
Gentlemen's Agreement, 171
"Georgiatown" study, 246–47
German American women, 24
Gildersleeve, Virginia, 111, 209
Gilman, Charlotte Perkins, 15–17, 23, 51, 55, 64, 298, 327, 390; compared to Margaret Sanger, 18–19
Gilson, Mary, 124
Glick, Paul, 395
Goldman, Emma, 18, 58
Gordon, Kate M., 38–39, 40
Grable, Betty, 153
Graves, Dixie Bibb, 116
Green, Edith, 208, 258
Greenwich Village, 21
Greer, Germaine, 302–303
Grier, William H., 307
Griffiths, Martha, 208, 258, 260, 324, 416
Grimké, Angelina W., 62
Gutman, Herbert, 10

H

Hadassah, 166–67
Hall, Adelaide, 62
Hall, G. Stanley, 17
Halsey, Elizabeth, 59
Hamer, Fannie Lou, 237, 241, 294
Hamilton, Alice, 33
Hampton Institute, 12
Harden, Mrs. Cecil, 209
Harding, Warren, 48

Harlem, 62
Harlem Renaissance, 62
Harper's magazine, 207
Harriman, Florence J., 115
Harrington, Michael, 244
Harris, La Donna, 294
Harris, Patricia, 243
Hasidim, 229
Hatch Amendment, 410
Hatch, Orrin, 408
Hayden, Carl, 144
Hayden rider: to ERA, 211
Hayes, Helen, 207
Haywood, William "Big Bill," 18
Hayworth, Rita, 153, 154
Head Start Program, 327
Heath, Mariwyn, 405
Heckler, Margaret, 261, 414
Heide, Wilma Scott, 294
Hellman, Lillian, 55
Helms, Jesse, 408
Hemingway, Ernest, 57, 311
Hennock, Frieda, 209
Henry, O., 71
Henry Street Settlement, 34
Hepburn, Katharine, 89, 154
Heritage: American Indian, 174–75; black community, 9; Chinese American, 168–69; Christian, 5–6; Japanese American, 171–72; Jewish, 161–62, 164–65; Judaic, 5; Mexican American, 178–79; Puerto Rican American, 224–25
Hernandez, Aileen, 293, 316, 352
Hickey, Margaret, 129, 207
High school. *See* Schools, secondary
Hirshberger, Ruth, 304
Hispanic Americans, 22, 24, 78, 177–81, 222–25, 352, 361, 370–73. *See also* Cuban Americans; Mexican Americans; Puerto Rican Americans
History of the Woman Suffrage Movement (Stanton, Anthony & Gage), 1
Hite, Shere, 314
Hobby, Oveta Culp, 209
Hodgson, James D., 261
Hoey, Jane, M., 209
Holbrook, Stewart, 88
Hollinshead, Byron, 217
Holmes, Hamilton, 221
Homemaking, 130, 203, 291
Homosexuality, 5, 298. *See also* Lesbianism
Honeyman, Nan Wood, 115
Hood, James, 238
Hoover administration, 176
Hoover, Lou Henry, 113
Hopi, 251

Horney, Karen, 200
Housekeeping: opportunity costs of, 396
Housewives, 202, 203, 289, 291–92, 298, 338
Houston Conference (IWY), 334–39
Howe, Julia Ward, 32
Hull House, 33
Human capital, 421
Human Sexuality: New Directions in American Catholic Thought (Kosnik), 312
Humphrey, Hubert, 207
Hunter, Charlayne, 221
Hurston, Zora Neal, 62
Husband's place, 31. *See* Male roles
Hyde Amendment, 411

I

Ibsen, Henrik, 302
Ickes, Harold, 110
Illegitimacy, 245, 344, 397
Illiteracy, 12, 13, 110, 253
Immaculate Heart of Mary, College of the, 358
Immigration Act of 1924, 170, 251
in loco parentis, 280–81
Indian Reorganization Act. *See* Wheeler-Howard Act
Innis, Roy, 241
Insurance benefits for women, 347
Integration, 221, 242. *See also* Segregation
Intermarriage, 250, 256, 309
International Women's Year Conference (IWY), 334–39
Interracialism, 108–110
Intra-uterine device. *See* IUD
Irish-Americans, 23–24
Issei, 171–74. *See also* Japanese Americans, Nisei, and Sansei
Italian Americans, 24
IUD, 310, 329

J

Jacobs, Helen, 90
Japanese Americans, 24, 171–74, 227–28, 250, 271, 373–74, 401
Jefferson, Mildred, 331
Jewish community, 161–67, 229–30; attitude toward abortion, 409; Conservative, 167; Orthodox, 164–65; Reform, 162–63
Jobs. *See* Labor force, female; Occupations
John Birch Society, 336
Johnson, Charles S., 62, 244
Johnson, Georgia Douglas, 62
Johnson, Lady Bird, 336
Johnson, Lyndon, 239, 240, 243, 261, 277, 327
Johnson, Owen, 21

Johnson, Virginia, 314
Jones Act, 223
Jones, Jennifer, 154
Jordan, Barbara, 336
Journalists, women, 90
Judaic heritage, 5
Jury duty, 211, 351

K

Kahn, Florence, 115
Kanowitz, Leo, 325, 326, 341
Kaufman, Alvin R., 310
Keating-Owen Act, 49
Kefauver, Estes, 144, 207
Kelley, Alice, 88
Kelley, Florence, 33, 34, 38, 49, 52, 53, 54
Kennedy administration, 256–57, 293
Kennedy, John F., 207, 238, 239, 243, 260, 277, 345
Kenyon, Dorothy, 209
Kierkegaard, Soren, 311
Kilpatrick, James, 404
King, Billie Jean, 289, 336
King, Coretta Scott, 336
King, Martin Luther, Jr., 237, 240
Kinsey, Alfred, 58, 314
Kirchwey, Freda, 90
Kirkpatrick, Jeanne, 414
Klamaths, 228
Klein, Viola, 204
Knowles, Gladys, 207
Koedt, Anne, 300, 301, 314
Kohut, Rebekah Bettelheim, 166
Komarovsky, Mirra, 87, 149, 202, 203, 279, 391
Koontz, Elizabeth, 262
Korean Americans, 373–74
Korean War, 192
Krafft-Ebing, Richard von, 17
Krol, Cardinal, 331
Ku Klux Klan, 167, 336
Kurland, Phillip, 325

L

Labor force: 1900–1920, 23–31; 1920s, 63–77; 1930s, 92–108; 1940s, 122–37; 1950s, 185–97; 1960s, 263–76; 1970s, 364–83; 1980s, 416–22
Labor force, female: demand for, 28–30, 64–70, 99–102, 124–27, 132–34, 185–91, 264–66, 364–76, 418–20; changes in, 1920–1930, Fig. 2-2, 67; changes in, 1930–1940, Fig. 3-7, 101; changes in, 1940–1950, Fig. 4-2, 133; changes in, 1950–1960, Fig. 6-2, 187; changes in, 1960–1970, Fig. 7-3, 267; changes in, 1970–1980, Fig. 10-5, 375

Labor force, female, marital status of: divorced, separated and widowed women, 135, 269, 377–78; married women, 28, 72, 74, 98–99, 128–29, 136, 192–93, 269, 377–78; single women, 28, 71, 96, 135, 268, 377–78, 417

Labor force, female, minority women in, 270–73, 369–74; American Indian women, 272, 373; Asian American women, 271–73, 373–74; black women, 28–29, 75–76, 103–106, 125–27, 137, 270–71, 369–70; Hispanic women, 271–73, 370–73

Labor force, female, occupations of, 66–68, 99–102, 133, 187–89, 263–65, 366–68, 375, 418. *See also* "Female" occupations

Labor force, female, part-time, 71–72, 195–96, 203–204, 273–74, 383

Labor force, female, supply of, 27–28, 70–77, 92–99, 128–30, 135–37, 191–97, 266–76, 377–83, 416–18; attitudinal factors in, 276; and elasticity of, 273, 382–83. *See also* Educational attainment; Population, demography

Labor force, primary, 250, 254, 419–20; defined, 418

Labor force, secondary, 251, 254, 419–20; defined, 418

Labor force, sexual division of, 26, 68–70, 102, 141, 189–90, 325, 418–20, 421–22. *See also* "Female" occupations

Ladies' Home Journal, 87

Landers, Ann, 312

Lanham Act, 140–41

Larsen, Nell, 62

Latch-key children, 140

Lathrop, Julia, 33, 48, 64

Lawson, Marjorie, 243

Laxalt, Paul, 412

Leadership Conference of Women Religious, 410

League of Women Voters, 48, 50, 55, 91, 144, 212, 294, 319, 334, 414

Legal status of women, 6, 8, 22, 341–45

Lehman, Herbert, 144

Lepper, Howard J., 151

Lerner, Gerda, 1

Lesbian feminism, 314–16, 391, 392

Lesbian rights, 316, 335, 337–38

Leuchtenburg, William, 63–64

Lewis, Hylan, 244, 247

Lewis, Oscar, 225, 244

LFPR: and age, 30, 74, 75, 96, 195, 270; and birth cohorts, 97, 98; and fertility rate, 396; and marital status, 194, 195, 269; and minority women, 249, 270–71, 372; and race, 75, 96; and school completed, 275; and wartime increase in, 130; 1900–1920,

26, 30; 1920s, 65, 73–75; 1930s, 95–96, 97, 99; 1940s, 130, 136; 1950s, 187, 194, 195; 1960s, 269–70, 270–71; 1970s, 364, 371, 377–80; 1980s, 416–17, 419

Life expectancy, 417–18

Life magazine, 144, 202, 203

Lifestyles. *See* Sex roles

Lippmann, Walter, 18

Little Rock, Ark., 221

Liuzzo, Viola, 240

Livermore, Mary, 32

Living-together-arrangement, 304, 312, 398

Lloyd, Cynthia, 421

Lochner v. New York, 34, 53, 54

Locke, Alain, 62

Lombard, Carole, 89–90

Long, Clarence, 266

Long, Rose, 116

Louis, Joe, 87

Lowell, Josephine Shaw, 34

Luce, Clare Booth, 209

Lucy, Autherine, 221

Luhan, Mabel Dodge, 17

Lundberg, Ferdinand, 200, 202, 391

Luta, Alma, 142, 143, 144

Lynching, 13, 14, 108–110

Lynd, Robert and Helen, 57–58, 87

M

McBride, Katharine, 149

McCall's magazine, 87, 206–207

McCarthy, Joseph, 208

McClendon, Rose, 62

McCormack, Ellen, 331

McCormick, Anne O'Hare, 90

McCormick, Ruth Hanna, 50, 115

McCulloch, Catharine Waugh, 38

McGovern, James, 20, 21

McIntosh, Millicent, 207

McKinney, Susan, 15

McKissick, Floyd, 241

McLaurin v. Oklahoma, 220

McNeer, Lenore, 339

McSherry, Louis, 140

Malcolm X, 241

Male egos, 87–88

Male and Female (Mead), 147

Male roles, 6, 87, 204, 245, 246–47, 253, 291, 301, 309, 392

Malone, Vivian, 221, 238

Manners and morals: revolution in, 55. *See* Sexual revolution

Manning, Alice, 142

Marble, Alice, 90

March-for-Life, 336, 408

Marital status, 72–73, 136, 193, 195, 267, 274, 378

Marriage, 10, 31; age at first, 204–205, 342, 394–95; critiques of, 5, 16, 18, 21, 169, 297–98, 338; demographic changes in, 394–95; rates, 132, 191–92, 204–205

Marriage for Moderns (Bowman), 147

Married women's property law, 342–43

Married women's property rights, 9, 22–23, 32, 295, 404, 413

Marshall, Thurgood, 243, 326

Marx, Karl, 18, 296

Marxism, 18, 295, 297, 303–304. *See* Socialism

Masculine mystique, 327

Maslow, A. H., 291

Masters, William, 314

Maternity: benefits, 308; leave, 293; legislation, 48

Matriarchal family, 246, 306. *See* Family

Matthews, Burnita Shelton, 52, 210

Matthews, Victoria Earle, 14–15

May, Catherine, 261

May, Henry F., 21

Mead, Margaret, 147, 201, 290

Meese, Edwin, 424

Memorandum on the Status of Negroes, 245

Menominees, 229

Men's groups, 212

Menstruation, 5, 162

Meredith, James, 238

Meriam, Lewis, 175–76

Meriam Report, 78, 175–76

Mesta, Pearl, 209

Metropolitan Opera Company, 110

Mexican Americans, 177–81, 222–23, 247–48, 271, 371, 401–402

Migration: of blacks, 13, 15, 25, 61, 145; of Chinese Americans, 168, 226; Cuban Americans, 248–49; Filipino Americans, 251; Japanese Americans, 171; Jewish Americans, 162, 164, 166; Mexican Americans, 179–81, 222; Puerto Rican Americans, 223, 224

Mikva, Abner, 262

Mills, Florence, 62

Mincer, Jacob, 421

Minimum wage laws. *See* Protective legislation; Wages and hours legislation

Minnesota, University of, 358

Minority women: American Indian, 174–77, 228–29, 251–56, 373; Asian American, 167–74, 225–28, 249–51, 373–74; attitude toward ERA, 352; blacks, 9–15, 61–63, 108–110, 125–27, 217–21, 237–47, 305–308, 369–70; educational attainment of, 401–402; Hispanic American, 177–82,

222–25, 247–49, 308–309, 370–73; Jews, 161–67, 229–30; plan for rights of, 337; values of, 390. *See also* specific groups

Miss America Pageant, 60

Mississippi Freedom Democratic Party (MFDP), 241

Mitchell, Juliet, 297–99

Modern Woman: The Lost Sex, The (Lundberg & Farnham), 200

Mojados, 222, 240–49

Moral Majority, 391, 416

Morgan, Robin, 296

Mormon church, 333, 335–36, 387, 406

Morse, Wayne, 141

Mortality rates, 191

Mosaic law, 5

Moses, 5

Moskowitz, Belle, 50

Motherhood, 15, 59, 166, 198–99, 291, 292, 338

Mother's pensions, 211. *See also* Social Security

Mount Holyoke College, 358

Movies, 57, 88–90, 152–54

Mowry, George, 64

Moynihan, Daniel P., 244, 245, 246

Moynihan Memorandum, 242

Ms. Foundation for Women, 409

Mucahy, Meta, 331

Muhammed, Elijah, 241

Muller v. *Oregon,* 35, 53

Munaker, Sue, 296

Murray, Pauli, 307–308

Myrdall, Alva, 204

Myrdall, Gunnar, 217, 244, 246

N

NAACP. *See* National Association for the Advancement of Colored People

NACW. *See* National Association of Colored Women

Nash, Diane, 237

Nation, The, magazine, 17, 21

National Abortion Rights Action League, 331, 408, 415

National Advisory Commission on Civil Disorders, 242–43

National American Woman Suffrage Association, 35, 48

National Association for the Advancement of Colored People (NAACP), 14, 109, 145

National Association of Colored Women, 14, 32, 108–109

National Association of Manufacturers, 49

National Association of Women Lawyers, 142

National Birth Control League, 58

National Black Feminist Organization, 308, 352
National Collegiate Athletic Association, 363
National Commission on the Observance of IWY, 334
National Committee to Defeat the Unequal Rights Amendment, 143
National Conference on the New Politics, 300
National Conference of Catholic Bishops, 331, 410
National Conference of Catholic Charities, 410
National Conservative Political Action Committee, 416
National Consumers' League (NCL), 34, 37, 48, 55, 91, 210
National Council of Catholic Women, 333, 336
National Council of Jewish Women, 32, 163
National Council of Negro Women, 109
National Council of Women, 109
National Education Association (NEA), 415
National Farm Bureau Federation, 49
National Federation of Business and Professional Women's Clubs (NFBPWC), 92, 107, 212, 334
National Industrial Recovery Act, 94, 106, 116, 210
National Labor Relations Act, 106
National League of Women Voters. *See* League of Women Voters
National Manpower Council, 189
National Maritime Union, 145
National Metals Trades Association, 127
National Organization of Women (NOW), 259, 293–95, 316, 319, 327, 330, 331, 332, 334, 339, 349, 350, 352, 387, 391, 400, 405, 409, 410, 414, 416
National Parent-Teacher Association (PTA), 32, 48
National Plan of Action, 336–39
National Right-to-Life Committee, 331, 336. *See* Right-to-Life Movement
National Urban League, 14
National War Labor Board, 141
National Woman Suffrage Association (NWSA), 32, 35, 141
National Woman's Party, 38, 39, 51, 54, 294. *See* Alice Paul
National Women's Political Caucus (NWPC), 294, 327, 334, 414, 416
National Women's Studies Association, 357
National Women's Trade Union League (NWTUL), 34, 48, 55, 91, 210
National Youth Administration, 109, 116
Native Americans. *See* American Indians
Natural rights, 37, 316
Navajos, 24, 176, 251–52, 253–54

NAWSA. *See* National American Woman Suffrage Association
NCL. *See* National Consumers' League
Negro Family: The Case for National Action, The (Moynihan), 244
Neo-Malthusian League, 19
New Deal, 91, 94–95, 100–101, 105, 106, 113, 116. *See* Roosevelt administration
New Left Notes, 296
New Left, 280, 295–97, 318, 326
New Negro Movement, 62
New Right, 393, 411–12, 414–16
New Woman, 19–21, 55, 61
New York City Bar Association, 112
New York Consumers' League. *See* National Consumers' League
New York Radical Feminists, 301
Newell, Barbara, 359
Newsweek, 130, 131, 144, 207
Niebuhr, Reinhold, 311
Niemi, Beth, 421
Nietzsche, Friedrich, 18
Nineteenth Amendment, 22, 47, 50, 51, 54
Nisei, 172–74, 227–28. *See* Japanese Americans
Niskanen, Bill, 423
Nixon administration, 243
Nixon, Patricia, 262
Nixon, Richard, 207, 242, 261, 262, 327–28
Norris, Louis William, 217
North Carolina Agricultural and Technical College, 237
Norton, Eleanor Holmes, 241
Norton, Mary, 115, 141, 208
NOW. *See* National Organization of Women
NPWC. *See* National Women's Political Caucus
NWTUL. *See* National Women's Trade Union League

O

O'Connell, William, Cardinal, 49
O'Connor, Sandra Day, 414
O'Neill, Eugene, 17
O'Neill, George, 311
O'Neill, Nena, 311
Occupation: black women, by, Fig. 4-4, 138; distribution by ethnic group, 1960–1970, Fig. 7-1, 272; distribution of women by, 1970–1980, Fig. 10-2, 366; distribution of women by race and, 1972 and 1980, Fig. 10-3, 369; employed women by, and race, 1950, Fig. 4-5, 139; employment by, 1960–1970 and 1970–1980, Fig. 7-1, 263; "female," 1940, Fig. 3-8, 103; "female," 1950–1960, Fig. 6-3, 190; female labor force by, 1950–1960, Fig. 6-1, 186; female labor

force by, 1960–1970, Fig. 7-2, 265; gainful workers by, 1930–1940, Fig. 3-6, 100

Occupations: blue collar, 134, 188, 365, 367–68, 370, 375–76; clerical, 68, 102, 105, 134, 264, 366–67; domestic servant, 23, 24, 76, 105, 132, 188, 368; farm laborer, 67, 76, 126, 132; nurse, 68, 127, 189, 264; professional, 68, 124, 134, 264, 365, 367; sales, 26, 71; secretary, 68, 189; teacher, 23, 68, 72, 189, 264; telephone operator, 25, 69, 189; white collar, 67–68, 102, 105, 124, 133–34, 188–89, 264, 365, 366–67, 368, 375. *See* "Female" occupations

Occupations for: American Indian women, 24, 252–53; Chinese American women, 24, 169; Cuban American women, 372; Filipino American women, 251, 373–74; Japanese American women, 24, 250, 271, 373–74; Jewish American women, 164–67; Mexican American women, 179–80, 223, 247–48, 272; Puerto Rican American women, 371–73

Occupational shares: constant share, expanded share: 1920s, 66–68; 1930s, 99–102; 1940s, 133; 1950s, 187–89; 1960s, 263, 265; 1970s, 366–68, 1980s, 418

Oedipus complex, 17, 199, 304

Office of Federal Contract Compliance (OFCC), 261

Oldfield, Fanny, 115

Open Marriage (O'Neill & O'Neill), 312

Operation Wakeup, 333

Oppression of women, 307, 308–309, 315, 392

Oral contraceptives. *See* Pill, The

Organizations, voluntary. *See* Women's clubs

Origin of the Family, Private Property and the State, The (Engels), 296

Other America, The (Harrington), 244

Owen, Ruth Bryan, 50, 115, 209

P

Parent's Magazine, 206

Parks, Rosa, 237

Parrish case. See *West Coast Hotel* v. *Parrish*

Parsons, Talcott, 147, 148

Participatory democracy, 200, 301

Passing (Larsen), 62

Patrilineal system, 316

Paul, Alice, 38, 39, 47, 51, 53, 54, 55, 91, 144, 211, 341

Paul, the Apostle, 5

Peace movement, 280

Peale, Norman Vincent, 206

Pearl Harbor, 122–23

Pendleton, Clarence M., Jr., 423, 424

Penis envy, 199, 200

Penn School, 12

Pensions for women, 211, 347–48. See Social Security

Pepper, Claude, 141

Pepper-Morse Equal Pay Bill, 143

Perkins, Frances, 115, 130–31, 135, 144

Peterson, Esther, 257

Phillips v. *Martin Marietta,* 259–60, 324, 326

Pickford, Mary, 57

Piety, female, 7, 8, 19, 162, 290

Pill, The, 268, 280, 306, 310, 329

Pima women, 24

"Pin money," 54, 92

Pittsburgh Courier, 145

Pittsburgh Press Co. v. *Pittsburgh Commission on Human Relations,* 269

Planned Parenthood of Missouri v. *Danforth,* 330–31

Planned parenthood movement, 310–11, 408

Plessy v. *Ferguson,* 9, 219

Political roles, 22–23, 50, 55–56, 113–17, 207–13, 317, 337, 413–16

Political status: of blacks, 9–10, 13; of women, 22–23, 351

Population: demographic changes, 27, 92–94, 128–30, 204–205, 266–76, 377–78, 393–94

Population, demographic factors: age, white women by age, 1900–1920, Fig. 1-1, 27; white women by age, 1930–1940, Fig. 3-1, 93; population by age group, 1950–1960, Fig. 6-4, 192; birthrate, 267–68; children under 5 years old, 1880–1940, Fig. 3-2, 94; divorce rate, 1921–1977, Fig. 6-9, 205, 268; fertility rate by race, 1940–1980, Fig. 6-10, 206; marital status, 1920–1930, Fig. 2-3, 72, 73; 1950–1960, Fig. 6-5, 193; marriage rate, 1921–1977, Fig 6-9, 205, 267; proportion of youths and elderly females by race, Fig. 3-4, 95

Populists, 9

Port Huron Statement, 295

Pound, Roscoe, 52

Powdermaker, Hortense, 244

Power of the Positive Woman, The (Schlafly), 339

Pratt, Ruth, 115

Pregnancy counseling, 357

President's Commission on the Status of Women, 343

President's Task Force on Women's Rights and Responsibilities, 327

Primary labor force, 250, 254, 419–20; defined, 418

2 2 0

Primary sector (of economy): defined, 28; 65, 131, 185–86, 187
Princeton University, 363
Pro-Life Action Committee, 331
Professional employment. *See* Occupations
Professional Women's Caucus (PWC), 319
Progressive Labor Party, 295–96
Progressive Movement, 33, 34, 37
Property rights of married women. *See* Married women's property rights
Prostitution, 8, 37, 59, 168, 310, 349–50
Protective legislation, 34, 38, 39, 52, 53, 54, 138–39, 140, 142, 143, 144, 150–51, 210, 258, 259, 324, 340
Psychology of Women, The (Deutsch), 290
"Psychology of Women, The" (Freud), 17, 199
Public Health Service Act, 329
Public policy, 137–45
Public roles of women: and educational access, 402–403; as office holders, 50, 115; as voters, 50–51, 115, 415–16
Pueblo women, 24
Puerto Rican American women, 223–25, 248, 271–72, 306, 371–72, 401–402
Punishment of women, 350–51
Puritan heritage, 5–6
Purity crusade, 8
Purity, female, 7, 8, 290

Q

Quicksand (Larsen), 62

R

Racial discrimination, 13–14, 125, 127, 145, 167
Racial segregation. *See* Segregation
Radcliffe College, 358
Radical feminism. *See* Feminism
Radical feminists, 299–305, 314, 316, 318, 319, 391–92, 410
Radical students, 281
Randolph, A. Philip, 125
Rankin, Jeannette, 22, 39, 50
Rape, 348–49
Rappaport, Nathan, 301
Rawalt, Marguerite, 294
Reagan administration, 405, 411–12, 424
Reagan, Ronald, 408
Redstockings, The, 300, 301
Redstockings Manifesto, 300
Reed, John, 18
Reid, Charlotte, 261
Relief Society (Mormon), 335
Religious Coalition for Abortion Rights, 331, 409

Rensselear Polytechnic Institute, 147
Repplier, Agnes, 20
Reproduction, 303, 327, 328–29. *See* Birth control
Republican Party, 92, 143, 405, 411–12
Reuben, David, 311
Rhode, Ruth Bryan Owen, 209. *See* Ruth Bryan Owen
Rickover, Hyman, 277
Right-to-Life Movement, 334, 335, 336
Riots, 238, 241, 242
Robins, Margaret Dreier, 4, 34, 425
Robinson, Patricia, 306
Robinson, Ruby Doris Smith, 305. *See* Smith, Ruby Doris
Roche, Josephine, 209
Rockefeller, John D., Jr., 310
Rodman, Henrietta, 18
Roe v. Wade, 330, 338, 407, 409–410
Rogers, Edith Nourse, 50, 115, 208
Rogers, Ginger, 153
Rogers, Robert, 88
Role models, 111–12
Roles. *See* Sex roles
Roman Catholics: and abortion, 331, 333, 336, 353, 409–410; and birth control, 329
Roosevelt administration (Franklin), 114–15, 176
Roosevelt, Eleanor, 109, 113–14, 144, 207, 208, 209, 211, 257
Roosevelt, Franklin D., 109, 125, 131, 137–38, 141, 209
Roosevelt, Theodore, 37, 390
Rosenberg, Anna, 209
Rosie the Riveter, 122–23, 125, 130
Ross, Nellie Tayloe, 50
Rossi, Alice, 210, 292, 294, 357
Rubenstein, B. B., 313
Ruffin, Josephine St. Pierre, 15
Rupp, Leila, 2
Russell, Rosalind, 154
Rutgers Clinic, 19
Rutgers University, 358
Ryan, Mary, 64
Ryder, Norman B., 268

S

St. George, Katharine, 208, 211
Sanger, Margaret Higgins, 18–19, 57–58, 310
Sanger, William, 18
Sansei, 228, 250. *See* Japanese Americans
Sarachild, Kathie, 300
Sarah Lawrence College, 112, 358
Sartre, Jean-Paul, 311
Schaffer, Gloria, 336

Schecter, Solomon, 167

Scheinfeld, Amram, 199

Schlafly, Phyllis, 333, 336, 338, 339–41, 352, 368, 391, 393, 405, 410, 411, 412

Schlesinger, Arthur Maier, Sr., 1

Schools: colleges, 79–80, 110–11, 146, 214, 215, 356–64, 402–403; curriculums of, 80, 111, 214, 278; democratization of, 77–78, 130; elementary, 11–12, 77–78, 110, 400; impact on American Indians, 175, secondary, 12, 77–79, 110, 130, 146, 278, 400; social function, of, 78–79

Schwartz, Bernard, 325

SDS. *See* Students for a Democratic Society

Seaton, Fred, 229

"Second emancipation" thesis, 125, 127

Second Sex, The (Beauvoir), 292

Second Stage, The (Friedan), 392

Secondary labor force, 251, 254, 419–20; defined, 418

Secondary sector (of economy), 65, 131, 186, 188; defined, 28

Segmented labor market, 66, 418–20. *See* Labor force, sexual division of

Segregation, 61, 105–106, 127, 212, 218, 220, 237–43

Self-realization, 291, 311

Selma, Alabama: march on, 240

Seneca Falls Convention, 8, 37

Seneca Falls Declaration, 8, 32

Settlement house movement, 33–34, 37, 91

Sex is destiny, 304, 325. *See* Anatomy is destiny

Sex discrimination, 53, 293, 342; against women faculty, 364; analysis of, by Martha Griffiths, 324; analysis of, by Sam Ervin, 324–25; in colleges, 281, 358; and Education Amendments Act, 363; and Equal Pay Act, 257–58; in job market, 345; in punishment, 350–51; and Richard Nixon, 261; and Title VII, 258

Sex roles: American Indian women, 175, 177, 255; black women, 10–11, 62–63, 244–47; Chinese Americans, 69–70, 168, 226–27; Japanese Americans, 172, 250; Jewish Americans, 161–62, 164, 229; Mexican Americans, 181, 222–23, 309; Puerto Rican Americans, 224–25

Sex roles: and advertising, 154–55, 206–207; critiques of, 31–32, 88–90, 148, 204, 292, 304, 316–19, 390–91; critiques of, by: The Feminists, 301; Friedan, 290–92; Gilman, 15–16; Lesbians, 316; Mead, 290; radical feminists, 392; Schlafly, 340; and the depression, 87; and education, 78, 147–50, 279–80, 402–404; and employability of women, 197

Sex and the Single Girl (Brown), 312

Sex and Temperament (Mead), 147

Sexual division of labor. *See* Labor force, sexual division of

Sexual exploitation, 25, 37, 297. *See* Oppression

Sexual liberation, 298, 309–312; and Germaine Greer, 303; and lesbianism, 314–15; and Margaret Sanger, 59; and Shulamith Firestone, 303–304

Sexual preference, 316. *See* Lesbian rights

Sexual revolution, 55, 60, 280, 309–310, 312

Sexual segregation, 105–106, 420. *See also* Labor force, sexual division of

Sexual stereotypes, 337

Sexuality, female, 17, 302, 304, 313; attitudes toward, 309–310; and the college woman, 280; and the Flapper, 57–58; views of antifeminists, 392–93; views of Freud, 17–18, 199; views of Gilman, 16; views of Jewish tradition, 161–62; views of New Left, 298; views of Old Testament, 5

Shaw, Anna Howard, 38

Sheppard-Towner Act, 48

Shipman, Gordon, 88

SIGNS, 357

Slavery, impact on blacks, 9

Slee, Noah, 310

Smeal, Eleanor, 336

Smith, Alfred E., 50

Smith v. *Allwright,* 219

Smith College, 111, 112, 358

Smith, Howard, 258

Smith, Jean, 241

Smith, Margaret Chase, 208

Smith, Ruby Doris, 237, 241. *See* Robinson, Ruby Doris Smith

Smith-Hughes Act, 77

Smuts, Robert, 266

SNCC. *See* Student Nonviolent Coordinating Committee

Social feminism, 91, 140, 210

Social feminists, 33–35, 37, 38, 48–50, 52–53, 55, 143

Social Security Act, 95, 116; impact on female labor force, 269–70

Socialism: and Germaine Greer, 302; and Juliet Mitchell, 297–98; and New Left, 295–96; and Shulamith Firestone, 301, 303

Socialist Worker's Party, 295

Sociedad Funeraria Miguel Hidalgo, 179

Solomon, Hannah Greenbaum, 163

Southern Christian Leadership Conference, 237

Southern Council for Human Welfare, 218

Southern Regional Council, 218

Southern States Woman Suffrage Conference, 38–39
SPAR, 124
Spencer, Anne, 62
Sports, women in, 59, 90, 278, 363–64
Stage, Sarah, 392
Stanley, Louise, 51
Stanton, Elizabeth Cady, 32, 36, 308, 400, 413, 416
Stanwyck, Barbara, 153
Stapleton, Jean, 336
Status of women. *See* Woman's place; Legal status; Political status
Steffens, Lincoln, 17
Steinem, Gloria, 294, 334, 357, 406
Sterilization, 306, 329
Stern, Annette, 333
Stevenson, Adlai, 207
Stoddard, George D., 149
Stone, Lucy, 32
STOP ERA, 333, 336, 406–407
Strauss, Anna Lord, 209
Strecker, Edward, 199
Student feminism, 280–81, 356–58
Student Nonviolent Coordinating Committee (SNCC), 237, 241, 306, 307
Students for a Democratic Society (SDS), 280, 295–96
Submissiveness, female, 7, 8, 20, 289–91, 308
Suffrage, woman. *See* Woman suffrage
Sumner, Jessie, 115
Supreme Court, U.S., 9, 34, 35, 49, 53, 54, 117, 212, 219, 220, 242, 324, 329, 330, 339–40, 364
Sutherland, George, 54
Sweatt v. *Painter,* 220
Sweet, James A., 136
Szold, Henrietta, 166–67

T

Taft-Wadsworth Legal Status Bill, 143
Task Force on Women's Rights and Responsibilities, 261, 295
Tax equity for women, 348
Tenayuca, Emma, 180
Terman, Lewis, 58, 80
Terrell, Mary Church, 14, 109
Tertiary sector (of economy), 65, 131, 186, 188, 264, 365; defined, 28
There is a Confusion (Fauset), 62
Thomas, Edna, 62
Thompson, Clara, 200, 313, 391
Thompson, Dorothy, 90
Thompson, William "Big Bill," 48
Thorn, Charlotte, R., 12

Tidball, M. Elizabeth, 359
Tilden, William "Big Bill," 60
Time, 144
Title VII, 258, 259–69, 294, 412, 421. *See also* Civil Rights Act (1964)
Title IX, 363, 364, 411, 412, 421. *See also* Education Amendments Act
"To Form a More Perfect Union" ... *Justice for American Women,* 334
To Secure These Rights, 145
Togetherness, 206–207
Trotter, William M., 14
Truman, Bess, 144
Truman, Harry S., 145, 207, 209, 217, 219, 221, 243
Tuskegee Institute, 12, 13
Two-income families, 197, 327

U

UAW. *See* United Auto Workers
Unemployment compensation, 346
Uniform Marriage and Divorce Act: draft, 344
Uniform Parentage Act: draft, 344
United Auto Workers, 127, 145, 319
United Nations Commission on the Status of Women, 144
United Rubber Workers, 145
United Service organization, 124
United States Chamber of Commerce, 423–24
United States Civil Rights Commission, 424
United States Employment Service, 127, 137, 138–39
United States ex rel Robinson v. *York,* 350
United States v. *Darby,* 117
United Steel Workers, 145
University of Chicago, 111
Upton, Harriett, 48
Urbanization, 6–7, 130, 181
USO. *See* United Service Organization

V

Values: of black women, 388; of Chinese Americans, 168–69; of conventional women, 388–89; of the Flapper, 55–56; of Jewish women, 164, 165; of minority women, 390; of older women, 389–90; of white working women, 389; of working class women, 388
Van Buren, Abigail, 312
Vassar College, 111, 112, 358, 359
Veblen, Thorstein, 23
Victorian Lady, the, 8, 9, 21
Vietnam War, 296
Vietnamese American women, 373, 374

Villard, Oswald Garrison, 14
Voting Rights Act, 240

W

WAC. *See* Women's Army Corps
Wacs, 127, 153
Wages and hours legislation, 34, 53, 116, 211.
  See Protective legislation
Wages, women's, 422–23
Wald, Lillian, 33, 34, 166
Wallace, George, 220, 238
Walling, William English, 14
Walsh-Healy Act, 94, 141
War Manpower Commission, 139, 141, 143,
  151–52
War on Poverty, 327
War and violence, 327
Ward, Ada, 62
Ward, Michael, 396
Waring, Mary, 109
Washington, Booker T., 12–13, 14, 209
Washington County v. *Gunther,* 424
Washington, Margaret Murray, 15
Waters, Ethel, 62
Waves, 124, 127, 153
Wayne, John, 87
WEAL. *See* Women's Equity Action League
Weaver, Robert, 243
Weeks, John, 48
Weeks v. *Southern Telephone and Telegraph,*
  259
Weisstein, Naomi, 296
Wellesley College, 111, 112, 358, 359
Wells-Barnett, Ida, 14
West Coast Hotel v. *Parrish,* 117, 210
Westinghouse Electric Co., 425
Westoff, Charles, 268
Wetbacks. See *Mojados*
Weyrich, Paul, 393
Wheeler-Howard Act, 176
White Citizens' Councils, 221
White collar occupations, 67–68, 102, 105,
  124, 133–34, 188–89, 264, 365, 366–67,
  368, 375. *See* specific occupations
White House Conference on the Emergency
  Needs for Women, 114
White, Lynn, Jr., 140, 217
White Rose Working Girls' Home, 15
White supremacy, 38
Widowhood, 10, 343, 394. *See* Population,
  demographic factors, marital status
Wifehood. *See* Marriage
Wilkins, Roy, 240
Willis, Ellen, 300
Willis, Frances E., 209

Wills (Moody), Helen, 90
Wilson, Woodrow, 40
Winters, Shelley, 144
Wise, Issac Mayer, 163
WITCH, 299
Wollstonecraft, Mary, 77, 337
Woman in America, The (Lifton), 292
Woman and the New Race (Sanger), 58
Woman Rebel, The, 18–19
Woman suffrage, 8, 22, 32, 35–37, 39–40,
  413–14
Womanhood, character of, 387–90
Womanhood, Cult of. *See* Cult of True
  Womanhood
Woman's Era, The, 15
Woman's Home Companion, 207
Woman's nature. *See* Freud; Freudians
Woman's place, 4–9, 15, 16, 87–92, 150–55,
  193–94, 199–201. *See* Sex roles
Women: image of, 152–54; political concerns
  of, 211–12; in public office, 50, 114–16,
  207–210, 243, 414–16
Women Against Rape, 357
Women and Economics (Gilman), 15, 17
Women Incensed at Telephone Company
  Harassment (WITCH), 299
Women and Men (Scheinfeld), 199
Women USA, 414–15
Women's Army Corps, 124
Women's Bureau, 48, 51, 54, 55, 92, 127, 140,
  262. *See* Anderson, Mary; Koontz, Elizabeth; Peterson, Esther
Women's Campaign Fund, 416
Women's centers, 357
Women's Christian Temperance Union
  (WCTU), 8, 32, 48
Women's clubs, 8, 32, 108–109, 210, 388;
  compared to men's clubs, 212
Women's colleges, 111–13, 148–49, 215–17,
  279–80, 358–59
Women's Equity Action League (WEAL), 294,
  319
Women's Equity Bill, 332
Women's history: defined, 1–3
Women's Independent Taxpayers, Consumers and Homemakers (WITCH), 299
Women's International Terrorist Conspiracy
  from Hell (WITCH), 299
Women's Joint Congressional Committee, 48,
  210
Women's liberation, 297–99, 308, 323, 339
Women's movement, 54–55, 318–19, 330; and
  birth control movement, 310; and black
  women, 305–308; and college women,
  403; and Chicana, 309. *See* Feminism;
  National Organization of Women

Women's rights, 8, 92, 256–57
Women's sphere. *See* Sex roles
Women's status, 9–11, 22–33, 293–94, 341–42, 351, 410–13. *See also* Woman's place
Women's studies, 281, 357
Women's Trade Union League. *See* National Women's Trade Union League
Woodhull, Victoria, 303
Woolley, Mary, 209
Work: attitude toward, 8, 23, 71; dual career pattern of, 97, 204; meaning of, for women, 420–22; role of part-time, 71–72, 195–96, 203–204, 273–74, 383; propriety of, 26, 123–24, 368; reasons for, 30, 92, 136; terms of, 345–47
Workmen's compensation, 346
Workweek: reduction of, 130

World War I, 15, 25, 39–40, 166–67
World War II, 122–30, 137–43, 144–45, 146–49, 150–54; impact on minority women, 170, 173–74, 177, 180, 253
Wright, J. Skelly, 242
Wylie, Philip, 88, 198, 199

Y

Yippies, 295
Young Socialist Alliance, 295
Young Women's Christian Association (YWCA), 32, 48
Young Women's Hebrew Association, 32, 163, 166–67
Young, Virginia Heyer, 246–47